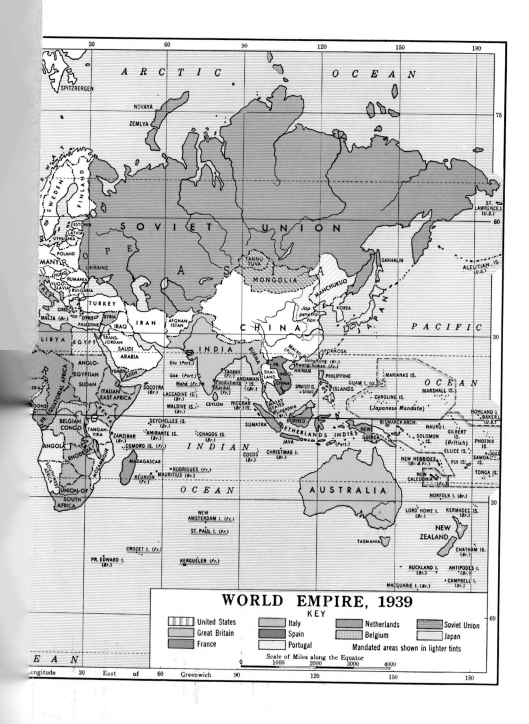

WORLD EMPIRE, 1939
KEY

United States	Italy	Netherlands	Soviet Union
Great Britain	Spain	Belgium	Japan
France	Portugal		

Mandated areas shown in lighter tints

Scale of Miles along the Equator
0   1000   2000   3000   4000

EUROPEAN COLONIAL EXPANSION

SINCE 1871

By MARY EVELYN TOWNSEND, Ph.D., PROFESSOR
OF HISTORY, TEACHERS COLLEGE, COLUMBIA UNIVERSITY,
WITH THE COLLABORATION OF CYRUS HENDERSON
PEAKE, Ph.D., ASSISTANT PROFESSOR OF CHINESE,
COLUMBIA UNIVERSITY

EDITED BY WALTER CONSUELO LANGSAM

J. B. LIPPINCOTT COMPANY
CHICAGO   PHILADELPHIA   NEW YORK

Foreword

IT IS universally recognized that a conflict of empires is basic to the second World War, as it was to its predecessor of 1914–1918. Again and again Hitler has declared his determination "to break the British empire," which constitutes but a louder and less euphonious echo of William II's demand for "a place in the sun." Japan's aggression in the Far East and in the Pacific is actuated by her desire to displace the Western powers from that entire area and to become imperialist master there instead; while Mussolini has unceasingly announced it as his intention to restore the Mediterranean as a "Roman Lake." Whatever else the second World War also becomes, whether expressed in terms of totalitarianism against democracy, a social revolution against the established order, the demands of a "master race" for world conquest, its fundamental issue remains the struggle for colonial or overseas possessions that has been in progress during the last seventy years. For colonial empires signify power, prestige, economic advantage, trade, markets and raw materials, wealth—whether real or imagined. And it is from competition over these vital elements of national life that international rivalries have inevitably arisen and have as invariably led to war.

Such being the case, a fresh survey that strives to present an account of the modern colonial overseas empires constructed by the European powers since 1871 is perhaps appropriate, since even a limited knowledge of that history would seem essential to the understanding of the present crisis. The emphasis of this book, however, is not primarily upon the effect of expansion upon diplomacy and world politics, for that story has been often told by former studies, but rather is it upon the peoples concerned, the effect of imperialism upon indigenous cultures, the native policies of the colonial powers and the nationalist movements which these policies have engendered. In view of the rapidly rising resentment of native peoples against imperialism in every area where it has been practised, it is timely, perhaps, to shift the emphasis from the great colonial powers where it has so long resided, to the so-called "backward peoples," from the colonizers to the colonized. Their bitter struggles against their colonial masters have, it should be remembered, also resulted in many wars. Altogether, imperialism, whether viewed from its effect upon Europe or its results in Africa, the Near East, the Middle East or the Far East, cannot escape the major responsibility for war.

Primarily, this book is designed for a college textbook for use in college courses which deal with modern European expansion overseas since 1871. The subject, inevitably, however, embraces Japanese expansion in the Far East and in the Pacific, as well as that of the United States, and a specialist, Cyrus H. Peake, has contributed Part V dealing with the far eastern area. It does not include in this edition, as it well might did space permit, the expansion of the United States in the Western Hemisphere. In addition to the practical use for which it is predestined, the volume may, it is hoped, possess also an appeal for that general reader interested in the westernization of these great colonial areas and stimulated by the present world crisis to analyze those causes which have disturbed "peace in our time."

Grateful acknowledgment is due Professor Walter C. Langsam for his invaluable criticism of the text and for his laborious proof-reading. The courtesy of the *Foreign Policy Association*, the *New York Times*, and the *Newspaper PM Inc* in granting permission to reproduce maps and charts is also herewith acknowledged. A valuable contribution to the book was made by Clarence Pontius and Julian Clark, who prepared the black and white maps included.

MARY EVELYN TOWNSEND

Contents

vii

PART I

The Mechanics of Modern Expansionism

Unrolling the Map of Modern Empire: A Preview of Contemporary Colonial Expansion

KINDS OF COLONIES AND THEIR DISTRIBUTION

THE EXTRAORDINARY extent of colonial expansion is one of the most impressive phenomena of this modern age. The contemporary map of the world is fairly dominated by a rainbow of colors—red, green, orange, blue, purple, yellow—which have overflowed their national boundaries and spread over continents and seas outside their own.

Furthermore, a comparison of the map at the beginning of the second World War with that of 1871 will show that this tidal wave of expansion into extramural areas reached its peak during the last seventy years. Prior to that date, indeed, history can exhibit no such universal nor widespread extension of influence and control on the part of great states overseas or overland. The great empires of the ancient world, of Assyria, Persia, of Alexander the Great and of the Roman Caesars pale into insignificance before it. Even the far-flung colonial settlements of the golden age of expansion in the sixteenth and seventeenth centuries, established by Portugal, Spain, Holland, France and England in Africa, the Far East and

3

the New World, fail to equal the size and sweep of those areas of expansion belonging to the recent period since 1871. During scarcely more than two generations, 11,000,000 square miles of Africa were annexed; China and her dependencies were forced into the long painful process of disintegration under foreign penetration which is still in progress; the settlements of the East India Company were enlarged and extended into the vast empire of India; the independence of Turkey, Persia and Afghanistan was reduced to a shadow; and hardly a coral island in the South Pacific remained unclaimed. A great drama affecting a redistribution of the world's surface was being enacted during this brief span of years, a drama on which the curtain has not yet been rung down.

Doubtless the pre-eminence of modern colonial expansion, its universality and magnitude, is in the main owing to the unique alliance of the state and private enterprise which characterized the late modern period and distinguished it from its predecessors. In the ancient and medieval worlds the state alone, were it represented by a Darius, a Hadrian or a Charlemagne, was responsible for extending the bounds of empire; while in the early modern period, private enterprise, in the persons of Henry the Navigator, the Cabots, the Conquistados, or the Jesuit missionaries, took the lead; their efforts were later aided and abetted by the state, it is true, but their achievements were the results primarily and principally of their own initiative and execution. In the years since 1871, however, an extraordinary co-operation of the state and private enterprise has taken place, and never before have their interests been so closely identified. It has been the age of industrial capitalism, and wherever the capitalists penetrated, the state has stood ready to protect and foster their adventures abroad with all the improved modern machinery of force, diplomacy and economic control at its disposal. So invincible proved the alliance that the modern map of empire is the result. And the recent era, moreover, has not only excelled in the pre-eminence of its own expansion, but it has witnessed also the retention and consolidation of considerable colonial territory acquired in the early modern period, so that the map of modern empire is indeed an impressive one.

Beginning to unroll this 1939 map of modern colonial expansion first at Africa, we see that vast continent dominated by two colors: first, the British red spanning its eastern half from the Cape of

Good Hope to the borders of the new independent state of Egypt, but recently released from imperial control, and claiming considerable sections along the west coast, such as South West Africa, Nigeria, and the Gold Coast; and, second, the French green, completely coloring the northwest corner, including Morocco, Algeria, Tunisia, along the Mediterranean Sea, and stretching southward, through West and Equatorial Africa, bordering on the Gulf of Guinea and the Atlantic Ocean. These two predominant colors are intermittently relieved by the vivid blue of the Belgian Congo in the centre; by the yellow of Portugal along both east and west coasts at Mozambique and Angola; by the deep orange of Italy on the coasts of the Mediterranean at Libya, of the Red Sea at Eritrea, and of the Indian Ocean at Somaliland, then united with Ethiopia in the solid orange block of Italian East Africa; and by the insignificant purple of Spain in Rio de Oro on the west coast, in Spanish Morocco and in the Canary Islands. In short, the entire African continent appeared to be pre-empted by the European powers whose variegated national colors gave it the aspect of a gay and intricate patch-work quilt.

Unrolling the map further to the east along the Mediterranean Sea, the red-hued British islands of Malta and Cyprus emerge, as do also the orange-tinted Italian Rhodes, with other islands of the Dodecanese group, lying off the Turkish coast. Then, the Asiatic continent appears. Its hither section, whose coast stretches along the Mediterranean, known as the Levant or Near East, is mainly colored by British red: a pale-red in Palestine and Trans-Jordan which corresponds with the French pale-green in Syria and Lebanon, the pale color indicating mandates not annexations, for these areas were awarded as "trusts" not as colonies to their respective "mandatory" powers, not "mother countries," according to the post-war interpretation of imperialism as contained in Article 22 of the Covenant of the League of Nations; a deeper red on the Suez Canal, under British domination, and along its left bank where lie the British protectorates of Yemen, bordering the vast Arab state of Saudi Arabia, and of Aden, situated at the eastern outlet of the Red Sea into the Indian Ocean. Also, faint traces of British red may be detected in areas from which it has but recently disappeared: in the kingdom of Iraq, formerly the mandate of Iraq; and in Saudi Arabia where the major aspects of British protection ended in 1928.

As the outspread map brings the Middle East of Asia into view, the same dominance of British red appears, only spread with a larger brush. A deep shade covers the vast empire of India, stretching from the Himalayan and Hindu Kush Mountains to its southern tip at Cape Comorin, flanked by the island of Ceylon; and a less bright shade in those areas under British influence which represent the approaches to the Indian empire, in Tibet, in Sinkiang, and in Koweit, the zone at the mouth of the Tigris and Euphrates rivers on the Persian Gulf. In the Middle East as in the Near East there are also faint traces of the British red: in the independent kingdom of Iran (Persia) formerly under British and Russian dominance; and in the kingdom of Afghanistan, where British influence before the first World War was acknowledged by Russia.

Finally the completely unrolled map of Asia reveals the Far East with its many colors of European penetration. Here again British red appears in Burma, adjoining India; in the elongated peninsula with its British-controlled Federated and Unfederated Malay States, as well as in the Straits Settlement, including Singapore; and in the scattered British concessions in China, now so seriously threatened by Japan, at Shanghai, Tientsin, and the British colony of Hongkong off the south China coast, as well as in the commercial interests in the Yangtse Valley and in the former leasehold of Weiheiwei, surrendered in 1930. Here too, the French green is prominent in the south: in the long stretch of French Indo-China, which includes Cochin China, Laos, Tonkin; in the leasehold of Kwangchow-wan in China and in the concessions in Yunnan province, all, like the British interests, gravely jeopardized today by China's chief enemy.

Further to the north of China, the yellow of this newly expanding country, Japan, appears, spreading solidly through Korea or Chosen, Manchoukuo, Formosa, southern Sakhalin, Jehol, Charhar, Shansi, Hopei, threatening to engulf all the northern and eastern provinces of China proper. Here it is today coming into conflict with another color that was there first previous to the first World War: the brown of the U.S.S.R. This extends over the vast Siberian territory north of the Amur River, in the coastal area around Vladivostok on the Pacific, in the island of Sakhalin and in a lighter brown shade of influence in Outer Mongolia which constitutes its heritage from the old Russia, as well as spreading less deeply over Inner Mongolia and casting its reflection upon parts of Tibet, Sinkiang and China.

But there still remains more of the map of the eastern hemisphere to be unrolled, the South Pacific or Oceania, which presents a veritable galaxy of color. North of the equator, Japanese yellow is prominent in the Marshall, Pelew, Marianne and Caroline islands, the former German possessions awarded as mandates after the war to Japan and still held despite her withdrawal from the League of Nations; Uncle Sam's red, white and blue appears in the Philippines, now promised independence, as well as in Guam and Hawaii; and the deep blue of the vast Netherlands colonial empire, extending south of the equator also, predominates in Sumatra, Borneo, Java, the Celebes, New Guinea, all acquired before 1870.

South of the equator, British red monopolizes the scene again: in the dominions of Australia and New Zealand; in the former Bismarck and Kaiser Wilhelm archipelagoes and Samoa, taken from Germany in 1919 and held as mandates; in the Fiji and Ellice groups. While here also, French green claims many islands such as Tahiti, the Society group, the Hebrides islands, Caledonia, the Marquesas, which were all gained before 1870.

In order to obtain the complete picture, the map of the western hemisphere should also be unrolled though it is outside our immediate story. For here are found extensive witnesses of empire acquired during the glorious age of early modern expansion, as well as recent acquisitions, mainly those of the United States. The first area to be revealed lies along the link connecting the Eastern and Western hemispheres, the Panama Canal Zone, acquired by lease by the United States government in 1904. Then appear the Caribbean Sea and the West Indies, which, like the East Indies, exhibit a rainbow of national colors, all painted there before 1870, with the exception of Cuba, Puerto Rico, Haiti, the Virgin Islands of St. Thomas, St. John, St. Croix, now belonging to or under the influence of the United States. Here early British acquisitions exhibit many red spots among the islands: Jamaica, the Barbados, St. Kitts, the Bahamas, the Windward islands, and, further north, Bermuda; while French green appears in Martinique and Dutch blue in Curaçao, Aruba and Guiana.

Again, the British red spans the northern section of the western hemisphere in the vast Dominion of Canada, from Nova Scotia in the east to British Columbia on the Pacific. British dominion possesses an almost complete monopoly here, broken only by two tiny pin-points of green represented in the French islands of St. Pierre and Miquelon on the east coast and by the red, white and blue of the United States in Alaska and the Aleutian islands, acquired in 1867. And from this extreme northwest corner of the American continent, Alaska reaches out to the eastern hemisphere again, separated from it only by the Bering Strait. So does the map of empire unroll around the world.

ANALYSIS OF THE MAP OF MODERN COLONIAL EMPIRE

Types and Kinds of Colonialism

Unrolling the map has revealed all sorts and kinds of colonial holdings indicated by an assortment of labels. These, in turn, indicate the degree of ownership, control or influence exercised by the colonial powers. Hence, it is important to define them so that we may recognize and understand them. For modern colonialism, especially, manifests itself in a multiplicity of forms, guises and masks. These range all the way from outright annexation, like the Belgian Congo or the former German East Africa, to the so-called protectorate like French Morocco, shading down to the spheres of influence or interest, such as those areas in the Near East, over which the great powers exercised control before the first World War or the Yunnan province in China gained by France; and finally, to the leasehold or naval base, such as British Weiheiwei and Russian Port Arthur, or the financial adviser or lender, well illustrated in the role played at first by Great Britain in Persia and by France in Tunisia.

Precise definition, at the outset, both of the term "modern colonialism" or "colonial expansion," and of the manifold types into which it has crystallized may assist later understanding. For these expressions, together with "imperialism" and "economic imperialism," have been bandied about rather loosely in current literature and made to apply to expansion movements of every kind in every age. Here "colonialism" or "colonial expansion" is employed to describe European expansion in the latter half of the nineteenth and the twentieth centuries which carried European influence into those areas mainly peopled with non-Europeans; and which established an economic and political control to a greater or less extent over those areas. The word "imperialism," commonly applied to this period of overseas expansion, has not been selected because it has come to connote a particular kind of colonial rule—generally exploitative—which often has characterized this modern movement, but not always.

Colony. Turning now to the types or forms of modern colonialism, the colony first demands definition, for we exclude the dominion which today occupies the status of an independent nation within the British Commonwealth of Nations and so no longer directly concerns us. For a dominion contains a dominant population homogeneous with that of England, owes allegiance to the crown only, exercises complete autonomy in domestic affairs and in foreign policy since the passage of the Statute of Westminster in 1931.[1] A modern colony, on the other hand, has come to mean a territorial unit, geographically separated from a state but "owing allegiance to it in some specific and tangible way," rather than a settlement of the subjects of a state beyond its frontiers, as historically it originally meant. In our contemporary world the "exploitation" colony has thus superseded the "settlement" colony, just as the expression "colonial power" has displaced "mother country." The modern colony is a geographic area held for political, strategic or economic advantage. While it may afford an opportunity for emigration, it receives the goods, the improvements, the ideas, the customs and the culture of its European power in far greater quantity than it does her nationals.

The administration of a colony also differentiates it from other forms of expansion: it is always ruled by a governor who is a national of its colonial power, directly responsible to the colonial ministry or to the foreign office. Whatever forms of local government or autonomy exist, such as native councils or native officials, are completely subordinate to the governor representing his government in Europe. Outstanding examples of these colonies are British Nigeria, Italian Libya, French Somaliland, French Equatorial Africa and Madagascar.

Crown Colony. A slight modification of the colony is the crown colony, a survival of a type of administration existent in

---

[1] There are at the present writing five dominions in the British Commonwealth of Nations: Canada, Australia, New Zealand, The Union of South Africa and Eire. For a brief description of each, see: Green, J., *The British Empire Under Fire.* Foreign Policy Association, Headline Book, No. 24.

the early British Empire. The governors of these are named by and are responsible to the colonial ministry in London, as in the other colonies, but are "advised" by assemblies or councils of British residents elected or appointed. The Gold Coast, Gambia, Sierre Leone, Kenya in Africa belong to this group as do also other older colonies, such as those in tropical America, and Hongkong, Malta, Ceylon.

The Protectorate. A protectorate, on the other hand, is an area which has surrendered by treaty to the colonial power the control of its foreign relations or the direction of its domestic affairs, to a greater or a less degree, in return for a guarantee of protection. Usually, such an arrangement takes place between a relatively backward state or section and some stronger power which exercises authority but permits the native ruler to remain in nominal command. Often the stronger power obtains the right to intervene in the internal policy of the weaker state only in certain circumstances or, indeed, is able to impose intervention, but does not exert such control in normal times. When such is the case, a veiled or semi-protectorate is said to exist.

The establishment of a protectorate is generally a compromise measure, often leading to outright annexation. Its practice was found to be an excellent substitute for military action and occupation in furthering imperialistic aims and a convenient method of preventing the dangerous interference of another colonial power. This was especially necessary in the scramble for Africa, and the French term, *occupation en protection,* reflects the system. Establishing protectorates, indeed, became a habit in the late nineteenth and early twentieth centuries and immense areas in Africa and the Orient were claimed in this convenient way. To mention some important examples only: Zanzibar, the Malay States, Morocco, Nepal, Tonking, Tunisia. There are many kinds of protectorates, weak and strong, and no two are exactly alike. Often a weak state seeks protection when in danger and allows a colonial power to intervene in certain circumstances, a relationship which is often termed a veiled or semi-protectorate. The protectorate, however, tends to disappear in the contemporary world, developing either towards or into a colony, or into independence like British Egypt.

The Mandate. A new form of colonialism, the mandate, became in Africa and Asia the rival of the protectorate. Inaugurated by the League of Nations Covenant in 1920, the mandate system represents a compromise between the idea of annexation and the ideal of international co-operation as applied to the disposal of the extra-European territories formerly belonging to Germany, except Kiaochow in China, and to Turkey. Some of these areas had already been annexed and secured by secret treaties. The term mandate injected the concept of trust or tutelage into colonial administration, to be exercised by advanced states towards backward territories entrusted to them under the League. Article 22 of the League Covenant recognized three types of mandates, whose differentiation depended upon the degree of advancement or civilization enjoyed by their respective inhabitants. It is the responsibility of the "mandatory" so to foster self-determination in the A group that they will rapidly emerge from transitional protectorates to independence; to administer the B group as colonies in such a manner as to protect the inhabitants from slavery, militarism, liquor, drugs, and definitely to promote their welfare; and to govern the C group as "integral portions of contiguous colonial areas."

Of the A mandates, Mesopotamia or Iraq graduated from British tutelage and emerged (1932) as an independent nation, member of the League; and Syria secured the promise of similar freedom from France in 1939. On the eve of the present conflict, however, the mandate's constitution was suspended and Syria was placed under a French high commissioner. The B class consists of Germany's former holdings in middle Africa: Tanganyika territory, now British; Togoland and Cameroon, held by Britain and France; Ruanda-Urundi, a small piece of former German East Africa, held by Belgium. While the C mandates, practically annexations, are found mainly in the South Pacific where those islands south of the equator are held by Australia (New Guinea and the Solomon Islands), by New Zealand (Samoa), by Great Britain (Nauru); and those north of the equator by Japan (Marshall, Caroline, Marianne, Pelew). In addition, former German Southwest Africa, now held by the Union of South Africa, is a C mandate.

Naval Bases, Franchises, Leaseholds. On the lower levels of modern colonial control, naval bases, franchises and leaseholds are devices that generally consist of small areas situated at ports or bays, seized at some crisis of weakness or goodwill on the part of

Area, Population, Trade of the B and C Mandates [2]

PRESENT MANDATORY	ENTRY INTO FORCE OF MANDATE	AREA [1a] (000's square miles)	POPULATION [1b] (000's omitted)			IMPORTS [1a] (Old U.S. gold dollars) (000,000's omitted)		EXPORTS [1a]	
			European	Asiatic	Native	1929	1937	1929	1937
Tanganyika (B) — Great Britain	July 1922	374	8.5	33.4[3]	5,096.2	19.6	11.0	18.1	16.4
British Cameroons (B) — Great Britain	July 1922	34	0.4	....	817.6	1.0	0.8	1.5	1.5
British Togo (B) — Great Britain	July 1922	13	0.04	....	293.7	0.3	[7]	1.0	[7]
South West Africa (C) — South Africa	December 1920	323	31.0	....	328.5	14.6	6.9	17.1	10.9
French Cameroons (B) — France	July 1922	166	2.3	0.07	2,338.8	7.6	5.4	6.7	7.4
French Togo (B) — France	July 1922	20	0.4	0.06	762.9	4.0	2.1	3.3	2.0
Ruanda-Urundi (B) — Belgium	July 1922	21	0.9	0.6	3,385.7	1.7	1.4	0.4	1.8
New Guinea (C) — Australia	December 1920	91	3.2	1.7	500.0[6]	4.2	3.8	5.6	7.3
Nauru (C) — Australia [2]	December 1920	0.01	0.2	1.1	1.6	0.5	0.5	1.7	1.3
Western Samoa (C) — New Zealand	December 1920	1.1	0.6[4]	0.5	51.2	1.4	0.5	1.4	0.9
Marianne Caroline, & Marshall Islands (C) — Japan	December 1920	0.8	0.08	51.6[5]	50.5	3.3	3.2	3.5	4.3
Total		1,043.91	47.62	89.03	13,626.7	58.2	35.6	60.3	53.8

[1] Chief Sources: (a) *League of Nations Statistical Year Book, 1936-7;* (b) R. R. Kuczynski: *Colonial Populations,* Oxford University Press, 1937.
[2] Nauru is a British Mandate administered by Australia.
[3] Chiefly Indians.
[4] There are also 2,453 half-castes.
[5] Chiefly Japanese.
[6] Areas under Government control only.
[7] Not available separately.

[2] From International Studies Conference, *Peaceful Change: Colonial Questions and Peace,* p. 291.

the native government. They afford footholds of complete sovereignty to the colonial power to do with them as it wills. The
leases or terms of leasehold run for a definite or indefinite period.
They are best illustrated by those ports, Kwangchow-wan, Weiheiwei, Port Arthur, seized before the first World War by France,
Great Britain and Russia, respectively, in China; as well as by
Kiaochow and part of the Shantung Peninsula leased (1898) to
Germany for ninety-nine years. They often served as nuclei for
further penetration and control.

Spheres of Interest and Influence, Concessions. In such definitely limited zones, states established preferential or exclusive
rights of economic development, control and exploitation. Often
this was done by agreement between two colonial powers, as
when Russia and Great Britain divided Persia into three zones
in 1907: a southern or British sphere of influence, a northern
or Russian sphere of influence, and a third or neutral zone
in between the two. Railroad construction played a great part
in extending spheres of interest where the colonial power exercised more economic than political rights as in the spheres of
influence. Such were the rights granted to Germany along the
route either side of the Bagdad railway in Turkey and along
railroads constructed into hinterlands from naval bases like those
to Russia at Port Arthur on the Yellow Sea and to Britain at
Koweit on the Persian Gulf. Again, the right to build railroads
constituted concessions and franchises, which proved effective
forms of imperialist penetration. Russia's concessions, wrested
from China, to continue the Trans-Siberian railway across Manchuria to Vladivostok, her Pacific port, known as the Chinese
Eastern railway, as well as to construct the famous South Manchurian railway, a branch of the Chinese Eastern railway running south to Port Arthur, were examples.

Sometimes economic concessions took the form of granting
the control of customs to the colonial power. China began to do
this in 1842 and not until 1929 did she regain the right to adjust
her own tariff schedules. So effective an instrument for penetration did customs control prove that it became a favorite technique
widely practised, notably in Egypt and the Turkish states in
North Africa by the European powers, and in South and Central
America by the United States.

Extraterritoriality. Economic concessions, spheres of influence, franchises brought, of course, many foreigners, merchants and business men, into these so-called "backward" countries where they found the existing legal system inadequate or unsuited to their use. Often, as in the Turkish Empire, justice was interwoven with religion, with the Mohammedan code, and everywhere, especially in China, it was not geared to the industrialization of the West. Hence the Western powers wrested from these countries the right of extraterritoriality, the privilege whereby their nationals might be tried by Western law and by Western courts. In this complete surrender of one of their sovereign rights, the right to administer justice, which sometimes included an abrogation of taxing power also, these "backward" countries only laid themselves open to a wider penetration and control. How detrimental this right of extraterritoriality was to their national integrity is illustrated by the haste with which such states as Turkey, Egypt, Persia renounced it when their nationalist movements delivered them from European imperialism.

Advisers, Residents. Inasmuch as concessions, franchises, spheres of influence and their like require individuals to direct and control their relations with the native governments, there developed special advisers and residents who became assertive instruments of expansion. Their technique is well illustrated in all its potentiality by the French in Morocco or Tunisia, the British in Egypt, the Russians in Persia and the Germans in Turkey before the first World War, where bankers, engineers, financiers, army officers, experts of all kinds, "advised" native rulers so freely that they fairly honeycombed their rule with foreign influence.

The Chartered Company. An additional "pre-colony" technique is the chartered company, like the crown colony a survivor from the sixteenth and seventeenth centuries; but, today, too weak a control to be employed in an age of nationalistic colonial competition. Such was the Royal Niger Company which acquired Nigeria and handed it over to the British government in 1900; the British South African Company which opened up and governed Rhodesia until 1906; and such is the one surviving example today, the British North Borneo Company, chartered in 1882.

Thus we see modern colonial expansion assuming many forms and a variety of masks, many of which we shall encounter and recognize in the ensuing discussion. One more or less constant rule concerning them may be discerned: in the less-developed

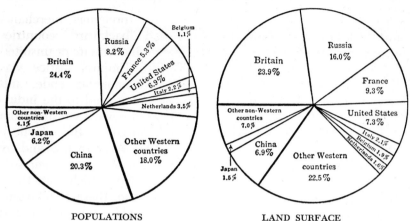

POPULATIONS   LAND SURFACE

From "A Place in the Sun" by Grover Clark. By permission of The Macmillan Co., Publishers

POLITICAL DIVISIONS OF THE EARTH IN 1935

areas, the thoroughgoing annexations, the full-fledged colonies will be found; while among peoples of long-established civilizations, the subtler and more indirect forms of colonialism will prevail. Thus, in the South Seas, and in Central Africa where the untutored native has no choice but to make his mark on the dotted line, vast areas can be annexed outright as colonies; while in North Africa, China, in the Near East, advice, loans, military or naval aid, economic bargaining of all kinds, must be employed as entering wedges of imperialistic control. Once established, the entering wedge, be it loan or concession, advice, protection or punitive expedition, may lead to something more permanent. Consequently, these minor and less obvious forms of colonial penetration are evolutionary in character; skilful hands may and do finesse them into rich colonial holdings. The ensuing survey will afford numerous examples of all these varied types of penetration and control which have here been briefly defined and indicated.

Distribution of Colonial Empire

Next to its extent and variety, the most impressive fact about the modern colonial map is its unequal distribution in area, in population and in resources. There were at the beginning of the second World War seven European and one Asiatic colonial powers,

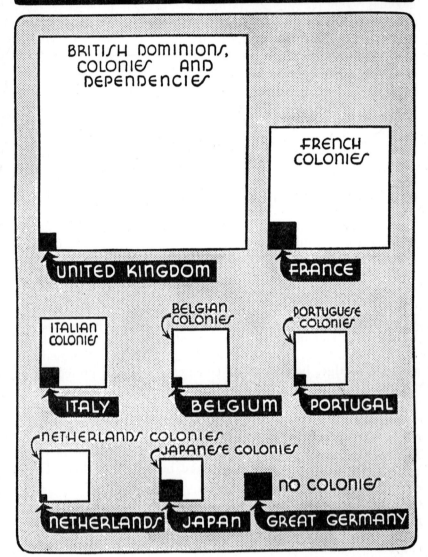

THE "HAVES" AND THE "HAVE-NOTS"

Great Britain, France, Italy, Belgium, the Netherlands, Portugal, Spain, Japan; one semi-colonial power, the U.S.S.R., and one ex-colonial power, Germany. All these might then have been classified into the *Haves,* the *Have-Beens* and the *Have-Nots.*

The Haves. The Haves were, of course, Great Britain, France, the Netherlands and Belgium. They held their huge empires intact, had announced their refusal to part with so much as a square inch of them, and were feverishly increasing their defenses. Of them, Great Britain held the lion's share. With 94,000 square miles at home, she claimed 13,100,000 square miles of colonies (including dominions). The United Kingdom constituted only .2 per cent of her holdings, while 16 per cent lay in Asia, 23 in Africa, 27 in Oceania, 33 per cent in the Americas and 1 per cent in Europe. Certainly it was true that the "sun never sets upon the British Empire, every part of which has a place in the sun part of every day."

These vast possessions contained 470,000,000 people in contrast to the 46,500,000 at home. Three hundred and sixty-one millions were in India, about 75,000,000 in the dependent areas and the remainder in the dominions. Most of the dependent peoples were non-Caucasian and represented the greatest diversity of race, culture and religion. It follows that just as Great Britain held the most territory, she controlled the bulk of the resources.

France ranked second as a contemporary colonial power. Her huge empire of 4,300,000 square miles would have contained the home country twenty times. Her share of the world's total area was 9.3 per cent. All her colonial empire except Algeria, a few trading posts in West Africa and in India, a vague hold in Cochin China, the so-called *colonies anciennes,* and Tahiti, Caledonia, Reunion, were acquired after 1870. Of her holdings 87 per cent were in Africa, 1 per cent in the Americas and in Oceania, 4 per cent in Europe and 8 per cent in Asia. Nearly all are in the hot, tropical climates and with the exception of North Africa, inhospitable to whites. Her empire contained 65,000,000 inhabitants as compared with 42,000,000 at home in France.

Belgium came third. The Belgian Congo, occupying 8 per cent of the African continent, was nearly eighty times the size of its motherland, representing a proportion of 940,000 square miles overseas to 11,800 square miles in Europe. Thus a population of 8,300,000 controlled one of 13,000,000 in Africa. All of Belgium's empire was acquired after 1871.

The Netherlands was the fourth and last of the *Have* powers. With only 13,200 square miles in Europe and a population of 8,500,000, she controlled a colonial empire of 790,000 square miles, sixty times as large as herself, and a population of 66,000,-000, eight times her own. All this was in Oceania and the West Indies and belonged not to the late but to the early modern period of expansion.

The *Have-Been* colonial powers, Portugal and Spain, displayed only the remnants of their past glory but even here the disproportion in distribution was evident. *Portugal,* with but 35,500 square miles in Europe and a population of 7,000,000, still ruled over 7 per cent of the African continent, 810,000 square miles, more than twenty-two times as extensive as herself. There her colony of Angola alone is larger than the old Germany, France, the Netherlands, Denmark and Switzerland together; and Mozambique, Portuguese East Africa, is larger than Texas.

Spain, the poorer of the Have-Been powers, controlled only 128,615 square miles in Northern Africa, Morocco and Guinea. This represents only a tattered remnant of that vast, rich colonial empire which in the seventeenth century was the pride of the Hapsburgs and the envy and threat of Britain. It serves, perhaps, as a warning of what history has in store for even the greatest and the most powerful oversea conquerors.

The Have-Nots. With the holdings of the Haves and Have-Beens in mind, the situation in 1939 of the Have-Nots will appear clearer. They were Italy, Japan and Germany. The first two were Have-Nots because they were unsatisfied with the little colonial empire which they had; the last one, Germany, because it had none whatever. Owing to a delayed national development, postponed to the last quarter of the nineteenth century, these Have-Not powers were unable to acquire any colonies before 1871. While the Haves were well-launched upon the modern era of expansion, the Have-Nots were still engaged with internal struggles of unification and stabilization. Thus, they all got off to a late start in the recent colonial race and discovered that all the best and most desirable areas had been occupied; hence they were compelled to take what was left.

Italy, with a homeland of only 120,000 square miles on which

Colonial Empires of the World in 1939 [1]

	The Haves				The Have-Nots			
	Great Britain[1]	France	Belgium	The Netherlands	Italy	Japan	Germany 1914	Germany August, 1939
Area in Square Miles	94,000	212,600	11,800	13,200	120,000	148,000	210,000	226,000
Population	46,500,000	42,000,000	8,300,000	8,500,000	43,800,000	70,000,000	67,500,000	80,000,000
Area of Colonies in Square Miles	13,100,000	4,300,000	940,000	790,000	1,400,000	576,000	1,100,000	0
Population of Colonies	470,000,000	65,000,000	13,000,000	66,000,000	10,000,000	59,000,000	13,000,000	0
Total % of World Land Surface	23.9	9.3	1.9	1.6	2.2	1.5	2.4	.4

[1]Figures include dominions.

[1] Figures in round numbers.

live nearly 44,000,000 people, controlled a colonial empire of but 1,400,000 square miles, sparsely populated with about 10,000,000 inhabitants. Much of it was tropical and desert land which had been considered worthless by the other powers. It amounted to twelve times the size of her own small country and failed utterly to fulfil her dreams of empire.

Japan, far worse off than Italy, occupies an area of 148,000 square miles and has a population of 70,000,000 excluding the virtual protectorate of Manchoukuo. Her colonial empire (including Manchoukuo) of 576,000 square miles was already populated by 59,000,000 and barely equaled four times the size of her own country. She is now in the process of a vast expansion. What its outcome will be, only the future will reveal.

Germany before the first World War, a nation of 67,500,000, living on an area of 216,000 square miles in Europe, possessed a colonial empire of 1,100,000 square miles overseas, with 13,000,-000 natives. Most of it was situated in Africa, where it occupied 8 per cent of the continent, and in Oceania.

When the second World War began, the new or Greater Germany numbered 80,000,000 and had increased its territories to 226,000 square miles. But its flag floated over no single overseas colony.

Distribution of Colonial Resources—Raw Materials and Foods

The unevenness of distribution in lands and people was naturally matched by that of resources, of raw materials and of food. The basic materials of modern industrialism are generally considered to consist of the minerals: coal, iron, oil, copper, lead, zinc, tin, manganese, aluminum (bauxite), asbestos, graphite, potash, phosphate, antimony; and of the vegetable products, cotton, rubber, wool, jute (sisal), silk, olive oil, palm oil, sago bean. The essential foodstuffs of contemporary civilization are reckoned as wheat, rice, coffee, cocoa, tea, beef and mutton, dairy products, sugar, citrus fruits, bananas, tobacco.

Here again, the Haves had it. Great Britain held the largest share. In industrial products she controlled more than half the rubber, tin, copper and palm oil of colonial production, as well as a fair supply of petrol, graphite, phosphates, bauxite. France was well provided with all the colonial nickel, three quarters of all the phosphates and of the olive oil, some graphite, tin and rubber; the Netherlands controlled more than half the colonial aluminum, an excellent supply of rubber and of tin, some supplies of oil, phosphate and palm oil; and Belgium possessed considerable palm oil, some copper and tin.

On the other hand, the Have-Nots' possessions were poor in the raw materials of industry. Italy, the poorest, had some olive oil and the prospect of more, together with the unconfirmed mineral resources of Ethiopia, such as copper. Japan was better off with soy beans, some silk, iron ore, graphite, a little cotton. The old Germany had in her oversea areas sisal (jute), some asbestos, phosphates, and a little lead and copper; the 1939 Germany, of course, had nothing.

The same situation prevailed with regard to the food stuffs: the Haves had them. Again, Great Britain controlled the largest share, 80 per cent of the cocoa, over half the tea and about half the cane sugar, nine-tenths of the citrus fruits and nearly half the bananas. Next came the Netherlands with nearly half the tea, a little coffee, tobacco and cane sugar; then France with rice, cane sugar, tobacco, cocoa and some bananas. But the Have-Nots were especially poor in food supplies, except Japan, who had developed rice in her colonies which supplied her with thousands of tons a year, and who had also cane sugar and bananas. Italy was negligible in this respect. The old Germany received a very little coffee and some cocoa; the Germany of 1939, nothing.

Besides these bare figures of land and peoples, these lists of commodities and products which convey the practical and tangible aspects of the maladjusted colonial situation, there are the imponderable elements without which the picture is incomplete. Chief among them is the fact that all the Have-Nots represent countries now experiencing a tremendous upsurging of newly awakened nationalism and unity, accompanied by unusual increases in population, a veritable burgeoning of industrialization, and an unprecedented technological development which demand raw materials and economic outlets. Add to this the belief in autarky or national self-sufficiency, which has been given new life by the totalitarian philosophy, as well as the doctrine of superiority of race and culture, inherent in Nazi ideology. With these in mind, one gains a clearer idea of the acuteness of the colonial problem arising from the inequality and maladjusted distribution of territory, which has been one object of this survey. Whether or not this uneven allotment of colonial possessions is in the end an advantage or a disadvantage for their possessors is not the question here in this chapter; the purpose of which has been to set forth the map of modern empire as it existed at the beginning of the second World War.

The course of the war during 1940-1941 carried the struggle into Africa, the Near, the Middle and the Far East. Significant changes in the occupation of colonial territories were made. The British seized Italian Africa; the Germans invaded North and West Africa, the Near and Middle East; while Japan advanced upon French Indo-China. No permanent settlement, however, guaranteed any of these occupations, and the final outcome regarding any future allocation of colonial possessions remains uncertain.

Colonial Production as a Percentage of World Production [2]

Raw Materials	British [1]	French	Belgian	Italian	Portuguese	Dutch	Japanese	Spanish	Mandates
Antimony	...	0.5	...	...	...	...	...	0.2	...
Bauxite	5.2	...	...	...	...	7.9	...	...	...
Chrome	...	12.7	...	...	...	...	...	...	...
Copper	12.7	...	8.6	...	...	...	...	...	...
Iron Ore	1.2	1.5	...	...	...	...	0.4	0.3	...
Manganese	13.1	0.2	...	...	...	0.4	...	...	...
Nickel	...	9.0	...	...	...	...	...	...	...
Tin	35.4	1.0	3.7	...	...	16.8	...	...	...
Tungsten	11.2	1.9	...	...	...	...	2.5	...	...
Zinc	1.4	0.5	...	...	...	...	...	0.5	...
Petroleum	0.8	...	...	...	...	2.9	...	...	...
Coal	0.1	0.1	...	...	...	0.1	0.3	...	...
Rubber	56.7	2.0	...	...	...	37.4	...	...	...
Graphite	10.5	7.5	...	...	...	...	...	...	...
Phosphates	3.4	41.9	...	...	...	1.1	28.0	...	5.6
Pyrites	3.2	0.2	...	...	...	...	...	...	...
Gold	1.8	0.7	1.4	...	...	0.3	1.7	...	0.5
Cotton	1.5	...	0.4	...	...	...	0.5	...	0.6
Wool	0.2	2.0	...	...	...	...	...	...	0.1
Silk	...	...	...	...	...	...	...	...	0.2
Hemp	...	...	...	...	...	...	2.9	...	0.2
Copra	24.6	1.8	1.2	...	1.9	30.5	6.0	...	5.6
Ground Nuts	6.0	13.7	...	...	0.9	3.8	2.0	...	0.9
Olive Oil	...	11.2	...	0.4	...	...	...	...	1.3
Palm Oil	48.4	7.1	13.9	...	2.3	22.0	...	...	5.1
Sesame	3.9	0.6	0.8	...	0.3	0.4	0.8	...	1.2
Cane Sugar	18.9	1.4	...	...	0.2	4.3	4.4	...	0.3
Tea	25.7	0.2	...	...	...	19.7	2.4	...	...
Cocoa	56.3	6.8	0.2	...	1.8	0.2	...	1.8	6.6
Tobacco	0.3	1.6	...	...	1.8	2.5	...	...	0.1

[1] Dominions excluded.

Moresco, E., International Studies Conference, *Peaceful Change: Colonial Questions and Peace*, p. 131.

CHAPTER TWO

Who Unrolled the Map of Modern Empire and Why

THE PIONEERS OF MODERN EXPANSION AND THE FORCES BEHIND THEM

MANY AND VARIED were the pioneers of modern colonial expansion: merchants and missionaries, traders and travelers, engineers and explorers, scientists and soldiers, consuls and diplomats. They all contributed to the unrolling of the map of empire. Each interested European state furnished representatives of almost every group; hence, to describe one or two examples of each group is to picture all, irrespective of nationality. For whether British, French, German, Belgian or Italian, these agents were all actuated by like motives, impelled by similar influences, which were in turn produced by identical forces operating in Europe during the last quarter of the nineteenth century; forces so universal as to be best analyzed later after the human examples of their creation are clearly before us. Nothing, perhaps, illustrates more clearly the common background of modern colonial expansion than does the close relationship of its national pioneers. They are counterparts one of another, and each is a type.

24

The Merchant

Representative of the merchant is Adolph Woermann of Hamburg. Son of the ship owner Karl Woermann, who in the early 1860's had established trading stations in Gabon, Liberia and the Cameroons, he realized what his father had then foreseen: the rich, commercial possibilities of the West African coast. He was sent abroad at twenty as future partner in the Woermann firm "to learn and to wander." From 1868 to 1874 he visited China, Japan, the East Indies, North America and Africa, in which latter continent he discerned the greatest opportunity and decided to concentrate the firm's energies. Gradually, he replaced the sailing ships of the house by steamships and in 1882 established the first regular steamship service between Hamburg and West Africa, the Woermann line, which was still running at the outbreak of the second World War.

In spite of the territorial holdings of the French along the west coast, Woermann built up a commercial empire there and laid the foundations for the future German colony of the Cameroons whose acquisition during the 1880's was largely owing to his initiative. He became a member of the *Reichstag* where he was able to influence government subventions for the line. For his "national service," he was rewarded by Bismarck with an appointment to the *Kolonialrat*. From this strategic position he could bind more closely and effectively trade, colonies and the government.

Woermann's type can be duplicated again and again among the initiators of modern colonial expansion: in his compatriots, F. A. Lüderitz of Bremen, founder of German South West Africa, in William O'Swald, early explorer of trading footholds in East Africa, and in Godeffroy, another Hamburger, who laid the foundations of German Samoa; in John Holt, Hatton and Cookson, British merchant pioneers in West Africa; in those early and venturesome French merchants in Annam; and in the Rubattino company, which secured the first footholds in Italian Eritrea by acquiring a port in the Bay of Assab in 1869.

The Explorer

Truly representative of those explorers who first started upon their own initiative and adventure and then became agents of the expansionists is Savorgnan de Brazza, founder of French Congo. Of Italian parentage, he was sent to France to be educated in a naval academy. He became naturalized, joined the French navy and fought in the Franco-Prussian War. In 1874, his warship visited the mouth of the Gabon River on the West African coast, where he fell in with some French explorers returning from the Ogowe River. Fascinated by their tales, de Brazza left the navy and returned to lead his own expedition up the Ogowe. On this trip he discovered the Alimu and Likonia rivers, but not until he returned to Paris and heard of Henry Stanley's exploits on the Congo River did he realize that his newly found streams were tributaries to that great waterway. Anxious to secure some of the Congo basin for France, de Brazza returned in 1880, where he proceeded to run a race with Stanley, employed on a similar errand by the Belgian king, Leopold II. Pushing through to the upper Congo he stole a march on Stanley and founded Brazzaville on Stanleypool, saving one bank of the river from Belgium. He concluded treaties with a chief, Makoko, thus laying the foundations for French Congo to which he returned in 1883, by government order, to open up further the new colony.

Playing much the same rôle for Germany in East Africa was the adventurer-explorer Karl Peters. This impetuous and erratic son of a mild Saxon pastor had never settled down to a profession, apparently finding the strictures of such a life in his well-ordered Fatherland much too prosaic. While on a long visit to his uncle in England he had become thoroughly imbued with the national necessity for imperialism, but even more with the exciting and romantic adventures which it so glamorously offered to its pioneers. Returning home in 1883, he strove to find support for his many plans of colonial adventure, which ranged all the way from founding a colony in Brazil to helping the Boers against England, but which ultimately, owing to the influence of Count Pfeil, an African explorer, resolved upon East Africa as a goal.

Upon the strength of a hastily formed company's financial support, Peters, Pfeil, Jühlke, and a merchant, Otto, set sail for East Africa in the autumn of 1884, with all the glamour of romantic adventure that secrecy, an alias, and the disguise provided by workmen's clothes could afford. When they arrived in Zanzibar, they found a telegram from Bismarck refusing imperial protection in advance to their adventures. Replying that they begged the government to keep its "protection" until it was asked for, they proceeded unmolested into the interior, as no one else, English or German, had the slightest suspicion of their real errand. Their technique with the native chiefs was simple and direct: it consisted of a judicious distribution of childish presents plus an injudicious application of grog. In the happy and somewhat hazy mental state produced by the grog, the chiefs listened to the treaty articles drawn up by Peters and read to them in the unknown, sonorous German tongue; then the German flag was ceremoniously raised and saluted with a salvo of gunshots; and the impressed and slightly befuddled chiefs obediently affixed their marks on the dotted line which signed away their rights.

So effective did this method prove that Peters was back again within ten days on the coast, carrying in his pocket a dozen treaties which covered the districts of Useguha, Ukami, Nguru, and Usagara, a region of about 60,000 square miles—the nucleus of German East Africa.

Matching the exploits of a de Brazza and a Peters, France had her Caillé, de Chaillu and others; England her Sir Harry Johnston, Grant, Baker, Speke and an innumerable company; Belgium her Henry Stanley; and Germany her Nachtigal, Rohlfs, Barth and Hornemann.

The Capitalist Promoter

It is perhaps among the British that the best examples of the capitalist promoters or business men are found, of whom Cecil Rhodes is the most famous prototype. His story is well known to almost every schoolboy and needs no repetition here, especially as we shall encounter him later in British Africa. The career of George Goldie Taubman, however, while not so familiar, is replete with the same characteristics of business acumen and executive drive; and resulted, not, to be sure, in anything so grandiose as the Cape-to-Cairo plan, but in Britain's second largest holding in Africa—the vast Niger colony with its 20,000,000 people and its area three times as great as the United Kingdom.

The son of an army officer, young Taubman was himself an officer in the Royal Engineers and as such had spent some time in Egypt and other parts of Africa. In 1877, he inherited several thousand pounds' worth of shares in small trading companies doing business on the Niger River and journeyed thither to see about their security. Impressed by the existence of so many firms and their consequent ineffectiveness, Taubman, like Cecil Rhodes and all modern big-business executives, determined upon amalgamation and proceeded forthwith to achieve it. With untiring energy he brought about the consolidation of all the British companies trading on the Niger River. Then he bought out the French and the governing rights of many chieftains, negotiating over four hundred treaties with these potentates along the lower Niger. This merger allowed him to point to his own company as the only one doing business in the area and so he applied to the government for a charter. His application coincided with the Berlin Conference over Central Africa which Taubman himself attended as the expert on the Niger River. The charter was granted to his company, first known as the National African Company but later as the Royal Niger Company.

Taubman's work was not completed, however; again, like Rhodes, he aimed at monopoly and was obliged to ward off the encroachments of both France and Germany. The former claimed the Lake Chad region and also pressed in from Dahomey; the latter planned to secure the basin of the lower Niger. The Anglo-French agreement of 1893 delimited France's boundary and also granted a strip to Germany to arrest the latter's advance. With this concession and with Bismarck's fall, Germany's activity in these regions ceased. One other obstacle remained, the hostility of the great Mohammedan empire of Sokota under the Emir Nupe. This was overcome in the traditional manner with the aid of a staff of British officers, Mauser bullets and machine guns, and the Royal Niger Company became the master of a vast riverain dominion in Central Africa—Nigeria. In 1900 the company transferred its territory to the British government, which in gratitude knighted Sir Goldie Taubman.

In the same capitalist-promoter class as Taubman and Rhodes belong Alfred von Kaulla and George von Siemens, backers of the Bagdad railroad, and the Mannesmann brothers, promoters of German mining rights in Morocco—all men who through their manipulation of trade, capital, economic concession and governmental influence developed into the great empire builders of our modern age.

Closely related to them are the bankers: individual captains of finance and firms like Julius de Reuter, an Englishman who founded the Imperial Bank of Persia in 1889 to lend money to the shah for mining; like Bleichröder and von Hansemann, who formed the German New Guinea Company and co-operated with Bismarck to advance German interests in the South Seas; like the British Hongkong and Shanghai Banking Corporation which appealed (1898) to the foreign office for the support of the British Minister at Peking in obtaining railway concessions from the Chinese government; the Russo-Chinese Bank which assisted the Chinese to pay the indemnity to Japan after her victory in 1895 and so acquired concessions for railways and telegraphs in China; and the Banca d'Italia or the Banco di Roma which so successfully "penetrated" Tripolitania by promoting investments in olive oil, soap factories, sponge fisheries and other enterprises.

The Missionary

Less direct agents of expansion, although equally effective, were the missionaries, of whom the Catholic Cardinal Lavigerie might well be selected as a type. A professor of ecclesiastical history at the Sorbonne, then bishop of Nancy, he was invited by the governor of Algeria, Marshal McMahon, to occupy the See of Algiers, just elevated to an archbishopric. For almost a quarter of a century Lavigerie labored in French Africa, where he became cardinal and primate in 1884. He devoted himself to two lines of endeavor: the establishment of French Catholic missions and missionary orders and the crusade against the slave trade. To carry on his crusade against slavery he founded the famous order of *Péres Blancs* who continue today to wear their picturesque white cassocks and red fezzes; also the White Brothers and White Sisters. Through them he organized missions in the Sahara, the Sudan, in Tunisia and in Tripolitania. In 1898 Pope Leo XIII gave him a rescript to evangelize all Central Africa and a decade later Bismarck vigorously championed his campaign against the cruelties of the Arab slave trade as a strategem to win Catholic Center votes for colonial budgets. His was a power to be reckoned with in Africa; a power which advanced immensely the colonial penetration of France and enhanced her political prestige. The cardinal's activities in Tunisia drew from Gambetta the celebrated comment: *"L'anti-clericalisme n'est pas un article d'expor-*

tation." Indeed, France's colonial rivals said of him that hand in hand with his desire to spread religion among Arabs, Berbers and Negroes, went an equally ardent desire to make them French-protected subjects.

Missionaries of other nationalities were just as eager as Cardinal Lavigerie to make native peoples German, British, Italian, Belgian, as the case might be; and expansionists of all countries let no opportunity slip to employ missionaries, dead or alive, to advance the "kingdom," not only of God but of nationalism and of economic power overseas. The Church Missionary Society supplied money to the British East African Company to enable it to remain in Uganda; Dr. Fabri, Inspector of the Rhine Mission, pressed the government again and again for protection of its work in South West Africa. The avenging of the murder of a Spanish missionary bishop by a Franco-Spanish naval squadron in 1857 led to France's first holdings in Cochin China; while Cristoforo Negri, an official in the ministry of foreign affairs in Turin, wrote as early as 1857 to the missionary Mgr. Massaia, apostolic vicar in the Galla region of southern Ethiopia, suggesting the convenience of entering into political and economic relations with the leading chiefs of those districts.

The Consul

Even more direct agents of modern colonialism than those hitherto described are the consuls or diplomats whom the European states assigned to near and remote points overseas to protect and promote the trading interests of their adventuring nationals. Very naturally, these officials acted to advance the political as well as the commercial interests of the home country; indeed, they were of the first to sense the necessity for political power in order to protect the commercial interests from encroaching rivals. Such a functionary was Théodore Roustan, a diplomat of exceptional abilities and energy, who was installed as French consul in the city of Tunis. Roustan had enjoyed a lifelong experience in the French consular service in the Near East. Born in 1834, he was first attached to the consulates in Beireuth, Cairo, Smyrna, then consul-general to Alexandria in 1867 and later French commissioner in Palestine. Appointed consul in Tunis in 1874, he brought to the task of winning both the bey and railroad concessions for

France a wealth of knowledge and a diplomatic technique in dealing with Oriental potentates. In Tunis he found the situation of France compromised by England and Italy, which exercised considerable influence over the bey. Roustan, however, capitalized the occasion of an uprising of a native tribe in Algeria against the French which threatened to spread into Tunisia and was the chief diplomatic factor in preparing for the establishment of the French protectorate in 1882.

Roustan's type was duplicated everywhere in those early years of modern expansion. The German consuls in Samoa and Australia gave Bismarck no peace in the early seventies with their insistent urgings that Germany speedily annex some point in Samoa or the Fiji Islands in order to protect German trade. Indeed, when the chancellor himself finally determined upon a colonial policy he made skilful use of consuls as tools in the game of scramble for Africa. Often colonial possession was determined by whose consul could get there first to stake out claims. This was true in West Africa, where consul Nachtigal out-manoeuvered consul Hewitt and the German colonies of Cameroons and Togoland eventuated to form unwelcome enclaves in British holdings in West Africa. Likewise, Signor Filonardi, Italian consul at Zanzibar, prepared the way by his clever "protection" of the sultans of the coast for Crispi's claim to Italian Somaliland in 1889, taking his cue from the British consuls at Zanzibar, among whom Sir John Kirk is justly famous.

Especially in the Far East, which was not so susceptible as a more backward Africa to the methods of direct colonization, the diplomat played a peculiarly important rôle. An outstanding practitioner of such diplomatic technique was Sir Harry S. Parkes, who gave a lifetime of service to advancing British imperial interests in that area. Going out to China at an early age, he began his career in the British consulate at Canton in 1841 when only fifteen years old. After the bombardment of Canton in 1857, due to the refusal of the Chinese to allow Europeans to settle within the walls of the city, Parkes was one of the three commissioners appointed to control the government of Canton. His efficient rule, based upon his knowledge of the language and familiarity with administrative difficulties, succeeded in inducing the British merchants to return to the city. Shortly after, he was made responsible for the selection of the new ports conceded by the Chinese to the British through the Treaty of Tientsin (1858), and assisted in establishing consulates at Chinkiang, Kiukiang and Hankow. In 1865, the British appointed Parkes as minister to Japan, where he succeeded in reorganizing British commercial interests in accordance with the opening of Japanese ports to commerce after the 1858 treaties. After nearly twenty years of highly successful service, Parkes left Japan in 1883 to become minister to China, where he won British commercial advantages in Korea and opened additional cities and ports to British trade. His last public service, which crowned a long career, was the acquisition of Fort Hamilton as a coaling station for the British fleet in the north Pacific.

The Soldier

Doubtless the most effective instrument of expansion in any age is the soldier. But the modern period seems to present peculiar opportunities for military leadership leading to important administrative posts. Not slow to accept such challenges in fullest measure was Sir Frederick Lugard, himself later a student and writer in the field of contemporary colonialism.

The son of an Anglican clergyman, he early selected the army as his lifework. Serving first in India he shortly transferred his activities to Africa and took part in the campaign for the Sudan. British East Africa was to owe him much although West Africa was destined to demand from him the greatest services to the empire which crowned his long career. Commanding an expedition against the slave trade in Nyasa, Captain Lugard finally brought that area under the control of the East African Chartered Company and became its first administrator. When competition for western Nigeria with the French became threatening in the early nineties, he was ordered to the Nigerian frontier where his skilful handling of native chiefs enabled the Royal Niger Company to score over the French. His work in pacifying the country won for him, now colonel, the post of first high commissioner of the northern Nigeria, where he organized the West African frontier police, subdued Ashantiland, overthrew various local emirs, and rose to be brigadier-general. Upon the amalgamation of northern and southern Nigeria, Sir Frederick became its first governor-general, 1914-1919.

Lugard's distinguished soldier-administrator service for empire is duplicated by that of many others: Gordon and Kitchener in Egypt, Lyautey in Morocco, Leutwein in the Cameroons, Marchand in the Sudan, to mention but a few.

The Engineer

Significant of the dominant part played by modern industrialism in recent expansion is the engineer. For it is he who has conquered the seemingly insuperable obstacles to white domination over the so-called "backward" countries by the practical application of modern science, has thrown iron rails across continental mountain ranges and sandy wastes, has spanned tumultuous rivers with the suspension bridge, and by hydraulic engineering has literally caused the floods to cease and the desert places to blossom as the rose—or the rice.

William von Pressell, the eminent German engineer, is typical of this group. Having constructed important mountain railways in Switzerland and the Tyrol, von Pressell established an international reputation and in 1872 became technical adviser to the sultan to develop railways in Turkey. Studying the whole situation, he envisioned a vast system of railroads extending from the borders of Austria-Hungary to the Persian Gulf: a system that would unite the scattered provinces of the Ottoman Empire strategically and politically; facilitate commerce by resuscitating the ancient caravan route from the Persian Gulf to the Mediterranean ports and connect the hinterlands with the markets; open up agriculture and penetrate the hitherto inaccessible mineral areas so rich in Mesopotamia and Anatolia. His dream became that of William II and the German expansionists and eventuated in the great imperial enterprise of the Berlin-Bagdad Railway, of which we shall hear more later.

In von Pressell's class as pioneers of expansion belong all the engineers who planned and executed those iron backbones of colonial penetration: the Cape-to-Cairo Railway, the Trans-Siberian Railway, the Chinese Eastern Railway and the like.

Similar to them also are those noted irrigation engineers, builders of the Assuan and Sennar dams on the Nile. One of these, Sir William Willcocks, said of Mesopotamia: "With the Euphrates and Tigris rivers really controlled, the delta of the two rivers would attain a fertility of which history has no record. The flaming swords of inundation and drought would have been taken out of the hands of the offended Seraphim and the Garden of Eden would have again been planted."

The Patriot-Expansionist

Finally, the patriot-expansionist who urged the acquisition of overseas annexations primarily in order to secure national prestige and greatness should be included among these agents of colonialism. There were many such and they were present in each interested state. To cite Sir John R. Seeley, their classic exemplar, will be to convey an idea of the service rendered by their group. One of the best known literary apologists of British imperialism, he wrote, as professor of history in Cambridge University, the kind of history calculated to charm the emotions of the protagonists of a greater England, and he harbored no other interest in colonies. In 1883 he published *The Expansion of England* in which he pointed out that the colonies were really an expansion of the English state, that imperial expansion constituted the British historic mission and that an England shorn of empire was to him synonymous not only with national degradation but with national ruin, for the future would belong to big states and England without a colonial empire would become a third-rate state in a world of empires. The book sold 80,000 copies in two years and exerted a wide influence in arousing expansionist sentiment not only among British leaders and statesmen who, like Lord Rosebery, accepted it as a guide to policy, but also among the general public whose patriotic pride it challenged.

What Seeley and other British writers accomplished for colonialism in the English language, Alfred Rambaud, professor of history at the Sorbonne and Paul Leroy-Beaulieu, professor of economics, achieved in the French tongue, and such nationalist historians as Treitschke in the German. "Every virile nation," asserted Treitschke, "has established colonial power," a theme destined to be elaborated in every possible variation and in almost every European tongue by the academic patriot-expansionists throughout the modern period of colonization overseas, even unto our own day. In the utterances of the dictators may be found the most exaggerated and flamboyant expression of the idea.

FORCES BEHIND THE PIONEERS—THE DYNAMICS OF EXPANSION

Turning now to the causes or forces present in each country that were responsible for these many pathfinders of expansion and their exploits, we find them to be basically two: the economic and the psychological, which happened to coincide at the beginning of this era. These were the second industrial revolution with all its works, and a self-conscious nationalism compounded of racial, cultural, religious, political and economic elements, all of which clamored for expression.

The Second Industrial Revolution

Just as the commercial revolution of the sixteenth and seventeenth centuries had required an industrial revolution, a shift to machine industry, in order to supply the needs of its far-flung markets overseas, so the second industrial revolution, itself hurrying country after country in both the eastern and western hemispheres into the machine age of the mid-nineteenth century, demanded in its turn more outlet markets and sources of raw material to satisfy the iron monsters, the machines; more food to still the hunger of increased populations produced by industrialization and withdrawal from the land; more opportunities for the investment of capital created by its own activity; and wider fields for the application of the science and techniques which the revolution itself had stimulated. Moreover, new and strange raw materials lacking in Europe were demanded by the new industry: increased machinery and locomotion demanded lubricating and fuel oils both vegetable and mineral; rubber was needed for tires; soap was in greater demand; textile fibers for electrical instruments; manganese, chrome ore, phosphates, lead, copper, gold.

In all these respects modern colonial expansion would seem to have possessed a certain economic inevitability. Free trade, *laissez-faire*, the cosmopolitanism of a Cobden began to fade in the scramble for markets; protection, national self-interest, neo-mercantilism loomed on the horizon. The cycle was rapidly completing itself: first, widespread industrialization; then keen competition and a race for markets; then protection, tariffs, colonies.

An essential corollary of this accelerated economic development was the rise of industrial or capitalistic democracy. By the

decade of the eighties, it had placed the business middle class in
direct or indirect power in those states where industry had supplanted agriculture as the economic basis of wealth. Naturally
it followed that these "captains of industry," manufacturers of textiles and machinery, shipbuilders, bankers and financiers, should
influence the government, if necessary, in the direction of their
own business interests; expressions, such as "the flag follows
trade," became a commonplace. When Henry Stanley, for instance, returned from Africa to report on his discoveries in the
Congo, he recognized this fundamental fact, for when he put his
case before the Manchester Chamber of Commerce he said:
"There are 40,000,000 of people beyond the gateway of the Congo
and the cotton spinners of Manchester are waiting to clothe
them." Continuing, he remarked that one Sunday dress alone for
each native would mean, annually, 320,000,000 yards of Manchester cloth. Stanley knew that he was appealing to the class in a
position to vote credits and influence their foreign ministers to
promote British expansion in Central Africa had they so willed.[1]

As for the foreign ministers and statesmen, they, ever responsive
to public pressure, were either already convinced of the political
and economic exigency of overseas activity, like Gambetta, Ferry
and Bismarck, or became easily converted like Rosebery upon
reading Seeley's classic *The Expansion of England*. At any rate,
they too became "apostles of expansion," often leading their governments into adventurous and daring exploits abroad in order to
deflect the minds of the peoples from domestic social ills, for
reasons of patriotism or for personal glory. As for the peoples of
Britain, France, Germany, Belgium, Italy, they, then as now, had
little to say in foreign policy and were dazzled by the appeals to
patriotism, religion and humanitarianism, by the "Land of Hope
and Glory" complex, or by the pleasure of tracing the extension of
their national possessions on the map of Africa or Asia.

Nationalism

In addition to the economic necessity, there was the psychological necessity for expansion. An exaggerated national self-con-

---

[1] The Manchester Chamber of Commerce had not yet awakened to the
economic situation in Africa and at this time did not "will," so that Stanley
carried his opportunities to Leopold of Belgium, who took advantage of them.

sciousness both begetting and begotten by a cultural and racial rivalry, as well as by an economic and political competition, entered an acute stage during the last quarter of the nineteenth century. This rising tide of nationalism was, moreover, sung by poets, expounded and exploited by historians, biologists, by religious and racial enthusiasts. Tennyson, Kipling and others were embroidering poetically the theme of empire for

"All the loyal hearts who long
To keep our English Empire whole";

and missionary zealots were singing

"Can we whose souls are lighted by wisdom from on high,
Can we to men benighted the lamp of life deny?"

At the same time Treitschke for Germany, Rambaud for Russia, Leroy-Beaulieu for France and Seeley for England were urging each for his own nation its historic mission of expansion; and Houston Stewart Chamberlain led the way as a protagonist of "Nordic superiority" to those "lesser breeds outside the law." Indeed, with the blow inflicted upon revealed religion by the triumph of Darwinism, it seemed as though the cult of nationalism were exalted to take its place; nationalism, itself, became a religion and was clothed with something of the same mysticism and romanticism.

Union of Nationalistic Romanticism and Industrial Materialism

Nationalistic romanticism united consequently with industrial materialism to demand colonial expansion: the former to satisfy its urge for power, prestige, adventure, a sense of superiority, a religious humanitarianism; the latter to translate these idealistic terms into the realism of increased business and trade, which in an industrial age is the only language that defines a "first-class" power. Just as romantic nationalism clothed the crass materialism of expansion with a beautiful idealism, with the concept of "the white man's burden," with humanitarianism and uplift of the "little brown brothers," so materialism with its "economic necessity" advanced the national arguments of "surplus population," outlets for capital and a bursting overproduction. In other words, Christianized Hottentots could be introduced to straw hats and tooth-brushes. It also pointed out to the idealists the necessity for self-sufficiency, for monopoly in the control of those raw materials which science was making so important. To control rubber, oil, sugar, palm oil, coffee, metals, minerals, phosphates, meant an expanded and a more secure nationalism. Economic materialism glorified monopoly as romantic nationalism. In short, psychology and religion and economics united to produce a demand for colonial expansion that brooked no resistance.

So it transpired that the idealists, scientists, missionaries, explorers, became allies of the materialists, the traders, promoters, capitalists, diplomats; and served with them as pathfinders of the new colonial movement. Thus a David Livingstone, actuated in the beginning by purely idealistic and spiritual motives, initiated a train of events ending with the practical "promoter" work of a Henry Stanley and the sordid materialism of a Belgian Congo; a Dr. Fabri, inspector for the Rhine mission, extended his oversight of things spiritual to things commercial and carved out not so much the contours of the kingdom of God, as those of the kingdom of German South West Africa; while two Roman Catholic missionaries, emissaries of their Holy Church, murdered by Chinese bandits in Shantung province, provided the foundation of a German naval base in the Far East. Even more obviously, a grateful France recognized her debt to her gallant soldier-explorer Marchand by a diplomatic bargain that secured her African empire; a not-so-grateful Bismarck realized the expediency of utilizing the pioneer work of an adventurous Karl Peters; while a wise England shaped her foreign policy to gain from the extensive explorations of her Sir Harry Johnston.

Opposition to Expansion

The compelling force of the new colonialism may be measured only when placed in its historic setting: the general and widespread opposition to any form of expansion which dominated western Europe during the first three quarters of the nineteenth century. The present movement sprang from a decidedly negative if not hostile background, as far as public and private opinion was concerned. Since the beginning of the nineteenth century, the shift in economic opinion from mercantilism to *laissez-faire* had produced among the great powers a lull in their enthusiasm for colonies, which had dominated the seventeenth and eighteenth centuries, if not a positive aversion to them. By 1800 the colonial monopoly of the sixteenth, seventeenth and eighteenth centuries had been broken. Both Spain and France were out of the race and England, in possession of the largest share, had temporarily lost her appetite for more, especially when she remembered the loss of her American possessions. Embarked upon her free-trade era and intent on building up her unprecedented industrial supremacy, Great Britain heeded the words of Adam Smith and rested content with her already far-flung possessions which had been materially increased by the treaty of Vienna. As her industry prospered along with her *laissez-faire* (unrestrained capitalism) and she became the "work-shop of the world," apathy towards colonies changed to active anti-expansionism; even to a movement aimed at the ultimate disruption of the empire. The "little Englanders" numbered among their leaders the best brains of the country: men like Gladstone, Bright, the young Disraeli; members of the colonial office itself not only opposed further expansion but advocated the voluntary and peaceful separation of the colonies from the mother country. They visualized England's colonial mission as that of creating free, independent communities in all parts of the world enjoying the benefit of British institutions. Indeed, the senior members of Gladstone's cabinet, Lords Derby, Northcourt, Selbourne and Harcourt, heartily fought imperialistic expansion, opposed only by the two radical members.

In France, opposition to her original colonial tradition was fully supplied by the indifference to colonies generated in the work of her eighteenth century philosophers, especially the Physiocrats; by the ensuing era of economic liberalism; and by the ideas of "liberty, equality, fraternity" which discouraged coercion and suppression at home and abroad. Moreover, the bedraggled appearance and unprosperous condition of those remnants of her first colonial empire lent support to anti-expansionism. The *colonies anciennes*, a few sugar islands, the fragments of St. Pierre and Miquelon, five towns in India, these held no allure for further overseas ventures. The total commerce of this "colonial empire" equalled about 600,000,000 francs a year, one third of which was in foreign hands; while the cost to France, Algeria constituting the largest item, amounted to about 30,000,-000 francs annually. Add to this the failure of the Mexican project in the sixties, the victory of democratic theory in the Third French Republic of the seventies and adequate explanation of French repugnance to colonies is obvious—a popular repugnance which always existed among the people even in the great age of expansion.

In Germany, likewise, the government of the lately united nation was opposed to colonies because unready for them. Before 1870, the official attitude of the German states had, like that of France and England, been one of *laissez-faire* towards individual effort in colonization, of merchant, trader or explorer. Sporadic and scattered attempts had been made to induce both the single and the combined state governments to take some action but they had all come to nothing. After unification and the establishment of the empire, the time for official action seemed more than ripe to the colonialists; but throughout the seventies Bismarck warded off their importunities and successfully avoided the adoption of a colonial policy before he had set his united Germany in order.

For quite the opposite reason, satiety of rich possessions, the Netherlands rested from further acquisitions. She was very active in trade with her vast colonial empire but was not, apparently, desirous of acquiring more. As for the remaining countries, little Belgium's potentiality as the ruler of a future colonial empire sixty times her own size had not yet, before 1870, been dreamed of; Italy and Japan were as yet too young in nationalism and had no inkling of their future imperialistic destinies. Even Russia's insatiable desire for the Dardanelles and the Near East had been temporarily lulled by her defeat in the Crimean War.

No doubt can exist that the idea of colonial expansion was unpopular with the European states, their governments nor their peoples before the last quarter of the nineteenth century. Nevertheless, so strong were the roots of the new colonialism embedded in the economic, political and cultural trends of the age, that the time was not far distant when it would overthrow all resistance and itself dominate the international scene.

READINGS

Barnes, H. E.   *World Politics in Modern Civilization*, 1930.
Bodelson, C. A.   *Studies in Mid-Victorian Imperialism*, 1925.   Abstract, philosophical.
Clark, G.   *The Balance Sheets of Imperialism*, 1936.   Statistical survey.
Green, J. F.   *The British Empire Under Fire*, 1940.   Foreign Policy Association.   Recent summary.
Hobson, J.   *Imperialism*, rev. ed. 1938.   Excellent, critical.
Hocking, W. E.   *Spirit of World Politics*, 1932.   Excellent.
Horrabin, J. F.   *An Atlas of Empire*, 1937.   Excellent.
Husain, M.   *The Quest for Empire. An Introduction to the Study of the Contemporary Expansionist Policy of Japan, Italy, Germany*, 1937.   Well balanced.
Langsam, W. C.   *In Quest of Empire: The Problem of Colonies*, 1939.   Foreign Policy Association.   Concise summary.
Moon, P. T.   *Imperialism and World Politics*, 1926.   Basic.
Muir, R.   *Expansion of Modern Europe*, 1925.   Old but useful.
Viallate, A.   *Economic Imperialism and International Relations*, 1923.   Useful.
Woolf, L.   *Economic Imperialism*, 1920.   International and anti-imperialist.
Wright, Q.   *Mandates under the League of Nations*, 1930.   Complete treatment.

PART II

Modern Colonial Expansion in the African Continent

CHAPTER THREE

Africa's Invitation to European Expansion

GEOGRAPHY AND RESOURCES

THE CONTINENT of Africa is no longer "dark" and is far from being "unknown." No square mile of it remains unpainted by the color of a great power, be that color laid on with a light or a heavy stroke. (Possibly Egypt may be excepted.) When Italy captured her Ethiopian empire, the last citadel of the African fell. Even Liberia, the so-called Negro republic, occupies a special position, owing to the interest, political, economic and sentimental, taken in her independence by the United States. Travel bureaus include Africa in their scheduled tours. Big-game hunting no longer inspires the thrill of danger and adventure, so perfected has become its technique, so standardized and accurate the equipment. Recently two men with motorcycles crossed the continent at its broadest part. The French are building motor roads through the once trackless Sahara, and Mussolini attempted to reclaim the sandy wastes of Libya. One can attend the cinema in Timbuctoo; ride through parts of the jungle in a Ford; and penetrate the mists of this once "darkest Africa" by gazing down

45

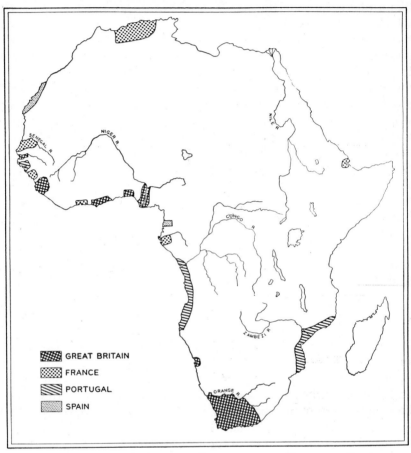

AFRICA ABOUT 1870, SHOWING POSSESSIONS OF EUROPEAN STATES

from the soaring liners of Imperial Airways, Linea del Impero or of Air France.

This startling transformation has been wrought since 1871 and is the product of modern colonialism with its capitalistic power and its scientific technique.   In 1871, an inaccessible and inhospitable continent jealously guarded Africa's indigenous treasures of gold, diamonds, rubber, ivory, ebony, copra, cocoa, groundnuts and palm oil; its potential resources of sisal, coffee, cotton, grazing lands and waterpower; and its natural highways of commerce, its sweeping rivers and vast inland lakes.   For Africa is like a plate rising on the edges to ranges of hills and mountains which roughly parallel the coast and repel invasion. Even its rivers are disappointing as entrances to the interior: they are guarded by deltas at their mouths that hamper navigation and by rapids and falls further up where the rivers break through the continental mountain ranges. Impenetrable, fever-infested jungles, savage and often cannibalistic tribes, interminable desert stretches, a mountainous east coast affording few harbors—Norway has a longer coast line than all Africa—and a low-lying, marshy, death-dealing west coast, known as the "white man's grave," effectually limited alien settlement. Only a narrow strip along the north coast between the Mediterranean Sea and Sahara, the southern tip of the continent at Cape Colony and Natal, and scattered trading posts and former slave stations along the west coast, were occupied by outsiders: Turks, Boers, British, Portuguese and a few French and Spaniards. With these exceptions, Africa in 1871 belonged to the Africans and the Arabs; the so-called indigenous peoples dominated the continent.

The Natives, Their Lands and Climate

Who are these Africans, the natives? It has long been customary in accounts of colonial expansion to neglect the indigenous peoples for the alien invaders. Naturally, the exploits and triumphs of the colonizing powers have dominated colonial history. The natives have sunk into obscurity just as they themselves, their lands, their resources and their cultures have fallen before their mighty and industrialized European conquerors. Recently many signs bear witness that this subjection, this abnegation of self and possessions, is not so complete nor final as would appear on the surface. To mention but a few indications of this fact: the triumph of the Egyptian nationalists; the Arab nationalist movement profoundly shaking northern Africa and the Near East, a veritable mass unrest; the stubborn resistance of certain Ethiopian tribes to Italian conquest; the crucial struggle in Kenya over the lands; the strength of the "Destour" or "Constitution" party among the Moslems in Tunisia; the strike and boycott for economic freedom on the Gold Coast; the assertion in the British White Paper of 1923 that the "interests of the natives must be paramount"; and the growing interest and research in social anthropology that is gradually changing the superiority complex of the conquerors. Assuredly all these signs indicate a surging native self-consciousness that cannot be ignored by students of the problem of empire. In the words of a famous social anthropologist, such students need to "know the natives." Let us turn to a brief survey of them.

The present population of Africa is the result of a series of immigrations which drove before them and in some cases exterminated the primitive peoples, the Bushmen, Hottentots, Pygmies who once existed far more abundantly and over a more widespread area than now in equatorial and southern Africa. Indeed, the Bushmen are all but extinct except in South West Africa and the Congo basin. Whence and under what pressure came these migrating peoples is largely a matter of speculation as is the time of their coming; but it is certain that across the land bridge into Egypt poured Asiatic Negroes, Caucasians, Malays, Polynesians, Hamites and Semites as well as a variety of folk from Asia Minor, Syria, Mesopotamia, Arabia, Turkey, whose later arrivals are of historic record. The result of these mass movements and displacements of the primitives has been to establish a diversity of peoples even more diffuse and numerous than in Europe—a racial diversity that matches the variety of geography and climate, both of which render Africa structurally lacking in cohesion and unity. To review the main characteristics of this domain, both physical and human together, is perhaps to acquire a more accurate picture.

The Southern Tip

Beginning in the south at Cape Colony a high plateau, reaching an elevation of 4,000 feet in places, stretches from the east to west. Covered with vegetation and situated in the temperate zone, it affords a rich agricultural life for the Boers. These people are the descendants of those early Dutch settlers who, themselves originally aliens, had achieved after three hundred years' occupancy, almost a native status in relation to the British, newcomers in 1815. Outnumbering the Boers almost three to one in 1871 were the non-European peoples: East Indians or Asiatics; the so-called Cape colored, a mixture of Asiatic, European and native; and a majority of native Africans who, coming out of central

Africa probably during the preceding five hundred years, had all but exterminated the aboriginal Hottentots and Bushmen. They consist mainly of Zulus or Kaffirs, Basutos and Bechuanas, all branches of the Bantu division of the Negro race, the youngest and toughest strain in Africa which dominated the sub-continent before the coming of the white man. This Bantu group is composed of Negro stock mixed considerably with Hamite, a straight-nosed and lighter-skinned people related to our own Caucasian type. Indeed, no full or true Negro tribe is found in South Africa. The Zulus were well-organized under their own kings and very warlike, as the long series of "Kaffir" wars fought in this region by the British bears witness. Together, these natives form an intelligent group of Negro stock, hunters and agriculturists for the most part, now completely submerged by the dominant Boers and British.

Equatorial Africa

The salubrious southern highlands, celebrated for their grass-covered veldt, merge into equatorial Africa, popularly known as the jungle: a tropical and sub-tropical region with its swamps and dense entanglements, its rank vegetation and teeming animal life, the vivid description of whose crocodiles and cobras has obscured the picture of its human inhabitants. Originally probably occupied by Pygmies, the Congo regions were conquered by the Bantu peoples who for self-preservation unified their various clans into native states ruled by able chiefs. Although depopulated and decimated by the well-organized Arab slave trade from the east and the European slave hunts from the west, firmly established states under powerful, native sovereigns were still in existence there in the 1880's. N'Tolela of San Salvador ruled the lower Congo; Putu Kasongo, the Kuango basin; the Balsabu people dominated a kingdom in Kasai; and powerful kings or chiefs ruled Ruanda and Kivu. This same tropical forest belt continues along the west coast occupied today by disorganized Negro groups with no large-scale central kingdoms, as formerly, before the coming of the white man. Such independent villages under local tribal control are found along the Ivory Coast, in Gabon and in French Guinea, although, today, they have forfeited all their real autonomy and live under alien centralization.

The Sudan

North of the tropical belt and stretching across the entire continent from Cape Verde on the west to the Nile Valley is the Sudan, the so-called "land of the blacks." More livable than equatorial Africa, it forms a rich agricultural region with its plains, grasslands, forests, rivers and steppes and supports a race of capable Negroes who from early days led a settled life and established organized kingdoms. Here dwell a medley of Negro tribes who vary from the shapely and self-respecting inhabitants of the uplands, with much Semitic and Hamitic blood, to the deteriorated but pure Negro peoples of the swamps on the Gulf of Guinea. Indeed, the real Negro today is largely confined to the region bounded by the Niger River and Senegal, although typical Negroes as individuals occur almost anywhere in Africa. Long contact with the Mohammedans of the north through commerce and conquest resulted in a high civilization with a stronger political organization for this region. Evidences of these once remarkable kingdoms remained in the 1880's and 1890's in the well-knit empires of the sultans of Sokoto and of Gando; in the tenacious power of the emirs with whom the Royal Niger Company wrestled and finally signed treaties; and in the strong states of the Wadi and Azande sultans of the upper Ubangi regions.

Besides these groups dominated by the Mohammedans in this area there were many mixed races, closely akin to the Moors, such as the Fulani, Tworegs, Ouolofs, as well as negroid peoples who established and maintained independent states. Typical of these were the Yorubas occupying the hinterland of Lagos, supposed to have come originally from upper Egypt. When the Europeans invaded their lands, the Yorubas, numbering about 5,000,000, had reached a high political and cultural stage of development, were agriculturists and lived in well-constructed walled cities, one of which, Ibadan, contained a larger population than Harlem in New York City. Their paramount chief was a sort of emperor under whom semi-feudal, military rulers presided over the states comprising his empire.

Illustrative also of the self-conscious independence of the peoples of this region is the history of the Ashantis of the Gold Coast and their "Golden Stool" or king's seat, a symbol of nationhood, by which the king or chief holds his authority. Among these people there is no such thing as divine right but each chief holds his authority by consent of the majority of the people who can "de-stool" him at will. When the British were conquering this region, they demanded that the Ashantis deliver up the "Golden Stool." Their refusal precipitated a long and bitter war during which the "stool" mysteriously disappeared. In 1922, in order to strengthen their prestige in Ashantiland, the British made the diplomatic gesture of restoring the "stool" which had as mysteriously been re-discovered. On that occasion, the king of the Ashantis said to the British representative: "The 'Golden Stool' is very great. It contains the soul of a nation." As the British and French discovered to their great cost this entire "land of the blacks" possessed strong rulers, efficient organization and a high civilization rooted deep in history.

The Northern Coastland

North of the Sudan stretches the desert belt occupied by the Sahara and the Nubian and Libyan deserts, directly across the continent from the Atlantic Ocean to the Red Sea. These arid wastes divide the "land of the blacks" from the "white man's" country which today extends along the entire coast of North Africa. The deserts are inhabited by Arabs, Berbers and, to the south, the Sudanese Negroes. Forming a transitional racial zone, this region is almost as changing with its nomadic population as is its physical aspect of shifting sands, scattered oases and misty, nebulous mirages.

Emerging from such an exotic backdrop is the Mediterranean littoral extending from Egypt to the Pillars of Hercules, as different from the rest of Africa as is literally "black from white." Geologically and climatically more like southern Europe than central Africa, this narrow coastland lies in the temperate zone, is suited to white settlement and cultivation, and forms the southern shore of that great highway of ancient medieval and modern commerce, the Mediterranean Sea. Consequently it has been in contact with Asia from prehistoric times and with Europe for at least two millenniums. Colonizing Phoenicians and Greeks, conquering Greeks, Romans, Vandals, Arabs and Turks and, in the modern period, British, French, Spaniards, Italians have all occupied this narrow fringe, almost as disconnected from the rest

of Africa as the lands from whence they came. Superimposing
their successive cultures and civilizations upon it with their capitalization of its unique agricultural, commercial and strategic resources, all these non-Africans have but added a racial and cultural isolation of North Africa to the already existent geographical
and climatic differences, thereby materially increasing African
disunity.

East Africa

To this general survey from South to North Africa must be
added a special description of country and people along the
eastern part of the continent, the land of the high mountains
and great inland lakes. A territory of great natural beauty with
Mount Kilimanjaro rising to 19,000 feet, Mount Mera to 15,000
feet and the Usambara range running down to the coast, it contains the sources of the Nile, Lakes Victoria, Tanganyika and
Tana. Here are situated the huge plains and rolling, dry bush of
Tanganyika Territory, the high, cool uplands of Kenya, the little
hills of Uganda clothed in intense tropical greenery and, off the
coast, the beautiful islands of Zanzibar and Pemba.

Geographically and climatically suited to white settlement, this
eastern region early attracted Asiatics who, like the sultans of
Zanzibar and Witu, organized powerful states, promoted a far-
flung slave trade and a monopolistic clove trade, and gave an
oriental, near-eastern character to their lands. It also invited
migration and settlement of native Negroes who established strong
independent kingdoms, such as the Bantu in Uganda; the mixed
Hamites and Semites in Abyssinia, whose king claimed descent
from Solomon and the Queen of Sheba; and the Watusi in Belgian Ruanda. These peoples are not pure Negro (the true or
full Negro is not found in East Africa) but rather mixed with
a considerable degree of Hamite, akin to the Caucasians and
ancestors of the Egyptians. Less Hamitized, lighter and less
negroid are the handsome and physically attractive Masai, the
industrious, sociable Kikuyu in Kenya and the ancient Baganda
nation which ruled for thousands of years over Uganda, the most
highly organized kingdom in tropical Africa. Of the Baganda,
Lord Lugard remarked that no purely pagan tribe has ever developed so extraordinary a social, political and even legal system.

All these peoples are as closely related in blood and physical type to men of southern Europe or of the Near East as to the Negro of West Africa. They have invaded East Africa within the last thousand years, driving out the primitives; and have differentiated these high, salubrious areas in population and civilization from the lowlands of the east where Nilotic peoples prevail.

It will be seen even from this brief survey that the African natives may not be dismissed as "savages" or as "niggers." To quote Julian Huxley: "All the peoples of Africa, save perhaps the Pigmies and the Bushmen, have an elaborate social organization which contains many admirable features. They have their systems of law and justice, of ownership, of council, of morals, of village and tribal administration, even in some degree of education and notably of mutual aid. Sometimes, large and elaborate kingdoms with a more or less feudal organization and even with official historians have come into existence. . . . The basis of organization is the clan and the outlook which resulted from that fact as well as many other of their ideas is so alien to our own that many Europeans never enter the African's mental atmosphere, never grasp the meaning of his institutions and ideas. This will overlook one half of native life and find the other ridiculous or incomprehensible." [1]

That the native, on the other hand, finds the white men, his conquerors, incomprehensible or ridiculous is a fact rapidly being established by anthropologists as they penetrate deeper and deeper into the life and art of primitive peoples. As one of them has recently shown, the African "primitives" gave way to the white men at first but now they are beginning to know him.[2] Their artists portray him honestly in caricature, in portraits, in the abstract; and in the honesty of the conception there exist humor, amusement and sarcasm. The fine bronze castings of the Bungi of Nigeria, the wood-carvings and terra-cotta work of the Congo tribes, the plastic models of the West Africans and multitudes of similar art forms often reflect what the black man has observed in his white conquerors: the greed of the merchant; the mechanical stupidity of the soldier; the prideful arrogance of the official; the sometimes helpless piety of the missionary; along with the fear, the awe and the terror which the conqueror inspires.

---

[1] Huxley, Julian, *Africa View*, p. 15.
[2] Lips, J., *The Savage Hits Back.*

REASONS FOR SPARSE SETTLEMENT IN 1871

With something of the geography, climate and peoples of Africa in mind, reasons to explain the sparse settlement of Europeans there in 1871 are not hard to discover. Even by 1876, only 10 per cent of the continent was under white occupation. Modern science had yet to provide the facilities whereby the white man could penetrate the jungles with his steel rails; could transport the munitions to break down and destroy the strong, well-organized native kingdoms; could combat the deadly, tropical diseases with his medical knowledge. The Turk maintained his age-old rule from Egypt to the Pillars of Hercules along the Mediterranean shore, with the exception of French Algeria and Morocco; the Arab was entrenched on the east coast and the Boer in Cape Colony; while strong, well-established native empires and kingdoms held their separate sway in Abyssinia, the Sudan, in Uganda and in the Congo. The disunion of Africa: its mixture of peoples, races, topography, geography and climate, formed a real obstacle to penetration.

More potent, perhaps, than any other reason for the sparseness of European settlement in 1871 was the fact that Europe did not need Africa—yet. Her development had not quite reached the expanding point; but, as noted previously, definite economic, political and cultural forces were at work to precipitate that need in the future. Meanwhile the pathfinders of expansion, the traders, missionaries, explorers, scientists, were already in Africa preparing that continent's response to Europe's demands when the time should arrive. By 1871, the sources of the Nile had been discovered by Burton, Speke and Baker; the Niger traced to its beginnings and its outlets by Caillé, Clapperton and the Lander brothers; the Lake Chad regions explored. Heinrich Barth and Paul du Chaillu had penetrated the hinterland of the Cameroons and the great northwest; a German scientist, Fretsch, had studied the mineralogy of Morocco. British missions had long been active in Nigeria, in Madagascar; the German Baseler Mission was in South West Africa; the Bremen Mission in Togoland; while French Catholics had long since carried the Cross even into the Congo. Besides signs of reviving life in the old trading centers, British, French and Portuguese, new commercial activity was astir: the British in South Africa, in the east and on the west coast where the Royal Niger Company was establishing its monopoly; German traders from the Hanse towns had won footholds on the east coast where the Woermann Line ran a packet; the French governors in Senegal were becoming sensitive to the need of a hinterland for their scattered parts. In short, the response to an external demand for colonial penetration was well-prepared in Africa should the compelling impetus arise.

National Interest in Africa Supplants the International

Late nineteenth century nationalism, compounded of economic, political and cultural ingredients described above, supplied the requisite stimulus. After 1871, missionary activity, trading ventures and even scientific inquiry in Africa came to assume a distinctly nationalistic character. While hitherto the opening up of the "dark continent" had evoked international interest strongly tinged with an altruism and a humanitarianism that emphasized its cosmopolitan character, after 1871, approximately, the era of universal scientific exploration and of humane objectivity ended and the age of nationalistic partition set in. The background of this change may be observed concretely in the growing revolt against liberalism in England, the shifting temper of Anglo-German relationship and the increasing economic rivalry of these two powers. The "little Englander" policy of a Gladstone who, believing that the inevitable separation of colonies from the mother country should be voluntarily and peacefully permitted, was giving way to the cold logic of national interest voiced and practised by the imperialists, Disraeli, Salisbury and Rosebery. Serious competition from German industrialists and travelers was making itself felt; ground was being lost in some foreign markets and in the home markets for some products. Germany was promoting the protectionism of Bismarck who, by 1880, had definitely aligned himself with the "national interest" school, established as early as 1841 by Friedrich List in his *National System of Political Economy* which advocated a strong colonial policy in all its phases. Indeed, during the eighties, Anglo-German economic, naval, colonial and national rivalry, which was to rise to its calamitous crescendo in the decade before the first World War, was taking deep root. Specifically indicative of the change from the international to the national attitude towards Africa was the work of the Geographical Congress summoned in 1876 at Brussels by Leopold II of Belgium, that shrewd and early protagonist of modern colonial expansion. Highly intelligent, interested in science, exploration, modern industry, he seemed to sense before other European statesmen the unlimited opportunities for economic gain afforded by the uncut melon of central Africa. Upon Leopold's invitation, scientists, explorers and travelers representing seven states assembled to discuss the opening up of Africa to civilization, termed by Leopold "a crusade worthy of this century of progress." The result was the formation of the International African Association for the Exploration and Civilization of Central Africa; commercial or economic motives were not mentioned. It was not to function internationally, however, as its name implied, but nationally through committees formed by each state. Indeed, its machinery is one of the best concrete evidences of the transition from the mid-century idea of humanitarian internationalism to the modern reality of selfish nationalism. Even more significant still, England formed her own national committee having no connection with the association at all. As one student of this conference has suggested, the international character of the association was but a cloak for furthering nationalistic ends.

Other signs of a shift from the cosmopolitan-international to the competitive-national attitude towards Africa were not wanting at this time. Voices arose, singly at first, and then multiplying to form a veritable chorus, calling for national colonial action and eventually drowning out the anti-expansionists or winning them over. In England, the influence of the anti-colonial school culminated at the end of the sixties while that of the imperialists superseded it during the seventies and eighties. The voices of Froude, Foster, Tennyson, Jenkins and Wilson were forerunners of the more confident imperialists such as Seeley, Lord Rosebery, Dilke and Disraeli. The Royal Colonial Institute was founded in 1868 with the purpose of winning support for a "United Empire" and of combatting the "little England" ideal of Gladstone, who believed in inevitable imperial disintegration; while the Imperial Federation League took shape in 1884 under the initiation of William Forster. As suggested before, a change was sweeping over England: her industrial monopoly was being challenged and her halcyon days of *laissez-faire* were fast receding as the Victorian era marched to its climax. In Germany, the rising colonial cult constructed by publicists, merchants, explorers, economists during the forties, fifties and sixties culminated in two stirring books: Fabri's *Does Germany Need Colonies?*, a rhetorical question answered with a resounding affirmative; and Hübbe-Schleiden's *Deutsche Kolonisation,* in which the author emphasized the life-and-death nature for Germany's future of a strong expansion policy. While in France, Leroy-Beaulieu wrote: "Colonization is for France a question of life or death"; the study of peoples, customs, cultures overseas was taken up with enthusiasm; and Jules Ferry and Gambetta discounted popular apathy towards colonization and demanded an active and far-reaching program of expansion.

More effective than mere demands for nationalistic expansion overseas was its spectacular dramatization by Leopold II when he sent Henry Stanley back to the Congo in 1879 to seize what he could of it before some other power got ahead of him. The shrewd Leopold had lent a more favorable ear than had the Manchester Chamber of Commerce to Stanley's account of the rich, economic potentialities of Central Africa which he had so carefully estimated as he searched for the lost David Livingstone. It will be recalled that Livingstone, that stubborn Scottish missionary, sent out by the London Missionary Society as an emissary of the then-prevailing objective humanitarianism towards the "heathen," soon turned explorer after he reached Bechuanaland in 1840. Absorbed in important discoveries in the region of the Zambesi River and of the territory later called Rhodesia, he became altogether the explorer in 1858. By that time, acting upon the conviction that European settlement alone could promote the civilization of central-eastern Africa and put an end to the Arab slave trade, that "open, running sore," he advocated the three C's, commerce, colonization and Christianity, and practically prepared the way for them by searching for a route into the interior. It was during his explorations to find the sources of the Nile that news from him ceased and Henry Morton Stanley, commissioned by James Gordon Bennett of the *New York Herald*, was sent to find him.

Stanley was well-fitted for the task: born in Wales as John Rowland, brought up in a workhouse, he had knocked about the world, finding his way finally to New Orleans where he was adopted by Henry Stanley, a cotton broker. He fought on both sides during the Civil War and then turned to journalism, to which he contributed one of the most memorable newspaper stories by finding David Livingstone in the Lake Tanganyika region of Central Africa. But Stanley found something else besides Livingstone: he discovered and publicized the vast economic possibilities of the Dark Continent. No one has done more to advertise its vast riches or to incite the ensuing international rivalry over their acquisition, than Stanley.

To be sure, Leopold dispatched Stanley back to Africa in 1879 as an agent of and under the auspices of the *Comité d'Etudes du Haute Congo*, a section of the newly founded International Association. But the Belgian king really financed him and, moreover, kept his mission a secret, with the result that the other members of the International Association were suddenly confronted with a Stanley Pool and a Leopoldsville, certainly not "internationalized" trading posts along the coveted Congo River. In alarmed response, France immediately sent her de Brazza, Germany her Nachtigal and England began negotiations with Portugal to guarantee her alleged "sovereignty" over the mouth of the Congo. The national "scramble" for Africa was on.

This story of the "lost" Livingstone and Stanley's successful search for him as recounted in his *Through Darkest Africa* is known to every schoolboy, and its real significance resides not in the narrative but in the picture it reveals of the motives, processes and results of modern colonial expansion. It not only draws them all together and presents them, as it were, in a microcosm but it differentiates between the fundamental and the superficial, between the real and the illusory, between the actual reasons for national imperialism and its apologetics. We see the missionary and humanitarian Livingstone becoming the nationalistic explorer; the adventurer and explorer Stanley turning into a keen, economic imperialist; the scientist, geographer Leopold transformed into a shrewd empire builder; while the whole story is shot through with intimations of the coming struggle for political prestige and national colonial rivalries, only dimly sensed by the powers at that time. It is customary to attribute the opening up of Africa to Livingstone, Stanley and Leopold II; but they chanced to be the instruments of vital forces already underway in Africa and Europe which were destined to inaugurate modern colonial expansion. A Karl Peters, a Marchand, a Ferry might just as well have substituted for them.

The Berlin Act

Final evidence of the inauguration of the era of nationalistic partition of Africa may be found in the Berlin Conference which met in Berlin in 1884 and produced the Berlin Act. The Conference originated in the resentment felt by the other powers against the Anglo-Portuguese treaty of 1884 which provided for Anglo-Portuguese control over navigation on the Congo. France and Germany, especially, considered their trade and interests in the Congo to be seriously threatened. Bismarck, now thoroughly aroused to Germany's colonial interests, issued invitations to a conference in co-operation with France. Its purpose was to consider freedom of trade in the Congo basin, freedom of navigation on the Congo and Niger rivers and the regulations of the colonial game in the African continent. For by this time, it was universally recognized that the era of partition had arrived and the Berlin Act of 1885 is symptomatic of the change.

Its main provisions emphasized nationalistic competition by definitely settling immediate difficulties and dictating the rules for future occupation; while vague and indefinite statements kept alive the illusion of internationalism and humanitarianism. Thus Portugal was denied control over the Congo's mouth but compensated with territory on the south bank; the Congo "Free State" under Leopold, the final metamorphosis of the International Association of the Congo, was recognized; the right of Europeans to extend their control over African territory regardless of existing non-European racial, political, social control or institutions was established; and, as the final irony, it was laid down that land to be legitimately claimed in future must be effectively occupied. On the other hand, the Act vaguely declared the neutrality of the Congo basin by leaving such neutrality optional to its future government[3]; created a commission with no power or money to maintain freedom of trade therein; and piously denounced the slave-trade without providing any means of destroying it. Thus, the Berlin Act reflects the realities of nationalistic, rival interests which triumphed over the ghosts of international altruism and humanitarianism. The complete document consists of sixty thousand words of which only two hundred were devoted to the natives; words concerned in no way with the black man's rights

---

[3] Leopold later exercised this option and declared the Congo neutral.

but devoted chiefly to slavery, from which the white men hoped to deliver him, and to his "welfare," with which they hoped to endow him.

With this international document the national game of colonial expansion in Africa was not only officially recognized; it was regulated and its rules defined and accepted by all. Let us now turn to its exciting prosecution.

READINGS

Beer, G. L. *African Questions at the Paris Peace Conference,* 1923. Detailed, technical.

DuBois, W. E. B. *Black Folk Then and Now,* 1939. Sympathetic.

Harris, N. D. *Europe and Africa,* 1927. Useful, factual.

Harris, N. D. *Intervention and Colonization in Africa,* 1914. Old.

Hertslet, Sir E. *Map of Africa by Treaty,* 1896. Basic source.

Hoskins, H. L. *European Imperialism in Africa,* 1930. *Berkshire Studies in European History.* Good, brief.

Huxley, J. *Africa View,* 1936. Comprehensive.

Johnston, H. H. *A History of the Colonization of Africa by Alien Races,* 1899. Old but useful.

Lucas, C. P. *Partition and Colonization of Africa,* 1922. Limited value.

Woolf, L. S. *Empire and Commerce in Africa,* 1920. Anti-imperialistic.

Wrong, M. *Land and Life of Africa,* 1933. Brief, popular.

CHAPTER FOUR

British Africa—Kinds of Colonies—How Held and How Acquired

Present Holdings

BRITISH AFRICA, in 1940, occupied 4,203,000 square miles of territory, more than one-third of the entire continent, and constituted 30 per cent of the area of the total British Empire. Beginning at the southernmost boundary of Egypt, now independent, these vast holdings stretched the entire length of Africa, embracing the Anglo-Egyptian Sudan, Uganda, Somaliland on the Red Sea, Kenya Colony, Tanganyika Territory, the Rhodesias, Bechuanaland, Nyasaland and the Dominion of South Africa, which was enlarged after the first World War by the addition of the Mandate of South West Africa, formerly a German colony.

This extensive area varies in climate from the tropic jungles of the Sudan and the hot deserts along the Red Sea to the salubrious highlands of East Africa; from the arid wastes of Bechuanaland to the high plateau of South Africa. It includes a chain of lakes which feed the great rivers of Africa, a fertility and altitude which make it suitable for white settlement, and rich minerals. Indeed, the Cape-to-Cairo territory constitutes the best part of Africa; it is the very backbone of the continent and it holds the key to its commerce.

But the Cape-to-Cairo stretch did not include all the British share in Africa. In the other half of the continent were found the holdings on the west coast, of which Nigeria is the prize. Almost four times the size of the United Kingdom, this colony lies wholly within the tropics. From its coastline along the Gulf of Guinea, it extends for miles inland west and north, reaching Lake Chad in its extreme northern boundary. Britain's other West African colonies lie further east and north, also along the southern Guinea coast: Gold Coast, Sierra Leone and Gambia. Survivals of a past age of trading posts and slave stations, they still serve as important ports and outlets for those commodities of the present industrial era which have superseded human cargoes, and facilitate a great prosperity, if a less gruesome one. Here also are situated the mandated territories, formerly German: Britain's share of Togoland, an enclave between the Gold Coast and French Dahomey; and of Cameroons, which lies between Nigeria and French Cameroons.

From the beginning of the age of modern expansion, the pattern of this contemporary British Africa just sketched in all its immensity had already appeared at three strategic points, West Africa, Cape Colony and Egypt. Its history since 1871 mainly concerns the development of these nuclei and the connecting of the last two into one unbroken continental stretch, the realization of the Cape-to-Cairo plan, which the first World War brought to completion.

BRITISH WEST AFRICA: *Nigeria, Gambia, Sierra Leone, Gold Coast, Mandated Territories, Togoland, Cameroons*

Nigeria

AREA: 338,593 square miles
POPULATION: 19,918,516
TRADE:[1] *Imports:*   £8,632,000
       From U.K.: £4,713,000
       Exports: £9,525,000
       To U.K.:   £4,647,000
(includes figures for Cameroons)

---

[1] Figures for the trade of the British colonies are taken from the *Statistical Abstract for the British Empire*, 1929-38. Those quoted are for the year 1938. Figures for bullion or specie are not included.

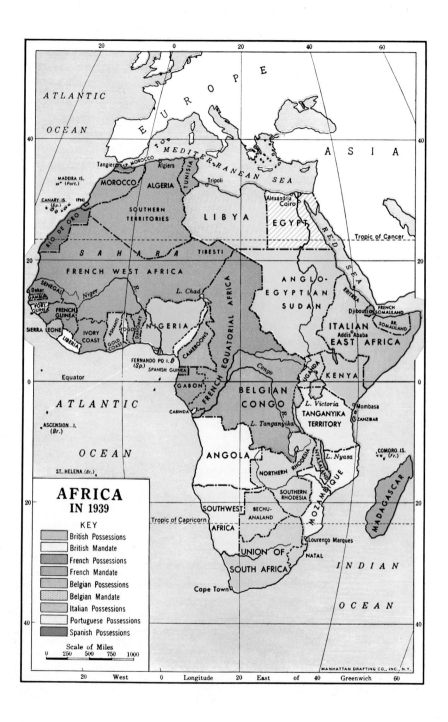

ATLANTIC
OCEAN

EUROPE

ASIA

MEDITERRANEAN SEA

Tangier SP. MOROCCO
Algiers
Tripoli

MADEIRA IS.
(Port.)
MOROCCO ALGERIA TUNISIA

CANARY IS. IFNI
(Sp.)

RIO DE ORO

SOUTHERN
TERRITORIES

LIBYA

Alexandria
Cairo
EGYPT

RED SEA

Tropic of Cancer

SAHARA

TIBESTI

FRENCH WEST AFRICA

SENEGAL Dakar GAMBIA
PORT. GUINEA
FRENCH GUINEA
SIERRA LEONE
LIBERIA
IVORY COAST ASHANTI GOLD COAST TOGO DAHOMEY
NIGERIA

Niger R.
L. Chad

CAMEROONS

FRENCH EQUATORIAL AFRICA

ANGLO-
EGYPTIAN
SUDAN

ERITREA

FRENCH
Djibouti SOMALILAND
BR.
SOMALILAND

ITALIAN
Addis Ababa
EAST AFRICA

FERNANDO PO I.
(Sp.) SPANISH GUINEA

Equator

GABON
CABINDA

Congo
BELGIAN
CONGO

Congo R.
L. Tanganyika

UGANDA
KENYA

L. Victoria Mombasa
TANGANYIKA
TERRITORY ZANZIBAR

ATLANTIC

OCEAN

ASCENSION I.
(Br.)

ST. HELENA (Br.)

ANGOLA

NORTHERN RHODESIA

L. Nyasa

COMORO IS.
(Fr.)

NYASALAND

MOZAMBIQUE

SOUTHERN
RHODESIA

MADAGASCAR

AFRICA
IN 1939

KEY

British Possessions
British Mandate
French Possessions
French Mandate
Belgian Possessions
Belgian Mandate
Italian Possessions
Portuguese Possessions
Spanish Possessions

Scale of Miles
0 250 500 750 1000

SOUTHWEST
AFRICA BECHU-
ANALAND

Tropic of Capricorn

UNION OF
SOUTH AFRICA

Cape Town

Lourenço Marques
NATAL

INDIAN

OCEAN

MANHATTAN DRAFTING CO., INC., N.Y.

20 West 0 Longitude 20 East of 40 Greenwich 60

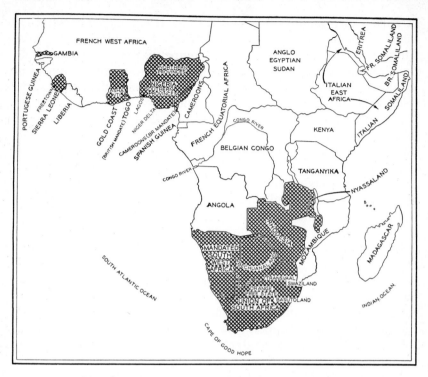

BRITISH WEST AFRICA AND BRITISH SOUTH AFRICA

Next to India, Nigeria is Great Britain's most valuable economic colonial possession. It comprises the basin of the Niger River, its tributaries and many deltas, an extensive sea coast as well as an inland lake, Lake Chad, thus forming an economic unit of commercial potentiality. Richly agricultural with a tropical climate hostile to white settlers, it is a land of native, peasant farmers and of European traders. The plantation system is unknown. Its principal crops consist of cocoa, cotton, palm kernels and groundnuts, the latter two yielding quantities of valuable oils and fats. Nigeria produces more food for home consumption than any other West African colony and, with the Gold Coast, one half the world's cocoa, while its exceedingly prosperous trade indicates its commercial importance to Great Britain with which, as it may be seen, half of its commerce is conducted. The control of the agricultural products, their marketing and distribution, is entirely in the hands of Europeans, mainly the great trading companies who likewise manage the importing and distribution of manufactured goods. These companies, like the Niger Company, now a subsidiary of the Unilevers Company, have divided the country into commercial zones where they fix prices, regulate production and manage trade relations between Africans and Europeans.

How Governed.   Nigeria is both a crown colony, on the coast at Lagos, and a protectorate inland.   Both units are amalgamated into a centralized control under a governor assisted by two lieutenant-governors and residents, the governor's special representatives and advisers at the courts of the native chieftains.   There is also a legislative council, which consists partly of elected or nominated members and partly of official members, the latter being in the majority, and which contains four elected Africans.

Nowhere is the British system of "indirect rule" more developed. Here a sort of "native state" structure exists in which the chieftains exercise considerable autonomy in local affairs.   They have their own courts, treasuries, police (unarmed), and vocational, medical, public works and other departments, free from the open control of the colonial, imperialist apparatus but at the same time subordinated to and dependent upon the central government for its authority.

How Acquired.   It was from Lagos at the outlet of the Niger River, seized by the British in 1851 in their fight against the slave trade, that Nigeria was developed.   British explorers had already set their seal upon the region: Mungo Park had first reached the Niger at the beginning of the nineteenth century and with the Lander brothers explored its tributaries, opening the way for European traders; the Clapperton expedition had penetrated the Lake Chad region and the basin of the lower Niger in the 1820's; while Major Lainy, in the same decade, reached the forbidden city of Timbuctoo.   But it was the trader and the merchant of the new age who became the real pathfinders of British colonization here as in so many places.   For Britain possessed certain great advantages at the beginning of the new colonial era: she controlled great markets, took the lead in power machinery and operated a great merchant fleet.   Moreover, the old demand for slaves as a trade commodity was rapidly being replaced by new needs, such as palm oil and the oil-yielding groundnuts which Africa could produce as readily as she had produced slave labor.   Social changes at home were creating an expanding market for soap and vegetable oils, while the new machinery, the railways and the steamships required lubricants in great quantities.

As the age of colonial competition dawned, therefore, the British traders determined to develop what they already possessed in West Africa. Blocked by the government-inspired encroachments of the French from penetrating the hinterlands of their three northernmost stations at Gambia, Sierra Leone and on the Gold Coast, they focused their efforts of expansion about Lagos. This station provided an excellent base from which to explore and exploit the many mouths of the Niger River debouching at this point through its delta. Here on the Oil Rivers they established trading posts and factories with the result that many commercial companies sprang up and prospered.

The story of Sir Goldie Taubman's exploits in amalgamating these separate companies into the Royal Niger Company, which, in turn, constructed the great Nigerian Empire, has already been related. But after the imperial government assumed control of the company's achievements in 1900, it pressed on with more expansion. The high commissioner, Colonel, later Sir, Frederick Lugard, undertook the task of pacifying the area north of the territory already occupied by the Royal Niger Company. Here its agents had already commenced the conquest of the powerful Mohammedan emirates who were strongly united into the Fulani Confederacy, which stubbornly resisted the British attempt to wrest all trading privileges from it. Only with ruthless and difficult fighting and the aid of superior forces and munitions was Lugard able finally to overthrow these once-mighty emirates of Sokoto, Kano, Katsina and Zuria, and establish the northern Nigeria protectorate in 1903.

Gambia and Sierra Leone

AREA: 4,069; 27,925 square miles
POPULATION: 197,811; 1,768,480
TRADE: *Imports*:   £277,000; £1,367,000
    From U.K.:   £127,000; £ 905,000
    Exports: £256,000; £2,158,000
    To U.K.:   £ 67,000; £1,227,000

Gambia and Sierra Leone have the distinction of being the two smallest colonies in British Africa. Nevertheless, despite their insignificant size, Sierra Leone controls the best navigable waterway on the west coast, namely, the upper reaches of the Niger River which extends 250 miles inland, while Gambia dominates the best roadstead. Like Nigeria, these two small settlements excel in native, agricultural produce which takes the form chiefly of palm kernels and groundnuts, so valuable for vegetable oils, and which constitute 96 per cent of Gambia's total export. Important, also, as trade depots, they enjoy a great prosperity. Unlike Nigeria, however, they lack hinterland because of the strongly entrenched position of the French in this area. But that does not prevent them from possessing a significant strategic value, for, on the one hand, they guard the terminal of the Benguella railroad which, traversing the African continent, connects the Atlantic and Indian Oceans; and, on the other, they provide the most important base, Freetown (Sierra Leone), along the West African coast for the British navy, which must protect the trade routes to South America, South Africa and to the East via the Cape of Good Hope. In this respect, Freetown serves the same purpose for the British as Dakar in French West Africa does for the French.

How Governed. Gambia and Sierra Leone are administered alike: their coastal regions, containing their capitals, Bathurst and Freetown, are crown colonies under governors aided by legislative and executive councils; their inland territories are protectorates governed by commissioners, European officials, aided by native chiefs and headmen appointed by the governors.

How Acquired. Gambia is the oldest British settlement in Africa, established in the sixteenth century as a slave station, while Sierra Leone, nearly as old, was originally visited by the Portuguese in the fifteenth century, and became the first British crown colony. After the abolition of the slave trade in the early nineteenth century, Sierra Leone developed into a settlement for freed slaves, for whom its capital, Freetown, became a center. As a consequence, these settlements lost their function as slave depots and sank into such unimportance that the British contemplated withdrawing from them entirely. For the systematic and extensive encroachment of the French upon their hinterland, during the 1870's, threatened also to render these two small colonies completely useless. The discovery, however, that they were capable of proving profitable markets and exchange stations for the commodities of a new age as they had been for those of the old led to their being retained by Britain as enclaves within the French territory.

The Gold Coast

> AREA: 78,802 square miles
> POPULATION: 3,230,550
> TRADE:[2] *Imports:*   £7,657,000
>   From U.K.:   £4,289,000
>   *Exports:*   £6,409,000
>   (exclusive of bullion)
>   To U.K.:   £2,550,000

Sometimes referred to as the "African Jewel" in the British crown, the Gold Coast possesses great mineral wealth, especially gold, diamonds and manganese. Celebrated for its alluvial gold from prehistoric times, the colony has exported this precious metal since the fifteenth century and, since 1900, has yielded £50,000,-000. Manganese constitutes its next important mineral, especially as the munitions industry has accelerated the demands for its products. The African Manganese Company's mines are some of the largest in the world, for Britain has taken care to provide herself with these essential supplies nearer home than those found in India.

In addition, the Gold Coast is agriculturally rich, like its neighbors, and produces palm oil, copra, cotton in large quantities and, above all, cocoa. During the first quarter of the twentieth century, the story of Gold Coast cocoa-raising is one of well-nigh unbelievable success. The first shipment abroad was made in 1891, amounted to 80 pounds and was vlaued at £4 sterling; by 1926, the crop had risen to 230,000 tons valued at £88,000,000. Although prices have fallen off in recent years, the output reached as much as 244,097 tons in 1932. Its cultivation is entirely in the hands of native farmers for the hot, damp climate prohibits white settlement as it does in the adjacent colonies. Europeans, consequently, are not the producers but rather the managers of the Gold Coast products. They devote their energies principally to mining

---

[2] Includes that of the mandated territory of Togoland.

operations and to trade and have met with phenomenal success in both as the above figures clearly reveal. The trade, it will be noted, is about 50 per cent with the British homeland.

How Governed. Like the other West African colonies, the Gold Coast consists of a crown colony, the coastal region, ruled by a governor aided by a legislative council; the Ashanti protectorate and the protectorate of the Northern Territories are under resident commissioners responsible to the governor. The governor may legislate for the protectorate independently of the council. A modified form of native indirect rule also exists. Each chief wields a certain amount of autonomy in local affairs in accordance with the laws and customs of the tribe. He and his native council are responsible to European political officers.

How Acquired. Like its neighbors, the Gold Coast colony is a survival from the British settlements of the sixteenth century which played such an important rôle as slave stations. During the seventeenth century, it experienced a bitter struggle between the British and the Dutch who fought for possession of the forts and trading posts along the coast, a struggle which was not settled in favor of the British until the latter part of the nineteenth century. Quarrels between the native tribes, the maritime Fantis and the inland people, the Ashantis, provided the British with an opportunity to penetrate the hinterland, which they did not hesitate to capitalize by inciting war among these factions in order to press their own advantage. But the warlike Ashantis inflicted a crushing defeat upon the British, who had temporarily allied themselves with the Fantis, and seriously weakened thereby the hold of the alien invader. As a result, the British government almost determined to withdraw entirely from the Gold Coast. As usual, however, a committee of merchants having interests here came to the rescue; they held on to the forts, cultivated closer friendship with the Fantis and promoted their own trade. So successful were they that towards the middle of the century (1844) the imperial government returned, negotiated a treaty with the Fantis as their allies and friends and not as a conquered people. Finally, the colonial rivalries of the 1870's led the British to buy out the remaining forts of the Dutch, while the French advance in Dahomey and the German seizure of neighboring Togoland in the eighties incited the complete conquest of the Ashantis and of the northern territories. The latter opposed a valiant but unsuccessful resistance, even dispatching a mission to London in 1894 to discuss terms with the imperial government. The colonial secretary refused to hear the Ashantis but advised them to submit in the face of force. The utmost effort was required to suppress them and only after a stubborn struggle were they ultimately conquered.

MANDATED TERRITORIES: *Togoland and Cameroons*

AREA: 13,041; 34,081 square miles
POPULATION: 341,254; 817,616
TRADE: [3]

British Togoland is akin in character to its nearby territory, Ashantiland, and the Gold Coast. Because of its bad climate and the absence of highlands, it has perforce been left to native peasant farmers who produce crops similar to those of its neighbors and in the same manner.

British Cameroons, on the other hand, situated in the fertile, equatorial zone, is a land of cocoa and cotton plantations managed by Europeans. When under German control, the government confiscated most of the highland territory and parcelled it out to white settlers and joint-stock companies. Expelled during the war, the former German plantation owners have been permitted to return and take up some of their former holdings.

How Governed. Togoland and Cameroons[4] are mandates of the B Class, which, according to Article 22 of the League of Nations Covenant, are described as follows: "Other peoples, especially those of Central Africa, are at such a stage that the Mandatory must be responsible for the administration of the territory under conditions which will guarantee freedom of conscience or religion, subject only to the maintenance of public order and morals, the prohibition of abuses such as the slave trade, the arms traffic and the liquor traffic, and the prevention of the establishment of fortifications or military and naval bases and of military training of the natives for other than police purposes and the defense of the

---

[3] Togoland's trade included in the figures for the Gold Coast, p. 67. Cameroons' trade included in the figures for Nigeria, p. 62.

[4] The name "Cameroons" is derived from a Portuguese word meaning "shrimps" or "prawns." Hence the "River of Prawns" or the Cameroons River, so named by Portuguese explorers.

territory, and will also secure equal opportunities for the trade and commerce of other members of the League."

For administrative purposes, Togoland has been placed under the governor of the Gold Coast Colony; while Cameroons has been incorporated into the neighboring colony of Nigeria.

How Acquired. Both these territories were the first to fall under Allied occupation early in the first World War and in 1916 were divided between England and France by a secret convention. With the allocation of the Mandates in 1919, almost one third of former Togoland, and one sixth of Cameroons were allotted to Great Britain.

BRITISH SOUTH AFRICA: *Union of South Africa, Mandated Territory of South West Africa, Bechuanaland, Basutoland, Swaziland, Rhodesia, Nyasaland.*

The Union of South Africa

AREA: 472,550 square miles.
POPULATION: Europeans, 2,034,534; Non-Europeans, 7,913,661
TRADE: *Imports:*   £95,612,000
From U.K.:   £41,446,000
Exports: £29,041,000   (exclusive of bullion)
To U.K.:   £10,730,000

Since 1910 one of the dominions of the British Commonwealth of Nations, the Union comprises the two old British colonies of the Cape and Natal and the two former Boer republics of the Transvaal and the Orange Free State. It lies between Cape Town, Durban and the Limpopo River, embracing an area which is eight times that of England and Wales. Geographically, this region constitutes a great, high plateau, three fifths of which rises to an elevation of from 3,000 to 5,000 feet above sea level; it is situated in the south temperate zone and is a land of prevailing sunshine. Thus the Union is a healthful and suitable place for European settlement. Cattle farming and sheep raising are pursued with success; cereals and fruits are raised in large quantities. But greater than its agricultural riches, South Africa possesses vast mineral wealth: the gold-mining industry in the Transvaal is the largest in the world; the diamond mines in Kimberly and near Pretoria are far-famed; coal and baser metals remain to be exploited.

The Cape has long been termed the "tavern of the seas" for its geographic position has made it a haven for many and various peoples: European and Asiatic, black, white and yellow, Afrikander or Boer, British, Bantu, Indian and Cape colored. Its racial question or "color bar" constitutes perhaps its most serious problem complicated by the accompanying land and labor difficulties. These are intensified, in turn, by the presence in South Africa of a strong feeling between conquered and conqueror, by the insistent demand for native rights and by the results of a growing impact of industrial capitalism on a large scale.

How Governed. The present government of the Union of South Africa resulted eventually from the Boer War (1899-1902) and was established January 1, 1910. It rests upon a federal constitution drafted in 1908 by a national convention in South Africa and approved by the British parliament as the South African Act in 1909. Thus it represents, in the first place, the will of the white people of South Africa made effective, in the second place, by the British parliament. The document provides for a federal government with power, as in England residing in parliament, and consisting of the governor-general, the agent of the king, the senate in which each province is represented by eight senators, and a house of representatives elected by popular, manhood suffrage, which, however, excludes the natives except in Cape Province. The lower house of the Union, which has always been dominated by the Boers, is supreme. Each province in the Union has its own government: a popularly-elected provincial council with legislative powers limited to such local concerns as education, hospitals, roads, local government and taxation within a restricted field; an administrator appointed by the Union government, and an executive committee. The power of the provincial government is, however, subordinated to that of the Union.

Chief among the Union's problems are: the demand for native franchise existent only in Cape Colony and even here recently curtailed by the Act of 1936 which withdrew from the natives the right to elect a native to the provincial council; the allocation of representation between Dutch and English; and the predominance of Boers in the government, some of whom wish complete independence. The reorganization of relationship with England brought about by the Statute of Westminster of 1931 whereby South Africa now possesses dominion status in the British Commonwealth has partially met the latter demand. Indeed, the Union of South Africa, itself, is a colonial power, for it administers the mandate of South West Africa assigned to it in 1919.

The Mandated Territory of South West Africa

AREA: 317,725 square miles
POPULATION: European, 30,000; Non-European, 359,516
TRADE: *Imports:*   £2,417,000
       From U.K.:   (not given)
       Exports: £3,547,000
       To U.K.:   £1,667,000

As a result of the first World War and conquest by Union troops, the former German South West Africa was awarded to the Union of South Africa as a C mandate. Geographically and climatically similar, it forms a natural, contiguous extension to the Dominion and is as much of a "white man's country." Because of the arid character of its high plateau, South West Africa is not so suitable for agriculture but mainly valuable for stock-raising; it also possesses some mineral wealth; its seaboard is almost harborless.

How Governed. According to the terms of the C mandates, South West Africa is administered as "an integral portion" of its mandatory. Hence the Territory is under an administrator, assisted by an executive committee and an advisory council. Some measure of self-government is provided by a legislative assembly, partly nominated and partly elected by European male suffrage. The Native Administration Proclamation of 1928 provides for a Chief Native Commissioner for the hearing of native cases, and deals with native control.

Although hers by virtual annexation, the Union of South Africa finds herself not entirely secure in her control of South West Africa. Here Germany's campaign for the return of her colonies has focused its intensity and Nazi diplomatic intervention in behalf of Germans has assumed a firm stand.

Bechuanaland

AREA: 275,000 square miles
POPULATION: 266,756

Basutoland

AREA: 11,716 square miles
POPULATION: 650,000

Swaziland

AREA: 6,704 square miles
POPULATION: 156,715

Geographically, these areas are part of the Union of South Africa but politically independent of the Dominion government. They constitute the remains of unconquered Africa brought under British protection by solemn agreement between blacks and whites. Bechuanaland is a district of arid deserts and grasslands lying directly north of the Union; Basutoland is a mountainous country situated like an island in its midst; while Swaziland on the southern border of Portuguese East Africa, forms a section also rich in minerals, gold and tin.

How Governed. All three regions, entitled High Commission Territories, are administered as protectorates under the direct rule of the imperial government represented by a resident high commissioner for South Africa. He wields absolute legislative and executive powers. Resident commissioners, magistrates, police officers, all Europeans, function in a lower protectorate assisted by native councils. A form of partial "indirect rule" prevails: native chiefs, sub-chiefs and headmen are used to carry out the orders of the European officers and a degree of local autonomy exists.

Rhodesia, Northern and Southern

Northern
AREA: 290,323 square miles
POPULATION: 1,377,889

Southern
AREA: 150,344 square miles
POPULATION: 1,289,000

TRADE: *North*	*Imports:*	£ 5,168,000	
Rhodesia:	From U.K.:	£ 2,227,000	
	Exports:	£10,127,000	
		(exclusive of bullion)	
	To U. K.:	£ 3,974,000	
TRADE: *South*	*Imports:*	£ 9,607,000	
Rhodesia:	From U.K.:	£ 4,845,000	
	Exports:	£ 6,116,000	
		(exclusive of bullion)	
	To U. K.:	£ 2,026,000	

This immense tableland stretching northward to the Zambesi River is of great value for its agriculture, its minerals and the opportunity it affords for white settlement. Southern Rhodesia, especially, with its fertile plateaus, uplands and salubrious climate, is suitable in every way for Europeans. That they have not been slow to appreciate this fact is witnessed by their occupation of over half of the best lands, the natives occupying reserves set apart for them, thus creating a serious land problem. Agriculture abundantly yields maize, citrus fruits, tobacco, wheat and some cotton. Northern Rhodesia lies in the tropics and part of it is at a much lower altitude than the South. Here too, the natives are confined to reserves but the land problem is not so acute for many are permitted to work in the mines and on European farms; indeed a labor rather than a land problem exists here, as mining develops. Both Northern and Southern Rhodesia are rich in mineral deposits: gold, asbestos, chrome ore, coal and copper. Northern Rhodesia is now one of the greatest copper-producing countries in the world. Between 1930 and 1935, British capitalists are said to have invested £25,000,000 in the mining industry in this colony.

How Governed. Northern Rhodesia is a crown colony administered by a governor assisted by an executive council; Southern Rhodesia is a self-governing colony half way to dominion status within the British Commonwealth of Nations, due to the dominance of white settlers and their vast economic interests. It exercises full autonomy in local affairs. The same system of native "indirect rule" prevails in Southern Rhodesia as in the Union of South Africa.

Nyasaland

AREA: 37,596 square miles; 10,353 square miles water
POPULATION: 1,603,257
TRADE: *Imports:*   £833,000
    From U.K.:   £381,000
    Exports: £975,000
    To U.K.:   £883,000

Next to Northern Rhodesia and bordered on the east by Lake Nyasa, this highland region of Nyasaland is similar geographically to Southern Rhodesia. Consequently, the country is one of white plantations: coffee, raised especially in the Shire uplands, cotton

and tobacco. Because of its hospitality to white settlement, Nyasaland contains more alienated lands than any other East African
colony. For this reason and also because it falls within the belt
of the devastating tsetse fly, acute land as well as labor problems exist. The natives are not pent up in reserves as in Rhodesia
but nevertheless must keep to special areas which are becoming
all too inadequate.

How Governed. Styled a protectorate, Nyasaland is really administered as a crown colony. Its governor is assisted by an executive council of four members who with four other Europeans make
up the legislative council. It is the latest colony in which a degree
of native indirect rule has been introduced. In 1933, native courts
and treasuries were set up to be administered by the chiefs.

How Acquired. Since the acquisition of all these units just described, which constitute British South Africa, was a planned and
connected process, the history of each is the history of all; hence
they must be treated together.

As stated above, the pattern of contemporary British Africa had
already begun to appear in its major outlines by the year 1871
and South Africa constituted its second point after the settlements
on the west coast. There Britain controlled both Cape Colony,
which had been taken from the Dutch in the settlement of 1815
and constituted a prize of the Napoleonic wars, and Natal, which
had been annexed in 1843 as a result of the trek thither by the
Boers, Britain's rebellious and emigrating subjects. The incom-
ing of British colonists into Cape Colony after 1815 had occasioned friction with the original Dutch settlers and about ten
thousand of them had emigrated northeastward, establishing settlements in Natal and further northward along the Orange and
Vaal Rivers. Always attempting to extend her sway wherever her
rebellious subjects trekked, Great Britain had succeeded in Natal
but failed in the Orange Free State and the Transvaal, whose
existence as independent Boer republics she had acknowledged
in 1852 and 1854 respectively. Thus by 1871, two British colonies
and two Dutch republics outlined the political future of South
Africa, where, as in West Africa, British explorers had well prepared the way for British expansion. Here in the regions to the
north of Cape Colony, Burton and Speke had discovered Lake
Tanganyika in 1858; James Grant had traced the Nile to one of its
sources in Lake Victoria in 1862, and Samuel Baker to its other

source, Lake Albert, in 1864; David Livingstone had followed the
Zambesi River to its beginnings, thereby exploring and surveying
much of later Rhodesia, discovering there various affluents of the
Congo River.

As in West Africa likewise, the trader, promoter, the business
men were to be the effective agents of expansion; but unlike West
Africa, or indeed any other part of the continent, larger and more
grandiose opportunities for promotion, stronger compulsions for
expansion were here at work. Briefly they were: the discovery of
gold and diamonds; the already germinating British commercial
interests in Egypt and East Africa which exerted a magnetic
attraction of north upon south to reach further and further up and
to establish lines of communication—the inception of the Cape-to-
Cairo dream—; and finally, the pressure to exert political and imperial prestige against rival powers, who, themselves influenced by
the same wave of expansion, threatened to crowd in and block
the way.

British expansionists were not slow in meeting simultaneously
these separate challenges and all the agents of colonialism co-operated to spread the British red northward, while in no part of
Africa were the services of the home government and its military
arm requisitioned quite so intensively and continuously to further
their plans. Finally the government itself, converted from its
"little Englander" viewpoint, threw itself, under the leadership of
Salisbury, Rosebery, and Chamberlain, wholeheartedly into the
colonial venture, at first following, then marching with and finally
leading the imperialists.

It is true that the expansion of South Africa northward was
owing to the combined action of merchant and missionary, soldier
and diplomat, promoter and politician but, as was true in all the
British African colonies, business and commercial interests dominated and the promoter and empire builder led. For Cecil Rhodes,
merely a "younger son" of an Anglican divine, in search of his
health, arrived in Capetown in 1870 and when he died in 1902,
no fewer than seven colonies or protectorates had been added to
the original two; the British boundary had been pushed north as
far as the Great Lakes and west to Portuguese Angola and German
South West Africa; an area considerably larger than that of
France, Belgium, the Netherlands and Switzerland combined,
had been added to the British oversea empire, and the Cape-

to-Cairo dream had not only been formulated but initiated into a growing reality.

To Cecil Rhodes, the empire builder, was due, more than to any other agent, this unprecedented expansion of South Africa. It was he who foresaw the possibilities, who framed the ambitious program, who supplied the capital, who perfected and employed the most advanced methods of imperialist technique. Arriving in South Africa as an observant boy of seventeen, about the time of the famous diamond discoveries, his coming coincided with the beginning of a momentous change in the history of that country. And Cecil Rhodes quickly grasped the nature and importance of the change. He remained one year on his brother's cotton farm but soon felt the lure of diamond digging and rushed off to Kimberley to seek a more spectacular fortune. There he proved himself a clever and successful manipulator in the buying and selling of claims and in the amalgamation of companies. Joining another successful diamond dealer from Hamburg, the two built up a powerful company, the DeBeers, Ltd., which came to possess a virtual monopoly of one of the two chief diamond fields and developed into one of the largest financial corporations in the world. Head of his company at the age of thirty, Rhodes had amassed a large fortune. But this was only the beginning of his plans. Employing the company's profits to buy out or force out competitors, he constructed a huge trust, the DeBeers Consolidated Mines, which by 1890 controlled 90 per cent of the world's supplies of diamonds. Meanwhile, he had applied the same methods of trust building to the gold-mining interests in the Transvaal and had established the Gold Fields of South Africa, Ltd., a company whose capital increased by a million and a quarter pounds in six years although it never obtained a monopoly of gold production.

It was the profits from these two companies which Rhodes used to paint the map of Africa a British red and to initiate the realization of the Cape-to-Cairo dream. For Rhodes believed in the creed of British imperialism with apostolic fervor and regarded it as his mission in life to bring as much of Africa as he could under the British flag, confining his attention especially to that highly desirable portion which stretched from Cape Colony to Egypt. "All this is to be painted red; that is my dream," he once remarked, running his fingers over a map of Africa from the Cape to the Great Lakes. He believed that whatever nation controlled this "backbone" of the continent would dominate Africa. "Give me the centre," he said, "and let who will have the swamps which skirt the coast." A chain of British settlements, therefore, the railway and the telegraph were to constitute the means of realizing the dream. "If this telegraph is made," he asserted, "it will also give us the keys to the continent." Then, he predicted, "we shall get through to Egypt with the telegraph and subsequently with the railway. . . . We shall not relax our efforts until by our civilization and the efforts of our people we reach the shores of the Mediterranean." This, in substance, constituted the magnificent Cape-to-Cairo dream.

But Cecil Rhodes, the dreamer, not only "thought in continents" and conceived expansionist plans of a magnitude never before imagined; Cecil Rhodes, the realist, set a new pattern for colonial acquisition that came to characterize much of the modern movement: a combination of ruthless exploitation, of sharp business practices, of finance capitalism, mixed with political and diplomatic manipulation. The result was irresistible. In the words of a native chief, who had bitter reason for knowing: "Rhodes ate up countries for his breakfast." The achievement of this vast expansion program which South Africa represents today demanded three separate campaigns, often carried on simultaneously: one against the Boers; one against the natives; and one against the opposition of the government, both in Cape Town and at home in London, generally dubbed "Grandmama" because of its annoying delays.

Bechuanaland

The acquisition of Bechuanaland in 1885 just north of Cape Colony, provides an example of this triple campaign in action. It also illustrates the new type of expansion, best termed long-range planning, perhaps, which was looking far beyond the immediate advantage and "thinking in continents." Bechuanaland possessed little intrinsic value, consisting largely of arid wastes, but in it Cecil Rhodes and others with him saw the "Suez Canal" to the north. For through this area and, consequently, along the western boundaries of the two Boer republics, the Orange Free State and the Transvaal, ran a great trade route to the interior called the "English" or "Missionaries" road, a well-marked track used by explorers, hunters, missionaries, traders, and constituting also the main approach to the Tati gold fields. This entire northward passage ran a great danger of being blocked by Boer, German or Portuguese expansion which would effectually bottle up all the dynamics of British expansion inherent in Cape Colony.

With the assistance, therefore, of Mackenzie, the missionary, and Robinson, the high commissioner of the Cape government, Rhodes determined, first, to "beat the Boers" in the "race to the north." This he accomplished by the simple means of using his influence in the Cape government to stiffen its stand on the London Convention of 1884 which barred the Transvaal Republic from extension into Bechuanaland. Then, he frightened the British by playing up the bogey of German advance in that area and, finally, won the intervention of four thousand British troops whose ruthless campaign reduced the native chiefs as well as the Boer intervention to submission.

Rhodesia

Rhodesia, on the other hand, affords a perfect illustration of Rhodes' campaign against the natives and the exploitation which they suffered at his hand. North of Bechuanaland stretched the high plateaus of Matabeleland and Mashonaland, reputedly rich in gold, a reputation which had occasioned a rush of prospectors, concessionaires and traders. Such a situation afforded Rhodes the opportunity for the practice of his masterly technique in amalgamation, combination and bargaining, upon which he had originally built his vast fortune in Cape Colony. With the co-operation again of the Cape government, owing to his influence therein (Rhodes became a member of the Cape parliament in 1883) he succeeded in his business combine and, like Taubman in Nigeria, formed his own company, the South African Company, Ltd., which swallowed up all competition. In 1889, he won, against Lord Salisbury's original opposition, the charter for his company. It granted the rights for twenty-five years over a vast and purposely undefined area, "to acquire by any concession, grant or treaty, all or any rights, interest, authority, jurisdiction and powers of any kind or nature whatsoever, including powers for the purposes of government or the preservation of public order."

Meanwhile, through his agents Rudd, Thompson and Maguire, Rhodes had already signed treaties with King Lobengula, ruler of the Matabeles, Mashona and Makalako tribes, which secured not only rich mineral concessions but promises to refrain from dealing with any other European states. In one of these transactions, Lobengula, induced to agree to concessions which he did not understand, discovered too late that he had bartered away all the mineral wealth of his kingdom for 1,000 Martini rifles, 100,000 ball cartridges, a small steamboat and £100 sterling payable on the first of every lunar month. Whereupon, he addressed a complaint to the great white queen herself. Her reply was to send a deputation to King Lobengula, consisting of "a military band and the three tallest of her Life Guards." [5] They bore a message which sanctioned the mineral concession and informed the king that a royal charter had been granted the South African Company.

With the support of the imperial government, the company could proceed with its exploitation. Its agents provoked a war with the Matabeles, Lobengula's people, in order to employ the company's forces against him and annex his lands. In despair, the tribe rebelled but was suppressed and its king driven out.

Unhampered, the company carried on its undertakings, pursued cattle breeding and secured a monopoly in railway as well as mining rights. Indeed, it completed the first section of the Cape-to-Cairo railway as far as Vryburg by 1890, thereby enabling that grandiose project, the highway of Cecil Rhodes, to assume definite shape and form.

Nor did the company's activities in Southern Rhodesia prevent it from spreading the British red in Northern Rhodesia where Sir Harry Johnston and other travelers were already at work in pursuance of Johnston's plan to cover as much of Central Africa as possible. Johnston became administrator of the company for this northern area. The combination here of two such empire builders as Rhodes and Johnston was irresistible, especially as vague claims on the part of Portugal, Germany and even Belgium, threatened to prevent this region from forming a link in the British chain.

By 1891, the police of the South African Company had driven out or captured the agents of the Portuguese Mozambique Company and signed a treaty with Chief Umtassa in Manicaland;

---

[5] Raphael, L., *The Cape-to-Cairo Dream*, p. 166.

Rhodes had bought up a grant to the dominions of Chief Lewanika in Barotseland; and the British government had signed the Anglo-Portuguese Treaty which secured the Barotse kingdom, as well as most of Manicaland, country healthy and suitable for white settlement, to Great Britain as spheres of interest, leaving to Portugal Gazaland, the more unhealthful coastal area.

This establishment of Northern and Southern Rhodesia drove a wedge between Portuguese East Africa on one side and the Belgian Congo on the other, touching Lake Tanganyika and German East Africa in the north, whose boundaries were settled in the Anglo-German agreements of 1890, 1893. After its first battles with the home government in London, the company and its exploits were heartily supported by the Colonial Office, especially Joseph Chamberlain who openly defended its practices in the House of Commons.

Nyasaland

Meanwhile Rhodes had realized that there remained one more stretch of territory between the Zambesi River and Lake Tanganyika still outside British control: the region around Lake Nyasa. For some years this area had been the scene of British interests: the Scottish missionary society had planted stations there, following Livingstone's explorations; the African Lakes Trading Company had secured treaties from the chiefs and was operating a steamer on Lake Nyasa; and a quarrel invoked by the Arab slave trade had lined up Britain on the side of the natives against Portugal, her rival, who supported the Arabs. Lord Salisbury was keenly interested in furthering British control and had sent H. H. Johnston, another Cape-to-Cairo dreamer, there in 1889 for that purpose.

Such was the state of affairs when Rhodes' attention was directed towards the territory. Johnston and Rhodes joined hands. Johnston secured Rhodes' financial aid with which to execute British expansion in the shape of a pledge of £10,000 a year to defray the cost of administration of the area; in return, Johnston influenced Salisbury's support for the charter of the South African Company. The company took over the African Lakes Company, reduced to bankruptcy by the native war, together with 2,700 square miles of territory. The British government declared Nyasaland a protectorate at the close of 1889 and the boundaries were settled with Portugal in the aforementioned treaty of 1891. The acquisition of Nyasaland admirably illustrates the interaction of explorer, missionary, humanitarianism, trade, capitalist promoter, government and diplomacy in spreading the British red; and, together with North Rhodesia, also marks the meeting place of the Cape-to-Cairo dreamers, who were working from the north as well as the south.

The Union of South Africa

Rhodes' triumph over the Boers in Bechuanaland was only the beginning of his long struggle with them. But its outcome marked a change in his original attitude of compromise and co-operation towards them. At first, Rhodes had firmly believed in a confederation of all the South African states, to be called the United States of South Africa, which would constitute an autonomous unit within the British Empire. To further the idea he meticulously practiced conciliation of the Dutch and, wherever possible, a reconciliation of their interests with Britain's. Indeed, it was a Dutch constituency which sent him to the Cape parliament in 1883 and a Dutch vote that maintained him as prime minister later. This shrewd empire-builder believed that it was only through alliance with the Boers that he could promote his northward expansion.

In the pursuit of this co-operative policy, Rhodes completely underestimated Boer nationalism and the strong determination of their president, Paul Kruger, to form a great independent republic north of the Orange River, an ambition which had assumed definite shape among Boer leaders in 1881. For, in that year, the Dutch Boers, resisting the British attempt to reassert their claim to sovereignty over the Transvaal, an effort begun in 1877, inflicted a decisive defeat upon a British force at Majuba Hill. The succeeding Anglo-Boer agreement, the Convention of Pretoria, guaranteed autonomy for the Transvaal but in vague and ambiguous terms. The Boers, resenting these, especially the clause of the Convention which reserved sovereignty to the crown, asked for a treaty instead. The British refused and replaced the Convention of Pretoria with the Convention of London, signed in 1884, which did little but increase the ambiguity of the Transvaal's status. The effects of this dispute, both political and psychological, helped measurably to make the Boers nationalists first and Cape Colonists second, a fact which Rhodes with his plans for co-operation failed, at the time, to appreciate.

The course of events, however, soon forced him to recognize the reality of the Boers' aim for economic and political independence. Their aggressive action in Bechuanaland and their schemes for developing a railway from Delagoa Bay to Pretoria ran counter to his railway plans and revealed the impossibility of co-operation with them. Then, in 1886, the discovery of gold in the Witwatersrand in the Transvaal, bringing an influx of non-Boer gold-diggers into the country, immensely stimulated Boer nationalism, arrogance and pride in what they considered as their own country. Into the Transvaal, particularly about Johannesburg, there poured a horde of miners and speculators, largely English and Welsh. By means of heavy taxation and government restrictions of all kinds, the Boers sought both to profit financially from the mines worked by these aliens and also to limit the flood of Uitlanders, as the British and others came to be called. This policy gave rise to constant friction and misunderstanding between Boer and non-Boer and thus, by the 1890's, Rhodes came to perceive that his plan of co-operation with the Boers was doomed to failure, that President Kruger was blocking his schemes both for a British South Africa under Britain and, more important, his project of northward expansion, the Cape-to-Cairo dream. He also became convinced that Germany and Portugal, the neighboring colonial powers, sympathized not with Britain but with Kruger and the Boers against Britain.

As a consequence, active hostility replaced conciliation as a deliberate policy. Rhodes espoused the cause of the Uitlanders in their very real grievances against Boer rule in the Transvaal. These grievances were many: the levying of excessive taxation upon the essential dynamite which was made a Boer-government monopoly, as well as upon the transport of coal, machinery and food supplies; the fixing of onerous customs duties upon essential commodities; the obstruction of efforts to establish railway communications with the Cape; and the failure of the exclusively Boer administration to provide adequate facilities for health, housing, education for the heavily-taxed strangers within its gates. Added to these burdens was the constant irritation of Boer truculence, of police regulations, of refusal to admit the Uitlanders to a share in the government commensurate with their numbers and economic status. To remedy their wrongs, which pressed heavily upon them as their stakes in the Transvaal increased in value, the Uitlanders formed a reform association, a national, constitutional union, which asked for political equality. Rhodes, the premier of Cape Colony, became spokesman of this union and gained the support of Joseph Chamberlain, Colonial Secretary in the Salisbury cabinet. Both Rhodes and Chamberlain thoroughly believed that the Boers constituted a serious menace to British supremacy in South Africa and determined upon the ultimate destruction of the Boer republics.

Rhodes and the reform movement encountered, however, a serious obstacle to their plans in the opposition of President Kruger. A hard-headed, old Dutch pioneer, who as a child had been on the first "Great Trek" of the Boers northward, he hated the British and bluntly refused the petitions of the Uitlanders. Rhodes, finally losing all patience with Kruger's obdurate attitude, stationed his right-hand man in the South African Company, Dr. L. S. Jameson, administrator of Rhodesia, with five hundred company police on the border of the Transvaal, and, in spite of his attempt to stop him at the last minute, was ultimately responsible for the disastrous Jameson Raid of 1895. It was Rhodes who, together with his colleague Beit, supplied the funds for an uprising against the Boers at Johannesburg.

The successful repulsion of the raid by the Boers, who beat down the Uitlanders and took them prisoners, inflicted the first serious check upon British expansion in South Africa, a check reinforced by the sympathy of Germany for the Boers as expressed in the famous "Kruger telegram," sent by Kaiser William II at the instigation of his foreign secretary. It congratulated President Kruger on "preserving the independence of his country" and publicized the real strength of German opposition to Great Britain in this region. The consequences of Boer success led directly to the Boer War and only through that costly, bitter and bloody struggle were British dominance in South Africa maintained, Rhodes' extensive gains secured, and the roads to the north kept open.

As for Rhodes himself, he was completely discredited and forced to contemplate the first great failure of his plans. The home government repudiated the Jameson Raid, censored Rhodes and appointed a British president for Rhodesia with direct control over the police force of the South African Company. But Rhodes was too great a hero of British imperialism long to remain under a cloud. In 1898, he was re-elected to a seat in the Cape parliament, won "Grandmama's" support in suppressing the revolt of the Matabeles in Rhodesia in 1896 and transferred his promotion of the Cape-to-Cairo plan away from its original base, Cape Colony, to the north where we shall soon meet him again.

The Boer War, 1899-1902

In the meantime the final contest between British and Dutch for South Africa became inevitable. The Jameson Raid represented the climax of Boer grievances against Britain, grievances political and economic which became more and more acute as the age of science and industry revealed the rich potentialities of South Africa. For the Boers resented not only Rhodes' annexations which hemmed them in, the British seizure of Tongaland in 1894 which blocked a Boer corridor to the Indian Ocean, the tremendous influx of British promoters and speculators into the Transvaal, but also the constant criticism of the oligarchical character of the Transvaal government on the part of the Uitlanders and the increasing British demand for wider franchise and extended rights in the Cape government. In short, Boer nationalism, at base rural and agricultural in its economy, was threatened by a rising British imperialism which sought to impose an industrial and urban economic order upon it. Paul Kruger, leader of a simple, farmer people, confronted Chamberlain, the sophisticated diplomat, and Cecil Rhodes, the protagonist of finance capitalism. Moreover, the Boers became convinced of a British plot to deprive them of their hard-won country and of a British desire for war.

Consequently, President Kruger prepared for war and was disinclined to suffer long the intransigence of the British over the franchise question in the Transvaal. For, although this conflict of British imperialism versus Boer nationalism was basically economic in character, the immediate precipitation of war was caused by a political dispute. There were at this time in the Transvaal 180,000 Uitlanders, and 80,000 Boers. The Uitlanders, British, Germans, Americans, owned two thirds of the land and about 90 per cent of the other wealth in the Transvaal; yet the Boers controlled the government and required a residence of fourteen years for the franchise. In June, 1899, President Kruger in negotiation with Sir Alfred Milner, high commissioner for South Africa and governor of the Cape since 1897, proposed a reduction of the fourteen required years to seven on condition that all future disputes be submitted to arbitration. This the British refused to accept and began to move troops towards South Africa, whereupon the belligerent Kruger issued a forty-eight hour ultimatum, October, 1899, which demanded the submission of all controversy to "the friendly course of arbitration" and cancellation of British military preparations. The British rejected the ultimatum and war broke out on October 11, 1899.

To the surprise of the British, the Boer War endured two and one-half bloody years. It was characterized by an overconfidence and lack of preparation on the part of Britain whose optimistic hopes for an early victory over the "Dutch farmers" was rapidly changed to pessimistic gloom; by the brilliant initiative and strategy of the Boer Generals DeWet and Botha; and by a guerilla warfare, whose long continuance strained the resources of the British Empire. It was estimated that Great Britain was obliged to put 350,000 men in the fields to defeat the Boer forces of probably fewer than 40,000. Finally, under the command of her ablest generals, Roberts and Kitchener, Britain vanquished the Boers, who were obliged to retire from Natal and Cape Colony and surrender Pretoria, the capital of the Transvaal, Johannesburg and Bloemfontein, capital of the Orange Free State. President Kruger fled, disappointed in not securing the active support of European allies, who, while hostile to the British cause, proved unwilling to carry that hostility to the point of armed intervention. Apparently the war was over at the end of the first year. But such was the character of Boer resistance that they continued their stubborn guerilla fighting until 1902 when peace was concluded.

The ensuing treaty of Vereeniging was a generous one, owing largely to the presence of a strong liberal opinion in Britain which denounced the government for having carried on an aggressive, imperialist war in South Africa against the Boers for the benefit of a capitalist group in England. According to its terms, the British government annexed the two Boer republics but promised them a future self-government, recognized the Dutch language in South Africa, and agreed to the levying of no special taxes to defray war costs. When the Liberals came to power in 1906, they redeemed the promise of self-government by granting it to the Transvaal in 1906, and to the Orange Free State in 1907, which prepared the way for the Union of South Africa. In addition, the British parliament made every effort to make the Boers feel that the British did not regard them as a conquered people. For even the imperialists had experienced a sharp lesson in the Boer War, which had cost the Empire 30,000 lives and $230,000,000. As Kipling wrote:

> "Let us admit it fairly, as business people should,
> We have had no end of a lesson: it will do us no end of good." [6]

READINGS

Cambridge History of the British Empire, vol. 8, 1936.

Dawson, W. H. *South Africa—People, Places and Problems,* 1925. Popular.

Hofmeyr, J. H. *South Africa,* 1931. Interesting.

Hofmeyr, J. H. "Germany's Colonial Claims: A South African View." *Foreign Affairs,* July, 1939.

Lovell, R. L. *Struggle for South Africa 1875-1899,* 1934. Detailed.

Lugard, Sir F. *The Dual Mandate in British Tropical Africa,* 1922. Good.

Millin, S. G. *Cecil Rhodes,* 1933.

Millin, S. G. *The South African,* rev. ed. 1934. Good.

Morel, E. D. *Nigeria,* 1911.

Raphael, L. A. C. *The Cape-to-Cairo Dream,* 1936. Careful monograph.

Walker, E. A. *A History of South Africa,* rev. ed. 1935. Excellent, up to date.

Walker, E. A. *The Great Trek,* 1934. Excellent.

Williams, B. *Cecil Rhodes,* 1921.

Young, F. B. *They Seek A Country,* 1937. Fictional account.

---

[6] For a detailed and excellent account of the Boer War, see Hall, W. P., *Empire to Commonwealth.*

CHAPTER FIVE

British Africa—Continued

BRITISH NORTH AFRICA: *Egypt until 1922, Anglo-Egyptian Sudan*

Egypt

AREA: 12,000 square miles; 370,000 square miles of desert
POPULATION: 14,000,000
TRADE:[1] *Imports:*   £43,333,938
    From U.K.:   £14,731,695
    Exports: £48,716,418
    To U.K.:   £23,037,260

E GYPT IS today (1941) an independent nation, member of the League of Nations; but her independence has been acknowledged by Great Britain only since 1922 and completely recognized as such since 1936. From 1914 to 1922 she was a British protectorate and before 1914, from 1882, a "veiled" protectorate. Nominally a Turkish province ruled by the khedive, who paid tribute and homage to the sultan, Egypt was actually adminis-

---

[1] *Statesman's Year Book,* 1923. Figures are in Egyptian £'s.

tered by British "advisers" and officials and was thoroughly "penetrated" both economically and diplomatically by British interests.
The only legal remains of her position as a protectorate consist
in the reserved British rights to maintain troops along the Suez
Canal and to occupy the airports at Alexandria and Port Said,
while an investment of two hundred million pounds and a prosperous colony of British subjects supply tangible witness of her
economic value to her erstwhile European protector.

Since the time of the Assyrians, the Persians and the Hittites,
this northeast corner of the African continent bordering both on
the Mediterranean and the Red Seas has been desirable to outsiders. No larger than the state of Vermont and hemmed in by
deserts, this narrow Nile Valley constitutes one of the most intensely fertile areas in the world and has cradled one of the oldest
and richest of civilizations. It is not so much for its inherent value,
however, that it has always been so attractive, but more because
of its geographic and strategic position. At the meeting point of
three continents and four seas, itself a land bridge to Asia, it has
controlled the routes of trade and communication from the day
of the camel to that of the airplane.

How Governed. Since Britain declared Egypt a protectorate
in 1914 as a war measure, the government from 1914-1922 par-
took of the nature of an annexation. Even the nominal rights
accorded by the Organic Law were abrogated. Promulgated in
1883 by the British so as to bring order out of the Egyptian
chaos and to facilitate their economic penetration and strategic
hold of Egypt, the Organic Law had allowed the khedive,
his ministers, council, and legislative assembly ostensibly to rule
Egypt; while the British consul-general and high commissioner
constituted the real government, reinforced by British advisers
and officials in charge of every department. But in 1914, all this
"visible government" disappeared: a puppet sultan replaced the
khedive, the legislative assembly was not convened, the press
was censored, all economic resources were requisitioned, and all
nationalist agitation suppressed. Egypt was ruled by a strong
British hand for Britain was at war.

How Acquired. Egypt supplied the third point in the pattern
of British Africa present in 1871; but unlike the other two, West
Africa and Cape Colony, it did not represent territory acquired

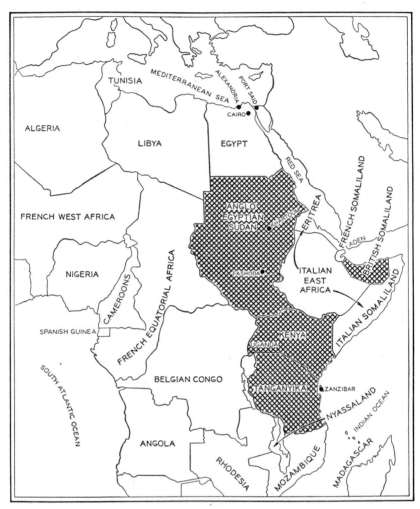

BRITISH NORTH AFRICA AND BRITISH EAST AFRICA

and occupied. Rather was it the first example encountered so far of modern expansion by the method of "sphere of interest," by economic penetration of which the agents are the "financial adviser," the "resident," instead of the explorer, the missionary or the soldier. For here Great Britain encountered not only the heirs to a great and highly developed early civilization but also the representatives of their overlords, the Turks who administered the territory under the sultan at Constantinople,[2] a situation requiring a far more subtle method of expansion than the simple one of dealing directly with the native African chiefs.

Britain's interest in Egypt in 1871 sprang from two sources: the traditional conflict in this region, indeed in the Levant generally, with France, dating concretely from Napoleon's defeat here in 1779; and the more tangible fact that Egypt occupied a vital position on the route to India and to Britain's extensive commercial interests in the East. Until 1871, Great Britain guarded her interests in this corner of the Mediterranean through diplomacy. After 1825, she had supported the Turkish government against its rebellious governor, Mehemet Ali, who looked to France for help in securing Egypt's independence. At this time, British statesmen were of the profound conviction that the only way to peace lay through the preservation of the integrity of the Turkish Empire and hence to the continuance of British "business as usual" in the Near and Middle East.

Secure in her control of the Cape route to India for the transport of goods and satisfied with the overland railway route from Alexandria to Suez which met her demands for a rapid postal service to the East, Britain blocked the project of a canal to the Red Sea through her influence with the sultan, whose consent to it was essential. For the canal was definitely a French project, based mainly upon science and sentiment. The engineer, Ferdinand de Lesseps, secured the preliminary concession in 1854 which represented the climax of a long effort. British statesmen considered, however, that the canal would cut off Africa from Asia, weaken the hold of the sultan in Egypt and threaten British commercial supremacy. They fought it with the weapons of diplomacy in the same manner in which they had hitherto expressed their vital interest in this area; they took no decisive step in Egypt itself.

But the opening of the Suez Canal in 1869 revolutionized Britain's position. Once there existed a canal connecting the Mediterranean and Red Seas, Britain could not afford to allow its control to rest in other hands, especially as its opening coincided

---

[2] Mehemet Ali, an Albanian adventurer and a soldier in the Turkish army, had become governor or Pasha of Egypt in 1806. He led a revolt against the Ottoman empire in 1833 but Turkey aided by Russia reduced Egypt again to subjection.

with the coming to power of an imperialistically minded prime minister in England. Hence Disraeli's haste in securing, with the help of the Rothschilds, 176,602 shares of canal stock, the considerable bloc owned by the khedive, for which Great Britain paid £3,680,000 in 1875. But that was only the beginning; to control the canal, it was necessary to control Egypt. Content until 1870 in preventing France from dominating at Cairo, it was now Britain's vital interest to control Cairo. The "economic imperative" of modern expansion changed Britain's rôle from passivity to energetic activity in Egypt.

As suggested before, the methods of expansion were quite different from those employed in other parts of Africa. Britain was not dealing here with illiterate chiefs whom she could force to sign treaties bartering away their birthright, but with oriental rulers of ancient civilizations, practiced in the arts of diplomacy and statecraft. One great advantage, however, adhered to Britain as to the other imperialistic powers, which set them far ahead of these older civilizations: Western industrialism and finance capitalism, which gave them so great an advantage over the so-called "decaying powers" as to permit the west to hold the east virtually at its mercy. There is something peculiarly appealing and tragic about those rulers of ancient civilizations who became the prey of modern expansionism. They stand, as it were, between two worlds, "one dead, the other powerless to be born": the old worlds of feudal, oriental splendor; the new world of modern industrialization. They, like Ismail Pasha of Egypt, were dazzled, bewildered, bewitched by the wondrous products of modern industry, by the miracles of its finance—fateful illusions like the mirages of their own sandy wastes which drew them further and further into an engulfing desert of debt and obligation to foreign capitalists.

For Ismail in Egypt envied the Western powers and determined to bring his country up to date in order to maintain its ancient splendor and prestige, a splendor that demanded modernity and renovation if it were to survive at all. Thus like his brother rulers along the North African coast, Ismail sunk greater and greater sums in "improvements": into the construction of the Suez Canal, into one thousand miles of railroads, and five thousand miles of telegraph wires; into bridges, harbor works and roads, one of which he built at great expense from Cairo to the Pyramids when entertaining European royalty in 1869; into the decoration of Abdin Palace which cost ten million francs; and into bribes to the sultan for independence. By the end of his reign, his country was some ninety million pounds in debt for a large part of which interest rates ran as high as 25 and 27 per cent. What happened in Egypt whither money-lenders, jobbers, smugglers, sharpers, all kinds of "jackals of finance" flocked, constituted a case of financial robbery to be duplicated later in other countries as a technique of the new expansion. It brought Ismail Pasha to bankruptcy and to exile.

The fact that Great Britain sent Stephen Cave to Egypt in 1876 to investigate the financial situation is significant both as a measure of her rapidly increasing interest in Egypt and as an example of one of the more subtle methods of the new expansion, the "financial adviser." The result of the Cave report led to the establishment of the International Debt Commission, the ultimate deposition of Ismail Pasha, and to the setting-up of the Anglo-French Condominium over Egypt.

While the Debt Commission was engaged in liquidating the financial situation and dictating an economical Egyptian budget designed to protect the European bondholder (British bondholders alone held £30,000,000 of the debt), an uprising broke out against Tewfik Pasha, Ismail's successor. Led by one Arabi, a peasant officer in the Egyptian army, the revolt was both military and national directed not only against Tewfik but strongly anti-Turk and anti-European. It threw the whole Egyptian question back into the international arena; but the powers refused to unite in any joint action, leaving England and France to send a naval expedition to Alexandria. The French, however, also withdrew, for the government was torn with indecision at home (the Freycinet cabinet fell when it asked for funds with which to defend the Suez Canal). France feared a quarrel with England and feared injuring its own interests in Algeria and in Tunisia by antagonizing the Moslems. Thus, the French ships sailed away and left Great Britain to bombard Alexandria, seize the Suez Canal and "restore order in Egypt."

Beyond doubt the Gladstone government, which had returned to power, possessed popular support for this Egyptian venture —Parliament voted for it 275 to 19; the "little Englanders" visualized at that time no empire here, and were sincere in their declared intentions to withdraw after Egyptian chaos had been reduced to order. Certainly their pronouncements on the matter were clear and explicit. But the "economic imperative" was too strong. British commercial interests, her imperial prestige and dependence upon the Suez Canal, the fortunes of her merchants already in Africa, the financial security of her bondholders: all demanded that Egypt be stabilized and occupied.

That it was occupied, we have already learned. For while the British set up an ostensible Egyptian government by the Organic Law of 1883 with the khedive ruling under the Turkish sultan, assisted by his ministers, a council, general assembly and native officials, able British "advisers" dominated the whole country. Sir Evelyn Baring, later Lord Cromer, consul general and high commissioner, actually ruled from 1883 to 1907 and is well-named the "Creator of modern Egypt." In the last analysis his stupendous and fundamental reforms and remarkable achievements laid the foundations of contemporary independent Egypt about which we shall hear more later.[3]

The Anglo-Egyptian Sudan

> AREA: 1,008,100 square miles
> POPULATION: 5,728,551; Europeans: 6,800
> TRADE: *Imports:* £6,421,000
>   From U.K.: £1,671,000
>   *Exports:* £6,025,000
>   To U.K.: £2,568,000

Stretching far to the south, the Sudan forms the hinterland of Egypt. An arid, equatorial region in parts, such as the Nubian and Libyan deserts, it also includes vast fertile uplands, steppe areas as well as dense forests and swampy riverine stretches. Forming a large section of that "land of the blacks," it is inhabited by Negroes and Arabs, the latter predominating in the north, the former in the south. Its highly prized value lies not only in its rich agricultural potentialities, its inherent resources, but in its strategic and geographical position: guardian of the sources of the Nile and essential link in the Cape-to-Cairo plan.

Today the Sudan represents one of Britain's greatest imperialist

---

[3] See pp. 212-213.

successes: engineering skill has enabled the north to produce the long staple Egyptian cotton under irrigation works, of which the Sennar Dam, nearly two miles long and ninety feet high is the latest achievement; railways penetrate everywhere; the Sudanese are trained for public service; trade is prosperous. Indeed, this once turbulent, uncivilized and unproductive area is today (1941) regarded as one of the promising spots within the British Empire. For those who justify imperialism, it is a model exhibit.

How Governed. As a so-called condominium under the British foreign office, the Sudan is jointly ruled by Britain and Egypt. The governor-general is appointed by the king of Egypt upon the recommendation of the British government.

How Acquired. As we have observed, it was essential for trade and prestige that Britain control Egypt but "Egypt was the Nile and the Nile was Egypt"; hence complete control must extend to the uttermost reaches of that river. British interests here dated from about the middle of the nineteenth century. A consular agent was stationed at Khartoum in the fifties and during the next decade the explorers Speke, Grant, Baker and his wife had aroused interest by their expeditions in the area. Speke had discovered the Ripon Falls and the source of the White Nile in Lake Victoria, while the Bakers discovered Lake Albert. Colonel Gordon himself explored the upper reaches of the Nile and traced the river from the Murchison Falls to the Karuma Rapids.

The Egyptians, of course, had been interested in the region from ancient times. The khedive Mehemet Ali had made extensive expeditions there and the extravagant Ismail had wasted huge sums in campaigns which met with ignominious defeat at the hands of the Abyssinians. Wherever the Egyptians annexed territory, they experienced great difficulty in governing it; their inefficiency and corruption only added to the unhappy lot of the people. Thus they adopted the custom of relying on foreigners to help them: Emin Pasha, a German adventurer, was one time governor of the Equatorial Province; Sir Samuel Baker was governor in 1869; and finally General Gordon became ruler of the entire Sudan in 1874. The British governors had attempted to abolish the Arab slave trade and stirred up further resentment among the people. In short, conditions in the Sudan were ripe for revolt: the oppression and long misgovernment of the Egyptians; the interference with economic interests in the north; the rise of religious fanaticism; the disturbance of the status quo occasioned by Arabi's uprising in Egypt and the consequent British occupation. The way was open for any adventurer to come in who promised the people deliverance from their oppressors.

Such a deliverer appeared in one Mohammed Ahmed, who styled himself a Mahdi or Guide of Islam and led a ferocious revolt against the Egyptians. British advisers counselled them to withdraw completely from such a disturbed area. General Gordon was engaged in effecting preparations for this withdrawal when he was beseiged in Khartoum by the Mahdi. There he was ultimately massacred with his entire force owing to Gladstone's, the "little Englander's," delay in authorizing a relief expedition, an event which involved the British, with or against their will, in the Sudan. The cry arose: "Smash the Mahdi and avenge Gordon." But Britain's forces were then too much engaged in India and she ordered a retreat to Wadi Haifa and a command to drop the Sudan.

Its conquest, however, was only postponed: for ten terrible years it remained in control of the Mahdists who conquered far and wide. By that time Britain had restored order in Egypt and Kitchener had reorganized the Egyptian army. The Italian defeat in 1896 by the Abyssinians shook the prestige of the European powers in North Africa and Britain determined to assert her might in the Sudan. At the battle of Omdurman in 1898, Kitchener shattered the power of the Khalifa Abdulla, who had succeeded the Mahdi, with a mixed British and Egyptian army. A convention with Egypt the following year established the Anglo-Egyptian Condominium. Then Great Britain, represented by Lord Cromer, pressed forward those purposes for which the Sudan was acquired: to guard the sources of the Nile and to continue the march of British domain south. With the aid of the engineers, Cassell and Willcocks, the great irrigation works which culminated in the famous Assuan Dam (1898-1902) were commenced, destined to triple the productivity of lower Egypt. Termed the greatest achievement of the British in Egypt, this huge dam, more than one mile long and ninety-six feet high (increased to one hundred and twelve feet in 1912), controls the floods and preserves a reservoir of water two hundred miles long. Engineers also succeeded in cutting through the "Sudd," the dense growths of floating water vegetation which often blocked the river, thereby linking up by steamer mail-service the Anglo-Egyptian Sudan with Uganda.

But British occupation of the Egyptian Sudan was not won by military campaigns and economic development alone: astute, clever diplomacy and international manoeuvering were essential. The Sudan was attractive to other powers besides England: France, Italy, Belgium, even Germany, were all interested in it. Indeed, it was here that the opposing ambitions of France for an east-to-west empire and of Britain for a north-to-south empire were inevitably to clash. The abandonment of the Sudan by Egypt to the Mahdi in 1884-1885 had excited the aims and ambitions of these powers, for they took the position that all former claims to this region had lost their validity since no "effective occupation" existed. Consequently a race for the Sudan set in.

Great Britain, sensing the danger both to her control of the Nile and her contemplated reoccupation of the area, strove to protect this seat of her vital interests as well as all the approaches to it. The Anglo-German Agreement of 1890, later described in more detail, barred Germany from penetration into the Sudan by its recognition of the British sphere of interest in Uganda and the Nile basin. The following year (1891) an Anglo-Italian convention designated their respective spheres in East Africa, Upper and Eastern Sudan and Somaliland. It placed Italy in part of the Eastern Sudan in order to guard Egyptian, otherwise British, interests there, yet carefully protected the upper Nile Valley from Italian encroachment. In addition it recognized part of Ethiopia as an Italian sphere, a buffer against French encroachment. In 1894, the Anglo-Congolese treaty dealt with the third rival, the Congo State. It provided for a lease to King Leopold of the so-called Lado Enclave along the upper Nile and the Bahr-el-Ghazal region, thus setting up a buffer state in the Sudan, and an ally against the French in the upper Nile Valley. In return Leopold recognized the British spheres as determined by the Anglo-German Agreement and leased, in turn, to Britain a corridor twenty-five kilometers wide, connecting Lakes Tanganyika and Albert, running behind the German sphere and affording the British a connecting link with their territories to the south. Because of German and French protests, however, this arrangement was finally withdrawn and other parts of the agreement modified as well.

But, though not a complete success, the Anglo-Congolese treaty illustrates the character of British effort to guard the Sudan.

In spite of these intricate arrangements, Britain could not prevent the French advance and, in 1898, news reached Kitchener that Marchand had raised the French flag at Fashoda in the upper Sudan. This was the one successful part of a much more extensive plan whereby two other French expeditions from the east, one from Addis Ababa in Abyssinia, and one from Jibuti, were all to converge and secure the upper Sudan for France.[4] The long-looked for crisis had arrived: either French west-east empire or British north-south empire must give way at Fashoda.

As usual, when the conflicting claims of rival powers collide in the colonial field, diplomacy and compromise afford a solution. Kitchener confronted Marchand and ordered down the French flag. When Marchand refused, Kitchener proposed the hoisting of the Egyptian flag. The soldiers then withdrew, throwing the Fashoda crisis onto the laps of the diplomats. Their solution emerged as the famous Fashoda agreement of 1899, the foundation of the later *entente cordiale* between Britain and France: France renounced all political rights in the Bahr-el-Ghazal, the upper Sudan, and England accorded her a favorable adjustment of her boundaries east of Lake Chad and a free hand in the southern hinterland of Tripoli. Thus, by military conquest and a series of treaties, Britain obtained the Sudan and secured her rights to the territory from the Egyptian border to the great lakes.

EAST AFRICA: *Kenya, Uganda, Mandated Territory of Tanganyika, Somaliland and Zanzibar Protectorates*

Kenya

AREA: 219,730 square miles; 5,230 square miles of water
POPULATION: 3,096,905 natives; 20,000 whites; 43,623 East Indians
12,166 Arabs
TRADE: *Imports:*   £8,802,000
From U.K.:   £3,671,000
Exports: £9,655,000
To U.K.   £3,267,000
(including Uganda)

---

[4] See pp. 120-121.

Kenya proper is an island of high and fertile land rising above a vast expanse of equatorial swamp and steppe. Coffee, cotton, maize and sisal constitute its best products; cattle raising is being developed and the wheat crop is expected to supply all local needs. Because of its moderate climate and potential production, it attracts white settlement, and after the first World War the British government invited ex-soldiers to emigrate there. About 2,000,000 acres of land were confiscated from the natives, divided into small estates and given to demobilized British army officers. Land reserves, claimed to be both inadequate and of inferior quality, were set aside for the indigenous population.

This situation has given rise to many problems: native agitation for land, difficulty of securing labor and discontent with the government which, it is charged, places the interests of the Europeans first. Indeed, Kenya is one of the most disturbed areas in the British African Empire.

How Governed. Both Kenya colony and Kenya protectorate, the strip along the coast, have the same governor and executive council, while the legislative council of the colony may legislate for the protectorate. The white-settled areas are administered by resident commissioners and the native reserves by district commissioners. Elected and official white members control the legislative council, although the East Indians send five representatives.

How Acquired. East Africa, the former name for Kenya, was the last section of British Africa to be secured before the mandates. The reason lay in the strength of Egypt's claims here, in the grip of the Sultan of Zanzibar plus that of the Arab slave trade upon the region, and finally, in the competition of the great powers. Nevertheless, England held a position of influence in the area prior to 1871. This was owing to the work of her explorers and scientists; to her East Indian trade connections which demanded the assigning of consuls, who later became advisers, to the Sultan of Zanzibar; and to her special position of ally and protector of Portugal which occupied a considerable section of East Africa and whose quarrels with the encroaching Arabian sultans Great Britain had arbitrated.

The decade of the eighties saw the collapse of Egyptian influence in East Africa, caused by the rising of the Mahdi and the consequent acceleration of the rivalries among the powers. Italy established her claim in Eritrea and Somaliland on the Red Sea, the German adventurer Karl Peters explored inland and signed treaties with the native chiefs, and French missionaries penetrated Uganda. All signs pointed to the necessity for British action.

As noted previously, Britain's trade in this region, linked as it was with the Indian trade, gave her a position of great advantage with the Sultan of Zanzibar. Indeed, so large a proportion of the Zanzibar trade was in the hands of British subjects, natives of India, that the British consuls possessed a golden opportunity to advance British interests as well as the crusade against the slave trade. No one made greater use of this than Sir John Kirk, who played off against one another and the sultan the rivalries of the other powers, Germany and France. He persuaded the sultan to sign a treaty abolishing the slave trade and finally to agree to the appointment by Great Britain of a number of salaried vice-consuls stationed throughout his domains.

Meanwhile, explorers were penetrating into the interior: Joseph Thompson traveled from Mombasa to Busoga; H. H. Johnston explored the region around Kilimandjaro in 1884 and signed treaties with the chiefs. Upon his return to England he handed these over to a committee of merchants, the nucleus of the Imperial British East African Company.

Just as the French had blocked England in West Africa, so did the Germans in East Africa. For Peters and Jühlke not only made treaties with the chiefs in the same region where Johnston had been, but followed them up with settlements so that in 1885 the German government extended its protection over these claims of the Society for German Colonization founded by Peters. Compromise between British and German interests remained as the only solution and Bismarck, desiring no break with England at this time, accepted Salisbury's proposal to delimit the sultan's domains. The ensuing agreement of 1886 marked out the German and British spheres of interest under the guise of protecting the "integrity" of Zanzibar. The sultan's sovereignty was limited only to his two islands, Zanzibar and Pemba, together with a strip of coastland, ten miles deep and about one thousand miles long, of which latter the German company was to have the southern six hundred miles and the British company the northern four hundred as spheres of interest. Behind the ten-mile strip, Britain and Germany divided the hinterland: German East Africa was to extend from the mouth of the Rovuma River on the south to the Umbe River and as far northwest as Victoria Nyanza; British East Africa was to include all the territory north of the Umbe River to the Tana River. The western boundaries, with the exception of Victoria Nyanza were left undetermined, which afforded both powers extended opportunities for expansion, that in turn led to another scramble later on.

Meanwhile the British East African Company, formed in 1887, went to work to secure the actual occupation of its sphere of interest: it gained control of the territory of the Sultan Burghask, between the Umbe River and Kipini; succeeded to the holdings in Witu after the failure of the German Witu Company; and won the award of the coastal islands in the German controversy. During the year 1887, the company signed treaties with twenty-one chiefs securing sovereignty for two hundred miles inland. Finally the Anglo-German Treaty of 1890 assigned Zanzibar and Witu definitely to Britain while the Anglo-Italian Agreement settled the Juba River as the boundary between British East Africa and Italian Somaliland.

Like the Royal Niger Company, the British East African Company had carved out a huge empire of approximately 200,000 square miles, providing not only a vast potential market for British goods but also, because of its high elevation and salubrious climate, a settlement colony for Britishers where coffee, sisal, grain and cotton could be cultivated. But the company had exhausted itself financially by its pioneer work and, in 1895, sold out its control to the British government for £250,000.

Stronger and possessed of more resources than the company, the government finally completed the pacification of East Africa and by 1896 had broken the last Arab power on the East Coast. In that same year, all this territory, except the islands of Pemba and Zanzibar, was united into the British East African protectorate. Finally, according to the Treaty of London (1915), which promised Italy compensation for possible British and French gains in Africa at German expense, Britain ceded to Italian Somaliland in 1924 a strip of East Africa, four hundred miles long and one hundred miles wide, known as Jubaland. Also in the year 1920, British East Africa became Kenya colony and Kenya protectorate, the name Kenya being taken from a huge mountain which rivals Kilimandjaro.

Uganda

AREA: 80,371 square miles; 13,610 square miles of water
POPULATION: 3,661,099; Europeans: 2,111
TRADE:[5]

A small country about the size of Britain, Uganda has been variously termed the "pearl of Africa" and the "key to the Nile basin." One of the most prosperous and advanced colonies in the whole of Africa, it lies in the highlands back of the lake district, is peculiarly fertile and suitable for white settlement. Cotton, coffee and tobacco constitute the major export crops, while the gold mining industry is rapidly developing under the auspices of the Tanganyika Concession Company, Ltd. But more important than its climate or its altitude, Uganda's position on Victoria Nyanza controls the source of the White Nile. With all these natural advantages, Uganda is inhabited by Bantu-Hamitic people of such a level of intelligence as to win from an anthropologist the title of the "Japanese of Africa." In the 1860's when the first white man entered Uganda, it was one of the most highly developed kingdoms. Lord Lugard said of the Buganda, the most ancient nation in the area, that no other tribe had ever developed so extraordinary a social, political and even legal system.

How Governed. Uganda is today (1941) a native protectorate administered by a governor aided by administrative and executive councils in which official members dominate. Three native kingdoms, Buganda, Taro, Ankole, retain jurisdiction over their local affairs. The king of Buganda, the most advanced native state, is called the Kabaka. By treaty with Britain he is officially styled "His Highness," flies his own flag and is entitled to a salute of nine guns on ceremonial occasions.

How Acquired. Naturally, such a prize as Uganda was early marked for acquisition. The first explorers, Speke, Baker, Gordon, Stanley, realized its strategic position and voiced the need for securing it. During the eighties, it became the focus of British, French and German ambition as well as the prey of all the technicians of colonial penetration: missionaries, traders, explorers, and finally soldiers with the Maxim gun.

---

[5] Included with Kenya; see page 98.

When, as previously noted, the Anglo-German Agreement of 1886 provided the opportunity for penetration into Uganda by its very indefinite determination of the western boundaries, there was already a triangular struggle for the territory under way among the Protestant missionaries from England, the first in the field, Father Lavigerie's White Fathers from France, and the Mohammedans. But the race for possession really began in 1887, under the guise of a relief expedition to rescue from the Mahdi Emin Pasha, governor of the Equatorial Province in the British Egyptian service. For Emin Pasha, German by birth, doctor by calling, whose real name was Eduard Schnitzer, had become a Turkish citizen and journeying through the sultan's domains had come in contact with Colonel Gordon, who dispatched him on a mission to Uganda. There he found himself in 1886 in the Equatorial Province holding out against the Mahdi, for Schnitzer was determined apparently to become an independent ruler. His appeal for help was answered by Stanley, equally determined to win the region either for England or for Leopold of Belgium. His choice fell on the former, however, since a large part of the funds for the expedition was supplied by MacKinnon, founder of the British East African Association. Meanwhile, the German East African Company, alarmed at a British expedition into the desirable hinterland, financed a German party led by Karl Peters and Wissmann to rescue this "native son" and German brother. The race for Uganda was on. It was won by Germany since Peters, learning on his arrival that Stanley had already relieved Emin, transferred the object of his rescue from Emin to the king of Uganda, Mwanga, who, having been deposed by the Mohammedans, was imploring British aid. With the help of one of the White Fathers, Peters secured a treaty placing Uganda under German protection.

Other and serious clashes occurred contemporaneously between Germany and Britain, their respective companies, pioneers, diplomats, throughout the entire region of East Africa: at Witu and along the Tana River, in Nyasaland where Salisbury blocked the application of the hinterland principle; in the region back of Victoria Nyanza, where Emin Pasha, parting from his rescuer Stanley, now became an agent for German advance. The need for some compromise became acute, especially as Britain desired Germany's support in Egypt and Germany, British weight in

Europe. The upshot was the famous Anglo-German Treaty of 1890, of which the reference to Somaliland, Nyasaland and South West Africa has already been noted. Here, Germany recognized a British protectorate over Witu and Zanzibar, except the coastal strip leased to the East African Company, transferred Uganda to the British sphere and recognized the basin of the upper Nile to the borders of Egypt as within the British interests. In return, much to the disgust of the colonial party, she received the island of Helgoland opposite Hamburg. Peters raged that "two kingdoms, Witu and Uganda, had been sacrificed for a bathtub in the North Sea."

This settlement of the contest for Uganda and the Nile basin with Germany did not, however, secure them finally for Britain. There remained two more steps to be taken before her hold on this territory, which later constituted so important a link in the Cape-to-Cairo scheme, was guaranteed: the recognition of the British title by more than one great power; and effective occupation of the area.

Since effective occupation only would lead to recognition, the British, through the agency of the Imperial British East African Company, became active. First, it was essential to win Mwanga, the ruler of Uganda, away from adherence to his treaty with Germany, which Peters had engineered and which the French missionaries supported against the British and Protestant claims.

Four months after the signing of the Anglo-German Treaty, the Imperial East African Company (Ibea) sent Captain, later Sir, Frederick Lugard into Uganda with a large force. It took him two years to reconcile differences of the three religious factions, sign treaties with all the chieftains and conquer the king, whom he forced to sign a treaty in 1892 bringing the kingdom directly under the rule of the company.

Meanwhile, support from the British for effective occupancy had been stirred up by a propaganda campaign carried on by the missionary societies, humanitarian organizations, chambers of commerce and the commercial and financial connections of the company in England, reaching a climax when Ibea, exhausted by the military expeditions and the attempt to construct a railway from Mombasa on the coast to Uganda, decided to withdraw from the area. Friends of the Protestant missions offered to finance the company for a year; MacKinnon contributed £20,000;

Lugard himself toured England pleading for the retention of Uganda; Cecil Rhodes offered to take over Uganda and to run it for £25,000 a year, which was refused, but his founding at this time of the Transcontinental Telegraph Company proved effective in adding Uganda as a link in the Cape-to-Cairo plan.

Finally Rosebery, the imperialist foreign secretary of the "little Englander" Gladstone, espoused the cause and the British government took over Uganda in 1894. But it was not until 1900 that the present area came under British protection. A formidable Islamic revolt inspired by the exiled Mwanga broke out in 1898. His defeat led to the extension of British authority over the remaining kingdoms by Sir Harry Johnston, high commissioner of Buganda. The unfortunate king was deported to the Seychelles Islands.

The Mandated Territory of Tanganyika

> AREA: 360,000 square miles; coastline 500 miles
> POPULATION: 5,140,368; native 5,131,240; white 9,128
> TRADE: *Imports:*   £3,448,000
>   From U.K.:   £ 928,000
>   *Exports:*   £3,461,000
>   To U.K.:   £ 657,000

Formerly German East Africa, Tanganyika, almost twice the size of the old German Empire, was Germany's prize colony and potentially extremely rich. Traversed by the long mountain chain in the eastern part of the Dark Continent which attains at Kilimandjaro the height of 19,720 feet, it is able to defy the tropical, equatorial climate. These highlands gradually descend to the coast and provide for Europeans healthful plantations with a wide diversity of cultivation. Cotton, rubber, tobacco, coffee, sisal, cattle may be raised with advantage. Besides, the territory possesses a long coastline with excellent ports on the Indian Ocean open to Eastern trade, as well as access to the inland lakes which form a gateway into the interior and to the Western commerce.

How Governed. Tanganyika Territory is a B mandate like British Togoland and Cameroons. It is administered as a protectorate with a governor responsible to the crown and a legislative council, partly nominated and partly official. A considerable body of British opinion considers Tanganyika a permanent possession.

The governor, Sir Donald Cameron, in his first address to the legislative council in 1927 said: "There is no provision in the Mandate for its termination. It constitutes merely an obligation and not a form of temporary tenure under the League of Nations. I make this statement with the full authority of His Majesty's government. . . . Tanganyika is a part of the British Empire and will remain so." In accordance with this attitude, a commission was appointed by the colonial secretary, L. S. Amery, to study the problem of closer union among Kenya, Uganda and Tanganyika. Its report, the Young Report, issued in 1929, favored an ultimate union of these three territories under a single governor-general. Although the British government abandoned the proposed plan in 1931-1932, the revival of a colonial campaign by Hitler in Germany, as well as the activities of the German *Bund* in Tanganyika Territory itself has tended only to reinforce the British opinion of permanent tenure.

How Acquired. The acquisition of the last block of territory which would complete the grandiose Cape-to-Cairo line was postponed until after the first World War. By 1914, the way was almost clear. To assemble rapidly the British gains to that date: Egypt and the Anglo-Egyptian Sudan, Uganda, formed a solid contiguous territory to the north of German East Africa; Rhodesia, Bechuanaland and the Union of South Africa completed the line in the south to the very Cape itself. Moreover, as we have seen, interference with the plan had been astutely prevented and the way cleverly guarded by the Anglo-Italian agreements of 1891 and 1894 which placed Italy in Ethiopia as an ally and buffer against the French, as well as in the Eastern Sudan to defend Egyptian and hence British interests there, at the same time guarding the upper Nile from Italian encroachments; by the Anglo-Congolese Agreements of 1894 and 1902 which secured the Congo as an ally against France as long as it was necessary, by the leasing of the Lado enclave along the upper Nile and with it Leopold's recognition of the British sphere; by the Anglo-French Agreements of 1898 and 1904 which eliminated France from East Africa; and, finally, by the Anglo-Ethiopian Agreements of 1898 and 1902 which allotted Great Britain a sphere of influence in western Abyssinia and the right to construct a railroad to connect the Sudan with Uganda.

In spite of all these intricate arrangements, the barrier of German East Africa remained in all of its immensity. How large it loomed as an obstacle to British imperialist plans may be judged by the fact that after the outbreak of the first World War, almost the first dispatch from South Africa expressed the hope that the end might see an "all red" Cape-to-Cairo Railway. Immediately the British carried the war into German East Africa, abrogating thereby the Congo Act of 1885 which established the neutrality of the Congo basin. Alone of all the German colonies, the war lasted here throughout the entire struggle, for East Africa was ably defended by General Lettow-Vorbeck to whose assistance some of the natives loyally rallied, and who did not surrender until after the signing of the armistice in 1918. In 1920, German East Africa was assigned to Great Britain as a B mandate, except for 21,255 square miles on the northwest boundary adjoining Belgian Congo, allocated as a B mandate to Belgium and known as Ruanda-Urundi.

By 1920, therefore, before Egypt achieved its independence, the British "red" stretched from Alexandria to Cape Town and the route for the famous Cape-to-Cairo Railway was clear. Today (1941) it stands, unfinished, with extensive gaps in the Sudan, in Tanganyika, in Kenya. Perhaps it never will be completed; the necessity for penetrating the hinterland no longer exists; air travel and motor routes proceed apace. As an imperialist dream, as a spur to economic expansion and penetration, the Cape-to-Cairo idea has already completed its work.

Somaliland and Zanzibar Protectorates

AREA: 68,000 square miles; 1,020 square miles
POPULATION: 347,383; 234,261
TRADE: *Imports:*   £1,521,000
    From U.K.:   £ 269,000
    Exports: £1,043,000
    To U.K.:   £   40,000   (from Zanzibar)

Somaliland is a small coastal area divided among Great Britain, France and Italy. The small British zone occupies part of the northeast horn of the African continent jutting into the Indian Ocean along the south side of the Gulf of Aden. The population is mainly Mohammedan. Britain declared it a protectorate in 1884 as part of her campaign for East Africa and guarding of the Sudan.

The Zanzibar protectorate consists of four small islands off the east coast, of which Zanzibar and Pemba are the largest, together with an insignificant coastal strip. Formerly, the sultans of Zanzibar ruled dominions stretching all along the mainland, were the center of the Arab power at the beginning of the nineteenth century and until recently dominated the trade of this part of East Africa. Gradually they were crowded out by foreign encroachments, the chief of which were the cession to Germany of the coastline territory in the Anglo-German treaty of 1890 and of the Benadir and Kishmayer coasts to Italy in 1904-1924. Britain took over the protectorate in 1890.

The islands, which are beautiful and fragrant with spices, possess practically a monopoly of the clove trade which was valued at £411,654 in 1927; they also provide ports of transhipment for the trade from the East. The city of Zanzibar, situated on its magnificent harbor, is the largest in East Africa.

How Governed. Both Somaliland and Zanzibar are governed as protectorates under governors-general sent out from England; the Zanzibar coastal strip is under the governor of Kenya.

READINGS

Beaman, A. G. *The Dethronement of the Khedive,* 1929. Revealing story.

Blunt, W. *Secret History of the English Occupation of Egypt,* 1922. Personal experience and documents.

Chirol, V. *The Egyptian Problem,* 1921. Authoritative.

Coupland, R. *The Exploitation of East Africa, 1856-1890,* 1939. Detailed.

Crabites, P. *Gordon: The Sudan and Slavery,* 1933.

Cromer, Lord. *Modern Egypt,* 2 vols., 1908. Firsthand account.

Dilley, M. R. *British Policy in Kenya Colony,* 1937. Good.

Leys, N. *Last Chance in Kenya,* 1931. Criticism of English policy.

Newman, E. W. P. *Great Britain in Egypt,* 1928. Clear and readable.

Young, G. *Egypt,* 1927. Authoritative.

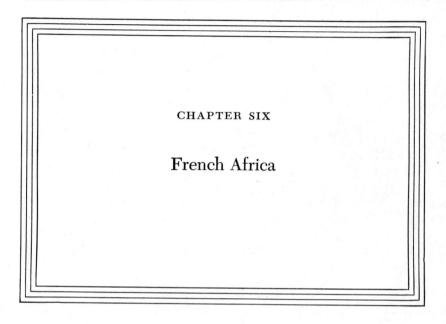

CHAPTER SIX

French Africa

HOLDINGS IN 1940

FRENCH AFRICA covers more than 4,000,000 square miles of territory, being twenty times larger than France herself. It occupies
one third of the entire continent, comprising a solid block or
"hump" in the northwest. Beginning with Algeria, Tunisia, and
Morocco extending east and west along the North African shore
of the Mediterranean Sea, it reaches south, nearly to the mouth
of the Congo River below the equator, and east to an irregular
north-south line formed by the western boundaries of Tripolitania, the Anglo-Egyptian Sudan and the Belgian Congo. The
north coastal plain lies in the temperate zone but the regions
south of it extend through the vast and arid areas of the Sahara
and the plains of the Sudan. These, in turn, merge into the
tropical colonies, many of which have a southern, coastal exposure
on the Atlantic Ocean and the Gulf of Guinea. They comprise
French West Africa, including Senegal, French Guinea, Mauritania, the Ivory Coast, French Sudan, Dahomey and the mandated
territory of Togo; and French Equatorial Africa, consisting of

THE FRENCH COLONIES

Gabon, Middle Congo, the Cameroons and the mandated territory of the Cameroons. In addition, there are Madagascar, a large island off the southeast coast in the Indian Ocean, Réunion, with its small island dependencies to the east of it, Somaliland along the west shore of the Red Sea and Obock, a coaling station thereon.

All this vast "second colonial empire" in Africa, except Algeria, a foothold on the Congo at Gabon, the trading posts at Senegal, Dahomey and on the Ivory Coast, together with the island of Réunion and the coaling station at Obock, has been acquired since 1870. Like British Africa, however, the present French empire was outlined in that year, at its essential points: at North Africa, at West and Equatorial Africa and along the eastern coast.

These scattered holdings supplied the pattern to the French government, which persistently and purposefully extended them and welded them into France's impressive African empire of 1940. For, unlike the British empire, French Africa was not an answer to the demands of the French people as a whole nor mainly to her traders, missionaries or business promoters; it was rather the consciously planned and strenuously executed endeavor of her own government.

FRENCH WEST AFRICA: *Senegal, Guinea, Ivory Coast, Dahomey, Mauritania, French Sudan, Upper Volta, Niger Colony, Mandated Territory of Togoland*

> AREA: 1,814,200 square miles
> POPULATION: 14,500,000
> TRADE: [1] *Imports:*   1,627,234,000 fr.
>   From France: 959,303,000 fr.
>   *Exports:*   1,416,120,000 fr.
>   To France: 1,122,558,000 fr.

This vast area of river basins, of forests and prairies, is mainly flat, humid and thoroughly unsuited to white settlement. The natives embrace many tribes and races and there is a group of about five million Moslems in the colony. Because of the climate and the unproductive quality of the soil, for the area is rich only in parts, the population is inadequate for the land, except in Guinea and Upper Volta, and is being further reduced by military conscription. It is of necessity a land of peasant farmers and a few native traders, the Ouloufs. European traders occupy the coast. The chief products are oleaginous—groundnuts, especially in Senegal—while cocoa and white timber form secondary crops. Immense effort has been expended upon cotton raising in the Sudan, but without great success, the major obstacle being lack of transportation and of man power. This lack of man power constitutes the chief difficulty in the development of West Africa, which in its fertile regions is a land of almost unlimited agricultural resource.

---

[1] Figures for the trade of the French colonies taken from the *Annuaire Statistique de la France*, 1938.

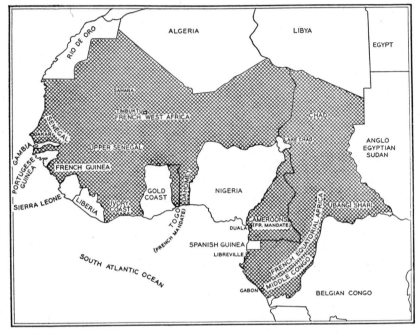

FRENCH WEST AFRICA AND FRENCH EQUATORIAL AFRICA

Senegal. Because of its age and size Senegal requires special treatment; for the early French settlements about the mouth of the Senegal River formed the nuclei of West Africa.

AREA: 75,000 square miles

POPULATION: 22,771 citizens; 1,187,830 subjects; 9,635 foreigners

TRADE: *Imports:*   1,016,800,000 fr.
        From France: 647,000,000 fr.
        Exports: 708,800,000 fr.
        To France: 632,600,000 fr.

    (including French Sudan and Mauritania)

The inhabitants of these original four communes also hold a peculiarly privileged position. For, due to the early liberalism of 1830, France conferred upon them the rights of citizenship. Thus these Senegalese communes are the only place in the entire empire where geographical position determines citizenship. The result is that they form isolated enclaves among groups of other natives not so enfranchised, resulting in discontent and friction.

Commercially, also, Senegal is important, ranking the highest in the entire colony. Indeed, its export of groundnuts far surpasses the value of all the products of the other colonies combined. Strategically also, it is invaluable to France. Dakar, the capital and trade outlet for the colony, overlooks those vital South Atlantic sea lanes, over which come such European necessities as Venezuelan oil, Brazilian cotton and Argentine meat and grain. A busy seaport with one of the safest and best harbors on the west coast, it is a convenient coaling and provision station, a regular port of call between Europe, Africa and South America. Already an important French naval base, it is also on the air route from western Europe to eastern South America.

How Controlled. The eight colonies of West Africa are united into a federation ruled over by a governor-general, sent out from France, having his seat at the capital in Dakar. Each unit has, in turn, its own lieutenant-governor responsible to the governor-general. In addition, the entire area is divided into ninety-eight *cercles* or administrative subdivisions, over each of which presides a French administrator who controls the smallest detail. The governor-general is advised by a superior council which includes some native notables, and the separate colonies have similar councils. Local autonomy is growing. Togoland, now a part of West Africa, is governed as a B mandate, but its administration is incorporated into that of Dahomey, its contiguous neighbor.[2]

How Gained. It has already been stated that all France found herself possessed of in Africa in 1871 constituted the beginnings of a strategically situated physical background, to which must be added a somewhat tarnished colonial tradition. The tradition sprang from the memory of the first great colonial empire and the eighteenth century struggle with England, represented by the neglected remnants of west-coast trading posts; and from the glamour surrounding Egypt and its environment, reminiscent of the glorious drama once enacted there by Napoleon I.

But neither the vague colonial tradition nor the more tangible physical background of Algeria and the beginnings of West Africa excited much interest in France in 1871. Indeed, the citizens of

---

[2] Togoland's trade: total imports—73,750,000 fr.; from France—12,294,000 fr.; total exports—66,530,000 fr.; to France—44,181,000 fr.

the Third French Republic were apathetic to colonial expansion
of any kind. Influenced by the anti-expansionism of the early
nineteenth century, by their own "forty years of accumulated failure in Algeria," they were rather absorbed by thoughts of *revanche*
and the recovery of French prestige in Europe. As one writer
summed it up: "There has never been an epoch nor a country
more indifferent to distant adventures than the Third French Republic and, paradoxically enough, the country sees its aversion to
colonies and its overseas empire grow at the same time by a
parallel progression."

On the other hand, the French ministers did not share popular
opinion. From the early seventies on, Gambetta, Ferry, Barthélemy,
Saint-Hilaire, and Étienne, more sensitive to the *Zeitgeist* and
becoming more and more alarmed by the spectacular scrambles
of Belgium, Britain and Germany in Africa, definitely planned and
promoted the second colonial empire. Their reasons or motives
were mainly three: the feeling of inferiority to Germany; the
ambition to make France again a great political world power; the
realization, not shared by the populace, that France's expanding
economic and political interests demanded colonies, for Ferry conceived of the four elements, industrialization, markets, colonies,
protection, as indissoluble. Twice, indeed, the Ferry ministry
fell on a question of colonial appropriations but, nevertheless, the
African empire marched on under the leadership of this "apostle
of the colonial renaissance" and his successors.

The French official plan, moreover, envisioned specific objectives that were pursued with relentless zeal. Grandiose in its
conception, it was no less than the union of the existing French
holdings in Algeria, West Africa and the Congo into one, solid,
French empire stretching from the Mediterranean to the Congo,
from the Atlantic to the Nile and to the Red Sea. Execution of
this plan demanded roughly three main lines of tenacious activity:
first, the consolidation and "effective occupation" of the scattered
holdings in the west coast and along the Congo River; second,
the establishment of some connection between these units and
North Africa; and last, the completion of the empire by the conquest of the eastern Sudan and the Nile Valley. French Africa
today reflects the success of these first two objectives; the third one
was obliged to abdicate before the ambitions of Great Britain and
her stronger might of execution.

French West Africa constitutes the achievement of part of the first objective and it would be more accurate to state that the real foundations of the second colonial empire were laid inconspicuously between the years 1830-1870 in West Africa rather than in Algeria, where they were ostensibly attempted in 1830. For while Algeria was being conquered, French explorers were tentatively probing the hinterland lying back of the French bases in Senegambia. Here French commercial tradition was strong. Merchants from Dieppe had gathered around the mouth of the Senegal River since the fourteenth century and there had been a French colony there since the sixteenth. After 1815, it was a lifeless settlement: the rubber trade languished, the slave trade was turned elsewhere, and France, disheartened by the defeat inflicted by Britain, despised her African settlements.

All was changed, however, in 1854 with the arrival of Governor Faidherbe, who really founded the colony of Senegal. He transformed a string of isolated posts into a large territory stretching from Cape Blanc to Gambia, a distance of about 700 kilometers, to which he gave a hinterland reaching back about 200 kilometers into the Senegal Valley. He also established a harbor at Dakar.

With Faidherbe's demonstration that it was thus possible to connect the hinterland with the ports, the results of the early exploration after 1815, such as the coastal settlements at Mellicouri in Guinea, Assine and Grand Bassam along the Ivory Coast, Porto Novo in Dahomey, as well as the island posts along the Niger, like Timbuctoo, assumed a new importance. In other words, it came to be realized that if the scattered West African settlements could be given a common hinterland, a rich trade might be opened up which would establish this region as an economic unit. Thus in 1870, France possessed not only the outlines of a compact block of organized territory in the Senegal Valley as far inland as Medina, together with the ports along the coast to Porto Novo, but her explorers had set the stage for linking these West African ports to a general hinterland and, as we have seen, her ministers envisioned the possibility and determined to realize it.

Their campaign necessitated a strategic as well as a physical race with the many rivals already holding so many advantageous positions in these regions, a race which soon became a scramble for the hinterland among French, British, German and Portuguese claimants. Space precludes mention of all the explorers, colonels, strategists and diplomats who won for France this objective. Reference only to the more spectacular aspects of the campaign may convey an idea of the energy and skill, the intensity of the competition and the tenacity of the official purpose with which it was waged.

Such are the union of Senegal and the Ivory Coast, pioneered by Captain Binger, who in a two-year journey traversed 4,000 kilometers from Bamaku on the upper Niger River to Assine on the Guinea coast; the link forged between the Senegal-Niger lands and Dahomey by Lieutenant Horst who traveled down the Niger River from Timbuctoo to the coast in an aluminum boat especially constructed in France and transported in sections to run the cataracts; the exploration of a 5,000-mile path from central Sudan to Lake Chad by the intrepid explorer Monteil, which demonstrated how France might reach this desirable body of water and thus link French Congo to French West Africa; and finally the work of all the various "missions" sent out by the government to unite these areas politically, militarily and scientifically.

In the wake of the traders, explorers, soldiers and scientists followed the diplomats and statesmen necessitated by the rival claims of those first in the field: like Great Britain in the Gold Coast and Nigeria, whose agents and commercial companies, such as the Royal Niger Company, were confirming and extending their preserves; like Portugal, who disputed the French holdings in Senegal near the Gambia River; like the German newcomers busily engaged in staking out their future Togolands and Cameroons. A series of skilfully negotiated treaties adjusted the dividing lines between French Guinea and Sierre Leone (1889); between Gambia, Gold Coast, Lagos and the French territories (1891); between British and French areas along the lower Niger (1898) and in the Lake Chad regions (1890-1899).

Strategy as well as military force were required in dealing with the natives. For, while the usual imperialistic methods mainly consisted in forcing overpowered and helpless chieftains to sign on the dotted line those blank treaties with which Europeans in Africa always find themselves equipped, the French discovered in this area able and shrewd emirs and sultans whose well-organized kingdoms of long standing imposed serious obstacles to the French advance. Like the Sultan of Segu, they all strove valiantly to protect their lands from the invaders. Samory, the most powerful of them, had consolidated an extensive kingdom on both banks of the Niger, but he, like the others, was obliged to bow before the superior arms and military science of the West.

By 1900, France had transformed her coastal stations with their limited hinterlands into one vast consolidated West Africa, extending from the Atlantic Ocean along the Senegal and Niger Rivers to Lake Chad, and connecting with her greatly expanded southern holdings along the Gulf of Guinea, namely, Guinea, the Ivory Coast and Dahomey. The dream of Faidherbe had been more than realized. Furthermore, after the first World War, in accordance with the secret treaty with Great Britain in 1916, French West Africa was enlarged by the acquisition of 22,000 square miles, about two thirds of former German Togoland, lying next to Dahomey, known today as the mandated territory of Togoland.

EQUATORIAL AFRICA: *Gabon, Middle Congo, Ubangi, Chari, Chad, Mandated Area of Cameroons*

AREA: 877,000 square miles
POPULATION: 3,200,000
TRADE: *Imports:*   295,756,000 fr.
     From France: 104,410,000 fr.
     Exports: 264,100,000 fr.
     To France: 183,722,000 fr.

As its name suggests, this colony consists mainly of a huge, unhealthful, tropical forest, back of which lies the agricultural lands of the upper Congo, which merge in turn into a pastoral, steppe zone, the entrance to the desert. But it is the forest zone that holds the treasures of rubber, timber and gums, and hence offered itself for exploitation from which it has cruelly suffered. Indeed, its history has been a tragic one of concession, monopoly and forced labor. Other resources in the agricultural area are cocoa, coffee, grain, and some copper in the Minduli mines.

But French Equatorial Africa today (1941) is in a state of economic stagnation—its population declining, owing to lack of food which is not sufficiently cultivated, the concession system, alcoholism, and sleeping sickness; its trade decreasing because of lack of transportation and of labor supply; its financial condition moribund. The colony presents a real problem for France. Since its creation it has produced almost always an annual deficit.

How Controlled. Like West Africa, Equatorial Africa is a federation, in this case of four colonies and one territory, Chari. It is ruled by a governor-general sent out from France and the lieutenant governor over each unit. Again, the entire area is divided into forty-four *cercles* and these are subdivided into one hundred and sixty-four smaller districts, each having its French head or native associate.

The mandated territory of the Cameroons is governed as a B mandate under the League of Nations. It is treated as an integral part of French Cameroons into whose administration it is incorporated.

How Gained. The acquisition of French Equatorial Africa represents the completion of the first and second objectives, so definitely planned by the government to construct an African empire: the consolidation and extension of the holdings on the Congo River and their connection with West Africa and the north.

In the early days, a situation similar to that in West Africa prevailed along the lower Congo River, the nucleus of Equatorial Africa. Merchants from Dieppe and La Rochelle had pioneered from the Guinea coast in the seventeenth century and established footholds in the Congo region at Gabon. Also, like the West African settlements, these languished until the 1830's when France intervened to end the slave trade, founded Libreville for freed Negroes and stimulated a busy commerce again in this region. Explorers became interested and, by 1871, tentative expeditions had revealed the possibilities of following the great rivers. These waterways invited exploration of the unknown interior and its resources, an invitation compelling in its mystery, its adventurous danger and its promise.

The first to meet the challenge seriously was Savorgnan de Brazza, the real founder of French Equatorial Africa. As recounted earlier, his first two voyages, commissioned by the French government, explored the Congo and stole a march on Stanley by cutting across from Gabon to the river. In 1880, he founded Brazzaville on the Congo opposite Stanley Pool and Francheville on the upper Ogowé River, a tributary. Rapidly signing treaties with the native chiefs, he claimed the northern bank of the Congo and part of the southern shore for France. Thus he secured a

French protectorate over a vast area between Brazzaville and the Ubangi River, which again challenged exploration and settlement. Just as Faidherbe originated the design of West Africa, so de Brazza inspired French penetration into the western Sudan and initiated what later developed into the government plan to connect Equatorial Africa with North Africa. His third journey, the *Mission de l'Ouest Africaine,* undertaken in 1881-1885, surveyed northward some 4,000 kilometers from the upper Ogowé River towards Lake Chad and thus pointed the way. Subsequent expeditions led by Paul Crampel and Lieutenant Mizan carried it further. In the nineties, the *Committee for French Africa* formulated and pushed the plan giving it strong official support. Finally, Casimir Maistre succeeded in making the round trip, mounting northward via the Congo and Ubangi Rivers to the basin of the Gribrinque River as far as Adamara and back by the Yola and the Niger Rivers.

As in West Africa, all those expeditions had brought the French into collision with the claims and ambitions of England, Germany and Belgium. Especially were the French disturbed by the Anglo-German Treaty of 1898, which settled the Nigeria-Cameroons boundary to Lake Chad. The French insisted upon the recognition of their prior rights of access to this inland lake from the south and their claim was conceded and incorporated in the Franco-Germany Treaty of 1894. During the same year, the southern boundary of French Congo was adjusted by treaty with the Congo Free State and the entire Congo-Cameroons frontier defined in a treaty with Germany in 1908. So was the second French objective of tying Equatorial Africa with French and North Africa achieved.

The third part of the great plan remained to be fulfilled: the conquest of the eastern Sudan and the Nile Valley. If realized, it would provide the inner provinces, already secured, with a river outlet; but, most important of all, it would complete the contemplated extension of the empire from the Atlantic Ocean to the Red Sea. "All Africa above the equator French" was the slogan.

Towards the realization of this project various factors favored the French in the 1890's: the northeastern portion of French Congo, unexplored and with no definite boundaries, bordered upon Bahr-el-Ghazal, a valuable district of Egyptian eastern Sudan; the Egyptian Sudan, south of Khartoum, lost to Great Britain in the insurrection of 1885, was under the corrupt and weak rule of the Mahdists; and France already possessed two footholds on the coveted Red Sea coast, Obock on the Gulf of Aden, acquired by purchase in 1862, and Jibuti in Abyssinia, established as a naval base in 1888. With the French penchant for connecting scattered holdings, it is small wonder that their plan included the building of a railway across Abyssinia to the Nile and expeditions to start from three points, Jibuti, Addis Ababa and French Congo, designed to converge in the Sudan and make it French.

Unfavorable factors, however, were also present, the chief of which was the Cape-to-Cairo dream. Great Britain was in sole possession of Egypt and was striving both by "effective occupation" and diplomacy to block France. By the Anglo-German Treaty of 1890, the Anglo-Italian Convention of 1891 and the Anglo-Congo understanding of 1894, she sought to win allies and buffers against the French. These obstacles only served to spur France on, and she hastened to put into execution her carefully planned operations. After a vehement protest to England against the Anglo-Belgian Treaty, resulting in its alteration in France's favor, the various expeditions were dispatched while the French military forces were concentrated in French Congo under Captain Marchand. He set out in 1896, successfully crossed the Nile, sailed south to Fashoda and took possession of the territory. At the same time Captain Clochette started from Abyssinia to join Marchand on the Nile. But he died en route and his expedition was forced to return on account of illness and lack of boats. A similar fate overtook the Ethiopian expedition which Legarde, the French consul at Jibuti had persuaded Menelik, the emperor, to equip in order to establish his claims on the Nile in co-operation with the French.[3] For these last had been striving hard for influence with Menelik, especially since the defeat of Italy at Adowa in 1896.

Confronted by the failures of his supporting expeditions, Marchand found himself in an extremely weak position at Fashoda with only about 150 men and inadequate supplies. Indeed, the French began to retreat diplomatically even before Kitchener confronted Marchand there. Delcassé informed the British ambassador, Lord Monson, in Paris that there was no Marchand mission in the political sense; that Marchand was only "an emissary of civilization." Buttressed by their conquests in the Bahr-el-Ghazal

---

[3] Raphael, L., *The Cape-to-Cairo Dream*, pp, 363-365.

and their reiterated claims to the Sudan, the British presented too insurmountable an obstacle to the continued prosecution of the French plan and Delcassé's government had no other course than graceful surrender. As we have already learned, the Anglo-French Treaty of 1899 effectually terminated the French ambition of a west-to-east African empire.

Although France thus renounced her grandiose dream of "north of the equator French" in the 1898-1899 settlement with England, she gained assurance of her possession of the western Sudan and of the permanent support of the British in creating her great northwestern empire. According to the Treaty of 1899, the details of the frontiers between the British and French spheres of influence in central Africa and the Sudan were determined. France lost the coveted Bahr-el-Ghazal, it is true, but retained the kingdom of the Wadai. This allowed her to round out her Sahara possessions south of Tripolitania, connecting them with the Lake Chad lands and these, in turn with the northern colonies. Thus, withdrawing from the lower Nile Valley, France concentrated upon those portions where she was supreme: she conquered Wadai; explored Borku, Tibesti and Ennedi; and, as we have observed, completed the conquest of the Lake Chad regions, perfecting by 1900 the long-planned connection between Equatorial Africa, West and North Africa. Little change occurred in the two latter regions before the first World War except for the surrender of 107,000 square miles of French Cameroons, undesirable and sparsely settled, to Germany in order to win her support of the French protectorate over Morocco. France recovered this region after Germany's defeat in West Africa by the Allies in 1918. She also gained 166,489 square miles of territory, about five-sixths of the former German Cameroons, in the allocation of the mandates.

FRENCH NORTH AFRICA: *Algeria, Tunisia, Morocco*

Algeria

> AREA: 722,000 square miles
> POPULATION: 7,234,684
> TRADE: *Imports:*   4,995,200,000 fr.
>   From France: 3,751,900,000 fr.
>   *Exports:*   5,638,800,000 fr.
>   To France: 4,706,700,000 fr.

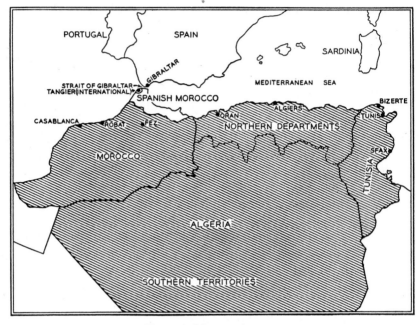

FRENCH NORTH AFRICA

France's prize colony extends along the Mediterranean coast
for six hundred and fifty miles between the protectorates of
Morocco and Tunisia. Fertile plains from fifty to one hundred
miles wide skirt the shore and are flanked by mountains whose
slopes bear rich forests and between whose ranges lie valleys
capable of raising cattle and grain. The mountains then rise to
a high, arid tableland. For two chains of the Atlas system, reaching to an altitude of 7,000 feet, divide the country from the Sahara
and protect the northern slopes from its hot and devastating
winds. Its salubrious climate, the success of its vinoculture, scientifically pursued on the coastal plain, its large French population
and trade (Algeria is France's best colonial customer), all contribute to its peculiar and valuable position in the French colonial
empire. For Algeria is regarded not so much a colony as a
prolongation of France, an integral part of the homeland. In the
1880's, when the plant disease known as *Phylloxera* attacked the
French vineyards, vinoculture was introduced into Algeria following the French emigration there. It has continued to flourish

so that the Algerian wine industry has become one-eighth that of France's. All over the wine-growing districts, peasants with Provençal accents drive ploughs between the vines. The neat village squares with their churches and their *mairies* might be anywhere south of Lyon. Indeed, if you remain north of the Atlas mountains you are not in Africa but in France. Besides its wine, Algeria produces cereals, cattle, phosphate and some iron. The native population is mainly Arab with some Berbers. To these Arabs, the French accorded as early as 1865 the right of acquiring French nationality and French citizenship with the result that French policy has raised up a French-educated, Moslem class, whose ambitions to be more French clash today with those of the European Algerians.

How Controlled. Unlike any other colony (1940), Algeria is literally a part of France, is divided into three French departments, and sends six deputies to the French Chamber in Paris and three senators to the Senate. This assimilation took place in 1871, the direct result of the establishment of the Third French Republic, which believed itself to represent the triumph of the republican idea and therefore everything belonging to it to be part of it. Algeria then came under the direct control of parliament and its *bureaux*. But this initial, extreme assimilation worked disaster: the governor-general was almost powerless because of the direct control from Paris, while local Algerian affairs were subjected to France's political and party exigencies. Algeria drifted into a veritable administrative paralysis. As a result, in 1896, the control was decentralized to the extent of cutting Algeria off from the Parisian *bureaux* (except from justice, public instruction and worship [for Europeans]) by setting up her own ministries of French officials within the colony itself and, in 1900, by giving Algeria complete financial autonomy. According to this latter arrangement, France pays only the military expenses and the interests on the railway loans, while Algeria must meet all the budget of the civil administration, receiving in return the proceeds of all the taxes. Thus, the government has worked out a kind of dyarchy: the administrative power is separated from France but not the legislative. The governor-general possesses full power and controls the north and more developed parts of Algeria by civil administration; the south by military force. He is advised by a council of government, consisting wholly of officials, analogous to an executive council in a British colony. There exist also a superior council and financial delegations. Both contain an elective element and in both Mohammedans are represented. The latter are demanding a wider franchise and a greater degree of representation.

How Gained. The conquest of Algeria by Charles X in 1830 constituted one of those autocratic gestures by which the declining Bourbons sought to justify their dynasty. Immediately precipitated by royal resentment against the famous *coup d'eventail,* the blow inflicted by means of a fly-swatter in the hands of the dey upon the French consul, it was caused at base by the economic struggle between French trade in the Mediterranean and Algerian pirates, and by rivalry between the Jewish banking houses of Bacri and Bushnor. Charles X, his ministers and military advisers pushed the conquest, to satisfy a passing craze for *la gloire,* to distract attention from his maladministration at home and to annoy England. The French people, with the exception of the commercialists and strategists, were apathetic in the extreme, and French control, obliged to prosecute almost perpetual war, vacillated for decades. Although Algeria is generally cited as the "beginning of the second French colonial empire," a generation of occupation exhibited little but a "barren use of force," resulting in the loss of about 150,000 soldiers and an equal number of colonists. In 1871, French nonexpansionists termed Algeria "a rock without water, a place where only air is found, and that is bad."

Tunisia

> AREA: 48,520 square miles
> POPULATION: Total, 2,608,313
>   French, 108,068; Moslem, 2,335,623;
>   Italian, 94,282; Jewish, 78,485
> TRADE: *Imports:*   1,559,600,000 fr.
>   From France: 966,600,000 fr.
>   *Exports:*   1,353,100,000 fr.
>   To France: 756,600,000 fr.

Tunisia has always been a tempting prize for any expanding empire because of its situation, its wealth of natural attractions and, above all, its strategic position commanding routes on land and sea. Here are well-watered valleys, mountain slopes covered with vegetation, a fertile coastal strip of vineyards and citrus orchards, large streams and even forests of oak, elm and poplar. Mountains containing some mineral wealth of iron, lead, zinc, copper, extend backwards into a central plateau whose richest possession is a vast deposit of phosphate. Northern Tunisia enjoys a remarkable climate, although it is exposed at times to the withering sirocco. The port of Bizerte on this coast has one of the finest natural harbors in the Mediterranean and is growing into an important naval base, ranking with Toulon and Brest, as well as an air base. Indeed, it has become the chief protection of routes in the eastern Mediterranean.

Tunisia became the major focus of Italy's demands, owing both to her disappointment in being crowded out of the area in 1881-1882 and by the presence of a large unassimilated Italian colony, nearly 80 per cent of whom have become Fascist. From the beginning, and until recently, Italians outnumbered French in Tunisia and formed, in contrast to the French who are predominantly transient, a group of permanent settlers engaged in agriculture, commerce, industry. The present status of these Italians rests upon the consular convention of 1896 permitting them to retain Italian nationality and to enjoy equal rights with French citizens. The attempt by the Franco-Italian Treaty of 1935 to extend this provision until 1965 has been abandoned by Mussolini's defiant denouncement of that accord in December, 1938, when he substituted an open demand for Italian annexation of Tunisia.

How Controlled. Tunisia is a protectorate which retains an oriental organization. It is governed by a native Moslem ruler, the bey, advised by a French resident general directly responsible to the foreign office and not to the minister of colonies. In accordance with the treaty between the native ruler and France, complete control over foreign affairs is vested in France, while she has a less defined influence in domestic concerns, largely determined by the personality and character of the resident general.

Notable political reforms were adopted in Tunisia in 1922, as a reply to the strong nationalist movement developing there during and after the first World War. These set up a series of economic councils, local, regional and national, which confer a considerable degree of economic self-government. Before the war Tunisia was termed an outstanding French success in government. As Sir Henry Johnston said of it: "The native dynasty has been strengthened rather than weakened, and Tunis may be pointed out as the best and wisest example of French rule over an alien race."

More recently the political problem in Tunisia became triangular: France is installed; Italy, looking to Africa for food, resources, and prestige, is demanding a territory long linked to Rome by association and situation; but the native Tunisians, whose youth is dreaming of a pan-Islamic civilization independent of Europe, want neither France nor Italy. These last are organized into a party, known as the *Destour*, meaning constitution, which is run by the educated Moslems. Since 1920 it has cultivated a growing resentment against the French and an increasing desire to be free.

How Gained. By itself, Tunisia would hardly have interested enthusiastic imperialists in the middle of the nineteenth century, for it was a sparsely settled and mostly an unsettled land. Proximity to Algeria constituted its chief attraction, while a quasi-independence from the Turkish Empire established under a weak line of inefficient beys further invited an easy penetration.

As in West and Equatorial Africa, France's first contacts in Tunisia were commercial; indeed, there are few centuries in the modern era when France's economic ties with North Africa did not exist. But after the conquest of Algeria, Tunisia naturally assumed greater importance geographically and strategically, as an extension similar to it in a temperate climate and suitability for white settlement; commercially, as affording expansion to Algerian trade; and politically, since the semi-independent rulers invited and welcomed France as an ally against the sultan.

The beys also welcomed French finance as they were extravagant administrators generally on the verge of bankruptcy. The first loan to Tunisia was floated in Paris in 1862, to be followed by many more with interest rising to the exorbitant rates of 12 and 15 per cent. Their borrowing marked the beginning of the beys' downfall. Mohammed Sadak's reckless spending during the seventies opened Tunisia wide to French, Italian and British penetration, and the ensuing rivalry hastened the French conquest, especially when Italy secured the British railway rights in 1880.

For a time, it appeared that Great Britain planned to extend her activities to Tunisia from Malta, but the Egyptian affair and need of French friendship essential for the Cape-to-Cairo plan dictated leaving Tunisia to France. At the Congress of Berlin in 1878, Lord Salisbury indicated that the French might have Tunisia as compensation for England's acquisition of Cyprus. And Bismarck, always anxious to allay France's *revanche*, remarked to the French Ambassador, St. Vallier, in 1879: "I believe the Tunisian pear is ripe and the time has come to pluck it. . . . The insolence of the Bey has acted like an August sun on this African fruit which may be stolen by another, if you leave it on the tree too long."

Supported thus by England and Germany, stimulated by her exclusion from Egypt and annoyed by increasing Italian settlement in Tunisia, France tightened her hold. As the seventies waned, she rapidly constructed a railway across the "no-man's land" between Algeria and Tunisia; replaced the French consul by a "diplomatic minister," the clever Roustan; and exploited to the utmost the internal corruption of the government and the spendthrift propensities of the bey. In 1881, border raids, utilized as an "incident," precipitated French action, and Ferry sent 35,000 Frenchmen into Tunisia as a "punitive expedition." The secret protectorate, provided for by the Treaty of Bardo signed in 1881 with the bey, became an open protectorate in 1883 by the convention of Marsa. Tunisia belonged to France.

Morocco

> AREA: 166,700 square miles
> POPULATION: 6,226,100
> TRADE: *Exports:* 2,126,800,000 fr.
> To France: 733,300,000 fr.
> *Imports:* 1,502,300,000 fr.
> From France: 676,200,000 fr.

The last of France's conquests in Africa, the capstone of her second French Empire, was reserved for the twentieth century. Significantly enough, Morocco is the *Mahgreb* of Islam, meaning the farthest outpost, the key of the West. Its situation on the northwest corner of the continent with frontages on two seas, its geology which makes it but an extension of the Iberian Peninsula and its climate, protected from tropical influences by the Atlas mountains, differentiate it from its neighbors to the east. Morocco provides good conditions for permanent European settlement and the cultivation of products little competitive with France's own. Besides, the country contains minerals, considerable copper, some silver, phosphate; invites commerce through its excellent harbors on the Mediterranean and the Atlantic Ocean; and offers an outlet for industry in its well-developed towns.

Because Morocco represents the extremity of the wave of Arab invasion, its inhabitants remain more than half Berber. Moroccan Arabs and Berbers are still a divided people: the one, town-dwellers, the other, a mountain race, who have given the reputation of hardiness, of toughness, to the country's inhabitants, about whom there is an Arabic saying: "The Tunisian is a woman, the Algerian a man, the Moroccan a lion."

How Controlled. Like Tunisia, Morocco is a protectorate governed under the same conditions. Nominally ruled by a native sultan, the country is virtually controlled by the French resident general. His control here has proved far stronger and more influential than in Tunisia, owing to Morocco or some part of it having been in a state of war since the beginning of the century; and also, to the remarkable ability and character of its resident generals, especially the first one, Marshal Lyautey, who remained in his post until 1926. Before the war he effected many administrative reforms but, at the same time, set the pattern for a native rule through native authorities from the grand vizier to the *caids* or tribal leaders, with the French as supervisors only. After the first World War, his extensive economic development further stabilized native self-government. Inspired by Marshal Lyautey, the equal of Cromer in Egypt, France administers Morocco today in the name not of France but of the sultan, and takes great care to respect native customs and religion. "Even the tourist, landing for a day from his cruising liner, cannot fail to see the chief symbol of this conception—the building of the French towns outside the old Moroccan cities, which still lead their lives as though Europe had never intruded on their privacy."[4]

Today there is a rising resentment in Morocco against France—as there is against Western control in every Moslem territory

---

[4] Monroe, E., *The Mediterranean in Politics*, p. 133.

except Algeria. Since the retirement of *Le Maréchal*, discontent has become rife and while not so organized as is the *Destour* movement in Tunisia, does cause talk of a "treaty" and of independence. Until the present, France has been able to stave off these demands; how long she can do so the future alone can tell.

How Gained. Morocco's many advantages help explain its late acquisition by France, for the country was a much-coveted prize strategically, geographically and economically. By 1900, French, Spanish, German and British interests had already either staked out claims, secured concessions or were jockeying for commercial advantage; like Constantinople, its position forbade conquest by any one power alone because so many wanted it. Consequently, it became the focus of international intrigue and the victim of diplomatic bargaining. To facilitate the latter, the weak ineffectiveness of its Mohammedan sultan, the rule of whose ancestors was so much more glorious than his own, predestined it for imperialistic penetration.

Early witness to the international jealousy Morocco excited was the Madrid Convention of 1880, which guaranteed "most-favored-nation" treatment to fourteen signatories, the United States included. During the two subsequent decades, Morocco, like Tunisia, appeared as "a rapidly ripening African fruit which no one power quite had the temerity to pluck." As soon as France essayed to pluck it, it became the apple of European discord. By 1901, Delcassé, no doubt observing that Great Britain's maritime commerce outstripped France's in Morocco by 7,000,000 francs per year, began to refer to the area as a "special interest" because of its contiguity with Algeria. At the same time France commenced to assist the sultan in suppressing native revolts occasioned by his oppressive rule and to lend him large sums. Sultan Abd-el-Aziz lived mainly for pleasure, levied heavy taxation on his subjects and borrowed recklessly abroad at exorbitant interest rates to meet the rising debts incurred by his indulgence in luxuries and products of the West. Apparently he had no sales resistance, for, while his country became more and more financially entangled, he amassed pianos and automobiles by the dozen, bicycles by the hundred, cameras, coaches, dolls, and even a zoo. Like Ibrahim Pasha of Egypt, he was the easy prey of the expansionist, the splendors of whose civilization completely dazzled and confused him.

But Delcassé's plans were not only favored by the internal situation in Morocco under its naive sultan, they were likewise facilitated by diplomacy. Germany's refusal of Britain's proffered *rapprochement* in 1901, part of which was a projected co-operation in Morocco, threw British influence on the French side with the result that the *Entente Cordiale* of 1904 settled the colonial difficulties of these two states all over the world and made them partners in future expansion. Specifically in Africa, France gave England a free hand in Egypt in return for the similar freedom in Morocco, the only condition being British insistence that Spain, not France, should occupy the northwestern corner of Morocco in the event of the sultan's loss of complete authority. For England naturally preferred a weak Spain rather than a strong France directly opposite Gibraltar. With England thus specifically bought off, Delcassé proceeded to bargain with Spain in regard to sharing north Morocco, and with Italy, promising her a free hand in Tripolitania. Thus, thoroughly protected diplomatically, as he thought, he moved on the defenceless young Sultan Aziz, already up to his neck in debts for foreign luxuries, with a demand for "reforms" by dispatching a French envoy to Fez. But, as is well known, Delcassé had failed to include Germany in his preparatory diplomacy—which neglect precipitated an international crisis, the kaiser's visit to Tangier and the Algeciras Congress of 1906.

For a time it appeared as though Delcassé's excellently laid plans had gone awry, but with the signing of the Algeciras Act of 1906 by twelve European nations, the United States and Morocco, France emerged as the real if not the nominal victor. To be sure, the act substituted international control for Morocco instead of the French protectorate and so appeared a tactical victory for Germany; but it gave France a partial control of the police power in Morocco, liable to broad interpretation. Most important of all, the congress had revealed the diplomatic strength of France—secure in her British ally, her Russian ally and in the friendship with Italy and the United States—and the weakness of Germany, isolated abroad except for Austria-Hungary, and disunited at home. For the kaiser opposed the expansion policy in Morocco, fostered by his foreign office under von Bülow and von Holstein.

The results of the Algeciras Conference served to open wide

the door of opportunity to France in Morocco, and she hastened to enter. When fresh disturbances broke out in 1907, she seized the occasion to send warships and to land troops. Germany's loud protest weakened into the conciliatory pact of 1909, whereby she recognized France's privileged position in Morocco for the guarantee of "the integrity of the Sherefian Empire" and "absolute economic equality for all nations." Finally, in 1911, the much "protected sultan," attacked by rebels, besought French aid and France, thoroughly prepared, hastened to Fez. This constituted a distinct violation of the Algeciras Act, and Germany, under the leadership of Kiderlen-Wächter, sent the gunboat "Panther" to Agadir with the reluctant consent of William II. But again the "Let-Morocco-be-French" policy of the kaiser triumphed in the divided councils of the foreign office, and Germany accepted the French protectorate over Morocco for a paltry 107,000 square miles of the French Congo. German Cameroons gained thereby a boundary on the Congo and Ubangi Rivers, but was obliged to recognize the rights granted the concession companies therein by France. The gain in territory fell far short of the demands made by German colonialists and, except for her mining rights and the privileges of the "open-door," Germany had abdicated in Morocco.

Between the years 1911 and 1914, France entrenched herself in her new protectorate. In 1912 she limited Spain's claims to include only the Spanish zone along the northern coast, 200 miles long and 60 miles deep, to be ruled by a Moroccan khalifa under a Spanish high commissioner, and the two small pieces of territory, the Ifni enclave and the Cape Juby area on the Atlantic Ocean in the extreme southwest of the country. Tangier with its surrounding 160 square miles was internationalized. The remainder of Morocco was French. The sultan accepted the French protectorate by a treaty in 1912. Nominally he was allowed to continue his rule, but a French resident general supervised the government, assisted by a large staff of French officials.

The real conqueror of Morocco, however, was the first resident general, General, later Marshal, Lyautey, who held the post until 1926. He translated France's treaty rights into occupation by military conquest, by his conciliatory policy and by his economic organization of the country. He subdued the serious rebellion occasioned by the establishment of the French protectorate in

1912 when the humiliated Sultan Mulay Hafid resigned his throne in favor of his brother; he pushed through district after district until by 1914 France controlled twice the area of 34,000 square miles occupied in 1911. During the first World War, in spite of German intrigue inciting the tribes to rebellion and the withdrawal of troops to Europe, General Lyautey not only maintained the frontiers intact but added 20,000 square miles of territory. Finally he evolved a comprehensive plan for completing the conquest and uniting Morocco by the building of transportation lines.

After the war France strengthened her hold on Morocco, since the Treaty of Versailles deprived Germany of all her concessions, mining rights and "open door" therein. But during the twenties she was compelled to exert a strenuous effort to maintain her supremacy against the rebellion of the Riffians, led by Abd-el-Krim, who was already waging a successful war against the Spaniards in Spanish Morocco. He had set himself up as "Sultan of Morocco" and bitterly resented French penetration into the Quergha Valley, the Riffian granary, and the consequent interference with his grain shipments. Both for this reason and also to justify his assumed prestige, he attacked the French, who were finally obliged to send General Pétain to force his surrender in 1926. France controlled in 1940 practically all Morocco except a few remote districts. With Morocco France completed her second colonial empire in Africa.

FRENCH EAST AFRICA: *Madagascar, Somaliland*

Madagascar and Dependencies

AREA: 237,776 square miles
POPULATION: 3,847,000
TRADE: *Imports:*   602,710,000 fr.
        From France: 454,303,000 **fr.**
        Exports: 819,397,000 fr.
        To France: 642,594,000 fr.

Quite outside the vast structure of French Northwest Africa, whose building we have just seen completed, lies the great island of Madagascar, larger than France itself, about 240 miles off the coast of east Africa opposite Mozambique. To it belongs the prosperous archipelago of the Comoro Islands, whose area is about 790 square miles.

The inhabitants are derived mainly from the Pacific Islands, mixed with Arab and Negro strains. Engaged chiefly in agriculture and stock-raising, they exhibit considerable skill in the irrigation and planting of their rice fields.

How Controlled. Madagascar and its dependencies are not divided into districts. Its rule is centralized under one governor-general, an advisory, administrative council, consisting of officials, four nominated Europeans and two natives. Since 1934 the *Délégations économiques et financières,* partly elected and partly nominated, serve as an advisory body.

How Gained. In common with all France's African colonies, her original interests here were economic when, in the seventeenth century, the East Indian Company established its stations.

Although these early settlements were sadly neglected during the eighteenth and early nineteenth centuries, France always cherished her traditional claims against the rival ones of Great Britain, whose missionaries and traders became exceedingly active. Both French and British passivity during the anticolonial periods allowed the island to fall under the rule of the native royal line of the Hovas, with whom the British element came to have considerable influence.

Naturally the situation was resented by France when her ministers became interested in Africa during the seventies. A *rapprochement* with the queen of the Hovas was attempted but failed. Ferry characteristically urged military conquest but found no support in the French chamber. However, as the result of the usual punitive expedition, a nominal protectorate was established over the island with the recalcitrant and independence-loving Queen Ranavalo in power. Moreover, British and German recognition of the protectorate was gained in return for French acceptance of the Anglo-German Treaty of 1890.

Despite the agreement, however, the proud Hovas remained hostile to French interests and favorable to British. France determined to conquer and annex the island since the still-unresolved race for position along the east coast between Germany and England jeopardized its position. In 1896 the conquest was completed with heavy expenditure of men and money. The queen was removed to another island and a governor-general installed.

Somaliland

AREA: 9,000 square miles
POPULATION: 70,000
TRADE:[5] *Imports:*   197,600,000 fr.
    To France: 20,500,000 fr.
    Exports: 133,700,000 fr.
    From France: 17,000,000 fr.

French Somaliland occupies part of the northeast horn of the African continent jutting into the Indian Ocean, along the Gulf of Tagura, and is separated from the British Aden protectorate by the straits of Bab-el-Mandeb. It extends only eighty miles inland, a mere fringe of territory, important only for its strategic value. The railroad running from its port Jibuti to Addis Ababa controls at present the only outlet to the sea from Ethiopia.

How Controlled. A resident governor-general administers Somaliland with a strong hand because of its strategic value. Recently his military staff has been increased and precautions taken to ensure its stability, for the control of Somaliland assumed especial importance with the establishment of the Italian East African empire in 1936.

How Gained. As now, strategy has always played the dominant rôle in French Somaliland. Its nucleus was the port of Obock, purchased in 1862 from a local sultan in order to provide a coaling station on the Red Sea. As national rivalry grew in the 1880's, so developed the need for greater French protection in this area. Then too, the Red Sea coast began to assume more and more importance as the dream of west-east French African empire emerged. In 1888, therefore, the French established Jibuti, near Obock, but possessed of a better harbor as a naval base, and planned to build a railway across Abyssinia to the Nile. The fact that Great Britain had closed Aden to French ships in 1883 during the Tonkin war in China had demonstrated to France the urgent need of a naval base of her own in the Red Sea and had made her more aware of the ever increasing British rivalry in East Africa. For British, French and Italian Somaliland are so many tangible witnesses to the triangular struggle for this part of the African continent.

[5] Figures for 1937.

READINGS

Anderson, E. K. *The First Moroccan Crisis, 1904-1906,* 1930. Detailed.

Knight, M. *Morocco as a French Economic Venture,* 1937.

Maurois, A. *Lyautey,* 1931.

Osborn, C. S. *Madagascar,* 1924. Travel book.

Piquet, V. *Histoire des Colonies francaises,* 1931.

Priestley, H. I. *France Overseas: A Study of Modern Imperialism,* 1938. Most recent and readable.

Roberts, S. H. *History of French Colonial Policy, 1870-1925,* 2 vols. 1929. Most complete and best.

Sloane, W. M. *Greater France in Africa,* 1923. Report of study trip.

Southworth, C. *The French Colonial Venture,* 1931. Evaluation of economic value.

CHAPTER SEVEN

Italian Africa

POSSESSIONS, 1940

WITH MUSSOLINI'S conquest of Ethiopia, Italian Africa covered 1,274,084 square miles of territory, only about one-ninth of the continent, illustrating why Italy is classed as one of the Have-Nots in colonial possessions. It comprised Libya on the south shore of the Mediterranean, and the recently created Italian East Africa, made up of Italian Somaliland on the Indian Ocean, Eritrea, lying along the coast of the Red Sea, and the newly acquired Ethiopia, a vast extent of territory stretching between them. To the Italian nationalist mind, these possessions form the scattered pillars, not the arches, of Italian Africa. For Libya, in the temperate zone of North Africa on the Mediterranean, is an isolated block of territory between Egypt and the French Empire, separated by the long reaches of the Anglo-Egyptian Sudan from the other Italian possessions in the east-central part of the continent; and Eritrea and Somaliland, until recently, were but narrow isolated fringes of territory clinging respectively to the shores of the Red Sea and the Indian Ocean, despite Francesco Crispi's dream to unite them.

This pattern of separateness which characterized Italian Africa reveals its history: above all, that Italy was a late comer in the African scramble; that it was obliged to "pick up the crumbs that fell from the rich man's table," in this case two rich men, Great Britain and France; and that, with the exception of the acquisition of Ethiopia, Italian Africa has always served as a pawn in the game of African imperialism, its extent and character entirely dependent upon the will of the other powers. For it must be remembered that Italy was not even a united nation when the era of modern expansion set in. During the 1870's, the new national government of Victor Emanuel II had its hands full welding all the diverse groups within the peninsula into Italians. The country was poor and backward; industrialization barely begun; a *national* urge for expansion as yet unfelt. It was easier to allow hundreds of thousands of citizens to emigrate in groups or individually to seek new homes in the well-established states of North and South America, favored by popular sentiment, than to organize a colonial empire with no administrative experience at hand nor surplus capital available in the country. Cavour had tried in vain to establish some Piedmontese interests in Tunisia; Italian missionaries had penetrated Abyssinia; geographers and merchants pointed out the advantages of a commercial depot along the Red Sea; but they met with no response from the yet unawakened people. "We sang to the deaf," cried Brunialti, a nationalist geographer.

Nor does the haphazard geography of Italian Africa alone reveal its history; the undesirable character of the possessions adds additional evidence, matching the disadvantages of their separateness. For Libya is largely an uninhabited desert of shifting sands with a small, fertile area along the coast, but containing no rivers; and Eritrea and Somaliland are barren, coastal places, tropically hot and unhealthful, only relieved by a restricted highland area of moderate climate in the interior and by their value as pivots and depots of trade with the East. In contrast, Ethiopia, won in apparent defiance of, rather than with the consent of the powers, not only affords a consolidation of Italian territory by linking up the East African possessions but contains considerable potential resources, agricultural and mineral, as well as opportu-

 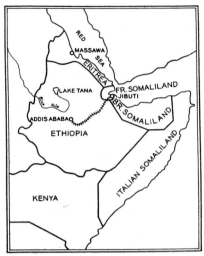

ITALIAN TRIPOLITANIA OR LIBYA   ITALIAN EAST AFRICA

nities for European settlement, its climate in some areas being generally considered the best in East Africa.

EAST AFRICA: *Eritrea, Somaliland, Ethiopia*

TRADE: [1] *Imports:*   2,447,057,000 lire
From Italy: 2,062,038,000 lire
Exports: 191,877,000 lire
To Italy: 114,845,000 lire

Eritrea and Somaliland

AREA: *Eritrea:* 46,320 square miles
Somaliland: 193,000 square miles
POPULATION: *Eritrea:* 620,000; *Somaliland:* 1,000,000

Because of their unfavorable situation and economic poverty, great effort and large sums have been prodigally expended by the Italian government upon these colonies, although the original idea of making Eritrea a field for white colonization has

---

[1] Statistics from *New International Yearbook,* 1939.

been abandoned since even its more temperate zone has proved unsuitable for European settlement.

Cotton raising has constituted the chief project here, as elsewhere in East Africa, for Italy, like Great Britain, wished to emancipate herself from dependence upon the American crop. In both colonies, the government has undertaken drainage and irrigation works, established experimental farms and granted concessions to individuals and companies. In addition, both colonies produce large quantities of oleaginous seeds: castor oil, linseed, sesame; and in Eritrea, coffee plantations are projected. Eritrea also is important for commerce, forming the natural outlet from Ethiopia and an exchange depot for goods coming from Arabia across the Red Sea. Indeed, this colony tends to be specifically a transit point for the exports from the Yemen to Europe and the Mediterranean lands.

How Governed. Prior to the conquest of Ethiopia, both Eritrea and Somaliland were governed as annexed territories, thoroughgoing colonies, each under an Italian governor and his subordinate Italian officials. On June 1, 1936, however, Mussolini issued a decree organizing them and Ethiopia into a single unit, Italian East Africa, over which he appointed Marshal Badoglio, the conqueror of Addis Ababa, the first viceroy. Under this organization, both Eritrea and Somaliland, each including some provinces of Ethiopia, have become two of the five regional governments under Italian governors and their subordinates. As such they enjoyed a measure of autonomy, always subordinate to the government at Addis Ababa in most matters of internal policy.

How Acquired. Italy's expansion into Africa, of which Eritrea and Somaliland represented the first meagre and sun-scorched fruits, was mainly the result of three forces: first, Italian historic tradition both in Africa and the Levant which manifested itself in the mid-nineteenth century by those commercial interests in the Red Sea who pressed the government to acquire a foothold there; second, the urgent nationalistic and economic need felt by the new nation—its rulers rather than its people—whose birth occurred at the same time as the dawn of modern expansion and the rise of economic nationalism; and, finally, the subtle diplomacy of England in using Italy as a buffer against France in East and Central Africa. All three of the forces coincided in the 1880's. In 1882 the Italian government, responding to the plea of commercial interests, although against the apathy and even hostility of the country as a whole, purchased the district on the Bay of Assab near the straits between the Red Sea and the Gulf of Aden, which had been acquired by the Rubattino Shipping Company as a coaling station in 1869. Macini, the foreign minister, stated in the chamber of deputies that Italy would "find the keys to the Mediterranean in the Red Sea," by which he meant that he envisioned the extension of the Italian sphere of influence from that point through the Sudan and Dafur to the Libyan hinterland, thus advancing northward from the south and southwest. Such an ambitious plan, however, was destined never to be executed although it was begun. Depretis, Mancini's successor, took possession of Massawa on the west coast of the Red Sea in 1884-1885, thus extending Italian occupation in the low-lying zone between the sea and the plateau, definitely encouraged by Great Britain. In 1890 all the various holdings in this area were united into a single colony, *Colonia Eritrea* or Red Sea colony.

Meanwhile, Italian explorers had become interested in East Africa and had observed that Somaliland was still unpre-empted by the European powers with the exception of the area about the Gulf of Aden, where the British had replaced Egyptian control. Immediately after the occupation of Massawa, the Italian government dispatched a cruiser to explore the mouth of the Juba River and the commercial opportunities along the Somali coast. The mission secured a commercial treaty signed with the Sultan of Zanzibar. Several years later, two other sultanates, Abbia and Mijertins, came under Italian protection and Francesco Crispi, who outdid all former premiers in colonial zeal, laid claim to twelve hundred miles of Somali coast from British East Africa to the easternmost tip of the continent at Cape Guadafui.

But Italian Somaliland was not actually occupied until 1891 by Captain Filonardi, the consul at Zanzibar, who formed a company to govern and develop the land. Despite an annual subsidy from the Italian government which also paid a rent, arranged by Great Britain, to the Sultan of Zanzibar for part of the coast, Filonardi's company failed as did likewise its successor, the Benadir Company. Unable to cope with the native insurrections, the Benadir Company yielded its control to the Italian gov-

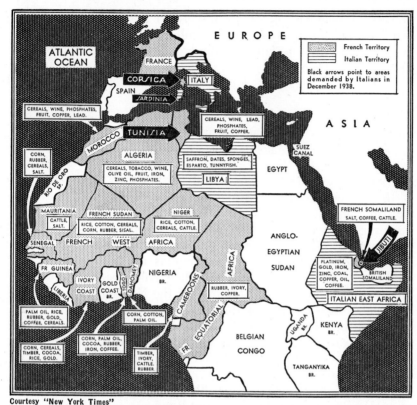

RELATIVE VALUE OF ITALIAN AND FRENCH COLONIES

ernment in 1906, when the whole area of the former protectorate received colonial status.

In accordance with the promise contained in the Treaty of London, 1915, Jubaland, consisting of about 33,000 square miles taken from former British East Africa, was added to Somaliland in 1924, a small compensation for the vast gains of Britain and France. As a result, effective occupation was extended over the Nogal territories and the sultanates of Obbia and Mijertins in the north. In the same manner Eritrea was aggrandized in 1935 by some strategically situated 300 square miles of French Somaliland, stretching north of Jibuti along the Red Sea and affording an outlet on the Gulf of Aden. This area was reoccupied in February, 1939, by France, both because Italy renounced the Italo-

Franco Agreements of 1935,[2] and as an answer to the Italian demands for Jibuti, along with the allotment to Italy of a further share in the French railway running from that port to Addis Ababa.

Ethiopia

AREA: 350,000 square miles
POPULATION: 10,000,000

About three times the size of Italy, Ethiopia is considered one of the prizes of Africa. Situated in the eastern highlands, its plateau ranges in altitude from 6,000 to 11,000 feet, enjoys in some regions a genial climate and possesses potentially rich agricultural and mineral resources. Whereas the lower country and deep gorges are hot, the higher regions are well-watered and salubrious. The chief river is the Blue Nile, issuing from Lake Tana—while many other tributaries of the Nile have their rise in Abyssinia. The fertility of the plain around Lake Tana as well as that of the Gojjam province is famous. Here the Italians hoped to grow flax in large quantity and coffee. Wheat can be cultivated on the slopes of the plateau; coffee, cotton and tobacco may be grown in the southwest.

The mineral resources, partially prospected but still unexploited, are believed to be large; but here opinions differ. Reports of mountains of copper, huge deposits of gold, great subterranean lakes of oil, have not so far been verified by those concessionaires who have attempted to develop them. Yet certain deposits do exist—such as salt in the plain of Danakil, containing virtually an unlimited supply; iron, mica, gold, platinum, precious stones, silver; and oil and coal are believed to exist. Prospecting for precious and other metals and for oil has been going on all over the territory. Twenty or more institutions and companies were reported to be so engaged, among them the Italian East African Mining Corporation, founded partly with German capital in 1937. In the absence of anything but Italian reports recently from the region, it is impossible to know the extent of their accomplishments.

---

[2] See p. 149.

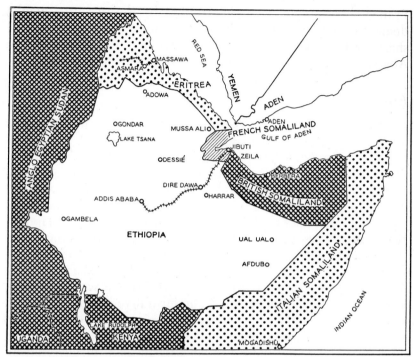

From Research Report, Foreign Policy Assn., September, 1935

ETHIOPIA: ITALY'S OBJECTIVE IN 1935

The same lack of accurate information surrounds the progress of the six-year plan for settlement, development, road engineering and education which was inaugurated in 1937, one year after the conquest, for which the sum of one hundred million lire was dedicated by the official Credit Consortium for Public Works. In 1939 it was reported that much had been achieved during the past three years: the military conquest almost completed; a vast network of roads created, 2,040 miles being ready by June, 1938; seventy-eight new post-offices opened; telegraph wires laid and the seats of the five local governments of East Africa linked to Addis Ababa, and the most distant corners of the colony served by air lines.

The actual settling of Italian colonies on the land began in 1938 when some six to seven hundred heads of families from Romagna and Apulia took up plots of from 75 to 125 acres. But the plans for further migration were interrupted by the unsettled condition of the country and the flareup of renewed resistance, so that by the end of the year Italy was discouraging further settlement there for the present. It was all too evident that much still remained to be done in Ethiopia by way of pacification. The people are less than one-half Abyssinian; the remainder, Gallas and Negro tribes along the west and south frontiers, with Somalis on the east. They carry on a guerilla warfare against the invaders and are themselves torn by tribal strife.

How Governed. According to the decree of June 1, 1936, Ethiopia became the core of the new East African Empire with Addis Ababa as the capital. Administered as a colony with all legislation and executive power concentrated in the hands of appointees of the home government in Rome, provision was nevertheless made for giving white colonists and natives some voice in the affairs of the empire. At the head of the central government stood the governor-general or viceroy, a vice governor-general and chief of staff whose major function it was to co-ordinate and direct the political and administrative action of the five regional governments into which the empire was divided. Each of these had its own governor and staff and enjoyed a degree of autonomy. Two consultative organs, the council of government containing the empire's highest officials, and the board of consultors, composed of prominent white colonists and six native chieftains, co-operated with the governor-general, but were subordinate to him as were the regional governments. Addis Ababa and its surrounding territory was not part of any of the five regions but occupied a position similar to the District of Columbia in the United States, with a special administration under its own governor.

How Acquired. The recognition by Great Britain of the Italian conquest of Ethiopia, in the Anglo-Italian Pact of 1938, represents the successful climax of a long struggle for this coveted territory, a struggle in which the major participants were Great Britain, France and Italy, and whose persistent recurrence has spanned almost half a century. The proud antiquity of the ruling Ethiopian dynasty, which claims descent from King Solomon and the Queen of Sheba, and includes among its king's titles "Conquering Lion of Judah," supplies one key to the length of the struggle; international, imperialistic competition provides the other.

As has already been indicated in the account of British North Africa, the expansionist ambitions of Britain, France and Italy were all converging upon Abyssinia and the eastern Sudan in the late 1880's. Britain needed to control the area essential to her Cape-to-Cairo plan; France desired it to realize her west-east African dream; and Italy, encouraged by her recent acquisition on the coasts of the Red Sea and the Indian Ocean, aspired to push into the Abyssinian hinterland and thus carve off the eastern tip of Africa as an Italian empire. Indeed, under the direction of the colonial-minded Francesco Crispi, premier of Italy from 1887 to 1896, Italian garrisons had been stationed along the Abyssinian frontiers where they touched those of Italy's newly established Eritrea, inevitably coming into conflict with the Abyssinians. But Italian penetration began in earnest in 1889, when Crispi supported with substantial armaments the claims of Menelik, a local chieftain or "king," to the throne of Abyssinia, and then proceeded to collect his bill upon Menelik's success in the shape of the ill-famed Treaty of Ucciali. According to this agreement, Italy granted Ethiopia a loan, free passage of arms through the port of Massawa and gained an extension of Eritrea back into the Abyssinia highlands, as well as Menelik's promise, according to the Italian version, to consult Italy in dealing with foreign powers. It was in this latter obligation that the Italian and Amharic versions of the treaty text varied—the Italian version binding Menelik to consult Italy; the Amharic text permitting him to do so if he chose. Italy's interpretation of the treaty amounted to the establishment of an Italian sphere of influence, really a protectorate, in Ethiopia, which was recognized and confirmed by England in 1891 as a move in her game against France.

Meanwhile Menelik, recognizing that his kingdom's independence was gradually being jeopardized by the encroachments and machinations of the European powers, formally denounced the Ucciali Treaty in 1893. Italy responded to this act of defiance by armed invasion which met disastrous and crushing defeat by Menelik's superior forces at the famous battle of Adowa in 1896, revenge for which became the slogan of Italian expansionists. After Adowa, Italy's lost influence in Ethiopia was replaced by that of Britain and France, to whom the emperor granted valuable favors in return for their protection: to the British, a sphere in western Ethiopia which guarded Lake Tana and the flow of waters in the Blue Nile, the first formal acknowledgement of Great Britain's interests on the headwaters of the Nile in Ethiopia, as well as a trading post near the Sudan border in the White Nile; to the French, the concession for a railway company to construct a railroad from Jibuti in French Somaliland to a point in the interior on the headwaters of the White Nile. Italy, indeed, appeared crowded out of the country. But in 1906, fearing disintegration of Ethiopia because of the supposedly imminent demise of its emperor, Britain proposed the Tripartite Agreement of England, France, Italy, to preserve the "integrity" of Ethiopia and, incidentally, to block the German advance in central Africa.

The 1906 treaty confirmed England's and France's already existing concessions in Ethiopia and admitted Italy to a sphere of influence in the region forming the hinterland of her possessions, Eritrea and Somaliland, through which she might construct a railway linking her two colonies, and a nominal sphere of influence over the whole of Ethiopia, subject to the British and French reservations. Also the French railway, running into the interior from Jibuti, was internationalized—the board of directors to include British, Italians and Ethiopians. The three powers further agreed that they would seek no special concessions which would injure the interests of the others. It will be noted here that while the spheres of interest of England and France had been acknowledged by the ruler of Ethiopia, those of Italy had not; they were dependent upon France and England, who had brought Italy in, as usual, as the pawn of their aims, to assist in preserving the status quo in Ethiopia. But the actual effect of the Tripartite Treaty of 1906 was to save Ethiopia from aggressive penetration by any of the powers from 1906 to 1934; in other words, it saved it for Italy, an effect quite unforeseen by its creators.

In the meantime, Italian nationalism had been growing and with it an appetite for imperialism; indeed Italy, although restricted in Ethiopia by the other powers, never renounced the dream of African empire. Always, she maintained close touch with the northern Mediterranean shore, which held for her the age-old memories of the "glory that was Rome's." Forced to submit to France's seizure of Tunisia (1881) into which she (Italy) had sent many colonists and merchants, she transferred her aims to Tripolitania (Libya), largely an uninhabited desert of shifting sands. Indeed, the first decade of the twentieth century witnessed an upsurge of colonial enthusiasm. Nationalists, such as Gabriele d'Annunzio and Scipio Sighele, wrote in the contemporary fashion that "imperialism is the necessity of nationalism. . . . it is the natural development of the instinct of power, of the desire for expansion." Premier Giovanni Giolitti yielded to political and economic pressure and, like his predecessor Crispi, led in the expansionist campaign to secure Libya, one of the few unoccupied areas in Africa. But even here, as we shall see, Giolitti was obliged to submit to Italy's again becoming the pawn of the powers of the *Entente*. It was owing only to the give and take between the colonial ambitions of her two rivals that she was allowed to acquire even Tripolitania in 1911.

It is no wonder then that Italy entered the first World War, discontented with only the crumbs of African empire that fell from the rich men's tables; or that she stipulated in the Treaty of London, her bargain with the Allies (1915), that if England and France acquired the German African colonies, Italy should be compensated by an extension of her colonies, Eritrea, Somaliland, Libya. But again she was doomed to disappointment and disillusionment: the only "compensation" received was a series of delayed, grudging boundary adjustments, mainly in desert areas. The first World War left her colonial ambitions unfulfilled; no mandates even were conferred upon her; of all the great powers, she alone received no appreciable colonial recompense for the sacrifices which she had endured, or such was her constant claim.

Post-war frustration in the colonial field coincided with the post-war rise of nationalism and Fascism, to which it supplied a contributory factor. And during the first years of the new regime, Mussolini devoted considerable attention to the colonial problems: "Destiny drives us towards the shores of Africa. Nothing, no one will stop the course of this destiny which represents the indomitable will of the Italian people," he declared after a journey of inspection around the Mediterranean; and later again, "Italy is able to civilize Africa and her position on the Mediterranean gives her the right and duty to accomplish this task. . . . We desire those who are satiated and who wish to retain their possessions to refrain from blocking the cultural, political and economic expansion of Italy."

In the pursuit of these objectives, therefore, the Italian government attempted to promote its sphere of influence in western Ethiopia and carry out those projects envisioned in the Tripartite Agreement of 1906, but here it met stern British resistance. Finally, with the aid of further bargaining and compromise, Britain recognized (1925) an exclusive Italian economic influence in western Ethiopia to be crossed by an Italian railroad, thus implementing the agreement of 1906, in return for Italian recognition of British paramount hydraulic rights in Lake Tana and the upper Nile, which included permission to construct a dam at Lake Tana. But the 1925 agreement differed noticeably, and to Italy's advantage, from that of 1906. For the latter was based on the principle of the "open door"; the former upon that of exclusive privilege, which emphasized no distinction between the urgency of British, French or Italian projects in Ethiopia.

The only interest not consulted in the 1925 agreement was that of the Ethiopians, whose regent, Ras Tafari (later Haile Selassie) vigorously objected to the Anglo-Italian arrangements and protested to League of Nations members, of which Ethiopia was one, that Ethiopia was being coerced against its own interests. Friction grew between the emperor and Italy, in spite of the signing of a twenty-year treaty of friendship, nonaggression, conciliation and arbitration in 1928 and renewed in 1934.

But with the beginning of the thirties, Mussolini evidently determined upon drastic action in Ethiopia. In 1932, Grandi, then minister of foreign affairs, gave warning in a ringing speech to the senate: "We cannot tolerate that Italy as a colonial factor be overlooked"; and Il Duce, himself, indicated Abyssinia as a field for conquest in 1934 when he pointed out that there was no room for expansion to the north or west; hence, "Italy must turn to the south and east." By the summer of 1934 also Italy was markedly increasing her armaments in her colonies; Ethiopia was reorganizing her military forces and conflict was imminent. In December, a clash occurred between the troops of an Italian outpost and the armed escort of an Anglo-Ethiopian boundary commission at Walwal near the Ethiopian-Italian Somaliland border. Mussolini decided that here was the needed "incident," mobilized 200,000 troops before the arbitration commission, appointed to fix responsibility for the clash, had submitted its report, and declared his intention to settle once for all the question of the Italian position in East Africa. Il Duce advanced two time-worn arguments for thus precipitately carrying the Italian sword into Ethiopia: the necessity for "restoring order," abolishing the slave trade and extending "civilization"; and the urgent economic need of Italy.

Both Great Britain and France found themselves caught between their African interests and the necessity of preserving "collective security" in Europe against the rising menace of Hitler. Consequently, they employed the possibilities of the League of Nations Covenant, as far as the latter did not conflict with their own national concerns, and the application of "sanctions," except on the most essential element, oil, in order to maintain their control of the situation. At the same time, however, France, it is strongly suspected, connived at Italian operations in Ethiopia in the Franco-Italian Pact of 1935, which fear of Germany in Europe induced her to sign. This Laval-Mussolini accord was supposed to liquidate all the colonial difficulties between France and Italy left pending by the Treaty of London (1915). It obligated Italy to consult with France in the event of Germany's threatened absorption of Austria, in return for which France ceded a slice of territory to Libya, a small area to Eritrea, a share in the French railway from Jibuti to Addis Ababa and extended special citizenship rights to Italians in Tunisia. In addition, it has been claimed that France verbally permitted Italy liberty of action in Ethiopia, although this was denied by Laval in the French chamber.

But the powers failed to control Mussolini either by their joint action within the framework of the League of Nations or by unilateral agreements outside it. Britain and France made one last effort to "find a formula" by advancing the abortive and ill-fated Hoare-Laval treaty proposals (1935) which attempted to protect their interests in Ethiopia along with Italy's and to perpetuate the old game. But it failed, and with its failure their fifty-year-long practice of "keeping Italy in leading strings" in Africa came to an end.

Meanwhile, Mussolini prosecuted the Italian campaign against Haile Selassie and Ethiopia with all the ruthlessness which an industrial twentieth-century power can inflict upon a primitive and undeveloped civilization. Both Adowa and Adigrat were bombed by Italian airplanes within the first three months of the war and both were captured without resistance. As a means of combatting a superior opponent, Haile Selassie pursued the tactics of delay and refusal to be trapped into open engagements. This forced upon the Italians the necessity of constructing roads through the difficult mountains and highlands in order to advance with their modern mechanized equipment. After three months, the Ethiopians collapsed before the new onslaught of machine guns, heavy artillery, poison gas, aircraft and tanks, which not only overpowered them but struck at their old routes and means of communication. Victory was proclaimed on May 9, 1936, after the taking of Addis Ababa on May 5 and of Harar, the second Ethiopian city, three days afterwards. While Victor Emanuel in Rome decreed that "the title of Emperor of Ethiopia is assumed for himself and for his successors by the king of Italy," Haile Selassie, the Lion of Judah, was on his way to exile in Europe on a British warship, leaving behind him his hard-pressed country which, by the Duce's decree of June 1, 1936, became the core of the new Italian East Africa.

But the decree of June 1, 1936, not only marked the Italian conquest of Ethiopia and the founding of Italian East Africa by the union with it of Eritrea and Somaliland; it meant the emergence of Italy as a great colonial power in Africa, a position confirmed by German recognition of the Ethiopian empire on the occasion of the cementing of the Rome-Berlin axis (July 1936) and, more significantly, by the Anglo-Italian Agreement of 1938. In the latter, Great Britain virtually accorded Italy the position of an equal in East Africa, especially in the clauses respecting the protection of their mutual interests along the Red Sea. It was from this position, buttressed by Germany and by Franco's victory in Spain, that Italy made further African demands: Tunisia, Jibuti, and shares in the Suez Canal (December, 1938).

Libya or Tripolitania

AREA: 684,764 square miles
POPULATION: 730,000
TRADE:[3] *Imports:*   882,058,000 lire
      From Italy: 786,456,000 lire
      Exports: 108,962,000 lire
      To Italy: 97,176,000 lire

---

[3] Figures for 1938. *Annuairio Statistico Italiano,* 1939.

Italian tourist literature grows eloquent in describing the charms of Libya for those seeking "new holiday resorts with unusual features, an excellent winter and spring climate, quaint customs and archeological remains of major interest." But these features hardly constitute a valuable colony. The fact is that Libya is known to be a poor land, in the main desert, without minerals, without water and without many inhabitants, about one to every square mile. It consists of the two ancient countries, Tripolitania and Cyrenaica, separated by 650 kilometers of dreary waste around the Bay of Sidra. Tripolitania in the west is mainly composed of light, sandy soil with underground water supplies, but not in sufficient quantities to be pumped for irrigation and the raising of crops on a large scale; but Cyrenaica is very different, with its small area of good land, red and black soil, and a few forested valleys. Not so hot as Tripolitania, it offered a future for cattle raising and for some products which Italy did not raise. Moreover, for years Libya was on the road to nowhere, for it lay on the disused caravan route from the Sudan to Europe. But when Italy conquered Libya, she was thinking mainly not of its inherent but its political and strategic value. "We knew it was no Eden. . . we went in there simply in order to be able to breathe freely in the Mediterranean—to avoid being stifled amidst the possessions and naval bases of France and Great Britain."[4]

Under Mussolini, however, great effort and vast sums of money were expended to make it an economic asset in produce and as a settlement area for Italians. In 1928 a policy of state-aided colonization regardless of expense was commenced, but in spite of lavish provision of capital to the small holders, the number of Italian agriculturists in Libya by 1936 amounted to only 13,000 when the Ethiopian campaign interfered with the plan. In 1938, however, after unsettled conditions in the new empire discouraged settlement, the home government adopted an ambitious four-year program designed to settle 80,000 Italians in Libya by 1942 at a cost of $100,000,000, and dramatized its inauguration by dispatching in one day a fleet of sixteen vessels from three ports, carrying 18,000 persons. Settlers were provided with homes complete down to matches to light the kitchen fire and a government subsidy for four years while they were bringing the desert, irri-

[4] Quoted in Monroe, E., *The Mediterranean in Politics*, p. 163.

gated with artesian wells, into production. Also, since the Ethiopian campaign, the through air line to Egypt and East Africa calls at Libya and a newly built road runs from the Tunisian to the Egyptian border. Although thus strategically increased in value under the late improvements, it remains a question whether production in Libya will ever pay for its extremely expensive colonization and irrigation. Barley, dates, olives, oranges, lemons and vegetables are raised, but, owing to the lack of rainfall, a good harvest can be expected only every four or five years. Principal exports are ostrich feathers, ivory, skins, sponges, hides, wool, cattle and horses.

How Governed. The Fascist dictatorship abolished the liberal measures of the Italian government whereby it set up in 1919 representative government in Libya: parliaments in both Cyrenaica and Tripolitania, citizenship for the natives and indirect rule. The two provinces were united under a single Italian governor and his staff and Libya became an annexed colony. In 1937, Il Duce himself visited the colony and declared that he was the "Protector of Islam." In the same year the government was reorganized with a slight extension of self-rule.

How Acquired. More than in the case of any other Italian colony, the acquisition of Libya illustrated the dependence of Italy's colonial empire upon the will and purposes of the great powers, no matter how pressing her economic need, her political and strategic exigency—a fact of great significance in the current colonial problem. As early as 1838, Mazzini, the prophet of a united Italy, claimed northern Africa for his country; but it was not until 1911 that Italy was able, as the latest comer, to secure the least desirable section of that Mediterranean coast; and then, only with the consent of the other powers and because of treaties of give and take, whose contrivance favored their own colonial aims.

Despite the elbowing aside of their young nation, Italians managed nevertheless to maintain close touch with the North African coast, hallowed for them by Rome's victory over Carthage and the traditions of the great commercial empire of the Italian city states of the Middle Ages. Impelled by population pressure at home, Italians in large numbers settled in Egypt, Algeria, Tunisia, and Tripolitania and there assumed a prominent part in the cultural and economic life. Royal schools for teaching Italian were established; the *Banco di Roma* and *Banca d'Italia* invested money in all kinds of business enterprises and were among the first to lend money to the extravagant beys who ruled over these provinces under the overlordship of the Ottoman Empire; and everywhere Italians competed with the Greeks in trade, with the British and French in finance and construction enterprises.

In 1862 a united Italy had begun to assert herself, especially in Tunis, only one hundred miles across the Mediterranean from Sicily, where the weak rule and reckless expenditures of the bey afforded so excellent an opportunity for financial penetration. By 1866, 2,000 Italians were settled there. Eventually a triple control of Tunisia's finances was established by England, France and Italy. Then Britain withdrew, having her hands more than full in Egypt and elsewhere, and in 1881-1882 Italy was forced to give way before France, a disappointment so bitter that it impelled her to seek admission in the Triple Alliance, whereby she hoped to realize her dreams of colonial empire under the aegis of the central powers.

In the meantime, Italy had sustained another blow: she returned from the Congress of Berlin, alone of all the powers, empty handed. As we have noted, she sought consolation in the Red Sea, not being strong enough then to follow up Freycinet's suggestion that she occupy Tripolitania as compensation for France's seizure of Tunisia. Her exploits in East Africa engaged her attention more and more and with England's encouragement, Crispi's dream of advancing into the hinterland of Tripoli from the south was growing stronger and stronger. Indeed, this colonial-minded premier secured in the renewal of the Triple Alliance Treaty in 1887 a proviso that, should the status quo be altered in the Balkans, Italy be permitted compensation even outside the Balkans, and from Germany a pledge of armed assistance to prevent France from taking Tripolitania. Also, the same year, Italy received a pledge from Austria in the Mediterranean agreement of England, Italy and Austria, to oppose any further extension of France's power in North Africa. But Crispi's dream was destined to be rudely shattered with the disastrous defeat of the Italians at Adowa in 1896 and by the ensuing Fashoda Agreement of 1898-1899 between France and England, which threatened to shut out Italy even from Tripolitania and to close the North African shore to her forever. Indeed, Rudini, Crispi's successor, renounced all the colonial ambitions which had been so tenaciously and fervently pursued by the latter, even in spite of parliamentary opposition, and turned to the consolidation of those lands left under Italian sovereignty.

This colonial inaction, however, did not long endure for, as we have already noted, Italy experienced with increasing intensity during the first decade of the twentieth century all those incitements to expansion common to the age: economic need, population pressure, hunger for power and prestige. Also, the expansionist aims and ambitions of the other powers helped to resurrect and again direct Italian colonial ambitions: France in Morocco, Austria in Bosnia and Herzegovina, Germany in Turkey and Russia at the Dardanelles and in the Balkans. Deterred by her alliance with Germany, rapidly becoming a close ally of Turkey—by fear of the other powers and the danger of opening the issues of the Eastern Question—Italy did not immediately assert herself in Tripolitania but contented herself with increased economic penetration, procuring from the Porte in 1905 the monopoly of all commercial concessions there. Meanwhile, Premier Giolitti, urged on by the expansionists, quietly negotiated diplomatic arrangements with most of the powers: with France the treaty in 1901, which guaranteed the French sphere in Morocco in return for an Italian sphere in Tripolitania, to which also Britain consented; and the Racconigi Agreement in 1909, promising Russia's support of Italy in Tripolitania in return for the latter's recognition of her claims in the Dardanelles.

Finally, the Agadir incident in Morocco, coupled with clashes between Italian and Turkish interests in Tripolitania, roused popular demand for its annexation to such a pitch that government action was precipitated. Italy notified both the Triple Entente and the Triple Alliance of its purpose, to which Britain and France gave hearty assent, but Germany and Austria counseled half measures. Unable to resist popular clamor, Italy demanded from the Porte not only the recognition of all economic concessions, which was granted, but also the right to plant Italian colonies in Tripolitania, which was refused. On the plea that Turkey barred Italian economic activity there, the government declared war in September, 1911, and Turkey, threatened by the Balkan War, was forced to sign the peace treaty at Lausanne in October, 1912. Italy gained the provinces of Tripolitania and Cyrenaica and retained the island of Rhodes and the Dodecanese group as a pledge of the treaty's execution, conquests not officially recognized until the signing of the Treaty of Lausanne with Turkey in 1923.

But the Treaty of Ouchy [5] (1912) conveyed "paper rights" only, which here, as in so much of African territory, had to be implemented by the pacification of rebellious Arabs and Berber tribes. It proved an expensive conquest and had to be achieved twice, for when Italy joined the Allies in the first World War, Germany and Turkey armed the Bedouin, who drove the Italians to the sea. Owing to internal disturbance at home, reconquest was only begun after 1922, Tripolitania not being pacified until 1923; Cyrenaica not until 1932. Even then, large sums had to be spent as now in policing the area and Rome in 1940 contributed two-thirds of the revenue of Tripolitania and three-quarters of that of Cyrenaica. Nothing that the colony is likely to produce promises to compensate for this outlay which the vast desert swallows, but the strategic advantage of Libya was considered worth its cost.

The colony was somewhat extended on various frontiers as compensation for African territory promised in the Treaty of London (1915). In 1919, a slight rectification of the boundaries was made at the expense of French territory; in 1925, the cession of Jurabub on the Egyptian-Cyraenican border was obtained; and in 1935, almost 45,000 square miles of French possessions in Tibesti were added.

READINGS

Barclay, T. *The Turko-Italian War and Its Problems*, 1912. Detailed.
Glanville, J. L. "Colonialism in the New Italy," *Arnold Foundation Studies in Public Affairs*, 1934. Brief overview.
Harmsworth, G. *Abyssinian Adventure*, 1935. Frank appraisal.
MacCartney, M. H. and Cremona, P. *Italy's Foreign and Colonial Policy, 1914-1937*, 1938. Biased.
Martelli, G. *Italy Against the World*, 1937. Best on Italo-Ethiopian venture.
Rey, C. F. *The Real Abyssinia*, 1935. Useful.
Villari, L. *The Expansion of Italy*, 1930. A defense.

---

[5] Referred to also as Treaty of Lausanne. Preliminaries of the treaty were begun at Ouchy, near Lausanne on Lake Geneva, and completed at Lausanne.

CHAPTER EIGHT

The German African Empire, 1884-1919
Belgian Africa[1]

POSSESSIONS IN 1914

COMPLETELY ELIMINATED from Africa immediately after the first World War, the German empire there consisted, in 1914, of 947,-578 square miles of territory, occupying about 8 per cent of the continent. For Germany was a late comer, indeed the latest of all, into the scramble for Africa. Like Italy's, her colonies were scattered and presented the appearance of mere insets in the map. No two of them were contiguous. East Africa, in the highland area, extending along the coast and inland to Lake Tanganyika, was separated by the vast Belgian Congo from the west coast possessions, Togoland, a small enclave between Nigeria and the Gold Coast, and the Cameroons, sandwiched between Nigeria and French Equatorial Africa. Down at the southern tip of the continent alongside the Union of South Africa on the western coast lay German South West Africa, again separated from the Cameroons by French Equatorial Africa, the Belgian Congo and

---

[1] Material in this chapter abridged, summarized, paraphrased or otherwise included from *The Rise and Fall of Germany's Colonial Empire* by Mary E. Townsend, with permission of The Macmillan Company, publishers.

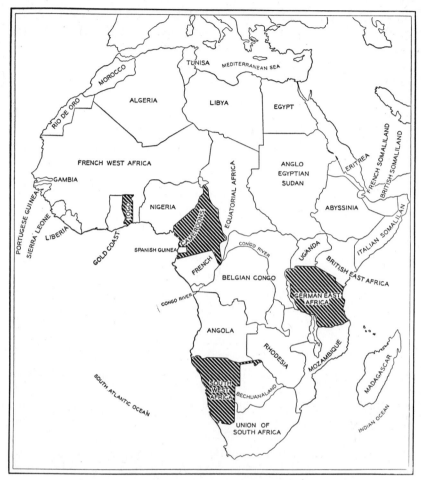

THE GERMAN AFRICAN EMPIRE, 1914

Portuguese Angola, and from East Africa by the great stretch of British territory, Bechuanaland and Rhodesia.

Like Italy's also, the geography and character of Germany's Africa revealed its history. She, too, got off to a late start in the colonial race; she, too, was obliged to take what was left against the opposition of England and France, upon whose superior power and prestige her position on the African continent, as well as her hopes for further expansion, were completely dependent. Unlike Italy, however, she was far stronger in Europe, more internally unified, and more influenced, in 1871, by a well-developed colonial cult or tradition. Moreover, she had taken a prominent part in the opening up of the Dark Continent with her early traders, missionaries, explorers and scientists. For all these reasons she was able to counter a more effective opposition to Great Britain, her most serious rival, both in activity on the spot in Africa and in the diplomatic field. Because of these advantages, Germany was able to secure her prize, East Africa, with its long coast-line, its salubrious climate and its potentialities for development and white settlement, and German South West Africa, with its strategic position, high plateau, opportunities for cattle raising and desirable climate. But the prior establishment of the French and British empires on the upper west coast prevented even her early trading connections there, or the astute diplomacy of a Bismarck, from securing anything except the most undesirable areas with limited coastal outlets unsuited to white occupation and, with the exception of agriculture, almost barren of resources.

In spite of all the disadvantages of geography and character inherent in her African possessions, Germany invested skill and huge sums in their development. The hope that the colonies would meet some of the pressing economic needs of the Fatherland was just beginning to be partially realized in 1914, and greater success was anticipated for the future, facts which are significant in view of Hitler's present colonial demands. To cite some of the most striking and concrete examples of her increased colonial production by 1914: the export of raw cotton from East Africa had increased ten times since 1902, while that of rubber from East Africa, Cameroons, and Togoland had quadrupled since 1908; the production of sisal hemp in East Africa had grown ten times greater between 1905 and 1914, so that it supplied all Germany's requirements and gave promise of soon supplying other countries. The output (including that from the South Seas) of vegetable fats and oils, so essential for soap, butter, lubricants, and food, had more than doubled since 1905; the cocoa crop had become one and one-half times greater during the five years 1909-1914; the number of bales of hides shipped from East Africa had increased eight times, and from Cameroons five times since 1910. In fact, the only serious disappointments in colonial production had been the failure of the great attempts to cultivate coffee in East Africa and tobacco in Cameroons. By 1919, however, colonies and hopes were lost.

As we have elsewhere recounted, Germany's entrance into the African continent had been well prepared by her pathfinders of expansion: explorers and scientists, traders, merchants and missionaries. Next to those of Great Britain and France, her interests and stakes in Africa came third in 1871. For while it is true that she possessed no territorial position, her trade and shipping connections as well as her missionary activity were very much alive. Ever since the eighteenth century and especially during the first half of the nineteenth, indeed, these spontaneous and individual enterprises had been at work, and it is owing to their efforts, rather than to any state or official action, that the foundations of Germany's colonial empire were laid.

Germany entered upon its united nationalism in 1871 singularly destitute of a state-directed colonial policy and its results, colonial settlements. And this was despite a rich colonial tradition built up throughout her history by the early migrations of her peoples into central and eastern Europe, by the economic expansion of the powerful Hanseatic League and its far-flung commercial settlements, by the activities of the firms of Welser, Fugger and others in the trading enterprises of the golden age of expansion in the West Indies and in South America, and, finally, by the ill-fated attempts of Prussia to establish a colonial empire. But the circumstances of her historical development all militated against a state-directed colonialism. They were: the political disunion and disorganization of the German states; the weakness of the Holy Roman Empire; the rise of strong nationalistic neighbors; the economic devastation wrought by the Thirty Years' War; and the absence of a strong middle class. To be sure, Prussia had attempted a state colonization. The Great Elector had formed an East India Company for trade with the East, purchased two ports from the Danes on the coast of India in 1650, attempted a settlement in the Antilles and sent out an expedition in 1676-1677 to reconnoiter the coast of Guinea, which resulted in gaining from the natives a protectorate on the Gold Coast between Axim and the Cape of Three Points. He then founded in 1682 an African Commercial Company to which he gave a monopoly of trade for twenty years. In 1683 the agent of the company, Frederick von der Groben, established a factory and built the fortress *Gross Friedrichsburg.*

But the Great Elector's Hohenzollern successors became too much involved in the intricacies of European politics and in their attempts to establish the hegemony of Prussia to continue a colonial policy abroad. So, with the failure of Frederick the Great's Asiatic Company in 1792, Prussia's attempts came to an end and with it a German state-directed colonialism.

More effective and successful, on the other hand, were the unremitting efforts of the individual, commercial colonizers, merchants and traders. With improved means of transportation after the opening of the nineteenth century and the destruction of the customs barriers, of which the *Zollverein* was the climax in 1834, German trade began to enter world trade. After 1830, the old commercial centers of the Rhine and the Hanse towns felt the tremor of a renewed activity which demanded colonies, not for settlement, but for economic development, the forerunner of modern colonization. Emigration had failed to establish German colonies in the strict sense of the word, because all the suitable places for settlements had been occupied by the other powers before Germany was strong enough to expand; commercial colonization was to succeed, on the other hand, because it demanded areas in the tropics which were, as yet, not entirely occupied.

The Hansa towns, in line with their old tradition, were the promoters of the new colonial expansion. Hamburg, Bremen and Lübeck had never entered the *Zollverein,* were free-traders, controlled the bulk of Germany's foreign trade, and had always kept alive the Hanseatic tradition. They gave their children ships for toys instead of the soldiers which amused their little Prussian cousins, and they sent their youth overseas in large numbers. Africa had been the scene of their first activity. As early as 1823, Hamburg had established factories on the west and southwest coast, the cornerstones, as they were to prove, of the German colonial empire. In 1844, the firm of Herz & Son had sent the first ship to East Africa, building up an export trade in cowry shells; it was succeeded by the firms of Hansing and O'Swald, which began by establishing a trade with the west coast at Lagos, and then concentrated their efforts in East Africa at Zanzibar in 1860. So great was their success that in June, 1855, a trade treaty was arranged between the Hansa towns and the sultan of Zanzibar, which was subsequently extended to the North German Confederation in 1869 and later to the German Empire. The Zanzibar trading coast became the most important in East Africa and, by the year 1870, the Hamburg firm of O'Swald was controlling most of the trade, its only serious competitors being the Indian firms under English protection. In Witu, also, Richard Brenner established such friendly relations with the Sultan Achmed, a Suehli prince, who had won independence from the sultan of Zanzibar, that he offered, in 1867, to make a trade treaty with the Prussian government.

The successors of the pioneer work of Hansing and O'Swald in West Africa were the Hamburg business houses of Witt and Busch and Gaiser. But by far the most active firm in West Africa, dividing and subdividing itself and radiating out in all directions, was that of the Hamburg firm of Woermann, of whom we have already heard. First entering Liberia in 1849, it penetrated and spread through the territories between Gabon and the Cameroons. It founded a factory in Gabon in 1862 and trading stations on the Cameroon River in 1864. Jantzen, a manager for Woermann, 1861-1871, and Thormählen, another agent, formed an independent firm, setting up a factory in Cameroons in 1875. Their trade grew enormously, and by 1879 they owned factories all along the coast. Later, in 1879, two other managers for Woermann, Wölber and Broehm, formed a partnership on this coast, thereby giving the house of Woermann a firm grasp on the entire district, and placing most of the commerce in its hands. Its packet boats carried on regular trade with all the West African coast.

Even the missionaries engaged largely in commerce in West Africa: in 1864 a stock company, with a capital of 700,000 M., was formed in Germany to support the commercial and religious work of the Rhine Barmen Mission at Otymbingue in South West Africa, where it had established a station as early as 1863. This company bought the land and buildings of the Walfisch Bay Copper Company and carried on an extensive business. In the same way, the Baseler Mission, working on the Gold Coast in Togoland since 1828, established in connection with its trade a large factory at Akra.

Besides the work of these pathfinders, as preparation for Germany's African empire, there existed in the Fatherland itself by 1871 a distinct colonial cult or theory of colonization. This had been constructed by publicists of all kinds and was fostered by the great emigration of Germans overseas which had been in progress for some decades. For, as the nineteenth century advanced, political economists, scientists, historians, explorers had all pointed out the necessity and advantage of colonial expansion. As early as 1817, it had been urged in the German Diet that the states take some action in directing the ever swelling volume of German emigration; later, the nationalist historians like Treitschke and Droysen echoed the same theme by advocating expansion and the projection of German nationality.

By the forties, the political economists entered the field. Such men as Roscher and Wappäus preached colonization for the overflow of population as well as for the benefit of trade, and demonstrated the value of colonies as new production and consumption centers. They were led by List, who broke with the prevailing *laissez-faire* and cosmopolitan school and urged colonialism as part of a national program. In his *National System of Political Economy* (1841), he advised a strong colonial policy in all its phases. Finally, scientists like von Humboldt, and explorers such as Fretsch and Mauch with their voluminous writings, played an important part in urging a policy of expansion and in creating a knowledge of the lands overseas. The existence of this colonial cult was apparent to the most superficial observer at the dawn of the empire. Never, indeed, can it be said of Germany, as it is so often observed of Great Britain, that she built up her colonial empire in a "fit of absence of mind." For while it may be an English characteristic to construct a policy *post facto*, it is equally a German habit to formulate *a priori* an abstract theory as a guide to practice.

BISMARCK INAUGURATES A COLONIAL EMPIRE: COLONIAL CURRENTS AND CROSSCURRENTS

With the advent of the Bismarckian era, the age-old deterrents to a national colonial policy—political disunion and economic weakness—were summarily removed. After the successive triumphs from 1864 to 1871, a united Germany overflowing with superabundant energy had emerged; and the intense nationalism and patriotism engendered by the wars of unification found a natural outlet in an enthusiasm for expansion. Now that Germany had become a nation, she, like the other great states of Western Europe, must express her self-consciousness in the extension of her nationalism to a colonial empire; she too must pass through her phase of oversea expansion, and the impression of her individuality upon other lands.

For Germany this newly aroused nationalism worked two ways, both centrifugally and centripetally, toward the encouragement of colonial foundations. For now, many of those emigrant Germans who had left the Fatherland in the days of its weakness and insignificance—the days of the Germanic Confederation—clamored to be united to a glorified Germany.

More important in its influence upon expansion than the removal of political disunion and the achievement of nationalism was, perhaps, the recovery of economic strength. Given a strong and united country after years of division and weakness, given the introduction of the Industrial Revolution with its consequent manufacturing and commercial boom, augmented by the billion-dollar war indemnity from France, and given the resulting overproduction of all kinds of commodities, what circumstances could be more favorable for colonial expansion? The era of security after 1870 developed industry and trade to a remarkable degree, as is too well established to need further exposition here; but the fact must be emphasized that "the commercial instinct is the origin of all colonial conquest," and hence there existed a veritable hothouse atmosphere for the culture of the colonial idea.

Voices from every phase of national life were not lacking to present all these circumstances to Bismarck in order to urge their demand for a national colonial policy. Naturally the eve of the treaty of Frankfort afforded a brilliant occasion for urging the cause of colonization as a means of strengthening the national economic and commercial welfare of the new empire. German merchants in Valparaiso, for instance, raised the question of taking possession of Patagonia; others advised seizing Madagascar, the Zulu Islands, the purchase of Danish St. Thomas. Many saw a golden opportunity to acquire colonies in the dictation of a victorious peace, and demanded that the treaty should include some of France's colonial possessions.

Even after the peace settlement, enthusiastic colonists did not lose hope, but took refuge in propaganda, appealing still to the national sentiment. Some advocated annexing the Fiji Islands, the Hebrides, the Philippines, while from America came German voices clamoring for the acquisition of Cuba, Sumatra, New Guinea and Pondicherry. In 1871, Samoa was proposed as a naval station; *Das Kleine Journal* and *Die Welt Post* supported the cause, and other pamphlets advocated Germany's interests in the East.

It would be an error to conclude, however, that German public opinion generally favored expansion in 1871. With few exceptions, official circles and the ruling class opposed a colonial policy because they feared friction with other powers and interference with the attainment of German hegemony in Europe. Their opinion was supported by the prevailing economic doctrine of the times, *laissez-faire*. The early seventies marked the ascendancy of the National Liberal Party in Germany which, although composed of the business men, still clung to free trade. Hence, to them, colonies as yet were an anachronism.

Whatever the currents and crosscurrents for and against colonial expansion, it was Bismarck who directed imperial affairs. Until 1875 he pursued, apparently, a policy of caution, evinced a decided unwillingness to encourage colonial undertakings by a consistent refusal of the many opportunities proffered by German merchants, consuls or native rulers, ranging from Brazil to South Africa, and vociferously expressed himself, the while, as fundamentally opposed to a policy of expansion. "For Germany to acquire colonies would be like a poverty-stricken Polish nobleman providing himself with silks and sables when he needed shirts," he stated in 1871. At the same time he did not altogether reject the importunities of traders for protection and the establishment of naval bases; he extended to them a "diplomatic guardianship" which meant an extension of the consular service in South America, Africa and the South Seas. Moreover, he invariably explained his refusal of the plans and petitions for direct protection and colonization by assigning three reasons: the weakness and unpreparedness of the new empire; fear of exciting the antagonism of foreign powers, especially England; and the lack of general support for colonialism within Germany itself.

After the year 1876, however, the chancellor discarded his caution and adopted a bolder line in favor of a colonial policy both at home and abroad. He initiated a series of commercial treaties, such as the Tongan and Samoan Treaties which inaugurated a definite system of overseas trade protection; endorsed the acquisition of naval stations; sharply demanded that England submit the claims of German settlers, evicted by her annexation of the Fiji Islands, to an international commission; and established with Britain a joint protectorate over Apia in Samoa. At home, he departed from *laissez-faire* and swung definitely over to trade protection by proposing the Samoan Subsidy Bill, designed to grant an annual subsidy to Godeffroy and Son, one of the pioneers of German expansion in the South Seas. Even the failure of this bill in the *Reichstag* did not deflect Bismarck from his policy of protection which he continued to pursue.

As the 1880's progressed, forces were at work both within and without the empire removing those deterrents to colonial expansion that had been hitherto specifically enumerated by the chancellor in 1875. In the first place, a strong national feeling, an impulse for colonization, had replaced the general apathy prevalent during those early years. Witness to this was a flood of propaganda literature, books and pamphlets, described above, setting forth the vital political and economic necessity for colonies, to which the rapidly rising emigration statistics gave immediate relevancy. But the best evidence was supplied by the organization of the movement for colonization into the *Kolonialverein,* founded in 1882. It united and co-ordinated into one society all the small groups and agencies working for the same objective, launched an official journal, the *Kolonialzeitung,* and enrolled 3,260 members during its first year.

In the second place, the international situation had changed completely: Germany's relations with France had materially improved since *revanche* had ceased to dominate the latter's policy and Bismarck had assisted Ferry in acquiring Tunisia; indeed, the chancellor was beginning to ask himself why France should not now become the ally of Germany rather than of Britain since the Anglo-French quarrel over Egypt, from which France entirely withdrew in 1883, appeared to be permanent. Again, the Triple Alliance and a more formal Three Emperors' League (1881) now guaranteed Germany's position in Europe and enabled her both to disregard England's sensitiveness in the colonial field and to abandon the support of her policy in Europe, from which there appeared no hope of securing any return. Finally, the international scramble for Africa, now well under way, revealed in all its stark reality the essential economic rivalry of the great powers, especially that of Britain and the new industrialized Germany. It provided, indeed, those grounds for a quarrel with Britain which led to the acquisition of South West Africa.

PRESENT POVERTY AND PAST TRADITION

South West Africa

AREA: 322,000 square miles
POPULATION: Native, 80,556; White, 14,830
TRADE:[2] *Imports:*   45,302,000 M.
        From Germany: 20,693,000 M.
        Exports: 28,573,000 M.
        To Germany: 3,193,000 M.

One and one-half times the size of the German Empire, South West Africa was Germany's first colony. Second in size and importance to East Africa, it attracted more white settlers than any other colony. They engaged principally in stock raising in the lofty plateau and also in the mining of copper, tin, gold and diamonds, which, under the scientific fostering of Colonial Secretary Dernburg after 1907, was materially increasing. The nature of the territory, however, required large sums of capital investment to develop; its inaccessible coasts demanded harbor construction; the high inland plateau so admirably suited to stock raising necessitated irrigation; its mineral wealth needed expensive machinery to make it available; and the vast stretches of the country, unconnected by natural waterways, made the construction of roads and railways on a large scale inevitable.

How Governed. First under the jurisdiction of the German South West African Company, formed in 1885, the colony came under imperial control in 1888, for the company soon found itself unable financially either to support a government, explore the interior or control the natives. It continually refused to accept the charter conveying sovereign rights with which Bismarck offered again and again to invest it according to his cherished plan of colonial government. Like all the other colonies, it was ruled by an imperial governor and his staff, while increased rights of self-government, owing to Dernburg's efforts, were being extended to the white settlers.

How Acquired. Bismarck embarked upon a definite colonial policy in 1883-1884 when he addressed himself in earnest to the demands of F. A. Lüderitz for the "protection of the flag of the German empire" over districts around Angra Pequena, a harbor on

---

[2] *Statistisches Jahrbuch für das Deutsche Reich,* 1913. Figures for 1911.

the coast of South West Africa which he planned to annex. This Bremen merchant, like so many of his kind, had long been active in the South African trade and was a leader of that group which had proposed to Bismarck in 1876 the founding of a German colony in the Transvaal. On that occasion, the chancellor had replied that a great nation like Germany could not, in the end, "dispense with colonies"; but, as much as he was in principle in favor of the acquisition of colonies, he hesitated "to embark upon colonization without adequate preparation and a definite impulse from the nation itself." Besides, he said that the international situation was unfavorably conditioned by the jealousy of France and the sensitiveness of England. Now, seven years after, Bismarck's response was quite different. He had Lüderitz confidentially informed that the government was in agreement with his demands, but that certain information must be obtained from England before a final answer could be given. Meanwhile, Bismarck addressed a courteous note to Britain (February 4, 1883) asking if England exercised any authority over the Angra Pequena region. "If not, Germany intends to afford her subjects in that region the protection which they need." The note conveyed the impression, however, that Germany "had not the least design of establishing a foothold in South West Africa," and would prefer to leave the responsibility of protection to England.

England replied to the note on February 23, 1883: "The Cape Colony government has certain establishments along the coast, but without more precise information as to the exact location of Lüderitz's factory, it is impossible for the British government to say whether it could afford this protection in case it were required."

The reply was evasive; and it appeared all the more so since England had already declared that this part of the coast was outside her jurisdiction. Indeed, when Bismarck had asked the British government, on November 4, 1880, to extend its protection to German missionaries in this region on the occasion of a native war, England had replied (November 29, 1880): "The British government cannot accept responsibility for anything occurring outside of British territory, which includes only Whale Bay and its immediate region." But the motive for British evasion becomes clear when it is realized that it was owing to the activities of the Cape government which was striving, against anti-expansionist sentiment in the British Cabinet, to effect an annexation of those regions now jeopardized by the German claim.

Meanwhile, Lüderitz took advantage of the delay in the negotiations to seize the harbor of Angra Pequena with its surroundings and to establish a trading post there, for whose protection he again applied at the German foreign office in August, 1883. By this time Bismarck, more determined than ever to carry through the affair to success, again asked Her Majesty's government whether it claimed sovereignty over Angra Pequena and if so on what grounds. Again England delayed her reply, having failed as yet to settle the insistent demands of the Cape colonists.

Finally Bismarck's impatience would brook no further delay: in November (1883) he officially repeated his question to the British foreign office, which replied that although British sovereignty had not been proclaimed along the whole country, but only at certain points such as Walfisch Bay and the Angra Pequena Islands, Britain would consider any claim to sovereignty or jurisdiction by a foreign power between Angola and Cape Colony as an infringement of her legitimate rights. Such a claim was preposterous and Bismarck demanded (December 2, 1883) by what right or title England could claim sovereignty over a territory formerly considered independent. But to this communication England made no response whatever.

Events rapidly moved to their climax. At home Britain's procrastination and evasion over Angra Pequena together with her continued postponement of the settlement of the Fiji Islands' controversy aroused keen resentment—a veritable Anglophobia, in fact, specifically encouraged by Bismarck's articles in the official press and his violent attacks on Gladstone, all of which immensely stimulated "that national impulse for expansion." Abroad the announcement of the Anglo-Portuguese Treaty, so threatening to French and German interests in the Congo region, precipitated their co-operation in calling the Congo conference and the completion of the Franco-German *entente*. The "unfavorable international situation" for the establishment of a German colonial empire disappeared. All that remained was for Bismarck to dispatch his official proclamation to Lüderitz on April 24, 1884, declaring his settlements to be under imperial protection. With this stroke, the German colonial empire was inaugurated and its first colony, South West Africa, was established.

Cameroons

> AREA: 197,498 square miles
> POPULATION: 3,326,132 Natives; 1,871 Whites
> TRADE:[3] *Imports:* 29,317,000 M.
> From Germany: 9,350,000 M.
> *Exports:* 21,251,000 M.
> To Germany: 16,872,000 M.

In the Cameroons Germany possessed a truly tropical colony. Its low coastal plain, lying in the so-called "white man's grave," rises to a well-watered plateau which in turn extends into high mountains in the east. Coffee, cocoa, rubber and tobacco thrive in its humid climate which is most unsuited to white settlement. Limited thereby to a plantation and commercial colony, it was, next to New Guinea, the least known of all the German colonies. Its pacification and exploration were thus delayed and for the most part entrusted to the concession companies.

The natives, exceedingly independent and jealous of their land rights, bitterly resented banishment to the reserves and gave the government continuous trouble, the colony rarely being at peace for some twenty years after its acquisition. Indeed, the military played the chief rôle in a successful attempt to penetrate the hinterland and to gain access to the natural resources of palm oil, groundnuts, ivory and rubber.

How Governed. Since the original commercial companies, like Woermann and Jantzen, confined their activities to trade and refused to incur any responsibility whatever for administration or exploration, the Cameroons was ruled from the outset as an imperial province. The government was obliged to maintain first the imperial commissioner and then the governor, his staff, and the military with no financial return from the commercial or concession companies, who enjoyed all the benefits and assumed a minimum of responsibility, a system which was exactly the reverse of Bismarck's plan.

Under Secretary Dernburg's reforms, the sphere of native administration was considerably enlarged; native treasuries even were set up in northern Cameroons to receive one half of the taxes. On the eve of the first World War, the governor was enthusiastic

---

[3] Figures for 1911.

over increasing the number of semi-independent "indirect government" units and in promoting other measures for native representation.

Togoland

AREA: 34,600 square miles
POPULATION: 1,031,978 Natives; 368 Whites
TRADE:[4] *Imports:*   11,427,000 M.
   From Germany: 2,715,000 M.
   Exports: 9,958,000 M.
   To Germany: 6,216,000 M.

The smallest, most prosperous and peaceful of all Germany's
colonies in Africa, Togoland, was the most successful and the only
self-supporting one. Sandwiched between the British in the Gold
Coast and the French in Dahomey, this little colony was only
slightly larger than the state of Bavaria in Germany. A numerous
and industrious native population cultivated the oil palm, groundnuts and maize and brought in rubber from the interior, while
foreign merchants carried on a lively trade on the coast. No native
uprisings have disturbed Togoland and no concession company
with exceptional privileges, financial, administrative or economic,
ever existed there. The richness of the land, able to support the
indigenous population of independent, peasant farmers, as in the
neighboring colony of the Gold Coast, rendered this territory outstanding in native production. White settlers confined themselves
to trade on the coast.

How Governed. Togoland was administered from the beginning as an imperial colony by an imperial commissioner followed
by a governor. Always it was considered a colony and never a
protectorate in the Bismarckian sense.

Native official machinery was not destroyed but was drawn into
co-operation with the German rule by placing upon it the responsibility for maintaining law and order. Dr. Dernburg did much to
enlarge the sphere of native administration.

How Acquired. From the middle of the nineteenth century
German merchants had been active on the West African coast. As
early as 1853 German missionaries and traders had established

---

[4] *Statistisches Jahrbuch für das Deutsche Reich,* 1913. Figures for 1912.

themselves in the English stations at Keta and Akra in Togoland and, in 1868, the Hamburg firm of Woermann had its own stations on the Cameroons River, later supplemented and extended by the firms of Thormählen and Jantzen. By 1880, the first German factories appeared in Togoland, founded by Broehm and Woelber of Hamburg, and the celebrated Vietor Sons of Bremen. In spite of the keen commercial rivalry of the British along the Gold Coast and on the river, almost one-half of the West African trade came to be controlled by the Germans in 1883, and Woermann had established a steamship line to Hamburg.

But trade in these regions was extremely difficult because of the English competition and the opposition of the natives in Cameroons, who did all they could to prevent penetration into the hinterland, the value of whose treasures they appreciated. Here the British maintained a Court of Equity to which all traders submitted, and jealous British merchants incited the natives, in 1882, to demand a British protectorate. Taking advantage of Great Britain's inertia in this respect, the chambers of commerce in both Hamburg and Bremen addressed a formal request to the imperial government demanding a warship, a consul, a naval station at Fernando Po and the establishment of a colony on Biafra Bay. Bismarck lent a ready ear to their petitions, sent the armored cruiser "Sophie" and promised to appoint a consul. After a secret conference with Woermann, April 30, 1884, at which Nachtigal's instructions to extend imperial protection over certain places in Cameroons, Togoland, and Angra Pequena were formulated, Nachtigal was dispatched on the "Möwe," with the sly scheme to outwit the British.

In the meantime, Lawson, a British agent, set himself up as king at Little Popo in Togoland, and was bending every effort to interfere with the German merchants. But, owing to the presence of the "Sophie," he was arrested and imprisoned on board. King Grigi and the princes of Little Popo, impressed by this "show of might," asked for German protection against the British, which was speedily granted on the arrival of Nachtigal in July, who signed a treaty with the king of Togoland and raised the German flag, for the first time in Africa, at Lowe and Bagida. Proceeding rapidly to the Cameroons River, Nachtigal hastily signed treaties with kings Bell and Aqua, placing under the German flag Belltown, Aquatown, Didotown and later Bimbia, Malimba and

Batanga. Scarcely had his orders been thus executed, and the coveted coast of Biafra Bay opposite Fernando Po been placed under German protection, than Consul Hewitt appeared on the scene with his British treaty forms; but he was a week too late, and was obliged to take refuge in addressing protests to the German government. Henceforth, he became known as the "too-late-consul." Finally, in the general colonial settlement of the year 1885, brought about by Bismarck's diplomacy, an agreement with England was reached and the boundaries of Togoland and Cameroons were determined to be later delimited by subsequent agreements with England in 1890, 1893, 1899; and with France in 1885, 1894, 1897 and in 1911, when 107,000 square miles of French Cameroons were ceded to Germany in return for her recognition of the Moroccan protectorate.

East Africa

> AREA: 393,500 square miles
> POPULATION: 7,645,770 Natives, 5,336 Whites
> TRADE:[5] *Imports:*   50,200,000 M.
>   From Germany: 17,433,000 M.
>   *Exports:*   31,418,000 M.
>   To Germany: 14,644,000 M.

Twice the size of the German Empire, Germany's largest and best colony was potentially very rich. This was owing to its physical character, situated in the healthful highland region of East Africa, which was hospitable both to white settlement and to the production of coffee, sisal, rubber, hides. Its geography and climate have already been described in some detail previously, since it is now Tanganyika territory, a British mandate.

The Germans made the best of their prize colony, where the application of their scientific methods showed, perhaps, the greatest results. During the ten years preceding the first World War East Africa's production of sisal hemp increased ten times, trade prospered, the extension of the railway running from Lake Tanganyika to the port at Dar-es-Salaam was completed, the Agricultural Experimental Station at Kibongoto was established and the world-famous Biological-Agricultural Research Institute of Amani enlarged.

---

[5] *Statistisches Jahrbuch für das Deutsche Reich,* 1913. Figures for 1912.

How Governed. First ruled by the East African Company, the colony soon became an annexed territory of the empire. For the company proved too weak both to quell native revolts and to cope with British rivalry, nowhere keener, as we have seen, than in this region.

An imperial governor with his staff held complete sway and directly under him functioned the district officials with similar assistants. Due to the high level of development attained by the indigenous population, among whom the Arabs formed a large group, native administrative co-operation was growing. Many of the original governing native bodies were permitted to function and methods and practices of self-government were on the increase.

How Acquired. The initial activity of Karl Peters, the founder of East Africa, has already been related and the story of his and his companions' adventurous explorations told. But he was building upon early foundations when he set out to win this territory, for Germany's interest dated as far back as 1844. Here her trade had met with unusual success, reaching the considerable sum of 3,500,000 M. in 1875, an amount three times greater than that of the English. Since that time the brothers Denhardt had penetrated far into Witu and had explored the Tana River. Appealing in the year 1882 to the government for support, they were referred to the ministry of the interior which had previously appropriated 5,000 M. for the Denhardt expedition because of its scientific value; but they were refused all imperial protection as had been the merchants and explorers in Zanzibar in 1874. Failing this, a private consortium was formed in Berlin which enabled Clemens Denhardt to purchase from Achmed, sultan of Witu, a strip of territory between the Tana and Zuba Rivers with full sovereign rights, a purchase designed to interfere with the activities of the Englishman, John Kirk, in that region and in 1888 included under the sovereignty of the East African Company.

In Zanzibar, events took quite a different course. There Germans had apparently done little since 1875 to build upon the substantial foundations already laid down by the merchants of the Hansa towns, although the expeditions of Sir Harry Johnston in the early eighties presented a serious challenge, and the English trade rivalry was keen. Suddenly Karl Peters appeared on

the scene in Berlin, reproaching the German government and the
colonial party for their neglect of imperialism in general, and
of the African continent in particular. After he had obtained the
imperial charter of protection from Bismarck over the 60,000
square miles which his original expedition had secured, he set
about other exploits to bring more of East Africa under the
control of his company for German colonization, later transformed
into the East African Company.

For East Africa amply fulfilled Peters' desire for adventure and
excitement. Added to the wild and unexplored nature of the
hinterland, there was in the coastal districts the well-established
authority of the sultan of Zanzibar as well as the keen rivalry of
England with which to contend. The sultan, not without encouragement from Kirk, the English consul, sent a formal protest
against the usurpation of the dubious rights which he claimed the
German East African Company had obtained by its flimsy treaties,
and began to mobilize. But Bismarck immediately replied by dispatching a small squadron of warships to the scene and a promise
to respect the sultan's independence, which at once silenced the
protest and established Germany in East Africa.

England, however—or rather the English agents—proved not
quite so amenable as the sultan, and the adjustment of German
and British claims and boundaries occupied several years. Immediately upon the receipt of its charter of protection, the German
East African Company had undertaken no fewer than eleven expeditions, which added considerable areas to its original holdings,
but brought the company directly into collision with both England
and France, who, it was now revealed, had guaranteed the independence of Zanzibar by a secret treaty in 1862. Commissioners
were appointed from the three nations to adjust the conflicting
claims and we have the alas, all-to-common spectacle of three
great powers dividing among themselves the territory of a little,
weak nation on the basis of protecting that little nation's integrity.

The decision reached in 1886, which has been explained in some
detail, gave to the German East African Company 600 miles of the
coastal strip, ten miles wide, and about 200,000 square miles of
the hinterland as spheres of influence. Germany completed her
area by leasing in 1888 the coastal strip bordering on her sphere
with its harbors and customs from the sultan and, two years later,
by purchasing the whole of his rights there for 4,000,000 M.

This addition secured her adequate seaports and the control of the coastal trade.

But the agreement of 1886 with England had left many other areas of rivalry unsettled; vast unexplored and unclaimed regions in the west, in the upper Nile, in Uganda remained. Peters, yearning for more excitement than the directorship of the German East African Company with its prosaic problems of administration now offered, set out to conquer new lands.

Opportunity offered in the guise of a relief expedition to rescue Emin Pasha, a German by birth, governor of the Equatorial Province in the British Egyptian service, who was reported besieged by the fanatical Mahdi in the regions of the upper Nile. That this expedition was but an excuse to checkmate the British and to acquire territories for Germany both in that section and in the coveted Uganda, the "pearl of East Africa," both Peters' own account and the records of the Emin Pasha Relief Committee show. Results could not possibly have been better planned. For on Peters' arrival at the gates of the Equatorial Province, he stopped to rest at the camp of two Englishmen, Jackson and Martin, who were temporarily away hunting in the bush. There he found waiting for them a letter from Stanley, containing the startling and somewhat disappointing (to Peters) information that he (Stanley) had found Emin Pasha. "What can have been the design of Providence in permitting me to advance so far, only to find my labors were in vain," exclaimed Peters, who shortly received an answer, however, by the simple method of reading further into the Englishmen's mail. Therein he found both an account of the distressing situation of the king of Uganda who, deposed by Mohammedans, was imploring the British to come to his assistance, as well as the proposition from Mackay, the director of the British East African Company, to Jackson, suggesting that this was the opportunity to conquer Uganda for the British. The "design of Providence" was clear: one object of rescue was substituted for another. It made no difference that Mwanga, unlike Emin, was not a German brother; Peters rushed to his relief, restored him to his throne, and concluded a treaty which placed Uganda under German protection. With the same careless disregard of consequences, Peters also invaded the French sphere of influence in Madagascar, as well as the Italian preserves in Somaliland—in the futile execution of this phantasmal dream to create a German "India" in Africa.

These irresponsible exploits of Peters were, moreover, duplicated by the erratic Emin Pasha who, having been rescued by
Stanley, deserted the British colonial service for the German, to
the amazement and disgust of the British. Disobeying the strict
orders of Wissmann, the imperial commissioner, he invaded British
rights in the region of Victoria Nyanza and soon afterward met a
violent death from the Arabs, whom he had stirred up against himself because they thought that he interfered with their trade in
slaves and ivory.

Meanwhile the German Witu Company had encountered the
keen rivalry and antagonism of the British East African Company
in Witu. Always on friendly terms with the sultan of Witu, the
Germans encouraged him to defy his superior, the sultan of Zanzibar, the friend of the English. Sworn enemies, the two commercial companies, backed by their respective sultans, created a
delicate situation, both local and international, for Witu was considered to be under the aegis of the German East African
Company.

Altogether, the agents and associates of the East African Company were seriously threatening the friendly relations of Downing
Street and the *Wilhelmstrasse,* which the chancellor had just
succeeded in re-establishing, and wished most earnestly to maintain. Consequently, we find Bismarck seeking again and again
to nullify the effect of these imperialistic adventurers in East
Africa by publicly disavowing all official responsibility for them,
and by continually assuring Lord Salisbury of Germany's good
will.

In addition to the international difficulties which the company
was creating for the German government, a serious native revolt
broke out in East Africa, a protest against the company's administration of the customs and its threat to the old and well-established Arab slave trade. The entire coast was in insurrection and
Bismarck was obliged to dispatch an imperial commissioner with
German ships, men and gold to quell the revolt and, ultimately,
to replace the rule of the company which had proved itself in-
capable both to control the natives and to cope with British
rivalry.

Finally, the Anglo-German Treaty of 1890 settled the boundaries of East Africa and dealt the German East African Company
its death blow as administrator, for it ceded to England, the hated

SUMMARY: ECONOMIC STATUS, GERMAN COLONIES, 1913-1914
THE AFRICAN COLONIES [6]

	GERMAN EAST AFRICA	SOUTH WEST AFRICA	CAMEROONS	TOGOLAND
Area—Square Miles	393,500	322,000	197,498	34,600
Native Population.	7,645,770	80,556	3,326,132	1,031,978
Whites	5,336	14,830	1,871	368
Chief Products ...	Rubber, Sisal, Hides, Coffee	Livestock, Hides, Diamonds	Rubber, Cocoa Palm Oils	Palm Oils, Rubber, Cotton
Minerals	Gold, Mica	Diamonds, Copper		
Chief Ports......	Dar-es-Salaam, Tanga	Swakopmund Lüderitzbucht	Victoria, Douala	Anecho, Lome
Railways	771 miles	1,222 miles	193 miles	203 miles
Exports	31,418,000 M.	39,000,000 M.	23,336,000 M.	9,958,000 M.
Imports	50,309,000 M.	32,500,000 M.	34,241,000 M.	11,427,000 M.
Revenue and Expenditure	54,760,000 M.	54,140,000 M.	15,340,000 M.	3,380,000 M.
Deficit or Subsidy.	40,940,000 M.	38,520,000 M.	6,940,000 M.	None

rival, the protectorate over the sultan and German claims in Witu, Uganda, and Nyasaland—all districts where the company had been most active. With the increasing encroachment of imperial control, it relinquished its sovereign rights and the East African protectorate passed under the administration of the empire in 1891.

Although the Anglo-German Treaty of 1890 was consummated by Caprivi, Bismarck had begun negotiations for it in 1889, as the most effective means of repudiating those dubious acquisitions, sponsored by the German East African Company, and of establishing friendly relations with Great Britain upon a basis which adventurers like Peters could no longer disturb. Its final settlement left to Germany the full possession of the coast of the mainland, hitherto leased from the sultan, and an extension of the boundary eastward to the great lakes Tanganyika and Nyasa. Germany also

[6] From Townsend, M. E., *Rise and Fall of Germany's Colonial Empire*, p. 265.

recognized, as has been stated, the British protectorate over
Witu and the Somali coast, transferred Uganda to the British
sphere of influence, and agreed to the British protectorate over
Zanzibar. In return Germany received the island of Helgoland
in the North Sea and the narrow corridor to the Zambesi River
on the west coast (Caprivi's finger). The treaty was popular with
the natives as a whole, but it raised a storm of criticism from the
colonial party, for it struck a severe blow at their interest, not
only locally in East Africa, but also at their hopes and enthusiasm
in Germany. "The acquisition of Helgoland blinds everyone to
the losses sustained. With a pen's stroke, England has acquired
a dominating position in East Africa. . . . Also we have lost the
coast." Even Stanley, the African explorer, exclaimed that "a
new pair of trousers had been exchanged for an old trouser but-
ton."

BELGIAN AFRICA

The Belgian Congo, Mandated Territory Ruanda-Urundi

AREA: 920,610 square miles
POPULATION: 11,000,000; White, 23,091
TRADE:[7] *Imports:*   1,137,091,689 fr.
From Belgium: 503,261,000 fr.
Exports: 2,486,995,485 fr.
To Belgium: 933,312,000 fr.

Belgium possesses a colonial empire in the Congo which is
eighty times as large as her homeland, one-quarter that of all
Europe, and amounts to about 8 per cent of the African continent.
This immense area, bounded on the north and west by the Congo
River, extends south to include all its left-bank tributaries and
east as far as Lake Tanganyika and the Mountains of the Moon.
An equatorial, tropical land of humid heat, dense jungles and
soaking rains, it is not conducive to white settlement but is immensely rich in the resources indigenous to its climate and latitude. Rubber ranked first among its resources until the destructive
and ruthless exploitation of the raw product carried on by Leopold II so reduced its output that today it cannot compete with
the plantations of the East. Now, copper mined in increasing
quantities in the Katanga region has become the chief export,

---

[7] Figures taken from the *Statesman's Yearbook*, 1940. Figures are for the
year 1937.

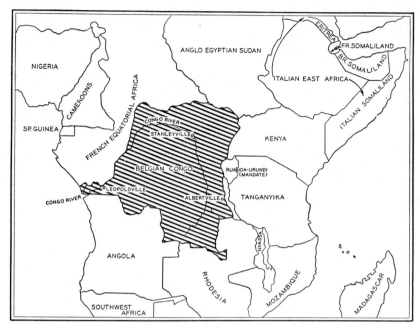

BELGIAN AFRICA

while the oily derivatives from the palm products used in the manufacture of soap, candles, margarine and other commodities occupy second place. Gold, diamonds and some tin are found and recently radium deposits have been discovered. The rich, well-watered soil of the Congo possesses potential resources also for the raising of cotton, cocoa, rice and plantation rubber, in whose development the country apparently has a great future, limited only by the securing of an adequate labor supply. For the area is as sparse in population as it is rich in products. The total, it is believed, now scarcely reaches 11,000,000 persons, of whom 3,000,-000 are concentrated in the mountains of Ruanda-Urundi, over which Belgium acquired a mandate after the first World War.

The colony's pressing needs are labor, capital and transportation, although the last is rapidly being remedied by the building of railways, motor routes and the establishment of air service. Trade is largely directed by non-Belgians, mainly British. American capital also has been fairly active in the Congo.

How Governed. The Belgian Congo was at first ruled absolutely by Leopold II of Belgium, who constituted himself sovereign of the Congo Free State, which was internationalized by the Berlin Act of 1885. But later the government was based upon the charter of 1908, framed by the Belgian parliament when it assumed control in that year. According to this document, the Congo constitutes a legal entity entirely distinct from the mother country with its own laws, treasury and monetary system. The governor-general is appointed by the Belgian king and is responsible to the Belgian parliament, which maintains the right of laying down general rules of administration and is represented on the colonial council. The governor-general is assisted by a government council with advisory powers only. The colony is divided into six provinces under commissioners and their councils, and these again into districts. Ruanda-Urundi is a B mandate, administered as a part of the Congo under its own vice governor-general.

How Acquired. The story of the acquisition of the Belgian Congo has already been recounted in its major outlines and more details regarding it will be found later in this book.[8] Briefly, to recapitulate, its occupation was due first to the discoveries of Livingstone and Stanley and then to the shrewdness and strategy of Leopold II, the Belgian king. So keen was his intelligent interest in the potentialities of Africa that he even anticipated Stanley's return to England bearing the news of the vast wealth of the Congo basin, by sending his agents to intercept the explorer's ship at Marseille and to beg Stanley to return to Africa on a secret mission in his interests. Although this first attempt failed, a later one was crowned with success. For Stanley, disappointed in England's apathy towards his discoveries and their opportunities, returned to Leopold, who at once dispatched him secretly to Africa in 1879. Nominally he went under the auspices of the Committee for the Study of the Upper Congo, ostensibly one of the national committees of the International Association—but, as we have seen, actually a group of Belgian business men organized by Leopold with a capital of a million francs with which to stake out the Congo.

After three years of adventurous toil and difficult pioneering through the jungle, in the course of which he was outwitted and

---

[8] See p. 195.

outdistanced, as we have earlier recounted, by de Brazza, in securing the north shore of the Congo River, he returned to Leopold in 1882 with the fruits of his labor. He had opened up the lower valley of the river for about 400 miles, established five trading posts or stations, chief of which was Leopoldville, on the Congo, and had connected them by roads. With such a record of success, he was at once sent back to secure the upper reaches of the river and within another year he had opened seventeen more stations, signed more than four hundred treaties with the native chiefs and established a protectorate for the International Association of the Congo, into which the Committee for the Study of the Upper Congo had by that time been metamorphosed, and over which Stanley now became governor.

All this activity in the Congo region had naturally aroused the interest of the other powers, especially France, whose de Brazza was a close rival of Stanley, and Great Britain, to whom Stanley, resigning his Belgian governorship, offered the region. Gladstone, then in power, rejected the offer, but nevertheless took measures to block Leopold by the very astute method of signing with Portugal the Anglo-Portuguese Treaty of 1884, which established a monopolistic control of the Congo River: the recognition of Portugal's sovereignty over its mouth, the establishment of an Anglo-Portuguese commission to direct its navigation, and the accordance to England of free navigation thereon. This would leave Leopold in possession of his territory but effectually close its outlet to the sea. As was to be expected, France's colonial-minded premier, Ferry, protested against the treaty. He then struck a bargain with Leopold granting him recognition of his territory in return for an option on it if he wished to sell; and lent a ready ear to Bismarck, who also protested the treaty and proposed a union of French and German commercial interests in the Congo against England, whom he was at that time attempting to isolate in Africa and in European politics by forming a Franco-German *entente*. The upshot of these negotiations was the calling of the Berlin Congress in 1884 in Berlin which, as we have seen, produced the Berlin Act of 1885 recognizing the International Association and its claims to the Congo and making optional a guarantee of its neutrality. Leopold became its absolute sovereign and changed its name to the Congo Free State, which was subject in no way to Belgium.

Leopold's first tasks were to adjust the boundaries of his vast domain, and buy out the foreign interests, which cost him heavily and which he partly met by borrowing from the Belgian government. He then turned to the ruthless and merciless exploitation of the Congo's resources, both material and human, described later, which gave to his rule that reputation for an unexcelled cruelty that has always blackened it and, as a result, colonialism in general. Mainly because of the international scandal which Leopold's unsavory regime created, the Belgian government assumed control of the region in 1908, which has since been called the Belgian Congo, and earnestly addressed itself to the task of righting the many wrongs endured under Leopold II's regime of twenty-three years.

In 1920 the Belgian Congo received as a B mandate the district of Ruanda-Urundi as a small share of Belgium's spoils of the first World War. Its 21,235 square miles rounds out the territory on the northeastern boundary, a highland district, thickly populated with about 3,000,000 inhabitants.

READINGS

GERMANY

Aydelotte, W. O. *Bismarck and British Colonial Policy, 1883-1885*, 1937. Detailed on South West Africa.
Calvert, A. F. *The German African Empire*, 1916. Fairly complete.
Peters, K. *New Light on Dark Africa*, 1891. Firsthand account.
Rudin, H. R. *Germans in the Cameroons, 1884-1914*, 1938. Special treatment.
Schnee, H. *German Colonization Past and Future*, 1926. German opinion.
Townsend, M. E. *The Rise and Fall of Germany's Colonial Empire, 1884-1918*, 1930.
Townsend, M. E. "The German Colonies and the Third Reich," *Political Science Quarterly*, June, 1938.

BELGIUM

Keith, A. D. *The Belgium Congo and the Berlin Act*, 1919. Objective—useful.
Lichtervelde, L. de. *Leopold II*, 1929.
Stanley, H. M. *Autobiography*, 1909.
Stanley, H. M. *Through the Dark Continent*, 2 vols. 1879.
Wack, H. M. *The Story of the Congo Free State*, 1905.

CHAPTER NINE

Results of European Expansion upon the Natives

Contrasting National Colonial Philosophies

THE ATTITUDES of the colonial powers towards their native subjects define the various philosophies of colonial rule. These
naturally reflect the character of the home government, the manner in which the colonies were acquired, the motives for expansion, as well as the particular brand of *apologia* advanced for
national colonization.

Great Britain regards the African natives as the recipients of
those great gifts of democratic administration, of the freedom of
institutions which she, as the "mother of parliaments," the stand-
ard-bearer of the liberal tradition in Europe, is best fitted to
bestow—indeed, which she considers she has a special mission
to disseminate, a sacred trust to carry to the backward peoples
and places of the earth. She has, therefore, always justified her
colonial acquisitions on these lofty grounds.

Moreover, Great Britain's colonies were gained as the result
of a spontaneous and national activity on the part of her people,
acting upon their own initiative and not incited primarily by the

government. This was due, of course, to England's geographical position, her need for expansion and for food, and her national temperament. The British government followed rather than led in the colonization process, giving rise to that aphorism, more or less true, that "the empire was acquired in a fit of absence of mind."

It follows then that the British attitude towards the native is one of superiority, of deep responsibility, of recognition that he must be helped and aided to a more abundant life by way of self-government, self-development and the adoption of free institutions under British guidance. The Englishman views the colonies as societies on their way to evolving their own lives and interests. He maintains an objective, aloof attitude toward the native, and dresses for dinner every night in the tropics to emphasize the fundamental racial distinction, even though he does not openly term the native's position inferior. While there is no sign of *camaraderie* with the native as among the French, yet there is a feeling of "live and let live," of respect and of recognition of native institutions. In recent years with the growth of the "indirect rule," of the application of the "dual mandate," the philosophy of native rights has been clearly enunciated. In 1923 a parliamentary white paper laid down in regard to Kenya, for example, that it was "primarily an African territory . . . . the interests of the natives must be paramount." [1]

France, on the other hand, has quite a different philosophy in regard to the native since, unlike Britain, her empire was acquired by persistent planning and by determined military conquest on the part of the government, and is considered to be an integral part of or extension of France. Again, unlike Britain she has been governed by a strongly centralized administration at home. The historic French attitude towards the native, therefore, has been "subordination," "assimilation" for the ultimate benefit of the mother country. Until recently France has regarded the African native solely from the point of view of his contribution to France, not from the angle of his own life and welfare. Since the colonies were thought to exist for the benefit of France alone, native welfare was to be fostered only insofar as it secured an advantage for France. There has been little of the "live and

---

[1] Parl. papers Cmd. 3234 of 1929.

let live" attitude in the theory and practice of French native policy.

At the same time "assimilation" has been influenced by the strong belief of Frenchmen in natural rights and in ultimate racial equality; by the absence of color prejudice as well as by a social ease and tolerance in human understanding of native life, conspicuously lacking among the British, who are rather the objective social analysts. It is because of this belief that, in theory, educated natives become citizens of France, not legally differentiated from her European citizens, while the mass of the native population remains subject. General provisions for citizenship are: ten years' service in French employ, ability to read and write French, evidence of good character and means of support. In addition, France has conferred citizenship outright upon the natives of Algeria and of the four communes of Senegal. In this way she creates an *élite* to whom all careers are open. Also, because of the same attitude, Frenchmen have not hesitated to marry widely among the natives and to enter into their life far more than any other colonizing power. "Going native" has not for them the same derogatory implication it has for the British. As Marshal Lyautey, resident general of Morocco said: "We do not regard the native population as an inferior race but as another race from ourselves."

Since 1919, however, the "assimilation" theory has been somewhat displaced, if only on paper, by the idea of "association." This may be said to be the French colonial expression of recognizing the aid rendered France in the first World War by native populations, and her acknowledgment of the new forces of democracy and nationalism unleashed during the post-war era.

According to the theory of "association," which so far exists more in theory than in practice, the colonies are to be strengthened and native well-being fostered to a degree limited only by considerations of national welfare for France. The natives are to be permitted to develop along their own lines, economically and culturally; native codes are to be allowed to remain and finally be embodied in new legislation; political decentralization is to be inaugurated and a growing self-government to be encouraged. As M. Sarraut has expressed it: "The working of the French colonial system, conceived for the benefit of both parties, no longer serves the spoliation of one race by another, but their 'association,' to use the happy phrase which has become our colonial motto."

Italy exhibits a somewhat contradictory native philosophy. Latin peoples generally are much more tolerant of indigenous populations than are the northern peoples, the British and the German, but Fascist ideology has gone a long way towards cancelling that attitude. The result is that Italy with her strongly centralized government at home regards her native populations in the same manner as she considers her own people, as so many subjects who exist for the good of the Fascist state. Racial equality is, of course, distinctly rejected: the natives are "inferior" and are to be recipients of Italian culture only to the extent that they may be able to absorb it. In the words of one of their own colonial authorities:[2] Although "the assimilation of Italian culture is certainly beneficent, it can only take place gradually, while absolute cultural equality with the Italians would breed aspirations and pretensions compatible neither with their true situation nor with the actual condition of the colonies."

At the same time, Italy has learned much from the colonial history of the other powers about the treatment of the natives. She aims at avoiding their mistakes and to prevent native uprisings. This practical policy, combined with her inherent social understanding, results in an unusual tolerance towards the customs, the *mores*, the religion of her African subjects. Towards the Arabs, especially, she is more tolerant than France.

Germany intensified in her treatment of colonial peoples both the absolutism of her home government and her sense of racial superiority when she first obtained colonies. In addition, her system was doubtless the most scientific of all and, in the pursuit of efficiency, was less concerned with human values, at least during the beginning years. With the Netherlanders and the Belgians she shared the exploitation theory and regarded the native population as mere chattels. The result was that cruelty, individual license and ruthless suppression characterized the first two decades of her rule as it is likely to in any colonial power. But it met with the scathing criticism and condemnation in the *Reichstag*, especially from the Social-Democrats and the Catholic Center Party, so that a reform was inaugurated with the election of a new colonial secretary, Dr. Bernhard Dernburg, in 1907. With his adoption of a really enlightened scientific colonization,

---

[2] Prof. Malvezzi de' Medici in the *Educational Yearbook. International Institute of Teachers College, Columbia University,* 1931, p. 649.

the natives came to be considered as assets to be protected and developed rather than as enemies to be exterminated. "The natives, gentlemen, are our wards. . . . We do not wish to exterminate but to preserve them. . . . This is a moral duty to which we stand pledged." So stated Dr. Solf, colonial secretary in 1912. Hence a thoroughgoing official paternalism, often strict and harsh but pre-eminently efficient and just, replaced cruelty and repression. The attitude of superiority remained but the Germans, like the British, accepted the responsibility or "trust" for the welfare of their native peoples.

Belgium has had no colonial native policy elaborated by its writers, but it may be said to be dominated by an official desire to remedy the damage inflicted upon the nation's reputation by the "scandals" of Leopold II's irresponsible rule; and by the aim of assisting European penetration of the Congo only if subject to the defence of the native's interests. The government has clearly and openly deplored the exploitation of the early decades, whose unequalled cruelties and horrors caused the civilized world to ring with cries for reform. The Belgian native philosophy until about 1915 meant a complete destruction of all that was vital in native life and the reduction of the mass to the level of a great black proletariat.

More recently the Belgian attitude has even abandoned "assimilation," which at first replaced ruthless exploitation, and has advanced to the firm foundations of development on native lines. "We absolutely break with the policy of assimilation. We claim that native society should freely develop after its own manner, its own nature, its own milieu. We must respect and develop native institutions, and not, as heretofore, break them," stated the minister of colonies in 1920. And the Belgian king, before ascending the throne in 1934, advocated in an important speech in the senate the establishment of a prosperous peasantry able to acquire property and to enjoy the economic freedom guaranteed by the Colonial Charter.

THE NATIVES' POLITICAL AND LEGAL STATUS—NATIVE POLITICAL RULE

With the foregoing differing national philosophies and attitudes towards indigenous populations in mind, let us survey Africa,

where we shall find as many kinds and varieties of native political
rule as there are European empires.

British Rule

Corresponding closely to the well-defined British position,
British Africa illustrates three types of government. The first is
dominion status, enjoyed throughout the Commonwealth of
Nations wherever English and other white settlers overwhelmingly predominate. It means the granting to such areas of economic freedom and political self-determination in all internal
affairs and, since the Statute of Westminster (1931), independence in external or foreign affairs. South Africa is the only country
in British Africa with full autonomy, although southern Rhodesia
is demanding it. But, as we have seen, in South Africa this political
independence refers only to the white population; the natives
are under the Native Affairs Department, whose minister is a
member of the Union Cabinet, and which maintains a modified
indirect rule for the nonwhite population.

In the rest of British Africa, two other types of rule prevail:
the direct or crown-colony system, and the indirect or protectorate
method. The principle of direct rule is the old one and generally
found in the earlier settlements where Europeans abound. In
practice it means that native peoples are to be administered in
every department from taxes to health and education services by
the central government, working through agents both British and
native appointed by and directly responsible to it.

Indirect rule, on the other hand, is the principle of governing
through native chiefs, regarded as an integral part of the
machinery of government with well-defined powers and functions.
It employs the existing institutions of the country where they are
adequate, molding them by careful guidance towards the greatest
possible freedom and development. In other words, indirect rule
is sort of a native-state structure with its own courts, treasuries,
public works, free from the open control of the colonizing power
yet dependent upon it for its authority. Lord Lugard first evolved
indirect rule in Nigeria, and he and Sir Donald Cameron, governor
of Tanganyika Territory, became its greatest champions. It obtains mainly in the hinterland and protectorate areas where the
majority of people still have strong tribal ties and recognize native

laws and customs, while direct rule prevails in the coastal areas of West Africa, among "Europeanized Africans," although both systems exist side by side in northern Rhodesia and in Nyasaland, Tanganyika Territory and Uganda. An important part of indirect rule is the fostering of native agriculture, skills, crafts and general economic welfare, so that indigenous peoples may become self-sufficient in developing their own resources without the imposition of the industrialization of the West.

Indirect rule is spreading rapidly in British Africa. Whether it will prove to be the panacea for existing evils of capitalist imperialism that its champions claim, remains to be seen. Its exponents argue that some such form of indirect rule or its modification, which strengthens the native social organism, rouses it from its century-old apathy and sets it growing into something stronger, is the only way to save the native from that disintegration incident upon the impact upon him of Western industrialization and to stabilize him; but its opponents see in indirect rule only another and more subtle method of securing the domination and exploitation by the whites over their subject peoples.

Militarization. The absence of militarization of the natives in their colonies also reflects the British native philosophy. No attempt is made to conscript the natives or to use the colonies as "reservoirs" of armed strength. The troops organized and maintained in all the British African colonies are militia, solely for the defence of the colony and for police protection.

Judicial System. In the same way the judicial system harmonizes with the outlook that recognizes native rights and customs. Nowhere is an extraneous code of justice, imported from the West, imposed on native peoples. For the most part, the civil code of British Africa is based on native customs, except those that are antisocial or which a civilized administration could not tolerate.

French Rule

In contrast to the British, French colonial government may well be described as centripetal where the British is centrifugal. In realizing "assimilation," France has leaned towards "subordination" in rule, towards uniform methods and meticulous supervision from the center. All the colonies were politically similar in that Paris had complete control over all matters of importance, a control vested in the ministry of colonies and its *bureaux*. At any time the French parliament might legislate for the colonies directly and these decrees were carried out by the central and local authorities who were responsible to Paris.

The keynote of French colonial rule in Africa was subordination, not autonomy. Indirect rule as practiced by the British, except in the case of the chiefs in North Africa, was unknown; nor did native councils exist to any extent except since 1926 in the Volta region of Equatorial Africa, in the Niger region of West Africa and in the panels of natives in the joint assemblies of the larger colonies. Beyond a purely advisory and minor participation, natives were not generally taken into partnership in French political, colonial government. The chiefs in French Equatorial Africa, for instance, had no administrative power, and none of the administrative units possessed their own treasuries. It is a significant fact that France employed twice as many colonial officials as England. Only recently have her ministers begun to realize the advantages of "association" rather than of "assimilation," but the change has not as yet been reflected to any noticeable extent in actual administration.

Militarization. No part of France's colonial rule is more indicative of her inherent philosophy than the militarization of the natives, which conscripts them and obliges them to spend twice the time of Frenchmen in military service.

It is well known, of course, that France regarded her African colonies as a "reservoir" of military strength and as a training ground for her regular army. She sought compensation in Africa for the difference between forty-two million Frenchmen and, now, eighty million Germans in Europe. African troops fought in the Crimean War, in Mexico and in the Franco-Prussian War as well as in those campaigns which won West and Equatorial Africa and Morocco for the French Empire. In the first World War, 680,000 African native soldiers fought for France.[3] In 1919, a decree of the French parliament obliged colonial territories to furnish a permanent contingent of 202,000 men and made native subjects liable to conscription for a term of three years. About 10,000 natives were yearly recruited from Africa. The number of conscripts was annually fixed by the minister of colonies

---

[3] Du Bois, W. E. B., *Black Folk Then and Now*, p. 378.

and prorated among the areas. Three months of the training had to be spent in France, often detrimental to health because of the climate and different way of life. The African soldiers were then assigned to companies and dispatched where needed.

Criticism, from Frenchmen themselves, centered on the colonial military policy. It charged that recruiting reduced the labor supply and absorbed the time of physicians so needed in constructive, protective medical work; that service abroad impaired the health of the native, who often disseminated disease upon his return, demoralized the demobilized and unfitted them for normal life at home. It is significant, in view of this criticism, that France altered her original military policy in the mandates. At first she insisted upon a broad interpretation of the mandate provisions, applied conscription and reserved the right to use such troops outside the territory of the mandate. But after 1925 she gave Togoland and Cameroons complete autonomy in this respect. They supplied a native militia for police duty and for guardianship of their territory. Only in case of a general war did France intend to conscript and employ native troops outside the mandated territory.

Judicial System. The administrative and military attitude towards the native very naturally tinctured the judicial. French courts administered justice in all the African colonies according to the French civil and criminal codes, although in the colonies acquired since 1880 there was a tendency to respect native justice and a compromise between French law and native law had been, in many places, achieved. French law, however, dominated, except in the mandate of Togoland, where a penal code had been given the natives along with the right of appeal.

Another evidence of the emphasis upon French supremacy is that only French administrative officers presided over trials of the natives. Europeans had French professional magistrates. This was contrary to the practice in the British and Belgian areas. Since 1924 France had placed all judicial power in the hands of European administrators, despite her original treaties with the chiefs which permitted them to retain their judicial rights. Inasmuch as many of the administrators were ignorant of the language and worked through interpreters, it was extremely difficult to render justice. Numerous abuses existed, and bitter complaints arose from this fertile field of misunderstanding.

Italian Rule

Italy differed as much from France as from England in her native rule. She followed neither the "assimilative" policy of France nor the decentralizing system of England, but maintained an absolute and rigorous control over her native peoples which clearly reflected the spirit of the home government. In the machinery of government the station agents were supreme; neither actual local autonomy nor divisions of administration with native chiefs existed. Often the same decrees and regulations that were in force in Italy applied in the colonies. At the same time great latitude was given native custom and practice, much more so than under French rule. Italy's indigenous peoples were permitted to retain their own religion, which was always carefully respected, their own usages and their own language, but entirely within the framework of Italian administration, which was ironclad in its authority.

German Rule

In any account of the political and legal status of Germany's natives, it must be remembered that all her colonies were located in the tropics and that therefore their inhabitants were for the most part at that stage of development where they could not stand by themselves as far as government was concerned. Consequently, in every German colony there was found an imperial governor and his staff, a complete civil service, a code of native law and a judicial system. Directly under the governor were the district chiefs assisted by smaller staffs on the model of his. This civil administration was supreme, for the military force in each colony was directly subject to the governor. Many of these colonial administrators were or had been military officers who tended to be strict and often unduly severe and cruel. During the latter years, before 1914, this situation was changing but it had existed long enough, doubtless, to account for the reputation for cruelty which German colonial rule bore in some quarters.

Besides the imperial officials, however, there were some organs and methods of self-government, or—more correctly—of co-operation with the alien administration. In East Africa, for example, in 1901 there were created district councils to meet with the district chief, on which the natives were allowed one representative; and this practice was followed in the other territories. Also, the government permitted many of the original native administrative bodies to remain. In East Africa, again, which because of its great size was still in 1913 understaffed, native assistance came to be greatly relied upon and the Arab system of ruling by means of alien native officials, known as *jambes* and *akidas*, was employed. As Sir Harry Johnston described it: "It is a fact that the German rule in East Africa was in no way unpopular during the decade or more before the [first World] war. The leading native chieftains were treated as we treat the rajahs in India, while the Arabs were so well satisfied with the German administration that they became their strong allies."

In Togoland and in Cameroons, likewise, the official machinery of the chieftains was not destroyed but, on the contrary, preserved and drawn into co-operation with the imperial rule by placing upon it the responsibility of maintaining law and order. Dr. Dernburg was especially interested in enlarging the sphere of native administrative power and did much to encourage it; and, following his example, Dr. Solf, in 1913, became enthusiastic over increasing the semi-independent "indirect government" units in Togoland and started to install them farther in Cameroons. In northern Cameroons, even native treasuries were established to receive half the taxes.

Judicial System. In regard to the administration of justice, "mixed courts" and to some extent the judicial right of the chieftains were recognized. In civil matters, the jurisdiction of the district chief was supreme but he was assisted by a native judge where native law was involved. But the system was incomplete by 1914 and led to considerable confusion and dissatisfaction. Dr. Dove, one of the most conspicuous colonial enthusiasts, stated in the *Reichstag* in 1914: "The whole system of justice is so undeveloped in our colonies that often the executive power and the judicial function are in the same hand. This must be altered as soon as possible." He welcomed the establishment in 1914 of the *Kolonialgerichtshof* in Germany as "one of the first steps towards a regulation of justice for ourselves as well as for the natives."

Militarization. Germany's colonial rule has been bitterly attacked in this respect because of the prominence of militarism in the mother country and because of the important rôle played by the military in subordinating native uprisings during the first two decades of her colonial history. But in 1914 there existed no fortified naval stations, no harbor fortifications, no military garrisons in the colonies. Germany supported no colonial army in the accepted use of the term, no colored troops outside the colonies; neither did she employ conscription of natives. Only the three largest colonies possessed protectorate troops, organized as military troops for protection and police duty.

Belgian Rule

Under the rule of Leopold II, who constituted himself absolute sovereign of the Congo Free State, the native possessed no civil rights whatever. He was but a nameless member of a vast black proletariat. With the assumption of control by the Belgian government in 1908, little change occurred in his status at first for, like the natives in the French colonies, he was subjugated and assimilated. A definite policy to destroy his institutions and to undermine the power and prestige of the chieftains was pursued and Belgian officials replaced the customary tribal authorities. The Charter of 1908 conferred civil rights of Belgian citizenship upon only a minority of soldiers, government workers and missionary-educated natives; the great mass were without rights.

Changed economic conditions, however, brought about by the termination of the drainage of raw rubber, ended the assimilation policy after 1917. Association has replaced assimilation, even faster than in the French colonies. Native organization is fostered, not crushed, and political freedom is growing along with the gradual elimination of economic slavery.

The Native's Economic Status—Land and Labor Policy [4]

Most of the colonial powers have ruthlessly deprived the native of his land and then, ironically enough, forced him to work upon it by making it impossible for him to live otherwise. These sequestrations enable the Europeans either to reap their natural re-

---

[4] For details on labor, see Orde-Brown, G., *The African Labourer,* Oxford University Press, 1933.

sources—gold, diamonds, phosphates, copper and other minerals, rubber, ivory, palm oil, timber, gums—or else to develop their agricultural potentialities—cotton, coffee, cocoa, grains, sisal. The justification advanced is that only the initiative, knowledge and industrialization of the West are able to realize Africa's incredible riches. We have read something about this land seizure and work compulsion in the accounts of European conquest, but now let us turn to a survey of its use and the treatment of the human factor—the laborer.

Great Britain, Belgium and the German Empire have all employed the planter or settler system of land development universally and on a large scale, while France and Italy, owing mainly to the nature of their colonies, have rather fostered native farming and individual cultivation. When carried to excess, as it often was in those first decades of modern expansion, and still is in some areas, this land system works tremendous hardship upon the native. It either crowds him off his most desirable lands onto ofttimes inferior and inadequate "reserves," or deprives him of all land. At the same time it inflicts upon him the Western labor system, often by means of direct or indirect "forced labor," resulting in the breaking of his tribal organization and customs, which brings social and moral disaster.

The Belgian Congo

In the Belgian Congo, the new Free State government in 1885 declared all "vacant lands" the property of the state and later decreed (1890, 1895) a state monopoly of rubber and ivory products which the natives were forbidden to sell except to agents of the state. Besides direct official exploitation of the "state lands," large tracts were granted as concessions to Belgians as well as to companies of other countries including American, in which the Belgian king reserved ownership of just more than one-half of the stock. In addition, Leopold II took possession of about 112,000 square miles of the choicest rubber forests as a private estate, *Domaine de la Couronne,* for himself, which in ten years yielded approximately 11,354 tons of rubber with a profit of $15,000,000.

Such ruthless seizure of lands was, of course, accompanied by forced labor induced by recruiting with the military arm; by taxes in rubber and ivory imposed upon the unwilling and work-resisting natives; by bloody punitive expeditions; by corporal punishment and mutilation; and by the taking of hostages, causing the breakup of families and long separation from tribal associations. Indeed, so notorious became the cruel atrocities in the Belgian Congo that Native Protection societies espoused the cause of the natives. Leopold himself was obliged to appoint a commission of inquiry, the British government demanded reforms and even the United States Senate became interested, which all contributed, as we have learned, to the Belgian government's taking over the Congo Free State from Leopold in 1908.

Many of the concession and labor evils still continue in the Belgian Congo, although the government since 1917 has made continuous effort to control them, combatting the interest of those nationals who are primarily concerned with the territory's economic development rather than with native welfare. The Belgian Congo Report of 1934 stated as the policy of the colonial government that settlement by Europeans is to take place only on sparsely settled areas. Since the first World War, concessions have been much reduced and areas are smaller, although some holdings are still extensive, the largest being that of the *Huileries du Congo Belge,* a subsidiary of Lever Bros., a British company. Under present regulations, concession owners may develop only such parts as cannot legally be claimed to be in native occupation, and there is nothing final about their grants. The concession policy in the mandated area of Ruanda-Urundi, where two large tracts had been allotted to companies, evoked unfavorable comment from the Permanent Mandates Commission which resulted (1929) in restricting the area granted as well as the time of occupation.

Due to the continuous legislation, labor conditions have been much improved, although Belgium reluctantly agreed to the Geneva Draft Convention of 1930 which pledged its signatories to suppress forced labor in all its forms. Compulsory labor may now be levied only by an administrative officer in emergencies, such as famine, epidemic and the like. Recruiting is strictly controlled, and concession companies are obliged to pay a minimum wage and maintain schools and dispensaries. Indeed, the standard of treatment which labor in the Belgian Congo is legally entitled to receive is now at least as high as in any other industrial area in Africa, but the universal conflict between the "interests" and the humanitarians proceeds.

Great Britain

Although not so notorious nor so publicized as those of the Belgian Congo, Great Britain's land and labor problems have caused and are causing her considerable difficulty, especially in the Union of South Africa, in Rhodesia and in Kenya.

When one recalls the campaign for conquest in South Africa, the competition of British and Boer, and the necessity to establish effective control by land confiscation, it is not surprising that demand for some final settlement of land allocation was postponed until after the close of the Boer War, in 1901. The answer came in 1913 with the passing of the Land Act by the Union, the aim of which was to divide the whole of the Union into native and European areas, and restrict further purchases by either class to their own areas. The result has been that a native population of 7,000,000 is legally entitled to occupy an area of some 34,000 square miles, while the remaining 440,000 square miles is either owned by or reserved for Europeans who number about 2,000,-000. Moreover, the land of the whites constitutes the best land. This situation bears heavily upon the native since agriculture is his basic means of subsistence, but overcrowding on the reserves often forces him into becoming a wage-earner.

South Africa's Labor Problems. The South African Union can number more labor problems than any other part of Africa due to its extensive mining, agriculture and industry in urban centers, as well as to its number and variety of races and peoples. To mention merely the major ones affecting the natives: unregulated agricultural wages; the restrictions upon native residence in the cities; the Color Bar Act of 1926 and other legislation excluding natives from positions of skill and responsibilities, thereby protecting Europeans from competition; the disparity of wages between black and white, especially in the mining industry, and in many others.

Complicating the land and labor problems in the Union of South Africa is the presence of about 170,000 Indians. Importation was stopped in 1911 and many thousands have been repatriated. Originally imported, beginning about 1860, as indentured laborers to work on the tea and sugar plantations of Natal, they have been subjected to all sorts of discrimination, political and economic. Some have become capitalists especially in Natal, but the great majority are poor artisans, laborers, with a sprinkling of retail traders and professional men. Despite Gandhi's agitation for their relief, during his long residence there, they are still victimized under the Color Bar Act and other laws regarding poll tax, trading prohibitions and land-purchase restrictions.

But while South Africa's land and labor situation has evolved by force of circumstance, Kenya's has been planned. That colony furnishes, with South Africa, the most serious problem of inadequate native reserves, although Rhodesia and Nyasaland provide other aspects of the difficulty whose description space precludes. In Kenya, as hitherto indicated, the question is tense with discontent, both because of the density of the native population and the attraction which its salubrious climate has for white settlers. The Crown Lands Ordinance of 1915 formally asserted that the natives had no titles to their lands, even to their reserves, all rights being vested in the crown. It also granted to settlers the right to obtain properties up to 5,000 acres for 99 years at the price of 1 d. per acre.

Then, as a means of providing for the demobilized soldiers, about 2,000,000 acres of land were confiscated shortly after the first World War under the Soldiers Settlement Scheme. Since land forms the very basis of the economic and social system of the natives, persistent agitation and open revolt forced the colonial office to institute an investigation in 1924 which resulted in the Crown Lands Amendment Ordinance of 1924, which set aside 30,908,800 acres of crown lands for native reserves; but it did not guarantee them, with the result that further nibbling by Europeans ensued and forced the passage of the Native Land Trust Ordinance by the Kenya legislature in 1930, hailed as a "Magna Carta." It failed to solve the land problem, however, due to the gold rush of 1932 and the consequent amending of the "Magna Carta," giving the government the right to annex "gold-bearing lands." To appease the natives, 2,500 square miles were added to the existing 50,000 square miles of reserves in 1934, as a result of the recommendation by the Kenya land commission. This again does not meet the situation which leaves 60,000 Kikuyu homeless and 1,029,422 of the Kairrando people living upon 7,114 square miles of reserves (averaging 136 per square mile), as compared with from 17,000-20,000 Europeans on 16,700 square miles. In short, about one quarter of the land in Kenya, representing most of the fertile, upland territory, is held by Europeans and is termed the "White Highlands." The Indians also are barred.[5]

The demand for cheap labor to work on the plantations has been as insistent in Kenya as elsewhere and many of the direct and indirect methods of pressure, such as the imposition of hut and poll taxes, which can be earned only by wage labor, and the discouragement of native production, have been applied. At one period after the war, instructions were sent out from Nairobi, the capital, to all district officers that "moral suasion" was to be employed to get the natives to leave the reserves to work on the private estates. As practiced it invoked a manifesto from the heads of the Anglican and Scottish missions to the effect that the open application of forced labor would be preferable. It has since been abandoned by order of the secretary of state, but the demand for labor in the Kenya colony is still acute and exerts its pressure throughout the colony. Wages on the European plantations are only 8 s. per month without food.

Besides her labor difficulties in agriculture, Great Britain is encountering an increasing number in industry as the finance capitalism of the West industrializes more and more of Africa. In North Rhodesia, for example, copper mining has precipitated among the natives a cataclysmic change from rural to urban life with its ensuing booms, depressions, unemployment and forced labor. Gold mining, which now employs on the Gold Coast about 40,000, in Sierra Leone about 12,000, is exerting an ever increasing pressure on the native to desert agriculture and the restricted environment of tribal life for such new opportunity as even the meanest wage-labor offers. In consequence, great agglomerations of humanity are arising on the mine fields, presenting all the problems incident to such transition between rural and urban existence.

On the other hand, Great Britain was one of the original signatories of the Forced Labor Convention of the International Labor Organization (1930) which pledges its adherents to suppress forced labor in all its forms within the shortest possible period, meanwhile permitting it only for public purposes and emergencies, and has notably enforced the mandate provision in this respect in Tanganyika Territory. Also, she has done more than

---

[5] Like South Africa, Kenya also has its "Indian problem." There are about 22,000 Indians, many of whom engage in trade. Since 1934, there have been five elected Indian members on the legislative council.

any other colonial power to encourage native production and to establish it upon a firm basis: by stabilization of the market as in West Africa, where the cocoa and groundnut cultivation has made such spectacular strides; by agricultural research education and the control of pests and plant disease, as notably in Tanganyika; by standardization of products, as in Nyasaland in cotton and tobacco production; and, finally, by the experiments in cotton growing in the Anglo-Egyptian Sudan, where co-operation between private company, native and government is being successfully achieved.

Germany

During the first twenty years of German colonization, the land was completely at the mercy of the colonial companies, to whom the government granted huge concessions and gave no thought whatsoever to native rights. So destructive and disastrous proved this policy that it incited many fierce native revolts, of which the worst was that of the Hereros in South West Africa, where the land companies had seized 32 per cent of their land—a revolt crushed by the government with the utmost cruelty. Reaction to such native treatment, mainly expressed by the Social Democrats in Germany, led to a reform movement at the end of the century upon which Dr. Dernburg, the first colonial secretary, built during the years after 1907. He promoted a land policy in favor of native ownership and production, which in East Africa resulted in the land law of 1907, prohibiting the sale to a white settler of any land that was already occupied by a native; and which in the Cameroons led to the law of 1910, restricting all land sales to "crown lands"—legislation which aimed to insure the native in the ultimate possession of his property. In East Africa, the result may be judged by the material increase in the amount of land under native production, although in some of the highland areas, notably in Moshi, a district capable of producing valuable crops of coffee and maize, Europeans tended to crowd the natives off the more desirable land in violation of the government policy. In the Cameroons, on the other hand, the application of reform was not so successful, owing doubtless to the stranglehold of the concession policy. The natives, generally, complained that the reserves were not large enough, that the poorer land was allotted to them, and that in a number of districts no native reserves were effected. How the natives felt in regard to their land rights may be observed in the Doualan controversy of 1913 when the German government expropriated land along the water front on which to build a model European city, moving four native villages back into the interior. The confiscation met the violent opposition of the Doualans, who employed a German attorney to defend their rights, and brought the case into the German *Reichstag*.

France

On the whole the French followed the policy of production by native farmers and not by large European plantations like the British and Belgians, exceptions being the concession system in Equatorial Africa, and, since 1918, the settling of French war veterans in North Africa. At first glance, this native-farmer system would seem to have left most of the land in the hands of its legitimate owners to develop as they will, but it possessed two major drawbacks: the granting of concessions to natives as well as to Europeans, which removed the distribution of land from the chiefs, the French becoming and considering themselves the chief's successors; and the blocking of agricultural improvement. The blocking of improvement is well illustrated in Algeria where, in contrast to the successful vinoculture of the Europeans, the bulk of agriculture was stagnant, because the natives refused to modernize age-old methods. In Tunisia, on the other hand, this difficulty was being overcome by instituting a system of European entrepreneurs and native tenants who received government aid, credit facilities and agricultural education. But we observed agricultural stagnation perhaps at its worst in those parts of West Africa where the land is extremely poor and the population thin. In many places the major crop, groundnuts, grown by natives on an individual area of about 740 acres, was steadily decreasing, owing to soil exhaustion. The government was stimulating fertilization for a second crop and urging the development of other oleaginous products—such as palm oil and kernels.

Although France maintained in each colony an agricultural experimentation station and facilities for native instruction, she had not gone nearly so far as the British in the scientific stimulation of native production, partly because of her system of peasant proprietorship which clung to old methods and lacked adaptability. Thus her twenty-year effort to develop cotton growing, in West Africa, in the Niger and Senegal Valleys and in the French Sudan, met with little success. Likewise, state aid to native agriculture in Morocco, which remains for the most part in a primitive state, has been far from sufficient.

As mentioned before, the one conspicuous exception to native landowning was the concession system in Equatorial Africa; minor concessions also existed in West Africa and forest concessions on the Ivory Coast. Established in 1899 in Equatorial Africa by granting forty companies land totalling about 140,000 square miles, more than one-half the total area of France, the system proved disastrous to the natives in two ways. It not only deprived them of their land and led to further confiscatory encroachments because of the vagueness of boundaries marking the concessions, but also deprived them of a livelihood and forced them to work for the companies at the latter's own price, because the companies received exclusive rights to "the whole of the products of the soil," which prevented natives even from selling forest products to traders and obliged them to collect rubber for the companies.

As an additional aid to this "forced labor," the government imposed a head tax payable in products. As a result, wages both for natives and Europeans were extremely low. André Gide has described the hardships and cruelties endured by natives in this area where at times they were fired on to force rubber collection and where a serious revolt occurred in 1927. Other writers have pointed out also "the gradual strangling of the life of these territories by a continuous exodus induced by hopeless poverty," especially into Spanish Guinea.

In 1930 a new system for the concessions which had received confirmation of their claims in 1920 was enforced. The main change consisted in withdrawing rights over the whole area of the former concessions and substituting the privilege of setting up oil factories, which control a monopoly of purchasing raw materials from the natives within a radius of thirty miles. The present situation remains somewhat obscure, but at least the trend seems to be towards further curtailment of monopoly rights.

But the concession companies have not been the only oppressor of native labor; they have had an all too active example in the government itself. The annual labor tax, the *prestation,* affected every native in a French African colony, obliging him to give a certain number of days' labor to the government, the maximum being twelve, while the *corvée,* an official institution, took natives from the villages and forced them to work on the roads, often herded into barracks under unhygienic living conditions.

Influenced partly by the terms of the mandates and by other humanitarian trends, the French government has supported some recent measures to curb forced labor. It was one of the signatories of the Slavery Convention of 1926 which undertook to "adopt all necessary measures to prevent compulsory or forced labor from developing into conditions analogous to slavery"; but has not, as yet, ratified the Forced Labor Convention of the International Labor Organization (1930), on the ground that it was out of harmony with French colonial labor problems. On the whole, however, forced labor may be said to be on the decrease: in North Africa where the labor legislation of France was gradually being applied there was no need to resort to it; in West Africa the demand was diminishing, the recent improvements in and about Dakar having been accomplished by voluntary labor.

Altogether, France had an extremely difficult labor problem in her African colonies mainly because of the sparse population in some of them, and because of the climate and lack of food and transportation. But her many difficulties have been surmounted in part by the employment of Italians in Tunisia and of Syrians in West Africa, and by the transplanting of whole villages and communities to work areas in West and Equatorial Africa, such as the contemplated transfer of blocks of Sudanese to the newly irrigated Niger Valley. Early abuses practiced in recruitment of labor power were being remedied by new decrees and the extension of control. The Blum administration stimulated such improvement by authorizing a mission of inquiry in French colonies to consider the co-ordination of labor and social policies.

Native Welfare Policy—Education—Health

Education

The history of African native education on the part of all the colonial powers has followed the same major outline. First, the

Christian missionaries, who, naturally, imported only that which they knew, gave the native a formal, standardized education, set in the Western mold, so that African children were learning the same things as their contemporaries in Berlin, London or Paris, without respect to their environment or to their need. Then, when the home governments came to the aid of colonial education in the form of grants and subsidies, they strengthened its Western tendency, for the very machinery of departments, syllabi, inspectors, examinations, was transplanted to Africa. The idea that education consisted in the imparting of a certain quantity of knowledge considered to be intrinsically valuable came to be more effectively realized. It is only in recent years that the new attitude towards education, adaptation to meet the needs of the people and their environment, has made any headway and that is still hampered by the presence or absence in the colony of European economic interests. When these interests are present, the education tends to develop the skills useful to the employer of labor and not those which might improve the whole basis of village life. Thus the natives may be trained as engine drivers in the Belgian Congo or as clerks in Tanganyika Territory, with no regard whatsoever to their own welfare. Indeed, only in one or two African territories has there been any attempt to envisage education as a broad, constructive program designed to develop native life, although this enlightened conception of educational aim is beginning to spread. And it is just in the acceptance and application of this new view that the variation in the educational policy of the various colonial powers may be illustrated.

Great Britain. In the older colonies such as South Africa, South Nigeria, the Gold Coast and Uganda, where the original system has become entrenched, the literary, formal education still predominates, but the wider application of indirect rule is militating materially against the spread of purely English language and culture, together with the idea that the treasures of Shakespeare and Milton alone can enrich native life. Thus in southern Rhodesia, the improvement of native economic life has, since 1929, been regarded as the most important function of education—an aim carried out by training in food production, pottery, tiling, manipulation of skins and hides, and continued by means of Jeannes demonstration schools, community demonstrators and the like. The same theory is being applied, since 1932, in northern Rhodesia and Nyasaland, which has recently produced a number of text-books in the vernacular, dealing not only with school subjects but with agriculture, child welfare and cooking. Likewise, the reorganization of the system in Tanganyika Territory lays much more emphasis upon the requirements of village life and the development of vernacular schools. Through the influence of Professor Julian Huxley, elementary biology has now become popular in the school program as encouraging hygiene as well as a rational explanation of natural phenomena hitherto ascribed to supernatural causes. Still, religious teaching occupies a larger proportion of the curriculum than in England. Standards of achievement in higher education are still set by the examination in the home country; the tendency to educate an *élite* for which there is little opportunity prevails; and the imposition, as in South Africa, of a complete elementary and secondary school course, similar to England's, still persists, even though barely 3 per cent of the pupils are able to pass beyond the elementary grades.

France. Nothing illustrates France's belief in "assimilation" more clearly than did her colonial schools. French language and literature, French history and the characteristics of French civilization were all regarded as the most important subjects of education. Indeed, the sole purpose of her preparatory schools, universal throughout her colonies, was to provide children from six to twelve years with a knowledge of spoken French, "the key to all opportunities," the initiation of the African to the world of the French people. In the words of G. Hardy, the director of the *Ecole Coloniale,* "A knowledge of French is the first essential to secure the unity of our empire." In short, the underlying principle of the French system was that the largest number of people possible should be brought into contact with the essential aims of French civilization; though only a minority, the *élite*, were expected to be sufficiently intelligent to assimilate much learning. And here, as in other aspects of French policy, it was only the *élite* who were really considered, and considered from the point of view of detaching them from their own culture and incorporating them into that of France. With this end in view, France created an elaborate system of higher primary schools, the *Écoles Primaires Supérieures*, both technical and academic, and the special training and professional schools, such as the teacher training institutes, the marine engineering, medical and veterinary schools.

The result of this principle, described as "instructing the mass and detaching the *élite*," has been to remove the leaders to another world and to create a gulf between the educated and uneducated natives.

Not until 1931 did a different attitude towards native education appear, when the then governor of West Africa, M. Brevié, outlined a program of education for the mass which aimed at a real evolution of native life. The whole educational system of French West Africa was being reorganized in accordance with these principles; indeed, the first normal schools for training village teachers and half a dozen experimental farm schools had been opened. France has been severely criticized for the "cultural imperialism" of her colonial education, for an overemphasis upon the literary rather than upon a practical manual training; but there were many signs of a coming change.

Italy. In the words of one of her own educators, Italy sought to adapt her system and methods to the different environments in which they operate, realizing realistically the diverse needs and intellectual capacities of the natives and profiting from the experience of the other colonial powers. The state sought to harmonize the instruction of the natives with their social development and the progress of each colony.

For this reason, the state delegated education in its oldest colonies, Eritrea and Somaliland, to the religious congregations which it subsidized. In Libya, the types of government schools included elementary schools for boys, giving a three-year course, and, in centers of more importance, higher courses of two years, institutes of instruction and handicrafts for girls, vocational schools, private schools. The curriculum was modeled on that laid down for the schools of Italy, modified to adjust to local needs, with great emphasis upon vocational training. Arab teachers taught in the same schools with the Italian teachers.

Belgium. From the beginning, the Congo Free State entrusted native education to the Catholic missionaries. They engaged in little but primary education until 1906, when a school for commercial assistants and three vocational schools were established to meet the needs of European interests. Lately the Belgian government continued this policy, subsidizing the missionary schools. These, it is true, concentrated upon the teaching of craftsmanship rather than upon literary subjects, not, however, with the aim of developing the native welfare as a whole, but rather to provide training dictated by the European employers. Indeed, Belgium holds apparently the same view as France, that the advancement of the native is best secured by detaching him from his native surroundings.

Germany. Like everything else in the development of the German colonies, the schools were not taken seriously in hand by the government until the "scientific era" began in 1907, and there was much to be accomplished. As in the other colonial empires, missionary societies had long prepared the way. Indeed, Germany began her educational work in Africa long before she possessed any colonies there, with the result that, by 1914, missions controlled four-fifths of all the colonial schools, although they had come to be heavily subsidized and consequently supervised by the government. Each mission station, Protestant and Catholic, established an elementary school to teach the elements of the three R's in the native tongue, practical work and some gardening, but in addition to these the missions, assisted by the government, were gradually adding higher schools and seminaries for the training of native teachers. The effect of the entrance of the government into colonial education, both by the introduction of its own schools and its supervision of the mission schools, was to broaden and to standardize the curriculum and to emphasize and develop vocational, manual education. By 1914 government schools were training native clerks, customs officials, telegraph operators, interpreters, carpenters, masons, and all kinds of mechanics and craftsmen, for it was becoming more and more evident that the solution of the native problem lay in practical rather than in abstract schooling.

Especially was this policy evident in East Africa, where there were six purely industrial schools, an increasing degree of native literacy and a growing number of clerks and stenographers in government employ—as well as in Cameroons, where the vocational schools trained the natives mainly to enter the service of Europeans. Here, only about 1.5 per cent of the natives were reached. In Togoland and South West Africa they had made little progress by 1914.

For the most part in all the higher colonial schools instruction was given in German, and despite its emphasis upon manual training, this was mainly designed for the benefit of European employers. As yet there existed no far-reaching conception of the function of education in the fundamental improvement of native life for native benefit.

All the colonial powers are open to the same criticism in regard to their education of the African natives: that they expend too little upon it in proportion to the other outlays of their colonial budgets. It is claimed that in none of the British colonies does the proportion of children receiving any kind of schooling rise over 20 per cent; that it costs £25 per annum to educate a white child in South Africa and £1.5s. to educate a black one. The Permanent Mandates Commission reported in 1937 that "it was struck by the smallness of the grant for education in Northern Cameroons . . . and finds inadequate the effort made to educate the natives in Tanganyika and South West Africa and over-adequate liquor consumption in Tanganyika and Togoland." The Belgian authorities admitted in 1930 that only about 25 per cent of the children had been drawn into their system, while only 2,800 children were being educated in 1930 in French Equatorial Africa.

Even though, as the Royal Institute of International Affairs reports, the expenditures for education have increased by 8 per cent since 1913 and "everywhere great efforts are being made, only part of the population in the African colonies receives sufficient education." Nevertheless, it is at least hopeful that the problem is, as we have learned, engaging the serious attention of all the colonial powers, who are coming to realize that a remodeling of African education to bring it into close relation with African life is one of the most urgent, although difficult tasks of current policy.

Health

If much requires to be accomplished in the field of education in Africa, more is demanded in the health services. The prevalence of disease in the tropical colonies; the high mortality statistics (even though incomplete), where it is estimated that infant mortality in the British colonies falls to 150 per thousand in only a few favored places; the failure of even the recently reorganized medical service in French West Africa to reach more than one-sixth of the population; the inadequacy of the present colonial health services even at their best; and the criticism of the Permanent Mandates Commission, all indicate the gravity of the situation.

The difficulties are, of course, stupendous, for nowhere is the transitional character of the African natives resulting from the impact of Western industrialism upon his tribal organization more fraught with maladjustment. Native medical practice has been proved unscientific and inadequate, yet European substitutes are not sufficiently developed to replace it; methods of village hygiene are unsuited to labor camps and to aggregations of natives in industry; primitive superstition and practices still block science; labor recruitment creates its own special problems of tribal and family disintegration; indigenous diseases are augmented by those imported by the white man; and the services supplied by the colonial powers to meet the increased need are far from adequate.

Like education, medical service was long carried on only by the missionaries, until, with the growth of scientific research into tropical diseases, the establishment of the Schools of Tropical Medicine in London and Liverpool, and the Institute for Tropical Diseases at Hamburg, as well as with the strengthening of national control, the colonial governments assumed the burden. What a burden it has proved and how insufficient have been the budget appropriations to carry it, their own reports—together with present conditions revealed in the colonies—illustrate only too well. Thus, the *Report of the Colonial Office Conference* (1930) stated that practice lagged far behind scientific knowledge in parts of the empire, attributing this lag to such conditions as pest-infested areas, insanitary and inadequate water supply and housing, native insanitary habits and customs and inadequate medical personnel —conditions all due in the last analysis to insufficient funds. In the French *Reports of the Economic Conference of 1935,* colonial medical authorities took the position that since the administration is unable to prov ide enough doctors and hospitals for their countless patients, it should concentrate on preventive measures against sleeping sickness, malaria, smallpox, hookworm and other scourges. But this policy, however essential, fails to relieve the urgent need of the present situation. The fact that all colonial expenditures for health have increased only five and one-half times since 1913 indicates where the major difficulty of the contemporary problem lies.

READINGS

Barnes, L.   *Caliban in Africa,* 1930.   Critical.
Buell, R. L.   *The Native Problem in Africa,* 2 vols. 1928.   Exhaustive.
Buxton, C.   *Race Problem in Africa,* 1931.   Challenging.
DuBois, W. E. B.   "Black Africa Tomorrow,," *Foreign Affairs,* Oct. 1938.
DuBois, W. E. B.   *Black Folk—Then and Now,* 1939.
Frankel, S. H.   *Capital Investment in Africa: Its Course and Effects,* 1938.
Hailey, Lord.   *An African Survey,* 1938.   Encyclopedic.
Lips, J.   *The Savage Hits Back,* 1937.   Study of native abilities.
Mair, L. P.   *Native Policies in Africa,* 1936.   Good, recent.
Mayhew, A.   *Education in the Colonial Empire,* 1938.   Principles and practices.
Morel, E. D.   *The Black Man's Burden,* 1920.   Anti-imperialist.
Orde-Browne, G.   *The African Labourer,* 1933.   Valuable.
Padmore, G.   *How Britain Rules Africa,* 1936.   Indictment of British rule.
Whittlesey, D.   "British and French Colonial Technique in West Africa." *Foreign Affairs,* Jan. 1937.

CHAPTER TEN

Results of European Expansion in Africa upon Nationalism and Internationalism

T HE RESULTS of European expansion in whatever area it has pene-trated overseas have been mainly and universally two: first, the stimulation of native revolts or nationalistic uprisings in resent-ment against the imperialist powers that threaten and weaken their position and prestige; and second, the creation of conflicting hostilities and antagonisms among the European powers them-selves that precipitate the formation of colonial compromises and deals, or else war, and that exert, therefore, a profound influence upon international relations and world politics. Let us examine these apparently inevitable consequences of colonial expansion in the African continent, turning first to the native uprisings.

NATIVE REVOLTS AND NATIONALISTIC MOVEMENTS

European expansion in Africa has been prolific of two kinds of uprisings against the colonial powers on the part of those people who live there: the one is carried on by the African natives; and the other by those first invaders of Africa who, having occupied the land before the present conquerors, come to regard themselves

211

as the legitimate owners and who therefore struggle against the depredations of the latest comers.

Native Revolts

Because of the primitive and undeveloped character of Africa's indigenous peoples, they have proved no match for their European conquerors as yet. Therefore the many native revolts which we have encountered in the course of our narrative, such as those of the Matabeles in Rhodesia, the Hereros in South West Africa, the Ashanti on the Gold Coast, the Doualans in Cameroons, besides a multitude of others like the revolt in the Belgian Congo in 1904, the Zulu rebellion of 1906, the mutiny on the Ivory Coast in 1923 and the turmoil in the French Congo in 1926, were all summarily and ruthlessly suppressed. Africa, indeed, has in the course of its history been literally bathed in blood because of its European conquerors. Even during the modern period, the late nineteenth and early twentieth centuries. minor revolts have been in progress all over the continent.

Although the native peoples have always lost in these conflicts and have been submerged by the ultimate triumph of their conquerors, their struggles have nevertheless left a heritage that is no less potent because it has, as yet, produced no actual fruits of success. For the results of the many revolts and the resentments and bitternesses which they have left in their train may be observed in the crystallization of the so-called African Nationalist Movement after the first World War. Undramatized, so far, like similar movements in India, China, Persia, among more advanced peoples, it nevertheless exhibits the initial symptoms of those popular upsurgings.

Among these symptoms may be cited the many organizations of African natives, ranging all the way from the tribal-religious movements like the *Watch-Tower Movement of East Africa* and the racial, single-objective associations such as *Native Farmers' Congress, Colored Citizens Union, African National Bond,* and the like, to the large, organized nationalistic groups, namely, the *African Native Congress,* the *West African Congress* and the *Aborigines Rights Protective Association.* All have their programs of political and economic rights, their missions and petitions to the home countries and legislatures.

The Italo-Ethiopian conflict gave a great stimulus to the feeling of solidarity among the blacks, who enunciated the slogan, "Our Flag is our Colour. An injury to me is an injury to all." This stimulus was expressed in words when a mass meeting of Kenyan African Natives passed a resolution in September, 1935, appealing to "all African natives and Colonial peoples of the world to take this Italo-Abyssinian dispute as the right opportunity of emancipation of the Colored peoples from the oppressive Imperialist Governments of foreign countries."[1]

It is true that from the nature of the situation in Africa these movements have as yet accomplished little, but they do, at least, indicate the presence of a nationalistic, racial consciousness in Africa. In the words of a French African-Soudanese leader before a congress of the colonial peoples of Asia and Africa in Brussels in 1927: "The Blacks have slept long; perhaps too long. But beware! Those who have slept long and soundly, when once they wake up, will not easily fall back to sleep again."[2]

Nationalist Movements and Revolts

Of more immediate importance, perhaps, because of their tangible successes, than the embryonic native movements, are the nationalist revolts of those groups who were early in Africa as conquerors themselves, against the late-comers of the modern period. Chief of these uprisings were the Boer War, about which we have already learned, the Egyptian national uprising, the Riff rebellion, and the rise of Arab nationalism.

The Egyptian Nationalist Movement. The Treaty of Alliance between the United Kingdom and Egypt, which was ratified in December, 1936, the abrogation of the capitulations in May, 1937, and the sponsoring by England of Egypt for membership in the League of Nations, brought to an end a struggle of more than fifty years in Egypt to develop a national unity which would be recognized by the world powers.

The first seeds of this nationalist movement had been planted by the Arabi rebellion or mutiny of the army against the new khedive appointed by England and France, when they assumed the Dual Control over Egypt in 1879. They forced their puppet khedive

---

[1] Padmore, G., *How Britain Rules Africa*, p. 364.
[2] *Ibid.*, p. 362.

to surrender all control over customs, trade and finance, reducing
his actual power to a shadow. Even when the Egyptian Assembly
of Notables demanded the right to retain that part of the national
revenue not required on the debt payment, he sided with his foreign patrons against them. It was, therefore, in opposition to this
supine ruler who had surrendered the national sovereignty to the
European powers, that Colonel Ahmed Arabi, officer in the Egyptian army and a scholar, organized a revolt with the demands that
all ministers should be dismissed, that a parliament should be
convoked, and that the army should be increased. The rebellion
was, of course, suppressed by Great Britain, who as a result increased her hold over Egypt. Nevertheless, it developed a feeling
of unity among the Egyptians which they had not felt before, and
stimulated a national movement which throve against all odds.

During the succeeding thirty years, 1883-1913, there were no
more internal revolts in Egypt but many factors combined to
foster a demand for political and economic freedom. The long
paternalistic "reign" of Lord Cromer, appointed consul-general
and high commissioner upon the termination of the Dual Control,
brought order out of chaos and unified the country. His many
reforms vastly improved, as we have seen, the economic, political
and social conditions of Egypt. The Organic Law of 1883 established a legislative council and general assembly. The budget
was balanced, the control of water was improved, the fellah was
greatly benefitted and attained a feeling of self-respect which he
had not ever felt before. Egypt, under the guiding hand of Great
Britain, was becoming a well-ordered, dependable nation. According to Lord Cromer himself, "The seeds which have now been
planted are those of true civilization."

Although his lot in life had been greatly improved, or possibly
because of that, the average Egyptian was not satisfied: the feeling of unity and the desire for self-rule increased. And the group
which demanded more of a hand in the governing of Egypt
was only somewhat appeased by the Organic Law, whose dis-
crepancies but whetted its appetite for more extended power.
Even the privileges of the Organic Law were curtailed when
Lord Kitchener, Lord Cromer's successor in 1911, exercised an
increasingly direct rule over the details of Egyptian administration.

Again the rising nationalism so general in Europe during the decade preceding the first World War directly influenced Egyptian nationalism. Especially was this true of the Young Turk movement, of which the effect was widespread throughout the confines of the old Ottoman Empire. Specifically the Egyptian leader, Mustapha Kamel, fearlessly and continuously criticized the British control in Egypt through his speeches and his newspaper, *Al Lewa.*

Britain's declaration of a protectorate over Egypt at the outbreak of the first World War and the consequent strangling of every vestige of freedom and independence brought the nationalist movement to a head. The legislative assembly did not meet and all nationalist demonstrations were suppressed. The Egyptians, particularly the farmers, became dissatisfied. In an effort to appease them the benefits of self-determination, one of the war slogans, were freely trumpeted by the press. Egyptian students, along with most of the rest of the world, became imbued with the idea and the belief gradually grew up that after the war England would put into practice what she had been preaching and relax her control over Egypt.

By the time the armistice was concluded Egyptian nationalist leaders were resolved to secure immediate autonomy for Egypt and the abolition of the protectorate. When British home authorities brushed aside the Egyptian request for autonomy without so much as permitting the leaders an audience, the nationalist party (the Wafd) led by Zaghlul Pasha appointed delegates to the Peace Conference. The delegates, among them Saad Zaghlul, were arrested and held as prisoners in Malta by Britain until the conference was over. A violent storm of protest ensued; riots broke out and bloodshed followed. During March and April, 1919, most of Egypt was in terrible turmoil. A delegation was sent by the Wafd to Paris to enlist the sympathy of France. General Allenby was delegated as British high commissioner to restore order in the country.

In December, 1919, Lord Milner headed a commission sent to Egypt to investigate conditions. As a result some relatively generous recommendations were made, but the Egyptian leaders disagreed with the findings in three points. In the first place, although they provided for recognition of the independence of Egypt under a constitutional monarch, there was no promise that the protectorate would be abolished. In the second place, they gave to British financial and judicial advisers in Egypt a greater degree of control than Egyptian nationalists were willing that they should have. In the third place, the validity of the entire arrangement was made contingent upon other foreign powers transferring their extraterritorial rights to Great Britain—a condition that might not be fulfilled for some time. The Sudan, of vital importance economically to Egypt, was excluded from the memorandum.

Later in 1921 negotiations were entered into concerning the terms of a proposed treaty to regulate Anglo-Egyptian relations. This draft treaty was an improvement in some respects in that it contained a definite promise that the protectorate would be abolished. The nationalist leaders objected because it would give British military forces free passage through Egypt and the right to maintenance for such periods and in such places as Great Britain should decide. It did not recognize Egypt's claim to sovereignty over the Sudan, its claim to the right to administer its own foreign affairs, or its claim to freedom from British interference in the department of finance and justice.

Although the British government considered their proposals as "liberal in character and far-reaching in effect," the nationalists refused to agree to them. There were strikes, a boycott and violent anti-British propaganda. Zaghlul himself was ordered to refrain from taking part in politics, and on his refusal was deported. The position was one of deadlock. Finally Lord Allenby was sent for by the British government and returned from London, February 28, 1922, with a declaration of independence for Egypt.

The declaration abolished the protectorate and stated that the following questions should be reserved to be discussed and settled by agreement between Great Britain and Egypt at some future time: the security of the communications of the British Empire in Egypt; the defense of Egypt against all foreign interests, direct or indirect; the protection of foreign interests in Egypt and the protection of minorities; and the Sudan. The sultan took the title of king and proclaimed Egypt a monarchy. Within a few days Sarwat Pasha formed a cabinet. A minister for foreign affairs was appointed. On April 3, 1922, a special committee was set up to draft a constitution which was enacted on April 19, 1923. When the election results showed the Wafd to be in the majority, Zaghlul, who had been in exile, returned as premier. A new parliament was elected in 1924, the first in ten years.

This parliament did not attempt to settle the points of dispute between the two countries because the leaders among the Nationalists refused to negotiate except on the basis of complete independence for Egypt and British withdrawal from the Sudan. Agitation against the declaration continued. Zaghlul Pasha went to London to talk with Ramsay MacDonald, but their conversations ended with no definite understanding having been reached.

The culminating event in a series of disorders in both Egypt and the Sudan was the assassination of Sir Lee Stack, sirdar of the Egyptian army and governor-general of the Sudan, November 19, 1924. Great Britain held the Wafd entirely responsible and seized this opportunity to insist upon the withdrawal of all Egyptian officers and troops from the Sudan and to increase the area to be irrigated in the Sudan to an unlimited extent. All popular political demonstrations were forbidden and an indemnity of 500,000 pounds was demanded. Pending the conclusion of a further agreement on the subject, the British financial and judicial advisers and the officials of the European department of the ministry of the interior retained their position and powers. British troops were used to force submission. The nationalist parliament appealed to the League of Nations, characterizing the British government's action as imperialistic aggression, but when Great Britain warned the League that this was purely a domestic problem no action was taken.

Parliament was dissolved by the king on December 24, 1924. In the general election which followed, all the non-Wafd parties joined forces and the Wafdists boycotted the election with the result that the new chamber contained no Wafd deputies. Ziwar Pasha formed a coalition cabinet of anti-Wafd ministers. However, when parliament met in March, 1925, it elected Zaghlul president, and his prestige was such that the support of the majority of the deputies for whatever policy he advocated was virtually a foregone conclusion. Siwar Pasha accordingly offered his resignation and when the king refused to accept it, obtained from him another dissolution of parliament. The election of May, 1926, resulted in a large majority of the Wafd in parliament. Zaghlul was again elected president and the demands of the Wafd for complete autonomy were continued until his death in 1927, after which the party became weaker.

In July, 1927, King Fuad and Prime Minister Sarwat Pasha

went to London to open negotiations for the settlement of the four points left outstanding in 1922. A draft treaty was drawn up which was taken back to Egypt in November. It was submitted to the Egyptian parliament in March, 1928, and rejected. Although Great Britain had been more generous in her concessions than before, the stumbling blocks in the way of an agreement were still: foreign relations, military affairs, the position of aliens resident in Egypt, and the Anglo-Egyptian Sudan.

With the return to power of a labor government in 1929 in England, the prospect for Egyptian independence brightened. Negotiations were carried on between Mr. Arthur Henderson, the new foreign secretary, and Mohammed Mahmud Pasha. Agreement was reached in regard to where British troops were to be stationed and the termination of the British military occupation. The status of the Sudan was to revert to that in force prior to the murder of Sir Lee Stack. The protection of foreigners was made into a treaty obligation of the Egyptian government instead of leaving the direct responsibility in the hands of the British government. Still these concessions on the part of Great Britain did not meet with the approval of the nationalist leaders. Negotiations were again opened in 1930 and another treaty was drafted. Agreement was reached on all points but one. Great Britain recognized Egypt's right to become a member of the League of Nations and each country was to send a fully accredited ambassador to the other. It also provided for a defensive alliance between the two countries. It was over the question of the Sudan that negotiations broke down. Great Britain wanted no change from the conditions stated in the convention of 1899, while Egypt was determined that it should be given more power. After effusive expressions of friendship on the part of both the British and the Egyptian negotiators, the Egyptians returned home.

On October 22, 1930, the king declared that the new constitution would take effect at the time of the next assembly of parliament. The Wafd decided to fight the constitution and refused to accept any treaty with Great Britain which was made by Sidky Pasha and his cabinet. The Liberal Constitutional Party joined the Wafd against the cabinet. Riots and strikes followed, but the elections were held and Parliament convened on June 21, 1931. However, the warring factions could come to no agreement and Egypt was ruled virtually by the king and his advisers.

On November 12, 1935, the Wafd withdrew its support from the government and led the agitation for again opening negotiations regarding a satisfactory treaty. The Italo-Abyssinian situation was focusing attention on Egypt, and Great Britain as well as the Egyptian nationalists were eager to come to a satisfactory agreement.

On December 12, 1935, the United Front leaders presented to the High Commissioner a note to be communicated to the British government requesting the opening of negotiations. The note listed the obstacles to the country's development as: the capitulations, the existence of European direction in the department of public security, the lack of an adequate army, and the exclusion of Egypt from the international concert. The British answer of January 21 "thought it desirable to begin with the categories which had given most difficulty in 1930," namely, military questions and the Sudan.

Preliminary negotiations opened in Cairo, March 2, 1936. This time the Egyptian delegation was made up of representatives of all the parties. The British delegation, led by Sir Miles Lampson, included naval, military and air experts. The draft treaty of 1930 became a basis for negotiations. A new treaty was finally drawn up on August 26 and ratified by both Britain and Egypt on December 22, 1936. This treaty gradually terminated Britain's military occupation of Egypt except insofar as British soldiers were needed to protect the Suez Canal. It provided for a military alliance, an alliance of friendship, cordial understanding, and good relations, and exchange of ambassadors between the two countries. Each country agreed not to adopt any alliance with another country inconsistent with the provisions of this treaty. Alexandria and Port Said were reserved by Britain as airplane bases.

At a convention in Montreux, May 8, 1937, an agreement between all the countries concerned and Egypt, to abolish the capitulations, was reached. And on May 27, Great Britain, in keeping with her agreement, presented Egypt's name to the League of Nations. The nationalists had triumphed and Egypt had become a sovereign state.

The Riff Rebellion, 1924-1925. Before the French occupation, Morocco had never been a homogeneous or stable state. Even the most powerful sultans had been forced to deal with independent tribes who refused to pay them tribute or acknowledge their authority. Among these peoples, the Berbers of the Riff mountains were the most independent. For the Berbers are a mountain people speaking their own language distinct from Arabic, having their own customs and characteristics and acknowledging only one bond with the Arabs, namely, Islam. They occupy, among other mountainous areas stretching round the whole sweep of the Atlas range, the so-called Riff, a chaotic and poverty-stricken province bordering the Spanish zone of Morocco. These tribes of the Spanish frontier were among the few left unpacified by Marshal Lyautey in his settlement of Morocco immediately before and after the first World War.

The caird or chieftain of one of these tribes, Abdul Krim, had been educated at the Moslem university at Fez and had served some time under the Spanish command in Spanish Morocco, where he had learned much about international politics and the rivalries of the Christian powers in that part of Africa. On assuming the leadership of his tribe after the first World War, he organized and united the other Berber tribes around him and inflicted a defeat on the Spanish general, Silvestre, at Anoual in 1921, confiscating guns and ammunition. With these and four million pesetas ransom money, paid for Spanish prisoners, as a nucleus, he constructed an effective military organization, even hiring the assistance of European officers.

By 1924, Krim had made himself absolute sovereign of the Riff, ruling with a military dictatorship. His plan was to extend his domain further towards the south in the direction of Fez, whose riches lured the mountain tribes. How great was his ambition to dislodge the French from that region may be seen in his statement: "I recognize that the French have given Morocco order, security, and economic prosperity; but I shall bring the same benefits, with the further advantage that I am a Moslem, and so it will be from a leader of their own faith, not from an Infidel, that the Moors will receive these blessings."

By many Moors throughout the Moslem world, Abdul Krim was considered an inspired leader; in Asia Minor they sold colored lithographs showing him as laying low the armies of the Christians. On the other hand, the sophisticated urban Moors in Morocco and the Young Arabs regarded him as an adventurer. Marshal Lyautey, however, thought it wise to take great precautions. He demanded reinforcements from France and Algeria and Marshal Pétain himself took part in the campaign. It was not until 1926 that the Riff rebellion was crushed.

While not a part of the Arab nationalist movement proper, since is was Berber in origin, the Riff rebellion contributed to general Moslem unrest in North Africa.[3] We have already noted the activities of the *Destour* party in Tunisia and the growing sentiment for independence among a group in Arabian Morocco. As yet the nationalist movement is not generally organized in Africa as it is in the Near East, where we shall learn about it in detail. Nevertheless, as we have seen, many causes for Arab unrest exist in Africa and the possibility of a general Moslem uprising presents a problem which the policy of every colonial power takes into account.

INTERNATIONAL RIVALRIES

The rivalries and antagonisms of the various powers in Africa which have resulted from their conflicting imperialist ambitions have already been partially indicated in the accounts of the separate colonial empires. Nevertheless, the full force of their competition and its effect upon European international relations may be appreciated only when considered as a whole. Nowhere may this relationship between cause and effect be more clearly observed than in the contemporary struggle in Africa which has formed a significant feature of the outbreak of the present European conflict in 1939. For there was nothing new about the colonial crisis created in 1938-1939 by the clamorings and strivings of Mussolini and Hitler for African colonies: Mussolini for Tunisia, Jibuti and shares in the Suez Canal; Hitler for the return of the "stolen colonies." It is as old as European imperialism in Africa, the rhythm of whose history has been international clash, crisis, compromise.

The only novelty in that recent situation existed in the crude, unvarnished baldness of the dictators' demands and the publicity of their ambitions. But that is the way the dictators conduct their foreign policy. Their statesmanship consists largely of oratorical,

[3] For an account of the Arab revival in North Africa, see Julien, Charles-André, "France and Islam," *Foreign Affairs*, July 1940.

shock-dealing speeches and sudden, breath-taking moves. Their voices are blatant, their demands "cold," their actions often crassly brutal. Not for them the dulcet, suave tones, the devious clever machinations, the smooth, quietly negotiated (although none the less brutal) deals of standard diplomacy. Mussolini and Hitler do not employ the polished and polite language of the foreign office; they employ, indeed, no foreign office in the British sense, for in the last analysis dictators are their own foreign ministers.

But these new methods so vociferously illustrated in the speeches of the dictators must not blind us to the old process of European imperialism in Africa, which is still at work. Always, since the "scramble for Africa" in the 1880's, the inevitable international rivalries and competitions have resulted. Again and again international war over Africa has threatened, and been averted only by compromises, by colonial deals, often hair-splitting in their details. Clash, crisis, compromise has been African history since 1871.

A glance at the map on page 223, both before and after the first World War, will show, as we have already learned, that four overpowering national ambitions have dominated the African continent for the last half-century. They were, of course, the British Cape-to-Cairo dream—fully realized since the first World War but at the beginning of the second World War threatened by Italy and Germany; France's west-east, Atlantic-to-Red Sea drive, checked by the British in 1898 and resolved by the Anglo-French *entente* into the French Northwest African ambition, which was realized but seriously resented by Italy; the German *Mittel-Afrika-Deutsch* plan—since the Treaty of Versailles, temporarily eliminated, but none the less alive, as indicated by Hitler's recent speeches and actions; and finally, the Italian East African plan which envisaged developing a vast Italian Northeast African empire. Obviously, all four of these ambitions mutually obstructed each other, which indicates why the African continent, since 1871, has been and still is a scene of the keenest national rivalry.

Considering first the British position, which reaches from Egypt to the Cape today as a result of the first World War, it is evident that here is one ambition realized. But, throughout the course of its building, that grandiose empire was threatened, as we have seen, in turn by France and by Germany. How did Britain manage these interferences and triumph in the end, temporarily

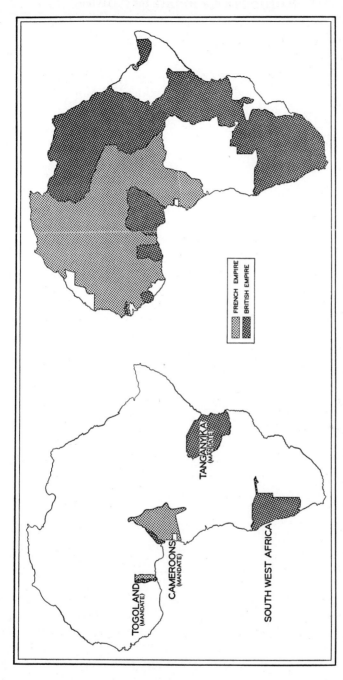

EFFECT OF THE GREAT WAR ON THE AFRICAN EMPIRES: THE ABSORPTION OF THE GERMAN EMPIRE BY BRITAIN AND FRANCE

at least? She employed the cleverest, most consummate and subtlest diplomacy—little force—until the first World War—a technique which proved so overwhelmingly successful that it is no wonder she stood aghast and bewildered before the distinctly unsubtle clamor and threatened violence of Hitler and Mussolini in 1939. Their methods were never her methods. Let us briefly recapitulate them.

From the very beginning, Britain's plan of uniting her South African Cape Colony with her holdings in North Africa was threatened by the French, who were determined to extend their equatorial Africa through the Sudan to the Red Sea. To prevent this fatal interference with her cherished scheme, Great Britain cunningly recognized the nascent ambitions of a newly united Italy who had caught the international epidemic of economic imperialism, and secretly encouraged the Italian development in East Africa as a bulwark against the French. In the early 1880's, consequently, Britain invited Italy to establish herself "somewhere in the Red Sea"—an invitation quickly answered by Italian seizure of the port of Massawa (1886) in what was later to become Italian Eritrea and also of those provinces which estabished Italian Somaliland. Likewise, the Anglo-Italian Convention of 1891 fostered the Italian dream of extending her sphere of influence through the Sudan to the Lybian hinterland and hence to an outlet on the Mediterranean. It placed Italy in the eastern Sudan and recognized Ethiopia as an Italian protectorate, a buffer state against France and her encroachments.

As a further protection against the French in this area, the British concluded the Anglo-Belgian convention (1894). This afforded to King Leopold and his Congo Free State the lease of a coveted section in the southeastern Sudan upon which France had had her eyes, in return for which Leopold leased to Britain a corridor of territory, twenty-five kilometers wide, running behind German East Africa and connecting British territory from Lake Tanganyika to Uganda, another link in the Cape-to-Cairo plan. These diplomatic maneuvers succeeded in forestalling France, but only for a time. When finally learned of, however, they resulted in whetting France's appetite for the Sudan, into which she proceeded to dispatch her famous expedition under Captain Marchand, whose meeting with Kitchener resulted in the Fashoda crisis, resolved by the celebrated Fashoda Agreement of 1898. It should be reiterated here that this compromise formed the basis of the ensuing Anglo-French *entente* of 1901-1905, which gave France a free hand in Morocco and England right of way in Egypt, as well as settled many other outstanding colonial difficulties. Since that date (except for the years 1923-1932, when it was nonexistent), this *entente*, which was based entirely on colonial issues, has exerted an enduring influence upon world politics. It affords a significant example of the effect of modern expansion upon international relations. So did England dispose of her first and most formidable rival in Africa, France.

The second serious rival was Germany. Germany's strongest and largest colony, German East Africa, lay squarely athwart the line of British march. But Germany was not only a passive hindrance, she was an active rival, for she too had begun to dream dreams of linking together her scattered possessions, Southwest Africa, Togoland, Cameroons and East Africa, into a *Mittel-Afrika* empire which would further block British plans as well as encroach upon the Portuguese colonies and upon Belgian Congo.

British diplomacy, however, was more than equal to the German threat. Playing upon the militaristic, aggressive tendencies of the new emperor, William II, Salisbury cleverly offered him the island of Helgoland, strategically situated off Hamburg in the North Sea (in British hands since 1815) for the German recognition of the British sphere of influence in Uganda, in the basin of the upper Nile to the borders of Egypt, and of the British protectorate over Zanzibar, Witu and Somali coast. In spite of the protests of German colonialists, the deal was consummated, with the addition of the cession to German South West Africa of a corridor to the Zambesi River, and Britain's Cape-to-Cairo plan extended and guarded thereby. A few years later, in 1894, and again in 1902, Great Britain by the Anglo-Congo Conventions not only won Belgium, as we have seen, as a buffer against France in the Sudan, but also as an ally against the German advance in middle Africa.

But German ambitions continued to threaten and in 1898 she gave alarming signs of designs upon the Portuguese colonies of Angola in the west and Mozambique in the east which, if realized, would seriously jeopardize British plans. Again British diplomacy handled the situation not only with compromise but, more subtly, with what appeared to be compromise and was not. The

Anglo-German Treaty of 1898 provided for the division of Angola and Mozambique into spheres of influence between Germany and England, should Portugal become insolvent and offer her colonies as collateral for a loan which she seemed on the point of doing. But the British got the best of the Germans because, unknown to. Germany, they practically nullified the treaty by secretly signing with Portugal the Treaty of Windsor the following year, which confirmed former treaties binding them mutually to protect each other's possessions and encouraging Portugal not to encumber her colonies by loans. The Germans wondered why the Portuguese failed to go bankrupt and revived the agitation for expansion in 1909. In 1912 a second Anglo-German treaty was negotiated for the joint division of Angola and Mozambique, but this time occupation was provided for, not upon Portugal's application for loans, but upon her failure to "keep order." The intervention of the first World War apparently prevented the terms of the treaty from being carried out.

At the outbreak of the war, Great Britain marched into the German African colonies, and the Treaty of Versailles with the subsequent allocation of the mandates threw the larger share of them into her hands. Indeed, as early as 1916 Britain and France signed a secret treaty dividing German Togoland and Cameroons in the event of victory. Her share of these on the west coast, together with Tanganyika Territory, former German East Africa, are held today by Britain as mandates, while former German South West Africa is held as a mandate by the Union of South Africa. Thus Great Britain effectually disposed of the German threat to her Cape-to-Cairo plan and the "menace" of a *Mittel-Afrika-Deutsch.* Just how much of a menace it was may be judged by those plans published as Germany's colonial war aims during the conflict by leaders of the colonial movement. A compact empire in Africa was contemplated, "so big that it would be capable of conducting its own defense in time of war." This domain would consist of the former German colonies plus the British, French, and Portuguese possessions south of Sahara and north of the Zambesi, including the islands off the coasts, such as Madagascar, the Azores, Madeira, and Cape Verde. It was pointed out that such a territory in Africa reaching from the Atlantic to the Pacific would enable Germany to dominate some of the most important trade routes of the world; that *Mittel-Afrika* would be at the very center of England's main arteries leading to South Africa, Australia, India, and, in German hands, would contribute to crippling the British Empire and would drive North American influence out of South America. In the light of the recent resuscitation of German colonial claims, these plans are significant since Germany is today demanding not only the return of her "robbed lands" in Africa, but also the lost opportunity to pursue her *Mittel-Afrika-Deutsch.*

Like Great Britain's, France's African empire was threatened in its construction by European rivals; and like Great Britain, France had recourse to diplomacy, compromise, concession—never force, until the first World War. How she dealt with Great Britain in the major clash in the Sudan, gaining thereby her rival as her ally, has already been recounted. Elsewhere, also, England and France had collided and found themselves again and again on the verge of war. But a series of skilfully and cleverly negotiated treaties adjusted the dividing lines between French Guinea and Sierra Leone, (1889); between Gambia, the Gold Coast, Lagos and the French neighboring West African territories (1891); between British and French areas along the lower Niger (1898); and in the Lake Chad region (1890-1898). Always, the remedy was compromise, "colonial deals" by which France and Britain disposed of the clash of their mutual aims.

Another inconvenient rival of France was Germany, mainly in Morocco, the Cameroons and in Central Africa. The Moroccan rivalry, where Germany possessed considerable economic interests (controlling 14 per cent of Moroccan foreign trade in 1898), resulted in three famous and serious international crises in 1905-1906, in 1908-1909, in 1911, when, as we have learned, war was averted only by the narrowest margin. That it was prevented at all was largely due to the nonbelligerent attitude of William II in sharp contrast to the bellicose mood of the German foreign office and the colonial party in Germany. For William II, intent upon German expansion in the Near East, subordinated his colonial aims in North Africa to the prosecution of the Bagdad Railway, the *Drang nach Osten,* for which he required both Turkish and French good will. He sought to win this by conciliation, not animosity, towards the Moroccan sultan and towards the French ambitions there, for which reason he caused Germany to back down before France in Morocco and lost the opportunity of valuable territorial gains in Central and West Africa, which

France was then prepared to surrender. "This wretched Moroccan affair must be brought to a conclusion quickly," the kaiser once said. "Let it be French and let us be done with the friction with France . . . now that great questions in the Near East are at issue."

The Moroccan crisis of 1905-1906, precipitated by the Anglo-French Moroccan Agreement, eventuated in the Algeciras Conference and its assurance to Germany of an "open door" in Morocco in return for French control of the native police force; the 1908-1909 crisis, caused by the penetration of French troops into Morocco, was resolved by the Franco-German Pact which guaranteed "economic equality" in return for French preponderance; and, finally, the 1911 crisis, provoked by French seizure of Fez, the capital, stung Germany into dispatching the gunboat *Panther* (the famous "Spring of the *Panther*") to the port of Agadir in Morocco, and ended by the French purchase of Germany's recognition of their Moroccan protectorate with 107,000 square miles—mainly jungle—of French Equatorial Africa, which was welded to the German Cameroons.

Thus, by compromise, did France dispose of her German competitor before the first World War; but, like Great Britain, she marched into German territory during the struggle and at its close regained the land with which she had bought Germany's consent to the Moroccan protectorate, and took over five-sixths of the former German colony of the Cameroons and almost two-thirds of Togoland as mandates under the League of Nations.

France had also to deal with Italy as a potential rival, although a much weaker one than Germany. Italy did, however, present a real threat to her interests in Tunisia; but this was a threat easily disposed of because of her superior resources, financial and military and, more important, because she had the other great powers behind her. Here, again, we may observe the part which bargaining and compromise played and the close connection between imperial interests and European politics. For England offered Tunisia to France at the Congress of Berlin as compensation for her taking of Cyprus, while Germany encouraged France's seeking compensation there for her loss of Alsace-Lorraine in Europe. But though France frustrated Italian hopes in Tunisia, her seizure of it in 1882 helped to drive Italy into the Triple Alliance, with whose aid she hoped to further her colonial ambitions in Africa. Again

France found it necessary to buy off Italy's possible interference in Morocco by the treaty or deal of 1901, which promised French support of Italy in Tripolitania as a *quid pro quo.*

With the cementing of the *Entente Cordiale* between the years 1901-1905, France secured Britain's help in controlling their joint rival, Italy, in Ethiopia. As we have already observed, they effectually stifled Italy's ambitions there by the Tripartite Agreement of 1906, wherein Italy's sphere of interest was held not directly from the Emperor of Ethiopia, as theirs were, but indirectly from Britain and France. Moreover, whenever Italy attempted either to implement or extend her supposed privileges in Ethiopia, she met resistance and obstruction on the part of her more powerful neighbors, now at one in preserving their own interests in Ethiopia against their common rival, Italy. So did France effectually balk Italian ambitions which might have interfered with the realization of her great African Empire. It was only the fear of a new, powerful Germany under Hitler in Europe that caused her to relent towards Italy in 1935 and allow Mussolini to proceed in Ethiopia. And then, as she and Great Britain both discovered, it was too late to hold him within limits.

It is obvious from the foregoing account that Italy's dream of a northeast African colonial empire originally conceived by Mancini and Crispi was doomed to be frustrated at every point, save in Tripolitania, by her potent rivals, Britain and France. Even her acquisition of Tripolitania was won by agreement and bargain with them and their ally, Russia, as evidenced by the Franco-Italian deal of 1901 and the Racconigi Treaty with Russia in 1909. Furthermore, this frustration, which Italy sought to end at the cost of her desertion of the Triple Alliance on the outbreak of the first World War, persisted. For the colonial compensations in Africa, promised by the Treaty of London, proved disappointing in the extreme with their inconsiderable cessions of territory and rectifications of frontiers. Their utter inadequacy determined Mussolini to conquer Ethiopia and end once for all Italy's subordinate position on the African continent. His success in this enterprise, which was encouraged and first recognized by Germany (1936), contributed to the forging of the Rome-Berlin axis which, in turn, created an alliance of two dissatisfied colonial powers in Africa. It illustrates again the close connection of colonial interest and European politics.

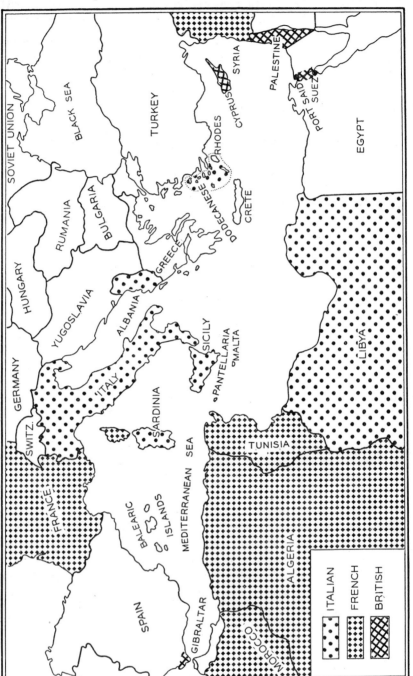

CLASH OF INTERESTS IN THE MEDITERRANEAN, 1939

For in all this story of compromise which Great Britain and France pursued before the first World War to settle their rivalries in Africa, this significant fact emerges: the compromises of these two most powerful states approached some degree of equality in their mutual give and take, but when they dealt with the weaker powers, Italy and Germany, they fobbed them off with the small end of the "concessions." Therefore the Have-Nots rose to demand their share from the Haves, and Italy led the challenge. Indeed, Italy became the most serious rival of Britain and France in Africa; the weak pawn of the 1880's grew into the dangerous competitor of the 1930's. With Italy's conquest of Ethiopia and the identification of her colonial demands with those of Germany in the Rome-Berlin axis, Italy loomed as the most menacing threat to both the French and the British African empires. Did Great Britain regret that she once encouraged those nascent dreams of an Italian East Africa? For it was Italy's position here, strengthened by the Rome-Berlin axis and by Franco's victory in Spain, that caused her to make demands for Tunisia, Jibuti, and shares in the Suez Canal. Furthermore, she used her newly acquired African prestige to strengthen Germany's claims. In return for German recognition of the Ethiopian empire (1936), Hitler was reported to have gained economic concessions in Africa. In 1937 Mussolini re-echoed Germany's colonial demands by declaring: "Germany must regain her place beneath the African Sun." Italy, indeed, in a double capacity, formed a great threat to the British and French colonial empires in Africa and to British and French political and commercial interests in the Mediterranean and the Red Seas.

With the first World War, the Haves threw compromise overboard and substituted force. They took what they wanted; they crowded Germany completely off the map; they refused adequate compromise and concession to Italy. They rounded out their vast African holdings, Britain occupying more than a third of the continent and France a third, and so fulfilled their dreams of empire. But they sowed the whirlwind and the day of reckoning was bound to come. In January, 1939, Hitler said: "The great German colonial possessions . . . have been stolen. . . . Either the wealth of the world is divided by force, in which case this division will be corrected from time to time by force, or else the division is based on the grounds of equity."

The gravity of the situation was also reflected in the formation of an Anglo-French front in Africa for the protection of their respective colonies. In answer to the German-Italian threat—both Premier Daladier and Colonial Minister Mandel proclaimed the imperial unity of the French empire; Britain recognized the parity of that empire with her own; and together they employed practical measures to defend it. Mandel planned to have French West Africa, Equatorial Africa and Madagascar supply a military force equal to that furnished by North Africa, thus doubling the available supply. Recent efforts had made it possible to transport these troops from the south over motor roads by three routes and it was estimated that this would oppose a powerful effective to the threatened plans of the axis powers to use Libya as a springboard for an attack on the Sudan and on the Lake Chad region. Also, to protect West Africa where it was feared Germany would attempt to regain her former colonies, Togoland and Cameroons, France speeded work on her port at Dakar in Senegal, in order to make it an important air and naval base which would defend British and French communications from attack from any position, such as the Canary islands.

By 1940, many signs indicated that the African continent would become the scene of international conflict and play an important and dramatic part in the second World War. By 1941 the struggle was well under way and its outcome uncertain.

READINGS

Anderson, E. N.   *The First Moroccan Crisis, 1904-1906*, 1930.
Harris, W. B.   *France, Spain and the Riff*, 1927.   Good.
Langer, W. L.   *The Diplomacy of Imperialism, 1890-1902*, 2 vols., 1935.   Indispensable.
MacCallum, E. P.   Rivalries in Ethiopia, *Foreign Policy Association.* Research report, 1935.   Excellent.
Martelli, G.   *Italy Against The World*, 1938.   Objective.
Symons, M. T.   *Britain and Egypt. The Rise of Egyptian Nationalism*, 1925.   Documented.
Work, E.   *Ethiopia: A Pawn in European Diplomacy*, 1935.   Good.

PART III

European Expansion in the Near East

CHAPTER ELEVEN

The Near East's Invitation to European Expansion and the Response of the Colonial Powers[1]

THE NEAR EAST, sometimes termed the Levant or land of the rising sun, affords as interesting a laboratory in which to observe the processes and the results of modern European expansion as does Africa. While the results of foreign penetration in both areas, however, will be discovered to be similar, the processes will be found materially to differ. For the character of the Near East, molded by its peculiar geography and age-old history, its unusual resources and its polyglot peoples, demanded of the colonial powers an altogether different approach and a far subtler and more varied technique.

GEOGRAPHY

In the first place, the area described as the Near East constitutes not one self-contained continent like Africa, but parts of three continents: a large slice of southwestern Asia, which constitutes

---

[1] Material in this chapter abridged, summarized, paraphrased or otherwise included from *The Rise and Fall of Germany's Colonial Empire* by Mary E. Townsend, with permission of The Macmillan Company, publishers.

its major part, a considerable edge of southeastern Europe and a corner of northeastern Africa, all lands converging on the eastern basin of the Mediterranean Sea. Today this area embraces in Asia and Africa the territory occupied by the Turkish Republic, the independent Arab kingdoms of Iraq, of Saudi Arabia, of the Yemen and of Egypt; by the mandates of Syria, of Lebanon, of Palestine, of Trans-Jordan; and, in Europe, by that fringe of the Balkan peninsula covered by the coasts of Greece, of Bulgaria, and the territory of the Turkish Republic; as well as the seas, islands and waterways of the region, which greatly facilitate intercommunication both with its respective parts and its neighbors. (There is no arbitrary delineation of the area described as the Near East. Here, Persia [Iran] which is sometimes considered part of the area is, for reasons later apparent, included in the Middle East.)

No area of expansion is so well supplied with connecting water routes extending hospitably in all directions as is the Near East. From its central basin, formed by the eastern Mediterranean and the Aegean Seas, one such waterway leads northeast through the Dardanelles, the Sea of Marmora and the Bosphorus into the Black Sea, and thence into eastern and northern Asia by way of the Caspian Sea and the great rivers, the Don, the Dnieper and the Volga; as well as into northern and central Europe through the rivers Danube, Dniester and Pruth. Another waterway leads southwest through the Red Sea, the Indian Ocean and the Arabian Sea, providing a link both with the Middle East by way of the Persian Gulf and the Tigris and Euphrates Rivers, and also with the Far East around the coasts of India. A third, the River Nile, empties into the southern portion of the central water basin and serves to connect it with central and eastern Africa. In addition to the unrivalled communications supplied by these waterways, still another is provided by the many islands with which the eastern Mediterranean and Aegean Seas are strewn. Here, single islands, like Crete and Cyprus, and chains and groups, such as the Sporades, the Cyclades, the Dodecanese, form so many stepping stones across the thresholds of the continents.

Again, the Near East presents no great difficulties of natural boundaries nor of climate, no impenetrable jungles, no malarial swamps nor obstructing deserts, as in Africa, and is therefore more inviting to would-be invaders. A girdle of highlands rises gradually from the Ionic shore of the Aegean Sea, develops into the Taurus and Zagros ranges which extend from west to east into the mountain country of Anatolia, Armenia and Persia between the Black Sea and the Caspian, stretching down to the Persian Gulf. The mountain chains running out from these ranges on the border of Anatolia form, it is true, considerable obstacles to transport and communication, but through the passes and along the coast there have always existed important routes leading to Cilicia, the Aegean Sea and into Armenia which have characterized Asia Minor as a transit area between West and East.

South of the mountain girdle lies the so-called "fertile crescent" formed by the Mediterranean plain and the green pasture lands in the northern Arabian steppe, which, in turn, merges into the desert lands of Arabia, Mesopotamia and Egypt. But the northern Mesopotamian desert, the old Assyria, is broken up by many rivers, especially the Tigris and Euphrates, which also form the Babylonian inundation region in southern Mesopotamia as does the Nile River in Egypt. Only central Arabia is barren desert, the coastlands of southern Arabia receiving ample rains from the Indian Ocean. As for the climate, its most distinguishing feature is the distribution of rainfall. For there are only two seasons: winter with its rains, severely cold only in the mountainous areas, and like southern California along the Mediterranean coast; and summer, the dry period, with a steady uniformity of dry, hot days, relieved by the inevitable drop in temperature at night. The area generally experiences no severe cold excepting in its highland girdle. Nature has no winter sleep; flora flourish in the fertile places all year round, retarded only by drought and by the hot desert winds of May and September.

STRATEGIC POSITION

It will be obvious from the foregoing description of its geography that the Near East possesses an unusual strategic position. Situated at one of the oldest and most important hubs of transport and communication in all history, it lies at the crossways of the world and holds the key to three continents. Like the Triboro Bridge in Greater New York, whose approaches lie in each one of the three boroughs and which serves to connect them all, so the Near East holds its stakes in Asia, Africa and Europe and forms a transit way among them. For this reason, the caravan routes of the ancient world and the trade routes of the Middle Ages met and crossed here: one from the Far East, coming by way of the Persian Gulf and the Tigris and Euphrates Rivers across to the Mediterranean coast and its harbors at Jaffa, Haifa, Beirut; another via the Caspian and the Black Seas through the straits of the Dardanelles into the Aegean Sea; another from northern Europe and the Baltic Sea, down the rivers emptying into the Black Sea; and still another from central and southeastern Europe down the Danube.

Here too, were located the bases of the far-flung Phoenician and Greek colonial empires, which pushed their contacts far outside the Mediterranean basin, south, north and west beyond the Pillars of Hercules. Here also, lay the centers of the vast Byzantine and Arabian commercial empires, as well as the focus and entre-dêpot of the trade of the Italian cities. In the extensive network of medieval commerce, the Near East continued to maintain its central position founded, as we have seen, upon the history of centuries. And when the modern age replaced the camel by the steel rail, later by the motor car and the airplane, the sail by the Diesel engine, the strategic position of the Near East as the passageway to three continents came to be further enhanced. Indeed, the eve of the modern periods of European expansion coincided with the rapidly developing importance of this area. Concretely, it guarded the route to India and to the Far East, both by way of the Persian Gulf and by the Suez Canal, the approaches to the Black Sea and hence to the Russian and Rumanian ports; and was just beginning to assume its guardianship of the outlet to the Mediterranean basin for these African colonial empires then in the process of creation along the Red Sea.

In other words, the strategic position of the Near East in 1871 was such as not only to invite but to demand the exertion of prestige and influence there if the political and economic interests of the European powers in the Middle and Far East, in Eastern Africa or in the Balkans, were to be protected or advanced—a necessity of which Russia and Great Britain had become aware early in the nineteenth century. The last quarter of the nineteenth century and the first quarter of the twentieth century, with their startling improvements in transportation and communication, were vastly to enhance the vital position of the Near East and hence to complicate the age-old "Eastern Question" as to what power should control and dominate the area—a question which has not yet been definitely answered.

Economic Resources

Like Africa again, the Near East in 1871 possessed rich actual and potential economic resources, whose value was becoming more and more conspicuous and enticing as the second industrial revolution continued to transform the world and to create an ever growing demand for foodstuffs and raw materials with which to feed its people and its machines. Agriculturally, parts of the area were, as today, extremely rich and capable of vast development through irrigation, through control of the floods of the Tigris and Euphrates Rivers, and by the application of other engineering and scientific techniques. Especially was this true in the fabulously fruitful uplands of Anatolia with its rich, black soil capable of intensive grain production, and on the plains of Mesopotamia or Iraq, the alleged site of the Garden of Eden, of whose land it is said that "if you tickle her soil, it will smile a crop." In ancient times, Iraq was an important center of cotton production, which might well be revived, inasmuch as it possesses an ideal climate for the purpose as well as a fair percentage of potash, nitrogen and phosphorus in its soil.

Even more inviting and challenging to the industrial powers of western Europe were the mineral resources of metals and fuel in Asiatic Turkey, raw materials most essential to modern industry as yet unappreciated and untouched at that time by the Ottoman Empire. Anatolia again was a veritable storehouse. Here existed deposits of chrome ore and antimony, indispensable materials in the manufacture of armaments, of copper, nickel, zinc, boracite, iron, mercury, sulphur, manganese, emery, and other abrasives, and of coal. Mesopotamia possessed oil in large quantities, later described by a German technical commission as a "lake of petroleum" of almost inexhaustible supply. Syria also contained oil in smaller quantity. Indeed, the oil deposits of Asiatic Turkey were believed to be vast. In addition, the undeveloped character of the area presented a large market of unrealized potentiality, a rich field for the investment of industrial capital. Altogether, the agricultural, commercial and extractive opportunities presented by the Near East were, in 1871, particularly alluring to the rising industrial capitalism of the colonial powers of western Europe.

THE PEOPLE

Unlike Africa, again, the Near East did not present to the European colonial powers in 1871 an area as openly hostile to expansion as far as its inhabitants were concerned. For here was not the home of primitive peoples as yet in the main untouched by the great movements of history, but rather the cradle of civilization itself in the valleys of the Nile, the Tigris and the Euphrates Rivers. Here the great ancient empires of Babylonia, Assyria, Persia, Egypt, Mycenae, Greece, Alexander the Great and, for a time, Rome, once rose and fell, conquered and were conquered, leaving in their wake their special contributions to modern man's heritage of politics, economics, art, thought, culture and social systems. From here sprang most of the great religious systems of the world: Judaism, Christianity, Zoroastrianism, Mohammedanism. Here lay the scene of the Hellenistic Age when Rhodes and Miletus were the busy marts of commerce and Alexandria the center of learning. Here, after the fall of the western Roman Empire in the fifth century, the powerful eastern or Byzantine Empire preserved the "glory that was Greece and the grandeur that was Rome," while the west was overrun by the barbarians, itself losing its Asiatic empire in the seventh century to the might of Islam, which spread in crescent shape down along the shores of the Mediterranean Sea, as far east as Persia, and south to include Arabia. This great Arab empire of Mohammed in Asia Minor, the center of learning, culture and civilization in its day, was overthrown in the eleventh and twelfth centuries by the Seljuk Turks from central Asia. These in turn were succeeded during the thirteenth century by the Ottoman Turks, whose descendants had come to rule most of the Near East by 1878.

Despite the glorious past of their homeland, the inhabitants of the Near East enjoyed little but its memory in 1871. In the first place, the population was polyglot in the extreme, made up of those innumerable peoples who had crossed and recrossed the transit area, some of whom had always remained. Hence the Ottoman Turks, themselves a mixed race, ruled over a medley of Arabs, Kurds, Armenians, Jews, Greeks, Bulgars, and others, each of whom considered that they possessed special and traditional rights to their own districts, even though apparently united to the all-embracing Ottoman Empire, a situation that rendered the interference of European powers particularly easy. In the second place, these heirs of a great tradition exhibited little of it in 1871. They were rather in a state of arrested development, political, economic and social, untouched for the most part by modern civilization. Ground down under the heel of their latest conquerors, the Turks, the majority lived as nomads in the desert areas or followed a primitive agriculture and handicraft. Only the merchants, the traders in the seaports and large towns even belonged in the nineteenth century at all.

The responsibility for the backwardness of the majority of the near eastern peoples in 1878 rested with the character of the governing power, the Ottoman Empire, which had been definitely on the wane since it reached its height in the seventeenth century. Then (1693) it had included, in Asia, all the territory bounded by the Black Sea, the Persian Gulf and the frontiers of Persia; in Africa, all the northern coast, except Morocco; in Europe, the Balkan peninsula, Hungary and the lands bordering on the Black Sea. The Mediterranean had become almost a Turkish lake. But the difficulties of holding such a vast realm together had proved too great and the Turks had gradually been driven back by the rising Christian powers of Europe and Asia and the Arabs of Africa. In the eighteenth century, they had been expelled from Hungary by the Austrians and from the northern shore of the Black Sea by the Russians, while Tripolitania, Tunisia and Algeria had become semi-independent under local rulers. Throughout the nineteenth century, nationalism had played havoc with European Turkey, pitting Balkan Slav against Asiatic Turk, Christian against Moslem, and resulting in the loss of most of the Greek peninsula, some of the Greek islands, Serbia, and the Rumanian provinces of Wallachia and Moldavia, and threatening further revolts.

By 1871, indeed, the Ottoman Empire amid the threatening menace of Christian rulers had become a shadow of its former self, although on the surface it presented the façade of an imperial domain. With its head at Constantinople, it extended, in Europe, straight across the Balkan peninsula from the Adriatic to the Black

Sea, including actual ownership of Albania, Macedonia, Thrace, most of the Aegean islands, and nominal sovereignty over Bosnia, Herzegovina, Novi Bazar, Bulgaria, eastern Rumelia and the island of Cyprus; in Asia, its homeland, it stretched from the Aegean Sea to the Persian Gulf and from the Black Sea to the Red Sea, embracing Anatolia, Mesopotamia, Armenia, Syria, Palestine, coastal Arabia; in Africa, it held the provinces of Tripolitania and Barca (Cyrenaica) and nominal sovereignty over Egypt.

This impressive extent of empire, however, was undermined by forces of disintegration which afforded just so many avenues of easy penetration and exploitation to European powers engaged in the quest for expansion. For the Ottoman Empire in 1871 was an anachronism politically, economically and socially, in a modern age. Against an ever rising tide of nationalism within its polyglot structure—Balkan, Arab, Armenian, Kurd, Greek and Jew—it opposed an old-fashioned imperialism symbolized by a sultan, at once secular and religious. For Abdul Hamid II (1876-1909) combined the rôles of Turkish tribal chieftain and of caliph or successor to Mohammed as civil and religious head of Islam. As head of the conquering tribal nation, he recognized other non-Moslem tribal nations within the empire, allowing them a degree of autonomy and an identity of culture and religion as long as they rendered homage and taxes to their Turkish overlords. These independent elements or states possessed in turn politico-ecclesiastical heads such as the Greek Patriarch, the Arabian Mufti, the Armenian Patriarch, the Grand Rabbi, each of whom exercised wide administrative and judicial powers, thereby increasing the general trend of disunion within the empire. Add, furthermore, Turkey's conglomerate and heterogeneous character, the circumstance of its vast extent in three continents and the consequent financial burden and physical difficulty of maintaining order or of subduing rebellion, a task further complicated by the absence of adequate transportation and communication, and the opportunities for alien penetration multiply. Incompetent, unscrupulous, corrupt and rebellious officials throughout the far-flung empire, over which the central government at Constantinople found it impossible to exercise supervision, afforded additional influences of dissension and disunion.

Economically and socially also, Turkey was behind the times.

This military religious empire still remained upon an agrarian, economic base in an age of industrialization and of science. The industrial revolution had not, as yet, penetrated its borders and a sparse and well-nigh stationary population made its meager living by means of a primitive agriculture to which modern methods of drainage, irrigation, fertilization and scientific cultivation were unknown. The wooden plow of the ancient Hittites was still used; the threshing floors and the wine presses described in the Bible constituted common usage. In spite of a considerable production of cotton, grain, opium, wine and tobacco, imports exceeded exports and plunged the government deeper and deeper into debt.

Industry was as backward as agriculture. Still in the handicraft stage, its far-famed production of luxury commodities, carpets, rugs, sheer fabrics, glass, enamels and steel, which had dominated the trade of the Middle Ages, was unable to compete with the mass production of the West and hence was being victimized by the machine. Capital, technical skill and directing ability were all lacking to bring Turkish industry up to date, while the absence of means of communication made markets inaccesible. Even local artisans, cobblers, tailors, weavers failed before the inroads of cheap machine-made Western goods, placing Turkey more and more in debt to the European powers. Indeed, by 1871, it is difficult to see how the invitation of the Near East to more extensive European expansion could have been resisted by the colonial powers. Let us therefore turn to an account of their response thereto.

INTERESTS OF THE EUROPEAN COLONIAL POWERS:
THE CONGRESS OF BERLIN (1878)

Unlike Africa, whose invasion by the colonial powers did not commence in earnest until the 1870's, the Near East had experienced long interference from them, at once diplomatic, territorial, economic and political. During the first half of the nineteenth century, such penetration had grown especially intensive. In fact by the 1870's, four powers, Russia, Britain, France and Austria, had come to possess such vital interests in the Near East as to become involved in serious conflicts, the latest

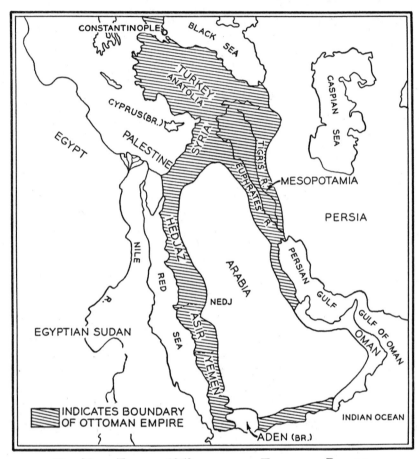

THE NEAR EAST IN 1878 AFTER THE TREATY OF BERLIN:
ASIATIC ASPECT

one of which they were engaged in settling at the Congress of Berlin in 1878 just as the modern period of expansion opened. It will be, perhaps, the clearest way of securing a picture of European aims, ambitions and designs upon the area to examine the decisions of that Congress, which are contained in the Treaty of Berlin. For this settlement virtually closes one chapter of European relationships in the Near East and opens the next one in which we are especially interested, the modern period.

The Congress of Berlin was called in 1878 at the insistence of Great Britain and France because Russia had upset the balance of

THE NEAR EAST IN 1878 AFTER THE TREATY OF BERLIN:
EUROPEAN ASPECT

power in the Near East, established in 1856, by again inflicting a decisive defeat upon Turkey. Pressed by urgent economic need to expand southward from the Black Sea into the broader currents of commercialism, Russia had been again pursuing her traditional foreign policy of pushing towards Constantinople and the possession of the Straits. For ever since the time of Peter the Great, her imperial interests had dictated expansion in this area both to secure a warm-water port and to increase her political prestige at the expense of the Turk, whom she alternately treated as friend and foe to gain her ends. Thus she had supported the sultan in 1833 against the uprising of his rebellious governor of Egypt, Mehemet Ali, for the reward of being permitted to station warships in the Straits; had proposed to England a joint dismemberment of Turkey in the 1840's; and upon the latter's refusal had embarked alone upon a campaign for the purpose in the 1850's in which her success had precipitated the union of Britain and France in the Crimean War against her. Her defeat in that war had resulted in the Treaty of Paris (1856) which neutralized the Black Sea, forbidding any nation to build forts on its shores or station warships in its waters. Thus Russia's ambitions in the Near East were forestalled and Turkey was protected by Great Britain and France from her attacks.

Now in the 1870's, renewed Turkish and Mohammedan persecutions of Balkan Christians, especially Bulgarians, provided Russia an opportunity to strike again at the Turk. For the peoples of the Balkan states were kindred Slavs and co-religionists (Orthodox Catholics) who regarded Russia as their big brother. This time, Russia had inflicted an overwhelming defeat upon Turkey, driving her almost entirely out of Europe, and had established herself in the eastern Balkans in "Greater Bulgaria" by the Treaty of San Stefano (1877), which she easily imposed upon her prostrate enemy. But her victory destroyed the status quo dictated by the Treaty of Paris in 1856, and hence the signatories of that treaty demanded a new settlement of the Near East.

Of the powers that met at the Congress of Berlin in 1878, Britain, Austria and France were the most vitally interested in preventing Russian dominance in the Ottoman empire. Because Russia was her imperial rival, Britain could not afford to have her on the route to India; she preferred a weak Turkey, whom she could control, at the Straits rather than Russia. So also did France, who had traditional, cultural and religious ties with the Near East and the Balkans, as well as rapidly expanding economic interests in the area. It was for this reason that they had both assisted Greece to win her independence from Turkey in the 1820's, and had posed as the protectors of the Balkan states to weaken Turkey; but whenever Russia threatened to overthrow Turkey, they rushed to her defense, as in 1856, and now, again in 1878, employing like their rival, the nationalist ambitions of the Balkan peoples to further their imperialist ends. Like Britain and France, Austria, too, feared Russian dominance in the Near East. Pushed away from the Adriatic by Italy in 1866, she aimed at pressing down to an outlet in the Aegean Sea at the expense of the Balkan Slavs, Russia's "brothers." Besides, the "Greater Bulgaria" violated an agreement she had made with Russia to prevent the setting-up of a large state in the Balkans.

In view of these interests in the Near East opposed to Russia's, it is not surprising that the Treaty of Berlin largely excluded her from the area and pushed her further away from the control of the Straits. Her recently won dominance in Bulgaria, Macedonia and the eastern Balkans was displaced in time-honored fashion by restoring there the ousted Turkey; and she was allowed to retain only Bessarabia, separated from Rumania, in Europe, and the provinces of Batum, Kars and Ardahan in Asia near the Black Sea. In short, Russia's influence and prestige in the Near East was reduced to a minimum.

On the other hand, Britain and Austria awarded themselves positions of influence to replace that of Russia. Austria received the two provinces of Bosnia and Herzegovina on her southern border as protectorates, which settled her determination to penetrate down through the Balkans at the expense of her Slav neighbors and indicated very definitely the direction. Great Britain gained the island of Cyprus in the eastern Mediterranean, the friendship of Turkey and all the political prestige which her prime minister, Disraeli, brought back from Berlin, of having settled the Eastern question to Russia's disadvantage. France received the promise, as we have hitherto seen, of Tunisia in Africa as compensation; Italy, nothing at all; and Germany, no tangible gain, unless it were to be found in the prominence accruing to Bismarck, who presided over the Congress as its "neutral" chairman, the "honest broker," as he termed himself. It is clear, however, from subsequent events, that Germany threw in her weight at the Congress on the side of Austria in the Near East, a pattern which she was with some reservations to follow until 1918.

EUROPEAN COLONIZATION IN THE NEAR EAST, 1878-1914

The terms of the Treaty of Berlin thus materially altered the situation of the colonial powers in the Near East and ushered in a new era of expansion there, the modern period. Russia, discouraged by the failure of her long effort to reach the Straits and by the loss of her hard-won influence in the Balkans, retired temporarily from the scene. Instead, she sought compensation and an economic outlet in the Middle and Far East as witnessed by her strenuous activity in Persia, in eastern Siberia and in Manchuria during the next two decades. Not until after 1907 did Russia enter seriously again into her campaign of expansion in the Near East. Great Britain and France also withdrew from the European aspect of the area, considering it "settled" by the Treaty of Berlin, and shifted their interests to the southeastern corner of the Mediterranean Sea where the cutting of the Suez Canal, completed in 1869, was emphasizing the importance of Egypt and adjacent lands in Africa and Asia Minor. It has been said that, in the language of the European chancellories, the Eastern Question with its eternal problem was "put on ice" after the Congress of Berlin; actually, the interest in it as a sphere of expansion was transferred to its Asiatic area, where a dying Ottoman Empire enticingly invited penetration by the rapidly increasing industrialism and commercialism of the Western colonial powers.

A New Colonial Power Appears—Germany

This change in the situation opened the way for a new power, Germany, to construct a colonial empire of political and economic control in the Near East, from which, under Bismarck's guidance, she had hitherto refrained. At once the backbone and symbol of this empire in Asiatic Turkey was the famous Bagdad railway. An outstanding example of the projection of a transcontinental line, a favorite technique of modern expansion, it was similar to the Cape-to-Cairo plan, the Trans-Siberian railway, or to those enterprises in the Western hemisphere, the Union Pacific or the Santa Fé railways.

As early as the 1850's the British, ever concerned with the problem of communication with India, had planned a railway to run from Alexandretta on the Mediterranean coast to the Euphrates River, via Aleppo, thence to continue to the Tigris River at Bagdad and down to Basra on the Persian Gulf. Deflected, however, during the 1860's and 1870's by their growing interest in the Suez Canal, the British allowed the Mesopotamian project to lapse and thus provided the opportunity for German engineers and financiers to carry it on. First conceived by the latter in 1888, the project developed into one that became truly magnificent. The proposed road was to consist of a trunk line running from the Bosphorus to the Persian Gulf which, in connection with the existing railways in Anatolia and Syria, would link Constantinople with Smyrna, Aleppo, Damascus, Beirut, Mosul and Bagdad. The German plan was to establish a unified system of railways: to connect Turkey with Anatolia, the old homeland, with Syria and Mesopotamia as far as Persia, Arabia, and Egypt; to revive the once fabulously fruitful Anatolian uplands and to grow cotton in Mesopotamia; to gather the Anatolian mineral wealth of antimony, chrome, copper, iron, coal and to exploit the oil wells of Mesopotamia and Syria; to develop and control, in short, this valuable stretch of territory for Germany's economic and political benefit. The railway was to extend about 2500 miles, a longer distance than the Santa Fé line from Chicago to Los Angeles. When completed, it was to be linked with the railways of central Europe and thus establish a gigantic line, largely under German control, stretching from the North Sea to the Persian Gulf, the whole to be known as the Berlin-Byzantium-Bagdad Railway—the "BBB."

This ambitious and challenging project was the result of two major forces impelling German official expansion in the Near East, which Bismarck had always so carefully avoided. They were: the growing pressure of German economic interests in the Near East during the last two decades of the nineteenth century, and William II's reorientation of foreign policy, which was so different from that of Bismarck's as to merit the label "the new course." For the guiding star of Bismarck's foreign policy was the maintenance of friendship with Russia. He was thoroughly cognizant of Russia's age-old interests in and around Constantinople and realized that for Germany to make any moves in that direction would mean stepping on the toes of his valuable ally. Besides, he and his newly united empire had their hands entirely too full with internal problems in the 1870's to permit of any adventures in the Near East.

Nevertheless, German publicists and economists, such as List, had, early in the nineteenth century, recognized the possibilities of the Near East for economic expansion, so urgently needed by

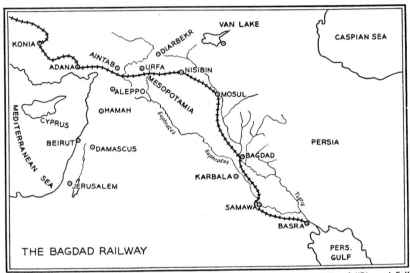

Adapted from map in "Macht und Ende des Deutschen Kolonialreiches," German translation of "Rise and Fall of Germany's Colonial Empire" by M. E. Townsend

PROPOSED PLAN OF THE BAGDAD RAILWAY (MAIN TRUNK)

the Germans, and had strongly advised the Prussian government to embark upon it. Their ideas were translated into practice by individual colonists, in spite of rejection by the government, with the result that many small agricultural colonies as well as schools, hospitals, missions and other German agencies were planted in the lands nearest Europe during the 1850's and 1860's, to which doctors, teachers, engineers attached themselves. These early endeavors prepared the way for the merchant and the investor who, after national unification in 1871, felt strong enough to compete in earnest with British and French agents already entrenched there—a competition rendered continually weaker by the waning of British and French influence in that region during the two decades succeeding the Congress of Berlin. As early as 1872, von Pressel, an eminent German railway engineer, was retained by the sultan to develop plans for railways in Turkey, and the bankers Bleichröder and von Siemens of the *Deutsche Bank,* and von Kaulla of the *Württembergische Vereinsbank* of Stuttgart became interested in his projects. In the year 1888, a German syndicate under the leadership of von Siemens was formed and gained a concession from the Ottoman government to continue the Haidar-

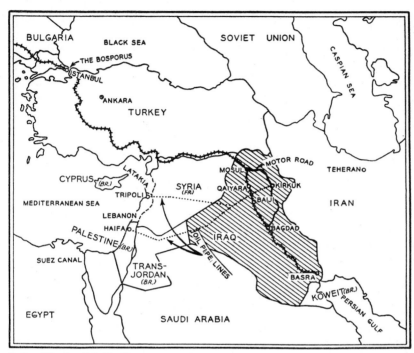

COMPLETION OF THE RAILWAY: THE MOSUL-BAIJI LINK

Pasha line, of which it had obtained control, to Angora with a conditional right of further extensions.

Naturally, the trader followed the investor and during the twelve years from 1888 to 1900, Germany's economic expansion into the Near East was one of the wonders wrought by her industrial revolution. Whereas, in 1888, the trade and finance of Turkey were practically monopolized by Great Britain and France, the Germans (in 1900) were by far the most active group in Constantinople and in Asia Minor. Hundreds of German salesmen were traveling in Turkey and during this period (1888-1900), Germany's imports from Turkey rose from 2,300,000 M. to 28,-900,000 M. and her exports from 11,700,000 M. to 40,900,000 M.[2]

Until the year 1898, the imperial government had played no part in this active, economic penetration of the Ottoman Empire.

[2] Earle, E. M., *Turkey, the Great Powers, and the Bagdad Railway*, pp. 36-37.

Bismarck, indeed, had taken every care to subordinate it to Germany's political relations both with the Near East and the other powers for fear of jeopardizing his system of alliances. But all this cautious and skillful diplomacy William II was to cast to the winds in his reckless pursuit of German expansion for world power. Always he seems to have realized the possibilities of the Turkish empire as compensation for Germany's limited colonial opportunities outside of Europe, although he appears to have formulated no definite plan for the political penetration of Turkey until 1898. Many signs, however, of his sympathy with the German-Ottoman economic *entente* were evident: his visit to the sultan in 1889 which resulted in a favorable Turco-German trade treaty; his utter indifference to the sufferings inflicted upon the Christians by the Turk; his presentation of his own portrait to the sultan; and the appointment of Marschall von Bieberstein, a protagonist of expansion, to the ambassador's post in Constantinople.

Finally, in 1898, William II paid a second and more spectacular visit to the sultan, on which occasion he dedicated a Lutheran church in Jerusalem with oriental pomp and ceremony and presented a gift of hallowed land to the Roman Catholic Church. In addition he pledged the eternal friendship of the German people to all Mohammedans, possessed with the idea that in time of war they would foment rebellions within the territories of Germany's rivals, Britain and Russia. Meanwhile, plans for the Bagdad railway proceeded apace in Constantinople and the following year, 1899, the Germans secured Turkey's promise of a concession to continue the Anatolian railway from Konia to the Persian Gulf.

As was to be expected, Germany's attempt to realize her promised concession of 1899 met with serious objection from the other powers interested in the Near East. They began to see that William II planned to employ the railway for political ends as a colossal mortgage for empire. To its early promoters and, indeed, to the mass of German people, at the beginning, the project was a vast business and economic undertaking and little else. Indeed, von Siemens and von Gwinner had earnestly striven to include British and French capital in its organization and control at the outset. They had almost reached an agreement whereby the board of directors was to consist of eight Germans, eight Frenchmen, eight Englishmen, and six others appointed by the Turkish government and the Anatolian railway company. But to the kaiser and his expansionist friends, such as Marschall von Bieberstein, the railway, "My Railway," as he called it, constituted an instrument for political expansion. "I trust my visit to the Turkish Empire promises the ultimate drawing together of these two nations," he said in 1898. One of the foreign office secretaries expressed the administrative view as: "With a bow to the British Lion and a courtsey to the Russian Bear, we will worm our way little by little down to the Persian Gulf."

Great Britain, therefore, opposed the project, and in 1903 Balfour, the prime minister, who was at first favorable to the railway, ultimately yielded to the pressure of British public opinion and rejected the plan of British co-operation; and Lord Lansdowne, secretary of state for foreign affairs, raised difficulties about the proposed terminus of the railway at Koweit, the only good harbor on the north shore of the Persian Gulf, by publicly announcing that his government would regard the establishment of a naval base or fortified port in that region as a grave menace to British interests, which "we would certainly resist with all the means at our disposal." Indeed, the German terminus at Koweit had already been effectually blocked by a secret agreement with the sheik to enter into no international agreements without the consent of the British resident adviser.

Like the English, the French bankers at first approved of the Bagdad railway syndicate and actually subscribed 30 per cent of the capital. But in 1903 Delcassé, submitting to the influence of French traditional near eastern policy and also to the pressure exerted by Russia, echoed Balfour's reasons for opposition in the French chamber, and prohibited trading in Bagdad railway shares on the Paris Bourse.

In the meantime, in spite of the widespread hostility from the powers, Germany had realized her tentative plan of 1899 by obtaining in March, 1903, a definite contract or concession from the Turkish government to carry through the Bagdad railway via Konia—Adana—Nisibin—Mosul—Bagdad—Basra to Koweit on the Persian Gulf, with branches to Aleppo in Syria, Urfa, Khanikin in Persia, and other cities north and south of the trunk line, with the important right to exploit all mineral resources found within a zone twenty kilometers wide on either side of the railway. The next step was to extend the line through the Taurus Mountains, then beyond through desert lands to Mosul, down to Bagdad along the Tigris River, thence down the Euphrates to Basra, and finally to the ultimate goal, the Persian Gulf—a project challenging in the extreme, involving as it did extensive tunnelling through solid rock, the throwing of steel bridges across mountain chasms and rivers, and the spanning of desert stretches by far-flung railway lines. But the continuation of the railway not only challenged imperialistic imagination, it challenged economic resource, for such an engineering project demanded immense sums.

Turkey promised to furnish the funds provided the Ottoman government could raise the customs dues from 8 per cent to 11 per cent. This proposal at once encountered the opposition of the powers, who by 1906 were uniting to block the railway in every possible manner. Fortunately, however, for its prosecution, Turkey's finances recovered sufficiently by 1908 to enable her to advance the required sum for the railway without raising customs dues, for which the consent of the powers was essential. In June, 1908, arrangements were made for issuing the necessary bonds and work on the railway was again resumed after a four-year pause. By September, Medina and Mecca had been reached and German officials were to be seen everywhere in that district. This success was short-lived, for the Young Turk revolution intervened, temporarily to postpone the continuance of the railway and to destroy Germany's influence in the Near East.

Eclipse both of her expansion program and her prestige, however, was of short duration, so firmly established was Ottoman confidence in her support at Constantinople, and so deeply rooted her power throughout Mesopotamia. It was not long before the Young Turks, in spite of the apparent greater congeniality of their new regime with Western nations, became convinced that Germany, after all, was the only great power who did not desire their dissolution. The concrete symbol of this renewal of friendly relations and consequent revival of the *Drang nach Osten* was the loan of $30,000,000, which the *Deutsche Bank* granted the new Ottoman government in 1910, with no conditions inconsistent with the dignity of Turkey.

This significant diplomatic triumph completely restored German prestige in Turkey to the position that it had formerly occupied, and prepared the way for its final triumph in regard to the rail-

way, namely, the convention signed on March 21, 1911, by which
Germany gained the concession for the last piece of the railway
and also a sub-line to Alexandretta. When the building of the
railway was again resumed after the delays imposed by the Young
Turk Revolution, *Punch* published a cartoon representing William
II as Haroun-al-Raschid seated upon a locomotive bound for Constantinople, behind him Kiderlen-Wächter, the foreign secretary,
as the engineer—bearing the inscription, "Hearty good wishes for
the success of the Bagdad R.R., from the Kaiser to Kiderlen-
Wächter."

But successful prosecution of the railway was unable to proceed until Germany could effect some sort of compromise with
her rivals, Great Britain, Russia and France, who continued by
every means to block her plans. So effective were their efforts,
that Germany had to sacrifice and curtail parts of the railway
project in order to advance at all. Thus in 1910, an agreement
was reached with Russia, the so-called Potsdam Agreement,
whereby Russia promised to cease obstructing the railway, and
Germany, recognizing Russia's predominance in northern Persia,
renounced plans for the gaining of railroad concessions there.

Meanwhile bargaining with Great Britain continued, facilitated,
it is true, after 1911, by the settlement of the Franco-German
clash in Morocco in the favor of the *entente*, but, at the same
time, complicated by the magnitude and growing importance of
Britain's interests in the Near East and by the menace of German
naval expansion. Finally, in February, 1914, after long and tedious
negotiations and the complete separation of the Bagdad question
from the naval issue, an agreement was reached by which the
German-Bagdad Railway Company renounced its existing right
to the building of the final stretch from Basra to the Persian Gulf.
It was to be constructed only after an understanding had been
reached by the German, English, and Turkish governments. The
harbors of Basra and Bagdad were to be built by a Turkish company, England to be allowed up to 40 per cent of the shares.
Germany was to obtain neither a harbor nor a railway station
on the Persian Gulf without a previous understanding with England, nor was she to have a financial interest in the construction.
Had the treaty gone into effect, Germany would have virtually
surrendered southern Mesopotamia and the Persian Gulf as a
sphere of interest, but gained the cessation of British opposition

to the Bagdad railway, so stubbornly maintained since 1903. The agreement was only initialed, and its final signing was interrupted by the outbreak of the first World War in August, 1914. More fortunate was the compromise with France. In February, 1914, the Franco-German convention, initiated by Franco-German banking groups, was signed whereby Germany recognized northern Anatolia and Syria as French spheres of influence and renounced control of the railways there in return for the cessation of French opposition to the railway.

On the eve of the first World War then, the Bagdad railway, the symbol of German expansionist ambition in the Near East with all it implied of political and economic control, had reached Adana in Cilicia—marking one half of the giant stretch from Konia to Basra. Westward therefrom, lines were under construction to the Taurus mountains, eventually to pass through these great gates to meet the tracks already laid to Burgulu; eastward the line was being constructed through the Amanus Mountains, where the costly tunnels had already been begun; a steel bridge had been thrown across the Euphrates; and the sections east of Aleppo had been completed almost to Ras-el-Ain in northern Mesopotamia. Besides this, the branch line to Alexandretta had been completed and opened to traffic, and rails had been laid north from Bagdad to Sadijeh on the Tigris. But more significant even than this great material advance, the Bagdad railway controversy with the other nations had been all but solved in 1914, and Germany's sphere of influence in Mesopotamia well-nigh satisfactorily adjusted to the balance of power.[3]

In addition to the Bagdad railway, other extensive German interests existed in the Ottoman Empire. German nationals held valuable concessions for public works in Anatolia. German churches, hospitals, schools and public buildings stretched in a long line from the cathedral on Mount Zion in Palestine to the palatial German embassy on the heights of Pera opposite Constantinople. Germany and Austria-Hungary took a far-reaching interest in the economic development of Turkey and extracted from her large quantities of raw materials for their home industries.

[3] During the first World War, the Germans and Turks constructed the difficult stretch of the road through the Taurus Mountains as far as Aleppo and pushing on towards Mosul, reached Nisibin. Also, the British built the line connecting Bagdad with Basra and ran a line up to the Persian border.

Austria-Hungary Contributes to the Pan-German Drive

Far behind Germany in achievement, yet active and ambitious was Austria-Hungary's penetration and expansion into the Ottoman Empire throughout the same period 1878-1914. Motivated by the urgent need of an economic outlet and her long tradition of struggle against Turkey in Europe, she limited her efforts mainly to the Balkan peninsula, where she attacked Turkey as an enemy rather than winning her, like Germany, as her ally.

The Treaty of Berlin had placed Austria in an advantageous position against Turkey by establishing her in the protectorates of Bosnia and Herzegovina, and she capitalized this opportunity to pursue her course by force and intrigue down through the Balkans. In 1907 she wrested a concession from Turkey to run a railway through the sanjak (province) of Novi Bazar which facilitated her southward inroad, and in 1908 deprived Turkey of Bosnia, Herzegovina and Novi Bazar by outright annexation. This serious blow against the Ottoman Empire, which was executed in the face of strong protest from Austria's ally Germany precipitated an international crisis. The result strengthened Austria's encroachment upon Serbia, the chief obstacle to her *Drang nach Osten,* and later enabled her to deprive Serbia of the fruits of her victory in the Balkan wars against Turkey by occupying the harbors of Scutari and Durazzo on the Adriatic Sea and by interference in Albania.

By 1914, Austria-Hungary had succeeded in gaining control of the communications between Vienna and Constantinople and from Belgrade to Salonika. She monopolized a large share of the trade of southeastern Europe, exerted a ruling influence in the economic development of the Balkan states and was proceeding step by step down to the Aegean Sea.

Great Britain and France Intensify Their Activities within the Ottoman Empire

Although Pan-German expansion appears to engage the center of attention during the period 1878-1914, largely because of its dramatic character, British and French penetration was not idle. The cutting of the Suez Canal on the eve of the modern period of expansion increased enormously the interest of Britain and

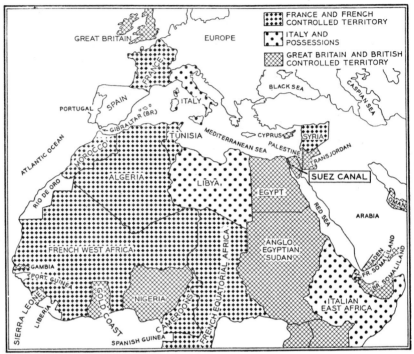

Adapted, courtesy "The New York Times"

CROSSROADS OF EMPIRE—THE SUEZ CANAL, SHOWING ITS STRATEGIC
IMPORTANCE TO BRITAIN, FRANCE AND ITALY IN 1940

France in northeastern Africa and its vicinity. Freed from the
menace of Russia, at the Dardanelles, temporarily at least, they
transferred their attention from the Balkans to North Africa and
Western Asia after the Treaty of Berlin.

But for Great Britain, this linking of the Mediterranean with
the Red Sea meant not only the quickening of her interest in
Egypt but in all lands adjacent to the Suez Canal. Awakened
to the necessity of guarding the life line of empire, she focused
her attention upon the Asiatic areas of the Near East. Indeed,
when Disraeli inaugurated his imperialist program in 1874, the
safe-guarding of the routes to India became a primary concern
of British policy. It was for this reason that her statesmen set
up a "temporary control" in Egypt in 1882 and increased their
watchfulness over all lands verging upon the route to the East.

At that time (1878-1882), Britain's only territorial holdings in the Near East consisted of Aden, the strategically situated peninsula on the south coast of Arabia, and the island of Cyprus in the eastern Mediterranean. The Aden colony had been appropriated as early as 1839 because of its importance on the long route to India around Africa and shortly afterwards, Aden protectorate had been acquired, adjoining it and stretching 600 miles along the Arabian coast. The only fortified point between Egypt and Bombay, Aden became a great fueling station and port of call, an emporium for the trade of the Arabian and African coasts. It guarded Suez from the south while Cyprus protected it from the north. The fruit of the Congress of Berlin, the reward for Britain's resuscitation of Turkey after her defeat by Russia, this second largest island in the Mediterranean Sea was first held only as a leasehold but annexed as a crown colony in 1914. It lies 266 miles north of Egypt and only 66 miles west of Syria— a perfect situation for the control of the eastern Mediterranean basin.

But Aden and Cyprus failed to suffice as adequate protection with the development of the short route to India. Newer areas of penetration and control within the Ottoman Empire were sought by Britain: from the east by way of the Persian Gulf into Mesopotamia and into the Arabian peninsula, where for three centuries she had taken the lead in trade and, during the nineteenth century, had entered into treaty relationships with the rulers of a group of states along the gulf, such as Koweit, the Bahrein Islands, the sultanates of Muscat and Oman and the sheikdoms of the so-called "Trucial sheikhs," all of which possess definite strategic value. From the west also, Britain endeavored to strengthen her position along the shores of the Red and Mediterranean Seas. In Palestine her preparations for its final acquisition took place. At the end of the century, a British company secured a concession to build a railway from the port of Haifa in two directions: one to Port Said, connecting Palestine with the Suez Canal, a project completed during the first World War, another to Mesopotamia via Damascus, which anticipated the all-British railway now planned from the Mediterranean to the Persian Gulf. In the 1890's also, the Palestine Exploration Fund, founded in England for archeological studies, did important preliminary work. It made a cartographical survey of the Holy Land, carried out by

THE NEAR EAST IN 1914

British officers, one of whom was Kitchener, later high commissioner of Egypt. These preparations assumed more significance as the German menace to the British position in the Near East grew more threatening in the years before the first World War. It was, indeed, to combat the German threat, especially, that Great Britain secured protectorates over the chieftains in and around Koweit at the head of the Persian Gulf, the proposed terminus of the Bagdad railway.

In addition, British subjects owned the Smyrna-Aidin railway and enjoyed special navigation rights on the rivers of Mesopotamia and other economic concessions. In 1908, the Turkish government commissioned Sir William Willcocks, a British engineer, to study navigation in Mesopotamia, and in 1913 assigned to a British corporation the reconstruction and development of the imperial navy yards at Constantinople. Meanwhile, British churches and schools scattered throughout Asia Minor, imparting education and training, made Britain popular with the peoples of Syria, Arabia, Mesopotamia and Turkey proper.

France's Expansion

In some ways, the expansion of France in the Near East during the years 1878-1914 was even more intensive than that of Great Britain, although she had no such immediate political interests to protect. As related above, France's connection in the Near East rested upon historic tradition and, to Frenchmen, appeared to span the centuries from the time of Charlemagne, whom legend represented as having received a protectorate over Palestine from Haroun-al-Raschid. More authentic were the glories won by French crusaders, the first capitulations secured in the sixteenth century, the right to protect the Christians of Lebanon, the Maronites, won by Louis XIV, and the exploits of Napoleon in Egypt. A treaty of 1740 fixed all these exclusive rights enjoyed by France in the Near East; Napoleon III defended them in the Crimean War, and they became matters of agreement at the Congress of Berlin. Besides, French liberalism supported the oppressed Balkan peoples against the Turk, and French Catholicism sympathized with the persecuted Balkan Christians.

It was for all these reasons that France had assisted Greece to secure her independence from Turkey in 1829; had supported the rebellion of Mehemet Ali against Turkey in 1833; and had joined Great Britain in the Crimean War assisting Turkey against Russia. Like England, she feared Russian domination in the Near East.

In addition, France's economic and financial stakes in this area were considerable in 1878 and increased during the latter part of the century. French funds built the ports and railways for the sultan; French bondholders held more than half of the Ottoman public debt. In Syria, France had acquired by 1914 a monopoly of the transportation and held all the railways except the Bagdad and Hedjaz lines. Here too, she strove to develop economic interests especially in the silk and fruit trades. By 1914, she controlled all the silk factories in Lebanon and was on the way to monopolization of cotton production in Alexandretta.

Religious and cultural penetration, likewise, was strong. Since the time of the crusades, French religious orders had carried on missionary and educational work which became intensified with the establishment of the Third French Republic. The Jesuits, expelled from France, increased their activity especially in Lebanon, while the government developed state schools in Syria which became agents of French propaganda. Indeed it may be said that by 1914, the educated classes throughout the Near East were thoroughly permeated with French culture.

Italy Demands Her Share of Expansion in the Near East

Like France's, Italy's connection with the Near East in 1878 rested mainly upon tradition, but it was older, less tangible and less practical. Her historic claim dated back to the Roman Empire and to the commercial empire held by the Italian cities in the Levant in the Middle Ages. The idea of the Mediterranean as a Roman lake, always present in Italian consciousness, was crowded into the background in 1878 by the pressing internal problems of the newly unified nation. To be sure, Cavour had lent the support of Piedmont to Great Britain and France in the Crimean War in the 1850's to prevent Russia's dominance at Constantinople, but this was purely a matter of diplomatic manoeuver to bring the case of the Italian states against their oppressor, Austria, before Europe. Piedmont had no interest whatsoever in the Near East at that time.

In common with the other powers in the 1870's, Italy held trading privileges and capitulations in the Ottoman Empire, but owing to her own late development and the entrenched position of her rivals, it was extremely difficult for her, a late comer, to acquire any more tangible footholds, and she came away from the Congress of Berlin empty handed. Her entrance into the Triple Alliance in 1882 secured for her, at least, the status quo as far as further Austrian penetration in the Balkans was concerned and assured her of compensation if Austria made further gains.

But with the opening of the twentieth century, colonial prizes were being won in the eastern Mediterranean and the Levant by the other powers and Italy's ebullient nationalism drove her to action. In the Tripolitan war with Turkey she occupied the Dodecanese Islands lying off the Macedonian coast, her rights of occupation being acknowledged until such time as Turkey withdrew her troops from Tripolitania. But Italy failed to acquire the islands outright before 1914, mainly because Britain and France, fearing the establishment of an Italian base so near their own interests, encouraged Greek aspirations to the islands and put spokes in the Italian wheel. Just as in Africa, Italy's colonial aims in the Near East were subject to the designs of Britain and France.

Russia Returns to the Near East

While the newcomer, Italy, was becoming interested in Near East expansion, one of the oldest aspirants for position there, Russia, returned. She had withdrawn from active penetration in the Near East after 1878 to follow her imperialist aims in the Middle and Far East. Nevertheless, she retained many of her commercial, religious and political interests there; she predominated in trade around the Black Sea and the Straits; exerted a special ethnic control upon the Armenians, part of whose country lay within her own border; and, despite the overthrow of her influence by Germans in Bulgaria in the 1880's, continued to intrigue in the Balkans for political dominance.

Finally, after her defeat in the Russo-Japanese War in 1905, Russia openly returned to pursue her aims and ambitions in the Near East, where she discovered a new rival, Germany. In Asiatic Turkey she engaged in a bitter conflict with Germany concerning her trade interests on the Persian border and obstructed, together with Britain and France, whose ally she had become, the Bagdad railway. Even the Potsdam Agreement which she reached with Germany about the railway succeeded in only temporarily compromising their rivalry. She also made a bold, though fruitless attempt to win the Straits[4] and in the Balkans adopted an aggres-

---

[4] See p. 330.

sive role by encouraging the Slavs against Austria and supporting the Balkan League against Turkey. The revival of Russian expansionist policy in the Near East during the years immediately prior to 1914 rivaled, indeed, in intensity any former period of her activity there.

THE DISINTEGRATED TURKEY ASSISTS EUROPEAN EXPANSION

Finally, European expansion in the Near East during the period under review was immeasurably assisted by the increasing disintegration of a weak and crumbling Ottoman Empire. For Turkey had sustained one vital blow after another during each decade from 1878-1914. Rehabilitated by the Treaty of Berlin, she was restored in Bulgaria but was driven out by the Bulgarians themselves in 1885; in 1882 she lost Tunisia; in 1893 Crete revolted and she had to be rescued again; in 1908 Austria drove her out of Bosnia, Herzegovina and Novi Bazar, and the Young Turk movement in the same year struck at her from within; in 1912 she lost Tripolitania and was driven almost entirely out of Europe territorially as the result of the Balkan wars, 1912-1913.

Meanwhile, internal disintegration in her government proceeded apace. Throughout the period since 1878 the European colonial powers had been gradually assuming control of her administrative, financial and economic life. Foreign business enjoyed special rights and privileges and was immune from Turkish law, while all foreigners enjoyed capitulatory rights and their own law courts. Tariffs were fixed by special treaties with the powers and much of the taxation was under their control. As early as 1881, the Public Debt Commission was formed to protect the interests of foreign creditors of the Turkish government. Composed almost entirely of foreign bondholders and responsible entirely to them, its council of administration exercised complete direction of the assessment, collection and expenditure of designated revenues. By 1914, German army officers were drilling the Turkish army, British naval officers reconstructing her navy, French financiers controlling Turkish banking. Theoretically an independent state on the eve of the first World War, the Ottoman Empire was in fact a protectorate of Europe. It awaited only the collapse of the ramshackle structure for the colonial powers to move in and establish territorial possessions.

THE EMPIRES IN THE NEAR EAST, 1919-1941

By 1941, three European colonial powers had succeeded in establishing territorial claims in the Near East, temporary though they might be. Great Britain held her mandates of Palestine and Trans-Jordan, and her mandate of Iraq until 1932. France held her mandates of Syria and Lebanon, and Italy her colony, the Dodecanese Islands, which lie in the eastern Mediterranean Sea off the cost of the Turkish republic. But these colonial territories have existed only since the first World War, for prior to 1914 European expansion in this area took the form of political, economic, financial and cultural penetration rather than of outright annexation. The first World War forms, then, the dividing line between these two types of colonialism in the Near East since it occasioned the total collapse of the crumbling Ottoman Empire, which permitted the invaders to enter and stake out territorial claims. It must be remembered, however, that these present holdings rested upon those foundations so firmly laid by all six of the European powers between the years 1878-1914 and before. Indeed, the contemporary occupants, Great Britain, France and Italy are, after all, the residuary legatees of all that extensive disintegration within the Ottoman Empire formerly achieved by Russia, Austria, Germany and themselves.

BRITISH COLONIAL EMPIRE—*Mandates of Palestine, Trans-Jordan, Iraq (until 1932)*

Mandate of Palestine

AREA: 10,358 square miles
POPULATION: 1,350,000
TRADE:[5] *Exports:*   £ 5,020,000
    To Great Britain: £ 3,305,563
    Imports: £11,356,963
    From Great Britain: £ 1,535,417
    (Including Trans-Jordan)

---

[5] *Statesman's Yearbook*, 1940. Figures for 1938.

Internationally famous in the contemporary world as the scene of a bitter and grim struggle among Arabs, Zionists and British, Palestine was assigned to Great Britain as a Class A mandate at the San Remo Conference of the Allies in 1920, an act approved by the League of Nations in 1922. A tiny country about the size of New Hampshire and Rhode Island, it lies between the Jordan River and the eastern littoral of the Mediterranean Sea. Along this coast extends a plain 150 miles long and 15 miles wide, capable of rich fertility, having excellent harbors at Jaffa, Haifa, Acre and Gaza. In the center rises the mountainous region of Judea, the backbone of the country, while the eastern border drops sharply into the depressed valley of the Jordan River and the Dead Sea, 1300 feet below the level of the Mediterranean Sea. The rainfall is rather scanty, the sun blazing, and, except for the coastal plain, much of the country is, or was until recently, barren sand, swamp or rocky hills.

Primarily an agricultural land, largely dependent on irrigation, it produces in large quantities citrus fruits, grapes, and olives which are cultivated intensively for soap oil. Other crops include wheat, barley, Turkish tobacco and, of late years, a high quality of vegetable products under irrigation. Minerals found are limestone, sandstone, and in the valley of the Jordan River and the Dead Sea, sulphur and salts.

Before the first World War, Palestine was a backward country, almost primitive. The Arab population was static, held down by disease, conscription and the harsh Turkish rule. In 1922, the total population numbered 757,000, of whom there were 673,000 Arabs, Moslem and Christian, and 84,000 Jews. Since 1922, Palestine's population has almost doubled, now numbering 1,350,000.

Owing to the tremendous immigration of the Jews into Palestine since 1935, which raised their number to 30 per cent of the total population in 1938, the economic aspect of the country is undergoing a rapid transformation. The intensive activity of these newcomers has made prosperous the agricultural settlements and country towns, as well as created flourishing industrial centers at Tel Aviv, the new Jerusalem, and at Haifa. The Jews have drained swamps and planted orange and grapefruit trees in what was once a sandy waste; they have developed new industries, cement, brick, flour, oil and soap; they have built large electric power stations and have developed new suburbs for their urban populations. The value of the fruit exported from Jewish plantations reached $10,000,000 in 1936, and it is estimated that Jewish capital invested in Palestine amounts to $75,000,000. All this development which is making a new Palestine contributes to the discontent and rebellion of the Arabs, who regard the land as primarily theirs and the Jews as alien invaders.

For, while Palestine possesses so few visible assets and is not impressive physically, it has been a bone of contention since the dawn of history, largely because of its geographical position and its religious associations. Turks and Tatars, Babylonians and Assyrians, Persians, Romans and Crusaders have all fought over this area. In the first World War Great Britain used it as a theater of campaign against Turkey. On the eve of the second World War, Arab, Jew and Briton were engaged in a desperate struggle—just short of warfare—for its control.

How Governed. Palestine is governed as a Class A mandate under the Permanent Mandates Commission, agent of the League of Nations. Its status so defined accords Great Britain full powers of legislation and administration but demands that she shall be responsible "for placing the country under such political, administrative and economic conditions as will secure the establishment of a Jewish national home and the development of selfgoverning institutions, and also for safeguarding the civil and religious rights of all the inhabitants of Palestine, irrespective of race and religion." For the A mandates are in theory merely transitional protectorates designed to guide states into independence, somewhat confused as to whose independence—Arab or Jew—in the specific terms of the Palestine mandate.

The country is ruled by a British high commissioner with the aid of an appointive advisory council; but, because of nationalist strife and constant disturbance, it came directly under the rule of the British military arm even before the outbreak of the present European conflict in the autumn of 1939. Great Britain has made several attempts to fulfil the terms of the mandate in regard to preparing Palestine for self-government by proposing various constitutional measures. Her efforts, however, have been blocked by the conflicts of the Arab nationalist movement and Zionism, whose history in detail is reserved for the next chapter.

The Mandate of Trans-Jordan

AREA: 34,740 square miles
POPULATION: 300,000
TRADE:[6]

Once part of the Palestine mandate assigned to Great Britain in 1920, Trans-Jordan was split off in 1922 and placed partially under Arab control with Abdullah, second son of Hussein, of Arabia as emir or governor. Britain took this step partly to offer compensation to the Arabs for their loss of Syria to France, and partly to prevent their claiming of Palestine.

As its name indicates, the country is a small area lying east of the Jordan River bounded on the north by Syria, on the east by Iraq, and on the south by Saudi Arabia. The land consists largely of barren desert and lava, except for a thirty-mile strip between the Jordan and the Hedjaz railway which traverses it; the population is made up chiefly of nomad Arabs. Nevertheless, Trans-Jordan is important strategically, for it forms the British land and air bridge between Palestine and Bagdad and hence is of paramount interest in British communications with the East. A motor road now extends from Jerusalem to its capital, Amman.

How Governed. Like Palestine, Trans-Jordan is an A mandate but, unlike its neighbor, it enjoys a degree of autonomy under an Arab prince as emir, and is not bound by the clauses in the Palestine mandate regarding the establishment of a Jewish national home.

Abdullah, brother of King Feisal I and great uncle of King Feisal II of Iraq, rules the country under the supervision of Great Britain. The most politically active of Hussein's sons in his youth, Abdullah was a prominent figure in the Arab revolt against Turkey. Technically not a king because of Trans-Jordan's special mandatory status, he is an emir, meaning the governor of a tribe or province. According to an agreement with Britain in 1928, an organic law defines his authority. There is a council of advisers and a legislative assembly of twenty-five members. But in effect, the British high commissioner for Palestine, who maintains an agent at Amman, the capital, rules Trans-Jordan.

---

[6] Included in figures for Palestine.

Mandate of Iraq (until 1932)

AREA: 140,000 square miles
POPULATION: 3,670,000
TRADE:[7] *Exports:*   £4,000,000
      To Great Britain: £1,708,000
      Imports: £8,000,000
      From Great Britain: £4,822,000

The name Iraq is Arab for Mesopotamia, the "land between the rivers," which embraces the whole Euphrates country in southwestern Asia and includes the former vilayets (provinces) of Basra, Bagdad and Mosul. It occupies the legendary cradle of the human race and is regarded by some scholars as the original Garden of Eden. Bounded on the north by the Turkish republic, on the east by Iran, the south by the Persian Gulf and on the west by the Syrian and Arabian deserts, it is as large as the states of New York, New Jersey, Pennsylvania and Ohio together.

Situated on a high alluvial plateau, Iraq is an undeveloped and under-populated country whose soil is of extraordinary potential fertility. Occupying about the southeastern half of the so-called fertile crescent, the country lies in a setting of desert waste and sterile mountains. But, although fairly rainless, it is well watered and fabulously productive. Engineers estimate that the Tigris-Euphrates Rivers could irrigate 7,000,000 acres in winter and 3,000,000 in summer. The chief crops are wheat, barley, rice, dates, tobacco. Flocks of sheep are raised in the north and wool and skins form a considerable export.

Most important of all, however, Iraq is one of the great oil-producing countries of the world, especially in the north in the Mosul district. Here Britain had established strong oil interests before 1914, represented by the Turkish Petroleum Company, which was practically the British government. It was the oil interest that caused Britain to insist that Mosul be included within the boundaries of the mandate when Iraq was allocated to her as a Class A mandate at San Remo in 1920. Mosul really belonged in the French sphere of interest but Britain compensated France by granting her a quarter share in the stock of the San Remo Oil

---

[7] *Whitaker's Almanac,* 1930. Figures for 1929.

Company, according to the San Remo Oil Agreement signed in 1920.

It was the oil interest also that contributed to a serious dispute between Britain and the new Turkish republic in 1923 over Mosul. For the Turkish government granted the Chester concession to the Ottoman-American Development Company, which conveyed oil and railway rights, a portion of which impinged upon Mosul. The quarrel was carried to the League of Nations, which awarded Mosul to Iraq, thus guaranteeing British oil interests there, for the British-controlled Turkish Petroleum Company obtained from the British-controlled government of Iraq a seventy-five-year concession to exploit the oil resources of the provinces of Mosul and Bagdad. Oil is pumped from the Mosul fields to the Mediterranean in a double pipe line: one egress at Haifa in Palestine under British control, the other at Tripoli in Syria under French protection.

The people of Iraq are fundamentally Arab and Moslem, although essentially hybrid since, due to Mesopotamia's long history, they carry elements of Persian, Kurdish, Armenian and other bloods. More than 40,000 Jews live in Bagdad alone and 70,000 in the whole country. For nearly seven centuries, the Arab-Iraqi has been under the iron heel of conquerors superior only in military force. The result has been to retard his development and about seven-eighths of the population, still under tribal rule, are Bedouins or nomads of the desert, subsisting on the milk of mare, sheep and goat.

How Governed. Iraq is no longer a mandate but an independent state, member of the League of Nations and allied to Great Britain by the Treaty of 1932, which accords the London government specific military, diplomatic and financial privileges. Iraq, unique among mandates, never accepted mandate status, so strong was her hostility to British rule. Instead, she signed in 1922 with Great Britain a treaty which paved the way for ultimate independence in 1932. Meanwhile, Feisal, son of Hussein of Arabia, deposed by the French as Arab king of Syria, became king of Iraq under British protection. It was he who guided to ultimate victory the Iraqi nationalist movement, the history of which will be related in the next chapter. Feisal died in 1933 and his son and successor, Ghazi, was killed in an automobile accident in 1939, leaving his infant son, Feisal II, to rule under a regency.

The government is a constitutional monarchy, hereditary in the family of Feisal. There is a senate, nominated by the king, a chamber of deputies elected by suffrage, in which some seats are reserved to special communities such as Jews and Christians, and a ministry responsible to the legislature appointed by the prime minister, who is selected by the king. There are no political parties and the bureaucracy is extremely powerful. When Iraq joined the League of Nations she was obliged to guarantee protection of minorities, freedom of conscience and religion, and the rights of foreigners before the courts.

THE FRENCH COLONIAL EMPIRE

Mandated Territory of Syria and Lebanon

AREA: 60,000 square miles
POPULATION: 3,630,000
TRADE:[8] Imports: £69,182,000
From France: £ 7,172,000
Exports: £42,012,000
To France: £ 8,235,000
(in Syrian pounds)

These two Levantine states, the Syrian and Lebanon republics, were allocated to France in 1920 at the San Remo Conference as Class A mandates. Always among the most advanced and troublesome of the mandated areas, they finally achieved, in 1936, a hard-won release from mandatory status, to eventuate in 1939. But because of the important rôle of the Near East in the second World War, they became the central focus of France's mobilization there in 1940.

About as large as the state of Michigan, Syria and Lebanon lie east of the Mediterranean Sea with Iraq further to the east, Palestine and Trans-Jordan to the south and the Turkish republic to the north. The area constitutes an important part of the land bridge connecting Europe, Asia and Africa and hence is populated by a vivid mixture of races which have crossed it. Twenty-nine or thirty religions or races—for here religion becomes indistinguishable from nationality—all affiliated with those of Asia, are found.

---

[8] *Statesman's Yearbook,* 1940. Figures for 1937.

Here are various sects of Moslem Arabs as well as dissident Moslems, such as the Druses and the Alawis or Alaouites, about 500,000 Christians including the Maronites of Lebanon, a number of the Greek Orthodox faith, some Greek Catholics, Armenians, Syrians, and Chaldeans. The outstanding characteristic of Syria and Lebanon is their sectarianism.

Because of this diversity of peoples, the mandate was divided into four states or sections. These are Syria proper, created in 1925, including Damascus, Aleppo, Homs, Hauran, Hama and Dair-es-zor; Great Lebanon, made independent in 1920 with its capital at Beirut; the Alawis or Alaouites on the north coast, at first united with Lebanon, Aleppo and Damascus in the Syrian federation, but separated in 1924 and reorganized as the republic of Latakia in 1930; and finally Jebel Druse, a tiny mountain state in the southern interior, strategically valuable as a defense against Pan-Islamism.

A fifth section, the province of Alexandretta, including the city of Antioch, situated on the northeastern boundary adjoining the Turkish republic, was originally part of the mandate. It was detached from Turkey when Cilicia was returned to her in 1921. It occupies part of the site of the ancient Hittites, whom the Turks regard as their ancestors, and contains a population which is about 40 per cent Turkish.

When the Franco-Syrian Treaty of 1936 promised Syria and Lebanon ultimate independence, the Turkish republic insisted that Alexandretta become autonomous also and sent troops into the province. The matter was referred to the League of Nations council, which defined Alexandretta's status in a Statute and Fundamental Law agreed to by France and Turkey in May, 1937. It permitted the district to become autonomous under its own legislature, with Turkish as the major official language but at the same time remaining under Syria. The arrangement failed to work, however, and riots incident upon the election of the legislature as well as international tension in 1938 led the disputants to come to an agreement without benefit of the League. The Franco-Turkish Treaty, accordingly, granted internal autonomy to Alexandretta, placed it under "Franco-Turkish administration with French and Turkish troops as a joint defense force," and promised it independence as soon as Syria achieved that status. The newly elected legislature then proceeded to substitute the Turkish "Hatay" for the Greek "Alexandretta." But the republic of Hatay proved to be one of the earliest victims of the diplomatic preliminaries of the second European struggle, and most of it was ceded to Turkey in the Franco-Turkish pact of June, 1939.

Principally agricultural, Syria produces wheat, barley, cotton, wool, silk, some copper, brass and leather goods; Lebanon adds citrus fruits and olive oil, wine and milk. Until recent years, industry was carried on by the traditional crafts mainly in textiles, inlaid furniture, metal and leather work. Syria was always the center of a textile industry doing an extensive export trade. Recently modern manufacture has begun to replace the handicraft system, unable to withstand the competition of Western methods; wholesale machine production is driving out the home industries. The mineral wealth is inconsiderable although oil prospecting is in progress in Syria. Strategically, the mandate is extremely valuable. Airports are situated at Aleppo, Beirut and Damascus, and France had in Syria the base of a transcontinental air system.

How Governed. Like Palestine, Syria was governed as a class A mandate under the League of Nations. Theoretically merely a transitional protectorate, its government was so designed as to guide it, an Arab state or states, into complete independence. Indeed, the French mandate is more specific in this regard than the British, for it expressly stipulates not only that "an organic law or constitution shall be framed" in agreement with native authorities, but also that the mandatory shall "enact measures to facilitate the progressive development of Syria and the Lebanon as independent states."

When France took over the mandate, however, she adopted the policy of "divide and rule" both to satisfy the intense sectionalist demands and to make the country easier to handle by splitting Arab nationalism into pieces. Thus there ensued the division into the states or sections described above, each of which has its own constitution and administration within the mandate, but over all of which rules the French high commissioner. In 1936 the Franco-Syrian Treaty promised the mandate independence within three years under French military supervision as provided for Iraq by Great Britain, and also agreed that France would sponsor its membership in the League of Nations. But the treaty was not ratified by the French chamber and the French military continued to constitute the supreme power in the French Near East.

Both the Franco-Syrian Treaties of 1936 as well as the constitutions of the four states within the mandate represent the long and stormy struggle of nationalism in Syria.

THE ITALIAN COLONIAL EMPIRE

The Aegean Islands: Rhodes and the Dodecanese Group

> AREA: 765 square miles
> POPULATION: 135,000
> TRADE:[9] *Exports:*   21,851,000 lira
>   To Italy: 14,809,000 lira
>   *Imports:*   157,421,000 lira
>   From Italy: 122,124,000 lira

Italy's territorial holdings in the Near East, representing the spoils of the first World War, were confirmed to her by the Treaty of Lausanne, the final Allied settlement with Turkey. They were insignificant and, to Italy, entirely unsatisfactory since they consisted only of a small archipelago of fourteen islands, belonging or adjacent to the Dodecanese group in the eastern Mediterranean Sea. They included the islands of Rhodes, Patmos, Cos and Castellorizo, and lay close to the Anatolian coast of the Turkish republic, to whom they geographically belong. Racially, however, they belong to Greece as their population is overwhelmingly Greek with a small percentage of Turks and a few thousand Spanish Jews.

Economically and commercially, the islands were of little importance since they possessed only limited areas of arable ground and industries of no great consequence, principally carpets, olive oil, wines and artistic pottery. The Italians, however, developed agriculture in Rhodes and Cos, famous for the cultivation of grapes, olives, tobacco, oranges and other fruits. Large sums of money also were expended in Rhodes in order to increase the tourist traffic attracted by the thermal springs.

Italy valued the islands most because of their strategic position:

[9] *Annuario Statistico Italiano,* 1939. Figures for 1938.

they are to the Dardanelles what Cyprus is to the Suez Canal; they afforded a foothold and an air base in the eastern Mediterranean; and they supplied a point of departure for Italian economic penetration of the Near East. For all these reasons, Rhodes was heavily fortified and in 1935 was made a hospital and munitions center.

How Governed. Like all Italian colonies the Aegean Islands were ruled by an Italian governor. Because of their strategic importance, however, they were directly under the foreign office instead of the colonial office. The islands of Rhodes and Cos possessed their own municipal governments.

Spheres of Influence Acquired Since 1924. Italy's dissatisfaction with Dodecanesia as inadequate spoils of the first World War led her to compensate herself for further territorial acquisitions by the establishment of spheres of influence in the Near East. This she accomplished by a vigorous campaign of economic, commercial and cultural penetration. In 1926 her East African interests led her to entrench herself on the eastern side of the Red Sea in Yemen and Asir as a make-weight against Great Britain's influence there and as retaliation for the latter's strangle hold at Suez. Thus Italian credits and material supplies to the kingdom of the Yemen afforded Italy an interest in this region which was recognized by Great Britain in the Anglo-Italian Agreement of 1938.

Indeed, in 1934, Mussolini specifically designated the Near East as one of Italy's "historic objectives," denying territorial aims, but emphasizing a "natural expansion which will lead to a closer co-operation between Italy and the nations of the Near and Middle East." The forms which this "natural expansion" assumed were numerous: the strenuous fostering of trade which by 1939 she had nearly succeeded in balancing here, and which amounted to about 10 per cent of her total trade; the designation of Bari on the heel of the Italian peninsula, an old clearing house for eastern goods, as a starting point for Italy's "pacific expansion" into the East, and its conversion into the site of the annual Levant Fair, of the Royal Institute for Commercial Research and the center of broadcasts in Near East languages; the subsidization of Near East shipping and air services; increasing investment and banking business; and the development of a cultural and missionary propaganda.

THE ACQUISITION OF THE RECENT COLONIAL EMPIRES

With the above picture of the recent colonial territorial holdings in the Near East before us, let us turn to the story of their acquisition. It was the first World War itself, as we have seen, that provided the opportunity for the colonial powers to take possession of those areas which they had so long ear-marked as their own. They achieved their objectives in two ways: first, by planning carefully in advance with the aid of secret understandings among themselves the distribution of the spoils of victory; and, second, by carrying the war against Germany and her ally, Turkey, into the Near East itself, and, in the case of Britain, by deliberately winning, through promises of future independence, the Arabs and Jews as allies.

Four major secret treaties, entered into by the colonial powers, arranged for the disposal of this part of the moribund Ottoman Empire, in the event of victory. The first of these, the secret treaty of March, 1915, among Britain, France and Russia, assigned Constantinople and the Straits to Russia, and designated Asiatic Turkey for France and Great Britain, to be disposed of between them by a later agreement. Before this was consummated, a Franco-Russian understanding, the Sazonov-Paléologue Agreement of April, 1916, awarded Russia 60,000 square miles of Turkish Armenia, and reserved the region stretching southwest from this area to the Mediterranean, including Syria, for France. Next, France and Britain settled their claims in the Sykes-Picot Agreement of May, 1916. France was to have Syria with its hinterlands, reaching up to the Russian zone in Armenia and a "zone of French influence" stretching eastward across the Euphrates and Tigris Rivers to the Persian border; Britain was to have all the territory south of the French sphere as a zone of influence, except that Mesopatamia would be under British administration, and most of Palestine would be "separated from Turkish territory" and subjected to a special regime to be determined by agreement among Russia, France and Great Britain.

This arrangement meant that the land bridge stretching from the Mediterranean to the Persian Gulf was parcelled out into five sections. One was to be under French administration, and one under British, while the inland portion of the territory was divided into British and French spheres of influence, although included in Britain's pledge to the Arabs in 1915. Already by the secret treaty of London (1915) whereby Italy had been won to the side of the Allies, she had been promised "a just share of the Mediterranean region adjacent to the province of Adalia" and full sovereignty over the Dodecanese Islands occupied in 1912. The secret treaty of St. Jean de Maurienne, April, 1917, defined the "just share" as the right to annex approximately the southern part of Anatolia and a sphere of influence north of Smyrna. By these arrangements, the colonial powers effectually disposed of most of Asiatic Turkey among themselves except for the northern half of Anatolia.

In the meantime, other plans were being made for the future of the Near East. The British government, realizing from the outset that Germany allied with Turkey could employ Syria and Palestine as a base for an attack on the Suez Canal and arouse all Islam there against Britain, had set about winning allies in the region. First, exploiting the nationalist revolt of the Arabs against Turkey, which she had been encouraging for some time, Britain won Arab support by the Anglo-Hedjaz Treaty of October, 1915, signed with Hussein, Sherif (chief) of Mecca. This treaty and the correspondence relative to it contains the famous MacMahon pledge that promised British support of Arab independence, not only in Arabia (Hedjaz), but in the whole land bridge linking the Mediterranean Sea and the Persian Gulf, with vaguely defined exceptions in regard to British and French spheres of influence there. Second, hard pressed by the war, Britain secured Zionist aid against the enemy by the equally famed Balfour Declaration of 1917 according to which she promised to establish in Palestine a "national home for the Jewish people," qualified, to be sure, by the statement that "nothing shall be done which may prejudice the civil and religious rights of existing non-Jewish communities." These two promissory notes obviously conflicted with each other as well as with the Anglo-French agreements. As we shall later learn, they led to a serious quarrel between France and Britain and to war between France and the Arabs; they snarled Anglo-French relationships at the Peace Conference in 1919 and continued to give trouble in later years, especially in Palestine.

Contemporaneously, while all these arrangements between the Allies themselves and among Great Britain, the Arabs and the Jews, were in the course of negotiation, the war against Turkey was being successfully waged owing largely to the wholehearted co-operation of the Arabs. At the end of 1916, the sherif of Mecca had proclaimed the independence of the Arab kingdom of the Hedjaz. The Arab revolt began in earnest and coincided with the attack on Turkey by the colonial powers. Moreover, a vital link between the Arab and Allied causes existed in the person of T. E. Lawrence, a British colonel, who was the moving spirit in the negotiations between the Arabs and Britain and later became the hero of the "revolt in the desert." Lawrence was a young Oxford University graduate engaged in archaeological excavations in Syria and Mesopotamia before the war and had been won to the cause of the Arabs, among whom he made many friends. He joined them and devoted his energies to their movement, helped them foment and lead a "nationalist revival," organized their armies and conducted a brilliant campaign both in Arabia and further north where he co-operated with Feisal, eldest son of Hussein of Arabia and with the British armies.

Together, British and Arab forces succeeded in effecting the collapse of the Ottoman Empire in Arab lands. General Maude conquered Mesopotamia (Iraq), with the help of Anglo-Indian troops, and placed it under a British high commissioner; Arabia (the Hedjaz) won its independence and King Hussein became its ruler under British protection; and General Allenby captured Jerusalem and occupied Syria and Palestine. Unfortunately for French claims to Syria, the Allied army which invaded the Near East was almost entirely British and Arab since the French had their hands full on the western front. Thus General Allenby's victory left all the territory over which the foregoing agreements had been made in British hands. Consequently, in fulfilment of their promise to the Arabs, who had so nobly supported them, the British left Prince Feisal in Damascus as virtual ruler of Syria, the majority of whose population desired independence and union with other Arab lands. By 1919 then, the Turk had been driven out of Arabia and out of all the land bridge extending from the Mediterranean Sea to the Persian Gulf. The British and the Arabs were in possession of this territory. It still remained, however, to effect a peace with the Turk, a task fraught with far greater difficulty than had been the conquest of the moribund Ottoman power.

For five years the Allies haggled over the spoils, entangled in their own intrigues and quarrels, hampered by Britain's promises to the native peoples, and delayed by the nationalist uprising within Turkey itself. Sharp and acrimonious debates occurred at the Paris Peace Conference over the colonial spoils of the war in which the imperialist ambitions clashed with the fifth point of the Wilsonian fourteen points, which called for "a free, open-minded, and absolutely impartial adjustment of colonial claims, based upon the strict observance of the principle that in determining all such questions of sovereignty, the interests of the populations concerned must have equal weight with the equitable claims of the government whose title is to be determined."

A solution was found, however, in Woodrow Wilson's proposal for a League of Nations, Article 22 of the Covenant of which set up a system of mandates which defined the colonial territories taken from Turkey and from Germany by the war as "trusts," not annexations. According to this scheme the Turkish territories were to be Class A mandates, "territories which have reached that stage of development where their existence as independent nations can be provisionally recognized subject to the rendering of administrative advice and assistance by the Mandatory until such time as they are able to stand alone." The adoption of this plan enabled the Allies to get their promised colonial areas but under a new label.

Hence, after long negotiations[10] between Britain and France, territorial, financial and economic, the Supreme Council of the Allies meeting at San Remo, April, 1920, three months before any settlement with Turkey had been reached, assigned Syria and Lebanon to France, Palestine and Iraq to Great Britain, all as Class A mandates under the League of Nations. But France had still to fight for her mandate, for the British at San Remo withdrew from the triangular struggle for Syria and left the dispute to the French and to Feisal. General Gouraud, sent out in 1919 to replace the British High Command in Syria, rapidly dispersed Feisal's supporters with the 90,000 troops under his command and occupied Damascus by July, 1920. Feisal fled to become king of Iraq under British protection. Also, France was obliged to go to

---

[10] See p. 333.

war with the nationalist Turks to obtain Cilicia and northern Syria and to put an end to Turkish encouragement of Feisal.

Meanwhile, the peace with the Ottoman Empire had been delayed by these Allied quarrels and by the Turkish nationalist movement. But in August, 1920, three months after the Allies had assigned themselves so much of Turkish territory as mandates, they forced upon the sultan the ill-fated Treaty of Sèvres, a veritable blueprint of European imperialism in the Near East. It confirmed most of the prior arrangements of the powers: deprived the Ottoman Empire of all its Arab possessions, assigning Syria to France, Palestine and Mesopotamia to Britain, the Hedjaz and other Arab states to the Arabs; it recognized Armenia as a free and independent state, and Kurdistan as locally autonomous; it opened the Straits to the trade of the world, placing them and adjacent territory under an Allied commission; gave to Greece many of the Aegean Islands, part of eastern Thrace and the temporary administration of Smyrna with its hinterland; and gave to Italy Rhodes and the Dodecanese Islands, although she promised to recede them to Greece.[11] In addition, Turkey was required to liquidate all German property rights within her territory and turn over the proceeds to the reparations commission. This, of course, included the Bagdad railway, for the Treaty of Versailles had obligated Germany to "recognize and accept all the arrangements which the Allied and Associated powers may make with Turkey . . . with reference to any rights, interests and privileges whatever which might be claimed by Germany or her nationals."[12]

Nothing, indeed, was left to Turkey but Anatolia and a corner of Europe; and even spheres of influence in Anatolia were outlined for France and Italy by an agreement signed the same day as the Treaty of Sèvres by Britain, France and Italy. But this "document of European imperialism" was destined not to endure; it was repudiated and finally destroyed by the counterforce of a

---

[11] See p. 337.

[12] All German rights within the former Ottoman Empire were thus dispersed among the powers who succeeded to the administration of these territories. Thus, today, the Bagdad railway is broken into three sections, under the three separate administrations of the Turkish republic, of France in Syria and of Iraq in Mesopotamia. In 1936 the Iraqi granted a concession to the British Oil Development Company, which has tapped a rich field south of Mosul, to complete the missing link in the railway from Nisibin to Baigi on the Tigris. The work was to be completed in three years. It is now about finished.

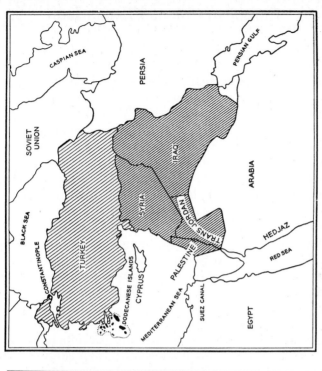

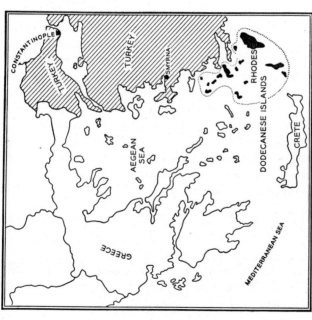

Lands Lost by Turkey to the European Colonial Powers by the Treaty of Lausanne

rising wave of nationalism in Turkey itself, a nationalism induced by the imperialism which the Treaty of Sèvres so accurately reflected. For Mustapha Kemal,[13] an experienced and revolutionary Turkish army officer, aroused an energetic group of nationalists, rallied them at Angora, established the Turkish republic replacing the sultanate and set about tearing up the Treaty of Sèvres. It was, in fact, the harsh terms of the treaty followed by the invasion of the colonial beneficiaries thereof into Turkish territory that ignited the spark of political and religious nationalism into a blaze which swept the country. All impatient to realize their spoils, the French invaded Cilicia, the Italians Adalia, and the Greeks, backed mainly by the British, attacked Smyrna.[14] With astonishing vigor and speed, the nationalist armies expelled the invaders, while Mustapha Kemal practiced a shrewd diplomacy in winning support from the Russians; in making separate peace with Italy and France, thus separating the Allies; and finally in negotiating a new settlement for the Near East, the Treaty of Lausanne (1923).

In contrast to the Treaty of Sèvres, the "document of imperialism," the Treaty of Lausanne is a testament to modern nationalism for it was agreed upon, not dictated, and reversed the position of Turkey and the colonial powers. The Turkish republic regained Constantinople and eastern Turkey as far west as the Maritsa River, while the zone of the Straits was demilitarized and opened to all nations in time of peace and, when Turkey was a neutral, in time of war. She also regained all Anatolia, Cilicia, Adalia and Smyrna in Asia but relinquished Syria to France; Palestine, Trans-Jordan and Mesopotamia to Britain; the kingdom of the Hedjaz and other Arab kingdoms to the Arabs. In the Aegean the Dodecanese, Rhodes and Castellorizo were ceded to Italy; Turkey retained Imbros, Tenedos, the Rabbit Islands; and the remainder went to Greece. In addition the capitulations were abolished, all claims for reparations arising out of the first World War renounced, foreign control over customs relinquished and no restrictions placed on Turkey's naval, military or air forces. With the Treaty of Lausanne, the European colonial powers had gained, it is true, territorial holdings in the Near East. But all these, except the Dodecanese Islands, were mandates, not annexations.

---

[13] See pp. 286 ff.
[14] See p. 290.

whose tenure was temporary, because of the rising strength of nationalist movements in the Near East.

READINGS

Earle, E. *Turkey, The Great Powers, and the Bagdad Railway*, 1923. Pioneer study.

Harris, N. D. *Europe and the East*, 1926. Useful.

Hubbard, G. E. *Eastern Industrialization and Its Effect on the West*, 1935.

Kohn, H. *Nationalism and Imperialism in the Hither East*, 1932. Valuable analysis.

Marriot, J. *The Eastern Question*, 3rd ed., 1930. Valuable.

Townsend, M. E. *The Rise and Fall of Germany's Colonial Empire, 1884-1919*, 1930.

Toynbee, A. J. *The Western Question in Greece and Turkey: A Study in the Contact of Civilizations*, 1923. Authoritative.

Wilson, A. T. *The Suez Canal: Its Past, Present and Future*, 1933. Thorough study.

Wolf, J. B. *The Diplomatic History of the Bagdad Railroad*, 1936.

CHAPTER TWELVE

Results of European Expansion in the Near East

NATIONALISTIC REVOLTS

Among all the areas in which modern European expansion has been active, the Near East affords the best laboratory in which to observe its results. Here are to be found more numerous and more successful uprisings of native peoples than have occurred either in Africa or in the Far and Middle East. Again, these nationalist movements directed against European imperialism are not only many but varied in their stages of development. They range all the way from the successful ones which have emerged into the independent states of Turkey, Egypt and Iraq, to those on the verge of triumph in Syria and Lebanon, to those at the height of their conflict, in Palestine, and, finally to the minor struggling groups, the Greeks in Cyprus and in the Dodecanese Islands. Thus, the result of European expansion in the Near East presents a veritable "fever chart" of nationalism, which fluctuates as rival empires struggle with and succeed one another in the region. Indeed, nationalism, itself, has here become an effective tool of imperialistic conflict since its satisfaction has often been offered as a reward for the support of empire against empire.

The Turkish Nationalist Revolt

The first nationalist movement effectually to throw off European domination in the Near East was the Turkish revolt of 1919-1923. It affords one of the clearest and most direct examples of the effect of imperialism upon nationalism, and its complete success acted as a powerful stimulant to its own former subject peoples, the Arabs, when they came to grips with European imperialism. Immediately precipitated by the invasion of the Greeks, supported by the Allies, and by the imposition of the Treaty of Sèvres, the four-year struggle brought to a climax a long process of nationalistic development within Turkey. Yet when Mustapha Kemal Pasha rallied his countrymen at Angora, drew up the Nationalist Pact and refused to accept the "document of imperialism," he was initiating a "new nationalism," in the sense that he was combining internal revolution with the expulsion of the European invaders. Earlier nationalistic movements, such as the rise of Turkish intellectualism in the nineteenth century, the attempt at constitutional reform in 1876 and the Young Turk revolt of 1908, were mainly caused by the misrule and corruption of the sultanate rather than by the pressure of European penetration; their major aims were directed at the awakening of national sentiment, internal reform and the establishment of freedom, rather than at the expulsion of the foreigner.

Nevertheless, insofar as these earlier strivings towards nationalist consciousness were influenced and animated by Western contacts, they, together with the revolt of 1920, were in a different sense the product of Western expansion. For no Eastern country had come into closer contact with western Europe than had Turkey; the leaders of Turkish thought had been quicker than others to grasp the significance of the institutions of the West, its commercialism and industrialism; so much so, indeed, that when the time came they modeled their new Turkey more nearly after European examples than did any other new nation. The fact that the Turks possess a relatively less glorious past has made them particularly hospitable to a Europeanization which has, in turn, acted as a boomerang against European imperialism so deeply and subtly entrenched there. It has been truly said that "everything in contemporary Turkey which has life in itself . . . can be traced back to some Western stimulus and will be found to be a reaction against Western influence, when not an emanation from it." [1] Thus, in two ways, European penetration of Turkey directly stimulated its nationalist movement.

A test both of the strength of Europeanization in Turkey and native hatred of alien domination may be found in the circumstances surrounding the final nationalistic revolt. It arose out of a period when the country had sunk to the very nadir of its existence as a political entity. The years subsequent to the signing of the armistice of Mudros in 1918 which closed the first World War marked the all but final expiration of the "sick man of Europe." His territory was reduced by the Treaty of Sèvres to northern Anatolia; the Committee of Union and Progress of the Young Turk party, set up in 1908, had fled the capital; parliament was dissolved and with it all hopes of reform scattered; even Constantinople itself was in complete confusion, nominally under a tottering sultan, humiliatingly dependent upon the Allies for protection. It seemed as though the death knell of Turkey was about to strike.

That this calamity was averted and that, instead, the torn and shattered remnant of the once great Ottoman Empire was rescued from complete disintegration and resuscitated into the new Turkish republic, constitutes one of those apparent miracles of the "new nationalism." And, like so many of these modern movements, Turkish regeneration was due to the leadership of a dynamic and commanding personality, the "colossus of Turkey," Mustapha Kemal Pasha—Mustapha being the name given him by his parents, Kemal, meaning perfection, bestowed by his teacher of mathematics, and Pasha, equivalent to general, acquired by the brilliant rôle which he played in the Dardanelles campaign during the first World War.

Born in Salonika, a gay, garrison town, in 1880, of a Mohammedan family reputedly with Jewish blood in its veins, two major influences shaped his illustrious career. Soldiery and revolution set the pattern for the two lines he was to follow in conducting the nationalist revolt: the military and the political. Graduated from the staff college in Constantinople at twenty-two, he saw active service in the Turkish army here and there throughout the empire: in the Tripolitan War, in the Balkan wars, and in the first World War, where he won distinction in checking the British at the Dar-

---

[1] Toynbee, A., and Kirkwood, K., *Turkey*, p. 3.

danelles and came to enjoy the reputation of a military hero in Turkey and in Germany. At the same time he had early felt the rise of nationalism and democracy in the Balkan provinces, read revolutionary literature and became an eager young radical in the Turkish nationalist reform movement, writing pamphlets and poems of an incendiary nature. He was arrested upon his graduation from the staff school in Constantinople and sent into political exile by assignment to a cavalry regiment in distant Damascus. His military career brought him into close contact with the evils of the sultan's rule, and always he introduced reforms in the army and stimulated rebellion, which involved him in many escapades. In 1908 he joined the Young Turk movement and was chief of staff to the commander of the army which marched on Constantinople to coerce the sultan into granting constitutional reforms. But he came to despise the Young Turk revolt as it relapsed into reaction and disappointed his hopes. Thus he fell into the position of a powerless oppositionist to the movement. Hating its leaders, he turned away from political activity to the study of militarism and reform, yet held himself ready to capitalize any opportunity that arose to undermine their authority and the weak regime which succeeded them.

Such an occasion appeared after the signing of the Armistice in 1918. Mustapha Kemal threw over his command in Palestine and hastened to Constantinople, determined to form a nationalist party strong enough to deal with the Allies and salvage at least some of the Turkish homelands. With some scheming, he managed to be sent by the Constantinople authorities (with British consent) as army inspector to Anatolia, where a Kurdish national revolt was in progress, which he took charge of and turned to account. Here in the heart of Anatolia he organized, with the help of other patriots, the National Organization, with two centers, one at Samsun and one at Smyrna. In the meantime, Greek troops, supported by the Allies, landed in Smyrna in May, 1919, pillaged the city and began to plan for the establishment of a Greek Pontus republic. This invasion, symbolic of all past European penetration of Turkey and representing the clash of Greek and Turk, stimulated the national movement, so solicitously fostered by Mustapha Kemal, into a thoroughgoing revolt, which, according to the pattern of its leader's preparation, followed two paths to victory: political and military.

A Political Revolution.   The reaction to the Greek invasion was the calling of the first nationalist congress at Erzerum in July, 1919, from which the National Organization emerged with a program of action.   It was followed by a second and more representative congress in September at Sivas which widened the scope of the movement and promulgated a declaration stating the general principles upon which the subsequent National Pact was based. An executive committee was also appointed at this meeting, of which Mustapha Kemal was elected president.   After the adjournment of the congress, the latter continued to meet and established permanent headquarters at Angora, chosen for its remote, yet militarily secure position.   "Ancyra" or the "Anchor" in ancient Greek, this town lay hidden in the mountain fastnesses of Anatolia, yet was in rail and telegraphic communication with Constantinople. It provided an ideal spot where a revolutionary and unconstitutional party could carry on its secret work against the legitimate government.

Here in October, 1919, a National Assembly, at which were present the deputies of the national party duly elected to the parliament of the sultan's government at the recent general elections, accepted a document known as the National Pact which was virtually a Turkish Declaration of Independence drawn up by Mustapha Kemal.   It emphasized the following principles which later became the bases for the major terms of the Treaty of Lausanne: self-determination as applied to all the areas of the old Ottoman Empire where large numbers of Turks remained; the security of Constantinople for Turkey and her right to have a say in the opening of the Straits to world trade; the assurance of the rights of minorities in Turkey; and finally, the abolition of the capitulations and all restrictions inimical to Turkey's development.   This National Pact was then carried by the party deputies to the parliament in Constantinople and on January 28, 1920, was "legally adopted by the legal parliament sitting in its legal capital," an action which constituted a major triumph for the nationalist movement.

As was to be expected, this triumph was of short duration, for in March, 1920, the Allies attempted to break up the nationalist movement and to protect the sultan.   Under the command of General Milne and with the consent of the French commander, who, however, was absent from Turkey, Allied troops, mostly

British, occupied Constantinople, arrested about forty nationalist leaders and carried them off to a British prison camp in Malta, just as they had Zaghlul, the Egyptian nationalist leader. At first glance, the Allied attack seemed to strike a killing blow to the nationalist movement, but in the long run it gave it its final stimulus; for if the nationalists lost their leaders, the British lost their prestige, angered all Turks by their occupation of the capital and weakened the sultan by protecting him. As has often been said, "If the Greek landing at Smyrna created the Turkish national movement, the British support of the sultan at Constantinople made its fortune."

From that time on the nationalist party gathered into its hands the reins of power and took charge. Its remaining deputies fled Constantinople and established a reconstructed parliament in Angora which was called the Grand National Assembly in defiance of the "legitimate" parliament convened by the sultan at the old capital under the protection of the Allies. Of these two governing bodies in Turkey, the former, purporting to represent national sentiment, became an effective instrument of government; but the latter, symbolic of the old regime under Western influence, declined into impotence, well illustrated by its later acceptance of the humiliating Treaty of Sèvres in August, 1920. On April 23, 1920, the Angora National Assembly, adopting a firm stand against imperialism, declared that it "will preside over the present and future destiny of Turkey, so long as her Caliph-Sultan and her Eternal City shall remain under the dominion and occupation of foreigners. . . . The Ottoman people, considering that all its rights have been violated and its sovereignty encroached upon, has assembled at Angora and appointed an Executive Council . . . which Council has taken in hand the government of the country."[2]

The first task of the National Assembly was to elect Mustapha Kemal president of the Assembly and commander-in-chief of the nationalist army; then it proceeded to construct an instrument of government. This document, the Law of Fundamental Organization, adopted by the Assembly in January, 1921, stated that sovereignty belonged to the people and no longer lay in the hands of a single monarchial individual. The sovereignty was to be vested in a new assembly, a single chamber, to be elected every

[2] Toynbee and Kirkwood, *op. cit.*, p. 89.

two years, which would have legislative and executive powers, the latter through its ministers; at the head was to be a president elected by the assembly. This instrument became the basis of the regular constitution of the Turkish republic which was declared in 1923, after Turkey's successful war against her European invaders. To this conflict we must now turn since it constitutes the second means by which Turkish nationalism won its independence.

Expulsion of European Invaders. The Greek invasion of Turkey-in-Asia in May, 1919, was charged with dynamite as far as the struggle of Turkish nationalism against European imperialism was concerned. For, in the first place, the Greeks represented the Allis and all their traditional designs upon Turkey and its resources; second, they themselves were not only closely associated with Turkish penetration and exploitation, but had lately formulated far-reaching plans for a Greater Greece at Turkish expense. Many Greek nationals had settled in Turkey-in-Asia, especially around Smyrna; Greek merchants exercised a tenacious hold upon the financial and commercial business of its coastal towns; they dominated the cereal trade from Odessa to the west and the British cotton trade eastward; the Young Turk revolt had, in vain, attempted to boycott their trade. Supporting this material hold in Turkey was the nationalist dream of re-creating the Greek Empire and of making the Aegean a Grecian lake. This dream seemed on the verge of realization when the Allies promised Greece, in return for her assistance in the first World War, Thrace, Turkey's province in Europe (down to the Chatalja line) and the greater part of the province of Aidin in Anatolia with its seaport, Smyrna. Had this plan been realized, Greece would have expanded her area about 41,000 square miles, plus most of the Aegean Islands. It was this situation which the Allies were capitalizing when they invited the Greeks to land in Smyrna, both to forestall the Italians and to protect their own interests by crushing the Turkish nationalist movement.

For over a year, 1920-1921, three Greek armies, backed by British loans and the British navy, carried on a vigorous campaign in Thrace and in Anatolia; the French fought the Turkish nationalists in Cilicia on the border of Syria; and the Italians invaded Adalia. Mustapha Kemal met this assault with characteristic military boldness: he struck at the French and the Italians;

in the east he recovered from the Armenian Republic of Erivan the provinces of Kars and Ardahan for Turkey; and he threatened the Greeks. Although he won the title of Ghazi, the conqueror, the Greek armies succeeded in defeating the nationalists, pushing far into Anatolia and capturing the city of Brusa.

The tide turned during the next year, however, in favor of Turkey, owing to Mustapha Kemal's diplomatic strategy and a growing rift among the Allies. He gained friends both in the east and in the west. In September, 1920, a treaty of friendship was signed with Soviet Russia which developed into the offensive and defensive military alliance of March, 1921; in the same month, an alliance was concluded with Afghanistan and in October, 1921, an entente arranged with Persia. The last two treaties rallied Islam and religious fanaticism to the support of the new Turkey, while the U.S.S.R. brought it much needed material military aid. Meanwhile, in the west, France withdrew from the conflict for various reasons: war-weariness, lack of sympathy with the Greeks after the fall of the liberal leader, Venizelos, and the resumption of the throne by the pro-German king, Constantine—as well as jealousy of her ally, Britain, whose naval strength bade fair to give her preponderance in any future settlement. In October, 1921, she recognized by treaty the Turkish nationalist government and restored Cilicia to it. Italy, also, never in favor of the Greek expedition, realized Turkey's growing strength and withdrew to the Dodecanese Islands, hoping at least to salvage them from the struggle. Even Britain became less enthusiastic and adopted a "benevolent neutrality" towards the Graeco-Turkish war.

This gradual withdrawal of the Allies left the campaign to the Greeks, who pursued it with great success, almost reaching the nationalist capital, Angora, in August, 1922. Against them, Mustapha Kemal launched a supreme offensive in his attack at the Sakharia River, which met with surprising success, considering the war-weary Turks, better equipped with nationalist fervor than with military supplies. Within ten days the Greek army was driven back through Anatolia, and Smyrna was regained on September 8. Only Great Britain's declaration that she was "prepared to do her part in maintaining the freedom of the Straits and the existence of the neutral zones" prevented Mustapha Kemal from crossing the Straits. Instead, an armistice was signed at

Mudania in October and the "revisionary" peace congress met at Lausanne in November, 1922.

The resulting Treaty of Lausanne,[3] signed July, 1923, proved, as stated above, to be a document of nationalism where its predecessor, the Treaty of Sèvres, had been a blueprint of imperialism. Turkey emerged with her homelands, Anatolia, Cilicia and Adalia intact; she regained Constantinople, and advanced her frontier in eastern Thrace to the Maritsa River, including the city of Adrianople (Edirne), and, in addition, a small district to the west of it embracing a bridgehead and railway center, Karagach; and she reclaimed in the Aegean the Rabbit Islands and the islands of Tenedos and Imbros. Altogether, the reborn Turkey covered an area of 295,000 miles with a population of 13,000,000. Other nationalistic features of the treaty settlement were the complete abolition of the capitulations, the absence of any restrictions on the country's military or naval forces and the release from any claim for reparations. A separate Graeco-Turkish convention also provided for a "compulsory exchange of Turkish nationals of the Greek Orthodox religion established in Turkish territory, and of Greek nationals of the Moslem religion established in Greek territory." Thus, the Treaty of Lausanne proved to be a fulfilment of the Turkish Nationalist Pact: Turkey won racial boundaries, release from the shackles of European imperialist domination and national independence.

"Turkey for the Turks." All that remained was to organize the new state, a process already begun. Before the signing of the Treaty of Lausanne, Turkey had been declared a republic (November, 1922), and the outlawed sultan, Mohammed VI, accused of high treason, had fled to Malta. After the conclusion of the settlement, the Turkish republic was officially declared (October, 1923), the sultanate and later the caliphate were abolished and Ghazi Mustapha Kemal was elected first president. A modern parliamentary dictatorship superseded the outworn religious monarchy and the Turkish constitution, ratified in 1924 and amended in 1925 and later, became its charter. According to this document, the sole lawful representative of the nation is the Grand National Assembly, elected by all citizens over eighteen. The assembly exercises legislative power directly, while its executive authority is represented by the president whom it elects every four years. He

[3] See p. 282.

appoints the prime minister, who in turn selects the cabinet from among the members of the assembly. Turkey became a republic, her national religion Islam, her official language Turkish, her capital Angora.[4] In theory, the Turkish government is exceedingly democratic and in principle the sovereignty of the national assembly is a constitutional fact; in practice, however, Turkey developed a dictatorial government operating through the people's party, a one-party system with aggressive leadership under Kemal Atatürk, the latter title, meaning Father of the Turks, bestowed by the grand national assembly.

For fifteen years, 1923-1938, Kemal Atatürk ruled the reborn Turkey, prosecuting a fundamental revolution based on the principles of republicanism, secularism, nationalism, modernization or westernization of industry and agriculture, and controlled economy. Virtually every phase of life, political, social, economic and religious, underwent a transformation in the direction of nationalistic uniformity that was truly startling. All foreign elements[5] were gradually eliminated either by Turkification and suppression, as in the case of the Kurds, or by legislation directed against the former economic and social position of foreigners in Turkey. When President Mustapha Kemal Atatürk died in 1938, the first stage of the Turkish nationalist revolution had been effectively accomplished; to his unanimously-elected successor, Ismet İnönü, was left the responsible heritage to achieve the final stage, consolidation of "Turkey for the Turks."

The Arab Nationalist Movements

With the exception of the Turkish, Greek and Zionist revolts, all the other nationalist movements in the Near East are part of the great Arab national awakening which swept not only this area but North Africa as well, and formed one of the most significant factors in the history of modern colonialism. Because of its far-reaching importance, let us consider it first.

The region affected by Arab nationalism comprised about three and one-half million square miles and embraced about

---

[4] The name of Turkey's capital was officially changed to Ankara, the Turkish form, in 1929. Similarly, Constantinople became Istanbul, and Smyrna, Izmir.

[5] In the Greek-Turkish exchange of populations, about 1,000,000 were sent to Greece and 400,000 to Turkey.

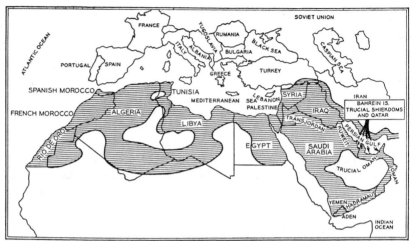

Adapted, courtesy "The New York Times"

COUNTRIES IN THE ARAB SPHERE

forty million Arabs. Its major manifestations occurred in Syria, the Lebanese republic, Palestine, Trans-Jordan, in the four independent states of Egypt, the Yemen, Saudi Arabia, Iraq; its influence reached throughout North Africa into Libya, Tunisia, Algeria, Morocco and even into the narrow fringe of British-protected Arab principalities along the southern and eastern coasts of the Arabian peninsula.

The movement itself represented a mighty resurgence of Arab nationalistic consciousness, with the objective of establishing a vast Pan-Arabia whose center should be the Near East, where it was planned to add Syria, Lebanon and Palestine to the already existing independent states. Once, the Arabs were undisputed masters of this vast area. From the eighth to the eleventh centuries they made it a center of culture and of notable contributions to the sciences of mathematics, medicine and astronomy, as well as to literature and philosophy. But they were obliged to give way to relentless invaders: first came the Seljuk Turks, later the Christian Crusaders who made temporary inroads; Egyptians and Mongols followed; and then the Ottoman Turks established themselves at Constantinople at the beginning of the modern age, from where they ruled over the Arabs for more than four hundred years until the first World War, allowing their lands to lapse into apathy and decadence. Finally, as we have seen, upon this tottering and corrupt imperialism of the Ottoman Empire, the European powers began to impose their sway, bringing the rising industrialism and commercialism of the modern West which, at first, completely submerged the Arab lands and turned them into deserted backwaters.

But the European colonial powers brought something more than alien political and economic domination to these Arabian lands under nominal Turkish sovereignty, during the modern period: they introduced "Europeanization" that has come to have a portentous social, economic and political effect and has proved a boomerang for European expansion. Early in the nineteenth century, nationalist ideas from the West reached Arab lands after the Napoleonic wars, while the short-lived rule of Mehemet Ali in Egypt stimulated anti-Turk sentiment. A renaissance of Arabian history and literature set in: schools carried on Arabic studies, an Arabic dictionary appeared in 1867, an Arabic encyclopedia in 1870 and Arab newspapers were founded in Egypt and in Syria. At the same time, missionaries, foreign educators, merchants, engineers, all agents of European expansion, disseminated the Western ideas of nationalism and democracy and prepared the way for the impact of the wave of "self-determination" released by the first World War and the Wilsonian fourteen points. Revitalized, also, by Western industry, science and humanism, the Arabs awakened to national consciousness and set about modernizing themselves in the European pattern in order to recreate their territories into independent states, politically and commercially, and to free themselves from the dominance of foreign powers.

The first formal nationalist organization was the Arab National Committee founded in Paris in 1895. Its leader was the Egyptian patriot, Mustapha Pasha Kamel, and its objective, the creation of an Arab state independent of Turkey, embracing both the Arabian peninsula and territories north of it. This national committee gave rise to a Committee of Decentralization with its headquarters in Cairo, and to a widespread network of nationalist clubs, secret societies and committees, all opposed to Turkish domination. The Young Turk revolution against the sultan in Turkey proper in 1908, among whose leaders was an Arab officer, greatly encouraged the nationalist Arabs, who hoped for the establishment of home rule in the Arab provinces as a result; but the return of the

Young Turks to imperialist repression embittered the Arabs and strengthened the nationalist movement. As a result, an Arab nationalist congress met in Paris in 1911 and demanded complete independence for lands under Ottoman control.

The outbreak of the first World War in 1914, with its eventual slogans of democracy and rights for small nations, immensely stimulated Arab nationalism: a mass conversion to democratic and nationalistic ideas ensued. Turkey's power was attacked and British treaties with Arab leaders elevated Arab nationalism to the status of Allied war aims. Britain won three Arab allies: the rulers of Asir, of Nejd in the Arabian peninsula and, finally, Sherif Hussein of Mecca, to whom the British pledged their support of Arab independence throughout the peninsula and greater part of the fertile crescent. We have already seen how the co-operation of British arms brought about Turkish defeat and Arab victory in the Hedjaz, in Iraq, and even in Syria. Let us now turn to some of these specific examples.

Establishment of Saudi Arabia

Illustrative of the strength of Arab nationalism was the composure of differences between the various Arab chieftains in the Arabian peninsula and its emergence into a consolidated state, Saudi Arabia, under Ibn Saud in 1934, with British influence reduced to a coastal fringe at Aden. The first effective step towards independence had been taken in 1916 when Hussein, sherif of Mecca, subsidized and supported by the British, won the revolt against Turkey and assumed the title of king of the Hedjaz. With the appointment of his son, Abdullah, as emir of Trans-Jordan and the election of another son, Feisal, as king of Iraq, his position seemed secure. But he lost the support of Great Britain by refusing to recognize the mandatory regime in Palestine, and stirred up trouble in Arabia by assuming in 1923 the title of caliph, after the deposition of the caliph at Constantinople by republican Turkey.

The result of his action was a revolt led by the emir Ibn Saud of Nejd, the leader of the powerful Wahabis, the reformist subdivision of Islam, the "Puritan Mohammedans," strictest interpreters of the doctrines of the Prophet. To save Mecca, the holy city, from invasion, King Hussein abdicated both the caliphate and the kingship, giving way to Ibn Saud who, since 1924, has either overcome his rivals in the peninsula or signed treaties of friendship with them.

Ibn Saud's great accomplishment was the unification of the Arabian peninsula, a few peripheral states and Aden colony and protectorate excluded. In 1927 he signed a treaty of friendship with Britain, the first friendship treaty ever granted by Great Britain to a modern Arab state on terms of equality without reservations inimicable to the independence of the state concerned. In 1932 he gave the country his own name, Saudi Arabia, and it stands under his direction today, an outstanding triumph and bulwark of the Arab nationalist movement.

Syrian Nationalist Movement

When France took over her mandate of Syria and Lebanon, she found herself confronted by Feisal installed as Arab king at Damascus with British support, an unusual diversity of peoples with which to deal, and a thoroughly organized nationalist movement. Prior to the war, indeed, Syria had been a veritable hot bed of Arab nationalism. More under European influence and therefore more advanced than any other Turkish province, Syria faced West not East, and was permeated with French culture, religion and economic interests, such as silk, textiles and railways. Moreover, many Syrians, having emigrated from the homeland, were living in Egypt, where they founded the first modern Arabic newspapers and co-operated with the Egyptian nationalist movement, and in the Americas and Australia, where they came to associate desirable standards of living with democratic institutions, which they took as a model for the homeland. For all these reasons Syria was especially hospitable during the opening years of the twentieth century to the formation within her borders of all types of nationalistic committees and organizations. Besides the Arab Brothers, the Lebanon Union, the Society of Decentralization and others, there was the Syrian National Committee. All these people desired their own united and free state, official recognition of the Arabic language and selection of local officials and judges from the native inhabitants. These local movements were encouraged by the general Arab renaissance, described above and directly identified with it.

With this background of organized nationalist feeling in Syria, it is clear why the Syrians supported Feisal when, with British consent, he established himself in Damascus as virtual ruler in 1918. Further confirmation of their desire for independence appeared in the report of the American Inquiry Commission, the King-Crane Commission, sent by President Wilson to investigate the situation during the peace conference, as well as the statement of the Syrian National Congress (1920) submitted to that group. For they both revealed that the majority of Syrians desired complete political independence and union with other Arab lands; failing that, they preferred the United States first, as mandatory, and, second, Great Britain, and France not at all.

But France insisted on her "rights" in Syria, guaranteed by the Sykes-Picot Treaty, despite the difficult situation obtaining there. In order to handle it, she began her mandatory rule in 1920 by the forceful expulsion of King Feisal, as we have already learned, and then by the adoption of a policy of "divide and rule," which called forth the bitterest opposition from the Syrian people and a desire for unity as well as freedom. Following King Feisal's defeat, the French partitioned the country: they created the state of Greater Lebanon, taking from Syria the seaport of Beirut, her access to the sea, her most fertile plains, which they added to the mountainous state of Lebanon. These regions were principally inhabited by Mohammedans and the French plan was to unite them with the Christians of Lebanon, which had always constituted the heart of French control. Also, they created out of the coastal region north of Lebanon the state of the Alawis or Alaouites and the province or sanjak of Alexandretta, thus depriving Syria of her whole seacoast, leaving her a state with her face turned only to the desert. Internally, the French also partitioned Syria by separating the states of Damascus and Aleppo and by creating the independent state of Jebel Druse. But the desire for union was too keen and the French government was obliged to meet it, first, by setting up a federation of Damascus, Aleppo and the Alawis, and then in 1924 dissolving the federation and allowing Damascus and Aleppo to unite in a single Syrian state, and the Alawis to return to their former separate existence.

Henceforth Syria was composed of five different states, in which France set up representative councils with exceedingly limited powers, together with a federal council for matters of common concern. This was her method of fulfilling her obligation under the mandate to prepare the Syrians for independence, an independence which they already considered should be theirs. Lebanon, whose tie with France was closest, received a provisional constitution in 1922 with a governor appointed by the French High Commissioner; and was permitted to adopt the French tricolor as her flag, with a Lebanese cedar in the center. The Syrian federation was given its own green and white flag but with the colors of the French republic in the corner; Syria, indeed, had to wait for eight years before it could fly the Arab national colors with no mark of France thereon.

Partition and the meager rights vouchsafed in the representative councils resulted only in the exacerbation of discontent, the growing impression that France supported Christians against Mohammedans and a keener desire for unity and freedom. The character of the French administration also added fuel to the flame of nationalistic revolt. At base, it was a military rule which suppressed personal and political liberties, maintained a network of spies, and supported pro-French officials, ignorant of native languages, who employed the French tongue, even in the law courts. It also struck a blow at Syria's economic integrity by introducing a depreciated currency. Finally, in 1925, the revolt broke out, led by the proud and independent tribesmen of Jebel Druse, the Druses, whose protest against injustice resulted in the imprisonment of their delegates invited to Damascus by General Sarrail. The uprising spread throughout the country and lasted for three years. Atrocities occurred on both sides: villages were ruthlessly burned, vital communications destroyed, rural life was rendered unsafe by fierce guerilla warfare, the dead bodies of insurgents were exhibited in the streets of Damascus by the French, and twice that city was bombarded by their tanks and airplanes, which caused great excitement throughout the entire Arab world. Indeed, the horrors of modern warfare as carried on by the mandatory power were so great as to lead the Permanent Mandates Commission of the League to suggest that "the mandatory authorities should not have recourse to such measures of suppression as the bombardment by airplane, incendiaries, destruction of villages and collective fines except in cases of absolute necessity." Besides these measures of violence, other French methods of suppressing the revolt contributed directly to Syrian nationalism.

For the French employed Armenian and Circassian auxiliary troops and armed the Lebanese Christians against the Mohammedans and Druses.

After eighteen months of reckless and cruel warfare, even the French became convinced of the seriousness of a people's struggle for national freedom. The iron-handed General Sarrail was recalled and de Jouvenel, a civilian parliamentarian, took his place. He introduced a constitution in Lebanon, which had not joined the revolt, as evidence of France's desire for reform. It established Lebanon as an independent republic within the French mandate, having its own president, senate, chamber of deputies and ministry. De Jouvenel also entered into negotiations with the executive committee of the Syro-Palestinian Congress in Cairo and with the rebel leaders in Syria, both of whom submitted the same demands for Syria. These were: the substitution of a Franco-Syrian Treaty for the mandate, complete internal autonomy, a freely elected national assembly to draft a constitution and the union of all Syria with the exception of Lebanon. Of these demands, internal autonomy was secured in 1930 when Ponsot, who had replaced de Jouvenel as high commissioner, issued a constitution for Syria after the nationalist constituent assembly, convened by him in 1928, had been dismissed because it demanded absolute independence. This constitution was more liberal than that of Lebanon (1926) because of the overwhelming strength of the nationalist movement. It constituted Syria as an independent, sovereign republic within the French mandate with a president, chamber of deputies and ministry, and, finally, with the Arab national flag.

Syria's new constitution also provided a nationalist government which could negotiate with France for independence. Consequently, in 1933, owing largely to the example set by the British Treaty with Iraq, 1932, a Franco-Syrian Treaty was signed by the Syrian premier and Damien de Martel, Ponsot's successor as high commissioner. It promised Syrian emancipation from mandate status as soon as the country could qualify for League membership. But the Syrian chamber rejected the treaty because it failed to guarantee territorial integrity, financial and military independence from France, and also because of nationalist discontent with the bad economic situation induced by the drop in trade of the depression years. As a result, France withdrew the treaty, prorogued the Syrian parliament and ordered the dissolution of the nationalist party.

But France found herself unable to withstand the strength of the Arab nationalist movement both within and without Syria. The success of Egyptian nationalism in 1936 revived the Syrian campaign for independence and a general strike in Syria brought about the re-establishment of a nationalist cabinet with French permission. Finally, the Léon Blum government in France reopened negotiations and signed treaties of alliance and friendship with Syria and Lebanon in September, 1936. Planned to come into force within three years, they were to replace the mandate, as soon as Syria and Lebanon were admitted to the League of Nations as sovereign, independent states, and to remain in force for a period of twenty-five years, renewable by consent. Modeled on the Anglo-Iraqi Treaty of 1932, they are practically alike, except that France's military rights were more definitely laid down. She was to retain a garrison both in Jebel Druse and in Latakia (formerly the state of the Alawis) for five years; and she had the right to maintain military forces of all kinds in Lebanon for twenty-five years and in Syria for five years. Although ratified by the Syrians and Lebanese representative chambers, they continued to await ratification by the French chamber and fell into a state of suspension because of the European conflict beginning in 1939.

The Nationalist Movement in Iraq

The independent state of Iraq represents the third triumph, after Egypt and Saudi Arabia, of Arab nationalism in the Near East. Moreover, it is the "first graduate pupil of the league's tutorial school for backward peoples peparing for statehood and membership in the family of nations"[6]—the first mandate to achieve independence. Twelve years after it was assigned to Great Britain as a Class A mandate (1920) it became an indeperdent state. Indeed, as we have already learned, it never even accepted the real status of mandate.[7]

Compared to Syria, Iraq stood at the other extreme as far as conditions conducive to the growth of nationalism were con-

---

[6] Foster, H., *The Making of Modern Iraq*, p. 1.
[7] See p. 270.

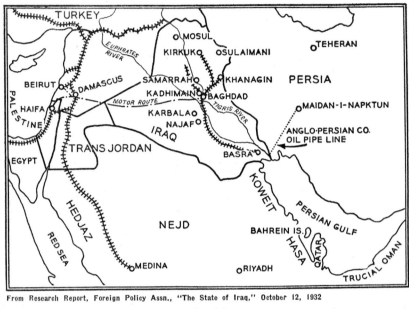

From Research Report, Foreign Policy Assn., "The State of Iraq," October 12, 1932

IRAQ AND ITS NEIGHBORS

cerned. Backward, internally, both in economic development and in the character of her people, the state stood more or less isolated, without much contact with the West. Thus, it is all the more remarkable that Arab nationalism so early triumphed here. Its victory is owing more to the universal, primal and religious character of the Arab revolt against age-old repression and to the leadership of its first, imported king, Feisal, than to the work of an organized, indigenous nationalist movement within the country. A nationalist organization was formed in Iraq in 1913, assisted by propaganda and funds from Syria. Its leaders, some of whom had served in the Turkish army, were encouraged by the establishment of an Arab kingdom set up in Syria under Feisal in 1920. They therefore became active in seeking Iraq's independence under the same sherifian family of Hussein and chose Abdullah, his second son, for their king. But it was Feisal himself, driven out of Syria by the French, who organized, stimulated and directed the unruly and unarticulated Iraqi national revolt. He, it has been said, constituted in his own person the "Wafd" of Iraq, the dominant expression of the independence movement. Born in the desert and brought up among the Bedouin, Feisal became the great leader and symbol of Arabian nationalism, both in spirit and practice.

It was the coincidence of the French attack upon Feisal in Syria and the assigning of Iraq to Great Britain as a mandate in 1920 that precipitated the nationalist revolt and shifted the center of Arab nationalism from Damascus to Bagdad. So hostile were the Iraqi to British control that a general appeal went out to the tribes for Islamic unity, and an insurrection started in the northwest against British provisional military control which had obtained since the war with Turkey. It rapidly spread throughout the country, but the importation by the British of reinforcements from India and news of the collapse of the Syrian Arab kingdom terminated the revolt. Its serious nature, however, led the British to substitute indirect for direct rule. Sir Percy Cox was sent out from England to "help the people of Mesopotamia form a national government," which was set up under a native premier. Meanwhile, the Cairo Arab conference discussed the re-partition of Arab countries and assigned Abdullah as emir of Trans-Jordan, and Feisal, who was under British protection since his expulsion from Syria, as king of Iraq.

King Feisal thus became the compromiser between the opposition of the Iraqi to British rule and the British decision to establish indirect rule in Iraq. Consequently he succeeded in negotiating, instead of the acceptance of the mandate, the signing of the treaty of alliance with Great Britain in 1922, which defined a degree of control similar to that proposed in the rejected mandate, but obtained Great Britain's pledge to support Iraq's admission to the League "as soon as possible." The next year, after peace with Turkey had been ratified, Iraq secured reduction in the years of the alliance from twenty to four and a provision that the treaty would terminate when Iraq joined the League. Other agreements of 1926 and 1927 defined Iraq as a kind of protectorate under Britain with its own King Feisal I, who with his council was subject to the British high commissioner, while British advisers were present in most of his administrative departments.

One provision of the 1926 agreements, however, was that Britain should continue the mandatory regime in Iraq for twenty-five years, a stipulation imposed by the Council of the League of Nations in 1925 when it decided that the province of Mosul

should be included within the frontiers of Iraq. This decision
of the League Council terminated the dispute between Turkey and
Britain over the Turkish-Iraqian frontier, since the Treaty of
Lausanne had merely stated that the frontier should be "laid
down in friendly arrangement to be concluded between Turkey
and Britain within nine months." But "friendly arrangement" failed
since Britain contended that Iraq should include Mosul because it
formed the natural frontier and would provide an unrestricted
grain supply, while the Turkish republic countered that Britain
during the war had occupied only about one-quarter of the area,
had advanced northward since 1918 without military provocation, and, further, that the population desired Turkish control.
The fact that Mosul is rich in oil was not mentioned but was
present as a strong factor beneath the surface both of Mosul itself
and of the discussions concerning it. After careful investigation of
the question by a commission composed of a Swede, a Hungarian
and a Belgian, whose report raised legal questions in regard to the
nature and binding character of the decision, which were in turn
submitted to the World Court, a settlement was finally reached.
Meanwhile clashes between Turkish troops and those of the mandate had occurred and Turkish atrocities were reported to have
been inflicted upon the population of Mosul; this influenced
the deliberations of the League Council. With unanimity the
Council awarded Mosul to Iraq on the conditions that Britain's
control over the mandate be extended, as mentioned above, and
that certain rights be guaranteed to the Kurdish minority.

By 1930 the strength of Iraqi nationalism, built up by King
Feisal, demanded the withdrawal of foreign control, a demand
which coincided with considerations of British imperial policy.
Consequently, in 1927, a new treaty was signed in which Britain
agreed to recognize the independence of Iraq within five years
and to support her application for admission to the League. Iraq,
in turn, promised to lease three new air bases to Britain and to
permit a British military commission to train the Iraqi army.
Thus the way was prepared for the final settlement of 1932. In
that year, Iraq was admitted to the League of Nations after
accepting a list of guarantees drawn up by the mandates commission in regard to the protection of minority rights, freedom
of conscience and religion, and the rights of foreigners before
the courts. The old treaty of alliance of 1922 was abrogated and

a new treaty was signed with Great Britain to endure for twenty-five years. According to its military terms, Iraq obligated itself to provide "for the permanent maintenance and protection . . . of the essential communications" of Great Britain by granting sites for British air bases at Basra and in the interior; "to provide all possible facilities" for the movement of British troops across Iraq, and to utilize only British military instructors. Other terms of the treaty include financial arrangements concerning joint ownership of public works and railways, as well as a mutual undertaking that neither power should adopt a foreign policy which might create difficulties for the other.

It will be noted that Great Britain's chief concern in Iraq was to secure British lines of communication to India and the East, for the country held a position of strategic importance. Already connected by air and motor car with the Mediterranean, it would soon be linked also by railways, since junction with the transport systems of Syria and Turkey apparently was only a matter of a few years. This would enhance Iraq's value both as a hinterland to the Mediterranean ports and as a transit area to the East.

With Iraq's entrance into the League (1932) it became nominally an independent state, but actually it still remained under British military, financial and diplomatic tutelage, which in the opinion of many observers reduced its status to the position of a puppet state. Despite that, however, the country has made headway towards national consolidation. Parliamentary self-government, the establishment of popular education, the perfection of the army, and the creation of modern industries have gone a long way towards welding the heterogeneous population into a unit. National integration, however, still remains a basic problem in Iraq. About one-eighth of the population of the country rules the remaining seven-eighths and attempts to reduce its Bedouin hosts to settled life and order and to revive the long-departed glory of such cities as Bagdad, Nineveh and Babylon.

The Arab Nationalist Movement in Palestine

In Palestine, no Arab nationalist uprising occurred comparable to those recounted in Syria and in Iraq. Nevertheless, the mandate came to witness one of the most crucial tests of the Arab movement, complicated as it was first by the mandatory's pressing strategic need of the territory and its great reserve military strength upon which it could draw, and second by the serious counter claim of Zionism, Jewish nationalism, which continued to grow with the rapid increase of anti-Semitism throughout the world.

Arab nationalism in Palestine rests upon two major foundations: "the natural right of a settled population, in great majority agricultural, to remain in possession of the land of its birthright; and the acquired political rights which followed from the disappearance of Turkish sovereignty and from the Arab share in its overthrow, and which Britain is under a contractual obligation to recognize and uphold."[8] In addition, these two motives of self-determination and self-preservation have been immeasurably strengthened, first, by the general Arabian renaissance with its appeal to nationalistic, political, cultural and religious unity; and second, by the extraordinary rise of Jewish nationalism owing to the Balfour Declaration, the accelerated Jewish immigration resulting from the Hitler persecutions and the economic revolution achieved by Zionism in Palestine itself.

Thirteen hundred years' occupation of Palestine, during which time Arabs have formed the most numerous inhabitants, constitutes the Arabs' basic claim to the country, which for them is also hallowed by their religious origins and in which are situated many of their holy places. This claim became more insistent when Palestine was included in the plans for a Greater Arabia, an Islamic union, which had their rise at the beginning of the twentieth century and were advanced by numerous committees and organizations opposed to Turkish domination. This resurgence of Arab nationalism coincided, it will be noted, with the tightening of British control in the eastern Mediterranean prior to the first World War.

Again, the contradiction between the British and Arab interpretations of the Anglo-Hedjaz Treaty of 1915, the so-called Mac-Mahon pledge, continues to excite Arab nationalism. When it was signed, the British imposed two limitations in the text of their promise to free Arab territories in the land bridge between the Mediterranean Sea and the Persian Gulf for the Arabs, in return for the latter's support in the war against Turkey.

---

[8] Antonius, G., *The Arab Awakening*, p. 391.

The first imposed a geographical limit, excepting from Arab control those portions of Syria lying west of the districts of Damascus, Homs, Hama and Aleppo, the so-called Damascus-Aleppo line; the second indicated the existence of French interests in the territory which they, the British, would be obliged to respect. The British have always claimed that the geographical exception, accepted by the Sherif Hussein, included Palestine; the Arabs assert just the contrary, that Palestine lies generally west of Damascus, to be sure, but more south than west, and forms also their only outlet to the sea, which they would never have renounced.

The controversy over the MacMahon pledge[9] still continues mainly because it is probable that the British and the Arabs never came to a clear understanding of just what the pledge did cover. Nevertheless, Arab nationalism has prospered upon the charge of British "betrayal" of the pledge.

But, according to the Arabs, British failure to redeem the Mac-Mahon pledge does not constitute the only "betrayal"; they find a second in the Balfour Declaration of 1917, which promised to establish in Palestine a national home for the Jews, and which was later confirmed in the terms of the British mandate over the country. As this promise to the Jews constitutes such an important stimulant to Arab nationalism, we pause to inquire into the origins and progress of Jewish nationalism or Zionism in Palestine.

Zionism: the Jewish Nationalist Movement

In 1914 about 80,000 Jews resided in Palestine, where they had fled from persecution mainly in Russia and eastern Europe. For although the Hebrew national life had ended in Palestine as long ago as A.D. 135, the Israelites had lived there for over 1200 years, more than a millennium before the advent of the Arabs. Here Judaism had taken form, here were their holy places, and here Jews all over the world hoped and prayed someday to return, led by a Messiah as they had once been led by Moses into the promised land.

But it was not until 1897 that the political movement known as Zionism got under way. In that year, a Viennese Jew, Theodor Herzl, founded the Zionist organization at Basle, Switzerland,

[9] The MacMahon-Hussein Correspondence was published by the British government in London, March, 1939.

where he had summoned a Jewish congress. The program adopted by the congress set forth the establishment of a national home for Jewish people in Palestine as its object, and henceforth Zionism became, like other modern nationalistic movements, mainly a political movement with a strong admixture of religion.

British official connection with Zionism dates from the negotiations between Balfour, the British foreign minister, and Dr. Chaim Weizmann, prominent Zionist leader,[10] which culminated in the Balfour Declaration of 1917; but British sympathy and activity for this persecuted race spans the whole period of modern history. The idea of settling the Jews in Palestine first found expression in Cromwell's day, and idealists since have frequently voiced the project, so that British support of Jewish hopes has enjoyed a long tradition, based primarily on liberal and religious sentiments. The Balfour Declaration, however, constituted a political bargain. Britain, hard pressed in the war, desperately needed allies in the Near East, needed a friendly people occupying an outpost of the Suez Canal, and needed to forestall proposals to the Jews from the enemy. The Zionists, on the other hand, like the Arabs, felt the necessity of planning for the future, of seizing the opportunity afforded by the hoped-for collapse of the Ottoman Empire, and the pressure of gaining support for their long-cherished objective. For these considerations, they were more than willing to support the Allied cause. It should be noted, however, that the Balfour Declaration did not commit the British government to the recognition of Palestine as the Jewish national home but only "to view with favor" the establishment of *a* Jewish national home *in* Palestine, provided, also, that the "civil and religious rights" of non-Jewish communities were to be respected, a provision likewise repeated in the terms of the British mandate for Palestine.

So, it would seem, did Great Britain strive to reconcile her promises to the Arab and the Jew. But for the vagueness of the terms concerning a "national home," the Jews also are responsible, for Jews everywhere have not supported Zionism with unanimity. Many Jews are "assimilationists," believing that they should lose

---

[10] Weizmann was born in Russia, educated in Germany and became a lecturer in chemistry at the University of Manchester in 1903, which was in Balfour's electoral district. During the first World War, he discovered a cheap process of extracting acetone, an ingredient of TNT, from horse chestnuts.

their separate identity in whatever country they live, co-operating with the population of that country, while others, convinced of the value of maintaining a spiritual and cultural center in the Holy Land, reject political domination. In fact, within Zionism in Palestine itself are several political parties.

However, in spite of splits among its members, Zionism has continued to grow in Palestine, accelerated by the mass refugee movements of 1936, 1937, 1938. The Jews in Palestine now constitute over 30 per cent of the population and, as recounted elsewhere,[11] they have effected an economic revolution both in the rural and the urban areas, owing to the enormous sums of capital poured into the country by world Jewry, which can command the best science and skill for agriculture and industry. While this has meant prosperity for the Jews, it has brought distress, the Arabs claim, to them, particularly to the *fellah* or peasant as well as to the small merchant. The more than 200 Jewish agricultural settlements containing 97,000 people occupy 324,000 acres[12] of land, depriving, say the Arabs, their own population which has increased from 673,000 in 1922 to over 900,000. The Jews also crowd the cities: 75,000 live in the new suburbs of Jerusalem which they have built and 50,000 in the seaport of Haifa, in each of which two cities 50,000 Arabs also make their home. The resulting struggle for economic advantage has, therefore, become an important asset of both Arab and Zionist nationalism.

Again, the unprecedented immigration to Palestine has strengthened the political organization of Zionism. Two political bodies exist to advance its interests: the Jewish Agency, set up under the mandate to co-operate with the British government, represents the World Zionist Organization in Palestine, but includes since 1929 non-Zionists united in their concern for the national home; and the governing body of the Palestine Jewish community itself. These organizations have done much to build up a social, cultural and religious life which fans a strong nationalistic influence especially in the schools, hospitals and other agencies. To a greater extent than the Arabs, the Jews are able to draw help from outside: World Zionism is a greater practical asset to the Jews than is Pan-Arabianism to the Arabs.

---

[11] See p. 266.

[12] The area of cultivable land in Palestine is generally estimated to be about 2,000,000 acres.

The Arab Nationalist Movement (continued)

Returning to the Arab nationalist movement, it now is clear why this inevitably conflicts with Zionism in Palestine and why the Arabs were alarmed when Britain took over the mandate. At once, nationalistic organizations sprang up in every town and village; the Congress of Palestine Arabs was formed with the youthful leader, El Husseini, at the same time Mufti (priest) of Jerusalem, as its president, who became the spearhead of the movement. Until 1925, the congress pursued a policy of non-co-operation with the British government as long as it adhered to the Balfour Declaration; since 1925, its program has become more and more positive—first a demand for democratic popular representation, then cancellation of the mandate and independence. During both periods Zionism has been ruthlessly attacked, the more violently as Jewish immigration and activity have threatened the Arabs' economic and cultural position in Palestine.

Illustrative of the negative obstructive tactics pursued by Arab leadership immediately after the first World War, is its response to the attempt of the British government to fulfil its obligations under the mandate to provide opportunity for political development by promulgating a constitution in 1922. This provided for a legislative council to consist of the high commissioner and twenty-two deputies, ten to be appointed by the commissioner and the remaining twelve (eight Arabs, two Christians and two Jews) to be elected by a system of primary and secondary elections. Since this arrangement failed to give the Arabs the absolute majority in the council, to which they considered they were numerically entitled, they refused to vote at the elections. Hence the constitution never went into effect and Palestine continued to be ruled by the decrees of the British high commissioner, Sir Herbert Samuel, a Jew, whose appointment further excited Arab nationalism. Meanwhile, Britain adopted a policy of Arab conciliation: all religious affairs were turned over to a supreme Moslem council, headed by the Mufti of Jerusalem, agricultural taxes were reduced, and improved social services and economic conditions were encouraged. But these failed to remove the basic causes of Arab discontent and led to a stiffer, more dynamic Arab policy.

In 1929 the Arabs broke out in open rebellion. An economic crisis, precipitated by the heavy immigrations of the years 1925,

1926, and the rapid encroachment of the Jews upon the land, coincided with a religious crisis occasioned by a fierce dispute over the famous Wailing Wall in Jerusalem. The Wall, supposedly composed of stones from Solomon's temple, constitutes for orthodox Jews the holiest spot on earth; but it is also holy to Moslems since it adjoins one of the most sacred of their shrines, the Mosque of Omar, at one wall of which the winged steed of the Prophet Mohammed is said to have been tethered during the night of his miraculous ascension to heaven. Mohammedan property, the Jews have always been permitted access to the Wall, but on the Day of Atonement, 1928, they placed a screen there to separate the men from the women. To the Arabs, this act was symbolic of Jewish encroachment in Palestine and their leaders fanned religious fanaticism into political agitation. Jews were massacred in many sections of the country, while troops and warships were rushed by the British government to quell the disturbances.

The usual commissions of investigation followed, resulting in the report of the British Shaw Commission and the Hope-Simpson Report which included a thorough land survey. Both appeared to favor the Arabs for they recognized specifically their grievances against the Jews and against the British government, which permitted the Jews to buy up large portions of land, to enter in large numbers and to import Jewish workmen instead of employing landless Arabs. The result was the publication of the Passfield White Paper by the colonial office which, while reaffirming Britain's obligation to both groups, took an even more pessimistic view than had the Hope Report of the future possibilities for Jewish immigration and land settlement. It reached this conclusion: "It can now be definitely stated that at the present time and with the present methods of Arab cultivation there remains no margin of land available for agricultural settlement by new immigrants, with the exception of such undeveloped land as the various Jewish agencies hold in reserve." Meanwhile, the government continued the suspension of Jewish immigration to Palestine, begun at the end of 1929.

Both the Hope Report and the White Paper aroused intense Zionist opposition towards Arabs and British. Zionists challenged the conclusions of the Hope Report in regard to the amount of cultivable land and condemned the anti-Jewish line of the White Paper. The British attempt then to "interpret" the White Paper and soften its anti-Zionism aroused, in turn, the fears of the Arabs, who felt their gains were being snatched from them. Indeed, all British efforts to resolve the causes of the outbreak of 1929 seemed but to increase the tension between Jew and Arab and to contribute to those forces which were to result in the more serious uprising of 1936.

As the 1920's advanced, new causes accumulated to urge Arab nationalism to assume a more positive stand. Then, after 1932, came the unprecedented immigration of German Jews fleeing the Hitler persecutions. Large numbers of these constituted the élite of the population: doctors, scientists, artists, business men, bringing all their available funds to invest in Palestine, for in 1932 the British had relaxed the immigration restrictions and allowed merchants and farmers with a capital of $2,500 to enter, as well as a Jewish labor quota of 4,500 for six months. Thus it appeared that the Jewish effort in Palestine was assuming the character of a permanent home on a sound economic basis. By 1935, the number of Jews had nearly doubled since 1933. Tel Aviv, the Jewish city, was increasing in population at the rate of 12,000 a year; about 4,000 new industrial enterprises had been established, including brick, cement, soap and oil, flour and potash works; great power plants had harnessed the Jordan to supply cheap current to the country; and the harbors at Haifa and Jaffa were deepened and improved. Moreover, the selective immigration brought an unusual proportion of young and highly intelligent Jews, passionately conscious of a national mission. A Hebrew University was established at Jerusalem.

At the same time, a new wave of Arab nationalism swept the Near East created by Mussolini's aggression in Ethiopia and the Arab victories in Iraq in 1932, in Egypt in 1936 and in Syria. It intensified the ever present Arab terror of submergence in Palestine. In 1935, all the Arab parties formally presented the high commissioner with three main demands: the establishment of democratic government, the prohibition of the transfer of Arab land to Jews, and the immediate cessation of Jewish immigration along with the formation of a committee to determine the absorptive character of the country. All these were refused. Instead, a plan was proposed which provided for a council with only restricted powers but with a large majority of members elected roughly in proportion to the relative numbers of the three religious

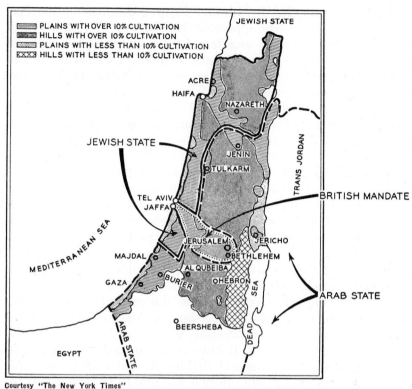

PLAINS WITH OVER 10% CULTIVATION
HILLS WITH OVER 10% CULTIVATION
PLAINS WITH LESS THAN 10% CULTIVATION
HILLS WITH LESS THAN 10% CULTIVATION

Courtesy "The New York Times"

PROPOSED PARTITION PLAN FOR PALESTINE (1937)

communities, Christian, Moslem, Jew. Under this plan Arab influence would have been predominant. But the plan was opposed when it came up for debate in the British parliament in 1936, on the ground that conditions were too disturbed and the people too untrained as yet for self-rule in Palestine.

The Arab answer was renewed anti-Jewish riots and the setting-up of an Arab higher committee, with the Mufti as president, which called a general strike. The most serious nationalistic disturbances, accompanied by terrorism, took place in Palestine and lasted until October, 1936. Jewish colonies were persistently attacked, trains derailed, bridges blown up, roads and telephone wires cut off. By September, twenty thousand British troops were estimated to be in Palestine.

Meanwhile, another British investigating commission, the Peel Commission, had been appointed to discover the basic causes of the disturbances, to ascertain legitimate grievances against mandate rule and to make recommendations. Its report, issued in July, 1937, contained the famous partition plan for Palestine, which has been likened to King Solomon's judgment in regard to the child claimed by two women. Divide the living child in two, said Solomon, and give half to one and half to the other. Partition Palestine, said the commission, among its three claimants, Britain, Arab, Jew. After stating that it found most of the Arab grievances unjustified and that "the establishment of the Jewish National Home had so far been to the economic advantage of the Arabs as a whole," the commission concluded that there was an "ever widening gulf between Arab and Jewish nationalism," which it declared to be irreconcilable. Hence, it presented a plan which offered a chance of ultimate peace. It proposed to divide the country into three political units: a Jewish state in the northwest, including the coastal plain, Galilee, the ports at Haifa and Tel Aviv, occupying about one-fourth of the present mandate, with a Jewish population (1937) of 250,000; an Arab state consisting of most of the remainder of Palestine, which was to be linked with Trans-Jordan; and a third, British section, a wedge-like corridor, including both Jerusalem and Bethlehem and stretching to the Mediterranean Sea at Jaffa. Britain was also to be responsible for the holy places of Nazareth and the Sea of Galilee in the Jewish state. The Arab and Jewish states were to be sovereign and independent, and to enter into military alliances with Great Britain on the Iraq model; a new mandate was to be devised for the British zone.

A drastic proposal, full of dangers and difficulties, the partition plan was acceptable neither to Arabs nor to Jews and raised a storm of protest. The Jews, however, agreed to negotiate. The major objections of the Arabs were that the Jews would receive the most fertile part of Palestine which would include an Arab minority of about 225,000 and that, whereas the Arabs demanded all or nothing, instead of which the "richest zone is to be given to the Jews, the holiest to the British, the most barren to the Arabs." The Jews objected that here would be "Zionism without Zion" (Jerusalem); that there would be only about 258,000 Jews in the Jewish state, the other 100,000 scattered in towns under British control; and that the Jewish state would be a "small island in a great Arab sea." Zionists raised the cry of "betrayal" and the Arabs that of "self-preservation." Britain, it was pointed out, was acting to preserve her own imperialist interests, inasmuch as her zone contained the center of communications, rail, air, and of military force; also that she retained Haifa, a naval base.

Although the British government first announced support of the proposed plan, it became more and more hesitant to push the proposal against the rising opposition. The mandates commission of the League recommended another study of the Palestine problem, a suggestion endorsed by the League Council and Assembly, to whom the House of Commons had submitted the whole matter. Accordingly, a new commission was sent out in 1938 and reported unanimous opposition to the partition plan. Meanwhile, the Arabs had determined to fight the partition plan and had inaugurated a new reign of terror not unencouraged by foreign influences, especially Italian. The Mufti, whom the British had determined to arrest, eluded his pursuers and escaped to Syria. By summer, the rebellion had all but paralyzed the country, and British authority seemingly collapsed in many areas. In November, Britain withdrew the partition plan and summoned a conference of Arabs and Jews at London, the Jews to be represented by the already existing Jewish Agency, the Arabs by the Palestine Arabs as well as by representatives of neighboring Arab states.

As was to be expected, the Round Table conference, convened in London in February, 1939, proved a complete failure because of the impossibility of reconciling the two diametrically opposed claims of the Arabs and the Jews, which remained what they had been from the beginning. The Arabs demanded an Arab state allied with Great Britain, cessation of Jewish immigration and of sales of land to Jews, and annulment of the Balfour Declaration; the Jews demanded fulfilment of the Declaration and the ending of restrictions on immigration and the sale of land to Jews. Discussion was further hampered by the fact that not until after two weeks had elapsed would Arabs and Jews sit in the same room and, more seriously, by the absence of the Palestine Arabs, who refused to attend at all. The failure of the conference proved the practical impossibility of settling the Palestine problem by agreement, and in March the government suspended the conference and announced it would draw up its own plan.

This plan, entitled the "final step" in Palestine, was published in May, 1939. In it, the British government announced its intention to establish an independent state in Palestine after a transition period, a state in which the Jews would not be permitted to exceed one-third of the total population unless the Arabs agreed to further immigration after 75,000 Jews were admitted during the next five years. During the transition period, Britain was to retain the mandate, see that the Jews had complete equality of political and economic rights and allow the high commissioner to limit land sales to Jews in certain areas.

In spite of the hopes of Malcolm MacDonald, the British colonial secretary, the plan brought no peace to Palestine. Both Arabs and Jews opposed it and sporadic violence broke out again. Moderates among the Arabs indicated their willingness to accept the proposal as a basis for further negotiation; but the extremists rejected it in its entirety as did the Jews, some of whom referred to it as an "attempt to create a Ghetto in the Promised Land." In July, 1939, it was reported that Britain would soon adopt a scheme whereby Palestinians would have a share in the government by dividing the country into six districts, two under Jewish, four under Arab heads; also, six department heads to be appointed in the central government in similar proportion. British advisers would function along with these appointees and three Britishers would occupy key posts in the central cabinet. The outbreak of the European conflict in September, 1939, however, ended all plans of self-government for Palestine.[13]

Minor Nationalist Movements—The Greeks

Finally, account must be taken of those minor nationalist struggles on the part of another submerged group, the Greeks, which have been in progress in the Near East. Compared to the major movement just discussed, they appear unimportant. Insofar as they represent parts of larger repercussions to European expansion in this area, they are significant in rounding out the picture of nationalistic unrest in the Near East.

---

[13] In February, 1940, the British government put into effect the land sale restrictions of the latest plan for Palestine. They divided the country into three zones: one in which sales to non-Arabs were prohibited; one in which they were prohibited except under certain conditions such as extension of irrigation; and one in which Jewish purchases of land were prohibited.

Like the Arabs, only in smaller numbers, certain Greek populations came under the domination of the European colonial powers
during the modern period of expansion. The gradual weakening
of Ottoman imperialism and the substitution of European control
was the basis of this—a process which frustrated nationalistic
hopes and fired anew the spirit of revolt. Cyprus and the Dodecanese Islands provided the two scenes of Greek suppression.

The Island of Cyprus.   Great Britain, it may be remembered,
gained the island of Cyprus as a leasehold in 1878 by the Treaty
of Berlin, a reward for the rescue of Turkey after her defeat by
Russia, and annexed it in 1914. A most convenient point of departure for the exercise of control in the eastern Mediterranean, its
main mission was the guardianship of the Suez Canal. Between
1935 and 1940 it became one of Britain's most important naval
harbors and air bases in the Near East.

Chiefly agricultural, Cyprus is only about 30 per cent cultivated
and its material development was sadly neglected, because
it belonged to a satiated colonial power. As a result poverty
remained widespread, the economic level low and discontent
rampant. This condition was aggravated by the long quarrel over
revenues, for the British collected from the Cypriots both the
amount of the rent which, as leaseholders (until 1914), they had
agreed to pay Turkey, and the cost of administration of the island
as well. Nor did they pay Turkey the rent directly but used it to
fund their own interest on the Turkish debt. This practice was
not changed even when they annexed Cyprus: the title of the
so-called Cyprus Tribute was merely altered to "share of Cyprus
of Turkish Debt Charge." Britain continued this until 1927 when
she undertook to make an annual grant-in-aid to Cyprus equal to
the exact amount of the Tribute collected, but receiving in return
£10,000 annually from Cyprus towards imperial defense.

The population is Greek with only about a 20 per cent Turkish
minority. Britain's policy drove the people under the influence of
Greek priests and moneylenders. Greek nationalist societies flourished, vaunting their Greek fatherland and the great Greek civilization, celebrating independence day and talking of union with
Greece. In 1931, cumulative grievances precipitated a crisis: further quarrels over the revenue, the unfulfilment of the governor's
promises for economic reform made in 1927, and Britain's refusal
of the Cypriots' request to be united with Greece. An insurrection

broke out and the government house was burned. Troops from Egypt suppressed the rebellion and restored order, while the legislative council of the crown colony was suspended and its powers were conferred upon the governor. Although the Cypriots enjoyed far more freedom in speech and action than did their compatriots in Rhodes, Greek nationalist discontent still smouldered. Yet fear of Italy (since 1935-1936) and the present insecurity in the Mediterranean occasioned by the European conflict goes a long way towards reconciling the Greek population to British rule and consequent British protection.

The Dodecanese Islands. With a majority of Greeks in the population and a small percentage of Turks, Italy faced the same problem in the Dodecanese Islands. National sentiment here was as strong as in Cyprus although revolt was incipient and not actual, owing to the authoritarianism of Italian rule.

Present-day repression and certain historical factors intensify Greek nationalism here, however, which grows stronger with secrecy. The inhabitants joined in the war of Greek liberation in the nineteenth century, hated the Turks and have never ceased to agitate for union with Greece. During the tumult of the Balkan wars when hopes of Greek Irredentists ran high, a conference of island leaders was held on Patmos in 1912. It proposed the establishment of an "Aegean state" and enunciated the permanent wish of the Aegean islands to be united with Greece. Italians, however, occupied the islands as a result of the Tripolitan War but hopes were raised again when Britain and France, in spite of promises to Italy, manoeuvered their acquisition by Greece in the settlement with Turkey in 1920. Once more, however, these hopes were dashed when Italy took possession in 1923 by the Treaty of Lausanne and proceeded to make up for lost time by prosecuting an active program of improvements in the islands.

More prosperous than the Cypriots, since Italy has poured money into the islands and has built up an excellent shipping and tourist trade, the Dodecanesians may appear lulled into resignation, preferring prosperity to liberty. Yet, whatever they are unable to express is constantly voiced for them in the hatred of Italian rule kept alive by Greeks in Athens, in Alexandria and by their own people who live in exile. Although small in number, these exiles are able to maintain an organization and, at times, even a press.

READINGS

Antonius, G.   *The Arab Awakening*, 1939.   Comprehensive, pro-Arab.

Foster, H. A.   *The Making of Modern Iraq: A Product of World Forces*, 1935.   Documented.

Kohn, H. A.   *History of Nationalism in the East*, 1929.   Excellent.

Kohn, H. A.   *Western Civilization in the Near East*, 1936.

MacCallum, E. P.   *Nationalist Crusade in Syria*, 1928.   Usable.

Main, E.   *Iraq*, 1934.   Impartial.

Main, E.   *Palestine at the Crossroads*, 1937.   Unusually fair and thoughtful.

Philby, H. St. J.   "The Arabs and the Future of Palestine," *Foreign Affairs*, Oct., 1937

Popper, D.   *The Puzzle of Palestine*, Foreign Policy Association, 1938. Handy and reliable condensation.

Price, C.   *The Rebirth of Turkey*, 1923.   Journalistic, popular style.

Samuel, Viscount.   "Alternatives to Partition," *Foreign Affairs*, Oct., 1937.

Sidebotham, H.   *British Policy and the Palestine Mandate*, 1939.

Stein, L.   *Syria*, 1926.   Survey.

Toynbee, A. J. and Kirkwood, K. P.   *Turkey*, 1927.   Reliable.

Webster, D. E.   *The Turkey of Atatürk*, 1939.   Sympathetic.

Wortham, H.   *Mustapha Kemal of Turkey*, 1931.

CHAPTER THIRTEEN

Results of European Expansion in the Near East—Continued

INTERNATIONAL RIVALRIES

THE NEAR EAST has again become one of the most important foci of world politics as the latest chapter of the age-old struggle between its many conflicting interests unrolls before us. For, just as it provides the scene of more nationalistic revolts than have occurred in any other area of European expansion, so too it has produced a greater number of competitive imperialist interests which have exerted an effective and far-reaching influence upon the relationships among the European states involved there and upon international diplomacy in general.

Here, on the eve of the second World War and during its first weeks, Britain and France exerted their utmost efforts in jockeying for position against their opponents, the U.S.S.R. and Germany, and scored an initial success in winning the Turkish republic as their ally, by the Tripartite Mutual Assistance Pact of October 19, 1939, which gave them not only Turkey as an ally but opened the Black Sea to Allied fleets. They then sought to strengthen their tie by favorable trade agreements (the British were forced to smoke

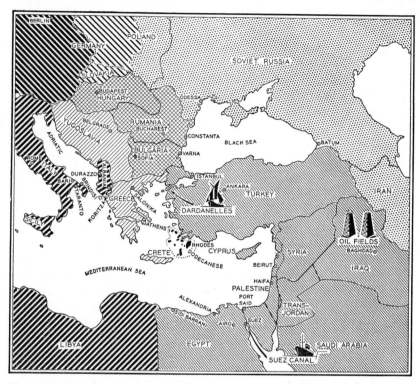

CONFLICTS OF EMPIRE IN THE NEAR EAST ON THE EVE OF THE SECOND
WORLD WAR: BRITAIN AND FRANCE VERSUS THE AXIS POWERS

Turkish rather than American tobacco), loans and other economic
means; and they strove to secure the support of the Balkan states,
with two of whom, Greece and Rumania, they signed treaties of
protection. At the same time they employed every means to prevent Italy from joining their enemies and to maintain the sympathy and assistance of the Near Eastern peoples, the Arabs and
the Jews, residents of their mandated territories, and of the allied
states of Egypt, Iraq and Saudi Arabia. As a further measure of
precaution, they massed troops in Syria, Palestine, Iraq and
Egypt and increased the guard at the Suez Canal.

On the other hand, the U.S.S.R. and Germany separately endeavored to extend their conflicting influences in the Balkan
peninsula and in Asiatic Turkey, to counteract Allied political and
economic strength and to encourage Arab nationalism against

Britain and France. The Soviet Union emphasized her special interest in Bessarabia, her province lost to Rumania in the first World War (1918), and gave evidence of a feeling that it would not be to her advantage to allow a too dominant Germany in the Balkans. Germany strove to hold Italy to the Rome-Berlin Axis and struggled against Allied economic efforts to control Rumania's oil and grain resources, as well as to preserve free access to the latter's Black Sea ports. For it was through these convenient entrances to the Balkans that supplies from the Russian Caucasian oil fields at Baku and at Grozny, as well as from her vast granaries might be shipped to defeat the Allied blockade.

Thus, in 1940, as in 1878, at the beginning of the modern period of expansion, five European powers were struggling for dominance in the Near East; but the powers, as well as the pattern and the stakes of the struggle, had undergone many changes. For in 1878, Britain, France and Austria had been united in their rivalry and their expansionist aims against Russia; in 1940 Germany, not active then in the contest, had taken Austria's place —indeed, had absorbed it. Fired with ambition to regain the control symbolized by her erstwhile Bagdad railway and determined to pursue her political and economic drive to subdue the Balkans and gear them into her national economy, she stood totally opposed to the interests of Britain and France, and, also, to the accession by Soviet Russia of dominance in southeast Europe, although she was allied to her. Further, the transformation of the old Russia with its backward economic regime into the industrialized and agriculturally developed Soviet Union had placed a greater, more powerful and potential rival to all the powers here in the Near East, especially in view of its unpredictable, nationalistic foreign policy. Finally, the fifth power, Italy, negligible in 1878, had become an important factor in the contest with her ambitions for extension of influence in both the eastern Mediterranean, which presents probably the most vital area for her expansionist hopes (particularly as regards the Suez Canal, through which passes the only route to the new Fascist empire in East Africa), and in the Balkans, where the Italian objective had been to preserve the status quo, at least where such disturbance would be unfavorable to Italy. Hence, her interests stood definitely opposed to those of Britain and France in the Levant and to the dominance of either Germany or the U.S.S.R. in the Balkans.

But not only have the expansionist powers, their relationships and positions thus shifted, the whole pattern of the contest in the Near East has altered. In 1878 the contestants were struggling over the moribund Ottoman Empire, its scattered possessions and its subject peoples. Today that dying empire has completely disappeared, its place in Europe taken by the stronger Balkan states, aggrandized and rid of her control; and, in Asia, superseded by the new, vigorous Turkish republic and two new and independent Arab states, Iraq and Saudi Arabia. These have risen upon the ruins of the former Turkey and have attained a position where they submit less readily to the old nineteenth century European dominance and penetration and demand the treatment of equals, or near-equals, in the game of power politics.

Once again, the stakes of the contest in the Near East have become considerably enhanced in importance and significance since 1878. The rapid strides of modern industrialism and commercialism, of transportation and communication have increased the value of Asiatic Turkey, its economic resources, its strategic position, its transit facilities. Britain possessed the largest stakes to defend in the area, although France's interests, too, had become more extended and consolidated than in 1918, not only in Syria but in her commercial, financial and general economic connections. Indeed Britain, with her allies, Iraq and Egypt, and France controlled in 1940 most of the elaborate network of roads, railways and air communications which has replaced the desert wastes and difficulties of terrain, those well-nigh insurmountable obstacles in the waging of war in 1914-1918. Britain, in Iraq, had fallen heir to the former imperialistic achievements of Germany, in the shape of parts of the Bagdad railway, the last link of which she was engaged in completing from Mosul to Baiji. When this is ready it will be possible to entrain at London and arrive at Istanbul without changing cars, and then, after crossing the Bosphorus, proceed straight to the Iraqi capital at Bagdad, which means that military supplies can then be sent direct to Iraq to guard the oil fields there.

Many similar projects had already been completed or were in course of construction: for example, a 600-mile motor road extended from Haifa and Damascus to Bagdad; a new road had recently been built from Suez through the Sinai peninsula into

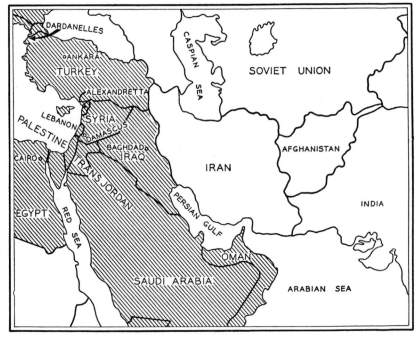

THE NEAR EAST IN 1939 IN RELATION TO THE MIDDLE EAST

Palestine; the railway line from Kantara on the Suez Canal to Haifa had been completed since 1918 and lines connecting the Syrian railways from Aleppo, via Tripoli, with Iraq were planned by the French; air bases were found at Tripoli, at Aden, Cairo, Ramla in Palestine, Amman in Trans-Jordan, Dhiban and Basra in Iraq. Finally, British control had been strengthened over the Suez Canal by the Anglo-Egyptian Treaty. All these transit facilities had become more vital than ever as Britain's life line of empire, and to France, as well, since they guarded the western approaches to her colonial empire in the Far East. Likewise, Britain and France through their mandates and Britain's allies controlled the oil resources of the area, upon which they were more dependent than any other product of the Near and Middle East. Britain drew about one-quarter of her petroleum imports from the fields of Iran and Iraq: 20 per cent from Iran in 1938, and about 5 per cent from Iraq. France counted on obtaining 41 per cent of her total oil supply here and took 39.5 per cent from Iraq in 1938.

As for the trade interests in the area, the advantage had come to lie by 1938-1939 with Germany rather than with Britain and France. Near Eastern products had assumed the position of an important asset in the economy of the Third Reich, not so much for total quantity, since imports from here represented only 3.8 per cent of all imports in 1938, but rather in the kind of specially needed commodities. For example, Turkey sent 33.3 per cent of its chrome ore to Germany, Cyprus 95 per cent of its copper ore, Greece and Turkey supplied 36 per cent of the German tobacco import, and Turkey, Greece, Iraq and Iran, 20 per cent of its cotton requirement; and nearly all the countries of the Near East provided quantities of foodstuffs.

Italy, also, as we have observed, had been rapidly developing her shipping and trade in the Near East. Like Germany's, her turnover during the preceding years had not been large, amounting only to 10 per cent of her total trade, yet it was important because her exports here, principally textiles, paid most of the bill for her imports, which included the supply of about one-half of her oil and about one-fifth of her iron and cotton. By 1939, Italian shipping had also come to possess a strong stake in the Levant: it headed "the list of foreign callers at most of the ports" and accounted for about 30 per cent of the vessels entering and leaving Turkish ports as against 18 per cent of British craft. This increase in shipping constituted one of the bases for Italy's demand for shares in the Suez Canal, controlled by the British and the French. Indeed, of the thirty-two directors of the Suez Canal company, nineteen were French and ten British, one Dutch and two Egyptian, while Italy claimed 16 per cent of the number of ships and 13 per cent of the tonnage passing through the canal. These statistics give weight to her other argument for membership in the canal's control, the strategic one, which had assumed greater importance after her acquisition of Ethiopia, and was expressed by one of her leaders in these words: "Italy is stretched like a bridge in the very centre of the Mediterranean. . . . Not only her liberty but her very life depends on those who hold the keys of Gibraltar and Suez."

Finally, besides possible territorial, economic and strategic encroachment in the Near East on the part of their major rivals, Russia, Germany and Italy, Britain and France had also to fear the penetration into these regions of political ideas and systems, hostile to their own, which might incite against them and win from them their allies, the Arabs and the Turks. For the new Turkey, although an ally of Britain and France, was, as we have learned, deeply indebted to the U.S.S.R. for assistance during its turbulent, formative years after 1919, in throwing off the shackles of Western imperialism and freeing itself from the control of those very powers with whom it stood allied. Arab nationalism also was in debt to Soviet help, and German Nazi propaganda had been tireless in both Turkey and among the Arabian peoples to win them from Allied support, while Italian Fascism in the person of Mussolini had posed as a rival of Britain and France in the guise of a protector of Moslems, and has sought by means of radio barrages and secret agents to destroy native loyalty to British and French colonial rule.

Such then, in brief, was the picture of the international rivalries existent (1940) in the Near East which had emerged as the result of the modern period of expansion there. But it should be remembered that the disturbed state of the Near East was but the latest version of its long history as a theater of interracial, interimperial, interreligious and international struggle which has rarely ceased for any extended period of time. In the ancient world, there were the contests of Egyptians against Assyrians, of Persians against Greeks, of Alexander of Macedon against the Asiatic potentates, of Rome against Greece. The Christian Crusades of the Middle Ages attempted without success to wrest the Holy Places from the infidels, while, at the same time, the powerful Italian city-states vied for the economic and commercial advantage here with Arab and Turk, and with each other. After the conquest of Constantinople by the Turks in 1453, the Christians capitulated for the time being and Turkish sway steadily encroached into the European part of the Near East, submerging the entire Balkan peninsula and the islands of the Aegean Sea. European powers, led by the Habsburgs, were constantly engaged in warfare with the Ottoman Empire, which from the end of the seventeenth century gradually receded from Europe with sporadic re-invasions. During the nineteenth century, these re-invasions were mainly due to the interference of the European powers, for Turkey, herself, was too weak and corrupt to maintain her own position. But the powers, preferring to see a weak Turkey in this strategic stronghold rather than one of their own European rivals, alternately resuscitated and weakened the "sick man of Europe" as suited their own expansionist ends.

In this imperialist struggle, in which the Ottoman Empire became the battledore and shuttlecock of the colonial powers, Russia, as we have recounted, became her consistent enemy after the middle of the nineteenth century and Britain and France her friends, who rescued her from Russia in the Crimean War in the 1850's and again after the disastrous Russo-Turkish War of the 1870's. They also encouraged the nationalist ambitions of the Balkan peoples, as they had done in the case of the Greeks, Serbians and Rumanians, only insofar as such support contributed to their own prestige and position without injuring Turkey too seriously, while Russia threw the whole weight of her assistance behind the "Slav brothers" whenever such policy attained her objective of injuring Turkey and so advancing Russian dominance both in Asia and in the Balkans. It was her supreme and victorious effort in this direction which brought about the convening of the Congress of Berlin by her rivals in 1878.[1]

After the Congress of Berlin, as has been already explained, Russia's withdrawal to the Far and Middle East, as more hopeful zones of expansion, afforded Germany her great opportunity to penetrate into Asiatic Turkey and left Austria, her ally, freer to pursue her advance down through the Balkan peninsula. Germany's outstanding success in the prosecution of the Bagdad railway and the consummation of a Turkish alliance established her as a new and portentous factor in the international situation in the Near East, while Austria came to occupy a more aggressive and dominant position in the Balkans. Hence, by the time Britain and France had compromised their rival positions in Africa, settled the Egyptian question in favor of Britain and the Moroccan question in favor of France—had, in short, cemented the *entente cordiale* and were ready to turn their attention again to Asiatic Turkey—Germany loomed there as a far greater menace to their interests than had Russia before 1878.

It was this situation, German dominance in Asiatic Turkey, which surprised and threatened Russia also, when she returned to the Near East after her failure in the Russo-Japanese War in 1905. But Russia found not only her traditional interests in Turkey

---

[1] See pp. 244 ff.

jeopardized by Germany and Slavic influences at the court of the sultan superseded by Teutonic; she also awakened to the triumph of Teutonic influence over Slav in Bulgaria and to the growing activity and ambition of Austria directed in the western Balkans against Slav nationalism. Altogether, these circumstances provided the common ground of imperialist interest between herself and the entente Allies, Britain and France, and contributed materially to the patching-up of Anglo-Russian rivalries in Persia and in the Middle East. The result was the Anglo-Russian Convention of 1907,[2] an agreement which completed the Triple Entente of Britain, France and Russia, since Russia and France already were tied by the Dual Alliance of 1894, and Britain and France bound by the *entente cordiale.*

By the year 1907, then, the tug of war for dominance in the Near East became squarely one between the powers of the entente, Russia, Britain and France, and those of the Triple Alliance, Germany, Austria-Hungary and Italy. For, even though their particular imperialist aims developed separate strains and stresses among the members of the same group and sometimes threatened seriously to divide the allies, in the main they coincided until 1914, thus setting one group against the other. For example, Germany's ally, Austria, was as intent upon the *Drang nach Osten* in the Balkans, which ran counter to Russia's interests in that region, as Germany was in Asiatic Turkey, where her drive opposed similar aims of Russia and of her allies, Britain and France. But their methods were contradictory and so failed to render their joint effort more effective than it was. For example, Germany made a friend of the Turk, and Austria attacked him as an enemy. Following the advice once given by Bismarck, Germany did not want to endanger her own policy by "pulling Austria's chestnuts out of the fire." As for Italy, the third partner in the Triple Alliance, her expansionist interests also were directed against those of the entente allies. She had joined the Triple Alliance in 1882, largely because she saw in it a brighter hope of attaining her rapidly growing expansionist aims, so frustrated by France and Britain in North Africa, although by 1907 she had come to recognize Austria as her rival in the penetration of the Balkans. Yet she yearned for expansion in Asiatic Turkey, where her ally Ger-

---

[2] See p. 368.

many was powerful, as well as for a position in the eastern Mediterranean, always opposed by the entente powers, Britain and France.

The International Conflict in Asiatic Turkey

Following the course of this struggle of imperialist rivals first in Asiatic Turkey, we note that even in 1906, before the Triple Entente was complete, Britain, France and Russia had begun collectively to thwart German progress in building the Bagdad railway by opposing Turkey's raising of the customs dues from 8 to 11 per cent in order to fund her share of the construction work. By 1908, the "entente net," woven against Germany in the Near East, was complete. For at the meeting of the Russian Czar, Nicholas II, and the British king, Edward VII, at Reval in that year, the Russian minister, Isvolski, the pan-Slav who was intent upon reviving Russia's traditional aggressive policy in the Near East, introduced plans for co-operation of the allies against the Bagdad railway, which France and Britain had been engaged individually in opposing, since 1903-1904, by means of intrigue with the Ottoman government. How well these allies of the entente succeeded in curtailing the scope of the railway and in compromising their rival commercial, strategic and imperialist interests with Germany's in their several agreements, entered into between the years 1910-1914, already has been related in detail.[3] On the eve of the great war in 1914, then, largely owing to the initiative of Great Britain, international tension caused by imperialistic rivalry was temporarily held in check by the Anglo-German, the Russo-German and the Franco-German "colonial deals." These agreements, it is true, effected a compromise of colonial interests in Asiatic Turkey between the powers of the Triple Entente and Germany, but the balance of power thus created was very delicately poised.

International Conflict in European Turkey—the Balkans

In European Turkey, or the Balkans, compromise was even more difficult because the conflicting interests and expansionist ambitions of the Balkan states were added to those of the great

---

[3] See p. 255.

powers and often cut across them. Here Isvolski took the initiative in intriguing with the Balkan Slavs against Austria-Hungary, Germany and Turkey. Indeed, it may be said that Russian intrigue here, especially in Bulgaria, had really never ceased even while Russia's interest was focused in the Far and Middle East. Isvolski accelerated it, however, and his zeal in the revival of Russia's aggressive policy became so great that he even plotted with the rival Austria for mutual aggrandizement. In the notorious Buchlau bargain of 1908, Austria was to annex her protectorates, Bosnia and Herzegovina, and Russia was to be permitted to send her warships through the Straits.

Austria's successful annexation of these provinces, carried through in defiance of her ally, Germany, who resented the blow to her partner, Turkey, is illustrative of the strain between their two methods of pursuing the *Drang nach Osten*. It produced Germany's forced acquiescence in Austria's course. For Russia's allies, too, objected to her share of the bargain; their imperialist interests would not permit Russia to profit by the opening of the Straits, hence Isvolski returned empty handed to St. Petersburg. Germany stood by Austria, her ally, because she possessed no other partner upon whom she could thoroughly rely, while Russia accepted her loss because her allies would not support her. Thus the crisis passed, but it left far-reaching results: Pan-Germanism had won over Pan-Slavism and the Triple Alliance had made a significant gain over the Triple Entente in the imperialistic struggle in the Near East; but the deep scars of resentment inflicted upon Russia stung her to further and bolder expansionist efforts.

Bitterly disappointed, Russia attempted to compensate herself by concluding with Italy, in 1909, the Racconigi Agreement in which she consented to Italy's attack upon Turkey in Tripolitania in return for Italy's promise to "regard with benevolence" Russia's interests in the Straits. This move, together with Russia's support of the Balkan League against Turkey, made Russo-Turkish ill-will deeper than at any time since 1877 and forced Turkey to seek even more a protector in Germany. Thus Russia's disappointment and loss in 1908 contributed to Austrian and German gain, which materially increased the tension between the Pan-Slav and the Pan-German struggles for dominance in the Near East and seriously threatened the balance of power.

Illustrative of these rival imperialisms is the position which the expansionist powers assumed in the ensuing Balkan wars when the Balkan states attempted to throw off Turkish dominance in the first Balkan War (1912) and then quarreled over the spoils in the second Balkan War (1913). In both conflicts Russia encouraged the winning side: first, the Balkan League against Turkey; and then Serbia, Greece, and Rumania against Bulgaria. The Central Powers and Italy sided against the Balkan League in the first war and with Bulgaria against her enemies in the second conflict. Indeed, Austria and Italy deliberately prevented Serbia from realizing her promised spoils after the first Balkan War by occupying the Adriatic ports of Scutari and Durazzo; and, after the second, by setting up with the other great powers, who feared a conflict there, the independent state of Albania with a puppet German prince as king under their protection. Meanwhile, Germany was extending the Teutonic influence throughout the Balkans by her dominance at the courts of Bulgaria, Rumania and Greece, the queen of which last country was William II's sister. Against this Pan-German influence, Russia actively plotted especially in Rumania and Serbia with Slav nationalism and its secret societies, whose intrigues led eventually to the murder at Serajevo in June, 1914, and precipitated the outbreak of the first World War—a war due largely to the rivalry of conflicting expansionist ambitions here, in Turkey-in-Asia and in Africa.

Renewed International Conflict in Asiatic Turkey

During and immediately after the World War of 1914-1918, these expansionist aims and their international repercussions shifted from the Balkans to Asiatic Turkey, where the promised spoils of the Ottoman Empire appeared especially enticing. As we have learned,[4] the Allied powers prepared at once for their partition by a series of agreements: first among themselves, the Treaty of Constantinople, the Sazonov-Paléologue, and Sykes-Picot treaties; then, with Italy, the Treaty of London, and with Greece, the treaty by which she joined them in the war; and, finally, the agreements made by Britain with the Arabs, the Anglo-

[4] See p. 276.

Hedjaz Treaty, and with the Jews, the Balfour Declaration. Some of these arrangements conflicted with each other, notably Britain's commitments to France and to the Arabs, and the Allies' promises to Italy and to Greece. Hence, at the conclusion of the war, the attempt to implement them could not but precipitate serious rivalries and disagreements among the Allies themselves, of which the most significant were those between Britain and France and among Britain, France and Italy.

British-French Colonial Rivalry. The original deals made by Britain and France for their division of the Turkish spoils were upset by the defection of Russia from the war in 1917, which left more to be divided between them. This circumstance, together with the pressing necessity upon Britain to satisfy the Arab claims, which she had done so much to stimulate, and to reconcile them with the somewhat vague promises made to France in the Sykes-Picot Treaty, led to a serious rift between the two allies. This quarrel [5] came to a head in 1918-1919 but it had its origins prior to the war, despite the bonds of the entente, for even then British secret active support of Arab nationalism against the Ottoman Empire formed a serious threat to French pretensions in Syria. Realizing this, France had assumed a determined stand when the Balkan wars upset the balance of power in the Near East and when propaganda from Egypt was then directed towards winning Syria for Britain. The resulting Grey-Cambon Agreement of 1912 assured France her traditional "rights" in Syria but failed to allay all her fears. For Britain was meanwhile keeping close touch with Moslem leaders in Beirut and Damascus, waiting apparently for Arab nationalist sentiment to ripen and so afford an opportunity for intervention—a policy confirmed later by the famous Anglo-Hedjaz Treaty or MacMahon pledge of 1915.

With these threats to her position in Syria in mind, it is not surprising that France attempted to secure herself there by blocking out early in the conflict the areas over which she was to have control and thus patching up the imminent dispute between the allies—a dispute which was to break out again when the original settlements which included Russia were altered by her disappearance from the struggle and France's claims were jeopardized by those of the Arabs. Thus when France attempted

---

[5] See p. 279.

to realize her "rights," in Syria, a three-cornered quarrel was precipitated among British, French and Arabs, the outcome of which we have discussed.[6]

But other disagreements, also, aggravated the Anglo-French dispute of 1918-1923. These arose out of keen rivalries over petroleum and transportation interests and a divergence of policy in dealing with the Ottoman Empire and its successor, the Turkish republic. Until 1923, all these conflicting interests, territorial, commercial, economic, political and strategic in the Near East, separated the "Allies." In 1920, at the conference of San Remo they reached a compromise: an economic agreement accorded France 25 per cent of the oil output in Mesopotamia, any native government or interests 20 per cent, and Great Britain 55 per cent; and the British government was to use its influence to secure for the French 25 per cent of the oil taken out by the Anglo-Persian Oil Company. For this, France agreed to transfer Mosul (originally included in the French sphere of influence) with its oil to Great Britain. Closely connected with this was the political agreement also signed at San Remo, April, 1920,[7] which allocated the mandate over the whole of Syria, including even Damascus, then under the rule of Britain's ally, King Feisal, to France, and Palestine and Trans-Jordan to Britain. This political and strategic compromise was further strengthened by Allied co-operation and agreement in regard to the terms of the Treaty of Sèvres,[8] which was imposed upon the Ottoman Empire in August, 1920; and by the Tripartite Agreement of Britain, France and Italy, immediately following.

The Treaty of Sèvres confirmed France's gain of Syria and Britain's of Palestine inasmuch as Turkey was now officially deprived of these territories. The Tripartite Agreement defined additional spheres of influence for the rivals: for France, territorial interests in Cilicia and along the west border of Kurdistan bordering on Syria; for Britain, no additional territory, but a confirmation of her special rights in the mandated territory; equal participation of the rivals (along with Italy, the third party) on international commissions created to carry out reforms in Turkey; tariff reciprocity in their respective spheres, joint diplo-

[6] See p. 333.
[7] See p. 279.
[8] See p. 280.

matic action to maintain their positions; and shared transportation rights in the Anatolian, Mersina-Adana, and those parts of the Bagdad railway lying in Turkish territory, which were to be unified and operated by a joint company, including these two rivals and Italy. Furthermore, Britain and France signed another secret compact in December, 1920, which defined the future boundaries of their respective mandatory territories and arranged for the adjustment of railroad rights in Palestine and Syria in connection with the building of oil pipe lines from Iraq to the Mediterranean Sea. Altogether, by the close of 1920, Britain and France had fairly well composed their differences, political, economic and strategic.

But this apparent Anglo-French accord was short-lived. The rise of the Turkish nationalist government and its stiff resistance to European imperialism drove a wedge between the two allies. The main difficulty arose from the fact that Britain advocated a belligerent attitude towards the new Turkey, encouraging and supporting with her navy a Greek offensive in Asia Minor, while France, at first endorsing the Greek invasion, gradually inclined to a recognition of the Angora government and finally signed a separate peace with its leader, Kemal, in October, 1921, for reasons which have been enumerated.[9] This Franco-Turkish separate peace excited bitter British resentment and again for a time divided the "Allies." But continued Turkish nationalist victories over the Greeks and Italians altered the British attitude also, prepared the way for a revision of the Treaty of Sèvres and finally produced Anglo-French accord in the Treaty of Lausanne, 1923. The necessity of making a "negotiated peace" with the Turkish republic once more drew the "Allies" together if only for mutual support against this astonishing new power in the Near East, allied with Soviet Russia.

After Lausanne, Great Britain and France, in the main, co-operated in the Near East. There existed many reasons why they should co-operate: they were both mandatory powers with similar responsibilities and the same pressing necessity of dealing with Arab nationalism; they possessed joint strategic, commercial and economic interests, especially in oil, railways, control of the eastern Mediterranean Sea; and they were both forced to guard the route

---

[9] See p. 291.

to their Far Eastern empires. Finally, the rise of Italian expansion in the Near East threw Britain and France close together after 1935, as we shall presently observe. In concluding the account of their rivalry, up to this point, it is interesting to note that it follows the same general pattern as the Anglo-French colonial quarrel in Africa: first, acute competition at many points, almost leading to war; then, a studied compromise of interests, involving territorial and economic bargains, which, in turn resulted in a consolidation of strength and a drawing together against the encroachments of other colonial powers. In Africa, these were Germany and Italy; in the Near East they were the same, Germany and Italy. We already have observed Anglo-French co-operation in weaving the entente net against German expansion here before and during the first World War and shall presently return to trace its revival after 1918. In the meantime, let us follow the course of Anglo-French rivalry with Italy in this area both before and after 1914.

Anglo-French-Italian Rivalry. Just as in Africa, Britain and France always opposed Italian encroachments upon what they considered to be their preserves in the Near East, although a keen desire for any such encroachment did not appear until after the beginning of the twentieth century. Hence their policy of exclusion became especially evident in 1911-1912, when Italy carried her conflict with the Ottoman Empire in Tripolitania over into Asia, Turkey's homelands, and proceeded to blockade the Hedjaz coast in an effort to harrass Turkey itself. Poincaré, the French prime minister at the time, fearful of Italian penetration into the eastern Mediterranean, impressed upon the Italian ambassador in Paris that France considered Syria her own preserve and took other measures as well to prevent Italian influence from increasing in the Near East. When Italian troops occupied the Dodecanese Islands belonging to Turkey but mainly populated by Greeks, both Britain and France tried to prevent the occupation from becoming permanent by urging the Greeks to resist. They also encouraged Greece in the Balkan wars of 1912-1913 to increase her possessions in the Aegean Sea as a makeweight against Italian influence in the eastern Mediterranean. Until 1914, then, Italian aspirations in the Near East had been consistently discouraged by her two rivals.

But need of Italian support in the World War of 1914-1918

obliged the Allies to accede to her colonial demands. In the Treaty of London (1915) they accorded her full sovereignty in the Dodecanese Islands, which she had continued to occupy since the Tripolitan War, and also recognized that: "Italy is interested in the maintenance of the balance of power in the Mediterranean, and, in the event of a total or partial partition of Turkey-in-Asia, she ought to obtain a just share of the Mediterranean region adjacent to the province of Adalia." It is noticeable that they failed to include her in their subsequent arrangements among themselves for the distribution of the spoils. Italy got word, however, of the Sykes-Picot Treaty between Britain and France and demanded her "just share." Hence, there followed the secret Treaty of St. Jean de Maurienne, April, 1917, signed among Britain, France and Italy, which promised Italy approximately the southern third of Anatolia, together with a sphere of influence north of Smyrna. This would give her the towns of the provinces of Adalia and Konia and thus raised her hopes for the control of western Asia-Minor including the important seaport of Smyrna.

It was only the exigencies of the war in which the Allies, Britain and France, feared that Italy might sign a separate peace with the central powers that led them to consent thus to an aggrandized Italy which would alter the balance of power in the Mediterranean Sea. But they guarded themselves against the eventuality of any such danger by their favorite method of supporting Greek claims against Italian as a counterpoise. Again, the exigencies of war played their part: the Allies held out as a definite reward to Greece for its services in the war against Turkey, which it joined in 1917, definite assurances that Greece would receive Thrace, including Adrianople, down to the Chatalja line, together with the greater part of the province of Aiden in Asia-Minor, including Smyrna. Fortunately for British and French interests and their objective, the exclusion of Italy, they were able to declare a flaw in the Treaty of St. Jean de Maurienne which hinged on the fact that Russia's consent to it had never been obtained. Therefore, they declared it invalid, turned a favorable ear to the demands of Venizelos, the Greek premier, who was clamoring for Greece's "nationalist interests" at the peace congress, and instead sent the Greeks to occupy Smyrna. As Lloyd George relates the Allies' action in his memoirs: "There was a race between the Italians and the Greeks as to which should be the first to land in Smyrna.

Prompt action taken by Wilson, Clemenceau and myself enabled Venizelos to get a Greek force into the town while the Italians were hesitating."

Meanwhile Italian foreign policy, owing to post-war internal troubles and the breakdown of state authority at home, became, after 1919, "retreatist" and conciliatory. Italy, for a time, seemed to abandon her ambitions in the eastern Mediterranean and to be ready to renounce not only Adalia but the Dodecanese Islands as well, in the face of Allied support of Greece and her aims as opposed to theirs. It was largely for this reason that the Allies were able to effect an Italian-Graeco agreement in which Italy ceded Dodecanesia, which the Treaty of Sèvres awarded her, to Greece. Indeed, the only recognition of Italy's claims made by the Allies was to include her in the Tripartite Agreement consummated immediately after the Treaty of Sèvres, according to which her special interests in southern Anatolia, including the coal basin of Heraclea, were affirmed.

But Mussolini's rise and the success of Fascist nationalism completely reversed Italy's "retreatist" policy in the Near East. The agreement for the transfer of the Dodecanese Islands to Greece was declared lapsed because of the nonratification of the Treaty of Sèvres by Turkey; the injustice of the Allies' insistence upon the invalidity of the Treaty of St. Jean de Maurienne was bitterly condemned, as was likewise Britain's partiality to Greece. Most indicative of the changing temper was the invasion of Adalia by an Italian army to secure the promised sphere of influence in Asiatic Turkey. It met with more defeat than victory, however, at the hands of the Turkish nationalist army, whose superior strength and that of the movement back of it the Italians were among the first to realize.

The Italians also recognized the fact that Allied struggle against the Turkish republic was being fought mainly in the interests of British and Greek imperialism, that the British were using the Greek armies as pawns in the game, and that they themselves could make better terms in the end by ceasing to fight. Consequently, they withdrew the Italian army and made a separate peace with the Turkish republic, concluded in 1922. It provided for the collaboration of Angora and Italy in regard to certain Italian plans for railroads, mines and public works within specified provinces in Asiatic Turkey and preserved Italy's special rights in the Heraclea coal basin. In the words of Count Sforza to the Italian parliament, it secured "a vast zone in Asia Minor open to Italian economic penetration without any political aims," and the "sincere and cordial co-operation of Turkey which is convinced of the honest and loyal intentions of Italy." This sentiment, however, was of short duration for, after the British abandoned the campaign against the Turkish republic, thus deserting the cause of the Greeks, the Italians were able to reassert their claim to the Dodecanese Islands and succeeded in gaining full recognition of their sovereignty over them in the final settlement with Turkey, the Treaty of Lausanne in 1923.[10]

Meanwhile, a second aspect of Anglo-French and Italian imperialist rivalry was in progress in the Balkans. It can be only briefly reviewed here but should be included to understand the keenness of national competition caused by expansionist aims. Here, the claims of Yugoslavia and of Greece were supported by their allies and patrons, Britain and France, against those of Italy both at the Paris Peace Conference and afterwards: first, in the famous quarrel over Fiume, the Adriatic port, demanded both by the Italians and the Yugoslavs; and, second, in the Graeco-Italian struggle over boundaries in Albania. The former quarrel, dramatized by the sudden departure of the Italian delegation, headed by Orlando, from the Paris Peace Conference, and by the spectacular occupation of Fiume by the Italian nationalist d'Annunzio, was finally settled by direct negotiation of the two participants in the Treaty of Rapallo (1923). It awarded the city of Fiume to Italy and Port Baros and a fifty-year lease of part of the Fiume harbor to Yugoslavia, a settlement satisfactory to neither side.

The second quarrel between Greece and Italy nearly precipitated war, since some Greeks killed an Italian general and other members of the boundary commission in Albania and in retaliation the Italians bombarded and occupied the Greek island of Corfu. The crisis was referred to the League of Nations, which turned it over to the Council of Ambassadors in Paris. Italy was obliged to evacuate Corfu and Greece to pay an indemnity for the Italian victims of the boundary commission and to guarantee the punishment of their murderers. The immediate issues of these two rivalries, Italo-Yugoslav and Italo-Greek, were thus settled, but

---

[10] See p. 292.

the part played by Britain and France in their settlement, which seemed to Italy designed to thwart her expansionist aims, always rankled. Mussolini declared at the time that he had long recognized it to be Britain's policy to support Greece because her geographical position made her a useful ally, while Italy, because of her geography, could be even more useful to Britain than could Greece.

It can be easily understood how the outcome of the peace settlements of 1919-1923 and their aftermath proved disappointing in the extreme to Italy and how bitter was her "frustration." Her government never forgot nor allowed the people to forget the Allies' nonfulfilment of their promises contained in the Treaty of London regarding accessions in the Near East, nor their policy of supporting Greek claims in the Levant, and both Greek and Yugoslav claims in the Balkans, at the expense of what it regarded as Italian "rights." The all too obvious result was an increasingly insistent acclaim, publicly voiced by Mussolini, of expansionist aims directed towards the East, followed up by a vigorous and intensive campaign of economic and political penetration of the Levant, by assertion of power in the eastern Mediterranean and by a striving for dominance in the Balkans, especially in Albania.

The conquest of Abyssinia strengthened Italian prestige and enhanced Italian stakes in the Near East, while adherence to the Rome-Berlin Axis increased the need for Italian influence in the Balkans and aggravated the colonial rivalry with Anglo-French interests in the eastern Mediterranean. This rivalry became so acute in 1938 that Britain and Italy included a series of compromises affecting their respective rights in and around the Near East in the Mediterranean Agreement of April of that year, as basic to the major purpose of the agreement to maintain the status quo in the Mediterranean Sea. These were in the main: mutual recognition of the British sphere of influence in Saudi Arabia and Aden and the Italian interests in the kingdom of Yemen, together with the provision that it was to their common interest to permit no other power to acquire a privileged position in these, the Arab states, which guard strategically the entrance to the Red Sea; and the mutual reaffirmation of the 1888 convention which guaranteed free use of the Suez Canal in time of war as well as in time of peace. Like so many of their predecessors, these undertakings constituted a colonial deal of the familiar type.

Actually the compromises of colonial interests effected by the Mediterranean Agreement were slight and superficial; they failed to strike at the root of the inequalities between British and Italian expansionist interests in the Near East and favored the stronger power at the expense of the weaker. Rather did their inadequacy and insignificance whet Italy's appetite and accentuate her position as a Have-Not state. Consequently, becoming more and more estranged from Britain and France by the diplomatic contests over the war in Spain and emboldened by the successes there of the Axis powers, Italy suddenly came forth in November, 1938, with her demands for shares in the Suez Canal and a greater dominance in the eastern Mediterranean Sea. This was followed by her lightning military occupation of Albania in the spring of 1939—both acts hardly in accord with the Mediterranean Agreement regarding the preservation of the status quo in that sea. Thus as the outbreak of the European conflict in the fall of 1939 approached, the colonial rivalries of the Allies and of Italy were reaching an acute stage and playing their part in determining upon which side of that great conflict Italy would enter.

Finally, the result of increased tension between Anglo-French and Italian colonial aims in the Near East just reviewed was, as ever, to cement more firmly the co-operation of Britain and France in maintaining their joint colonial interests in the area. Illustrative of the close integration of their objectives in this respect was their policy towards the Turkish republic which consistently endeavored to win her from German and Russian influence. For this reason they both acquiesced in the Montreux Straits Convention (1937) and accorded Turkey's request for a revision of the Treaty of Lausanne insofar as it permitted her to refortify the region of the Straits; France did not block Turkey's efforts to detach the province of Alexandretta from her mandate, Syria, for a time re-christened by Turkey the Republic of Hatay,[11] while both powers strove increasingly for Turkish trade agreements and economic alliance. The climax of this policy was reached in the signing of the Anglo-French agreements with Turkey in May and June, 1939, which were transformed into the Tripartite Mu-

---

[11] See p. 273.

tual Assistance Pact of October, 1939. Thus, as 1940 dawned, Britain and France stood united in the Near East, as in Africa, in close political, economic, military and strategic co-operation in mutual defense of their colonial empire against their traditional rivals, Germany and Italy.

READINGS

Howard, H. N.   *The Partition of Turkey: A Diplomatic History, 1913-1923,* 1931. Solid, documented.

Langer, W.   *The Diplomacy of Imperialism, 1890-1902,* 2 vols., 1935.

Monroe, E.   *The Mediterranean in Politics,* 1938.   Clear, useful.

Shotwell, J. and Deák, F.   *Turkey at the Straits,* 1940.   Fine outline.

Sillani, T.   "The New Balance of Power in The Levant," *Foreign Affairs,* Jan., 1939.

PART IV

European Expansion in the Middle East

CHAPTER FOURTEEN

The Middle East's Invitation to Its Expansionist Neighbors and Their Response

Adjoining the Near East lies another area especially attractive to its expansionist neighbors, the Middle East. It consists of an irregular, triangular block of territory occupying the middle, southern section of the Asiatic continent. The Caspian Sea, Asiatic Russia and two parts of the former Chinese Empire, Sinkiang and Tibet, form its extended northern boundary. The Turkish republic, Iraq, the Persian Gulf and the Arabian Sea border its long, diagonal, western side; and China, Thailand, the Bay of Bengal and the Indian Ocean outline its shorter and irregular eastern edge. Today, Iran (Persia), Afghanistan and the border provinces of British India constitute roughly the uneven base of the triangle which is set slightly askew, while the vast peninsula of the Indian Empire, itself continental in size, forms the apex.

Unlike the Near East, the Middle East is contained in one continent, Asia, instead of sprawling over three; but it resembles the former area in that it is bordered by many waterways which have greatly facilitated its accessibility to penetration from outside. These are the Caspian Sea, the Persian Gulf, the Arabian Sea, the Indian Ocean and the Bay of Bengal. From a geographical and strategic viewpoint, therefore, the Middle East forms the continuation of the Near East as a vast transit area between West and East into southern Asia and into the Far East, while it includes the immediate approaches to the Indian Empire and India itself. It constitutes also, unlike the Near East, a compact geographical unit distinctly defined in the north and south by the natural boundaries of mountains and seas. Lofty mountain ranges, the Zagros, the Elburz, the Hindu Kush, the Pamirs and the Himalayas, the last three among the highest in the world, rise like a wall to separate the Middle East from Asiatic Russia and the Chinese republic, while its seas and gulfs make up the entire southern border. No natural barriers protect the eastern and western approaches to the area; they lie exposed to easy access. For the waterways situated on the east, south and west function not as deterrents to, but as means of, communication and render the entire territory peculiarly hospitable to the inroads of the European powers, especially to those having stakes in the Near and Far East.

In the same manner as the southern waterways, the Caspian Sea on the north, a border sea, has invited the invader, Russia, to cross its smooth surface and to enter. Even the high northern mountain wall has proved no protection, for the western part of the area, that occupied by Persia and Afghanistan, is situated in the "narrowest waist" of Asia. This meant that an obstacle of less than one-third of the entire width of the continent, at this point, lay between Russia and her advance to the sea with its warm-water ports. Such a favorable geographic situation inspired Russia to scale the tremendous mountain barrier and to pursue her direct route to the Persian Gulf and the Indian Ocean. As early as the sixteenth century, Czar Ivan the Terrible blazed a trail towards these natural barriers for Russia's southern march, which the mighty mountain wall has since then entirely failed to block. Similarly, Alexander the Great in both his land and sea expeditions demonstrated to Europeans the accessibility of the Middle East and its excellent communications with the Near East.

The Middle East resembles the Near East not only in its geographical and strategic position, being part and parcel of the same transit area between East and West, but it is like the Near East in its political structure in that it was the seat of the great empires of the past. Here before the Christian era, the mighty empires of

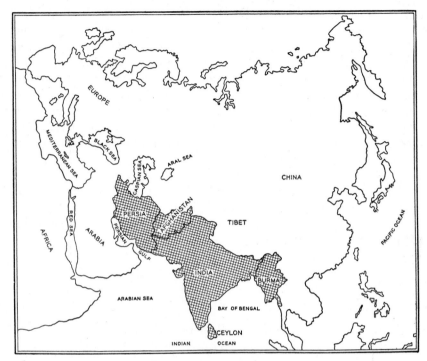

THE MIDDLE EAST, 1871

India and of Persia held their sway. Their age-old civilizations, world-renowned in political and economic organization, in art and in literature, flourished in this region, along with fundamental and enduring religious, philosophic systems and cultures, such as Zoroastrianism, Mohammedanism, Buddhism and Hinduism. Consequently, at the beginning of the modern period of expansion in the nineteenth century, Persia and India presented special obstacles to the expansionist powers, albeit they had by that time become mere ghosts of their past glory.

Yet, at their centers, these empires could not be dealt with as were the undeveloped peoples of Africa or of the South Sea Islands. Other and more skilful techniques involving economic, financial and commercial penetration had to be employed by their would-be invaders, to whom the weaknesses of their social and political structures afforded, as in the case of the Ottoman Empire, just so many avenues of approach. At the same time, these central units of the Middle East, India and Persia, were bordered by territories and provinces, such as Afghanistan, Baluchistan, the Punjab, Turkestan, Pamir and many others which were occupied by backward, sometimes savage, and undeveloped peoples, who were peculiarly subject to easy military aggression on the part of colonial powers. Hence, both methods of expansion, the indirect, penetrative system which we have so closely observed at work in the Near East, and the direct, territorial conquest were required and consequently employed by expansionists in the establishment of their control over this area.

As we turn now to examine in detail the two major units which occupy the area, Persia and India, it will be well to keep in mind the general, geographic, strategic and political concepts, here so briefly reviewed, of this irregular, triangular territory, the Middle East, as a whole.

PERSIA (IRAN, SINCE 1935)

Geography

At the beginning of the modern period of expansion in 1871, the kingdom of Persia proper occupied, as it does at present, about 628,000 square miles stretching from Asiatic Russia and the Caspian Sea on the north to the Persian Gulf and the Arabian Sea on the south; from Mesopotamia, now Iraq, on the west to Afghanistan and Baluchistan, now a province of British India, on the east. Over Turkestan, a district lying to the northwest, situated between Asiatic Russia, the Caspian Sea and Afghanistan, Persia exercised a vague control as she did, also, along certain areas on the Baluchistan frontier. One of the fastnesses of the Moslem world, the country was (and is today) remote and inaccessible, yet highly strategic, for it is situated on the highway that runs between Asia and Europe as well as on the route to Russia's southern outlets. To Russian eyes, it formed a pathway to India and warm-water ports; to British, a barrier between India and the advance of the Russian Bear.

Topography, Climate, Soil

Her topography, climate and the character of her soil explain Persia's remoteness. A tableland, whose altitude varies from 3,000 to more than 5,000 feet, surrounded and crossed by mountain ranges, composes most of the country; the remainder consists of a great depression sinking towards the west and the Persian Gulf. More than half the plateau is constituted of desert land and the rest is divided between almost treeless and uncultivable mountain ranges, wooded slopes around the Caspian Sea and a rich, arable plain in the northwest. The mountains act as storage reservoirs for the snows whose waters in the summer pour down through streams to the plains. In the depression towards the west, salt deserts abound, towards which run the small rivers of the plateau. Temperatures range from the heat of the dry Persian Gulf coast to the extreme cold of the mountain plateaus with an equable and delightful zone in the center. Rainfall is high on the Caspian coast, scanty along the Gulf of Persia, and the one navigable stream in the entire country, the Karun river, is in the southwest. Consequently, agriculture in the arable land is dependent upon irrigation and oasis farming, and such is the predominance of mountainous and arid soil that only about one-fifth of the land is under cultivation. Natural transport facilities have always been lacking and the nature of the terrain imposes great obstacles to road and railroad construction. In 1871, camels, mules and donkeys spent weeks on the road transporting goods to the ports on the Persian Gulf, the Caspian Sea, into Turkey to the Black Sea, or out through Bagdad on the Tigris River.

Resources

Nevertheless, Persia, despite her forbidding exterior, possesses a wealth of economic resource that was only beginning to be appreciated at the end of the nineteenth century. Even her disproportionate area of arable soil produced easily wheat, rice, barley, maize, tobacco, cotton and sugar, although, generally, her agriculture was underdeveloped owing to a lack of railways and the absence of a comprehensive program of improvement in irrigation and scientific method. Along the Caspian Sea, all kinds of fruits, vegetables, and rice grew in abundance; and the grapes, melons, plums, peaches and pears of the province of Azerbaijan were, as now, unsurpassed. Wool and silk culture had long flourished, supplying the hand looms which wove the world-famous rugs, carpets, shawls and tapestries of exquisite craftsmanship and design. Native industry also exploited the turquoise mines of Khorassan and the pearl fisheries of the Persian Gulf. But in industry, as in agriculture, the output was limited and actually shrinking in volume because of the increasing failure to gear it to the demands of modern economy.

Minerals

Persia's most valuable assets, from the viewpoint of expansionists, lay in her mineral wealth, which was practically untouched at the end of the nineteenth century. This included gold, iron, coal, copper, sulphur, mica, arsenic, and salt, but, above all, oil. For, aside from agriculture, oil is the chief undeveloped asset of the country. The oil belt lies about two hundred miles northeast of the Persian Gulf in the southwest section of the country. By 1909, it had become evident that the Persian field was one of the richest in the world and by 1940 Persia (Iran) was estimated as the third among oil-producing countries. Remote and barren, Persia was found to be a veritable treasure house of petroleum, perhaps the most desired commodity of the Western, industrialized world. Thus, already valued for its strategic and commercial position in the nineteenth century, it added its newly discovered economic wealth to the alluring invitation which it extended to the expansionist powers.

People

Another factor which increased Persia's attractiveness to alien invaders was the character of her population. Numbering about 12,000,000, her people reflected the remoteness and backwardness of the country and contributed to its disunion and vulnerability. Largely primitive, they were in 1871, and in 1940 for that matter, villagers and nomads with the nomadic group predominating. Poverty, lack of education and a national apathy have prevented their development as has also their backward and fanatical religion, for they are mostly Moslems of the Shia sect.[1] The true Persian or Iranian is Aryan by race and so differs from the many

[1] The Shia sect is a "factionist" group of Mohammedans who, unlike the Sunnis or "traditionalists," do not acknowledge the first three caliphs as do the majority of Moslems.

other near eastern peoples who are Semitic. Artistic, skilled in craftsmanship, highly intelligent and capable of great development, they are heirs to an ancient and celebrated culture which has successfully resisted assimilation by its many conquerors. Peoples of pure Iranian or Persian stock who speak the Persian language survive only in the eastern and central parts of the country; elsewhere a variety of ethnic groups occur. The northeastern section bordering on Russian Turkestan is the home of people of Turkish origin; along the Persian Gulf live Arabs and some of Negroid descent; the western provinces contain Kurds and Armenians. This mixture of peoples was brought about by Arab, Turkish and Mongol conquests to which the country was subjected from the tenth through the eighteenth centuries and has contributed materially to its weakness, disunion, backwardness and accessibility to foreign intervention.

Historical Background

In common with so many other countries of the Near and Middle East, Persia's status as a third-rate power in the nineteenth and twentieth centuries contrasted unfavorably with its once great imperial position in the ancient world. For the empire of Persia, the land of the Lion and the Sun, is one of the oldest and most famous monarchies of the world. The sixth and fifth centuries before Christ witnessed the period of its greatness under its conquering rulers, Darius and Cyrus. By 550 B.C., its domain extended from the Aegean Sea to the Oxus and Indus rivers and included all Asia Minor, Mesopotamia, Afghanistan and Egypt. A world empire, it was renowned not only for its power but for its political and economic organization as well as for its creative civilization. Darius' post road, for instance, was a transportation wonder of the times; Persian architecture, as exemplified in the ruins of Susa and Persepolis, Persian poetry and artistic achievement provide living proof of the country's vitality. The Persians were one of the few peoples who defied and defeated the Roman armies and, even though partially conquered, enjoyed a recrudescence under the Sassanian kings from the third to the seventh centuries. Then, like all transient lands, Persia fell a prey to the invaders, Arabs, Turks and Mongols (under Genghis Khan), many of whom remained and left their imprint upon the land.

Victim of conquest, of invasion, of numberless wars and struggles for its existence against enemies from without, Persia nevertheless maintained a continuous existence as a nation. It emerged, however, in the modern period a weak state, just when the nations of western Europe were rising upon their nationalistic, commercial and industrial strength, ready for fresh conquests overseas.

Political, Economic and Social Weaknesses

Persia was obliged to contend not only with attack from without; she suffered in addition from cruel, rapacious and corrupt rulers who, by the last quarter of the nineteenth century, had reduced her government almost to complete impotence.

The Kajar dynasty, which ruled Persia from the end of the eighteenth century to 1925 when it was overthrown by the nationalist movement under the leadership of Reza Khan, was no exception to its predecessors, who had plunged the country into anarchy, strife and bloodshed. Its founder, Agha Mohammed, had established his rule by usurpation and characterized it by cruelty, tyranny and repression. His successors did not equal him in these respects but neither did they exert themselves to resuscitate and improve conditions. Rather, they permitted the country to sink into an impoverished apathy while enriching themselves and the palace ring surrounding them by means of foreign loans and the ruthless exploitation of their country's resources and people. The Persian shahs ruled absolutely, exercising their power through ministers, often corrupt, incompetent and interested only in graft and personal gain. The National Council was merely advisory and was rarely consulted. Supporting the monarchy was an upper or aristocratic class mainly self-seeking and irresponsible; between them and the mass of illiterate, tax-ridden, poverty-stricken people, there intervened no strong, virile middle class to fight for popular rights. The priests or *mullahs* controlled education and exerted great influence over the masses. But they were fanatically backward, too conservative and jealous of their own privileged position to work for reform. Thus, social and economic stagnation combined with political impotence to render Persia peculiarly vulnerable to the expansionist ambitions of her strong and imperialistic neighbors.

AFGHANISTAN

Geography, Peoples, Resources

Even more remote than Persia, geographically, economically and socially in 1871, was Afghanistan. It lay, a broad wedge of territory, between Persia on the west, British India on the east and south, and Russia on the north. This "land of rocks, stones and sanguinary feuds" contains about 250,000 square miles of mountainous terrain whose general elevation rises about 4,000 feet; although on its northern frontiers, which are flanked by the Pamir and Hindu Kush mountains, this figure rises to from 14,000 to 25,000 feet. Afghanistan's area falls about 20,000 square miles short of that of the state of Texas but compensates vertically for what it lacks horizontally. Her inhabitants in 1871 numbered about 10,000,000, most of whom were Mohammedan warlike mountaineers, who through the centuries have made continuous forays and invasions into Persia on the west and into India on the east.

The country was, and remains, chiefly agricultural. Wool, skins and a profusion of fruits, such as pomegranates, figs, mulberries, quinces, apricots and peaches, form its chief products. Some copper, lead and iron are found in the country. There are no railroads and merchandise is transported by camel and pony along the seven important trade routes.

The attraction of Afghanistan for its expansionist neighbors, Russia and Britain, did not reside in its inherent qualities but in its strategic position: as a transit area for trade and communication; a buffer state for the protection of India; a direct route for Russia to India and to an outlet on the Arabian Sea. Its inherent qualities, however, such as its backwardness and its remoteness, rendered it easy prey to invasion and alien control; even its high mountain barriers failed to succeed in protecting it.

From the foregoing description, it will now be clear that this section of the Middle East, Persia and Afghanistan, presented an especially desirable field for expansion to its two neighbors, Russia and Great Britain. That they were not slow to respond to the invitation lying so close to their very doors, the following account will disclose: first, by presenting the contemporary interests of Britain and the U.S.S.R. in these regions, which interests will be

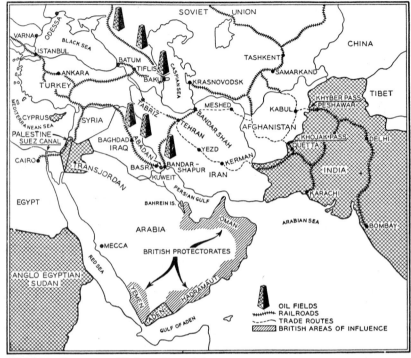

Adapted from the newspaper PM, Inc., with permission

BRITISH INTERESTS IN THE MIDDLE EAST, 1940

found to have shrunk almost to nothing compared with what they were in 1907-1921; and then by relating how these interests were achieved and then lost.

PRESENT-DAY EXPANSIONIST INTERESTS OF GREAT BRITAIN AND THE U.S.S.R. IN IRAN (PERSIA) AND AFGHANISTAN

In 1940, both Iran and Afghanistan were independent states. Since asserting their independence in 1921 they succeeded in freeing themselves in a truly remarkable manner from the shackles of Russian and British imperial control by which they were bound as almost helpless victims from 1907-1921. Whatever traces remained, therefore, of British and Russian expansionist interests in these two states represented but pale shadows of the economic

and political subjugation which once enveloped them so completely.

British Interests in Iran

British interests in Iran consisted in 1940 of certain rights to exploit petroleum and a flourishing export and import trade, especially in the south around the Persian Gulf. The agreement of
1933 which the Iranian government concluded with the Anglo-
Persian, later the Anglo-Iranian Oil Company, defined in exact
terms the Company's concessions in Iranian oil. It represented,
indeed, a distinct triumph of Iranian nationalism for it succeeded
in greatly curtailing British privileges in extracting the nation's
most valuable product, although the oil company still was controlled by the British government. In 1931, Iran began to attack the British monopoly represented by the Anglo-Persian Oil
Company, whose far-reaching concession dated back to 1901, and
subordinated it to ultimate, if not immediate, national control.
For the 1933 agreement conceded the three chief demands of the
Iranian government: first, it cut the area of the original concession
to exploit 500,000 square miles of Persia (four-fifths of the country) down to 200,000, with the proviso that this would be limited
after 1938 to 100,000 square miles and that Iran would have a free
hand in the granting of further concessions; second, it increased
Britain's obligation to employ and train Iranians in the extraction
of oil, so that all workmen and, as far as possible, all engineers
should be Iranian and the company should pay £10,000 a year
for training young Iranians in England; and finally, the securing
of increased royalties for the Iranian government by changing
the system from a share in the net profits to a specific rate per ton
of oil, with the proviso that it never fall below a certain amount
(£750,000) a year, which had the effect of raising Iran's income
from the company to over £2,000,000 in 1934 as against £306,-
872 in 1931. It was further agreed that after sixty years all the
company's property would revert to Iran. By 1940 Britain drew
about one-quarter of her oil supply (24.6 per cent) from the fields
of the Near East, Iran and Iraq, and the larger amount from Iran
which, in 1938, supplied 20.2 per cent of this total.
British trade in Iran continued in spite of the curtailment of
many former monopolies and privileges. Britain continued to be

Iran's best customer although of late years German economic influence grew rapidly. In 1937-1939 British commercial interests exceeded those of any other country, and amounted to 49 per cent of the total trade of the country inclusive of oil exports.

Soviet Russia's Interests in Iran

While Britain was forced to relinquish most of her imperialist grip upon Iran through the latter's self-reliant activity in recovering the elements of lost sovereignty, Soviet Russia renounced at one stroke all expansionist interests held by czarist Russia in Persia by signing in 1921 the Russo-Persian Treaty. Pursuant to its professed belief in anti-imperialism, the Soviet government condemned, in the first articles of the treaty, the entire Asiatic policy of its predecessor and proclaimed "all treaties, conventions, and agreements concluded by the late czarist government with Persia and tending to the diminution of the rights of the Persian people null and void." Thus the new Iran received as a birthday present from her northern neighbor all rights to loans granted by the old Russia to Persia as well as to customs and other revenues which had been mortgaged to secure such loans; and all Russian property in Persia—the Bank of Loans, the railway from Julfa to Tabriz, the roads built by Russia, the navigation properties on Lake Urumiah, the Russian telegraph and telephone lines, the port of Enzeli with all its goods and power station.

In addition, all private concessions which had been granted to Russian subjects were cancelled, with the one exception of the Caspian Sea fisheries; and all capitulation privileges were surrendered by the Moscow government. In short, the new Russia surrendered to the new Persia practically everything which the old Russian government had claimed within the old Persia. The one great exception was the tariff. The treaty of 1921 had provided that the old tariff which dated from 1903 and was highly preferential to Russia should continue, pending a new agreement. Finally, after several efforts to establish trade co-operation with the Soviet government, a trade agreement was signed in 1931 on terms which were decidedly advantageous to the U.S.S.R. Therefore, exclusive of the oil exports to Britain, Soviet Russia became Iran's principal customer, which gave her a growing economic grip upon the country.

Together with her trade, the Soviet's principal interest in Iran today is ideological. Russian agents are numerous throughout the country and propaganda is rife. It is also claimed that Russian money finances groups opposed to the present national government.

British and Russian Interests in Afghanistan

In Afghanistan, Britain controls at present no important special interests. They consist, at most, of British restrictions upon Russian special privileges in the country, of the guarantee against the shipment of arms and munitions to India and of the mutual free exchange of goods without the payment of customs duties. As for the interests of the U.S.S.R., they too amount to little since the former pressure of the czarist regime upon Afghanistan has likewise been removed. Indeed, opposition to the Western powers has been even more vigorous here in this remote country than in Iran, an opposition about which we shall hear more in a later chapter.

How Russian and British Expansion in Persia
and Afghanistan Was Achieved

The startling contrast between the limited interests of Britain and Russia in contemporary Iran and Afghanistan and their former economic and political grip upon them can only be appreciated by an analysis of the Anglo-Russian domination over these states, which reached its climax in the years 1907-1921, and by an account of how it was achieved.

Russian Expansion into Persia. The Russo-Persian Treaty of 1921, just previously mentioned, represented a complete reversal of the imperialist policy of czarist Russia towards its neighbor, Persia, as well as a renunciation of what it had been engaged in securing to the detriment of that country over a period of three hundred years, with the exception of its territorial aggressions and some aspects of its commercial control.

The most active and fruitful period of Russia's penetration and exploitation of Persia itself took place during the modern period of expansion, since 1871; but her approaches to the country and her strategic position thereby gained for further depredations were secured throughout the previous two hundred and fifty years, the achievements of which must be briefly considered as a prelude. Peter the Great and Catherine the Great pushed the frontiers of Russia to the south into that region lying between the Caspian and the Black seas, which included the old kingdom of Georgia, the mountain districts of the Caucasus range and the Caspian Sea provinces. All this territory had long been debatable ground among Russia, Turkey and Persia and subject to the attacks and intrigues of the rulers of all these three states. Consequently, it became the scene of Peter's and Catherine's campaigns, conquests and reconquests as well as of counterattacks from the Persian shahs. Finally, at the close of the eighteenth century, Catherine succeeded in occupying the Caspian provinces and only her death in 1796 saved Persia from further losses then.

But in 1801, the kingdom of Georgia was incorporated into the Russian Empire by the abdication of its king in favor of Alexander I of Russia; in 1813, Persia was obliged to cede the area north of the Caucasus Mountains lying between them and the Caspian Sea, including the ports of Derbent and Baku, and in 1828, the provinces south of the Caucasus which, during the next quarter century, were colonized and Russianized and finally incorporated into the Russian Empire in 1864 as Transcaucasia. The middle of the nineteenth century, therefore, found Russia well established on Persia's northwestern boundary, a position which was further strengthened by her acquisition of the neighboring Turkish provinces of Kars, Batum and Ardahan, which were accorded to her by the Treaty of Berlin in 1878.

Meanwhile, Russian advance on the northeastern border of Persia to the east of the Caspian Sea had not only kept pace with that on the west and northwest but had antedated it and far outdone it in scope and conquest. This push into the "heart of Asia" can be traced to the conquests of Czar Ivan the Terrible who, in the sixteenth century, conquered Kazan and Astrakhan, huge districts in central Asia, lying between the Chinese Empire and the Caspian Sea. During the two succeeding centuries, Russia's southern and eastern march into Asia continued, for, while the western European nations were expanding across the Atlantic Ocean and into the new world, Russia's "course of empire" eastward and southward took "its sway." Advancing by way of the Ural River, along the shores of the Caspian Sea and from the Russian eastern outpost at Omsk, expeditions penetrated the great Kirghiz steppe, an arid plateau situated north of Turkestan, which borders directly upon Persia. By the end of the eighteenth century, an irregular frontier extending approximately 1200 miles across the Kirghiz steppe had been established. Along this stretch Russia built forts and established trading posts but found it impossible to stabilize the border. Hence, further conquest was demanded.

As answer, Russia's "big push" into central southern Asia began in the 1830's and continued without intermission for the next fifty years. Slowly but steadily and thoroughly, the Russian advance proceeded: first, Khiva and Bokhara were gained, then the sea of Aral, next the outposts of Tashkent and Samarkand. By 1873 the czars had annexed all this territory down to the Oxus River, so that the beginning of the period of modern expansion found Russia solidly ensconced territorially upon Persia's northeastern approaches as she was upon her northwestern border in the Caucasus.

Russia's Territorial Advance During the Modern Period Since 1873. After pushing her boundary down to the Oxus River in 1873, all that remained between the Russian Empire in central Asia and Persia proper was the province of Turkestan, over which Persia exerted her undefined control. Inhabited mainly by half-civilized people who, with the exception of the Turkomans, were completely untrained in war and defense, they presented an easy prey. Moreover, constant quarreling among rival chieftains within and the maraudings of tribesmen without, who continually preyed upon Russian commerce, invited conquest. Russia entrusted the campaign to General Skobeleff, who brought it to a triumphant conclusion in 1881, inflicting upon Persia thereby considerable loss of territory and prestige. The Russo-Persian Boundary Convention of 1881 assigned to Russia all the northeastern rim of the Iranian plateau north of the river Atrek and thus gave her access to the great mountain frontier of Persia.

Instead of proving an obstacle to Russian territorial advance, the mountain barrier challenged further effort, for beyond it lay the road to India and the pathway to a warm-water port on the Persian Gulf. General Komarov replaced General Skobeleff and Russia pressed on despite a protest from the British foreign office, which was becoming extremely alarmed at the march of the Russian Bear. For if Russia once crossed the mountain barrier of

Afghanistan, the unobstructed way lay open to India. Already, to forestall the Russian advance, Britain had taken several important steps: in 1873, an Anglo-Russian understanding had been reached regarding the boundary between Bokhara, which Russia had conquered, and Afghanistan; in 1878-1881, British troops had been sent into Afghanistan and a puppet prince, in British pay and under British control, as far as foreign policy was concerned, had been placed upon the country's throne.

None of Britain's precautions delayed the Russians, however. Taking advantage of Britain's troubles in the Sudan during the early 1880's, they occupied the famous town of Merv and other strategic centers within striking distance of the Afghan frontier in 1884, and gained possession of a mountain pass through which they poured on their way to Herat, the capital of Afghanistan. Britain, regarding this as an abrogation of the boundary agreement of 1873, sprang into action: Queen Victoria appealed personally to the Czar Alexander III to restrain the Russian aggression, and British troops dispatched by the government of India rushed to the defense of the Afghans. The "race for Herat" was on, but diplomacy won the day. A boundary commission, composed of British and Russian diplomats, met in St. Petersburg and produced the Russo-Afghan Boundary Convention of 1887, which fixed the northwest frontier line of Afghanistan from the Persian border to the Bokhara line. North of this Russia was permitted to keep her gains, and the decision gave her access to the principal passes and trade routes into northern Afghanistan. Her advantage thus secured was mainly owing to Britain's absorption in Africa and to Gladstone's unwillingness to fight.

But Russia's "appeasement" at Britain's hands in 1887 had the effect of inciting her to further effort to pierce the mountain barrier between her and India in 1891. This time her advance was bold in the extreme, for she struck at the Pamir plateau, in the extreme northeast of Afghanistan. This is a mountain region north of the Hindu Kush range, which rises to an altitude of 14,000 to 25,000 feet, and is known as the "roof of the world." The Pamirs lie directly opposite Chitral in northern India, only separated by a narrow strip of Afghanistan. Russia's attack was resisted by the Afghans, to whom Britain dispatched aid, and another boundary line was adjusted between Russian and Afghan territory and Russian and British spheres by the Anglo-Russian Convention of 1895. This agreement, the fourth in a long series between Russia and Persia (1881), and Russia and Britain (1873, 1887, 1895), marked the termination of the territorial encroachment of the Russian empire upon Persia and Afghanistan. As far as actual territorial aggrandizement was concerned, Russia now transferred her activities further eastward to central Asia, to Tibet and even to the Far East in order to obtain her long-desired objectives.

Russian Economic Penetration. But territorial encroachment was not the only method by which Russia was able to fulfil her expansionist ambitions in Persia which, during the modern period, aimed actually at incorporating this helpless state into her empire by the use of every available economic and political means. Hence, after the beginning of the twentieth century, she applied herself to the perfecting of her commercial penetration of the country which already was well under way by 1871. Such was the remoteness, the backwardness and the impotence of Persia, added to her lack of interest for any other European power except Great Britain, that Russia was able to exercise a free hand of ruthless aggression and exploitation. By 1907, northern Persia was completely within her control.

Commercial Penetration. The excellent strategic position obtained by depriving Persia of her northern provinces and establishing herself in the Caucasus on the west and in Turkestan on the east, just reviewed, afforded Russia an unequaled opportunity to dominate the trade of northern Persia, a domination begun 250 years before, when, in 1618, Russian merchants first secured the right to trade in Persia. By the opening of the twentieth century, she had about completed this process. The building of the Caucasus and Trans-Caspian railroads during the last quarter of the nineteenth century had brought the terminus of one Russian railroad just across the border of Persia's province of Azerbaijan in the west; of another, to the very edge of the province of Khorassan in the east; and, in the middle of the northern border, the control of the Caspian ports gave Russia access to the rich territory lying between the Elburz Mountains and the sea. For here, too, she had long been powerful: in 1735 her merchant ships won the right to navigate along the Persian shore, her merchants to build warehouses; and in 1818 her warships secured the exclusive privilege of operating in the Caspian Sea, "no other power to have a military flag" there.

Indeed, about three-quarters of the exportable products of

Persia had no other market than Russia because of her peculiar geographical situation, her remoteness and lack of transportation. Hence, sturgeon from the Caspian, timber from the forests, cotton, wool, carpets, silks, dried fruits, all poured into Russia on Russian terms. By 1897 it was estimated that the value of Russian trade with Persia amounted to £3,500,000 and by 1907 it had increased to £8,250,000—a gain of 137 per cent in one decade.

As early as 1828, after the war over the Caucasus, a reciprocal *ad valorem* tariff on imports and exports was established, and since no term for this agreement was stated, Persia was powerless to alter any tariff rate affecting Russia without the consent of the Russian government. Hence all such arrangements favored Russian interests to the loss and detriment of Persia. For example, in 1901 the shah, requiring a loan, negotiated a revision of the Russian tariff with the result that export duties, payable by Russia, were largely eliminated and low rates were placed on all commodities going to Russia. In comparison with British tariff rates of the same time, goods to Russia carried an average tax of 4.75 per cent, those to Britain of 26.77 per cent. Morgan Shuster, the American financial expert, who was summoned by the Persian cabinet in 1911 in order to bring some system into the archaic and anarchic Persian treasury, stated that the above tariff "[is] absolutely prejudicial to the interests of Persia, and is so grossly partial to Russian interests and trade as to render it the most conspicuously unsuccessful tariff in the world, from the viewpoint of the people in whose behalf it is supposed to be framed." [2]

Loans, also, as always, were employed by Russia to weaken Persia financially and to reduce the shah to the position of a mere puppet of the Russian government. The Bank of Loans (*Banque des Prêts de Perse*) was set up in 1889 as a rival to the Imperial Bank of Persia established by Baron Julius de Reuter, a British financier, to lend money to the shah and to finance the extraction of minerals. Russia and Britain thenceforth vied with each other in encouraging spendthrift and reckless shahs to borrow money at exorbitant rates of interest, not only as a means of winning concessions, monopolies, mining and railway rights and effecting an economic grip upon the country, but also of establishing political control. Russian imperial loans to Persia before the first World

---

[2] Shuster, W. M., *The Strangling of Persia*, pp. 313-314.

War amounted to nearly £5,000,000. (It was these loans which were cancelled by the Russo-Persian Treaty of 1921.) In return for them, Russia and her nationals gained all kinds of concessions and monopolies and, hence, economic and political power. These included: the right to construct a railway from the Russian border to Teheran, the Persian capital; the exclusive permission to prospect for oil and coal and other minerals in certain districts; and the monopoly to develop the sturgeon fisheries on the Caspian Sea. This last was granted to a Russian, Stepan Lionsosoff, in 1876 and renewed many times. The business of producing caviar developed so profitably that it came to occupy more than ten establishments on the Caspian coast. With its warehouses, docks, refrigerators and power houses, it expanded into an enterprise which would have done credit to any industrial city.

By the opening of the twentieth century, therefore, Russian economic penetration of northern Persia was nearly achieved; military and political domination, which had proceeded simultaneously with it, remained to be perfected. From the control of trade, customs, finances, justice and sometimes even revenues of northern Persia, it was but a step to complete subordination of the entire government, especially as the weakness and degeneration of the shahs and the utter corruption of their rule so greatly facilitated the process. But as this subjugation was achieved in the year 1907 in conjunction with Great Britain, it will assist in keeping the records clear to turn first to an account of this second great power's economic penetration and exploitation of Persia during the same period, before 1907, which we have just traced with regard to Russia.

British Colonial Stakes in Persia and Afghanistan Until 1907. In contradistinction to the Russian objective, which was to destroy Persia and Afghanistan and incorporate them into her empire, Britain's purpose was to preserve them for their strategic value. To develop and bolster them up as buffer states between India and Russia seemed to British statesmen the only way of making them serve as effective obstacles to the southern march of the Russian Bear. Thus, in 1889, Lord Salisbury said at a dinner in honor of the then reigning shah, Nasir-Din: "We desire above all things that Persia shall not only be prosperous but be strong, in order that she may pursue the peaceful path upon which she has entered in security and tranquility."

Unfortunately for Britain's objective, however, her policy was not pursued with the same continuity, relentlessness and consistency as that of Russia, especially at the end of the nineteenth and the beginning of the twentieth centuries when acute imperial problems, such as those in Africa and in the Far East, were engaging her attention elsewhere. Nevertheless, during the first three decades of the modern period of expansion, 1871-1901, Britain's dominance in southern Persia and Afghanistan became considerable, thanks to the activities of her merchants, consular agents and diplomats. These, in turn, were assisted by the government of India, whose viceroys, like Lord Curzon, so thoroughly appreciated the Russian menace to the north. Let us, therefore, learn how this commanding position of Great Britain in these regions came to be constructed.

British Commercial and Economic Penetration of Persia. British interests in Persia do not extend so far back as do those of Russia—about two hundred instead of three hundred years. It was in the middle of the eighteenth century that British merchants succeeded in establishing trading posts and factories along the shores of the Persian Gulf at Just and Bushire, and, in 1763, obtained special privileges for British traders from the shah. Since the time of Queen Elizabeth such connections had been sought in Persia but they had been rejected by the shahs or blocked by Russia. At first purely commercial, British interests soon became also strategic and diplomatic. For Napoleon I awakened realization of the importance of Persia as India's first line of defense by sending an envoy to the shah to arrange for passage of a French army across the country, so intent was he upon striking at Britain through India. To counter any such move, the government of India signed a treaty with the Sultan of Oman on the Persian Gulf whereby he promised to deny the French access to his territory and his ports, and also permitted the British to construct a fort and factory at Bandar-Abbas.

The growth of commerce thus facilitated by the acquisition of these posts in southern Persia as well as the ensuing increase of the caravan trade into India emphasized the importance of the whole area as it affected communication with and transportation into the Indian Empire. As a result, the British erected an extensive system of telegraph lines and stations throughout Persia connecting with the cable laid down in the Persian Gulf. By

1864, the central system had been completed and, since the plan had been executed with the full consent and co-operation of the shah, British telegraph officials were scattered with his permission throughout his country.

During the modern period of expansion after 1871, the growth of British economic hegemony in southern Persia almost matched that of Russia in the north. Shah Nasir-Din, bankrupt but fond of European travel and luxuries, was most generous with concessions of all kinds: the Karun River, Persia's one navigable stream, was opened to foreign trade which further favored British commerce; in 1889 an exclusive banknote concession was granted the British financier, Baron Julius de Reuter, which was followed by the right to open the First Imperial Bank of Persia under a British charter; mining rights were also conceded to de Reuter, who began to assume an influential position as financial adviser to the shah in extending loans. Perhaps the greatest commercial concession of all was the monopoly of the Persian tobacco trade gained by a British company in 1890, only one-fourth of whose profits was to accrue to the Persian government.

In 1901, British economic control was further consolidated by the extension of the telegraph system across Persia, stretching from Kashan and Yodz in the center of the country, to Karachi in India; and by the granting to William Knox D'Arcy, an Australian capitalist, of the exclusive right to exploit petroleum, natural gas and asphalt deposits from 500,000 square miles, which covered all but the five northern provinces of the country, in return for which he paid only £4,000 plus a moderate royalty. These concessions developed into the formation of the Anglo-Indian Telegraph Company and the organization of the Anglo-Persian Oil Company, both of which came to exert a strong economic grip upon Persia. The operations of the oil company revealed that barren Persia was, in reality, a treasure house of oil, a discovery that resulted in the British government's acquiring a controlling interest in the company by 1914.

British Interests in Afghanistan. In Afghanistan, also, the British had acquired a dominant position by the beginning of the twentieth century. But there again, unlike the Russians, their objective was to preserve rather than to destroy and they had no desire for territorial aggression. Before 1871, their first care had been to protect this mountainous and remote state from Persian invasion and to this end they had fought the first Afghan war, 1838-1842. By interfering in civil conflict between rival claimants for the throne, they succeeded in placing the country under British protection, providing the amir with an annual subsidy and otherwise assisting him to withstand Persia. Finally, in 1857, an Anglo-Persian Treaty secured the renunciation of Persian claims to Afghanistan and recognition of its independence, after which the country was left largely to its own devices and, under Gladstone, British vigilance was relaxed.

Britain's failure to guard her interests in Afghanistan afforded Russia her opportunity to penetrate the country and with the beginning of the modern period of expansion, after 1871, Afghanistan replaced Persia as a more serious threat to India's security. Spurred to vigorous action in order to displace Russian dominance, the British embarked upon the second Afghan war, 1878-1880. Lord Roberts' campaign therein finally succeeded in restoring British prestige and in placing a new ruler upon the throne, who set about reorganizing the country under British direction. During the next decade, 1880-1890, as previously related, the British ably assisted the Afghans in repelling the Russian invasion from Herat and the north and in fixing the frontier. By 1893, a treaty of alliance was signed which guaranteed British dominance in Afghanistan: it raised the amir's annual subsidy paid by Britain to $600,000, promised him assistance against external attack and adjusted the boundary between his country and India. Thus Afghanistan, as far as its foreign policy was concerned, became a vassal state of Britain.

Russia and Great Britain Unite to Partition Persia and Afghanistan. It will be clear from the foregoing account that by the opening of the twentieth century, Persia and Afghanistan had been so penetrated by Russian and British economic, territorial and political encroachments as to be ripe for almost complete domination. This was finally achieved between the years 1907-1914 by signing of the Anglo-Russian Convention (1907) and by the action of the Persian shah, who openly placed himself under the protection of Russia and allowed himself to be aided and abetted against his own people by both Russia and Great Britain. The Anglo-Russian Convention was one of the most famous colonial deals of the modern period and will be discussed later in its diplomatic connections, as will also the constitutional revolt

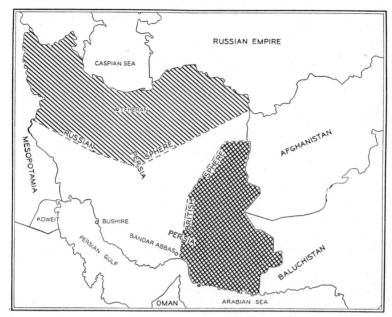

THE ANGLO-RUSSIAN CONVENTION OF 1907, AS IT AFFECTED PERSIA

of the Persian people in its relation to the Persian nationalist movement. But here, let us first concentrate upon the surrender of the Persian government to the expansionist powers.

The way was well prepared for such a surrender by the assassination of the shah, Nasir-Din, in 1896. His long hospitality to British and Russian interests, reckless borrowing and unscrupulous rule had completely undermined the state and brought it to the verge of bankruptcy with the result that his subjects finally became aroused against him. His violent removal accelerated the movement towards constitutional reform, already under way, and enabled the Persian people to wrest a constitution establishing a national assembly, or Medjliss, from his timid successor, who lived only a year. The latter's son, Mehemet Ali, who succeeded him, has been described by Morgan Shuster as "perhaps the most perverted, cowardly, and vice-sodden monster that had disgraced the throne of Persia in many generations." Apparently, he hated and despised his subjects and "became the avowed tool and satrap of the Russian government and its agent in Persia for stamping out the rights of the people." He refused to recognize the Medjliss, recalled the infamous Atabak, who had been exiled to Russia in 1903 for his dishonest participation in Russian loans, and authorized the formation of a Cossack brigade, composed of Russians and Persians under a Russian officer, for his protection.

It was in this turbulent state of civil war between the National Assembly and the Russian-protected shah that the Anglo-Russian Convention was signed in 1907. Taking advantage of Persia's difficulties and the suppression of its people, Britain and Russia closed in upon the helpless country as part of their plan to settle their differences in the Middle East and Central Asia. The agreement, despite its guarantee of the independence and integrity of Persia, systematically partitioned the country. It awarded northern Persia, comprising about one-half of the total area of the state, to Russia as her zone of exploitation, where Britain would seek no concession nor oppose any sought by Russia; it assigned southeastern Persia, amounting to about one-fifth of her territory, to Britain, where Russia would abstain from interference; and it fixed between the two a neutral zone open both to Russia and to Britain. Without any consultation with the Persian people, the Persian Cat, to cite *Punch's* cartoon of the agreement, was literally torn between the Russian Bear and the British Lion. Persia's absorption by her expansionist neighbors was well-nigh complete.

The Persian people, however, did not surrender without a struggle. The effect of the Anglo-Russian Convention was to spur them on to stern resistance, though this proved ineffective in the end, for the Convention enabled both Russia and Britain to intervene on the side of reaction. In the civil war which ensued between Mehemet Ali and his supporters and the Medjliss, Russian, British and British-Indian troops invaded Persia and helped escort the despised shah into Russian exile when deposed by the victorious nationalists. The two imperial governments then concentrated upon destroying the new shah and his regime set up by the restored Medjliss. They blocked its attempts to obtain help and money from other European powers and all its efforts for the reform and stabilization of Persia. In 1911, when the Persian government succeeded in obtaining the assistance of Morgan Shuster, an American, to reform and straighten out its tangled finances by appointing him Treasurer-General for a term of three years, Russia sent back Mehemet Ali and instigated a counter revolution. But this reactionary move again met defeat at the hands of the Persian nationalists, although Britain and Russia employed every intrigue to further its success.

Finally, however, realizing that the Shuster regime in Persia was under agreement not to recognize the foreign spheres of influence there, Russia decided to act directly. Her troops invaded the country and her government issued an ultimatum which demanded the removal of Morgan Shuster, an assurance that Persia would appoint no foreign experts to official positions without the consent of her two controllers, Russia and Britain, and the payment of an indemnity to meet the expenses of the Russian invasion. Britain's attitude throughout had been complete support of Russia and she urged Persia to yield. In December, 1911, the helpless state accepted the ultimatum in all its essential points and thus signed her own death warrant.

During the years 1911-1914, Persia fell more and more under the encroachments of her expansionist neighbors. In 1913, Russia gained the concession for the proposed Julfa-Tabriz-Teheran railway, and Britain for the construction of the railway from Mohammerah to Ispahan, neither of which, however, was ever built. Russian troops and colonists penetrated north Persia so that it became politically and economically a Russian province where even taxes were not paid to the legitimate government, while disorder in the British zone permitted further foreign aggression there. The weak and humiliated Persian government became again completely subservient. It was even obliged to promise that all moneys secured by loans would be expended only in agreement with Russia and Britain and that the country's rule would be in accord with the Anglo-Russian Convention. Upon the outbreak of the first World War in 1914, the complete dissolution of Persia and the annexation of its northern half by Russia appeared imminent.

British Dominance Replaces Russian in Persia, 1914-1921. The first World War, however, turned the tables in favor of British and not Russian dominance in Persia. The collapse of the old Russia and the Soviet revolution in 1917 enabled Britain to fall heir to northern Persia held as a Russian sphere of interest since 1907, an inheritance which Britain did not hesitate to claim. In 1916, a British-Indian army under Sir Percy Sykes had occupied and controlled southern Persia and then, together with a British force in the west, had conquered the invading Turks. Thus entrenched, Sir Percy Sykes entered Teheran, the capital, in 1917 and "accepted" from the shah the task of "restoring order" in Persia.

The result of Russia's collapse and Britain's military effort was the signing of the Anglo-Persian Treaty of 1919 which Britain imposed upon a supine, war-weary and pro-British Persian government. It represented the consummation of British expansionist efforts in Persia which had endured for over two hundred years. Among other restrictions, it arranged that British advisers were to be appointed to the important government departments, British officers were to train the Persian army, British capital was to build the railroads and other means of communication; Great Britain was to exert a controlling influence in revising the Persian tariff, and was to grant a loan in order to finance all reforms. At that time (1919) British interests in Persia already amounted to an economic hegemony. They included: a prosperous trade in the Persian Gulf and across the borders of Iraq, control of the Imperial Bank, the Ottoman Bank, the Indo-European Telegraph Company, the Anglo-Persian Oil Company and a number of minor interests. This economic dominance, supported, as it was, by the regime of capitulations and coupled finally with the strictures of the treaty of 1919, would have reduced Persia to the position of British monopolistic protectorate.

As it happened, Britain was not destined to realize her imperialistic triumph over Russia in Persia; Persian nationalism, whose rise will be recounted in a later chapter, snatched it from her. One of the first acts of the new and revolutionary government of Iran, set up in 1921 under Reza Khan, was to repudiate the humiliating Anglo-Persian Treaty of 1919 and thus to forestall the establishment of British political domination over the country. Following his bold stroke, the new leader directed his attention, during the ensuing decade, towards cancelling or curtailing all those privileges and concessions upon which rested Britain's economic grip with the result that, as previously described, her expansionist interests in Iran were reduced to the minimum.

In Afghanistan, likewise, Britain was obliged to withdraw before the force of nationalism. Encouraged by the collapse of czarist Russia and the nationalistic revolts of Turkey and Persia, the new ruler, Amir Amanullah Khan, declared in 1919 that "the government of Afghanistan should be internally and externally independent and free." Then, to implement his declaration and release his country from British control over its foreign policy and domestic affairs, which had been so firmly imposed upon it, he launched an attack upon British India. Defeated within a month by British-Indian troops, he retired but obtained as the price of future peace on the Indian border the recognition of Afghanistan as free and independent both internally and externally. A subsequent treaty with Great Britain signed in 1922 granted complete independence.

Thus there collapsed, within the short space of a decade, the very considerable structure of British colonial interests in Persia and Afghanistan, which had taken all of two hundred and fifty years to put together.

INDIA

By far the largest and most important section of the Middle East is the peninsula of India. Sub-continental in size and completely enclosed by high mountains on the north and enveloping seas on two sides, it forms a geographical unit by itself. Easily accessible externally because of its surrounding seas, the country is inaccessible and self-contained internally, for most of its rivers are navigable only on their lower reaches and its coasts lack bays and indentations. Ordinary maps fail to convey India's size in relation to other countries, but some idea of its vast area of more than a million and a half square miles may be obtained by superimposing it upon a map of the United States. Place India's northernmost boundary province, Kashmir, upon the Canadian border of North Dakota, and Cape Cormorin, the tip of her peninsula, would reach to Vera Cruz in Mexico; and the city of Karachi, in the western province of Sind, would coincide approximately with Salt Lake City, and Calcutta in eastern Bengal with New York. Thus the Indian peninsula extends north and south from the highest Himalayas to the Indian Ocean about 2,000 miles, and east and west about 2,500 miles.

Such a range of territory presents a wide variety of geographic and climatic characteristics which are startling in their contrast: the highest mountains in the world with their regions of eternal

snows, as yet hardly touched by man's encroachment, where
Mount Everest rises to 29,141 feet and the low fertile plains of the
three great river systems, the Ganges, the Indus and the Bramah-
putra with their torrid heat and teeming life; the scanty, annual
rainfall, at most three inches, on the scorching sands of a wide
desert area, and the torrential rains of Assam which fall to a depth
of forty feet per year; the rich and varied flora, exquisite in its
rare beauty, of the lofty plateaus like the vale of Kashmir; and the
dusty aridity of the treeless plains. The country lies about half in
the torrid and half in the north temperate zone, the climate being
generally tropical.

Resources

India is fundamentally agricultural and its hot, moist climate
produces a luxuriant and lush vegetation. Particularly is this true
of the rich alluvial plains of its river basins and of some sections
along the coast. Much of its soil is infertile, however, owing to
lack of moisture and to its geological age which, in relation to its
teeming millions, creates a serious population pressure for food.
About one-half of its total area is arable although only about one-
third is good soil. This land has always produced a variety of
crops—rice, sugar cane, wheat, jute, cotton, flax, indigo, wool,
leather—and possesses great potentiality through irrigation for the
cultivation of tea, coffee, rubber, opium, silk and tobacco, which
has been developed by European enterprise. Approximately 20
per cent of the area is forested and yields such valuable timber as
teakwood, sandalwood, satinwood and acacia.

With a range and variety of minerals, India is also well provided. Famous for its riches even before the days of Marco Polo,
it supplied gold, silver, diamonds and rubies to the Western world.
During the nineteenth century other products, also, began to be
discovered: petroleum, coal, lead, iron, tungsten, manganese, tin,
mica, copper and zinc, a long and valuable list of commodities
whose exploitation has, for the most part, been left to Europeans.

Industry

India's industry, until developed by the West, was primitive and
entirely in the hand-tool stage although possessed of exquisite

craftsmanship and beauty of artistry. The spinning wheel and the pit loom matched the simple agricultural equipment of sickle and plow, yet they produced textiles of gossamer fineness in the famous Indian muslins, which came to be known throughout the world; and the ancient potter's wheel and the smithy turned out artistic ceramics and ornamental metal work of rare quality.

Since most goods were fashioned and consumed within the same village, there was little internal trade in the old India. Means of communication were conspicuously lacking, even roadways. There were no railways in India until after the middle of the nineteenth century and but eighty-two miles of telegraph line as late as 1852. India was organized on a rural economy of a backward type; only a few cities of political, religious or commercial importance constituted any exception to her primitive pattern, even in the middle of the nineteenth century. This afforded a situation for the opening up of an almost illimitable market by an enterprising industrial power.

The People

In keeping with the country's tropical character and geographic differences, its people were and continue today to be numerous, diverse and varied in the extreme. Numbering over 300,000,000 in 1871 (now rapidly approaching 400,000,000), they constituted approximately one-fifth of the human race, and presented a galaxy of races, religions, languages, cultural and social levels, unmatched in any other country. There exist three chief original stocks: the dominant Indo-Aryan, of which the Rajputs represent the purest strain, living for the most part in the lowland belt or central India; the dark-skinned, often coal-black, Dravidians, probably the aborigines, who dwelt in the so-called Deccan or southern plateau; and the Mongols in Burma. Besides, there were the descendants of Afghan, Persian and Arab invaders, together with the various blendings of these with the indigenous peoples. As a consequence, variety of language outdid variety of race and India was, as now, a veritable Tower of Babel. About 265 vernacular tongues were further complicated by even more dialects. Hindui was spoken by nearly one-third of the population but there was no such thing as a national language. Consequently, the literatures of the various groups were inaccessible to one another.

Besides race and language, religion and socio-cultural differences divided India's people in 1871, as they still do, creating
sharp antagonism and further disunion. Hinduism and Mohammedanism commanded the largest number of followers, Hindus
outnumbering Mohammedans about three to one. The Mohammedans were the invaders; they never assimilated Hinduism and
continued to form the largest block of the followers of their Prophet in the world. But in addition to these two dominant religions
there were, as today, Buddhists, mainly in Burma, although scattered elsewhere, Sikhs in the Punjab, who form an autonomous
community which is also a military caste, Parsees or followers
of the Persian Zoroastrian faith, Christians, and followers of a
crude animism among the primitive tribes still existent in central
India. To multiply the religious differences, the major religions
were divided into sects, castes and sub-castes. Many of these,
especially among the Hindus, carry socio-cultural divisions. The
Hindu religion contains four major castes ranging from the highest, the Brahmins or "twice-born," to the caste below the fourth,
the pariahs or "untouchables," the outcasts; in addition there
are about 2,000 sub-castes determined, among other factors, by
occupation, locality, social custom, as well as by special religious
beliefs or philosophies fanatically adhered to. The Mohammedans
do not have castes in the Hindu sense, but they are roughly divided into the Sunnis, or orthodox, and the Shias or dissenters,
with variations in between.

Additional Indian disunion has always existed in the sharp
differences in wealth, in standard of living, in education and opportunity inherent in so vast a land and so numerous a population. At one end of the scale live the wealthy Maharajas, rulers
of the native states, surrounded by courts and trappings which
rival those of ancient potentates in luxury and splendor; at
the other end, the starving peasantry of the agricultural villages
and the destitute beggars of the cities eke out existence in inde-
scribable poverty. Again, on the top cultural level, the educated
minority enjoys the intellectual riches and refinements of an ancient civilization freed from the slavery of its ignorant customs by
the further advantage of Western education; but on the lower
level, the illiterate masses of India remain in bondage to all the
superstitions of the past.

Political Organization

Neither did India present any unity derived from political organization when the Western states first obtained their footholds in the sixteenth and seventeenth centuries, nor in the last half of the nineteenth century when Britain entered upon the completion of her vast imperial structure there. For India had been but a geographical expression throughout the entire period of modern history. In the sixteenth century it had been invaded by a dynasty of Moslem emperors, the Moguls. They established a court of oriental splendor at Delhi, a loose sovereignty over the princes and gave the country a semblance of unity. It was only a semblance, however, owing to the disparate elements of race, language, religion and culture, just reviewed, and also to the Hindu's loyalty to his own civilization. Moreover, during the seventeenth and eighteenth centuries, the Mogul empire declined so that India's development became just the reverse of that of the states of western Europe. They were emerging into unified national units, freed from the shackles of feudal separatism, while she was disintegrating into feudal states ruled by semi-independent princes who grew bolder and more powerful as the central government weakened. It was this situation which the great commercial companies, such as the French and the British East India Companies, capitalized, for it afforded them abundant opportunity to intervene between the warring princes, who embraced the opportunity to secure modern means of warfare as well as powerful allies. Indeed, the very weakness of India and its anarchic state suggested to the companies, which had first penetrated the peninsula for commerce and wealth, the idea of political domination so easily to be secured. It was the constant and competitive application of this policy of alliance with the Indian princes by the companies' leaders, both British and French, that involved Britain and France in the fateful colonial wars in India, which further weakened the country and established Britain as mistress there in 1763.

Subsequently, India's internal weakness could not prevent the success of the British East India Company in establishing itself as a great state within the country. Nor could the company withstand the ensuing, gradual extension of British governmental control over its administrative activity, as it became more and more involved in the responsibilities and consequences of its success. For it meant a reinforced attack upon India's already crumbling defenses, both by a stronger defense of the company's interests and by further territorial aggression. Thus, when the British government superseded the rule of the East India Company in India in 1858, India's power of resistance to the invader was reduced to the minimum, one-half of present British India had already been conquered and the remainder lay exposed to rapid acquisition.

As this brief survey has perhaps revealed, it is clear that India, more than any other area of expansion in 1871, extended the most alluring and unusual invitation for colonial exploitation. This was true not only because of the richness and variety of its resources and opportunities, its defencelessness inherent in its divisions, backwardness and political incapacity, but also because one-half of the peninsula had been already acquired by one power, Great Britain, which had virtually expelled all competitors and had earmarked the remainder as her own preserve. Let us therefore turn to an account of what has often been termed this colossal example of imperialism, and discover how it was constructed, and how it is today administered.

British India or the Indian Empire

AREA: 1,575,187 square miles
POPULATION: 370,000,000
TRADE:[3] *Exports:*   £122,476,000
           To U.K.:   £ 55,944,423
           Imports: £116,642,000
           From U.K.:   £ 36,550,000

Termed the "brightest jewel" in Britain's imperial crown, the Indian Empire is, perhaps, entitled to that designation for two reasons: first, because it forms an exclusive, monopolistic enterprise of one power and is thus unique among areas of expansion; and second, because it is so vast in size, rich in resources and consequently so economically profitable. By 1940 the glory of this "brightest jewel" was somewhat dimmed. The Indian Nationalist movement, about which we shall later hear, was mainly responsible for its loss of lustre as was also, fundamentally, the seeming failure of Britain's native policy, as revealed in India's backward

---

[3] *Statistical Abstract for the British Empire, 1929-38.* Figures for 1938.

social state, its population pressure and all-pervasive poverty, its extensive illiteracy and cultural lag. For it is against these conditions that the nationalist movement thrives as a living protest. And, in the words of a critical British commentator: "It is manifest to all but a minority of Englishmen that their direct rule over a subject dependency cannot continue. It is no longer a question whether self-government is desirable; it is inevitable. India's will to freedom is fixed."[4]

Territorial Extent and Population. Britain's Indian Empire is almost coterminous with India as a geographic unit and hence has been already described. It does not, however, occupy the whole peninsula, which embraces the independent principalities of Nepal and Bhutan in the north, situated in the Himalayas, between Tibet and India, the insignificant possessions of France[5] in the southeast, constituting the remnants of her empire there and amounting only to about 193 square miles, and also those of the Portuguese,[6] which cover about 1,467 square miles. Without Burma, which became an independent province in 1935, the Indian Empire possesses today an area of 1,575,187 square miles and a population which represents almost one-fifth of the human race (370,000,000) and increases by about 9,000,000 a year.

On the average, there are about 247 people to the square mile in India, although several areas have densities of 600 and a few rural areas of 1,000 persons per square mile. These figures nearly equal the average densities of the most thickly populated countries of the world, England and Belgium, which live mainly by industry and trade. They are not high, however, compared to those of Japan, where an agricultural population of 1,200 per square mile is not uncommon. It is because of the poorer and less certain rainfall that the saturation point is reached in India with a sparser population.

It must always be remembered that the Indian Empire consists of two parts: British India proper[7] and the Native or Princely

---

[4] Brailsford, H. N., "Indian Question," *Encyclopedia of the Social Sciences.*
[5] Pondichéry, Karikal, Chandernagor, Mahé, Yanaon.
[6] Gôa, Damão, Diu.
[7] British India in 1940 consisted of eleven major provinces: Bengal, Bombay, Madras, Bihar and Orissa, United Provinces of Agra and Oudh, the Punjab, the Central Provinces and Berar, Sind, Assam, and the North-West Frontier Province; and six minor provinces: British Baluchistan, Delhi, Ajmer-Merwara, Coorg, the Andaman and Nicobar Islands, Panth Piploda, which were delimited and put more directly under the control of the Central Government in 1912.

States. Representing that territory acquired by direct imperialist action, commercial penetration and military conquest, British India proper contains about 55 per cent of the whole area of the empire and 76 per cent of the people. The Native States, whose allegiance was gained by treaties, charters and alliances between Britain and their ruling rajahs, maharajahs and nizams, occupied about 45 per cent of the territory and contained 24 per cent of the population. Five hundred and sixty-two of them, they are scattered throughout the British territory and vary in size from the great and powerful ones such as Hyderabad with its 82,648 square miles and 14,500,000 inhabitants, Mysore with a population almost that of New York City, Kashmir (85,885 square miles), Udaipur and others, to tiny districts containing only a few villages, such as Sandur for example, with an area of only 161 square miles, Banku with five and Bibari with 1.65 square miles.

Britain's Major Imperialist Interests in India. Britain's interests in India remain today, as they were in the seventeenth century when she first went there, predominantly economic. While commerce was paramount throughout the eighteenth and part of the nineteenth centuries, industry, mining, transportation and finance came during the modern period of expansion, since 1871, to equal and in some respects to surpass trade. A brief survey of these major interests will perhaps convey some idea of Britain's enormous and valuable economic stakes in her Indian Empire.

Commerce. Since India is overwhelmingly an agricultural country with a vast population and at the same time possessed of rich present and potential resources, it has always presented an ideal area for the application of a mercantile policy by a strong colonial power able to impose tariffs or free trade, to adjust taxation, to preserve a favorable balance of trade, and to stimulate or to prevent native economic activity in order to serve its own ends. Never was this opportunity for economic exploitation greater than at the beginning of the modern period of expansion when the industrial revolution both transformed Britain into the workshop of the world and also so improved the means of transportation as to enable its products to be carried into the farthest outposts of empire. Especially after the cutting of the Suez Canal, factory-made goods streamed into India by sea, while the railways began to penetrate ever newer markets and to tap fresh sources of raw materials as they extended their steel tentacles into the remote areas of this vast sub-continent.

It can be easily understood, therefore, how all conditions conspired during the last quarter of the nineteenth century to facilitate the building up of a vast overseas trade with India, which was further increased by the British policy of destroying the indigenous handicrafts and flooding India with manufactured goods from the Lancaster mills. As a result the period 1875-1925 presented an almost fabulous tale of economic prosperity as far as trade was concerned. The following table [8] indicates the rapid rise of Indian exports and imports during the first quarter of the twentieth century, the bulk of which was with Great Britain.

VALUE OF TOTAL TRADE OF INDIA WITH ALL COUNTRIES
(in £ million)

	IMPORTS	EXPORTS
1903-04	91.6	115.4
1913-14	164.5	177.0
1920-21	400.5	309.8
1921-22	331.0	280.9
1922-23	328.0	334.3
1923-24	310.3	383.3
1924-25	375.7	424.1
1925-26	291.4	390.7
1926-27	211.8	234.9
1927-28	222.3	250.0
1928-29	225.5	259.1

During the period 1875-1913, India's imports increased almost 500 per cent and her exports about 350 per cent, while three-fourths of all India's sea-borne trade was under British control.

The years immediately prior to and after the first World War would seem to have constituted the heyday of Britain's imperial commercial advantage in India, especially in so far as that country provided a market for British exports. For, after 1918 and notably in the recent 1930's, there occurred a decided decline in the stream of British goods to India. The value of Indian imports from Britain which amounted approximately to £62,000,000 in 1913, dropped to £41,000,000 in 1934, to £39,000,000 in 1937, and to £36,426,883 in 1938. In other words, Britain's share in Indian im-

---

[8] *Statistical Abstracts for British India,* 1915, 1926, 1933.

ports decreased from 64 per cent in 1913-1914 to 47.8 per cent in 1926-1927. Again, before the first World War 70 per cent of India's supply of textiles came from England and 28 per cent from Indian mills, while only 35 per cent of her post-war supply was British and 61 per cent Indian. Three or four factors seemed to account for this trend: the growth of Indian industry, the production of cotton goods—a large item in Indian imports—in other parts of the empire, Japanese competition, and a general decrease in trade during the depression. The list of commodities imported by India from Britain confirmed the explanation with regard to the increase of India's industry, for during the post-war years they consisted of machinery, iron and steel at the top of the list, then motor cars and cotton goods in fourth place.

There is also a reverse side to the picture. It is noticeable that a change is taking place in the growth of India's imports over exports. Throughout the years since 1871, always the amount of India's imports has outweighed her exports to Britain, thus redounding to Britain's financial benefit and conversely constituting a serious drain upon India and her resources. Recently, however, Indian exports have materially increased. In 1934, they rose to approximately £32,000,000; and in 1937, to £64,000,000, which overtopped British exports to India. At first, the World War of 1914-1918 was responsible for this increase, but it has continued to grow. As India becomes more and more industrialized, the outlook for the development of a national trade, with the advantage accruing to India rather than to imperial Britain, brightens.

Industry, like commerce, has constituted one of Britain's major imperialistic stakes in India although its constant development strengthens Indian nationalism, that archenemy of British imperialism. The chief aim of Britain's policy during the last half of the nineteenth century was, it is true, to preserve India as a monopoly market for British goods and not permit her to compete with home production. Still, it was distinctly to the advantage of certain groups of British capitalists and financiers to promote industry in India where labor was cheap and unorganized, raw materials were immediately at hand, and where the consequent building of factories and extended means of transportation would bring increased business to Britain's metallurgical and machine trades. The result was that by 1890 India had developed a large factory industry, whose growth during the thirty years before the first

World War was constant. Cotton spindles more than doubled, jute looms increased four and one-half times, the average number of factory operatives employed daily increased from 316,816 in 1892 to 869,643 in 1914; in the eighties and nineties the coal and iron industries were built up and railways were constructed at about the rate of 800 miles a year. Then came the war and Britain's preoccupation with making munitions, on the one hand, and, on the other, there arose an enormous demand for cotton goods, jute, steel, wool, and leather manufactures. To India came the opportunity of meeting both the demand for those goods usually supplied by European imports and also the unusual need for producing the sinews of war. Such a stimulation of industry resulted in turn in a post-war boom accompanied by unprecedented expansion and extension until checked by the world depression. Profits, always large, became enormous. Cotton mills, whose dividends had ranged between 20 to 60 per cent, now rose to 100 per cent; the jute industry, one of the most prosperous, since 1900, earned between 1915 and 1924 an average annual profit which amounted to eight times its wages bill; coal companies whose returns had averaged 10 to 44 per cent rose to 75 per cent; tea plantations, always notable for large dividends, made from 50 to 96 per cent on their investments.[9]

The chief industries from which Britain, the government and the private investor, derives so great an economic advantage are cotton, jute, coal, iron, steel, engineering, finance and the plantation industries. British capital established, built up and controls all these except the cotton, which Indian capital originally started and in which it is now paramount. Indian capital also tends to share more and more in the jute, iron, steel and plantation industries of tea, coffee and rubber. In 1911, it was estimated that British capital investment in India amounted to £360,000,000; in 1929, it was reckoned at £573,000,000; and today, a moderate estimate would place it between £700,000,000 and £800,000,000 although an accurate computation is difficult. More British capital is invested in India than in any one other country and the present amount represents almost one-quarter of the total of British overseas investments. Indeed, the story of the industrialization of India with its railways, canals, tramways, banks, mines, planta-

---

[9] For recent development in industry, see Orchard, D. J., "India Enters the Machine Age," *Asia*, April, 1940.

Adapted from "Atlas of Empire" by J. F. Horrabin, by permission of Alfred A. Knopf, Inc., publishers

BRITISH INDIA AND THE NATIVE STATES

tions, factories and mills, is one which has only been suggested in this brief treatment, but sufficient perhaps has been said to indicate its unequalled value and significance.

Other interests of inestimable benefit to imperial Britain in India are many. Answers to the question of what Britain gets out of India would include among them: naval bases and ports; communications with her dominions in Australia, New Zealand, and with her holdings in the Far East and the Pacific; opportunities for careers and support of a large proportion of her own citizens in the Indian army, the police force and the civil service, imperial power, prestige and support. In the first World War India

Adapted from "Atlas of Empire" by J. F. Horrabin, by permission of Alfred A. Knopf, Inc., publishers

THE ELEVEN PROVINCES OF BRITISH INDIA

rallied to help Britain to the extent of contributing $500,000,000 to the Allied war chest, bought war loans to the amount of $700,-000,000 and sent 1,338,620 men to the fronts. What Britain has given India in return for all these imperial benefits will be discussed in the account of the Indian nationalist movement to follow.

How Governed. There exist two administrative areas in the Indian Empire corresponding to British India proper and to the Native States, although the new constitution or Government of India Act of 1935 has taken the first step towards federation. Better to understand this present constitution, it is essential to place it in its historic setting and thus briefly review the character of the imperial rule which preceded it in both sections of the empire.

In 1858, when the British government superseded the British East India Company, British India was placed by the Better Government of India Act under the direct, autocratic rule of the mother country, with no native Indian representation. The government consisted of a viceroy and two councils of state, one legislative and one executive, which were appointed by and responsible to the British cabinet and under the supervision of a member of the cabinet, the secretary of state for India and his council in London. Further to centralize and emphasize the imperial character of this rule the British parliament, under the leadership of Disraeli, the prime minister, declared India an empire and the British sovereign, then Queen Victoria, Empress of India in 1876.

No change interrupted this direct sovereign and autocratic government of India until 1909, when in answer to the demands of Indian nationalists,[10] the India Councils Act or Morley-Minto Reforms permitted the native election, by a highly restricted suffrage, of a minority of members of the viceroy's legislative council and of the advisory councils that were set up in six of the nine provinces of British India. Again, in 1919, the Montagu-Chelmsford Reforms increased the number of native, elective seats in both the viceroy's councils, and also the number of voters in provincial elections from 30,000 to 5,300,000; and established a system known as dyarchy or double government in provincial matters. This meant that in each of the legislative provinces, such matters as law, police and administration were reserved to the governors who were appointed by the viceroy, while more local affairs, such as health, agriculture, sanitation, education, were transferred to the provincial councils, which were now mainly elective. Despite these major reforms, the government of British India remained until recently substantially within the direct, imperial framework which had been originally set up in 1858.

The Native States.   Quite different was the character of the British rule as far as the Native or Princely States were concerned, although they too had been brought under imperial

---

[10] See p. 404.

control. Their native independent or semi-independent rajahs, maharajahs or nizams continued to govern their states directly under the sovereignty of Great Britain as represented by the viceroy or his agents. Although they are, for the most part, supreme in local affairs, Great Britain, the paramount power, has controlled their external affairs and their relations with each other. It has also exercised supervision over their internal policy, which varies from state to state, according to usage, agreements, charters and treaties, summed up in the word "paramountcy."

These native princes, Hindu and Mohammedan, rule for the most part despotically, except for the few enlightened among them whose number is increasing, and they are fond of surrounding themselves with courts of oriental splendor. Their group includes many picturesque figures as well as modern, educated rulers. Some wear rubies on their toes worth $100,000 apiece and surround themselves with fantastic luxuries; others are like the Maharajah of Mysore, who is an ascetic and spends his week ends in prayer and meditation; or the Nizam of Hyderabad, whose annual income is reputed to be $50,000,000 but who lives frugally in a shabby palace. Some have never been to school; others are poets, writers and scientists, and one is a doctor of medicine with a degree from Edinburgh. The present Indian constitution supersedes all prior administrative arrangements in India although it alters the position of Princely India least of all. First made public through a White Paper issued by the British government in 1933, it was carefully revised and favorably reported in 1934 by an Indian Joint Select Committee chosen from both houses of parliament, after which it became the Government of India Act by a vote in the House of Commons of 386 to 122 in 1935, and was inaugurated in India in 1937, although all its provisions were not made effective at once. Mainly the result of the work of the India Nationalist Movement, whose history appears in a later chapter, it represents the culmination, although to many Indians an unsatisfactory one, of a long struggle directed towards freeing India from British imperial rule.

The document provides for an eventual federation of British India and Princely India or Native States represented by a federal legislature of two houses. The upper house or Council of State is to consist of 260 members, of whom 104 are to be appointed by the princes, 150 chosen by the provincial upper houses or analogous electoral colleges, and 6 appointed by the viceroy; the lower house or legislative assembly is to contain 375 members chosen for five years, of whom 250 are to be selected by the lower houses of the provincial assemblies in accordance with definitely assigned numbers to the religious and special interest groups,[11] and 125 appointed by the princes. According to the original draft of the constitution, members of the lower house, representing British India, were to be elected directly by the Indian people, but the revised document withdrew this right and hence was considered less liberal. Another measure which won the criticism of being reactionary was the allotment of delegates to the federal legislature. As may be noted, this greatly favors the princes since they are given one-third of the membership of the council of state and well over one-third of that of the assembly, although the population of the states is less than one-fourth of the total for the Indian Empire. The Native States, indeed, have proved and remain a great obstacle to federation, because of the number and variety of their separate treaties with the Crown, in which it has been necessary to redefine the powers transferred by the States to the new federal government; and also because of their fear of losing their independence and autocracy.

Under the new constitution the executive, the viceroy or governor-general, remains head of the government aided by a council of ministers, with exclusive control of the three departments reserved to the federal rule, defense, foreign affairs and ecclesiastical affairs.[12] In addition, the new constitution vested special emergency powers in the viceroy to deal with domestic crises that might arise over matters of religion, minorities, currency, and justice for the foreign population. The list of these "discretionary powers," which would enable him to deal with his "special responsibilities" and which he may exercise without any "constitutional responsibility," includes the dissolving and summoning of the legislature, the promulgation of emergency ordinances having the effect of law, and the assumption by himself of all powers vested by law in any federal authority.

Besides formulating the central government, the constitution provided for eleven provincial governments, upon which it placed

---

[11] For example, 90 seats are assigned to Hindus, 82 to Moslems, 10 to labor, 9 to women, and so on.

[12] Foreign Policy Report, *The New Indian Constitution*, July 17, 1935.

the chief responsibility for domestic administration. The electorate for these provincial assemblies was increased to about 35,000,000 men and women and five of the provinces were to have upper houses. In the Native States the princes were left completely unhampered to make whatever arrangements for local government they wished. Although the Government of India Act represented a decided advance over any former provisions for liberalizing the government of the Indian Empire, it fell far short of the expectations and demands even for dominion status and, hence, met at first with dissatisfaction and opposition. Indeed, to the overwhelming majority of British Indians it represented an imposed constitution and was therefore completely unwelcome.

How Acquired. During the modern period of expansion since 1871, the construction of what now constitutes the Indian Empire followed two chief lines of activity: territorial acquisition mainly on the borders of the empire already acquired by the East India Company before 1858 and by the British government since that date; and the extension of British alliance and control over native rulers within India and over those neighboring states which form its "defences."

Territorially, the British government inherited from the East India Company in 1858 somewhat less than one-half of the present area, which constitutes the core or center of the Indian empire. How this was acquired from the seventeenth century onward must be briefly reviewed.

First, the discovery of the ocean route to India in 1498 by Vasco da Gama resulted in the Portuguese inaugurating a lively trade with the Indians in the sixteenth century. Establishing their factories at Calicut, an island off the west coast, and on the mainland, they were so successful that the Dutch followed their example. Then the British traders, hearing of the profitable commerce in finely woven silk and cotton, in opium, spices, gums, precious stones and other desirable commodities, arrived to join in the new enterprise, which soon became worthy of organized effort.

The effort materialized in the form of the British East India Company, which was founded by London merchants in 1600. It received a royal charter granting it a monopoly of British trade with India, which it retained, except for short suspensions, until 1813. By the year 1619, the company had founded four factories with Surat as its chief center on the west coast. Then in 1640 it established Fort St. George at Madras, which later became the headquarters for the factories on the east coast. Next, the island of Bombay, acquired in 1661 by Charles II as part of the marriage dowry of his wife, Catherine of Braganza, was transferred to the company in 1668, having replaced Surat as the seat of administration for the west coast settlements in 1667.

Until this time, the end of the seventeenth century, the aim of the British East India Company was solely trade; it exhibited no political or imperial purpose, no ambition for territorial aggression; but the very success of its rapidly expanding trade and commercial competition made it essential to oust its competitors if its prosperity were to continue. The Dutch and the Portuguese were easily disposed of but the French, whose East India Company had appeared on the scene in 1664, constituted important rivals. Inevitably the opposing companies became involved in Indian politics through the accident of the Franco-British world-wide wars of the eighteenth century, of which the struggle to obtain the upper hand in India formed so vital a part. The French, ably led by Dupleix, governor-general of the French factories from 1741, began to carve out an empire, employing with great success the technique of backing one native ruler against the other and using them as puppet rulers. Hence the British company needed to outdo them with the same strategy. Moreover, conditions were especially propitious for European penetration: the Mogul empire was rapidly disintegrating, invaders poured in from the north, and the struggles of Indian rulers, who were throwing off their feudal yoke, to extend their power afforded the companies unmatched opportunities to obtain land, power and trading privileges.

Robert Clive, originally a clerk in the East India Company, laid the foundations of British territorial expansion in India. He defeated the French at the battle of Plassey (1757) and gained control of the province of Bengal. The conquest was typical of the methods of the time, compounded of bribery, mutual ill-faith, Indian cruelty and British rapacity. Eventually the struggle ended with the complete defeat of France at Pondichéry in 1761, the elimination of the French East India Company and the dissolution of the dream of French empire in India. Five trading posts were all that remained of Dupleix's ambitious plan.

The resulting establishment of a practical British monopoly in India by the end of the eighteenth century marked also a momentous change in the status of the East India Company from that of a mere trading organization to an administrative power. Just as the territorial foundations of British India were laid in the latter half of the eighteenth century, so also was constructed the first machinery of imperial rule. Warren Hastings created law courts for Bengal, drafted a legal code and set up a council for the governor-general with the Regulating Act of 1773. Finally, William Pitt's India Act of 1784, which deprived the company of the right of appointing the governor-general and vested it in the British government, supplied the initial indication that the British people were to assume ultimate responsibility for India.

With the nucleus of a territorial empire in India so acquired by the beginning of the nineteenth century, it was only to be expected that the company would devote the next fifty years to its extension. Continual conquest ensued. Lord Wellesley subdued the Mahratta princes who represented the remaining heirs of the Mogul power in 1802-1804, and succeeding governors-general waged wars from the Punjab to Burma with the Sikhs, the Gurkhas, the Pindaris, the Afghans. Lord Dalhousie annexed southern Burma in 1847, and adopted the policy, known as the "lapse," of annexing the estates of any native ruler who lacked direct heirs. In this way province after province was gained so that British territory increased from 480,000 square miles in 1813 to 970,000 square miles in 1856.

What appeared an enormous extension of British rule in India proved, however, only the prelude to a vaster area of control for it resulted in the first serious uprising, the Sepoy Mutiny of 1857, against alien rule, which in turn precipitated the modern Indian Empire. Immediately caused by the protest of the Sepoys against the use of cartridges greased with cow and pig fat [13] served out to them by their masters, the British, and which they believed to be a deliberate insult to their religion and culture, the mutiny constituted the first crude expression of Indian nationalism. Essentially it was a revolt against the extinction of so many native dynasties, against foreign rule, against an alien culture, against Westernization. Its suppression required a force and a ruthlessness beyond

---

[13] The cow is sacred to Hindus. Moslems may not touch pork.

the resources of the East India Company to provide. Hence the British government superseded the rule of the company, and the British nation became sovereign of India.

Thereafter, the company's policy of annexation, so constantly pursued for 250 years, was abandoned in the center of India, partly because it had formed a major cause of the mutiny, and partly as a reward to those princes who had remained loyal to the Crown. For it was substituted the alliance of native rulers with Great Britain and the building up of the defenses of India by a series of annexations along the northeastern, northern and northwestern frontiers. Thus it was in these border regions that British expansion mainly focused after 1871.

During the decade of the seventies, about 15,000 square miles were acquired by annexing northern Burma to the east and several provinces of Afghanistan in the west, as the result of the second Afghan war, which adjusted scientifically the frontiers of India and gave Britain control of Afghanistan's foreign policy. Likewise, in the succeeding decade of 1881-1891, 90,000 square miles were annexed mainly from the barren wastes and arid plateaus of Baluchistan on India's western border which, together with the districts acquired from Afghanistan, were organized into British Baluchistan in 1887. By this conquest, the British secured control of the passes and routes into Afghanistan and Baluchistan from India and of a long strip of territory through which passes the great caravan route to Persia.

With the defenses on the east and west of India secured, the British next centered their efforts upon the northwestern frontier in the section lying between the Punjab, Kashmir and Afghanistan on the southern slopes of the Hindu-Kush Mountains, which had long been the scene of constant warfare and border raids. For the mountainous, inaccessible and remote character of the region, which is inhabited by warlike, wild and freedom-loving tribes, among them the famous Pathans, presented peculiar difficulties of conquest. Finally, however, in 1901, the district was subdued and organized into the North-West Frontier Province under a governor responsible to the viceroy of India. On the northeastern frontier also, especially along the Chino-Burmese and the Assam-Burmese boundaries, territorial acquisitions were made. Altogether the Indian Empire was enlarged about 123,000 square miles during the decade 1891-1901.

Besides these outright territorial acquisitions, more and more native states, among them important border districts like Kashmir and Sikkim, were brought under imperial rule. After 1901, a more effective control was established over them, so that they became increasingly dependent upon Great Britain and could be used to strengthen British authority in India.

Continuing the policy of building up the defense of India, the British government was especially assiduous after 1871 in forming alliances and signing treaties with those states which bordered India and constituted buffers between it and would-be invaders. Chief among these were Afghanistan, of which we have already heard, Tibet, and the kingdoms of Nepal and Bhutan. These alliances varied in the degree of sovereignty which their rulers conceded to Great Britain; but most of them relinquished command over their foreign relations to the British Crown, receiving protection and sometimes internal assistance in return.

Symbolic of Britain's great Indian Empire thus acquired were the dramatic evidences of her imperial rule which her government took especial care to emphasize. Among them may be mentioned: the constant reminder that Britain had fallen heir to the Mogul rule by the location of the center of government at Delhi, the ancient capital, instead of Calcutta where it had hitherto been; and the institution of the "durbar" or reception to the Indian princes on the occasion of the coronation ceremony of the British sovereign as emperor of India, accompanied by all the magnificence and splendor which Oriental trappings can bestow.

READINGS

See list at end of Chapter Fifteen.

Results of European Expansion in the Middle East upon Nationalism and International Relations

Nationalist Movements in the Middle East

LIKE THE NEAR EAST, the Middle East is rife with nationalist movements and in no other area of expansion does imperialism, which has been on so vast a scale, find itself in so definite a decline. The reasons which account for the intensified nationalism in this section of Asia are also similar to those which explain the same phenomena in the Near East, only here they are, if possible, more convincing. For these peoples, upon whom the expanding powers Russia and Great Britain have imposed their control and exploitation, inherit civilizations and cultures far older, longer established and, in many respects, much richer than those of their invaders. These native populations possess all the deep resources of their centuries-old historic traditions upon which to draw in their revolt against the aliens. More than that, the nationalistic uprisings in this area represent, even more than in the Near East, the fundamental contradiction of the East and West: Oriental civilization, still under the spell of the past, opposed to Occidental, which is so much a creation of the present; the mysticism

392

and spirituality of Eastern culture in rebellion against Western materialism and realism; the artistry and freedom of handicraft in contrast to the standardized industrialism of the machine.

Moreover, again as in the Near East, the first World War immensely stimulated nationalism in this area although in different ways. In the more advanced sections, where hitherto nationalism had been confined to the intellectual group and the rising bourgeoisie, the war precipitated a thorough popularization so that today (1941) it represents all groups, classes, regions and communities of the people as a whole, whatever may be their economic, social, religious or cultural status. In the more backward parts of the area a cruder, more embryonic movement, recent and hitherto restricted to a few at the top, has been seized upon by stronger rulers who have capitalized disorganized postwar conditions to impose a nationalistic independence upon their countries. The result has been that since 1921 the two most backward states of the area, Persia and Afghanistan, have successfully thrown off the shackles of colonial exploitation and freed themselves from European domination; and India's nationalism has developed into a dynamic, mass revolt against Great Britain, whose ultimate victory in some form is widely acknowledged to be only a matter of time.

The Indian Nationalist Movement

No clearer indication of the present strength of Indian nationalism may be found than in its attitude towards Great Britain in 1940, especially when compared with its position in 1914. Then, India responded unconditionally to the Empire's call. In 1940, nationalist India demanded complete independence with the right to secede from the empire, and insisted upon democracy at home.

When India adopted this position at the outbreak of the armed struggle in the fall of 1939, Great Britain at first replied that her demands were utterly unacceptable and that all political discussion would have to be postponed as the time was unpropitious for them. Ten months later, however, in August, 1940, Britain offered India dominion status, "a free and equal partnership in the British Commonwealth of Nations" and the framing of a new dominion constitution, after the conclusion of the war "with the least pos-

sible delay." Also, as an added concession, the viceroy of India
was authorized to invite immediately "a certain number of representative Indians to join his executive council as a token of Indian
partnership in the prosecution of the war."

The fact that Britain's promise failed to meet the National Congress' demand for complete independence for India, and that,
internally, the country as always was divided and torn by groups
with conflicting purposes should not be permitted to detract from
the significance of this patent triumph of the nationalist movement. It is true that Mohammed Ali Jinnah,[1] leader of the Moslem League, and the princes of India prefer dominion status
instead of independence, resent the claim of the National Congress to speak for India, and tend to throw the weight of India's
wealth and man power on the side of Britain as in 1914. But the
Indian problem is a complex one and its very complexity constitutes an indication of its strength rather than its weakness.

That such a promise has been secured from Great Britain in
the throes of a titanic struggle is but another proof of the virility
and effectiveness of the National Congress Party, which is the
dynamic, consolidated expression of Indian nationalism. By far
the best organized and most powerful group in India today,
it numbers over 3,000,000 members and constitutes the largest
party in every province of British India, except the Punjab, the
North-West Frontier and Sind. In the elections of 1937 when
the new constitution was inaugurated, it gained control of six
of the eleven provincial assemblies, a result which astonished
even the nationalists. The structure of the Congress is complex
and far reaching, building up from the village organization,
through the provincial congress committee to the All-India Congress Committee, which is a sort of parliament. At the top is the
president, chosen by the Congress Committee, who in turn selects
fourteen or fifteen associates as a cabinet. None of these men
receives any salary. But the National Congress Party is really
something more than a political group; it partakes somewhat of
the nature of a state within a state. Its members wear a uniform of
white homespun, form their own army, the Volunteers, maintain a
foreign department and propaganda bureau and have their own
flag, made of three stripes, saffron, white and green, with a spin-

---

[1] See Abbas, K. H., "Jinnah: The Enigma of India," *Asia*, August, 1940.

ning wheel. When it holds its annual, plenary sessions at which thousands of people congregate, it ceases to be a mere political party and becomes the organized expression of the aim and will of India. For its membership represents a cross section of the Indian people: Hindus, Moslems, rich, poor, high caste and pariah, prime ministers of the provincial governments, homeless radicals, reactionaries and socialists. It has been well likened to a "giant People's Front against the British raj." [2]

How has this national movement come into being and what, in more detail, does it want? Let us first consider this question by depicting the grievances of India against her imperial overlord, which will afford us a picture of Britain's native policy, and then by tracing the historical development, the failures and successes of Indian nationalism from its inception in the middle of the nineteenth century, throughout its various phases, to the entrenched position which it occupies today. The discussion of the former point, India's grievances, will in no way seek to evaluate Britain's rule in India with any degree of finality or state whether it has been a blessing or a curse—perhaps it has been both; but it will seek merely to present the facts with as much accuracy as possible.

India's Major Grievances. India's grievances against Great Britain, and they are legion, fall under three general classifications: the deprivation of political freedom, economic exploitation, and the failure to compensate a country which has proved so profitable to her with adequate measures for its material development or with sufficient social services for its human welfare. From our former discussions of native policies and national movements, all these grievances will be recognized as standard complaints voiced by nationalism against imperialism in every area. But the unusual size of India, its peculiarly favorable conditions conducive to exploitation, combined with its vast and unequaled opportunities, have sharpened and, at times, exaggerated the extent of the grievances. Nevertheless, they are, at base, intensely real and their validity is freely admitted by many Englishmen.

In the first place, the National Congress claims that Indians have an inalienable right to be free. "India for the Indians" is its cry. Upon deaf ears fall the British arguments that Indians are incompetent to govern themselves, that they are too divided,

---

[2] Gunther, J., *Inside Asia*, p. 427.

that the problem of races, princes, minorities, religions, are all too complex for them to manage. They retort that it is largely the British rule that has created and aggravated these difficulties, by accentuating the divisions, by playing off groups one against another for its own advantage, and that the only way to settle the matter is to allow the Indians to rule themselves.

On this point of disagreement regarding political capacity, the British cite, in general, the irreconcilable divisions in India and in particular the dismal failure of the Round Table Conferences held in London in the early 1930's to formulate a constitution for India when, at the first, the Congress Nationalists preferred to remain in jail rather than to co-operate. While on the matter of political inability, Gandhi, in a talk with the viceroy, remarked: "If we are deficient in the character and experience necessary to enable us to take over our own affairs, it is because you have never given us the opportunity to develop those qualities in practice. We demand responsibility." British rule, the nationalists claim, has never provided opportunity for normal political training in problems of administration. British officialdom assumes the burden of government, demanding only submission, docility and the performance of routine tasks from the native.

As for economic exploitation, the second major grievance, much has already been said in the description of Britain's commercial, industrial and financial stakes in India to illustrate its basis.[3] In this field, the nationalists assert, Britain has sucked dry the wealth of India, leaving the country impoverished, weakened, impotent in many ways. Countering the British argument that British capital has developed India, released her resources and opened up the country with railways, canals, irrigation works, they point to the tariff policy which has been directed for Britain's benefit and India's loss, to the low wages, to the primary purposes of the transportation systems which serve Britain's commercial and administrative ends rather than India's internal economy, to the tremendous burden of taxation and to the inadequacy of irrigation systems and of agricultural development. On the other hand, in fairness, it must be remembered that if India were independent and there were no exploiting

---

[3] See pp. 378 ff.

power, the country would be obliged to pay interest on the capital invested in the industries, transportation and public works, as well as salaries to foreign experts.

But an additional and unnecessary economic load is placed upon the country, Indians contend, by the tremendous cost of British officialdom and the British army, which is mainly borne by the native taxpayers and constitutes after all the machinery of imperial, administrative control, whose use, moreover, is not confined to India. For the Indian army is employed by Britain in imperialist wars in China, Abyssinia and Egypt, and the Indian government extends its administrative services to Aden, the Persian Gulf and other parts of Asia. Support of the army consumes about one-half of the Indian budget for the central government, $186,413,030 per year; and 8,000 European officials receive in yearly salaries the total of $70,000,000 as against $16,500,000 earned by 130,000 Indian officials.

In striking contrast to the wealth which Britain extracts from India, the nationalists place the country's overwhelming and, in some places, unimaginable poverty. "At least one-third of the population is perpetually hungry, while the overwhelming majority does not know the meaning of a satisfactory meal," states a recent writer.[4] Famines are recurrent, misery is widespread. It has been roughly estimated that for every pound ($5.00) which an average Englishman possesses, the average Indian owns one shilling, sixpence, or thirty-seven cents. In spite of its rapidly growing industry, India remains about 88 per cent rural. Almost nine-tenths of its population live in its 500,000 villages, which depend on the soil for livelihood. There is not enough land to satisfy the rapidly increasing population, and production is extremely low, owing to ignorance of agricultural methods and lack of improved machinery. Rents are high, taxation heavy.

Nor is the lot of the urban population any better. India's factories provide some of the worst working conditions in the world, many being situated in old, insanitary buildings, while her slums are notorious. Hours are long, generally twelve a day. The Factory Act of 1922, which limited work to ten hours a day and sixty hours a week, has never been enforced. As already indicated, wages are unbelievably low: below thirty cents a day for the

---

[4] Viton, A., *Great Britain: An Empire in Transition*, p. 71.

skilled, between five to ten cents a day for the unskilled workers. It has been estimated that for every $500 returned to the shareholders in Scotland by the Calcutta textile mills, $60 is returned in wages to Indians.

From these conditions of widespread poverty and suppression of the Indian masses arises the third main grievance of Indian nationalism, that Great Britain has returned to India so little in proportion to what she has derived therefrom. The Indians point to the British failure fundamentally to relieve the agricultural situation by research, education, modernization of methods and processes and by adequate irrigation. Extensive irrigation works have, it is true, been constructed and have increased the cultivable area, thus removing the threat of famine in large sections of the country. Although this is always cited as evidence of good administration, again, it is claimed that only a small proportion of the agricultural population has benefited thereby and that famine and plague continue to take their unnecessary toll of lives.

And as their bodies are starved, so are their minds, claim the Indians. As late as 1931, 84.4 out of every 100 men and 97 out of every 100 women were illiterate. The Simon Report (1930) revealed that out of the total amount of taxation in British India, the government spent 3 shillings, 4 pence per head for the army and less than 9 pence per head for education. In British India in 1928-1929, the government expenditure for education, for a population of 240,000,000, was under £10,000,000, while in Great Britain it was over five times as great for a population of 40,000,000.[5] As a result, as late as 1935, only about 4 per cent of the population was receiving any schooling, from primary class to university. Indeed, some of the Native States have a better record for education than has British India. A contemporary writer has summed up the situation: "The British have simply not been interested in raising the cultural level of the Indian masses or in introduction of a scientific civilization. Therefore, the total number of normal schools—the key plants in the production of teachers—was even in 1935 below six hundred; therefore, girls' education received only about two cents per head of the population; therefore, the total cost to all branches of government for

---

[5] Beauchamp, J., *British Imperialism in India*, p. 120.

each scholar, from infant to university student, has been less than three dollars a year." [6]

The general ignorance and cultural lag that has ensued is largely responsible for India's backwardness, especially as an undue proportion is expended for universities while the elementary schools are neglected. The same criticism, indeed, can be directed against British efforts towards native education in India as in many parts of Africa: it is not primarily planned for or suited to the needs of the people, their welfare or growth. Technical, vocational, agricultural education is neglected for the more conventional, formal and traditional British system which produces lawyers, clerks, white-collar workers, all serviceable to the British *raj*,[7] but not, it is claimed, designed or suited for the sound and wholesome development of the Indian community life.

Nor is Britain's record much better in the other social services, such as public health. The effects of climate, poverty, malnutrition, unemployment, bad housing and insanitary conditions are all too evident in India's vital statistics. The death rate in British India in 1930 was 26.8 per 1,000 as compared with 11.7 per 1,000 in England and Wales; the infant mortality rate was 232.2 per 1,000 for All-India, and 303 per 1,000 in the United Provinces (British India). The number of persons who suffer every year in India from malaria is not less than 50,000,000 and may easily exceed 100,000,000 in some years. In 1930, cholera, plague and famine took a toll of 434,000 lives; malaria and other fevers over 3,500,000; and respiratory diseases over 400,000. According to the report of the Director of the Indian Medical Service (1930), 13,000,000 of the population are suffering from venereal disease and tuberculosis is "increasing rapidly." Commenting upon his report, the *Manchester Guardian* stated:[8]

> The Report draws the general conclusions that India has a poorly nourished population, with an average duration of life of less than half of what it might be; that periods of famine or scarcity of food occur in one village out of five as a

---

[6] Viton, A., *Great Britain: An Empire in Transition*, p. 84.

[7] The Wardha scheme of education now being developed by the National Congress is designed as a remedy.

[8] *Manchester Guardian*, November 14, 1933, quoted by Beauchamp, J., *British Imperialism in India*, p. 118.

normal rule; that, in spite of the death rate, the normal population is increasing far more rapidly than the output of food
and other necessaries of life; and that malaria is present
throughout the greater part of India.

No one will deny that India presents a health problem of
staggering proportions with which it would be difficult for any
colonial power, no matter how good its intentions, to cope. For
a time, so much was there to be done that the government's
efforts met with decided progress and succeeded in extending
a considerable hospital service at various centers throughout
the country, but these have reached only a small percentage of
the population. The fundamental difficulty rests in the inadequate amount of money appropriated to the entire medical and
sanitary service. In 1913-1914, for example, $7,000,000 out of
a total budget of $280,000,000 was expended by the central and
provincial governments on health; even as late as 1931, only
2.77 per cent of the total budget was assigned to health as compared with 25.29 per cent to military and marine services.

British accomplishments in the field of social reform are even
more meager than in education and public health. For the protection of labor conspicuously little has been done. Not until
1881 were children under seven prohibited from working, and the
hours for children between seven and twelve limited to nine per
day. This was the first Factory Act, but it was not enforced any
more than has been the Act of 1922, which prohibits the employment of children below twelve years and sets eleven hours as
the working day for adults. These two Acts, together with the
Workmen's Compensation Act, constitute about all the protection for labor in India provided by Great Britain, a neglect which
has resulted in the development of a trade union movement characterized by militant nationalism. As for other social reforms,
aside from the decrease in child marriage, the abolition of *suttee*,[9]
and the prohibition upon parents to pledge their child's labor for
payment of debt (1933), and various other minor measures,
little has been done. But it must be remembered that it has long
been British policy to interfere as little as possible with established custom and religious belief, just as it has always been

---

[9] The volitional burning alive of a widow upon the bier of her husband.

orthodox Indian habit bitterly to resent and to obstruct such interference.

In addition to these three major grievances, Indians heartily resent the superior attitude of the British towards them, the Anglo-Saxon's prejudice towards persons of color—although India contains many of the purest Aryans in the world, the assumption that the British constitute "a ruling race" and that they rule, moreover, by a kind of "moral prestige." The fact that the British actually live this attitude in everyday life and do not merely hold it as an abstract belief affords a constant irritant. For the British in India have always surrounded themselves with a home atmosphere seeking to differentiate themselves from India: their homes, gardens, furniture, clothes, sports are British; they speak English and read English books and papers; they gather socially in British circles and British clubs, from which the Indians are as a rule excluded, except as servants; they exist, in short, as a race apart—a conquering race.

The enumeration of the above grievances, with which Indian nationalists have indicted the British rule, should not be permitted to obscure what the British claim to have done for India, but should, rather, be considered in relation to those claims. Among them are: that the British have brought political order out of chaos, have preserved a wide-reaching internal peace (until recent years), have established British justice and have placed the country under the control of an administrative system, the British civil service, which is unequaled in character. Furthermore, the British point to the material benefits which they have bestowed upon India, such as the 79,000 miles of government canals, the fourth largest railway system in the world, the largest irrigation works in any area and the forestry reservation, which has come to include about one-fifth of British India. While it is true that none of these achievements may be minimized, they must be examined in their relative benefits to the British and to the Indians as well as their cost to India.

Again, the excellence of the Indian civil service cannot be gainsaid in its own sphere. Generally characterized by a single-mindedness, a devotion to duty, a conscientiousness and a high sense of imperial purpose, and, on the whole, free from bribery, corruption and cruelty, it has not so much misruled as it has not ruled well in the larger sense of the term. Given a stupendous opportunity, the Indian nationalists point out, it has failed to grasp it. The British government's conception of administration has been limited and narrow; it has not conceived of social and economic improvement in India on a scale commensurate with the problems involved; even the two most fundamental problems, education and public health, have escaped it. Largely because of this neglect, together with the general inadequacy of the British imperial rule to meet and to satisfy the insistent needs, demands, yearnings and longings of a rapidly awakening country, the Indian nationalist movement has prospered and nationalism is undermining imperialism. Let us turn, therefore, to the historical development of the Indian nationalist movement.

Historical Development of the Nationalist Movement. While it is true that the cumulative effect of all these grievances described, which bear so heavily upon the Indian people today, has not been realized nor fully appreciated until within the last generation in India, yet a nationalist movement, an instinctive revolt against the alien invader, has existed since about the middle of the nineteenth century. It has already been remarked that the Sepoy Mutiny of 1857 possessed a far greater significance than just a rebellion of discontented mercenaries and represented the first outward expression of Indian national feeling. Even before this outbreak, petitions had been sent to parliament asking for the appointment of "respectable and intelligent natives" to the governor's council.

Although it is thus possible to trace Indian nationalism back to the Mutiny, the movement did not assume any practical importance until the founding of the Indian National Congress in 1885. Since that date, three main stages or periods in its growth may be distinguished: from 1885 to 1905, from 1905 to 1917, and from 1917 to the present. Each one of these will be found to be characterized by certain concrete evidences of new strength in India, as well as by a corresponding response from Great Britain in the nature of more and more concessions of constitutional prerogative. Let us therefore determine what each of these periods contributed to the national movement.

During its initial or preparatory stage, 1885-1905, Indian nationalism became organized into the Indian National Congress formed at Bombay in 1885 by a group of educated young men, many of whom had been trained at Oxford or Cambridge and

there absorbed nineteenth century ideas of democracy and nationalism. Its crystallization at this juncture may, among other
things, be attributed to the liberalizing efforts of the Gladstone administration, which was seeking to ameliorate such harsh measures
as the disarming of Indians and the gagging of the Indian press,
reforms which were being opposed by the European community in
India. Its actual founder is said to have been an Englishman,
an ex-civil servant whose liberalism dictated the belief that Britain
should take the lead in developing political institutions in India.
All of which confirmed the oft-quoted theory that the very gifts
of imperialism everywhere, conscious or unconscious, such as
education, industrialism, liberalism, Westernization, prove in the
end a boomerang to the colonial power. Certainly the history
of the Indian Nationalist Congress is illustrative. The seventy-two
members at the first meeting inaugurated an annual gathering
which has met without break, except when banned by the British
government 1931-1934, and which since 1919 has averaged an
attendance of more than 6,000, representing every province of
India.

At first, the Congress drew its membership largely from Hindus,
representing students, intellectuals and professional men. Other
groups, both the religious communities and the merchants, peasants, landlords and workers had little interest in it. Moslems, indeed, as a whole had nothing to do with it. Even when the All-
India Moslem League was formed in 1906, it was not at first so
enthusiastic about nationalism but was mainly communal. The
Congress' membership was divided into the moderates, who
sought by constitutional means to effect reform, and the extremists, who tended to adopt methods of terrorism.

A contemporary wave of reaction against European materialism, which deprecated European habits of life and thought and
formed secret organizations to drive out alien rule, strengthened
the movement. The Congress, however, managed by the intelligentsia, occupied itself mainly with protests against this
and that and was not, on the whole, a particularly effective
body. The fact that its membership was mainly confined to
Bengal and that the nationalist movement, as a whole, remained
as yet divorced from the masses, constituted its major weaknesses.
The Congress, indeed, during this period, may be characterized
as more liberal than national.

The Second Period of Indian Nationalism, 1905-1917. Throughout the second period of its history, however, the Indian nationalist movement overcame many weaknesses of its first stage. For,
during the years 1905 to 1917, it spread over all India, penetrated all communities, all social and industrial classes, and
wrested significant concessions from the British government.
Many factors both external and internal were responsible. Among
them were the victory of Japan over Russia in 1905, which lent
great encouragement to the Asiatic Indians in the consequent loss
of prestige on the part of the European whites; Britain's co-
operation in the despoiling of Moslem countries, especially in
North Africa, and the exclusion of Indians from British self-
governing dominions. Within India the distressing famines of
1896 and 1899 had contributed to unrest and Lord Curzon, the
viceroy, had culminated his autocratic rule with the partitioning
of Bengal, which incited a revolution. For the Bengali Hindus
interpreted the act as an attempt to set up a predominantly Moslem area in order to outweigh their influence and to break up
their unity—as but another example of Britain's policy, "divide
and rule," which it doubtless was.

The undoing of the partition and the introduction of the
Morley-Minto Reforms or Indian Councils Act of 1909 failed to
assuage aroused feeling. Although marking the first step in representative self-government, as we have noted,[10] John Morley himself declared that Britain would never surrender to the people of
India responsibility for its own government. It is true that the
Act established the elected element predominant over the official
element in the provincial councils, but not in the central legislature, where native influence remained powerless. Hence the result was to drive opinion in the National Congress over to the
left and to extend the demand for reform.

Meanwhile, another potent influence besides the political was
affecting the nationalist movement at this time. In common with
nationalism generally at the end of the nineteenth and the beginning of the twentieth centuries, Indians tended to exalt India,
its spirituality, its culture, its literature, in short to idealize and
romanticize their country, to explore its past and to find it superior
to other civilizations. An outgrowth of the earlier reaction against

---

[10] See p. 384.

materialism, it counted among its protagonists many distinguished names. What Tilak, Banerjea and the Moslem, Aga Khan, were to the earlier period, with their newspapers, schools, their scholarship and their literary work, Mrs. Annie Besant, Lajpat Rai, Chandra Pal and the Ghose brothers were to the second stage. Mrs. Besant, an Irish woman who became a theosophist in 1889 and went to India where she spent the remainder of her life, founded among her many activities the Central Hindu College, later the nucleus of the Hindu University at Benares, wrote a number of pamphlets attacking British imperialism, and founded the paper *New India;* Lajpat Rai promoted the society of Armja Samaj, whose object was to effect social and religious reforms by reviving the ancient Hindu doctrines with the slogan "back to the Vedas," and also served as the historian of the nationalist movement; Chandra Pal was a journalist and missionary for the Brahma Samaj, a Hindu reform sect; Aravida Ghose was a poet and popularizer of sacred literature of the Hindu, and his younger brother was a propagandist and promoter of vernacular newspapers. But whatever their varied methods, and most of them were active politically also, they were all part of that great host of Indian men and women who imparted to Indian nationalism a distinct spiritual quality. They maintained that Indian freedom must be evolved in harmony with her national history and her national characteristics; they believed that India had her own part to play in the long story of human progress, and they urged that India's power lay rather in the realm of the mind than in that of matter. In a way they performed the same service for Indian nationalism as Mazzini performed for Italian nationalism; they spiritualized and popularized it.

The way was well prepared, therefore, in 1914, both by the intense political discontent engendered by the disappointing reforms of 1909, and by the quality of the intellectual temper, for the effect of the first World War and its stimulation of national unity and desire for national freedom. India's response to George V's appeal in 1914 "to overthrow an unparalleled assault upon the continuity of civilization and the peace of mankind," unlike its reaction to the similar appeal of George VI in 1939, was spontaneous and overwhelming. India poured out her treasures of wealth and of men without stint and rallied loyally to imperial defense. At the same time her people listened with even greater enthusiasm to the Wilsonian doctrines of "democracy" and "self-determination," which fell as music upon the ears of long-suppressed populations everywhere. But her patriotism and enthusiasm did not smother the rising political dissatisfactions in India and the nationalist movement made significant progress during the war.

In 1915 the National Congress resolved: "The time has arrived to introduce further and substantial measures of reform towards the attainment of self-government." And in 1916, representatives of the National Congress and the Moslem League, meeting together for the first time, drafted a scheme for reform— a plea for home rule which the Nationalist Party would accept— and thus by *rapprochement* immeasurably strengthened the movement. At the same time Nationalists carried on a lively agitation for self-government, widened their membership and enlarged their scope. Everywhere excitement ran riot. To state that India emerged from the first World War in 1918 with high hopes for the future and with an exaggerated anticipation of reform, is mildly to describe her temper.

Nor were her people without foundation for these great expectations of national fulfilment. Partly out of gratitude for India's war contribution and loyalty, partly as a matter of expediency to meet the rising tide of discontent and altogether in tune with the idealism voiced by the alleged war aims, Mr. Montagu, the secretary of state for India, had stated in 1917: "The policy of His Majesty's Government is that of increasing association of Indians in every branch of the administration and the gradual development of self-governing institutions with a view to the progressive realization of a responsible government of India within the empire." As this statement was coupled with a promise of forthcoming reforms, the second period in the history of Indian nationalism closed climactically. A note of warning, however, that too much must not be expected, was sounded in the ensuing *Report on Indian Constitutional Reforms* issued by Mr. Montagu and Mr. Chelmsford, the viceroy, in the statement that reform must not be too radical.

The Third Period of Indian Nationalism, 1917-1940. The Government of India Act of 1919, known as the Montagu-Chelmsford Reforms, more than justified the apprehension that was felt concerning it. It fell far short of meeting the demands of Indian nationalism, was attacked in India even before its passage by parliament, and plunged the national movement into a period of turbulence which has characterized the third stage of its development and has not as yet subsided. The Act affected British India alone, not the Native States, and fundamentally altered the political situation. Its essential element was decentralization and the establishment of a system known as dyarchy. Decentralization was effected by the delegation to the provincial governments of such matters as public health, education, irrigation, criminal law, prisons and labor legislation. Dyarchy or double government meant that these functions or powers were divided, in turn, between the provincial governors with their executive councils, to whom were reserved police, law, administration, irrigation, land revenue; and the provincial councils, to whom for administration by ministers chosen by them were transferred such matters as education, health, agriculture, public works. Each of the provinces had a provincial legislative council, in which about 75 per cent of the members were to be elected. The number of voters in the provinces was increased from 30,000 to more than 5,300,-000, thus placing the proportion of enfranchized Indians at about 2.2 per cent of the population.

No dyarchy was established in the central government. There, as before, the viceroy or governor-general ruled, directly responsible to the British parliament, with his executive council and the two advisory bodies, the legislative assembly and the council of state. He appointed the provincial governors, possessed full control of finance, defense and foreign affairs for All-India and was also invested with emergency powers whereby he might issue decrees with force of law. In neither house of the central legislature, however, was there to be any longer a majority of British officials. The viceroy appointed twenty-six of the sixty members of the council of state, and thirty-four were to be elected by a highly restricted suffrage which permitted only about 18,000 persons to vote; and 103 out of the 144 members of the legislative assembly were also to be chosen by an electorate of fewer than 1,000,000.

Clearly, the Montagu-Chelmsford Reforms were not democratic. The British retained absolute control of the central executive and of that important part of the provincial executive dealing with the reserved powers, which were after all decisive. Furthermore, whatever concessions were made were, in the main, protected by all kinds of safeguards. It was claimed that the new scheme was designed as a political training for Indians, who would be thereby gradually incorporated in the business of administration "by the progressive realization of responsible government"; that it was therefore only transitory and experimental. Indeed, the Act itself provided for the reconsideration of further reforms after the next ten years.

The Montagu-Chelmsford Reforms of 1919, however, were doomed to failure. Born in an atmosphere of rebellion, they were both inadequate and came too late, as imperialism usually is too late in its understanding of its opponent, nationalism. Even before they were presented, the National Congress had condemned the proposals, as contained in the preliminary *Report* published in 1918, and had raised the cry for *Swaraj* or self-government. The British government failed to grasp the fact that the nationalist movement had emerged from its infancy and from the leadership of the intellectuals; it did not sense the effect of the war upon it, nor the rallying to its support of the masses of India who were now asserting their own demands and finding their own spokesmen. Consequently, in order to quell the riotings and violences occasioned by the opposition to the proposed reforms, the administration had recourse to its old methods of suppression and decreed the Rowlatt Acts, which empowered the authorities to make arbitrary arrests, to suspend jury trial, to deny the right of appeal and to inflict summary penalties. The severity of these Acts reflects the extent of India's unrest at this time when the dissatisfaction with the proposed reforms appeared to unleash the unrestrained expression of all grievances, political, social, economic,[11] accompanied by strikes, agitation and disturbances of every kind. These culminated in the Amritsar massacre of April, 1919, in the Punjab, which inflamed the entire country almost overnight and sowed the seeds of the present situation in India.

In attempting to restore order after a riot in which two English bank managers and a woman missionary had been murdered, soldiers, on orders of General Reginald E. Dyer, opened fire on a peaceful crowd (public meetings were forbidden) assembled to

---

[11] A demand was made at this time for a protective tariff against certain British products as an aid to Indian industry, which the Montagu-Chelmsford Reforms met in some degree.

protest against the repressive measures. They killed over 500, wounded several thousand, and departed without administering first aid. Although relieved of his Indian command, Dyer was later retired on full pension from the Indian treasury, presented with a sum of $100,000 raised by public subscription in England and won the support of the House of Lords against even a mild Commons censure of his conduct. Gandhi from his sick bed begged the viceroy to right the wrong done his people and not to allow the massacre to go unpunished. But there was only silence from official quarters and the Indian nationalist movement moved under new leadership and onto new grounds.

Gandhi, the New Leader. Mohandas K. Gandhi, the Hindu social and religious reformer, provided the new leadership. Born in 1869, in the small Indian state of Porbander, near Bombay, he came of an official family belonging to one of the high Brahmin castes. According to his own account, it was his mother "who would take the hardest vows and keep them without flinching," who exerted the dominant influence upon his character, both by her example and her exhortations. It was she who laid the foundations of his future asceticism by extracting a promise of complete abstention from meat, eggs and alcohol, as well as a vow of celibacy (he had been married at thirteen) when he left India to pursue his education for the law in the University of London.

He spent three rather uncomfortable and unadjusted years in England, where he had difficulty in finding palatable food to accord with his vows until he joined the Vegetarian Society and became a member of its executive committee. In spite of successfully passing his examinations, being admitted to the bar and learning the ways of the ruling race, he returned to India in 1892 a shy, inarticulate young barrister, unhappy over his future career. Soon, however, an opportunity arose to serve his firm in South Africa, where he went for a few months and remained twenty years.

It was Gandhi's long sojourn in South Africa that determined the future course of his life. From experiences afforded him there, he began to formulate his own personal philosophy, as well as his plans for social and political reform, the dictates of which he found opportunity to put to the test. There was at this time in South Africa a large population of Indian immigrants, many of whom had been brought there to provide cheap labor and who suffered from the deprivation of all kinds of political, economic and social rights. Their cause Gandhi sponsored and in time became the acknowledged leader of the South African Indians, meanwhile renouncing whatever advantages a career in his own country offered. As barrister at the supreme court in Natal, he found himself in a strategic position to study the position of his compatriots as well as some of the most pressing problems and difficulties of imperial rule. Here, too, in his tussles with the authorities and with his own people, he learned much of men and motives and acquired the skill and tact of a shrewd politician. Seizing also the opportunity to put his beliefs to the test, he persuaded the Indians of South Africa to disobey governmental decrees that were detrimental to their own interests and to undergo imprisonment, in which he did not shrink from joining them, himself going to jail three times.

Altogether, his South African experience made him a fervid champion of nationalism and helped him evolve the principles and methods of fighting for it, which later found their full development and application in India. Let us glance at their fundamentals. Compounded of religion, piety, gentleness, asceticism, will power and unwavering adherence to the cause of justice, Gandhi's philosophy may be said to combine the teachings of Jesus, Tolstoy, Ruskin and Thoreau. Treating himself with the utmost harshness, he has become absolute master of his own body: he walks barefoot, sleeps on a hard couch, dresses like his humblest compatriots and fasts for days at a time, recalling the severest asceticism and discipline of the Hindus. He is indifferent to science, rejects the mechancial and materialistic civilization of the West. In place of its complexity, he adopts the village community as the loosely organized unit of society and the spinning wheel as the symbol of the revival of hand industry, which he considers a cure for poverty and the ills of Western industrialism. Abhorring the use of arms, violence, or physical force, he substitutes the power of will, of personality, of right and justice. Consequently, he conceived of passive resistance or nonviolence as an active method of resistance to whatever he considers injustice. It was Gandhi's conviction that passive resistance, which is not, after all, passivity, if generally adopted and genuinely practised, would win in the end over brute force. It was this theory which he began to apply practically in South Africa, and which was later to appear in India as non-co-operation, civil disobedience, the silent protest or *hartal*.

In 1914, this wizened, forty-five year old ascetic of insignificant physique, clad in loin-cloth and sandals, returned to India to assume control of the Indian nationalist movement. Displaying apparently none of the outward signs of leadership, he was to capture by his charm, his sincerity and saintliness the imagination of the masses of India, over whom he wields today an almost unbelievable power. For there he found, in 1914, conditions which enabled him to galvanize the inarticulate millions of India into action and to popularize the Indian nationalist movement.

The turbulent events of 1917-1919 provided, as we have seen, the opportunity for the emergence of Gandhi's leadership of the nationalist movement. The moderates lost control of the National Congress and, in 1920, he was named dictator with a practical mandate to devote every effort towards *swaraj*. Even the Moslems, disaffected by Britain's share in the dismemberment of Turkey by the Treaty of Sèvres, joined him. Immediately the campaign of non-co-operation, of nonresistance, was launched. British goods were boycotted, British cloth was burned, the repressive Rowlatt laws were not obeyed, students refused to attend schools, cases remained untried in the law courts, and the bewildered British found themselves unable to deal with literally thousands of young Indians who besieged the jails demanding to be arrested. But the movement got out of hand, despite Gandhi's abhorrence of violence and force. Unprecedented riotings and turbulence ensued, culminating in the disturbances which greeted the Prince of Wales' visit to India in the fall of 1921 and the Chauri-Chaura episode of 1922, when an Indian mob burned to death a group of police in their barracks. Gandhi, horrified by this repudiation of all his teaching, terminated the entire campaign. The same year, 1922, he was sentenced to imprisonment for six years, but was released in 1924 after an operation for appendicitis. Meanwhile the moderates assumed control of the National Congress and the national movement declined, to sink to its lowest ebb by 1926. Non-co-operation had apparently not succeeded.

During the years between 1924 and 1930, Indian nationalism indeed began to assume more of a European aspect, contrary to the teachings of Gandhi and of Tagore, its great literary exponent, who, although separated by profound differences from Gandhi, yet was at one with him in the belief that the people supersede in importance the state and in the emphasis upon cultural over political nationalism. Both Gandhi and Tagore subordinated the idea of nationalism, as representing the political power and economic mastery of the state, to the less materialistic and more spiritual conception that nationalism means the well-being, development and unity of its people. Both Gandhi and Tagore exalted education—and an essentially Indian, not European, education—as a method of attaining this kind of nationalism.

Evidences of this European trend in the national movement were various between 1924 and 1930, when Gandhi again entered the arena. They were: the abandonment of non-co-operation, except for the boycott upon British clothing materials; the adoption of political compromise instead of resistance to British reforms; the promotion of protective tariff to encourage Indian industry instead of Gandhi's revival of native handcraft; and finally the substitution of military training for passive resistance. Chitta Das, India's greatest nationalist leader, 1923-1925, and head of the All-India Swaraj Party which was organized in 1924, attempted to restrain this trend but failed. Indeed, he contributed to it by advocating the suspension of non-co-operation and participation in the elections for the provincial legislative councils in order to demonstrate by opposition within those bodies how unrepresentative they really were. In 1924, the Swaraj Party demanded full responsibility for India in provincial affairs and in national matters save defense and foreign affairs, but the main agitation for home-rule was carried on in the legislative councils, both provincial and central, as set up by the Montagu-Chelmsford Reforms of 1919.

The dyarchic plan, however, did not survive its allotted trial period of ten years. Acknowledged as early as 1924 by both representative British and Indians not to have succeeded, the date for a re-examination of the Indian situation was advanced two years by the appointment of an interparty parliamentary commission in 1927—headed by Sir John Simon. The official exclusion of Indians from the commission angered the nationalists, who boycotted it, referred to it as the "Simple Simon" commission and rejected its offer to include, unofficially, selected Indians on "equal terms of joint conference."

As was to be expected, therefore, the publication of the Simon Report in 1930 was thoroughly unsatisfactory to the Indian nationalists, whose demands had by that time far outrun those of 1924. It studiously avoided any mention even of dominion status or independence for India, even though the National Congress, meeting in 1928, while the investigations were in progress, had demanded dominion status and given Britain just one year in which to grant it. Failing to take note of this rising temper of the movement, the Report advised an increase in the executive powers of the secretary of state for India, the governor-general and the provincial governors. More than that it proposed making the provincial legislatures a school where natives might secure "primary instruction and training in government," which was regarded as an insult by educated Indians. Altogether, the Report was greeted by a veritable howl of indignation, in which even the more conservative Moslems joined.

The result of the publication of the Simon Report was to bring to a climax the resurgence of nationalism underway during the three years of the commission's work. Gandhi again took the lead and in April, 1930, launched another campaign of civil disobedience, of which the most spectacular incident was the Mahatma's "salt march" to Dandi on the sea. Since salt was a government monopoly, the tax upon it was especially onerous to the poorer people. Leading a group of volunteers, Gandhi marched 170 miles to the Gulf of Cambay, to make salt, seizing upon this as a symbol of rebellion which all could understand. A general defiance of laws in India followed, accompanied by riotings and strikes; and the prisons became embarrassingly full. As the emotional temperature of nationalism rose, complete independence for India came to be the cry of more and more members of the National Congress, which by this time had come to be strengthened by a fresh group of young and able leaders.[12]

Confronted by a situation which the obviously glaring inadequacy of the Simon Report could not hope to meet, the British government, upon the suggestion of the viceroy, Lord Irwin, summoned a Round-Table Conference in London with the hope of reaching a compromise. On November 12, 1930, the

---

[12] Among these leaders were Mrs. Sarojini Naidu, the poetess, a passionate worker for Hindu-Moslem unity; Motilal Nehru, the Pandit or wise man; and his son, Jawaharlal Nehru, a socialist and one of the most influential men in India.

first of the three Round-Table Conferences of 1930-1932 met in London. Delegates from the three British parties, the Native States and practically every other group in India were invited to attend, but the National Congress preferred to remain unrepresented, and Gandhi remained in prison. He did attend the second Round Table in September, 1931, although the third one found him once more in prison in India.

The three conferences were, on the whole, productive of results, although they failed to effect that compromise and co-operation of all elements in the forging of an instrument of government for India, in which it was hoped they would succeed. The first accomplished many things, among them the bringing together of all groups in India and the breaking down for a time at least of those insurmountable barriers so destructive to Indian unity, for Moslems, Hindus, Native Princes, women, Brahmins and pariahs or members of the "untouchable castes" all met with their British masters to thresh out common problems; the adherence of the native princes to a federation with British India; and the winning of the principle of political equality of "the untouchables" with the Brahmins. The second Round Table broke up in fruitless wrangling and was considered by many to be a failure; the last one drafted, to be sure, a plan of government, but it was mainly the work of British committees appointed by MacDonald, the premier, to devise a plan to bridge the apparently irreconcilable divisions among the Indians, and especially to work out a solution of the minority problems.

The greatest difficulties which the Round Tables encountered may be summarized as follows: first, the perennial disagreement between Moslems and Hindus which, when it came to constructing a representative government, involved the question of protecting the Moslems, who form a minority of about 22 per cent of the population, from the domination of the Hindus, and meeting their demands for separate communal electorates and other safeguards; second, the reconciliation of British India and the Native States on the kind of federation to be established, a question complicated by the growing sympathy of a part of the subjects in many Native States with British India; and finally, the old controversy between Great Britain and India over the degree of self-government which India was to have. Nor was the work of these Round Tables facilitated by the incessant disturbances to which India was subjected by the violence and intransigence of the nationalists. For India reflected the disharmonies within the London meetings in the same way in which the latter mirrored the divisions, the conflicts, racial, religious, social, in India. The temperature of the national movement in India rose and fell in accord with the successes, failures and wranglings in London. In 1931, Gandhi launched another campaign of civil disobedience, precipitated by Lord Willingdon's, the new viceroy's, refusal to withdraw a number of especially repressive ordinances, and was again imprisoned. In 1932, conditions reached a crisis: during the first half of the year nearly 50,000 persons were arrested, among them Mrs. Naidu, the president of the Congress, and 400 other members. British aggravation was great since, in addition to the usual riotings, serious attempts were made upon lives of important officials. To increase the universal unrest, the wedge of difference, always present between Hindu and Moslem, was driven deep. Bloody and fanatical riots broke loose and hundreds of lives were lost. Economic distress occasioned by the world depression added its contribution of turmoil and bitterness.

Altogether it was this *impasse* in India itself, as well as the failure of the second Round Table, which exhausted British patience and impelled the government to assume the responsibility for the drafting of the bases of India's new constitution. A solution of the major difficulty was found in the scheme which provided for separate communal electorates, representing different groups, such as Moslems, Hindus, untouchables, Sikhs and Indian Christians, to each of which a certain number of seats was to be allocated. Although violently opposed by Gandhi, who saw in the plan the destruction of Indian unity, especially in the separation of Brahmins and outcasts or untouchables, adjustment was finally reached by the latter surrendering their right to have separate electorates and receiving in return from the Brahmins twice the number of seats which they originally had in the provincial legislatures. With this compromise, Gandhi came out of his "fast to death" for the untouchables and the British government issued a White Paper containing the proposed new Indian Federal Constitution in March, 1933.[13]

---

[13] See pp. 385 ff.

The effect of the Government of India Act of 1935 (the third major change in India's constitutional development within twenty-five years) upon the national movement was similar to that of its predecessors. It stimulated the opposition and increased the demand for radical reform by its failure to meet expectations. Nowhere was this more clearly indicated than by the Indian National Congress in their choice of a new leader, Pandit Jawaharlal Nehru, who became its president. Born of an aristocratic family, educated at Harrow and Cambridge, he has again and again asserted his belief that India's complete independence is India's true goal. He has publicly announced that he is "a socialist and a republican and no believer in kings or princes or in the order that produces the modern kings of industry." He is determined to destroy the power of the British rule, the ruling princes and the hereditary landowners whose property he would expropriate. He rejects Gandhi's idea of the simple life and advocates industrialism. Minimizing Hindu-Moslem communal strife as an obstacle to unity, he claims that it is more economic than religious, which gives him another reason for believing that "socialism is the only solution for the woes of India."

Nehru also believes in obstructionist tactics and was responsible for the Delhi Resolution passed by the Congress in March, 1937, which demanded that the governors of provinces give assurance in advance not to use their veto powers over legislation, else congress members would not accept ministerial posts in those provincial assemblies where they possessed a majority. Lord Linlithgow, the viceroy, criticized the congress for this attitude; the governors refused to accede on constitutional grounds; and the nationalists finally accepted ministerial responsibility.

During the years 1937-1939, the National Congress, while permitting its members to co-operate in the new constitution and abandoning its earlier plan of calling legislatures of its own if its demands were not met, relentlessly pressed its program for complete independence in opposition to both the viceroy, who favored the constitution of 1935, and to the moderates, like Gandhi, who prefer compromise and negotiation with the British for the ultimate attainment of dominion status. Its president who succeeded Nehru, Subhas C. Bose, and his adherents not only demanded complete independence but also advocated civil disobedience and other direct action as a means of attaining it.

On the other hand, there appeared various signs that the strain between India and Britain was lessening, that the national movement was coming to believe in evolution, co-operation and not revolution. Among them were: Congress majorities increased in from six to eight of the eleven provincial assemblies; Rajendra Prasad, a moderate, was elected president; 11,000 political prisoners were released by the government; Gandhi's influence again emerged in the Congress; and the former feeling of fellowship for Japan changed to resolutions of condemnation for Japan's actions in Asia.

The outbreak of war in September, 1939, however, revealed once more the obdurate strength of the nationalist movement as well as the tension within it of conflicting groups. The provincial assemblies under Congress control resigned, the All-India Congress Committee on October 10 reiterated the demand that India be declared independent and the Nationalist Party moved towards civil disobedience; Gandhi, leader of the moderates, counselled patience and moderation for all, postponed civil disobedience and worked for compromise with Britain; the Moslems split asunder, Jinnah, president of the Moslem League declaring, on the one hand, that Moslem India would be willing to fight for Britain, and a large group of independent Moslems demanding, on the other, that all Moslem Indians remain neutral in the war. Until 1941, the stalemate within the Indian nationalist movement had avoided a major crisis arising for Great Britain in India.[14]

The Nationalist Movement in Persia-Iran

As previously described, Iran is an independent state which emerged from the very depths of imperialist subjection, the first oriental nation to free itself from European domination.[15] Its remarkable attainment of independence was immediately secured both by the action of Soviet Russia in renouncing all former claims of the czarist regime upon it and by its own striking defiance of Great Britain in revising the Anglo-Persian Treaty of 1919, by which Great Britain had sought to keep the country in its accustomed subjection to her expansionist aims. But before it was possible either to profit from the Russian renunciations or successfully

---

[14] See pp. 394 ff.
[15] See pp. 354 ff.

to defy Great Britain, an internal revolution was essential to rid the country of the weak, corrupt and thoroughly incompetent rule of that Kajar dynasty which had burdened it since the eighteenth century.

Persia's situation was thus similar to that of Turkey under the misrule of the Ottoman sultans and, like Turkey, it produced a national hero in the hour of crisis after the first World War, Reza Khan. He rallied the latent nationalist forces within the country, deposed its weakling shah, destroyed at one stroke the treaty, which was the symbol of Britain's imperialist control; and then proceeded, as dictator, to weld a disintegrated and woefully backward people into a national unit so that Persia became, in 1935, an independent state, member of the League of Nations, under the ancient and racial name of Iran.[16]

In common with Mustapha Kemal of Turkey, Reza Khan rose from the ranks of the army to become the embodiment and instrument of nationalism. Little is known of his early career save that he was born in the mountains of Mazanderan near the Caspian Sea, of hillman stock, of poor parentage and, probably, like other peasant boys, tended the flocks and herds. Unlike Mustapha Kemal, he received little education and appeared almost illiterate when he first emerged into prominence. Enlisting in the Cossack division of the Persian army, which was under Russian officers, his height and strength, courage and soldierliness commanded the allegiance of his comrades. He soon became an officer and won distinction in the campaigns of the war, especially against Russia's inroads in the north. Because of his military reputation, he was chosen by the group of young nationalists, led by the journalist Zia-ed-Din, to overthrow the government and install a reformed administration. On the night of February 20, 1921, Reza entered Teheran, the capital, with 2,500 men and effected a bloodless *coup d'état*, setting up a nationalist government with himself as minister of war. In command of the armed forces, it was not difficult for him to consolidate his position, and to bring most of the country under his domination. In 1923, he assumed the office of prime minister, and began his reforms by inviting an American commission, headed by Dr. A. C. Millspaugh, to straighten out the finances and place the country on a sound financial basis.

---

[16] The Persians consider themselves the true Iranians, or Aryans.

Meanwhile, the nominal shah, Ahmed, who spent much of his time in Paris and on the Riviera in the pursuit of pleasure, gradually lost his prerogatives. Reza first persuaded the parliament or Medjliss to grant him wide powers independent of the shah and then, in 1925, while Ahmed was ill in a Paris hospital, to depose the Kajar dynasty. The new national assembly, convoked at Reza's behest, elected him sovereign of Persia with the title of Shah Reza Pahlavi, an Iranian name which he selected, with right of succession to his heirs. In the following year, he was crowned and became military dictator of Persia, the name of which was officially changed to Iran in 1935. At first, Reza Khan desired to make Persia a republic on the Turkish model but was blocked by the strongly conservative Moslem clergy, who resented Turkey's abolition of the Ottoman caliphate. While Iran's constitution, therefore, placed the legislative power in the parliament, the shah exercised his privilege to appoint the ministers and officials and, again following Mustapha Kemal, established a personal rule.

Under Shah Pahlavi, Iran, like Turkey, has undergone a complete political, economic and social upheaval and although still in a transitional stage, has made significant advances towards unification and modernization, in spite of its backwardness, unproductiveness, the primitive character of its people and the fanaticism of its Moslem religion. The government's direct attack upon the inroads of imperialistic exploitation has already been referred to,[17] the chief and most daring of which was the modification in 1932 of the concession of the Anglo-Persian Oil Company, a majority of whose stock was held by the British government. For, in spite of Britain's efforts to refer the question of Persia's right to cancel the concession of so many years standing first to the World Court and then to the League of Nations Council, Persian leaders stoutly insisted with all the strength of their new nationalism that the company deal directly with their own government. Their victory was complete in this respect, as it was also in the conclusion of the new concession treaty of 1933 in which they succeeded in embodying all three of their principal demands: the limitation of the area of the concession, giving to the government alone the right to grant further concessions; the

---

[17] See pp. 355 ff.

increased employment and training of Iranians in the oil business; and the securing of increased fees which were not dependent upon oil prices. Further curtailment of the hitherto extended privileges of imperialistic interference in Persian affairs consisted, as in Turkey, of the abolition of the capitulations and special privileges; the establishment of a national fiscal and tariff control, accompanied by the withdrawal of note-issuing power from the British Imperial Bank of Persia; the taking over of the telegraph lines from the (British) Indo-European Telegraph Company; and the prohibition laid upon foreign mission schools forbidding them to teach Iranian primary children.

One of the most significant changes wrought by the triumph of nationalism over imperialism was Iran's recovery of the control of her defenses and her foreign policy, so long in the hands of foreigners. The army was thoroughly nationalized and freed from the supervision of all those Russian generals, British officers and Swedish guards who had been so conspicuous under the old regime. Remembering, indeed, the country's bitter experience at the hands of Europeans, the Iranian government refused the request of Imperial Airways to establish landing fields within its borders and withdrew the concession from the German Junkers Company to operate in Iran. Determined to exercise its own national sovereignty, the new state submitted to no external dictation in establishing new relationships with the powers.

Reza Shah Pahlavi not only expelled imperialism in its many aspects but fortified his country against it by a constructive policy of unification and nationalization. As the embodiment of the new nationalism, as yet unrealized by a large number of his countrymen, he and his ministers undertook reorganization and modernization with an independence of spirit and thoroughness of execution startling to observe. Among their political and economic achievements were: the restoration of order throughout the country; reform of the finances, of the judiciary and legal codes; the promotion of industrialization, national trade, intensive farming; and the unifying of the country by means of a central railway system. In addition they decreed wholesale social reforms like those in Turkey regarding such matters as education, the Europeanization of dress, customs, weights, measures and the calendar. Unlike Mustapha Kemal, however, Reza Shah Pahlavi was not able to deal so drastically with the church nor to disestablish it. Islam remains in its Shiite form the state religion of Iran although its priests have become state officials under the latter's supervision. Only by compromise and conciliation was Reza able to deal with the original opposition of the clergy caste. The constitution contains a provision that no law can be enacted that conflicts with the canon law of the church and provides that the parliament must always contain five ecclesiastics, who are experts in canon law.

The dramatic nationalization and modernization of Iran under the astonishing Reza Shah Pahlavi represents the climax of a Persian nationalist movement which can be said actually to have begun only in 1906. Before that date, it is true, faint signs of a national awakening might be observed, although they amounted to little and accomplished less. As early as 1850, a few Persian officials had encouraged their young countrymen to study in Europe, the first Persian newspaper, *Iran,* was established in Teheran and other indications of an intellectual quickening appeared. But the oriental despotism which ruled Persia, supplemented by the power of an ignorant obscurantist and superstitious clergy, provided anything but an hospitable atmosphere for the flowering of a Persian renaissance. Shah Nasir-Din, indeed, added to his already long list of crimes against Persia by directly crushing out any attempt to revive Persian intellectual life or to permit it to be influenced by those outside of Persia who were striving for a united Islam. Yet the task of national reform devolved largely upon the scholars and those religious teachers who became champions of the people's rights. For the upper, noble class largely benefited from the exploitation of their country by the foreign powers, as they did also from the bribery and graft of the shah's corrupt rule; there existed no well-organized or economically strong middle class, while the mass of the Persian people were uneducated and inarticulate.

The outlook for reform brightened, however, with the opening years of the twentieth century. More frequent contacts with Europe increased the numbers of the group in Persia imbued with ideas of Western constitutionalism and liberalism, and the British liberal governments at first encouraged these leaders. A national party took definite shape, augmented by merchants from towns and cities who during the last two decades of the nineteenth century were awakening to the need of economic regeneration.

The resentment aroused by the granting of a tobacco monopoly to an English company resulted in a popular boycott in 1891 which had its unifying effect. The shah Nasir-Din himself was assassinated in 1896 by a revolutionary, and the Russian revolution of 1905 inspired hope and courage in oppressed Persia.

As previously related,[18] the way was well prepared for a national revolt in 1906. Shah Muzaffar, Nasir-Din's successor, proved too weak and timid to cope with the rising tumult but only increased it by renewed extravagance, reducing his country to insolvency, which he then sought to remedy by fresh concessions to Russia. The vicious circle of loans guaranteed by the mortgaging of national resources, leading, in turn, to deeper indebtedness and increased servitude to the foreign powers, continued. Taking advantage of the shah's incompetent weakness and the aroused temper of the people, the national leaders demanded a constitution by the direct method of retiring from the capital, Teheran, and refusing to return until it had been promised. Their "strike" succeeded: the first Persian parliament met in October, 1906, and drafted a constitution providing for a national council or Medjliss under whose control, finances, treaties, concessions and other vital matters were placed. The timid shah signed this document upon his deathbed and his successor, Mehemet Ali, swore to respect it.

Although the nationalist movement won a significant victory in the constitution of 1906, it was doomed to failure mainly because of the interference of the European powers, Russia and Britain, who, especially Russia, championed the cause of the shah and of the conservative court party against the liberals in the Medjliss. During the civil war [19] that ensued between that body and Mehemet Ali over the issue of constitutionalism versus autocracy, Russia, not the shah, was at first the real adversary of the Persian constitution. Then when the very disorganization of Persia, caused by the national revolution of 1906, played into the hands of her foreign masters and facilitated the Anglo-Russian Convention of 1907, which enabled Britain and Russia practically to absorb the country, the nationalist cause became hopeless. For the British liberal government now joined Russia as an enemy of Persian constitutionalism.

[18] See p. 367.
[19] See p. 368.

Nevertheless, as we have hitherto described, the Persian nationalists carried on the fight: they deposed Mehemet Ali and set up their own shah, Ahmed; they called in Morgan Shuster, an American expert, to reorganize the country's finances; they won the support of their countrymen in the outlying provinces; they organized the Medjliss or parliament upon the European model;[20] and they developed a truly national Persian press. But the difficulties confronting Persia's nationalism at this time were too great. The nationalist party was, after all, small and far in advance of the majority of the backward population, composed of peasants, tribesmen and nomads, long accustomed to a despotic rule, or merely a law unto themselves. The fiber of the country was weakened by economic exploitation, burdensome taxation, graft and corrupt government. Above everything else, the real rulers of Persia were the foreign powers, Russia and Britain. In the face of these insurmountable difficulties, the Medjliss was suspended after 1911 and the nationalist movement was rendered impotent in the face of the imperialistic grip upon the country, which threatened in 1914 to effect its complete collapse.

The Russian revolution of 1917, however, afforded the reform leaders their long-sought opportunity to accomplish what they had failed to do in 1906-1907. It both removed the czarist protection from the Kajar dynasty and imparted fresh energy, enthusiasm and practical assistance to the nationalists to effect the Kajar dynasty's final overthrow. Although the revolutionary movement of 1906 had apparently failed, for then imperialism had proved too strong for it, its ultimate success may be found in the triumph of nationalism in 1921. Not that the popular movement was able to achieve this victory by itself; it represented too small a proportion of this backward country. Nevertheless it was the little group of leaders, descendants of those of 1906, who called in the military arm in the person of Reza Khan, who in turn imposed nationalism upon his country and built up its defenses against a renewed imperialism. This he accomplished both by a fearless challenge of all alien privilege within Iran and by a program of rapid modernization in imitation of the U.S.S.R.

---

[20] Parties in the parliament were: the moderate and conservative progressive party (the majority group), the democratic party, and the radical progressives, whose left wing included representatives of the Armenian and Georgian socialist organizations.

Nationalism in Afghanistan

Although the most backward and primitive of the countries of the Middle East, Afghanistan joined her neighbors in revolting against imperialism and declaring a nationalistic independence. But its rebellion was distinctly the work of its rulers and not of its people.

Enough has been already related about the oppressive weight of the expansionist powers upon this mountainous, border country, which served as a battleground for their competitive aims, to demonstrate the remote background of its revolt. But three chief influences may be cited as directly responsible for the immediate precipitation of the declaration of independence by its new emir, Amanullah Khan in 1919, and the winning of British recognition thereto in the Anglo-Afghan Treaty of 1922.[21] In the first place, the collapse of Russia as a threat and the substitution, instead, of the Soviet government as an assistance to Afghanistan's nationalism was important. For the Soviet government aroused all the Near and Middle East to revolt against British imperialism, as well as rendered active encouragement thereto. Then, Britain just at this time gave further justification to such an attack by her treatment of nationalist Turkey which excerbated Moslem resentment, and this played a significant part in the "holy war" which Amanullah carried into India against her in 1921. Finally, like his father, Habibullah, who had been assassinated, Amanullah believed strongly in the reorganization, modernization and Europeanization of his country as a bulwark against foreign inroads. To this end, Habibullah, extremely jealous of his rights over internal affairs left to him by his treaty with Britain, had promoted schools, roads, progressive improvements of all kinds— a work which his son continued and one which made him desire independence.

Illustrative of the nonpopular aspect of Afghanistan's nationalism, however, was the constant revolt against their ruler's efforts to effect a unified secularized state, carried on by the Afghan tribes. For after Amanullah had secured his country's independence, he introduced, too radically for his backward people, Western ideas of education, administration, engineering and defense,

---

[21] See p. 371.

importing foreign experts to put them in motion. It was after he returned from a trip to western Europe, and attempted seriously to interfere with religious and tribal customs by replacing them with European, that the orthodox Moslem tribes, again revolting, besieged the capital, Kabul, and forced Amanullah's abdication and flight. Among other things he had attacked the power of the Moslem clergy, the mullahs, by decreeing a division of their land.

His successor, Mohammed Nadir Shah, after a struggle with pretenders to the throne, finally succeeded in re-establishing the royal family's rule by rescinding many of his predecessor's decrees and advancing more gradually along the road of secularized nationalism. He promulgated the "Fundamental Rules," which provided for the drafting of the laws by a royal ministry and their ratification by an elective council, but which declared Islam to be the state religion and Islamic law to be binding. Compulsory state elementary education was, however, established; slavery was forbidden; and Nadir's rule gave every promise of enlightenment. But he too fell a victim to assassination by an inflamed student in 1933. Succeeded by his young son, the real rulers of the country became his three uncles, Nadir's brothers. Afghanistan was admitted to the League of Nations in 1934.

THE EFFECT OF EXPANSION IN THE MIDDLE EAST UPON
INTERNATIONAL RELATIONS

Since expansion in the Middle East during the modern period concerned mainly two colonial powers, Russia and Britain, its effect upon international relations did not prove so widespread as in the other areas. Nevertheless the constant rivalry between these two powerful competitors exerted a significant and far-reaching influence upon world politics which it is important to review.

As previously related,[22] the long-standing Anglo-Russian competition for empire in the Middle East arose from diametrically opposed policies in that entire region: Russia's to destroy, annex and absorb all those territories which blocked her southward march to warm-water ports or to an attack upon India; Britain's to preserve, strengthen and protect such territories as buffer states and as defenses to her possessions, interests and lines of communi-

---

[22] See pp. 357 ff.

cation in middle and southern Asia. For generations, all through
the long years of empire building in the Middle East, these
conflicting policies had proved a chronic source of anxiety and of
danger. Even when Britain and Russia were allies in Europe
against Napoleon I during the early years of the nineteenth century, expansionist rivalry in the Middle East drove a wedge
between them. For in 1800 Czar Paul of Russia and Napoleon
planned together to invade Hindustan, while an envoy from
Napoleon visited the Persian court to arrange for the passage of
a French army through Persian territory to a rendezvous on the
plains of India with the Russian forces. Britain's answer to this
threat was, as we have previously noted,[23] the signing of two
treaties designed to guard her interests: one, the Malcolm Treaty
(1801) negotiated between the government of India and the
shah of Persia, which constituted an offensive-defensive alliance;
and the other between the government of India and the sultan
of Oman which obligated him to close his territory and his ports
along the Persian Gulf to the entrance of French troops. Both of
these treaties were aimed, it is true, directly at France, but indirectly also at Russia.

With the conclusion of the treaty of alliance between Czar
Alexander I and Napoleon I at Tilsit (1807), the Franco-Russian
threat to Britain and India in the Middle East became ever more
serious with the French influence in Persia tending to dominate
the Russian. But with Napoleon's downfall in 1815, Russia again
emerged as the chief rival, a position which she maintained with
ever increasing strength throughout the ensuing years of the
nineteenth century. Indeed, Anglo-Russian rivalry in the Middle
East matched that in the Near and Far East with the result that
the foreign policy of these two states, as far as it concerned Asia,
was consistently oriented to the fundamental concept of their
mutual competition and antagonism in all three of these areas of
colonial penetration.

During the last decades of the nineteenth century and the opening years of the twentieth, clashes between Russia and Britain in
the Middle East grew more and more frequent and serious as
the stakes of expansion everywhere rose in value. Besides, Great
Britain, at that time, had her hands full in Africa, compromising

[23] See p. 364.

on the one hand her colonial interests with those of France in the north, in Egypt and the Sudan, and, on the other, fighting for her imperialist position in the south against the Boers in the Boer War. Her preoccupation on the African continent afforded Russia an excellent opportunity to make headway in Asia, especially in central Asia, which she did not fail to capitalize. As hitherto described, the constant friction occasioned by Russia's drive for territorial acquisition in Afghanistan and along the border of India, which had disturbed British security during the 1870's and 1880's, had been allayed, temporarily at least, by the Anglo-Russian Convention of 1895.[24] But in common with all such compromises of expansionist ambitions, it proved non-definitive. For Russia, frustrated in Afghanistan, transferred her efforts to Tibet, seeking to make it a pawn in her game against her imperialist rival.

Here she instigated intrigues against British trade and British interest of all kinds by means of agents who worked under cover of certain religious orders, which possessed a close bond with their monkish brotherhoods in Russia, and also through the devious bypaths of diplomacy. Fostering the antipathy of the Dalai Lama, the religious, semimystical ruler of Tibet, towards Britain, these Russian agents taught him and his country to look to Russia rather than to Britain for protection, to repudiate the Anglo-Tibetan trade treaty of 1890, and to turn a deaf ear to all British attempts to communicate with Tibet. They even persuaded the Dalai Lama to return unopened all messages received from Lord Curzon, the viceroy of India. So effective were Russia's anti-British tactics that the government of India became obliged in 1904 to dispatch a military mission, under Colonel Younghusband, in order to secure British commercial rights guaranteed by the 1890 treaty and to discipline the recalcitrant Tibetans. Although the mission met with success, the need to send it revealed the strength of the Russian menace in this quarter, which only the outbreak of the Russo-Japanese War in 1905 and Russia's consequent preoccupation in the Far East served temporarily to relieve.

Meanwhile, Russo-British clashes in Persia became more and more acute at the turn of the century. Again taking advantage of a slackening of British watchfulness because of the Boer War,

[24] See p. 360.

Russia became daringly aggressive. Not content with her privileged economic position in north Persia, she sought to invade British prerogatives in the south and around the Persian Gulf. In 1900, she dispatched consuls into the province of Seistan, which adjoined the border of India, and also into Basra, Bushire and Bander Abbas, British stations on the Persian Gulf. At Bandar Abbas, a Russian gunboat attempted to establish a coaling station and Russian emissaries of all kinds visited and "explored" the gulf. As answer to this threat, Britain declared in 1903: "We should regard the establishment of a naval base or fortified port in the Gulf by any other Power as a very grave menace to British interests and we should certainly resist it by all the means at our disposal." To stiffen the declaration, Lord Curzon journeyed from India with an impressive array of warships which steamed up the gulf and effectually demonstrated British prestige in those quiet waters.

Besides these concrete and sometimes spectacular evidences of Anglo-Russian expansionist friction in Afghanistan, Tibet and Persia, must be placed, as additional proof, the obvious signs of Britain's official awakening to the threat of Russia's advance and the realization on the part of her statesmen that Anglo-Russian rivalry was reaching a dangerous climax. For the above quoted declaration, made for Britain by Lord Lansdowne in regard to the Persian Gulf, constituted only one symptom of the general stiffening of British policy towards Russian encroachment in the Middle East, which characterized the decade 1895-1905, and whose greatest protagonist may be said to have been Lord Curzon. Appointed viceroy to India in 1898, he carried with him to Asia strong suspicions of Russia's designs in the Middle East generally, and especially in the Persian Gulf, where just at this time Germany's projected Bagdad railway was focusing attention. Envisaging the establishment of the railway's terminus at Koweit upon the Persian Gulf, he feared the advantage that such an event might afford Russia, a fear which was augmented by a scheme for a railway from Syria to Koweit put forward by a Russian. Long interested in Persia, Curzon had written a book upon this country some years before in which he had pointed out that the concession of any port on the Persian Gulf by any power to Russia would constitute, in his view, "a wanton rupture of the *status quo* and an international provocation to war." Thus the agreement which he signed with the sheik of

Basra in 1899 which obligated the latter to cede no territory and to receive no ambassador from a foreign power without Britain's sanction was primarily a protection against Russia although it eventually, as we have learned, served as one against Germany and her plans for the penetration of the Near and Middle East.

From his vantage point in India, Curzon was in a position at the opening of the twentieth century to observe the pressure of Russia upon British interests at many points, a situation which he brilliantly analyzed in his famous dispatch of 1899 to the home government. Herein, among other penetrating observations he declared: "Closely pressing upon Persia and Afghanistan is the ever-growing momentum of a power whose interests in Asia are not always in accord with our own," and he advised that "we press for early action, for unless we bestir ourselves, there is good reason for fearing that the already trembling balance may be disturbed to our disadvantage." Two years later, in 1904, he again appealed in a personal letter to Lord Lansdowne for firmness on the part of Britain in Persia. Here, the overshadowing of British influence by Russia had reached such a point that British representatives at the shah's court grew to feel so hopeless and useless that, as one of them declared, he "felt like a jelly-fish in a whirlpool." "The Russian Bank at Teheran is rapidly cutting out the Imperial Bank," wrote Curzon. "Russian consulates are being established in all parts of the country. The Persian Cossacks under Russian officers have been greatly raised in numbers."[25]

A way out of this serious *impasse* caused by the acute conflict of Russian and British expansionist interests which became so evident during the opening years of the twentieth century was afforded both by the course of events and the customary diplomacy of compromise. For contributing to the solution of Anglo-Russian rivalry were the Russo-Japanese War, wherein Russia's defeat by Japan materially reduced her prestige in Britain's eyes; the Persian revolution of 1906 against the shah, which weakened the country's resistance, and facilitated partition; and finally, Germany's success in pushing the Bagdad railway, which menaced both British and Russian interests in the Near and Middle East, and threw the two countries together to defend them. Russia's defeat, moreover, frustrated her ambitions in the Far East and drove her to

[25] Quoted in Langer, W., *The Diplomacy of Imperialism*, II, 753.

accelerate her expansion program in the Middle East, where turbulent internal conditions in Persia and a pro-Russian shah invited the imposition of a more complete subjection of that helpless country.[26] This renewed aggression on the part of Russia forced Great Britain into the choice of active resistance or compromise with her rival. Britain chose compromise, urged on to her decision by the realization that Germany loomed as a greater menace to her expansionist interests than did Russia and that she needed Russia's assistance against her.

Again, the way for Anglo-Russian diplomatic *rapprochement* was already well prepared: Russia had become an ally of France in the Dual Alliance of 1894 and Britain and France had just succeeded in compromising their colonial clashes in Africa by forming the *entente cordiale* of 1901 and 1904; Lord Curzon himself had suggested in his dispatch of 1899 an agreement with Russia based on the principle of partition; and by 1906, King Edward VII, Sir Edward Grey and Isvolski, the Russian foreign minister, were heartily in favor of such a compromise. Indeed, such a step had been discussed by Edward VII and Isvolski (before he became foreign minister) during the Russo-Japanese War, but it could not be pushed until Russia came to terms with Japan. Britain pressed the matter far more than did Russia, where the conservative imperialists demanded that Persia be completely absorbed by their country. But Isvolski believed that such aggression would at once precipitate an Anglo-Russian conflict which a Russia weakened by foreign war and the revolution of 1905 could ill afford. Consequently, the British proposal of the partition of Persia into spheres of influence made in 1906 was adopted and the visit of a Russian fleet to Portsmouth foreshadowed the imminent Anglo-Russian agreement.

The Anglo-Russian Convention of 1907. When signed on August 31, 1907, the Anglo-Russian Convention included three agreements: one dealing with Persia which partitioned it into three zones of influence, Russian in the north, neutral in the middle and British in the south; one regarding Afghanistan, which Russia recognized as a British sphere of influence as long as Britain promised not to occupy or annex it; and one concerning Tibet. Since the first two settlements have previously been explained,[27]

[26] See p. 367.
[27] See p. 368.

and the fate of Persia and Afghanistan described, the third one regarding Tibet remains to be added. Both contracting powers agreed not to interfere with Tibet's internal concerns or attempt to secure special concessions such as railway, road or mining rights. They also concurred in recognizing the territorial integrity of Tibet under the sovereignty of China and mutually promised to conduct all negotiations with Tibet through China and to refrain from sending direct representatives of their respective governments to the Lama at his capital, Lhassa. Thus Tibet became a buffer state, a barrier between the Russian Bear on the north and the British Lion in India.

These three agreements over Persia, Afghanistan and Tibet, which constituted the Anglo-Russian Convention of 1907, compromised, if only temporarily, the expansionist interests of Britain and Russia in the Middle East and maintained Persia and Afghanistan almost completely subjected to the expansionist powers from 1907 to 1914. With the outbreak of the World War in 1914, Persia, although neutral, was overrun by Russian, British and Turkish troops and Russia and Britain sought to secure their hold arranged by the Anglo-Russian Convention. Consequently, in 1915 they signed a secret agreement, which was part of the Allied secret treaty of that year regarding Constantinople, wherein Britain was to be permitted to add the middle or neutral zone of Persia to her own southern portion and Russia to be allowed a completely free hand in the northern zone, which pointed directly towards ultimate annexation. Russia's withdrawal from the war in 1917, together with the collapse of the czarist regime, invalidated all these agreements, and attempts to compromise Anglo-Russian expansionist rivalry in the Middle East became unnecessary. As previously related, the Soviet government at first disclaimed all imperialist ambitions and renounced all old Russia's claims in this area, while Great Britain was forced, in the face of the establishment of Persia's and Afghanistan's independence, to curtail her penetration and control.[28] With the recrudescence of nationalist imperialism as a policy of the U.S.S.R., Anglo-Russian expansionist rivalry was again revived in the Near East, a dangerous antagonism which the outbreak of the European conflict in 1939 did much to aggravate. Thus, like so many of the colonial deals

---

[28] See pp. 355-366.

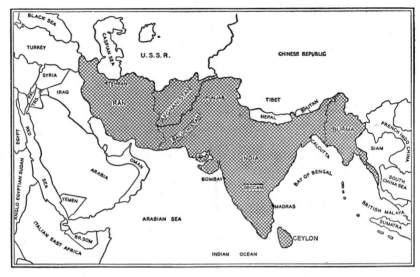

THE MIDDLE EAST IN 1939

hitherto reviewed, in Africa and in the Near East, the Anglo-Russian Convention failed definitely to compose conflicting expansionist ambitions but only held them in a precarious balance and postponed their ultimate settlement.

Not so indefinite, however, was the effect of the Anglo-Russian Convention of 1907 upon international relations, for here its influence was profound. The agreement brought Russia into partnership with Britain and created the Triple Entente. Although it included no military obligations and did not at first effect a closely integrated diplomatic partnership, it nevertheless supplied the missing link and completed the circle of Britain, France and Russia. Henceforth until 1917, these three powers were to stand together not only in defense of their expansionist aims in Africa, the Near East, the Middle East and the Far East, but also in European affairs, with such fateful consequences as the first World War was to demonstrate. But whatever the effect of the Anglo-Russian Convention of 1907 upon the Triple Entente and its activities, its chief significance resided in the fact that it added one more alliance to the international pattern whose roots lay in expansionist rivalries. Thus, the Triple Entente, including the Anglo-French Alliance and the Anglo-Russian Convention, rested in at least two-thirds of its foundations upon the unstable compromise of colonial ambitions.

READINGS

Andrews, C. F. (editor). *Mahatma Gandhi—His Own Story*, 1930.

Beauchamp, J. *British Imperialism in India*, 1934. Anti-imperialistic.

Brailsford, H. N. *Rebel India*, 1931. Social conditions described by a liberal.

Buchanan, D. *The Development of Capitalist Enterprise in India*, 1934. Reliable, objective.

Chirol, V. *India*, 1926. Authoritative.

Coatman, J. "India Today and Tomorrow," *Foreign Affairs*, Jan., 1940.

Gandhi, M. K. *Young India, 1919-1922*, 1923. His own story and philosophy.

Gandhi, M. K. *Young India, 1924-1926*, 1927.

Gunther, J. *Inside Asia*, 1939. Journalistic, detailed.

Ikbal, Ali Shaw. *Afghanistan of the Afghans*, 1928. On customs and traditions.

Kiralfy, A. "The Middle East on Guard," *Asia*, June, 1940.

McMann, Sir G. F. *Afghanistan from Darius to Amanullah*, 1929. A survey.

Merritt-Hawkes, O. A. *Persia: Romance and Reality*, 1935. Travel picture.

Millspaugh, A. C. *The American Task in Persia*, 1925. Post-war problems.

Muzumdar, H. T. *Gandhi versus the Empire*, 1932.

Nehru, J. *Toward Freedom*, 1941. A well-written autobiography.

Rolland, R. *Mahatma Gandhi*, 1924. Sympathetic biography.

Roth, A. "Triangular Conflict in India," *Amerasia*, Nov., 1940.

Roth, A. "Religious Conflict—Red Herring of India," *Amerasia*, Aug., 1940.

Sheean, V. *The New Persia*, 1927. Account of social and political change.

Shuster, W. M. *The Strangling of Persia*, 1913. Personal, detailed.

Ward, A. W. and Gooch, G. P. (editors). *The Cambridge History of British Foreign Policy*, 3 vols., 1922. Standard.

Wilson, A. T. *Persia*, 1933. Geographical, social, economic, political aspects.

Younghusband, F. E. *Dawn in India: British Purpose and Indian Aspiration*, 1930. Good survey.

PART V

European Expansion in the Far East

BY

CYRUS H. PEAKE

CHAPTER SIXTEEN

The Geographical, Cultural, Economic and Political Setting

GENERAL FEATURES

THE TERM "Far East" is here defined, partly from geographical and partly from political considerations, as including areas under the control of the former Chinese Empire, comprising China Proper together with Formosa and Manchuria, its dependencies, Mongolia, Sinkiang and Tibet, and its tributary states, Korea, Liu-chiu Islands, Annam, Laos, Burma and Siam. Included, also, are Eastern Siberia, Japan, the Philippines, the Malay Peninsula and the East Indies. This region occupies approximately (lack of accurate statistics for all parts of the area prevent the presentation of exact figures) 8,000,000 square miles or a little less than one-sixth of the area of the land surface of the world (less the Arctic and Antarctic regions) and has a population of about 650,000,000, which is roughly one-third of the world's total population. Comparing it with other regions of the world we find that it is more than twice the area of Europe and has nearly 200,000,000 more people; while it is only half the size of the Americas, it has almost three times as many people; and though only three-fourths of the

size of Africa, it has a population that is between four and one-half
and five times as numerous as that of the "Dark Continent."

Variety and contrast to an extent unsurpassed, if indeed equaled
in any other region of the world, are the key words descriptive
of the Far East. Topographically and climatically the region
abounds in striking contrasts. Towering mountain ranges, many
of whose peaks rise above 20,000 feet, encircle plateaus such as
that of Tibet, the so-called "roof of the world." These mountains,
averaging 10,000 feet above sea level, stand in contrast to the
nearby Turfan basin which lies 1,000 feet below sea level. Virtually uninhabitable deserts, such as parts of the Gobi and the
Takla Makan (the latter has been described as a "true" desert
and the "most formidable of all the dune-covered wastes of the
globe") located in the "dead heart" of Asia, contrast sharply with
the fertile Chengtu plain, China's "Garden of Eden," with its
population density of 2,150 per square mile; or the densely
populated island of Java in the tropics. Through this region flow
some of the great rivers of the world, such as the 3,200 mile long
Yangtze in China, which is Asia's Mississippi. In the Pacific, lying
within a few hundred miles of the mainland, stretches an almost
continuous chain of many thousands of islands reaching from
Kamchatka, at 50° N. latitude, to Sumatra, in the heart of the
tropics. Included within this chain are the islands of Japan Proper,
Saghalin, Formosa, the Philippines and the East Indies. On these
islands live 140,000,000 people—a population greater than that of
the United States.

It follows naturally that in a region of such varied topography,
extending as it does from the equator to beyond the Arctic circle,
the greatest extremes of climate should obtain. The hot, humid
lowlands of equatorial Java have an average annual temperature
of 78.6° F. with a rainfall of from 40 to 80 inches. Southern Burma
has an average temperature of 80° F. and in places an annual rainfall of nearly 200 inches. By way of contrast the arid deserts and
semiarid steppes of Mongolia and Sinkiang have the greatest
climatic extremes in the world. The rainfall averages less than 15
inches and falls in places to less than 2 inches, and temperatures
range down to 40° below zero during a winter season which grips
the land eight months of the year and is followed by only a
brief hot summer.

The great variety of topography and climate together provide

the conditions for the existence of an equally unexcelled variety
of plant and animal life. China, for example, has 9,000 flowering
plants, half of which are endemic. It has been aptly called the
"Mother of Gardens" from which Western peoples have secured
many of their loveliest flowers, shrubs and fruits. From the soils
of the Far East come about 90 per cent of the world's rubber,
over 70 per cent of the world's pepper, over 90 per cent of the
quinine, over 80 per cent of the kapok and over 70 per cent of the
camphor. Beneath the surface of the land it treasures in varying
amounts nearly all important minerals. Its resources of antimony
and tungsten are richer than elsewhere. China has supplied as
much as 80 per cent of the world's production of the former and 75
per cent of the latter. However, the Far East is relatively poor in
those basic minerals that undergird modern industry, such as oil,
iron ore and coking coal, which predestine the region to a relatively minor degree of industrialization compared with Germany,
England or the United States. The area as a whole is predominantly agrarian. Despite the potentialities for the development of
light industries, particularly textile industries, its relative paucity
of mineral resources inherently limits the development of heavy
industries. This, together with its great population, predetermines
the persistence of a predominantly agrarian economy in the
region.

Varied topography, climate and vegetation have contributed
the basic conditions which make of the Far East a vast ethno-
logical and anthropological museum of unparalleled richness. The
ruggedness of the terrain provides innumerable isolated valleys
and plateaus where successive migrations of peoples and tribes in
prehistoric and historic times have found refuge from flood,
famine and powerful enemies. In these areas they have found
well-nigh complete isolation for centuries. The region as a whole
not only presents a relatively high degree of isolation to modern
times in its world position, but within it there is an excessive degree of regionalization which has made it impossible for any one
race, language, culture, religion or political force to unite or dominate it. China came the nearest to achieving cultural and political
domination over the area.

The principal peoples in the area, representing in most cases
a blend of more primitive, aboriginal migrations, are the Indo-
Chinese group made up of the Chinese—who are quite as diver-

sified in racial make up and physical appearance as the Europeans —the Thai, Tibetan-Burmese, Lolo, Mo-so, Miao and Man; the Indo-Aryans, represented chiefly by the Russians and the Indians; the Ural-Altaians, made up for the most part of the Turks, the Mongols and the Tungus; the Austronesians, among whom are included the Mon, Kmer and the Malays. In addition there are the Koreans, the Japanese, the Ainu—the aborigines of Japan—and a few isolated groups of Negritos in the Philippines. There are to be found among these varied peoples of the Far East living examples of all stages of cultural and economic development from head-hunters in Formosa to the highly civilized and sophisticated Chinese; from primitive hunters and fishers and nomadic herdsmen to the progressive Japanese, who have transformed their nation into a modern industrialized power within a period of sixty years. These peoples of the Far East speak many different languages and dialects and in writing employ a varied form of script both phonetic and ideographical (e. g., Chinese characters). Among them are to be found religious practices ranging from primitive animism through more evolved Shamanism and Shinto-ism to Mohammedanism, Brahminism, Buddhism and Christianity.

It is not surprising, therefore, in the face of these overwhelming forces making for isolation and diversification, that no single group or nation has ever extended its political control throughout the length and breadth of the region. The Chinese empire under the control of the Mongols (c. 1260-1368) and under the Manchus (1644-1912) did for a time exercise varying degrees of control over a major portion of the area. But for the most part, from the dawn of history to the present, the Far East has witnessed the rise and fall of many regimes, countries and empires that were ruled by leaders of many different races and administered under widely varied types of government.

Generalization about the Far East as a whole in the face of this diversity of land-form, of climate, and vegetation, of race, culture, language and religion and of political organization and control becomes hazardous and misleading. If we are to acquire a clearer and more detailed picture of the land and the peoples of the Far East together with the products which they have wrested from the soil or made with the skill of their hands, which constituted in large measure the invitation to European and Japanese expan-

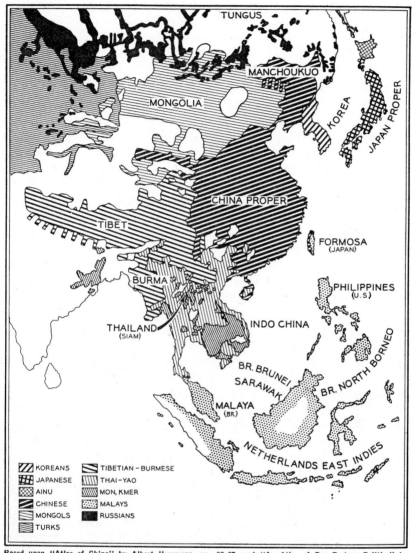

TUNGUS		
MANCHOUKUO		
MONGOLIA	KOREA	JAPAN PROPER
CHINA PROPER		
TIBET	FORMOSA (JAPAN)	
BURMA	PHILIPPINES (U.S.)	
THAILAND (SIAM)	INDO CHINA	
	BR. BRUNEI	BR. NORTH BORNEO
	SARAWAK	
MALAYA (BR.)		
	NETHERLANDS EAST INDIES	

KOREANS	TIBETIAN – BURMESE
JAPANESE	THAI–YAO
AINU	MON, KMER
CHINESE	MALAYS
MONGOLS	RUSSIANS
TURKS	

Based upon "Atlas of China" by Albert Herrmann, pp. 66-67, and "An Atlas of Far Eastern Politics" by
G. F. Hudson and Marthe Rajchman, p. 33

ETHNOGRAPHIC MAP OF THE FAR EAST, SHOWING DISTRIBUTION OF
PRINCIPAL PEOPLES IN MODERN TIMES

sion, it will be necessary to deal with the area country by country and region by region.

China

First let us consider China, which, under the empire, dominated the major portion of the Far East politically and culturally. Despite its relative loss of political and military power under the advance of the West and of Japan it still remains, because of its sheer size and advanced culture, a major factor in the political, economic and cultural life of East Asia and of the world. The area over which the Chinese republic claims sovereignty is coterminous with that held by the empire under the Manchus with the exception of the former vassal kingdoms of Korea, the Liuchius, Nepal, Burma, Siam, Annam and Laos as well as Formosa. The size of this area, which includes Mongolia, Manchuria, Sinkiang and Tibet, is about 4,277,260 square miles, which is roughly 500,000 square miles larger than the United States including its outlying possessions. The population may conservatively be estimated at 450,000,000 or about one-fifth of the world's population. In relation to the Far East as a whole it occupies over one-half of the area and has nearly three-fourths of the population.

These round figures, however, give quite a false picture of the density and distribution of the population within the area. China within the Great Wall or China Proper, has an area of only 1,532,795 square miles with a population over 400,000,000. Of this number about 24,000,000 are non-Chinese-speaking peoples. Most of these are mountain tribesmen representing various degrees of assimilation to Chinese culture in China's south and southwestern "colonial" provinces. The foreign population in China in 1935 numbered 1,485,979 of whom 1,213,531 were Japanese; only 200,000 Europeans and Americans resided there. The remaining area of Greater China, which is nearly twice the size of China Proper, has a population of only about 45,000,000.

China Proper shares, with the Far East as a whole, striking contrasts in topography, climate and vegetation. This situation and the very high degree of isolation afforded by the towering mountain ranges, plateaus, and deserts of the border regions to the north and west have combined to create almost complete economic, social and cultural self-sufficiency through the centuries.

Outside contacts and influences there were, both overland through central Asia and via the ocean, but these were not sufficiently powerful or significant to alter the basic characteristics and features of Chinese civilization. It was in these circumstances that the Chinese evolved one of the highest and most stable civilizations in the history of mankind. It still stands today, despite Western and Japanese invasions, the contemporary world's oldest continuous civilization.

The richness and variety of its soils and their products, as well as of the minerals within the soil, have enabled it to support a vast population at a relatively high degree of material culture. Marco Polo, one of the first Europeans to travel through the Far East, pictured the wealth of China in the thirteenth century in graphic and alluring terms in his account of his travels. For this he has been well called the "Columbus of China," awakening in the minds of the potentates and adventurers of a relatively poorer Europe of the late Middle Ages and early modern times a longing to sail to the shores of "Cathay" and tap the unlimited riches to be found there.

China Proper, contrary to the impression of most European travelers, who rarely go beyond the rich alluvial plains of north and central China or the Canton delta, is a mountainous, or hilly country. Only about 15 per cent of the total area is now cultivated and little hope is held that this tillable area can be appreciably increased in the future. The great majority of the population is to be found in the middle and lower reaches of the three great rivers, the Yellow River in the north, the Yangtze in central China and the West River in the south, all flowing down from the buttresses of the high Mongolian and Tibetan plateaus; and in the remote basin of the Red River in the western province of Szechuan.

Greatest of all the mountains of China Proper are the Kun Lun which reach eastward from Tibet almost to the Pacific, dividing China into two major geographical areas of great contrast in climate, agriculture and social environment. This cleavage lies along the thirty-fourth parallel, about half way between the Yangtze and the Yellow Rivers. Agriculturally, the distinction lies in the fact that, south of the division, rice cultivation predominates, while to the north, dry farming of wheat, millets and other sorghums constitutes the main cultivation. The contrast in economy is reflected in the life of the people—in their differing dialects, customs, costumes and architecture; yet they are all Chinese.

South and west China, which lie for the most part south of the Yangtze River, constitute the most mountainous portions of the country. Far to the west, near the headwater of the Yangtze, lies the province of Szechuan, the third largest of China's provinces and by far the most populous, having over 46,000,000 people. Surrounded by high mountains lies the basin of the Red River at its center, whose rich soil and humid subtropical climate support probably the densest agrarian population in the world. The potentialities of its vast market were a prime factor in causing the Europeans to demand shipping rights for a distance of 1,500 miles up the Yangtze to one of its leading cities, Chungking, which in 1938 became the capital of the Nationalist Government of China. Likewise it stimulated the rival imperialisms of France and England to acquire control over Burma and Tongkin respectively in order to command the gateways leading to this province by the shortest overland routes.

To the south and west of Szechuan lie the provinces of Kweichow and Yunnan, the latter bordering upon Burma and Indo-China. Topographically, these provinces constitute a spur of the great Tibetan plateau, averaging 4,000 to 6,000 feet above sea level. High mountains and deep gorges characterize most of the terrain, the level land averaging only about 5 per cent of the total. Economically and culturally, these provinces represent the most backward regions of China, having come last in contact with the expansion southward of Chinese civilization from the original home of the "Chinese" in the Yellow River Valley in the north. Of a total population of about 19,000,000 in the two provinces, nearly 13,000,000 are non-Chinese-speaking tribes who are still, for the most part, unassimilated to Chinese culture, and, in the remoter regions, under little effective political control. The mineral resources include tin—the most important—silver, zinc, mercury, lead, gold and antimony. The known existence of these, in estimated amounts since discovered to be greatly exaggerated, were an added incentive to the British and the French in the nineteenth century inducing them to expand their empires to the borders of Yunnan.

Southeast China is likewise distinctly hilly and mountainous, the level land not exceeding 10 per cent of the total area. The mountains run all along the south coast, creating many coves and excellent harbors in contrast with the low sandy regular coastline that predominates in North China. Hence the southern Chinese are more sea-conscious than those of the north. For some centuries the people of this region have carried on trade relations with the Philippines, the East Indies and Malaya. From the two coastal provinces of Fukien and Kwantung have gone most of the Chinese that have in the course of the past century migrated to all quarters of the globe. In this area a large proportion of China's tea and silk has been produced, the two principal items in China's trade with the Europeans down to the present century. Canton, located on the fertile delta plain of the West and other rivers, is the most populous city of the region. It was the principal port of trade with the Europeans from the coming of the Portuguese in 1517 to the opening of Shanghai to foreign trade and residence after 1842.

Shanghai, at the time of its opening to foreign trade in 1843, was a mere fishing village. It has since grown to be the greatest city in Asia and one of the six leading cities of the world with a population of over 3,000,000 in recent years. As a port it rapidly became the leading one in China and by 1929 ranked as the eighth among world ports. Its admirable location near the mouth of the Yangtze River, in whose valley live 200,000,000 Chinese, one-tenth of the human race, destined it to fulfill this rôle. Through Shanghai flowed, between the years 1924-1931, about 45 per cent of China's total trade, most of the exports being drawn from the rich agricultural region that lies behind it up the Yangtze River. Despite the high degree of urbanization of the area, two-thirds of the people are engaged in an intensive form of agriculture. The rich soils and a favorable climate have permitted two and sometimes three crops a year. Partly as a consequence of this and partly because China is still in the early stages of industrialization, the export trade from this region as well as from China as a whole has been composed largely of cultivated products of the soil.

This region is the most modernized and industrialized region in all China with the possible exception of Manchuria, while in and around Shanghai before 1937 were located most of China's modern factories. In view of these circumstances it is not surprising that the area has witnessed some of the sharpest clashes of the competing imperialistic interests of Europe and Japan with each other and with the Chinese. Long out-weighing North China in economic, commercial and industrial importance, it has in recent years gradually assumed leadership in the cultural, educational and, with the removal of the capital from Peking to Nanking in 1928, definite political leadership of the nation.

What we call North China today was the original home of the Chinese. It remained the dominant economic as well as political center of the empire until successive migrations and colonization in the Yangtze Valley raised that region to the "key economic area" by the time of the T'ang dynasty (618-906). Thereafter, the north retained the political, cultural leadership to the present century, partly as a result of tradition, but largely because of strategic reasons. The major defense problems of the empire, through the centuries, arose from the well-nigh continuous threats of invasion by the "barbarians" on the northern and western frontiers. The Chinese were by no means wholly successful in warding off these attacks. For nearly half of the two millenniums (*c*.221 B.C.–A.D. 1912) that the empire existed, China was ruled in part or wholly by these invaders such as the Mongols and the Manchus. Nor has the threat on the land frontiers wholly ceased. First Russia and now Japan have, since 1870, replaced the more primitive border peoples as invaders. Yet the coming of the Europeans via the sea has considerably altered the traditional defense problems of the country, whose solution lies not alone in the military and naval sphere, but in the political, economic and cultural spheres as well, involved as they are in the slow process of modernization which has been under way since the mid-nineteenth century. Hence the decision in 1928 to remove the capital from Peking to the more centrally located Nanking, in the heart of the Yangtze Valley, was not made without adequate justification.

North China is divided into two sections, the alluvial plain that reaches to the sea, and the loess—a fine, yellow, wind-blown silt—highlands that lie between the plains and the deserts of Central Asia to the north and northwest. The plain has been built up largely by the Yellow River, which has borne the soil down from the loess covered hills of the west and from the more distant mountains of Tibet. Despite the fact that it is the principal flood and famine area of China, 80,000,000 people live upon and cultivate its soil. The racial make-up of the Chinese of the region is highly complex, owing to the successive invasions of nomadic warriors who intermarried with the agrarian peoples of the plain. In physical appearance they are taller and appear more vigorous than the "true" Chinese of the south, but are, however, more conservative in outlook and temperament. About 90 per cent of the people are farmers cultivating a wide variety of crops including wheat, millet, kaoliang (a giant millet), barley, beans, corn, sweet potatoes, cotton, tobacco and various kinds of garden vegetables. The two largest cities of the area are Peking (renamed Peiping after removal of the capital to Nanking in 1928), and Tientsin, the leading port and the third largest one in China.

The region of the loess highlands covers parts of the northwestern provinces of China extending in the north to the deserts of Mongolia and in the west and south to the Tibetan plateau and the Tsingling mountains which branch off from it. While the yellow silt soil is exceptionally fertile, the small and uncertain rainfall makes cultivation hazardous and limits it largely to the wetter valleys. The principal food crops are wheat, millet and kaoliang together with a variety of vegetables and fruit. The cash crops are opium, cotton and tobacco. The total population at present is about 46,000,000. Among the people of the region are to be found representatives of the five major races—namely, the Tibetans, the Mongolians, the Chinese, the Manchus and the non-Chinese-speaking Mohammedans—that made up the old empire. Their existence was recognized in the five-barred flag adopted by the republic in 1912. The region is still relatively isolated owing to the difficult nature of the terrain and lack of modern means of travel through most of the area. It possesses together with Manchuria the richest mineral resources of China. Iron and other metals are found in some quantity, but it is in coal that its richest potential sub-soil wealth lies. It is the Pennsylvania of China, possessing nearly half the estimated reserves of the country, which in turn is surpassed only by United States and Canada in the total amount of its reserve.

Manchuria

The most important region of Greater China is that of Manchuria which lies to the northeast of the Great Wall. For over a thousand miles its northern and eastern borders are coterminous with the Far Eastern regions of the U.S.S.R. along the Argun, the Amur and the Ussuri rivers. To the east and south it borders upon Korea and to the west on Mongolia. The converging center of three empires—the Russian, the Chinese and the Japanese— the area has in the past fifty years been one of the "storm-centers" of Far Eastern politics.

The population numbers over 35,000,000 of whom 97 per cent are Chinese. It was the original home of the Manchus, who conquered and ruled China from 1644 to 1912. Until the early part of the present century they had discouraged Chinese migration to the area, but, after that date, to offset Russian and Japanese aggression, they threw open the country to Chinese colonization. The Chinese migrated there by the millions to settle upon its rich rolling plains. In topography and climate Manchuria affords a striking parallel to North America. To the east are heavily forested mountains, in the center a rolling plain similar to the plains of the Middle West, marked by increasing aridity as the mountains of the west are approached. The chief crops in order of importance are kaoliang, soy beans (the chief cash crop), millet, wheat and corn. Stimulating and heightening the clash of imperialisms in the region are the mineral resources. Some of the better iron and coal reserves of China are located there. Dairen, the chief port of the area, is second only to Shanghai in importance from the point of view of foreign trade. Its growth and position are a reflection of the rapidity with which a relatively high degree of development along modern industrial lines has occurred in Manchuria in the past forty years, largely under Japanese initiative and control.

Mongolia

Mongolia, China's dependency in recent centuries, is a vast area measuring nearly 1,000,000 square miles in extent or about one-third of the area of continental United States. Yet it has an estimated population of only about 6,000,000, which is a reflection of the aridity of its climate. Topographically, it is essentially a plateau from 3,000 to 5,000 feet in height. The Gobi desert, parts of which may be characterized as poor steppe land, divides the region into what the Chinese have called Inner and Outer Mongolia. Outer Mongolia is similar in topography, vegetation and climate to the regions of the U.S.S.R. which it adjoins. Politically too, as we shall see, it has been orientated toward Russia, particularly since the establishment of the Chinese republic in 1912. Inner Mongolia, adjoining China, has a better climate and more rain, permitting a gradual extension of Chinese agrarian economy into the area in recent decades, forcing the nomadic Mongol herdsmen off some of their erstwhile more fertile pasture lands.

Sheep, cattle, camels and horses are raised by the Mongols. They form the chief source of wealth and livelihood, and their wool and hides are the main articles of trade with the outside world. Imports include tiles, tea, wheat flour, textiles, tobacco and sugar. Industrially the region is backward, there being only a few small-scale factories, mostly under control of Chinese in Inner Mongolia or established under Russian initiative or assistance in Outer Mongolia. The minerals known to exist include gold, silver, copper, lead, iron, coal, graphite and lime, but amounts available are not large. The few mines that have been opened are largely under alien control. The Mongols, despite their nomadic existence under the leadership of Genghis and Khublai Khan, created in the thirteenth century one of the greatest empires of history—an empire which extended over a great part of Asia and on into Hungary and Poland in Europe. The Mongols have a small body of literature of their own written down in a phonetic script which was adopted in the thirteenth century. Their religion is Lamaism, the Tibetan form of Buddhism first adopted by Khublai Khan in the same century.

Sinkiang

Sinkiang, a dependency of China until 1884 when it was organized into a province, occupies an area of nearly 600,000 square miles. Bordered on the north, northwest and east by Russia, Mongolia and China Proper and on the southwest and south by Afghanistan, India and Tibet, it lies at the very center of the "dead heart of Asia." Despite the towering mountains and expansive arid deserts, some 3,500,000 people gain a precarious livelihood around oases and along banks of rivers and the less arid fringes of the deserts. The racial composition of the population is highly complex. Through it pass the two main historic caravan routes linking China with the rest of Asia. It has been well called, from the point of view of its central location, the "Switzerland of Asia." Over half the population is composed of a highly mixed people whom the Chinese call the Chantou or turban-wearing Turkomans, who adhere to the Mohammedan religion. Next in point of number come the Mongols, then the Kasaks, who are predominantly Turkish by blood and Moslem by religion. The Chinese number less than one-tenth of the population. They are prominent in the administration of the area and in conducting commercial relations, particularly with China Proper. The construction of auto roads within the area and the linking of the region to China Proper in recent years have been important factors in stimulating trade and developing resources of the area. Gold, silver, lead, copper, iron, coal, jade, salt and sulphur are found in some abundance. The small amount of adequately watered agricultural lands produce a great variety of crops including wheat, kaoliang, millet, beans, rice, fruit, tobacco and cotton. Strategic considerations, perhaps more than an interest in its trade and resources, have guided rival British and Russian political interests in Sinkiang as in its neighbor, Tibet.

Tibet

Tibet has an area of over 800,000 square miles, and a total population of between 4,000,000 and 6,000,000. It consists of a stretch of upland plains lying at a height of more than 12,000 feet surrounded by mountain walls rising to as much as 10,000 feet higher. These formidable mountain barriers have kept the country through the centuries relatively isolated, a land of mystery, and one of the last inhabitable areas of the world to be penetrated by the forces of modern imperialism and industrialism. The greater portion of the area is a scarcely habitable waste of frozen desert. The population is concentrated in the south and west around Lhasa, the capital, and in the east bordering on China. This latter area, comprising over half of the total area of the country, the Chinese government in 1928 formally divided into two new Chinese provinces of Sikang and Chinghai. Over the rest, or Outer Tibet, the British and the Chinese have contested in recent decades for dominant control and influence. Small quantities of peas, beans, barley and wheat are grown, but the chief occupation of the people is raising yaks and goats. The unknown mineral resources include gold, silver, copper, iron and petroleum. In exchange for wool, skins, furs, drugs and other products, the Tibetans secure from the Chinese tea, silk, cotton cloth, porcelains, wines and religious ornaments. From India they import finished goods including munitions. Tibet is a theocratic state, the political head or Dalai Lama sharing with the Panchan Lama ecclesiastical control, while both are regarded as reincarnated "living Buddhas." Lamaism, the Tibetan version of Buddhism, began to spread through the land in the seventh century of our era. The lamas or priests not only control the realm spiritually and politically but their lamaseries exercise a monopoly over trade and education.

Southeastern Asia

Southeastern Asia is cut off from China and India by high mountain ranges and steaming tropical jungle marshes. It comprises the broad peninsula of Indo-China made up of Burma, Siam and French Indo-China, and the long narrow Malay sub-peninsula, most of which is a part of British Malaya. Neighbors to the advanced and powerful civilizations of China and India, it is not surprising that the relatively more backward peoples of this area have, through the centuries past, been under the preponderant racial, linguistic, religious, cultural and political forces emanating from these two countries, as the name Indo-China suggests.

Burma. First let us consider Burma. Although it was until 1935 a province of British India it was historically, and is geographically and ethnologically, a part of the Far East. It paid tribute to the Chinese Empire up to the end of the nineteenth century. Its total area is 262,732 square miles. Although half the region lies outside the tropics, it is all a tropical country, climatically speaking. Topographically it is divided into three distinct regions. On the west running from north to south is the Arakan Yoma range, some peaks of which rise to over 10,000 feet, definitely cutting the country off from India. The eastern part of the country consists of the Shan plateau—3,000 feet in height. The central portion is a rich fertile basin through which runs Burma's chief river, the Irrawaddy. The rainfall varies from 20 to more than 200 inches a year. Heavy tropical hardwood forests extend over a wide area and timber is the third item of importance on the export list.

It is essentially an agricultural country, the cultivation of rice being first in importance. Sesame, millet, beans, groundnuts, cotton and rubber are also produced. The most important mineral product is petroleum, and some gold and iron deposits exist.

The 14,667,146 (1931) people of Burma speak many languages and represent many "races." The members of the leading races are called the Mons, the Tibeto-Burmans and the Thais. They are Buddhists by religion. They have been under the strong influence of Hindu civilization from the early centuries of the Christian era. Indians and Chinese make up the important alien elements. The Indians number about 1,000,000 and supply all the coolie labor. The Chinese, who number about 200,000, are concentrated in Rangoon, the principal port, and are mostly artisans, merchants and traders.

Siam. Siam or Thailand, as it has been officially known since June, 1939, lies between British Burma and French Indo-China. It owes its continued existence as an independent state largely to the decision of the British and French, at the end of the nineteenth century, to reconcile their dangerous competing imperialistic expansion in that part of the world by leaving the country as a convenient buffer area between parts of their empires. This decision was not reached, however, until after a large portion of the area of the country had been annexed by the two powers, leaving it with only about 200,000 square miles. Northern Siam consists of thickly forested parallel hill ranges. Central Siam, where dwell most of the people, consists of a rich highly cultivated plain. Eastern Siam is a huge shallow basin with an indifferent soil and an adverse climate. Southern Siam, consisting mostly of the northern part of the Malay Peninsula, is a land of beautiful scenery and possesses a rich soil. Bangkok, the "Venice of the East," is the capital. It has a population of over 600,000 and is situated near the mouth of the Menam River. It handles nearly all the foreign trade. The population of the country in 1937 was 14,464,489.

Minerals of various kinds occur, including tin, wolfram, gold, coal, iron, zinc, manganese and antimony. Rice is the chief product and makes up over 80 per cent of Siam's export trade. Teakwood is next in importance as an export item. Pepper, tobacco, betel nuts and rubber are also produced. The principal peoples are the Khmers and the Thais or Shans. The Thais conquered the area in the thirteenth century. From the early part of the Christian era they, like the Burmese, were under Hindu religious and cultural influence. They are now for the most part Buddhists. From the fourteenth century, Chinese institutional forms and codes were a model for the Siamese rulers.

French Indo-China. French Indo-China had an area of 285,000 square miles (until March, 1941, when it lost about 25,000 square miles to Siam), which surpassed that of France itself, and a population of 23,000,000, a little over half that of France. The political units roughly correspond to the geographical divisions of the region, which as a whole is divided into several great basins by chains of mountains and highlands that stem from the plateaus of Yunnan in South China. Annam is largely a mountain range running along the east coast. Tongkin is cut off from China by another range. Through it flows the Red River. To the west, cut off from the sea by the mountains of Annam, lies the more backward kingdom of Laos. Cochin China lies for the most part in the delta plains and marshes of the lower Mekong River to the south. Cambodia is a great fertile basin in the southwest. The climate is tropical with wet and dry monsoonal seasons.

Rice, the principal export item, is grown for the most part in Cochin China and Cambodia. In addition these two regions produce maize, sweet potatoes, beans, sugar cane, tobacco, rubber, coconuts, betel nuts, coffee, indigo and pepper. Annam's agricultural crops are similar to Cochin China's and Cambodia's, but in addition it produces tea and silk. More backward and inaccessible Laos exports teakwood, the logs being floated down the Mekong. Tongkin, the most densely populated region, contains most of the minerals. The coal deposits are especially large, while tin, graphite and zinc are also mined. Rice is its chief crop. Maize, sugar cane, coconuts, tea, coffee and silk are also produced. It is now surpassed only by the Netherlands East Indies and British Malaya as a producer of rubber. Hanoi, the capital of Indo-China, is located within its borders. Haiphong is its chief port and is connected by rail with Kunming, the provincial capital of Yunnan. French Indo-China is a young country, industrially speaking; consequently the imports consist largely of manufactured goods coming from France.

The peoples of French Indo-China have been under the influence of two powerful cultural streams from India and from China since the beginning of the Christian era. From India came cultural, religious and artistic influences which are still predominant in Cambodia and Laos. Consequently a variant form of Buddhism, which superseded earlier Brahministic influences, prevails. From China the influence lay in the political and institutional realms, particularly in Tongkin and Annam where Chinese legal codes and bureaucratic organization were adopted and the Chinese calendar officially used. Confucianism deeply penetrated the psychology of the people and molded their social institutions. Chinese characters were employed in writing, though a modified, less difficult form was developed.

Malaysia. The peoples and states of the Indo-Chinese peninsula, as we have seen, had developed their social, religious and political life and institutions, before the coming of the Europeans, chiefly under the influence of Indian and Chinese civilizations. As we move southward to the Malay Peninsula, the East Indies and the Philippines, we enter a different world where Chinese influence has been less marked, but where an earlier Indian influence had to contend with a later powerful Mohammedan political and cultural invasion. The majority of peoples living in these areas are Malays, more a linguistic characterization than a racial one. Racially, they are an amalgamation of various more primitive groups that found their way there in prehistoric times. The term "Indonesia" as applied to the islands of this region is indicative of the strong Hindu political and cultural influences that began to penetrate the region at the beginning of the Christian era. Buddhism supplanted earlier Brahminism after the fifth or sixth centuries. In one place, however, on the little island of Bali, the earlier Hindu cult survives to this day. Under the predominant Indian influence, Sanskrit became the official language. It was in use as far east as Celebes and as far north as the Sulu Archipelago in the Philippines. However, in eastern Java and in Bali a local written language developed.

The second cultural stream to flow through these regions, before the arrival of the Europeans, came with Mohammedan traders at the beginning of the fourteenth century. In time there came to be established Mohammedan states replacing the former Hindu political organizations. Mohammedan influence spread rapidly and by the end of the fifteenth century Mohammedan states were found in the Malay Peninsula, Sumatra, Java, Celebes, and in the Philippines. The Arabic language, spoken and written, found a secure foothold that it has maintained to the present in some parts of the Malaysian world. With these general remarks in mind by way of background, each of the three major political divisions of this "world," British Malaya, the Netherlands East Indies and the Philippines, will be considered in more detail.

Malaya. The term "Malaya," which applies to the areas on the lower part of the Malay Peninsula and adjacent islands, over which the British now exercise control, should be distinguished from the term "Malaysia," which applies to the East Indies as well as to the Malay Peninsula. The Malay Peninsula has a diversified topography with few areas of flat land. The east coast on the China Sea is stormy, while the west coast on the Indian Ocean is tranquil, and there most of the population dwells. There are two seasons—"a wet and a wetter," the rainfall averaging between 100 and 270 inches. In this hot, humid climate heavy forests thrive against which man must constantly struggle to keep clear the more suitable agricultural lands along the coasts. The three principal crops of the area are rubber, coconuts and rice. Rubber and tin are the chief export items and account for the prosperity of Malaya.

The Straits Settlements are composed of isolated tracts of land on and near the Malay Peninsula, including Singapore, Malacca and Penang, the chief trading ports, with an area of about 1,600 square miles and a population of 1,372,568 (1931). The population of Singapore and Penang is mostly Chinese, with Indians second. The Chinese are active as tin producers, truck gardeners and traders. The Indians supply most of the labor on rubber plantations. The native Malays occupy the rural areas of Malaya, being less active or enterprising than the Chinese and Indians.

The Federated Malay States consist of four small native Mohammedan states which fell under British protection in the modern period. The total area is 27,456 square miles and the population 1,324,870 (1921) of which number only 510,821 were Malays, 494,584 Chinese and 305,219 Indians, who are divided occupationally as in the Straits Settlements. The five native Mohammedan Unfederated States are each ruled by a sultan who acts under advice of a British adviser. Johore in the south is the largest and is more developed than the four northern states. It produces rubber, copra, tin and tapioca. Since the first World

War iron mining under Japanese control has developed in the Unfederated Malay States of Johore, Trengganu and Kelantan. In 1937 nearly 2,500,000 tons were produced, half of which was exported to Japan. The region constitutes one of the chief overseas sources of supply for the steel mills of that country.

Netherlands East Indies. The Netherlands East Indies include the greater part of the East Indies, excepting the north and northwest parts of Borneo under British rule, and the eastern half of the island of Timor under Portuguese control. It also includes the western half of the island of New Guinea, which geographically is usually linked with Australasia. This vast colonial area was the legacy of the Dutch East India Company, which conquered and ruled the islands until 1798 when their administration was taken over by the Netherlands government. The total area is 735,267 square miles, fifty-eight times the size of the Netherlands. The population is nearly 70,000,000. Of this number there are approximately 1,000,000 Asiatics, mostly Chinese, and 200,000 Europeans, mostly of Dutch descent. A majority of the people, an estimated 48,000,000, live on the islands of Java and Madura, which have an area of only 51,032 square miles. The remaining islands or "outer territories" as the Netherlanders call them, are much more sparsely populated and are still largely undeveloped economically, though great strides have been made in that direction in recent decades.

Java is one of the most densely populated agricultural regions in the world. This is due primarily to the richness of the soil and the nature of the terrain, which permits cultivation of 80 per cent of the surface. The north coast is for the most part an alluvial plain and there are located the chief towns and ports. The main mountain ridge of the island runs nearer the south coast. Rice is the chief crop of native agriculture, yet it must be imported in quantity to feed such a dense population. Other crops are maize, cassava (from which tapioca is made), sweet potatoes, groundnuts, soy beans, tobacco, sugar cane, indigo and tea. Batavia, the capital, Semarang and Surabaya, the chief ports, are linked up with the remote parts of the island by a good railroad system.

Sumatra with an area of 163,145 square miles has only begun to be developed in recent years. The population now (1941) is about 10,000,000, whereas in 1925 it was only 5,759,568. Topographically the island consists of a mountainous volcanic ridge lying to the west with broad stretches of undulating and low level land to the east facing the Malay Peninsula and the Pacific. On these lower levels rubber, tea, coffee, copra and tobacco plantations have in recent years rapidly developed. These crops, together with sugar and cinchona bark, out of which quinine is made, a product over which the Netherlands East Indies enjoy a virtual world monopoly, make up some of the principal items on the export list of the islands. Among the minerals produced are tin, coal, gold, silver and petroleum. Petroleum is the chief mineral produced, the wells of Sumatra supplying two-thirds of the output of the islands in 1938. The Netherlands East Indies supply most of the oil produced, though not consumed, in the Far East, a fact which is of political and strategic significance. Iron deposits are potentially fruitful. Within the past few years bauxite and nickel mining has developed.

Until a few years ago only the coastal fringe of the 115,000 square miles of the snow-capped mountains and dense, fever-ridden jungles of Dutch New Guinea had been explored. Many developmental schemes were under way in 1939 to settle Javanese on its fertile soil, to discover and exploit its possible mineral resources, particularly petroleum, and to grow cotton, rubber and coffee. Between New Guinea and the Celebes lie the Moluccas, the southern group of which are the Spice Islands which the early European explorers sought to reach in order to break the Venetian monopoly of spices in the European trade. While spices are no longer the major export of the East Indies, the Moluccas still remain an outstanding source of nutmegs, cloves and mace.

The Dutch portion of Borneo covers 206,810 square miles, about three-fourths of the island. The British portion is divided into three states as follows: British North Borneo with an area of 29,500 square miles and a population of 270,223 in 1931; Brunei with an area of 2,226 square miles and a population of 30,135; and Sarawak with an area of 50,000 square miles and a population of 442,900. The island produces timber, sago, rice, coconuts, coffee, fruits, spices, rubber, tobacco, tapioca, copra, as well as mineral oil, coal, iron and gold.

The Philippines. The Philippine Archipelago has 7,083 islands with a total area of 114,400 square miles. The areas of the two largest islands, Luzon in the north, on which Manila, the capital, is located, and Mindanao to the south, cover nearly two-thirds of the total area. Only 12 per cent of the total area is cultivated, though the amount suitable for cultivation is considerably greater. Heavily forested mountains cover 64 per cent of the surface. The population in 1939 was 16,000,000. Most of the people are related racially to the Malays and were converted to Christianity by the Spanish priests in the course of more than three centuries in which the islands were subjected to Spanish rule. The more primitive inhabitants of Mindanao, the Moros, still remain Mohammedans. Chinese have migrated to the islands in large numbers, particularly since the coming of the Spanish, and have been active as artisans and merchants. The number there in 1939 was 117,461. The Japanese have been coming in increasing numbers in recent years and by 1940 numbered about 30,000.

Both peoples are playing an important rôle in the economic life of the islands, while the Japanese threaten to play a political one. Production is predominantly agrarian. The principal crops in order of the amount of land devoted to their cultivation are rice, maize, abaca, coconuts, sugar cane, bananas, sweet potatoes, tobacco, mangoes and rubber. Gold, coal, iron, ivory, gypsum, limestone and nickel are the principal known or exploited minerals.

Guam. This island was acquired by the United States from Spain after the Spanish-American war of 1898, at the same time that the Philippines were secured. It has an area of 206 square miles and a population in 1930 of 18,509. It is strategically important as a naval station and as an air base, situated as it is between Hawaii and the Philippines. Copra and coconut oil are its principal exports.

Japan. The Japanese Empire, the Britain of the East, consists of a curved chain of 1,700 islands off the east coast of Asia stretching from the island of Formosa, which lies athwart the Tropic of Cancer, to the 50° north latitude, together with the Korean peninsula and the Kwantung leased territory in south Manchuria on the mainland. The climate varies from a subtropical warmth to the bitter winters and cool summers of the north. The total area is 260,252 square miles and the population in 1935 was 97,697,555. Japan Proper, comprising the main group of islands, has an area of 147,327 square miles. It is made up largely of volcanic mountains, and two-thirds of the area is forest covered. Only one-fifth of the total area is cultivable, yet on these islands live

70,000,000 people. The rivers are short and swift, and for the most part, unnavigable, but are useful as sources for electric power and for irrigation. Rice is the principal cultivated crop. It forms along with fish the two main items in the Japanese diet. The mineral resources are relatively poor, there being but little iron, lead, tin, gold, silver and petroleum, though there are fair amounts of coal and copper.

The island of Formosa, or Taiwan as the Japanese call it, has a population of over 5,000,000 and an area of 13,889 square miles. Most of the inhabitants are Chinese immigrants from the adjoining Chinese coast or their descendants. They occupy the lowlands in the western half of the island. The mountainous eastern half is largely inhabited by savage head hunters ethnologically related to the Malays or Indonesians. Japanese came to the island in increasing numbers after 1895, when it was acquired from China. They now number over 250,000. Most of the people as in Japan are Buddhists and Shintoists. The latter is the indigenous animistic religion of Japan, elevated in the nineteenth century to the status of an official national cult. The three principal crops are rice, sugar cane and potatoes, the first two of which are exported—chiefly to Japan Proper. Other important agricultural products are jute, ramie, tea, fruit, tobacco and camphor. The production of camphor is under control of a government monopoly and the amount produced reaches 70 per cent or more of total world production. The chief mineral products are gold, silver, copper, iron, lead, zinc, coal, petroleum, sulphur and phosphorus. The total annual production is small and is indicative of scanty reserves with the possible exception of the sulphur and phosphorus. Taihoku, the leading city and capital, is located at the northern end of the island.

The southern half of the island of Sakhalin, called by the Japanese Karafuto, was acquired from Russia in 1905. It has an area of 13,934 square miles. The vast majority of the 330,000 people on it are Japanese engaged in agriculture, fishing, mining and lumbering. The chief minerals are coal and petroleum. Most of the oil, however, is to be found in the northern half of the island, the Japanese exploiting a number of wells under lease from the Russians.

Korea (Chosen) is a peninsula having an area of 85,228 square miles. It is on the whole mountainous, the eastern part bordering

on the Sea of Japan being especially so. The lowlands lie along
the western half bordering on the Yellow Sea. The total population is about 23,000,000 of whom over 500,000 are Japanese. The
Koreans are a blend of racial stocks migrating there from northern
Asia with an admixture of Chinese from the beginning of the
Christian era. Their language belongs to the Turanian group, is
polysyllabic and possesses a phonetic script. Chinese characters
were introduced along with Chinese cultural, religious (Buddhism) and administrative influences and institutions, some of
which were in turn passed on to Japan. Korea is still primarily
an agricultural country though in recent years industrialization
has begun to develop under Japanese auspices. Rice is the principal crop, more than half of which is exported to Japan. The
Koreans eat mostly millet. Barley, wheat and rye are also
cultivated. Forests cover 73 per cent of the area. Gold is
the principal mineral mined, followed by coal and iron, copper, silver, lead, tungsten and zinc, but all in relatively small
quantities.

Eastern Siberia. That portion of the Soviet Union which lies
within the Far East, as herein defined, covers an area of about
2,000,000 square miles and lies for the most part east of the Lena
River. It has a population of between two and three million. On
the north it reaches to the Arctic Ocean and its southern border is
contiguous with that of Outer Mongolia, Manchoukuo and, for a
stretch of about ten miles only, it borders Korea. Coal is widely
distributed throughout the area, all grades being represented, including some of the largest coking coal (necessary for metallurgical purposes) deposits in Eastern Asia. Oil is found on the
northern half of the island of Sakhalin and on Kamchatka. Careful surveys by U.S.S.R. geologists have resulted in the discovery
of extensive iron ore deposits that place the region in the forefront
as concerns reserves of that mineral in the Far East. Manganese,
lead, zinc and silver are also found, and the region is rich in
gold. In the north lies the tundra with its perpetually frozen sub-
soil. The rest of the region has a variety of soils capable of producing all types of temperate agricultural crops, but it is still mainly
a forest region. There also exists a variety of fauna, particularly
fur-bearing animals, which are of great commercial importance.
Under the three Five Year Plans a rapid development of agriculture and industry has been under way, aiming at economic and

strategic self-sufficiency. Great improvement in transportation facilities has been achieved in recent years.

The peoples of this region comprise three groups: descendants
of prehistoric inhabitants; races that migrated northward from
Central Asia in the period between the third and the thirteenth
centuries, such as Tatars, Buriyats and Tungus; and the Russians.
The Russian expansion into Siberia began at the end of the sixteenth century. The advance wave of the migration reached the
Pacific within a century. The Manchus, feeling the threat of this
advance, used force to keep the Russians out of their native land
of Manchuria. This led to the Treaty of Nerchinsk of 1689,
China's first treaty with a Western power, which kept the Russians
north of the Amur. It was followed by the Treaty of Kiakhta in
1727, which together with the earlier one roughly delimited the
4,000-mile frontier separating the Chinese Empire and Siberia
along a line which for the most part approximates the frontier to
this day. Colonization of eastern Siberia by the Russians was
relatively slow until after the completion of the Trans-Siberian
railroad at the end of the nineteenth century. Unlike other European nations, which approached China from the sea, Russia
threatened China's integrity from the land side, thereby replacing
the "barbarians" of the past who down through the centuries had
harassed the frontiers and even ruled for many centuries the old
Chinese Empire.

It was in this varied and contrasting geographic, cultural and
political setting that the Europeans from the sixteenth century
on gradually extended their influence until the greater part of the
Far East was brought under their political, economic and, to a
considerable extent, cultural and religious domination. By the
middle of the nineteenth century they had well established themselves strategically for the more intensive period of conquest and
exploitation that was to follow.

The Coming of the Europeans to the Far East

The motives which led the Europeans to seek out the sea routes
to the East have been well epitomized in the expression "gospel,
gold and glory." The desire for gain led to an attempt to find
the direct sea route to the East and the increased trade which
would result. Religious zeal animated the missionaries who wished

to spread the Christian gospel among the "pagans." It also won wide-spread popular as well as kingly support to overseas explorations and ventures. Animating trader, missionary and sovereign alike were the prestige and glory which would accrue to them as individuals by sponsoring or participating in such expansion.

The Portuguese in the Far East.   The Portuguese were first to reach the Far East in modern times via the sea. They, as well as the Genoese, had been seeking to discover a sea route to the Spice Islands and the Indies to break the monopoly which the Venetians enjoyed in the sale of products from the East, chiefly spices, that they picked up at the eastern end of the Mediterranean. This objective, the Portuguese realized, could best be achieved by finding a direct route to the East where they could purchase the spices at the places they were produced more cheaply than the Venetians could buy them in the Mediterranean. Thereby could the Portuguese not only break the Venetian monopoly, but also establish their own monopoly in the trade.

Finally, in 1497-1498 Vasco da Gama rounded Africa and completed the first successful round-trip sea voyage from Europe to India. He was followed a few years later by Alfonso D'Albuquerque, who captured Malacca in 1511 and established the first outpost of European empire in the Far East. Five years later a Portuguese sailed to China on a prospecting trip, to be followed in 1517 by four Portuguese ships in search of trade. In 1542 the first Portuguese reached Japan, following upon which trading relations were established. Within half a century the Portuguese had successfully invaded the East. Their superior armament in the form of cannon and firearms enabled them quickly to break Muslim sea power in the Indian Ocean and to overcome local opposition wherever it arose.

The explorers and traders were shortly followed by the missionaries, whose influence was to be more than purely religious. It was also cultural as they became active agents in spreading elements of Western civilization to Eastern peoples. Consciously or unconsciously they introduced to the peoples of the Far East the scientific, economic, cultural and political techniques, philosophies and institutions of the "Christian" civilization of the West. At times consciously and at other times unbeknownst to themselves they were to advance the political interests of the nations they represented. Moreover, from the nineteenth century on, they were usually quite willing to rely upon the strong arms of their governments to maintain their positions in the face of repeated outbreaks against them on the part of the peoples and the governments of Far East countries. They, together with the traders, were by that time intimately associated with the expanding forces of European imperialism. At times the European governments and their official representatives in the region acted under pressure from them, trader and missionary alike, to protect and expand their interests. At other times attacks upon them became allegedly adequate excuses for further aggression leading to additional economic and political demands.

The Spanish Come via the New World. Next to reach the Far East were the Spaniards, both traders and missionaries. Deterred by the monopolistic claims of the Portuguese from reaching the East via Africa, they sought and found through Columbus another route by sailing directly westward. Stimulated and inspired by Marco Polo's account of the wealth of the Far East which he had read; diplomatically prepared by a letter from the sovereign of Spain to the descendants of the great khan of Cathay under whom Marco had served (the news of the fall of the Mongol power in China in 1368 having not yet reached Europe!); and emboldened by his distorted map of the world which revealed eastern Asia as extending eastward to a position actually occupied by the Americas, Columbus set forth upon his epoch-making voyage. To reconcile the conflicting claims which then arose between Spain and Portugal to the non-European world there was issued in 1493 a Papal Bull, later modified by treaty, which divided the world into two hemispheres, the Eastern to belong to Portugal and the Western to Spain. Thus Spain was to reach the Far East via the Atlantic and Pacific Oceans. The first successful voyage over the westward route set out under Magellan's leadership and resulted in the first circumnavigation of the world in the years 1519-1521.

Though Magellan himself reached the Philippine Islands, where he was killed by natives, it was not until after 1543 that the Spanish hold on the archipelago was well established. The Portuguese, however, and the representatives of other European nations later to arrive, were successful in limiting Spanish conquests to these and neighboring Pacific islands and in restricting Spanish trade largely to an indirect trade with other parts of the Far East.

Spanish galleons picked up cargoes at Manila and carried them to
Mexico and Spain. Spanish Franciscan and Dominican missionaries, however, were active in other parts of the Far East, particularly in China and Japan. In both countries they engaged in
heated sectarian quarrels with the Jesuits who had preceded them
under Portuguese protection. Their disputes became a source
of annoyance and even alarm to the Shoguns, the feudal rulers of
Japan, and to the Manchu emperors in China, leading them to
proscribe the preaching and practice of Christianity in the early
seventeenth and eighteenth centuries.

*The Portuguese and Spanish Positions Challenged by the
Dutch, English and French.* By the end of the sixteenth century
the monopolistic claims of the Portuguese and the Spanish to
trade and conquest in the Far East were beginning to be effectively challenged by the rising, more energetic states of northern
Europe, first the Dutch, followed by the British, the Russians and
the French. Not that they were to be completely driven out, for
the Spaniards held the Philippines until the war with America
in 1898, while the Portuguese still hold the little port of Macao
on an island near Canton and half of the island of Timor in the
East Indies. The English, French and Dutch sought direct trade
with the Far East through monopolistic trading companies chartered by their respective governments after 1600. Like the Spanish and Portuguese before them, they coveted the spice trade at
first above all else. As early as 1600 the Dutch garrisoned a
trading post on the island of Amboyna. It was the first step in
building up their East Indian empire, these islands becoming
from then on, despite the efforts of the English to drive the Dutch
out, the center of Dutch colonial empire in the Far East. From
these islands as a base they carried on trade with China and
Japan. Because of their willingness to divorce trade from religion,
even to the extent of "trampling upon the Cross" in the presence
of Japanese officials, the Dutch were the only Europeans allowed
to carry on a restricted trade with Japan during the years of the
seclusion policy in effect from 1638 until the opening of the
country to foreign trade and residence by Commodore Perry
of the United States Navy in 1853-1854.

After contesting unsuccessfully with the Dutch for control
of the East Indies, the English fell back upon India, where they
proceeded to build up an empire and a base for commercial and

imperial expansion in the Far East. The expanding political control which the British and other East India Companies attempted to acquire over the hinterland that lay behind their scattered trading posts was dictated by the desire to secure monopolistic control over the commodities of trade at their source. This placed them in a position to buy at the lowest possible prices by eliminating competing native middlemen. In addition they were placed in a position to increase production by maintaining "law and order" in the interior, improving communications and methods of production. With a gradual strengthening of their political and economic position they were able to take over an increasing share of the trade in Far Eastern waters formerly carried on by Far Eastern peoples themselves—a trade which had flourished off and on for a thousand years or more before the Europeans came. For these reasons increasing political domination tended ever to accompany European economic expansion.

The English entered the Japanese trade in 1613 by establishing a "factory" or trading post at Hirado. They were forced to close it in 1623 at considerable financial loss due to effective Dutch competition. They withdrew from the Japan trade until after the country was reopened in 1854. In China, the British East India Company was to attain an outstanding success. The first attempt to open trade, made in 1637, was a failure and only occasional voyages were made to Chinese waters after that for a time. Finally a factory was established in Canton in 1715. At last the China trade was put on a firm basis and the English quickly won that supremacy in the trade which they were to enjoy until the present century. The French made an entrance into the China trade only in 1699. Thereafter their trade with China was infrequent and of little value until the nineteenth century. The chartered companies of Sweden, Denmark and Prussia inaugurated trade with China in the eighteenth century, but like the French were unable to carry on any considerable trade until the nineteenth century. The Americans entered the China trade in 1784 immediately after the revolution. By 1820 their trade was second for a time only to that of the British.

Russia Comes Overland. The Russians were not to enter into trade with China via the sea until after 1858. Prior to that time they were confined by the Chinese government to trade by land at designated points on the frontiers separating the two empires. By the end of the seventeenth century Russian expansion and colonization in Siberia had reached the outer confines of Manchuria in the region of the Amur River. Further expansion into Manchuria, the homeland of the Manchus, who were then on the throne in China, was stopped with the signing of the Treaty of Nerchinsk in 1689, China's first treaty with a European power, which delimited the frontier along the watershed of the Amur and permitted trade. In the eighteenth century the chief trading center was at Kiakhta, further to the west. There a lively trade developed, the Chinese receiving European textiles, leather, tanned hides and glassware in exchange for silk, tea, porcelain, sugar, ginger, rhubarb and lacquered work. The Russians made several vain efforts to open Japan again to trade at the end of the eighteenth and early part of the nineteenth centuries, as did several other European nations. All such attempts were to fail until after Commodore Perry's arrival in 1853 and the conclusion of a treaty the following year. This led to the abandonment of the seclusion policy adopted by Japan over two hundred years earlier.

Early European Interests in China

It was the desire to control the spice trade that first drew Europeans to the Far East. Once there the possibility of opening up trade with China, from whence they might secure silks, porcelain and the highly prized *objets d'art* produced by skilled Chinese artisans, led them on to that country. Silk, which had been prized in Europe as early as the days of the Roman Empire, and later tea, the drinking of which spread through Europe in the second half of the seventeenth century, became the two chief items in China's export trade until near the end of the nineteenth century. While there were many Chinese products which the Europeans wanted, they were to find it difficult to provide products and manufactures, before the middle of the nineteenth century, which the self-sufficient economy of China needed or could not provide. There was much truth in Emperor Ch'ien-lung's assertion in his "edict" to George III of England, in which he refused the requests made by the Lord Macartney Mission of 1793 further to open China to European trade, asserting that his country possessed all things in prolific abundance and had no need to import the manufactures of outside "barbarians." The English did find a limited market for their woolens and the Americans for furs from the northwest coast, but all that they could sell to the Chinese fell far short of balancing the growing export trade. Hence they had to bring large amounts of silver specie to balance the trade until toward 1820. After that date increasing imports of opium into China for a time actually more than balanced trade in their favor, leading even to an exportation of silver from China.

This increased opium trade and export of silver, which had adverse economic consequences in China, became the major cause, from the Chinese point of view, for the so-called "opium war" or Anglo-Chinese War of 1839-1842. From the British point of view, which was shared by other Western traders in China, that war was fought primarily to force China to open the country further to Western trade and incidentally to the missionary. At first the Portuguese and other European traders had been allowed to trade at several south China ports, but after 1757 the trade was confined by imperial edict to the port of Canton. There until after 1842 foreigners were forced to deal with a small group of Chinese monopoly merchants called the *Cohong* and to carry on their trade under numerous and vexatious restrictions, as well as increasing and fluctuating dues and duties. Furthermore, the Chinese were demanding and securing partial legal jurisdiction over them, particularly in homicide cases. Where the life of a Chinese was involved, the Chinese rulers were demanding the surrender of a luckless foreigner, alleged to be guilty, for trial in a Chinese court, which usually resulted in the execution of the prisoner. This practice greatly outraged the European sense of individualistic justice. The British, after the notorious case of 1785, which arose out of the accidental slaying of a Chinese by a gunner aboard the ship *Lady Hughes*, were opposed to surrendering a single man to the tender mercies of Chinese justice. As a result of the treaties following the war of 1839-1842 the practice of European governments of exercising extraterritorial jurisdiction over their own nationals in China was recognized by the Chinese regime. In addition to these two developments leading up to the war, there was a third factor of psychological importance. The British demanded that the Chinese no longer treat foreigners as vassals or "barbarians," as they were called in official dispatches, but as equals. A long and bitter struggle centered in this question of equality and its closely related question of a proper audience. It was not finally settled to the satisfaction of the Europeans until the last decade of the nineteenth century.

As long as the British East India Company held a monopoly over the China trade open war over these issues was avoided. Those in control of the company were loath to take any action that would jeopardize their highly lucrative trade despite these handicaps. They were willing to adjust, compromise or "appease" in accordance with the circumstances of each issue as it arose. However, the days of the company's monopoly of the China trade were numbered. The monopoly expired in 1833. The growing commercial and financial interests of an industrializing England after 1770 brought increasing pressure upon the government not only to assist them in finding wider markets for their textiles and other manufactures in China and elsewhere, but to abolish the East India Company's monopoly of the trade so that all Englishmen might engage in the Eastern trade upon an equal competitive basis.

With the abolition of the China monopoly in 1833 the British government was brought into direct contact with the Chinese government. Replacing the company's representative in control of its affairs at Canton was a government-appointed superintendent-of-trade. It is not surprising that Lord Napier, the first official appointed to that post, should demand, as a representative of his sovereign, that he be granted an interview upon his arrival in Canton with the highest ranking Chinese official there. Nor is it surprising that the Chinese should refuse this request, unfamiliar as they were with the European concept of equal sovereign states and the corresponding body of diplomatic rules and procedures governing the relationships of such states. Two wars were fought and the greater part of the century elapsed before the Chinese court was fully to abandon, with all its ceremonial trappings, its concept of the universal Chinese Empire which had relations only with inferior vassal states and to accept the Western concept of equal sovereign states.

Position of the Europeans in China by 1860

The Anglo-Chinese War of 1839-1842 witnessed for the first time the effective application of force to bring China into the comity of nations and to open it further to commercial exploitation on a free, competitive basis. By 1860, at the end of the second war, in which France had this time joined England, China had been reduced from its lofty rôle of a "universal" empire not to full but rather to associate membership in the family of nations. For as a result of the treaties which were signed at the end of these wars—"unequal treaties" as later generations of nationalistic Chinese were to call them—the Europeans won "rights" which seriously infringed upon China's administrative sovereignty. The establishment of the regime of extraterritoriality, whereby Europeans in China were to be subject only to their own laws, and the setting up of concessions in the "treaty ports" which they administered and where they lived and carried on their business, were both serious curtailments of China's sovereign rights. These two basic features of the treaty system, which regulated and governed China's relations with the West and later with Japan, still obtained in 1941. Encroachment upon China's territorial sovereignty was slight up to 1860. The primary interest of the Europeans in China up to that time lay in exploiting the alleged "unlimited" market of the then 300,000,000 Chinese. Interest in China as a source of mineral resources, as a market for capital investment, or as an outpost of empire was on the whole to develop after 1860, except in a few minor instances.

In order to gain a clearer picture of the position the Europeans held in China as a result of the two wars it will be necessary briefly to summarize the pertinent provisions of the treaties and subsequent agreements which were signed by the victorious English and French and by other European nations who shared in the fruits of victory.

The Treaty of Nanking, signed August 29, 1842, brought the first war to an end. It provided for the cession to the British of the small island of Hongkong near Canton; the opening of Canton, Amoy, Foochow, Ningpo and Shanghai to foreign trade and residence where consuls were permitted to be stationed; the abolition of the *Cohong;* the imposition of a low and uniform import and export tariff to be fixed at about 5 per cent ad valorem; and equality in the relations between officials of corresponding rank of the two countries.

The other nations secured their "rights" through the most-favored-nation clause first included in the British Treaty of the Bogue, October 8, 1843, which provided in substance, para-

doxically enough, that there should be no most favored nation.
Its inclusion in the treaty is an indication that the British had
fought their war to open China equally to all comers. The
Chinese representatives had early in the war asked the British
if they would consent to an extension to the other nations of the
privileges which they were seeking. By throwing the country
open to all equally the Chinese and Manchu officials saw an
opportunity to employ a diplomatic stratagem which centuries
of precedent had proved to be of value—namely that of playing
one "barbarian" off against another. It was a strategy to be employed with varying and at times a surprising degree of success.
The British readily consented. As a result all the basic treaties
which other nations, including Japan after 1894, signed with
China were based upon this fundamental provision. Its effect
was to create among the foreigners in China a community of interests that led to a large degree of co-operation among them and
their governments in efforts to maintain rights and privileges
against Chinese opposition. At the same time the clause served
China beneficially in that it operated negatively to frustrate the
efforts of individual nations to secure special privileges or
concessions or even territory. It was the basic principle upon
which was to be formulated the Open Door policy first enunciated
by the United States government in 1899 and 1900.

The Americans in the Treaty of Wanghia, July 3, 1844, and the
French in the Treaty of Whampoa, October 24, 1844, inherited
these basic rights for which the British had fought. In addition
they acquired certain rights which the British treaties failed to
secure. The American treaty more carefully and fully defined the
extraterritorial regime under which the traders and missionaries
and all others were to live in China. It was formally stipulated
that they should be almost completely under the jurisdiction of
their own laws and courts in China no matter where they might
go, or in regard to missionaries, where they might live. The
French envoy, in accordance with his government's traditional
policy of protecting and promoting Catholic missions in non-Chris-
tian lands, secured the issuance of an imperial edict in 1844 which
granted toleration to the religion of the "Lord of Heaven," thus
rescinding the proscription edicts in force since the first part of
the eighteenth century. The following year, when the differences
between Protestantism and Catholicism were brought to the atten-

tion of the Chinese officials, the rescript was broadened to include Protestantism. The efforts of the Belgians to secure a treaty in 1845 failed, but an edict granted them the existing treaty rights. Sweden and Norway, one country at that time, were more successful, securing a treaty in 1847.

The Europeans were to have difficulty in trying to induce the people and officials of China to observe and fulfill all the "rights" granted under these treaties and agreements. This situation, together with the renewed pressure from the traders for a further opening of the country to trade and residence as well as the desire of the various governments to enter into more formal diplomatic relations with China by having a minister in permanent residence in Peking, was to lead to a second conflict that dragged itself out over a four-year period from 1856-1860. The principal provisions of the treaties and conventions that were signed at the conclusion of the conflict provided, in the first place, for the opening of eleven additional ports to foreign trade, including Tientsin near the capital and several "ports" far in the interior of the country, such as Hankow, 600 miles up the Yangtze River. It was further provided that Europeans and Americans might travel on business or for pleasure to all parts of the interior under specially issued passports. In addition clauses were added granting further protection to Christianity and extending permission, at least so the Westerners effectively claimed, to missionaries not only to preach in the interior, but also to buy and hold property. The extraterritoriality regime was better defined. The British secured the cession of a strip of land at Kowloon on the mainland opposite Hongkong to strengthen the island's strategic position. The Russians secured the right to trade via the sea and acquired with Chinese consent control over the territory to the east of the Ussuri River, which became the maritime province of Primorsk on which Vladivostok is located. Finally, permission was secured to station permanent envoys at the capital. To these privileges and rights under the treaties, there was added at this time the control over the collection of China's maritime customs by Europeans under a British inspector-general, aided by an international staff of officials.

By 1870 the Europeans had laid that firm foundation for their special position in China upon which they were to build their expanding commercial, financial, industrial, missionary and cultural interests. Other European and American nations which had not up to that time entered into treaty relations were to be able to do so if they chose, under the most-favored-nation clause.

This system of treaty rights formed the pattern for a similar series of treaties signed with Japan following Commodore Perry's formal opening of the country in 1854 in the decade from 1858 to 1868. By this time a number of ports had been opened to foreign trade and residence; the regime of extraterritoriality had been established; envoys were in residence at Tokyo; and Japan was forced by treaty to accept a limited 5 per cent import and export tariff. However, the Europeans made no infringements on Japan's territorial integrity. The Japanese government in 1873 voluntarily extended religious toleration, thus avoiding the incorporation of this right into the treaties.

Position of the Europeans in Southeastern Asia and the South Pacific by 1870

By the middle of the nineteenth century the Spaniards were still entrenched in the Philippines. The Dutch claimed the East Indies, the Netherlands government having taken over the East India Company's position in the islands in 1798 when the company ceased to exist. German traders and trading companies, like the famous Godeffroy Company, had penetrated into Samoa, part of New Guinea, the Solomon Islands, New Britain and a host of smaller islands in the vicinity. Effectively they paved the way for the acquisition by the German government during the 1880's of German Samoa, *Kaiser Wilhelmsland* (New Guinea) and the Bismarck Archipelago. The foundations of the extension of British and French empires into the Indo-Chinese and Malayan peninsulas were either securely laid or foreshadowed by the activities of the traders and missionaries and official emissaries of these countries by 1870. In the seventeenth century both the Dutch and the British East India Companies had entered into trade with Siam (Thailand) and Burma, breaking the Portuguese trade monopoly with Siam held in the preceding century. French influence, religious and commercial, became supreme for a time in Siam in the latter part of the seventeenth century. But the intrigues of the missionaries gradually aroused opposition, and in 1780 Catholic missionaries were banished by royal decree. The British in

EUROPEAN EXPANSION IN THE FAR EAST BY 1870

1826 secured a trade treaty with Siam which provided for free trade. But their request for extraterritorial rights was not conceded until 1855 when a treaty was signed based on the model of the China treaties with virtually all the same rights. In 1856 the United States signed a similar treaty with Siam, quite willingly granted by the Siamese who sought American aid to counteract the British threat through Burma and the French threat to the east in Annam. By the 1860's the British had fought two wars with Burma resulting in the annexation of lower Burma to British India. By 1885 the conquest of Burma was completed.

Losing out finally in both Siam as well as India, the French concentrated on building an empire in the eastern part of the peninsula. By 1867 they had securely laid the foundations of that empire in Indo-China. Their influence in the area dates from the end of the eighteenth century. Between 1843 and 1857 the political activities of French missionaries aroused the Annamese court to take measures to suppress them. Missionaries continued to be active in the country, however, leading to assaults upon them resulting, from time to time, in death. Naval expeditions were sent on each occasion to demand redress and an end to such activities. Finally in 1858 France and Spain united in sending a fleet to force these demands on the Annamese king. There followed eventually the Treaty of Saigon of 1862 whereby France acquired Saigon and the eastern province of Cochin China. The following year a treaty signed by the king of Cambodia substituted a French protectorate over that kingdom for one formerly held by Siam. Siam formally recognized this transfer of suzerainty in 1867. Then in 1867 France acquired the three western provinces of Cochin China. After two centuries of repeated but failing effort the French at long last had laid the foundations of a Far Eastern empire.

On the lower part of the Malay peninsula and the adjoining islands the British established a strategic naval and commercial outpost of empire. Penang near the northern end of the Malacca Straits was acquired by 1790. The next step was consummated in 1824 when the island of Singapore was obtained from the sultan of Johore. Sir Stamford Raffles, who was primarily responsible for taking the first step to acquire the area in 1819, prophetically asserted it to be ". . . the most important station in the East; and, as far as naval superiority and commercial interests are concerned, of much higher value than whole continents of territory." In the same year that it was secured, Malacca was obtained from the Dutch in exchange for some minor holdings in Sumatra. These three strategic points were combined together with Wellesley Province and the Dindings in 1867 to form the Crown Colony of the Straits Settlements. The extension of British protection over the Malay states in the hinterland then inevitably followed.

By the 1860's we find the Europeans well entrenched in the Far East for commercial expansion and religious proselytizing with the foundations laid on which to expand their earlier established empires, to extend their political, commercial and cultural interests, or to acquire industrial and financial spheres of influence and control.

READINGS

Bain, H. Foster. *Ores and Industry in the Far East,* 1933. Useful, balanced survey.

Bergsmark, D. R. *Economic Geography of Asia,* 1935. Has a good bibliography.

Cressey, George B. *China's Geographic Foundations,* 1934. The best descriptive survey.

Fellner, F. V., Ed. *Communications in the Far East,* 1934. Development of all forms in past century.

Field, Frederick V. *Economic Handbook of the Pacific Area,* 1934, Rev. Ed. in preparation. An indispensable reference work.

Hudson, G. F. and Rajchman, Marthe. *An Atlas of Far Eastern Politics,* 1938. Useful introductory work.

MacFadden, Clifford H. *A Selected Bibliography of Pacific Area Maps,* 1940.

Morse, H. B. and MacNair, H. F. *Far Eastern International Relations,* 1931. A useful textbook and reference work.

Roberts, S. H. *Population Problems of the Pacific,* 1927. Effects of European contacts on native peoples.

Stamp, L. Dudley. *Asia, a Regional and Economic Geography,* 1931. Rev. ed. 1935. The best general survey of the continent.

Steiger, G. Nye. *History of the Far East,* 1936. Best one-volume history of the whole Far East from earliest times to the present, with excellent bibliographies.

CHAPTER SEVENTEEN

China Proper Becomes a Semi-Colony

THE SHARPEST and bitterest struggles among the European nations in the Far East centered in their efforts to dominate the markets and control the economic resources of China. No one of them ever seriously planned to establish its hegemony over all that vast "continent" to the exclusion of the other nations. Only the Japanese in recent years have embraced that ambition with a view to exploiting the resources of the country for their own ends and dictating the terms upon which the Westerners shall do business with the Chinese. In China Proper the forces of European imperialism seemed to exhaust themselves before the country, like Africa, was carved up amongst them. The result was that throughout the modern period the fiction of China's territorial sovereignty and administrative integrity has been maintained. Yet the degree of control which the nations exercised within China and the special privileges which they held in derogation of its sovereignty reduced the country to what has aptly been called the status of a "semi-colony." In this chapter the varying stakes of fortune won and lost by the nations in China during the eighty-year period since 1860 will first be considered.[1] The second part of the chapter will recount how the nations acquired their special positions of control and influence in China Proper.

GREAT BRITAIN

TRADE: 1899— 53,900,000 Hk. Tls.[2]—11.7 per cent of total trade
1913—113,300,000 Hk. Tls. —11.4 per cent of total trade
1930—170,900,000 Hk. Tls. — 7.8 per cent of total trade
1939—168,723,000 Yuan—7.2 per cent of total trade
POPULATION: 1899— 5,562—32.4 per cent of the total foreign population
1913— 8,966— 5.4 per cent
1930—13,015— 3.6 per cent
FIRMS: 1899— 401—43 per cent of total foreign firms
1913— 590—15 per cent
1934—1,021—9.3 per cent
SHIPPING: 1899—23,300,000 tons—59.4 per cent
1913—38,100,000 tons—40.8 per cent
1934—58,800,000 tons—41.9 per cent
INVESTMENTS: 1902—$ 260,300,000—33.0 per cent of total foreign investments
1914—$ 607,500,000—37.7 per cent of total foreign investments
1930—$1,189,200,000—36.7 per cent of total foreign investments

As late as 1930 British investments exceeded those of any other nation. Japan at that time was a close second and since then has gone well into the lead if the large investments placed in Manchoukuo are included in the Japanese total. About 80 per cent

---

[1] The figures on investments, trade, firms, and shipping up to the year 1931 which follow are taken from C. F. Remer's excellent survey, *Foreign Investments in China* (New York, Macmillan Co., 1933). Permission to use this material has been kindly granted by The Macmillan Company, publishers. Figures on investments and trade since that time have been drawn largely from the *Far Eastern Survey*, a fortnightly publication of the Institute of Pacific Relations, New York, and from F. V. Field's *Economic Handbook of the Pacific* (1934), published by the same organization.

[2] The Haikuan Tael represented the customs unit of valuation. It was not a coined unit, but represented a value of about a Chinese ounce of silver. In 1899 it was worth about 75 cents; in 1913, 73 cents; and in 1930, 38 cents. It was replaced in March, 1933, by the standard silver dollar (Yuan) which had a value of $0.34 in January, 1934. Through 1939 it had an average value of 12 cents or less. The figures on investments are given in U. S. dollars.

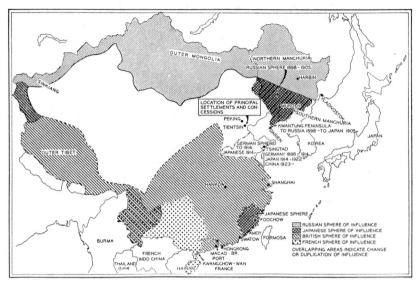

POSITION OF THE POWERS IN CHINA, 1898-1931

of the British investments were in the nature of direct business
investments and only 20 per cent were Chinese government obligations. Property held by British missions was estimated to be
about $10,000,000. Over 75 per cent of the business investments
were located in Shanghai, 9.3 per cent in Hongkong ($89,812,-
000), and 14.1 per cent in the rest of China. By categories 14 per
cent of these investments were in transportation, mostly shipping,
18 per cent in manufacturing, 12 per cent in banking and finance,
21 per cent in real estate, 25 per cent in import and export and
general trading enterprises, 2 per cent in mining, and 5 per cent in
public utilities. The main items of distribution of Chinese government obligations to the amount of $183,814,000 owed to British
investors were as follows: general purposes of the government,
$79,575,000; Chinese government railroads, $67,949,000; unsecured loans, $20,094,000; and obligations of foreign municipali-
ties in China, $14,235,000.[3]

---

[3] Details as to the companies, etc., which held these investments and the
purposes for which the loans were made by British interests as well as by the interests of the countries mentioned below, are to be found in C. F. Remer's
Foreign Investments in China, passim.

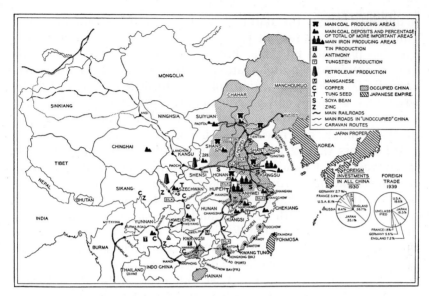

CHINA PROPER—POLITICAL AND ECONOMIC, 1940

While there was a revival of investment activity on the part of the British, as well as of the other powers, after 1930, the British total did not increase. There was a probable decrease due to a general decline in China's foreign trade, and to conditions arising from Sino-Japanese hostilities which were accompanied by increasing Japanese success in efforts to close the door on Western investments and trade. In north China Japanese pressure was especially severe on the British, but other interests were affected as well. Through the establishment of monopolies, export prohibitions, exchange control regulations, and tariff rigging, the Japanese were gradually undermining the position of the Western interests in the north and to a lesser extent in central and south China. Western or "free" China remained a promising field for occidental investments and business enterprises, but the amount invested was not great, due in part to continued fighting between the Chinese and Japanese. As a result of the outbreak of the European War in 1939 there was little possibility that the Western nations would be in a position to extend much further their interests in that region as long as the war continued.

The British, closely supported by the French and the Americans, maintained up to the outbreak of the war the semblance of a united front in the face of Japanese efforts to undermine their respective positions in China Proper. Various methods were employed ranging from diplomatic protest to financial support, such as a £5,000,000 stabilization fund established by the British to strengthen Chinese currency against the deteriorating effects of Japanese exchange control regulations, and the judicious deployment of military and naval forces in Chinese waters.

While less than 2 per cent of the United Kingdom's foreign trade was with China and only about 6 per cent of British overseas investments were to be found in that country, more was involved than these figures would seem to indicate. There was the potentiality for growth in trade and investment, a consideration of which always animated British policy. Then there was the question of prestige. To back out in the face of the Japanese advance would be to jeopardize the whole imperial economic and strategic position in the Far East and even in India. Whether the European war would result in the retreat of the British and the French, not only from China but from the Far East as a whole, or whether a compromise settlement would be made with Japan, possibly at the expense of China, remained an open question in the spring of 1941.

The British still retained in 1940 concessions at Tientsin and Canton, had a controlling voice in the International Settlement at Shanghai and participated in the administration of the foreign settlement of Kulangsu at Amoy. The International Settlement at Shanghai covered an area of 8.3 square miles and had a population of over 1,000,000. All but some 40,000 of these were Chinese, the rest being foreigners representing 46 different nationalities. The Settlement had its origin in the treaties of 1842-44, but was not set up in its contemporary form until 1869. It differed from a concession, which was an area granted by the Chinese government to a single nation on perpetual lease, in that it was an area set aside by agreement among foreign consuls and local Chinese officials within which foreigners might rent land from Chinese owners, paying an annual ground rent to the Chinese government and registering their deeds both with their own consulates and the proper Chinese authorities. Thus China's basic sovereign rights in the area persisted and the practise of the settlement's municipal council of governing the Chinese living in the area had no clear-cut legal basis. Members of the municipal council were elected by an oligarchical group of qualified voters numbering only 3,852 in 1935. They represented the predominant commercial and financial interests of the community. It was not until 1928, after years of agitation, that the Chinese ratepayers, who contributed more than half of the revenue of the municipality, were allowed to elect three members to the council. The number was increased to five in 1930, but this figure did not give them a majority for the British still held five seats, the Americans two, and the Japanese two.

While the council gave the area fairly efficient administration, allowing the city to grow despite periodic war in its environs, the share of the public services afforded the Chinese were woefully inadequate. Public schools were provided for only 3 per cent of the Chinese children of school age. Conditions among the industrial and laboring classes were bad. While perhaps better than in the adjoining native city they were far below standards in the countries from which the ruling elements in the city came. The settlement authorities contended that if they laid down stringent regulations governing working conditions, it would serve only to drive the factories into the adjoining Chinese areas. In recent years, however, the modernized nationalist government at Nanking had made attempts to raise working standards through factory acts and factory inspection. The municipal authorities co-operated with the government in this effort so as to improve conditions throughout the area of Greater Shanghai simultaneously.

The assumption by the foreigners of control over Chinese in the area necessitated the establishment of a Mixed Court in 1864. This court, which continued to exist until 1927, was a Chinese court presided over by a Chinese magistrate assisted and advised by foreign assessors with jurisdiction over civil, criminal or commercial cases in which Chinese were involved or cases in which they were defendants. Recently a nationalist China, resenting this usurpation of sovereign rights, induced the Settlement authorities to abolish the court and in 1930 a regular Chinese court was set up administering modernized Chinese codes. It was apparent that a strong nationalist government in China would not tolerate any longer than necessary a continuance of the foreign-dominated municipal government. Since 1931 the Chinese have not been pressing for surrender of the Settlement and all other special rights of foreigners in China. In their long struggle against the Japanese the continuance of the foreign position in the country served as a check to Japan's ambitions. As far as the Settlement was concerned, as late as 1940 it was the Japanese who were struggling to dominate the municipal council by securing a majority control by their nationals.

JAPAN

TRADE: 1899— 53,100,000 Hk. Tls.—11.5 per cent of total trade
1913—184,900,000 Hk. Tls.—19   per cent
1930—543,000,000 Hk. Tls.—24.7 per cent
1939—380,019,000 Yuan—16.5 per cent

POPULATION: 1930—255,686—70.6 per cent of total foreign population
1939—575,000 (exclusive of soldiers), 426,000 of whom were in Manchuria

FIRMS: 1899— 195—20.9 per cent of total foreign firms
1913—1,269—33.3 per cent of total foreign firms
1930—4,633—55.9 per cent

SHIPPING: 1899— 2,800,000 tons— 7.2 per cent
1913—23,400,000 tons—25 per cent
1930—45,600,000 tons—29.3 per cent
1939—Japanese shipping into Shanghai, Tientsin, and Tsingtao exceeded all others

INVESTMENTS: 1900—$ 1,000,000— 0.1 per cent
1914—$ 219,000,000—13.6 per cent
1931—$1,136,900,000—35.1 per cent
1939—Japan has invested upwards of $500,000,000 in Manchuria since 1931, which places it in first place as regards foreign investments in China.

Japanese investments in China constituted 81.9 per cent of Japan's total overseas investments in 1930. At that time nearly two-thirds of Japanese investments were concentrated in the South Manchurian Railroad Company in which the Japanese government held a controlling share. Of the direct investments in China Proper two-thirds were located in Shanghai. The direct business investments in all China totaled $874,129,500, of which 23 per cent were in railroads in Manchuria; 10 per cent in mining, of which 95 per cent was in Manchuria; 19 per cent in manufacturing; 8.4 per cent in banking and finance; 8.4 per cent in real estate; and 21 per cent in import and export concerns.

The total Japanese holdings of Chinese government obligations in 1930 was $224,077,619. Of this amount, about $100,-000,000 was in the form of unsecured loans granted mostly to the Japanese-controlled Chinese regime dominant in Peking after 1917 for a few years. By 1931 Japan had some $57,000,000 invested in cultural and philanthropic institutions in China, mostly schools, libraries and hospitals.

Accompanying Japan's growing military and political control in China since 1931 was the development of schemes for exploiting the natural resources of China accompanied by the establishment of light and heavy industries, plans for expanding the production of cotton and wool and the improvement of communications. In Manchuria some progress was made. In China little had been achieved by 1940. In both regions lack of capital was a retarding factor, while in China Proper continued warfare was a constant drain on the resources of Japan. The devices set up to carry on this exploitative work were highly monopolistic in character. Such for example was the North China Development Company, which formally opened for business in November, 1938. It was organized as a Japanese corporation capitalized at Yen 350,000,000, half of which was to be subscribed by the Japanese government and half by public subscription. All but 10 per cent of the shares were allotted to the great financial houses of Japan, such as the Mitsui and Mitsubishi. It was a vast holding company whose subsidiaries were to have a virtual monopoly in their control of railroads and ports, communications, iron and steel works, coal and cotton production. The subsidiaries were to be organized as joint Sino-Japanese concerns, but Japanese interests were to hold the controlling shares. By August, 1939, little progress had been made—only two of the eight subsidiaries having been organized. A similar company was projected to develop central China. It had made even less headway by that time. Lack of capital, continued Chinese resistance and Western opposition were still effective at the outbreak of the European War in 1939 in preventing Japan from establishing its complete political and economic hegemony over the greater part of China and making of that area a virtual Japanese colony.

UNITED STATES

TRADE: 1899— 43,700,000 Hk. Tls.— 9.5 per cent of total
      1913— 73,000,000 Hk. Tls.— 7.5 per cent
      1930—364,000,000 Hk. Tls—16.5 per cent
      1939—439,973,000 Yuan—18.6 per cent
POPULATION: 1899—2,335—13.6 per cent of the total foreign population
      1913—5,340— 3.6 per cent
      1930—6,875— 1.9 per cent
FIRMS: 1930—566 or 6.8 per cent of total
SHIPPING: 1939—6,500,000 tons or 4.2 per cent of total
INVESTMENTS: 1900—$ 19,700,000—2.5 per cent of total
      1914—$ 49,300,000—3.1 per cent
      1930—$196,800,000—6.1 per cent

American investments in 1930 comprised only 1.3 per cent of America's total foreign investments. The total of American business investments was $155,112,778. Two-thirds of these were located in Shanghai. The amount invested in transportation was 7 per cent of the total; in public utilities 23.4 per cent; in manufacturing 13.7 per cent; in banking and finance 16.8 per cent; in real estate 5.6 per cent; and in import and export businesses 31.8 per cent. American holdings of securities and obligations of the Chinese government amounted to $41,711,346. American missions and philanthropic societies had holdings to the amount of $41,-904,889.

American investments were only about one-sixth of those of Great Britain or of Japan. Investments made after 1930 did somewhat alter the picture. Two American utility concerns acquired a dominant interest in the power and telephone companies of the International Settlement and there were investments of about $2,000,000 in aircraft and commercial airlines in China. The government extended a cotton and a wheat loan and there was a loan granted by the government-supported Export-Import Bank in 1937 to enable China to purchase American locomotives. The three together totalled $27,051,412. In December, 1938, the Export-Import Bank again extended credit to the amount of $25,000,000 and a similar amount again in September, 1940, followed by an additional grant of $50,000,000 from the same source and $50,000,000 from the treasury's stabilization fund in December, 1940. These credits, while patently economic in character, also had their political overtones as they evidenced American moral as well as material support of the Chinese Nationalist Government's efforts to oppose Japan's goal of establishing its hegemony over China.

FRANCE

TRADE: 1905—22,700,000 Hk. Tls.—3.4 per cent of the total foreign trade
1913—46,000,000 Hk. Tls.—4.7 per cent
1930—59,700,000 Hk. Tls.—2.7 per cent
1939—43,948,000 Yuan—1.8 per cent
POPULATION: 1899—1,183—6.8 per cent of total foreign population in China
1913—2,292—1.4 per cent
1930—8,575—2.4 per cent
FIRMS: 1899— 76—8.1 per cent
1913—106—2.7 per cent
1930—186—2.2 per cent
INVESTMENTS: 1902—$ 91,100,000—11.6 per cent
1914—$171,400,000—10.7 per cent
1930—$192,400,000— 5.9 per cent
1938—$200,000,000

Investments in 1930 were distributed as follows: general purposes of the Chinese government, $76,268,367; railroad obligations, $13,864,000; business investments, $95,000,000; and mission property to a value of $21,707,200. About $40,000,000 was invested in Shanghai and some $32,000,000 in the Indo-China-Yunnan railroad. Since 1930 French capital operating through the *Banque Franco-Chinoise pour le Commerce et l'Industrie* advanced (Chinese) $7,000,000 in cash and (Chinese) $27,500,-000 in materials in a co-operative project with a Chinese concern to finance a railroad from Chungking to Chengtu in Szechuan province. In June, 1938, a French company was organized to construct a line from Nanning to Chennankuan on the Indo-China border with a capitalization of 9,000,000 francs.

In addition to the French concession in Shanghai, the French had concessions at Tientsin, Hankow and Canton. The area of the French concession in Shanghai, adjoining the International Settlement, was 2,525 acres. It had a population of 500,000 in 1940, all but about 20,000 of whom were Chinese. It was largely a residential area and was not important industrially and commercially. It was not a true concession as the area was not granted outright on a perpetual lease as in the case of the other concessions. However, unlike the adjoining International Settlement, it was administered like a concession in that there was centralized control by the French consul-general who was subject to check only by the French ambassador and the Foreign Office. The *Reglements* which governed the administration of the area were first drawn up in 1866 and were revised on several occasions. In origin they have the same vague legal basis in the treaties as in the case of the International Settlement regulations. The municipal council was merely an advisory body as the consul-general had complete veto power over it. In 1927 it was dissolved by him and replaced by a provisional commission. On this commission there were fifteen members, eight of whom were French, two representing other European nations, and five Chinese.

Some effort was made to care for the health of the Chinese largely through vaccination against communicable diseases. Educational facilities were wholly inadequate for the Chinese, there being only three schools with 2,000 students. The Chinese held no high positions in the municipal government. Despite an expenditure of 30 per cent of the budget on policing the area it was notorious as a hideout for renegade Chinese politicians, racketeers, opium smugglers and strikebreakers, and licensed prostitution existed. Cases involving Chinese and foreigners in which the Chinese were defendants and cases among Chinese themselves were tried in a Mixed Court as in the International Settlement until 1931, when the court was rendered. Modernized Chinese courts were then allowed to function in the area with Chinese judges on the bench rendering decisions independent of foreign assessors and in accordance with modernized Chinese codes.

Kwangchow-wan

The bay of Kwangchow in south China was secured by the French on lease in 1898. It comprised an area of 325 square miles with a population of about 250,000 of whom only about 250 were foreigners, the rest being Chinese. It was administered by the government of Indo-China and its budget formed a part of the budget of that administration. At the Washington Conference the French delegation agreed to "join in the collective restitution of territories leased by various powers in China" under certain conditions. Up to the outbreak of the European War in 1939, France had not found that those conditions obtained.

SOVIET UNION

TRADE: 1899—10,100,000 Hk. Tls.—2.2 per cent
  1913—67,400,000 Hk. Tls.—3.3 per cent
  1930—74,400,000 Hk. Tls.—3.4 per cent
  1937— 5,000,000 Yuan—.02 per cent
POPULATION: 1904— 40,000—42.5 per cent of the total foreign population
  1914— 65,000—37.8 per cent
  1930—140,000—32.1 per cent
INVESTMENTS: 1904—$246,000,000—31.3 per cent of total
  1914—$269,300,000—16.7 per cent
  1930—$273,200,000— 8.4 per cent
  1940—$ 50,000,000 (estimated)

The sale of the Chinese Eastern Railroad to Manchoukuo in 1935 followed by withdrawal of practically all Soviet interests in North Manchuria left U.S.S.R interests centered in Mongolia and northwest China, where they probably totaled less than $50,000,000 in value in 1940. While valued at $200,000,000, the road was "sold" under considerable pressure for about $47,-000,000. The sale fitted in with the avowed Soviet policy of liquidating former czarist Russia's imperialist adventures. In 1930 Russian investments were distributed as follows: $261,783,-000 invested in Manchuria, $5,258,250 in Mongolia,[4] and only $6,156,000 in China Proper. Of this investment 77 per cent was in transportation; 4.7 per cent in manufacturing; 11.9 per cent in real estate; and 4.5 per cent in import-export businesses. The Soviet government controlled 77.5 per cent of these investments, a higher percentage than in the case of any other country. Japan was second in this respect. In both cases this situation reflected the political character of the investments, and both countries in the modern period, Russia up to 1904-5 and Japan since, were considered the chief threats to China's territorial integrity.

---

[4] A further account of Russian investments in Mongolia is given on p. 547.

GERMANY

TRADE: 1905— 20,200,000 Hk. Tls.—3   per cent of total
   1913— 45,300,000 Hk. Tls.—4.7 per cent
   1921— 20,100,000 Hk. Tls.—1.3 per cent
   1930— 92,500,000 Hk. Tls.—4.2 per cent
   1939—132,264,000 Yuan—5.6 per cent
POPULATION: 1899—1,134—6.6 per cent of the total foreign population
    1913—2,949—1.8 per cent
    1921—1,255—0.5 per cent
    1930—3,006—0.8 per cent
FIRMS: 1899—115—12.3 per cent
   1913—296— 7.7 per cent
   1921— 92— 0.9 per cent
   1930—297— 3.6 per cent
INVESTMENTS: 1904—$124,300,000—20.9 per cent
     1914—$263,600,000—16.4 per cent
     1931—$ 87,000,000— 2.7 per cent

By 1914 German investments reached their highest point and were about equally divided between business investments and Chinese government obligations. As a result of the first World War these investments had shrunk to about one-eighth of their former value by 1921. There followed a rapid recovery in trade with the result that by 1931 Germany had reached its pre-war relative position. Investments increased from $35,000,000 in 1921 to $87,000,000 in 1931, all but $12,000,000 of which were business investments. After 1931 both trade and investments enjoyed further expansion. The concluding of the anti-Communist pact between Germany and Japan in November, 1936 (followed by German recognition of the state of Manchoukuo in February, 1938), opened the way for German investments there. In September, 1937, Otto Wolff, the large steel and iron concern, signed a £2,000,000 loan agreement with the Central Bank of Manchoukuo. German investments in China Proper between 1931-1937 totalled some $40,000,000. They were made to promote railroad construction and the building of a ferro-wolfram works near the Kiangsi tungsten mines.

Germany lost all of its concessions and special privileges in China (as will be discussed later) as a result of the first World War.[5] During the years from 1898 to 1914, when the Germans

---

[5] See pp. 506, 508.

occupied their concession at Kiaochow and held a special position in Shantung, they proceeded with characteristic efficiency and energy to develop the port at Tsingtao, by building extensive wharfs and modernizing the city. In the provincial hinterland they extended their railroads and opened and exploited natural resources, largely in the form of coal and iron deposits which were to be found there.

The investments of other European nations were small in amount and may be treated in a more general way. Belgium in 1931 had a total investment of about $90,000,000 of which $48,-000,000 was in the nature of Chinese government obligations. Total railroad obligations reached an estimated figure of $37,353,-482 in 1931. In August, 1936, the Belgian *Société de Chemins de Fer et de Tramways en Chine* agreed to advance credits to the amount of Bel. Frs. 450,000,000 to further extend the Lunghai railroad. Netherland investments in 1931 totalled $28,706,000 of which 10,000,000 were business investments and the rest obligations of the Chinese government. Denmark, Norway and Sweden together had a total investment of $2,886,750 in 1931.

SUMMARY OF FOREIGN INTERESTS IN CHINA

A few general statistics will serve to present a clearer picture of the fluctuating stakes held by the imperialist powers in "semi-colonial" China and bring out their relative relationships. The total foreign investments in China in 1931, the last year in which there is provided a full and competent estimate, made by Professor C. F. Remer, was $3,242,500,000. This figure represented a doubling of investments since 1914 and was four times as great as the investments in 1902. One of the outstanding characteristics of these investments was the high percentage of direct business investments, a proportion which rose from 64 per cent in 1902 to 78 per cent in 1931. In India, for example, the total business investments represented only one-third of the foreign investments, and in Japan only one-tenth. This situation arose directly out of the special privileges which the foreigners enjoyed in China, and the high degree of control which they exercised in the country over the tariff and the foreign trade.

The distribution of a major portion of these investments by

purpose or nature of the business was as follows: general purposes of the Chinese government, 13.2 per cent; transportation,
26.1 per cent; mining, 4 per cent; manufacturing, 11.6 per cent;
banking and finance, 6.6 per cent; real estate, 10.5 per cent; import
and export businesses, 14.9 per cent. Geographically 34 per cent
of the investments were located in Shanghai, 27 per cent in Manchuria and the rest were distributed more generally throughout
China. The distribution by country discloses that Great Britain held
the lead to 1931, having in that year 36.7 per cent of the total.
Japan was a close second, having 35.1 per cent, representing a
rise from practically no investments in 1902, whereas British investments held relatively the same position in 1902 that they did
in 1931. By 1940 Japanese investments in China (including
Manchuria) were greater than those of Great Britain. U.S.S.R.
investments declined from 31.3 per cent of the total in 1902 to
only 8.4 per cent for reasons given above.[6] The share of the
United States was only 6.1 per cent of the total; France, 5.9 per
cent, being a decline from 11.6 per cent in 1902; Germany, 2.7
per cent, representing a decline from 20.9 per cent in 1904; Belgium, 2.7 per cent; Netherlands, .9 per cent; Italy, 1.4 per cent;
and the Scandinavian countries, .1 per cent. Indicative of the importance of these investments to the general economy of the
various nations was the percentage of their total overseas investments which they represented. Japanese investments in China
represented over 80 per cent of the nation's overseas investments,
while in the case of Great Britain they constituted only 5.9 per
cent; France, 4.8 per cent; Germany, 4.3 per cent; and the United
States, only 1.3 per cent.

The above brief description and analysis of the status and
various holdings of the nations in semi-colonial China would have
little meaning apart from a knowledge of the methods employed
in the struggle to achieve these positions. This struggle was in
turn conditioned by two outstanding developments in the Far
East in the years since 1870, namely, Japan's successful rise to
the position of a world power and China's failure to achieve that
status. In what follows, therefore, there will be first discussed
some of the forces and historical developments which help explain how Japan was successful in meeting the West on its own

---

[6] See p. 487.

terms where China was to fail so conspicuously. Then there will be recounted the methods employed and the conflicts which arose out of the struggles among the powers to achieve their respective positions in China.

JAPAN'S EMERGENCE AS A MODERN STATE

Japan, by the 1860's, had been forced to enter into trading and diplomatic relations with the European nations on terms similar to those which earlier had been fastened upon China. Yet by 1899 Japan had won its freedom from the onerous unequal treaties when the Western nations relinquished their extraterritorial rights in that year and restored to the Japanese control over their tariff to become effective after 1910. Having achieved equality of status as a sovereign power, the country quickly forged ahead to the front ranks of the world powers when, in 1905, it brought to a successful conclusion its war with Russia. This rapid transformation from a secluded feudal society, which Commodore Perry found when he arrived in 1853, to the status of a modernized, highly militarized nationalistic state within a period of fifty years has been one of the outstanding "wonders" of the modern age. Even before the Japanese were successful in throwing off the shackles of Western imperialism they were competing with the Europeans for concessions in China Proper and in attacking and seizing the weakly held dependencies of Korea, the Liu-ch'iu Islands and Formosa.

Domination of State by the Military and the Oligarchs

How it came about that Japan was able quickly to reverse the tide of European expansion, which still partially submerges China, necessitates a brief survey of the contrasting historical, social and political forces at work in the two countries in the modern period. Such a survey will help to explain the predominant, initiating rôle which the militarists of Japan have played in the undeclared war on China and the attempted establishment of a "new order in Eastern Asia" since 1931. The commanding position which the militarists hold in the Japanese state, little hindered by weak political, moral or constitutional checks, is no new phenomenon in Japanese history. It has its historic origins deep in the roots of the past. We need, in the first place, only to recall that it was a feudal society with which the Europeans first came into contact in Japan—a society where military virtues were extolled and a military caste ruled. This society was finally abolished in its institutionalized forms, but not in its spirit, in the years 1868-1872. The modernized governmental, political, social and economic institutions which rapidly replaced the former social structure were organized, developed and controlled, not by a new class of people rising by revolution from the masses, but by this very ruling military caste, the former *samurai* and *daimyo* or knights and lords of the *ancien regime.*

That they should seek to preserve and maintain their former position and prerogatives under the new state is doubly understandable in the light of the world situation confronting them when they commenced to build their modern political and industrial state. The tidal wave of European expansion was undermining their shores and the only thing which would save them from the fate of Chinese, Indians or near eastern peoples was the rapid creation of a strong army and navy. This pressing and inexorable necessity bore its indelible mark on every program of reform which they undertook. Industrialization was for the primary purpose of building a strong army and navy. Telegraphs and telephone services were to be state monopolies to assure strict governmental censorship and to maintain secrecy in times of stress. The railroads were ultimately nationalized for the same reason.

When it came time to build their new political institutions, marked by the promulgating of a Prussian-modeled constitution in 1889 and the establishment of a parliament in 1890, it is not surprising that these ex-feudal military oligarchs should see to it that ultimate power would not slip into the hands of the rising "liberal" bourgeoisie who were organizing themselves into political parties and clamoring for a voice in the government. The military and naval services, for example, exercised a virtual veto power over the cabinet as the ministers of the army and the navy had to be high-ranking officers holding those positions only on approval of the high commands. Should the army or the navy high commands disapprove of the cabinet's policies, they could instruct their ministers to resign, thereby automatically forcing the downfall of the cabinet. Then again the power of the diet was curtailed at its very source by the adoption of a Bismarckian device which provided that the budget of the preceding year continue in the event either house refused to adopt a budget submitted by the government. A constitution was promulgated and a parliament set up immediately to serve as a splendid and attractive façade with which to impress Europeans with the modernity of the new regime and to justify the government's demand for cancellation of the unequal treaties. It achieved that purpose by 1899, as we have seen.

Growth of Liberalism and Democracy

Up to the first World War the military oligarchs and bureaucrats dominated the government almost uncontested. That war brought about a great expansion in Japan's industrial capacity. It resulted in a rapid increase in the size and strength of the bourgeoisie, whose interests were centered in the light industries, which were dependent upon a peaceful liberal world order as a prerequisite for the expansion of their international trade. They began by the end of the war to contest successfully for power, both economic and political, with the military oligarchs, the bureaucrats and the great *Zaibatsu* or monopolistic financial houses, such as the Mitsubishi and the Mitsui, which had risen to towering heights of financial and industrial power under the patronage of the government. There ensued a liberalizing of Japanese political institutions in the 1920's, as evidenced in the increased strength of the political parties, the rise of party-controlled cabinets accompanied by an increasing degree of responsible cabinet-controlled government, as well as the further democratization of the country through the passage of a universal manhood suffrage act in 1925. These liberalizing internal developments were reflected in the pursuance of a peaceful foreign policy. Military and naval budgets were curtailed. Japan was an active member of the League of Nations, signed the Kellogg-Briand Pact and the Washington Treaties, including the Nine-Power Treaty which aimed at preserving China's territorial and administrative integrity and giving that country the time and opportunity to emerge as a modern sovereign state.

Reaction in Japan

Alarmed by this progressive encroachment upon their monopolistic preserves of financial and political power by upstart bourgeoisie—whom they traditionally looked down upon with feudal contempt, and whose immoral connections with the "corrupt" political parties they vociferously decried—the bureaucrats, the militarists and the financial oligarchs, while struggling, compromisingly enough, amongst themselves, united in an effort to stem this "dangerous" development. The army took the lead. By 1931 a world situation had arisen which admirably fulfilled the prophecies of nineteenth century Japanese statesmen that a time of confusion must some day come in Europe which would be Japan's opportunity to follow its own course, not only ". . . to put meddling Powers in their places" but also to ". . . obtain the balance of Power in the East and thus compel others to esteem and fear us." The army renewed its drive to achieve its continental ambitions abandoned at the end of the first World War under pressure from the Western nations, in September, 1931. The effect on Japan's "home front" was to reinstate the militarists and the bureaucrats once again in the dominant seats of power which they had held in the decades following the Restoration of 1867-1868 when the emperor had restored to him his secular powers usurped by the feudal Shoguns centuries before.

CHINA'S RETARDED RATE OF MODERNIZATION

In marked contrast to Japan's amazing success in achieving modern statehood and in entering the ranks of the nations as an expanding imperialist power, is China, still struggling to achieve the status of an independent national state. The aggressions of the Western powers and more latterly of Japan have been important factors delaying China's progress toward national unification and economic and political modernization. In order to understand the activities and the position of these nations in China since 1870, it will be well to consider in outline the more important internal obstacles to reform and modernization that still operate in conjunction with the forces of imperialism to delay China's emergence as a modern state.

At first glance it would appear, from the geographical point of view, that the tasks confronting the Restoration leaders in Japan were much simpler in degree if not in kind than those faced by Chinese reformers. Japan's total area was less than that of any of the three largest provinces of China Proper at the time. While this served to simplify Japan's problems in degree as compared with those confronting the Chinese in their efforts to modernize the vast continental area which they occupied, yet it should be borne in mind that the actual as well as potential mineral wealth of Japan was not nearly so great as that of China. However important the geographical factor is in determining the contrasting rates of modernization of the two countries, it cannot in itself adequately explain the contrast. The explanation is to be sought in an historical and analytical examination of developments in the political, social and economic realms.

Contrast in Political Developments in China and Japan

In the political realm the contrast between the two countries was striking. The setting up of the Restoration government followed by the abolition of feudalism in Japan was accompanied by little fighting. By 1877 all armed opposition to the new regime was put down. Most of the feudal lords and their retainers voluntarily surrendered their fiefs and former feudal prerogatives and bent their energies in a successful effort to win a position in the new society and government comparable to that which they had held under the former regime. Loyalties formerly limited to the clans were quickly transferred to the newly restored emperor.[7]

The China of the nineteenth century, however, was a "universal" empire under the rule of an alien Manchu dynasty. In control of the state machinery were the Confucianistic literati who had relegated the soldier to the bottom of the social scale below the peasant and even the merchant. Well ensconced in their lucrative positions of power in a vast decentralized government, they, for the most part, turned a deaf ear and a blind eye to the demands of the times for modernization of government and of armament if they would preserve their empire from Western aggression. How striking in contrast they stood in their aloof

---

[7] For a further discussion of the rise of modern nationalism in Japan see pp. 556-559.

dignity and cultural conceit to the eager, alert and imitative Restoration leaders of Japan! True, a few enlightened viceroys in the provinces succeeded in establishing some modern arsenals and in laying the foundations for a modern army and navy. The defeat at the hands of the Japanese in 1894-1895, however, disclosed both the feebleness of this reform program and awoke larger sections of the bureaucracy and the intelligentsia to the necessity for more thoroughgoing reforms.

Meanwhile, the demand for reform had spread far down into ranks of the common people and the merchants, whence there emerged a revolutionary movement under the leadership of Sun Yat-sen which aimed both at the overthrow of the alien Manchus and the establishment of a republic. After a fatuous attempt to drive all the Westerners into the sea during the Boxer crisis in 1900, the court and the bureaucrats made a belated attempt to undertake a series of reforms along political, educational, legal and economic lines, such as was adopted by the Restoration leaders in Japan with marked success after 1868. However, it was too late. Revolutionary forces continued to grow, culminating in the overthrow of the dynasty and the establishment of a republic in 1912.

Weakness of the Chinese Republic

The setting up of the republic, however, fell far short of achieving that miracle of unity and centralization of power which developments following upon the Restoration had accomplished in Japan. China socially, economically and psychologically as well as politically was far from ready to carry forward a thoroughgoing program of reform under a highly centralized republican regime where the contestants for power worked peacefully through the ballot-box and political parties. While a few Western-trained men found positions in the successive republican regimes, their efforts at reform were largely neutralized by the remnants of the old-fashioned bureaucracy who clung to power; and in the provinces the conservative landed gentry remained dominant. Both groups, moreover, fell under the domination of semi-feudalized war lords who, basing their power upon the provinces, plunged the country into a long period of civil wars in their treacherous, personal struggles to seize and maintain control in Peking, the capital. Again in contrast to Japan, where the Restora-

tion was followed immediately by the abandonment of institutionalized feudalism, in China the political revolution of 1911-1912
opened the way for the emergence of semi-feudal regimes, dominated by upstart war lords who gathered around themselves
cabals of personally loyal retainers and a rabble following of
soldiery whose loyalty was guaranteed only by the full rice bowl.
Their petty quarrels and treacheries further weakened China and
made it a more facile tool in the hands of the competing imperialistic powers.

Progress under the Nationalist Government

Had the Japanese army leaders been able, at any time during
this period of war-lordism, which obtained up to 1927, to have
used force to follow up and realize upon the Twenty-one Demands
which their government had presented to China in 1915 with a
view to extending their hegemony over all of the country, it seems
very possible they might have successfully achieved their objective with only a fraction of the force which they were to employ
after 1931 in an effort to attain the same objective. For in 1927
a new modern China began in reality to emerge along political and
economic lines. In that year there was established in Nanking
the Nationalist government under the control of China's one
strong well-organized political party, Sun Yat-sen's Kuomintang.
Under the shrewd and effective military leadership of Generalissimo Chiang K'ai-shek, the war lord period was brought to a virtual end and China became united politically as never before
under the republic. The bureaucracy of the new government
was staffed largely with modern, Western-trained men who
carried through a number of important reform measures in the
decade between 1927-1937. The currency of the country was
nationalized and stabilized, while internal transit dues and other
heavy war-lord exactions were eliminated or reduced in the effort
to prepare the way for the development of a national economic
order under a centralized regime. Many other reforms were
initiated, including the improvement of communications and the
extension of a modern educational system. Animating and
strengthening this new movement toward national unity was the
rising spirit of modern nationalism.[8]

[8] For a further discussion of the rise of modern nationalism in China see pp.
561-565.

External Pressure as a Cause of China's Weakness

The causes for China's retarded rate of modernization and emergence as a modern sovereign state are not to be sought alone in the internal situation. While the forces making for internal disunity and weakness were a marked incentive to continued aggressions on the part of the European powers and of Japan as well after 1870, the continuing and increasing pressure brought to bear by the competing imperialist nations was in itself to present a well-nigh insuperable obstacle to the efforts of reforming Chinese to achieve political unity and build up a strong modern nation. Those same competing forces born of the second industrial revolution in Europe, which demanded a search for further markets in which to sell the surplus products of the factories, new sources of raw materials with which to feed the machines and places in which to invest the mounting profits accruing to their owners together with sentimental nationalists who gloried in expansion, were to make themselves felt in the most remote and formerly inaccessible regions of China and the whole Far East.

Trade Penetration

That China did not go the way of Africa, as it was widely believed it would during the period of "scramble for concessions" in 1897-1898, was due not to any effective physical resistance which China could present, though its clever diplomacy of playing one power off against another was an important indirect deterrent, but rather to the realization in European chancelleries that such a development was a serious threat to European peace. Also at that time interests of the Europeans, particularly of the British who still enjoyed the lion's share of the China trade, and of Americans as well, were still predominantly commercial. The long-established trading concerns of the countries continued to be primarily interested in China, the whole of China, as a market, as from the beginnings of European expansion in the sixteenth century. The dividing up of China into spheres of influence which might lead to the establishment of protectorates accompanied by the raising of preferential tariffs and transportation rates could only injure their China-wide trade. While in the last half of the nineteenth century industrial concerns and financial houses began to look upon China as a source of mineral resources and a place to invest surplus capital in the extraction of these natural resources and in railroad construction, the older trading interests continued to remain dominant in determining policy.

The China trade developed rapidly after 1870 as the machine-made products of the West began successfully to compete in quality and in price with the handicraft industries of the country. A further stimulant to the trade was given by the opening of the Suez Canal in 1869; the rapid supplanting of sailing vessels by steamships; and the opening of cable communications with Europe. These three developments, all occurring about the same time, served to speed commercial transactions and facilitate the movement of greater quantities of goods at lower cost, making it possible to take a lower profit per unit of goods sold and, in general, increasing the competitive nature of the trade.

In addition, a series of incidents arising from the murder of foreigners, or wars—as between France and China in 1884-1885 and Japan and China in 1894-1895—led to a further opening of the country to trade. The number of places where foreign business men could reside and carry on trade increased to thirty-two in 1899, forty-eight in 1913 and about eighty by 1930. The number of concessions in the ports, where the foreigners enjoyed control over the police and the municipal administration, had increased to twenty-four by 1914. Accompanying the increase in trade was the growth of foreign shipping in Chinese coastal and inland waterways, which far outranked native shipping.

Growth and Change in the Nature of the China Trade

A few figures will reveal the marked growth of foreign trade with China, the change in the nature of the trade and its distribution among the different nations. Between 1885 and 1914 China's foreign trade increased 600 per cent. By 1914 it amounted to U.S. $662,000,000. By 1928 it had more than doubled again, reaching the figure of $1,642,000,000. Since then there has been a decline due to the depression and the war with Japan. The changes in the nature and distribution of the trade and shipping were equally marked. In the 1870's tea and silk together accounted for more than 90 per cent of China's exports by value. In 1900 they formed only half and by 1928 less than a quarter of the value of the exports. By the first part of the twentieth century China had lost its dominant position as an exporter of these two commodities. The export list became more diversified, the principal exports in the 1920's being beans and bean products, which had displaced raw and manufactured silk as the leading export item; eggs and egg products; cotton goods and yarn, indicating that China was becoming a competitor with the textile mills of Europe and Japan; skins, hides and leather; ores, metals and minerals; coal, raw cotton, peanuts and wood oil.

The import list likewise underwent a striking change. By the last quarter of the nineteenth century the import of cotton goods took first place, displacing opium in 1885, the importation of which went into a gradual decline until it virtually disappeared from the list in 1917. Kerosene oil, the "light of Asia" for the lamps of China, became an increasingly important item of import, while the growing taste among wealthier Chinese for a wide variety of consumers' goods, such as window glass, soap, clocks, watches, foreign wines and liquors and wheat flour, were important factors in the expansion of the import trade. In 1929 over 6 per cent of the imports by value consisted of iron, steel, machinery and automobiles, reflecting the trend toward industrialization. The development of light industries may be seen in the marked decline in the imports of cotton yarn, from 20 per cent of the total imports around 1900 to less than 1 per cent in 1930.

The striking shift in the distribution of the trade controlled by the various nations is a fairly accurate reflection of their relative political interests and influence. The dominant rôle enjoyed by the British throughout the greater part of the nineteenth century was to be challenged by the rising interests of Germany, the United States and Japan, and to a lesser extent by other countries. By 1930 Japan had surpassed the British, taking over 26 per cent of the trade and also by the United States, which had 17.6 per cent of the trade in that year. The British were third with about 10 per cent, seconded by Germany, which had quickly recovered its markets lost during the first World War, with 5 per cent, while France had only 2.7 per cent. From 1931 to 1938 the United States had the leading position in the trade with China. In shipping tonnage, England still led in the 1920's, followed by Japan, China, the United States, the Scandinavian countries, Germany and France in the order named.

*The Scramble for Concessions and the Rise
of Spheres of Influence*

The threat to China's territorial and administrative integrity in
the period after 1870 came more from the general support
given by the competing imperialist governments to newly emerging industrial and financial interests seeking to develop China's
natural resources, to build its railroads, to establish modern factories and to make loans for political as well as constructive industrial purposes, than from a search to open wider markets. From
the days of Baron von Richthofen, a German geologist who, following travels in China in the years 1870-1872, wrote extensively
in an enthusiastic and exaggerated tone about the amount of resources in coal and iron, there emerged a vision of China as a second Eldorado. A sharp competitive struggle among banking and
industrial interests arose, which, backed by their respective national governments, sought to wrest from a reluctant China special
rights to exploit mines and to build railroads. They also competed in extending loans to a hard-pressed Chinese government,
at very handsome profits, to pay its mounting indebtedness arising from various indemnities or accepted for the purpose of reorganizing its national currency.

This struggle for concessions reached a climax in 1898 following China's defeat at the hands of Japan in the war of 1894-1895.
By that year China was divided into roughly defined "spheres of
influence" which threatened to become rapidly transformed into
virtual protectorates, a situation which, had it come about, would
have destroyed China's territorial integrity. The centers of these
spheres of influence were leased territories on a coastal seaport
from whence radiated a control over the hinterland in the form
of special concessions to build railroads and exploit mineral resources.

The French sphere lay in south China adjoining French Indo-
China. The base was the ninety-nine year leasehold at Kwangchow Bay and in addition a number of railroad and mining
concessions were acquired in the adjoining provinces. The Germans carved out their sphere in North China with a base at the
leasehold embracing the seaport of Tsingtao in Kiaochow Bay.
The Russians established themselves in Manchuria with a naval
base at Port Arthur under a twenty-five-year lease, with control

over railroads linking that port with the Trans-Siberian Railroad via the Chinese Eastern Railroad in North Manchuria, the rights to construct which having been earlier acquired (1895-1896). The British sphere lay in the broad Yangtze Valley, the outlet to which was Shanghai, where British trading and financial interests were predominant. In addition they had as a base Hongkong and adjoining territory on the mainland, having acquired an extension of their control over the whole Kowloon Peninsula through a ninety-nine-year lease granted in 1898. To counteract growing German and Russian influence in North China waters, the British acquired a lease over the seaport of Weihaiwei across the Yellow Sea from Port Arthur. The Japanese claimed as their sphere of dominant influence the province of Fukien which lies opposite the island of Formosa, which they demanded of China in the 1895 peace settlement. Italy tried in 1899 to secure a naval station on Sanmen Bay in Chekiang province but surprisingly enough was unsuccessful. In addition to mining rights the British acquired concessions to build 2,800 miles of railroads; the Russians, 1,530; the Germans, 720; Belgians, 650; French, 420; and Americans, 300.

Enunciation of the Open Door Policy in China

Alarmed by these developments, which threatened to lead to the imposition of preferential tariffs and railroad rates in favor of the nationals occupying these spheres, the commercial interests, particularly those of England and the United States, whose trade extended over the whole of China, made moves to frustrate such an eventuality. Basing his action on the most-favored-nation clauses and the uniform tariff provisions of the treaties, Secretary of State John Hay in 1899 issued, with the indirect support of the British, his first Open Door notes. These notes, while indirectly recognizing the spheres of influence, asked the interested nations not to discriminate against the trade of other nationals in their respective spheres. The governments addressed all more or less willingly consented. In July of the following year, it was feared that the presence of the Allied troops in Peking, sent there to rescue the foreigners from the Chinese Boxers, might lead to a decision to complete the break-up of China. Whereupon Hay issued a second series of notes calling upon the powers to respect

China's territorial and administrative integrity. The nations one after another replied favorably.

Thus was born the Open Door policy, the keystone in the arch of America's far eastern diplomacy. That China was to be given an opportunity to linger on as a political entity and an opportunity further to modernize and strengthen itself, was due not so much to a sincere belief in or adherence to the principles embodied in this policy as to the realization in the chancellories of Europe that sharpening imperialistic clashes in China were leading the nations rapidly along the road to war. The struggles in the Far East in these crucial years from 1898 to 1904 had a profound influence on the formation of those alliances and ententes which led up to the first World War.[9]

Financial Pressure

The more or less sincere adherence to the Open Door notes by the various nations by no means brought an end to their conflicting interests in China. The struggle from the opening of the century to the outbreak of the first World War in 1914 centered on the competing efforts of industrial interests and bankers to extend loans to the Chinese government and to develop railroad and other concessions. This phase of the imperialist struggle got under way right after the close of the Sino-Japanese War in 1895. French and Russian banking interests first made a loan to the Chinese government of £15,820,000 to help pay the indemnity forced on China by the victorious Japanese. The German and British governments protested the exclusion of their banking interests from this loan and, joining forces, induced the Chinese government to accept two loans totalling £32,000,000. The acceptance of these loans really marked the beginning of China's growing foreign indebtedness and partial fiscal subjection to Western interests. Prior to 1895 the total amount of China's foreign borrowing had reached the figure of only about $120,000,000, nearly all of which had been repaid by that date. After that year the amount of the Chinese government's foreign obligations increased rapidly, reaching the figure of $723,000,000 at the end of 1930. To guarantee payment on these loans, income from the

---

[9] For a further discussion of the effect upon international relations of these imperialist clashes in the Far East see pp. 575-578.

maritime customs revenue and certain of China's internal sources of income, such as the salt tax, were hypothecated. This meant not only a continuation but an extension of foreign control over the chief revenue-producing sources of the Chinese government, making it more than ever subject to the political interests of the various nations.

Railroad Concessions and Loans

Over a third of the above indebtedness was in the form of government railroad obligations. It was around the struggle to realize upon profitable railroad concessions, originating in the period of the struggle for concessions, that the sharpest conflicts arose in the period prior to the first World War. In the rush for these railroad concessions scant heed was paid to the vague spheres of influence which the powers were claiming. Furthermore, to have constructed railroad systems of varying gauges and types of material within each of these artificial spheres without linking them up with a well-planned national system of roads would have been highly uneconomic. At least that would be true as far as China Proper was concerned. In Manchuria, which constituted more of an economic and geographic unit, it was possible for the Japanese, who fell heir to Russian rights in South Manchuria as a result of the Russo-Japanese War of 1904-1905, to build up their own railroad system. This they were able to do without admitting Western capital despite the strenuous efforts of the American government, culminating in Secretary Knox's abortive scheme put forth in 1909 for neutralizing Manchuria's railroads, to hold the door open for American financial interests in that part of China. The Russians, too, were successful in keeping out all other interests in the restricted sphere left to them in North Manchuria, after the war with Japan.

In China Proper, however, a period of conflict over railroad concessions led to co-operation, as that between the British and Germans, who agreed to construct a line running southward from Tientsin to the Yangtze River opposite Nanking. Or again, in the case of the projected Hukwang railroads running northward from Canton to Hankow and thence westward into Szechuan province, the competing concessionaries united in 1908-1909 to form a four-power group consisting of British, French,

German and American financial interests for the purpose of constructing the line.

The International Financial Consortium

This four-power group then claimed a monopoly of extending loans to the Chinese government for currency reform and reorganization. Before any progress could be made toward currency reform and railroad construction, the political revolution of 1911-1912 occurred, which overthrew the monarchy and established the republic. The negotiations for the construction of the Hukwang railroads had been an immediate cause of the revolution. The provincially minded gentry of the provinces through which the proposed road was to run vigorously resented the intrusion of Western capital and the centralizing policy for nationalizing railroad construction adopted by the government. Much local unrest occurred and it was in the Hankow region that the revolution actually broke out.

Following the revolution the new republican government under President Yuan Shih-k'ai sought from the four national banking groups a reorganization loan. Negotiations began in February, 1912, but were not completed until April of the following year. Because of the political character of the loan, Japan and Russia demanded and secured admission for their financial interests in June, 1912. There was vigorous opposition in China to the monopolistic demands and control provisions which this Six-Power International Financial Consortium was demanding of the government. Having nowhere else to turn for the sizeable loan needed, President Yuan finally agreed to borrow £25,000,000. Meanwhile the Democrats had come to power in Washington; and President Wilson, soon after he entered the White House, withdrew the support of the American group as he held that the terms of the loan infringed seriously upon the administrative integrity of China and hence were not in accord with the Open Door policy.

Effects of the World War

By 1918, however, the Wilson administration was to reverse this policy. The outbreak of the first World War had led to a breakdown of the co-operative policy in China and a partial restoration of the old struggle for concessions. In effect the preoccupation of the European powers in the war left the field wide open for the Japanese. Quick to take advantage of the opportunity, the Japanese government forced upon the Chinese government the Twenty-one Demands in January, 1915. The Chinese, supported by Western, particularly American pressure, were able to induce the Japanese to withdraw for later consideration the more far-reaching of these demands, which would have made China virtually a protectorate of the island empire.

Nevertheless, the demands which Japan did force China to accept, under threat of an ultimatum in May, 1915, extended Japan's right and leaseholds in Manchuria and eastern Inner Mongolia from the original twenty-five-year period to a full ninety-nine years; provided for the turning over to Japan of the former German leasehold in Shantung and the mining and railroad concessions granted Germany in the former German sphere of influence; gave to Japan virtual control over the Hanyehping ironworks at Hankow, within the British sphere of influence; and secured an agreement from China not to alienate any portion of Fukien province, Japan's proclaimed sphere of influence in China Proper, to any other power. In addition, in the years from 1914-1918 the Japanese loaned an estimated total of $200,000,000 to China in exchange in part for additional mining and railroad concessions; but in large part these loans also were of a political character designed to maintain Japan's dominant influence over the Chinese government.

The Second Financial Consortium

Alarmed by these developments and the threat to the Open Door in China which they constituted, President Wilson reached the decision in November, 1917, to permit the reorganization of a new four-power financial consortium. It was only in October, 1920, that the final agreement among the banking groups of the United States, France, England and Japan was reached. These prolonged negotiations centered in the efforts of the American bankers, backed vigorously by the State Department, to induce the Japanese to throw open Manchuria and Inner Mongolia to the Consortium interests. Only after Japan had demanded and secured an agreement that its established railroads and certain projected mining and industrial enterprises in that region be closed to the Consortium was the final agreement reached.

The second International Financial Consortium was not to place a single loan in China. An increasingly nationalistic China was no more willing to become the ward of an international financial organization than of a single or a group of competing imperialist powers. Moreover, China was not to be as profitable and safe a place for investment in the years up to 1931 because of the almost continuous civil strife. By 1931 the nationalist government had well established itself with the result that China's credit status rose. The way was open for placing foreign loans that were more purely commercial and industrial and less political in character than the loans already granted. The struggle among the nations interested in China, particularly the United States, England and Japan, centered in competitive efforts to assist China in establishing a stable national currency which would be linked to the respective currencies of these nations. Thereby each hoped to be in a better position *vis à vis* the others in the competition for China's trade.

There was also a renewal of the efforts to participate in China's industrialization and modernization in general. The revived rivalry to finance railroad construction, after 1931, was without the serious political implications and consequent threat to Chinese sovereignty inherent in the earlier period of financial imperialism because of the emergence of nationalistic China under a relatively strong nationalist government. That government took the lead in initiating such construction and called on foreign capital to participate more under Chinese terms and control than formerly. Japanese capital was not sought because of the political character such loans would assume. Japan's military activities in China after 1931 were animated in large part by an effort to keep out this renewed flow of Western capital into China.

The Washington Conference

America's move to stop the Japanese threat to the Open Door policy in China, originating in the support given by the State Department to the organization of the second International Financial Consortium, achieved at least temporary political success at the Washington Conference of 1921-1922. As a result of the negotiations held at that time, treaties and agreements were signed which forced Japan to return its holdings in Shantung to China; to withdraw its troops from Siberia; and to give up, much to its regret, the Anglo-Japanese Alliance first signed in 1902, which had been of indirect aid in building up its continental position. Then, too, Japan signed with eight other nations the Nine-Power Treaty in which the principles of the Open Door were fully and carefully defined. The treaty was designed to give China the needed opportunity and time to build a modern sovereign state. In addition the Japanese navy against its will was induced to accept an inferior naval ratio of three to five in relation to the navies of Great Britain and the United States. In return, however, the United States agreed not to strengthen its naval position at Guam, the Philippines or in the Aleutian Islands, while England agreed to maintain the status quo at Hongkong.

China Recovers Some of Its Sovereign Rights

As a result of the conference Japan's continental position was virtually the same as it had been in 1914 on the eve of the first World War except that it was enjoying a normal and legitimate commercial expansion and a correspondingly greater share in China's foreign trade and shipping. And, in addition, its position in Manchuria had been broadened and strengthened by the extension of the time limit on the Kwantung leasehold and certain other concessions which had been lengthened from twenty-five to ninety-nine years. Encouraged by the achievements of the Washington Conference, China made marked progress toward complete national independence in the decade from 1921-1931. As a result of the war, Germany and Austria lost the special concessions and extraterritorial rights which they formerly held. In 1924 the Soviet Union voluntarily surrendered all the rights accorded czarist Russia in the unequal treaties and recognized China as a first-class power by appointing an ambassador, rather than a minister as did the other nations, to be in residence at the capital.

The successive Chinese governments, both at Peking to 1928 and at Nanking after that date, took up the question of treaty revision with the various nations one by one as their treaties came due for revision, and in a number of instances they were successful in concluding new treaties which restored the right of tariff autonomy and provided for a conditional abandonment of extraterritoriality. By 1930 full tariff autonomy was recovered. Considerable progress toward the elimination of the extraterritoriality regime was achieved by that time.

In addition to the return of the Russian, German and Austrian concessions, the Belgian concession at Tientsin was restored in August 21, 1929, and the British concession at Chinkiang in November, 1929. In March, 1927, the British government had already agreed to return the concessions at Hankow and Kiukiang. The British-leased territory at Weihaiwei was returned in April, 1930. In consonance with this trend and in response to a resurgent Chinese nationalism the foreigners, who up to this period had been ruling over the Chinese living in the concessions and the International Settlement at Shanghai, taxing them without any or at best inadequate representation on municipal councils, admitted the Chinese to a minority status on the councils of the British and French concessions at Tientsin, the International Settlement in Shanghai, and the French concessions at Shanghai and Hankow. Significantly enough, the Japanese in this period granted no such representation on the councils of their concessions and were the last to grant China tariff autonomy.

Japan Attacks Again

The nationalist government of China set up at Nanking in 1927 had by September, 1931, achieved notable progress by its "revolutionary diplomacy" as it was called, toward the recovery from the powers of all sovereign rights formerly surrendered. On September 18, 1931, the Japanese army, alarmed by the rise at home of political parties to positions of influence which threatened its erstwhile impregnable position in the Japanese state, and taking advantage of the world economic depression and the consequent preoccupation of the Western nations with the problems at home to which it gave rise, renewed its continental expansion hoping to achieve what the nation had futilely set out to attain during the first World War. A decade later that goal had not been clearly or finally won despite the expenditure of billions of yen and the sacrifice of millions of Japanese and Chinese lives. In Manchuria the army succeeded in setting up a puppet state wholly under its control. The new state was extended to include North Manchuria. All Soviet interests in that area centering on the Chinese Eastern Railroad were liquidated through an agreement to "purchase" the line.

In China Proper the Japanese had, by 1940, a tenuous hold over the northern and coastal provinces and the seaports. They established at Nanking in March, 1940, a shadowy, puppet regime whose power at the time did not extend beyond reach of Japanese bayonets. This feeble regime they formally recognized as the "legitimate" government of China on November 30, 1940. On the same day the Nanking government formally recognized the Japan-protected state of Manchoukuo. In the hinterland the armies of nationalist China under the leadership of Generalissimo Chiang K'ai-shek remained intact and a constant menace to the Japanese position. Foreign interests were still rooted at Shanghai, Tientsin, Hongkong and elsewhere.

The outbreak of the European war in September, 1939, seemed to make easier of attainment the objective of the Japanese in forcing the United States, France and England to recognize their hegemony over all China. Such was not the case, however, up to the beginning of 1941. Despite American interest and absorption in the European conflict, the Washington government maintained through 1940 a strong diplomatic policy in the Far East to uphold the traditional Open Door policy. The presence of a major portion of the American fleet in the Pacific, where it had been stationed most of the time since 1931, had a marked restraining effect upon the ultra-chauvinistic expansionists of Japan. The ever present possibility of an American entrance into the war against Germany was a constant check on the army objective of driving out Western interests in China or the navy's southward expansion policy which constituted a threat to British, French and Netherlands possessions in the Far East. The signing of the German-Soviet pact on the eve of the war was a further check upon Japan's ambitions at the outset of the war as it left Russia in a better position to deal with Japan in the Far East and, at the same time, to continue to send aid to the Chinese. China itself, by prolonging its resistance to Japan, which required the Japanese to keep an army of upwards of a million men on the continent, was serving indirectly to check an expansion in other directions, particularly toward the South Seas. If, however, the outcome of the war should witness the defeat of not only France, but of England, accompanied by the seizure or destruction of a major portion of the British navy and the consequent almost complete absorption of the Soviet Union in European affairs, it appeared that Japan's position in the Far East would be immeasurably strengthened. Particularly would this be so if in the event of the downfall of England it should become necessary to concentrate the American navy in the Atlantic, thereby leaving the Pacific to Japan. In that event the Japanese government's avowed goal of establishing a so-called "Monroe Doctrine in Eastern Asia" would emerge from the realm of possibility into that of probability. What such a development would mean not only for China, but also for Indo-China, Malaya, the Netherlands East Indies and eventually the Philippines, only the future would disclose.

Before considering more at length, however, the effect upon international relations of the struggles for positions of power and influence in the Far East, it will be necessary first to recount in the chapter which follows how the European nations, and the United States and Japan as well, acquired, governed and exploited their colonies, dependencies and protectorates in the Far East, a number of which they stripped away from the old Chinese Empire. Central as was China in the imperialist struggle since the mid-nineteenth century, rich prizes were to be won and lost in the areas adjoining China and among the islands of the Pacific off the coast of eastern Asia by the expanding powers in the same years that they reduced China Proper to the status of a semicolony.

READINGS

Bisson, T. A. *Japan in China,* 1938. A balanced account of developments since 1933.

Borton, Hugh. *Japan Since 1931,* 1940. A competent survey.

Friedman, Irving S. *British Relations with China, 1931-1939,* 1940. Detailed, documented.

Griswold, A. Whitney. *The Far Eastern Policy of the United States,* 1938. A critical account of the period since 1898.

Johnstone, W. C. *The Shanghai Problem,* 1937. A competent historical account of the International Settlement.

Johnstone, W. C. *The United States and Japan's New Order,* 1941. Emphasis on legalistic aspects.

Jones, F. C. *Shanghai and Tientsin*, 1940. The position of the Europeans in these two cities with special reference to their investments.

Kotenev, A. M. *Shanghai: Its Municipality and the Chinese*, 1927.

Latourette, K. S. *The Chinese: Their History and Culture*, 2 vols., 1934. A standard text.

Norman, E. Herbert. *Japan's Emergence as a Modern State*, 1940. Best comprehensive account.

Overlach, T. W. *Foreign Financial Control in China*, 1919. One of the best accounts of the struggle for concessions and the rise of the international financial consortiums.

Pollard, Robert T. *China's Foreign Relations, 1917–1931*, 1933. Useful for account of China's efforts to free itself from the unequal treaties during this period.

Remer, C. F. *Foreign Investments in China*, 1933. The only comprehensive treatment of the subject.

Vinacke, Harold M. *A History of the Far East in Modern Times*, 3rd Rev. Ed., 1941. The most satisfactory text covering both internal developments and international relations.

Willoughby, W. W. *Foreign Rights and Interests in China*, 2 vols., 1927. The standard reference work on the legalistic aspects of the subject.

CHAPTER EIGHTEEN

Colonial Policies and Forms of Control in the Far East Outside China Proper

THE COLONIAL policies and forms of control exercised by the European nations, Japan and the United States in the Far East, other than in China Proper, present highly complex and varied patterns. Not only were there striking differences in the techniques and objectives of colonial rule among the various powers, but there were also wide variations in the forms of administration employed simultaneously by some of the nations within their respective areas of control. Moreover, there were marked shifts in policy within a specific area over a period of time. For example, consider the contrast in ultimate objectives held by the United States with respect to the Philippines, and Japan with respect to its "Overseas Territories." The American government from the time of the acquisition of the archipelago promised the Filipinos their independence when they were prepared for it, with the result that they were legally assured of attaining that status by 1946.

Japan, on the other hand, never promised independence to the non-Japanese people in its "colonies." This difference has necessarily dictated an equally great difference in forms of administrative control. Or again consider forms of influence and

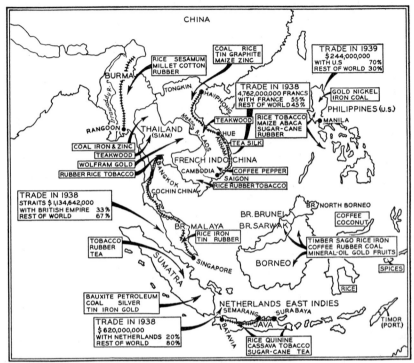

CHINA

RICE SESAMUM
MILLET COTTON
RUBBER

COAL RICE
TIN GRAPHITE
MAIZE ZINC

TRADE IN 1939
$244,000,000
WITH U.S   70%
REST OF WORLD 30%

BURMA

TONGKIN

HAIPHONG

TRADE IN 1938
4,762,000,000 FRANCS
WITH FRANCE 55%
REST OF WORLD 45%

GOLD NICKEL
IRON COAL

PHILIPPINES (U.S.)

RANGOON

THAILAND
(SIAM)

TEAKWOOD

HUE

RICE TOBACCO
MAIZE ABACA
SUGAR-CANE
RUBBER

MANILA

COAL IRON & ZINC
TEAKWOOD
WOLFRAM GOLD
RUBBER RICE TOBACCO

TEA SILK

FRENCH INDO CHINA

CAMBODIA

BANGKOK

COCHIN CHINA

COFFEE PEPPER
SAIGON
RICE RUBBER TOBACCO

TRADE IN 1938
STRAITS $ 1,134,642,000
WITH BRITISH EMPIRE 33%
REST OF WORLD   67%

BR. NORTH BORNEO

BR. BRUNEI

BR. MALAYA   BR. SARWAK

COFFEE
COCONUT

RICE IRON
TIN RUBBER

TOBACCO
RUBBER
TEA

SUMATRA

SINGAPORE

BORNEO

TIMBER SAGO RICE IRON
COFFEE RUBBER COAL
MINERAL-OIL GOLD FRUITS

SPICES

RICE

BAUXITE PETROLEUM
COAL   SILVER
TIN IRON GOLD

TRADE IN 1938
$ 620,000,000
WITH NETHERLANDS 20%
REST OF WORLD   80%

NETHERLANDS EAST INDIES

SEMARANG   SURABAYA

JAVA

BATAVIA

TIMOR
(PORT.)

RICE QUININE
CASSAVA TOBACCO
SUGAR-CANE TEA

Based in part on Philips' Series of Corporative Wall Atlases, "Asia Commercial Development," Denoyer-
Geppert Company, Chicago

POLITICAL AND ECONOMIC MAP OF SOUTHEAST ASIA

control maintained by the Soviet Union, which had denounced imperialists and all their works, in Outer Mongolia. There the Soviets intervened to set up a revolutionary government, which called itself independent though the Soviet government continued to recognize Chinese suzerainty over the area. With this Mongolian government they entered into close financial, economic and military relations.

The policies of the French in Indo-China, the Dutch in the Netherlands East Indies and the British in Malaya present examples of different types of colonial rule within the same area as well as shifts in policy as applied to the same peoples or native states. The differences may be summed up under the categories of the direct or "assimilative" type of rule and the indirect or "associative" type. These broad terms suggest the nature of the kinds of control to which they refer. Direct rule means rule over native peoples by officials who are appointed from above by the representatives of the ruling power. They carry on their work within a European administrative framework, ignoring if not destroying native social and political organizations. Extended into the cultural realm this type of rule is characterized by the assimilation or "Europeanization" of the "inferior" native peoples politically, economically and culturally. Direct rule in its administrative aspects was employed by the Dutch in the East Indies in the nineteenth century. The French pursued it both administratively and culturally in Indo-China toward the end of the nineteenth century. The Japanese adhere to it in both its aspects in their Overseas Territories.

Indirect rule in its modern and contemporary form began to develop toward the end of the nineteenth century and came into its own in the present century. Administratively it means the practise of governing native peoples through their own conservative, usually hereditary, rulers operating within the traditional framework of their indigenous institutions, modified to a greater or lesser extent to meet European needs and preconceptions. As applied to the cultural realm it means the opposite of "assimilation." Its application implies a respect for native languages, religions, social and political institutions and a slow, cautious adjustment of these to modern political, economic and industrial conditions. The Dutch, French and British have employed it for the most part in their Far Eastern domains. Japan applied it for controlling and exploiting nominally independent Manchoukuo and was by 1940 attempting to extend it to Inner Mongolia and the "occupied" parts of China Proper.

The emergence and application in varying form and degree of these two types of rule were determined in part by historical developments; in part by the relative degree of cultural and political advancement of the subject peoples; and in part by the changing economic interests of the colonial powers in their colonies. The tendency to shift from the more oppressive direct rule to the more liberal indirect rule in the present century does not necessarily imply that the ruling colonial powers making such shifts envisaged ultimate independence or even an autonomous status for their colonies or protectorates. The change began before modern nationalist sentiments had hardened into definite political movements in the colonies and long before a world-wide reaction, born of the first World War, denounced imperialism and asserted the rights of self-determination for all peoples. The European governments and colonial administrators were not slow to discover, however, that policies and controls formulated in accordance with this principle, and for other reasons to be indicated later, could be pointed to as partial justification for continued rule no matter how slow or long delayed were the steps taken to extend self-rule to the colonial peoples. Moreover, they were to find that indirect rule by its conservative, divisive appeal to the native-ruling hierarchies and regard for native cultural institutions were useful barriers to social and political revolutionary nationalist or nationalist-communist movements, whose strength increased greatly in all colonial areas after the war.[1]

Political and administrative expediency together with economic developments were primarily responsible for the adoption of indirect rule. Direct rule when applied to more backward and primitive peoples presented few difficulties from an administrative viewpoint. When, however, the European powers sought to apply it to more advanced peoples as in Indo-China and to a lesser degree in Malaya and the East Indies, they discovered that the problem of pacifying and policing them presented difficulty—particularly from an economic viewpoint. The co-operation of native ruling groups became imperative. Particularly was this true when towards the end of the nineteenth century the colonial powers sought to open up and develop the remote interiors of their colonies. The colonial areas since that time have no longer been looked upon only as a source of agrarian products such as spices, tea, or sugar cultivated by the natives in traditional ways, but as a source for minerals and as a market for European goods. In order to develop their colonies to the full it was necessary to extend "peace and order" to every part of the colony to make it a safe place for the investment of European capital in mines, railroads, industrial and processing plants, and to clear the jungles to establish large plantations where tobacco, rubber, sugar, etc., might be grown for European markets. Adequate supplies of native or imported Chinese and Indian labor had to be made available to work on these new enterprises. These laborers had to be energetic,

---

[1] For a further discussion of nationalist and communist movements in the Far East see pp. 554-575.

hence healthy, and fairly well content with their lot and conditions; and the population as a whole, in order to utilize European manufactures, needed to enjoy higher living standards than formerly. It came about, therefore, that colonial administrators began to take an interest in educating the natives, extending to them health and sanitary services and protecting them in their rights in property and person.

It is out of these administrative and economic developments in the colonies in recent decades that there has emerged the dilemma which perennially confronts with increasing intensity the colonial powers. To obtain the greatest economic benefit from their colonies they must improve the condition of the natives educationally and culturally as well as economically. Yet the further this process of modernizing native life proceeds, the more self-conscious they become culturally and politically, resulting in the growth of nationalist movements with their demands for increasing autonomy and ultimate independence. It is apparent that indirect rule is an uneasy and unstable transitional stage between direct rule and independence.

With these few generalizations concerning colonial rule and policy in the Far East in mind, it will be well now to consider in more detail how each country in turn acquired and administered its colonial areas, overseas territories, and protectorates acquired outside of China Proper since 1871.

THE NETHERLANDS

Netherlands East Indies

> AREA: 733,681 square miles
> TRADE: 1938—$620,000,000
> > Exports: $356,000,000
> > Imports: $264,000,000. Netherlands share
> > only about 20 per cent
> INVESTMENTS: 3,500,000,000 guilders [2]

How Administered. At the head of the government, located at Batavia, was a governor-general. He was assisted in his legislative and executive functions by a council of five members, two

---

[2] The Dutch florin or guilder has a par value of U.S. gold $.40.

of whom might be non-Dutch. As a result of the liberalizing tendencies born of the first World War and the growth of nationalist sentiments in the islands, a Volksraad or parliament was established in 1918, which at first was purely advisory in character. In 1922 under a new constitution it was granted legislative powers. It had sixty members of whom thirty-eight were elected. Of this number only twenty were natives, the rest being Dutchmen or representatives of other races, such as Chinese or Arabs, in the islands. The governor-general might enact laws over its head if necessary by an appeal to the home authorities. Moreover, the budget before having the force of law had to be approved by the states-general at the Hague. In 1929 it was decreed that thirty members of the Volksraad or one-half of the total number in that legislative body should be East Indians.

In response to the growing nationalist movement the legislature in 1937 unanimously petitioned the Dutch government to grant dominion status within ten years. Only two years later, following the fall of the Netherlands to Germany, in May, 1939, the colony was to achieve virtual if not legal semi-independent dominion status.

In local administration the Dutch, in the past fifty years, have favored indirect rule over natives through their own leaders. This was especially true among the more advanced natives of Java. In the sparsely populated islands or "outer possessions" Dutch officials intervened more directly. Nevertheless the chiefs of the various tribes were of the natives' own choosing. Except for the continued existence of two large native states and several small ones, the hereditary chiefs in Java were all set aside and replaced by natives who held the title of regents. They acted under the close tutelage of the Dutch residents, who in turn were directly responsible to the governor-general. The regents, who appeared in the eyes of the natives to be the real rulers, were usually members of the old ruling families and hence possessed much personal influence and control over the people of their territory. They were usually without much land and hence dependent upon their salaries, which in turn gave them a vested interest in the existing order of things. Justice was administered fairly, local customary or adat-law having been gradually introduced into the codes and their administration in accordance with the cultural attributes of indirect rule.

In consonance with a policy of decentralization and delegation of authority inherent in indirect rule, the island of Java was divided into three "governments," each comprising a number of "residences." There was a governor over each, advised by a provincial council in which the elected element was in the ratio of three to two.

Nearly nine-tenths of the population lived in self-contained villages controlled by a headman and council of elders. The Dutch were careful to preserve this village organization and never questioned the rights of the villagers to elect their own headmen and councils. The headmen were the local magistrates and collectors of the revenue.

How Acquired. The Dutch government inherited the East Indies from the earlier period of colonial expansion. The Dutch East India Company had consolidated its hold over portions of the area after 1600. In 1798, when the company was dissolved, the Dutch government took over the administration of the islands. The increased competition for colonies after 1870 led the Dutch to extend more effective control and administration over the nominally held outer possessions lest they fall into the lap of another colonial power.

Economic, Labor and Land Policies. The ruthless exploitative policies pursued by the company were carried on by the Netherlands government in even more intensive form in the nineteenth century under the so-called Culture System. This abusive system required the natives to devote a part of their time and of their land to the cultivation of export crops desired by the Dutch. Partly under the pressure of changed economic conditions and partly due to the growth of liberal and humanitarian sentiments and principles in Europe, the system was abandoned toward the end of the century. Since then measures designed to protect peasants and laborers have come into operation.

Natives could sell their tenure rights to each other, but never to a non-native. Outside interests might rent land from natives in Java but had to pay a rate which fully compensated the peasant for the loss of the crop he might otherwise have grown and in addition he received a wage for growing and cutting the crop which he grew on the land for the renter. In the less densely populated outer possessions, capitalists could more easily acquire large areas on which to develop tobacco, rubber or sugar plantations. All land not in private hands was declared to be public domain in 1870.

There was but a bare beginning in the way of labor legislation. Labor organizations were discouraged and even attacked as being allegedly dangerous and radical. However, the evils of contract labor on the large plantations, mostly in Sumatra, developed by outside capitalist interests, were, by 1940, largely eliminated.

The open door policy, both as regards trade and investments, pursued in the islands for about sixty years, hastened their development through the investment of several billions of guilders by the nationals of other countries. The effect of this policy was also reflected in the small share of the total foreign trade with the mother country, which was less than 25 per cent. As a small, weak country, militarily speaking, the Dutch were wise in adopting such a policy as it removed the economic excuse for threats to their control on the part of more aggressive nations. However, the depression and increasing Japanese trade competition led to the abandonment of the free-trade policy in 1933 accompanied by extensive regulation of trade, industrial development and price controls in favor of the mother country. This in turn led to strained relations with an expanding Japanese empire.

Taking advantage of the Netherlands' predicament after the German occupation in May, 1939, the Japanese brought increasing pressure to bear on the East Indies government to grant preferential economic concessions. A strong economic mission was sent to the islands by Tokyo in September, 1939. In November the Batavia government agreed, with the consent of American and British interests, to supply Japan with a greater share of the petroleum output of the islands during the ensuing year. It was held to be a price that had to be paid to secure the islands from a Japanese attack. However, the increasing strength of the British resistance in Europe and the speed of the American rearmament program seemed to strengthen the hands of the East Indian government in subsequent negotiations, and as late as the spring of 1941 a definite agreement granting further economic concessions to Japan had not been reached.

Social Services. In addition to protective land and labor policies the Dutch in recent decades made marked progress in improving the lot of the natives and other Asiatics in the islands through the development and extension of public health services,

education, the introduction of more scientific agriculture and the
building up of a popular credit system to protect native borrowers
against usurers. Increased security and health conditions resulted
in a striking growth in the population. In 1815 Java had a population of about 4,500,000, which grew to 34,500,000 by 1920, and
in 1940 was estimated at 48,000,000. The population of the outer
possessions increased from 7,374,611 in 1905 to about 25,000,000.
Another reflection of the beneficence of the Dutch rule, and the
Dutch have been colonizers *par excellence* among colonial powers,
was the relative absence of unrest and revolt among the masses
of the people. It was believed that the authorities could count
upon at least the passive co-operation of the people in case of an
invasion.

Nevertheless the Dutch were by no means in a hurry to educate
all the natives so as to prepare them for independence as was the
case with the United States in the Philippines. They aimed at
only a bare literacy for the peasant and working classes and
higher education for a select few largely for the purpose of filling
junior positions and clerical posts in the civil service. There was
an expansion of educational facilities after the first World War,
expenditures having increased more than fourfold since 1912. Yet
by 1928 only about 30 per cent of the children from six to nine
were receiving education and only 14.7 per cent of those between
six and thirteen years of age. In that year there were 1,513,000
in vernacular schools, 75,317 in Dutch schools, 6,462 in secondary
schools and 16,177 in professional institutions.

Defense Measures. Lying athwart Britain's imperial line of
defense, it is apparent that Dutch occupation of the Indies has
been, for over a century at least, on British sufferance. Up to
the end of the first World War the Dutch relied instinctively,
though not overtly, upon British protection. Japan's expanding
program since the first World War and particularly since 1932
became an increasing source of alarm. This led to the development of a relatively inexpensive and mobile system of defense
designed to harass a foe and possibly hold off invasion until
British or perhaps American naval forces could come to their aid.
For this purpose a fleet of cruisers, destroyers and submarines had
been constructed or imported by 1940 and the air forces rapidly
expanded. There was a small army of some 50,000 men available made up in part of natives. Small as this force was, it was

held to be sufficient, in co-operation with the British and the United States, to hold off a Japanese attack. With the prolongation of the war in Europe into the spring of 1941 there was increasingly close collaboration among the responsible authorities of the three countries to perfect co-operative plans for the defense of the whole area.

GREAT BRITAIN

British Malaya

AREA: 52,500 square miles
TRADE: 1938—Straits $1,134,642,000 [3]
          Exports: $579,649,000—$82,072,000 to U.K.
          $101,978,000 to other British areas
          Imports: $554,993,000—$102,332,000 from U.K.
          $100,419,000 from other British areas
INVESTMENTS: No accurate figures available. British investments probably in the neighborhood of £90,000,000; American $30,000,000

How Administered. The modern administrative period in Malaya dates from 1867 when the administration of the Straits Settlements was transferred from the India Office to the Colonial Office in London. Supreme authority over all Malayan units was vested, under the general supervision of the Colonial Office, in the governor of the Straits Settlements, which was a crown colony. He was at the same time high commissioner for the four Federated and the five Unfederated Malay States. He governed with the assistance of a united Malayan civil service, which, with the exception of a few Malay members, was exclusively British in personnel. In the Straits Settlements a colonial secretary carried on the general administrative work and was head of the civil service. An executive council advised the governor. It consisted of high-ranking officials and three non-officials, one of whom was a Chinese. The presence of the Chinese member reflected the important position which the Chinese in the colony held in its economic life, 75 per cent of the population of Singapore being Chinese. There was a legislative council of twenty-seven members. Thirteen were officials, making with the governor a

---

[3] Straits $ par value U.S. $.5678.

working majority for the administration. Only six of the twenty-seven were non-European members. Labor and the lower classes could secure no direct representation. This autocratic rule was little resented, however, as the people did not constitute a unit racially, culturally or economically, and their political consciousness was little developed.

The sovereignty of the nine Malay states remained legally intact under a series of treaties and agreements signed with the rulers of those states. British residents were provided for the Federated States and advisers for the Unfederated States. They were empowered to give advice which must be asked for and acted upon in all matters other than religion and local custom. Thus these protected states were in reality little more than colonies. Uniform orders sent to the British officials directing and advising them gave a unity of policy and administration to all of them despite the maintenance of a multitude of nominal sovereign states.

A federal administration for the Federated States was set up in 1896 accompanied by the formation of an elaborate secretariat under a resident-general whose powers soon surpassed those of the separate administrations under the residents in the four states. The consequent loss of local autonomy was causing the British difficulties, particularly in dealing with the more autonomous Unfederated States which feared the same centralizing, absorbing process might be extended to them. While a beginning was made in 1909 toward decentralization, or devolution as the British call it, it was not until after 1931 that really effective measures were taken. These resulted in the return of certain functions to the Federated States and in a modernizing of the state services and state councils. Progress toward the achievement of a Malayan federated union of all the nine states, which was the chief objective of the decentralization policy, had made little headway by 1940. The effort to establish a customs union in line with that policy had, up to that year, failed.

How Acquired. In 1867 the crown colony of the Straits Settlements was established. It comprised Singapore, Penang, Malacca, Wellesley Province and the Dindings. In 1935 the Dindings was returned to the state of Perak. During the years from 1874 to 1888 the four Malay states of Perak, Selangor, Negri Sembilan and Pahang came formally under British protection.

In 1895 they were joined together to form the Federated Malay States. In 1909 four more Malay states were added under a treaty which bought from Siam the rights of suzerainty formerly exercised by that state over them. These were the states of Kedah, Perlis, Kelantan and Trengganu. The largest of the Malay states, that of Johore, though for a century under virtual British control, came under formal British protection in 1914. These five last-named states have retained a larger degree of administrative autonomy than the earlier acquired states, and have been called in consequence the Unfederated Malay States.

Economic, Land and Labor Policies. A free trade policy was pursued by England to 1932. After that year the policy of imperial preference was introduced followed by the establishment of quotas in 1934 to check rising Japanese imports. Partially as a result of this there was a decline after 1934 in Japanese imports, when they comprised 2.9 per cent of Japan's total exports, to 1938 when Malaya's share of Japan's exports dropped to less than 1 per cent. Malaya's trade, however, is not naturally with the United Kingdom as its share was only about 15 per cent of the total trade before imperial preference was introduced. By 1938 it had risen to only about 17 per cent. The British Empire as a whole, however, absorbed one-third of the total trade in that year. That there was an open door for outside interests was reflected in the fact that in 1930 American private investments totalled about $30,000,000, while since the first World War Japanese concerns have been exploiting the iron ore reserves in some of the Malay states.

To protect the Malays against the loss of their land to immigrants, particularly Chinese, the government created large Malay reservations which can be alienated only to Malays and must thereafter remain in Malay hands. In the Federated Malay States all land not held under title was considered state land. The disposal of this land and the collection of revenue from it was under the control of the various British residents. The states retained all rights to minerals under the soil and special mining licenses were required to extract them. The residents could prescribe the type of cultivation applied to such lands. The Unfederated States on the whole followed the same regulations.

Strikes became common in Malaya after 1930. The lack of organization among the Indian laborers made compromise and bargaining with employers difficult. The government pursued a paternalistic policy operating through a department of labor and in accordance with a Malayan labor code. Through this policy they were carefully protected against grosser abuses. The Chinese coolies, being well organized, were better able to defend their own rights. The government adopted with respect to them more of a laissez-faire policy. The important position of the Chinese in Malaya led to the establishment of a Secretary for Chinese Affairs, assisted by a staff of Protectors of the Chinese to consider and deal with their problems and their relations with the Malays.

Social Services. While there was an increase in the amount of expenditures for medical, health and educational services after the first World War, an analysis of the budgets discloses that the government still considered its prime function that of maintaining the kind of law and order conducive to the encouragement of capital investment by assuring investors and exploiters of the valuable tin, iron and rubber interests security and returns. The colony contributed $100,000,000 for imperial defense after the first World War. This was many times what was expended to benefit the poor and the starving people in the area. While the amount spent on education doubled between 1924 and 1932 and had increased sevenfold since 1913, educational expenses were still less than 6 per cent of the budget and only 12 per cent of the children of suitable age attended English schools. The 1922 labor code required employers to provide schools for children of laborers on their estates. Under the inspiration of the nationalist movement in China, the Chinese expanded their own vernacular schools and began to use national language textbooks imported from Shanghai. In 1930 there were 339 such schools registered with the authorities with some 24,059 pupils enrolled.

Defense Measures. Singapore became after the first World War one the most vital points in Great Britain's imperial line of defense. On February 14, 1938, one of the largest and strongest naval bases in the world was formally opened. While the British were not able, due to developments leading to the war in Europe, to station a full-sized fleet there, it remained nevertheless a potential barrier to Japan's southward expansion. To the construction of this base and to imperial defense generally the colony contributed handsomely in proportion to its size and population. Annual contributions ran to about Straits

$5,000,000, while in the score of years after the first World War a total sum of about Straits $100,000,000 was provided.

British North Borneo, Brunei and Sarawak

British Borneo was divided into three parts. British North Borneo was a protected state administered by the British North Borneo Company under a royal charter granted in 1881. The governor of the state was appointed by the company, with the approval of the Secretary of State for Colonies, and was responsible to the Court of Directors in London. It had a trade in 1938 amounting to £751,463 in imports and £1,193,252 in exports. Brunei was placed under British protection by treaty in 1888. In 1906 general administration of the state was entrusted to a British resident who was a member of the Malayan civil service. The head of the state was a sultan. Free vernacular schools in the Malay language were provided by the state for 1,810 pupils. It had a trade in 1938 of £329,210 imports and £767,723 exports. The right to govern Sarawak was obtained from the sultan of Brunei by Sir James Brooke in 1842. In 1888 under agreement it was recognized as an independent state under the protection of Great Britain. Its foreign trade in 1938 amounted to Straits $22,371,939 imports and Straits $26,135,097 exports.

Hongkong

The crown colony of Hongkong was ceded to England by the Treaty of Nanking in August, 1842. Together with the subsequent leased territory on the mainland it covers a total area of 356 square miles. It had a population of over 1,300,000 in 1938. It was administered by a governor aided by an executive and a legislative council. Three Chinese were admitted to membership on this council. In addition to the University of Hongkong, the majority of whose students were Chinese, there were thirteen government schools for Chinese boys and two for Chinese girls. The total number of students in all schools in 1938 was 104,134. It was a free port. For defense it relied largely upon a volunteer defense corps and the China squadron of the fleet for which it was the headquarters. The Japanese threat to the British position in China led to rather feverish efforts to modernize and strengthen its fortifications.

Tibet

The effect upon developments in the Middle East of Great Britain's and Russia's conflicting aims in Tibet has already been discussed. Here the effect of their conflict in Central Asia upon China and China's relations with Tibet will be emphasized. By 1900 Britain had come to regard Tibet, as we have seen, as a strategic buffer state against Russian advance from the north. While the British had never denied Chinese suzerainty over the area, they had taken steps from time to time to interfere in internal Tibetan affairs primarily to keep the Russians out. Thus in 1904 as a result of a successful military expedition sent into the forbidden city of Lhasa, Tibetan authorities were forced to sign a convention which not only opened the country to British trade, but also stipulated that Tibet was not to pledge its revenues nor grant territorial or commercial concessions to any foreign power "without previous consent of the British government." This was followed by the signing of a convention between England and Russia on August 31, 1907, in which both parties recognized the suzerain rights of China in Tibet and agreed to deal with Tibet only through the Chinese government. Thereby they reconciled their conflicting interests in that area. With the downfall of the Manchu dynasty in China in 1912, British influence in the portion of Tibet nearest India mounted steadily. By agreement between British and Tibetan authorities in 1914, Tibet was divided into two regions: Inner Tibet nearest China, to be controlled by China, and Outer Tibet nearest India, to be "an autonomous state under Chinese suzerainty and British protection."

British ascendancy in Outer Tibet was evidenced by growth of trade with India, the partial modernization of the Tibetan army by British and Indian officers, the presence of British political officers in the country each year, and the staffing of the administration with Tibetan returned students from England. Stimulated and awakened by these contacts the Tibetans had, after 1920, moved to recover territory in Inner Tibet that had fallen under direct Chinese control. Thereby they hoped to restore the historic frontiers of their country. The Chinese authorities reacted by nominally setting up in 1928 the two new provinces of Sikang and Chinghai, made up in large part of former Tibetan territory. On January 1, 1939, a provincial government was formally established in Sikang. The Nationalist government of China, driven into the far west by Japanese armies, took a renewed interest in these frontier areas and was not only seeking to consolidate its direct rule over Inner Tibet, but was also attempting to recover a position of prestige and influence formerly enjoyed by the Manchus in Outer Tibet. As Lamaism, the Tibetan form of Buddhism, originally spread from here to Mongolia, the Chinese hoped to secure greater prestige among the Mongolian lamas and princes through a control over the Dalai Lama, or the ecclesiastical and secular head of Tibet and high priest for all followers of Lamaism. Chinese influence was seen in the selection and enthronement in 1940 of the new Dalai Lama, to succeed the one who died in 1933. While for over twenty years British influence had centered on the former Dalai Lama, it was not likely that Britain objected to Chinese influence working through his successor as it strengthened China's hands in dealing with the U.S.S.R. and Japan in Mongolia and Sinkiang as well.[4]

FRANCE

Indo-China

AREA: 285,000 square miles (1940)
TRADE: 1938—4,762,000,000 francs [5]
         Imports: 2,845,000,000 francs—France's share 57 per cent
         Exports: 1,917,000,000 francs—France's share 53 per cent
INVESTMENTS: No accurate estimates of total amount.
                     French investments have been estimated to
                     be as high as $600,000,000.

How Administered. The ministry of colonies in Paris had jurisdiction over the usually politically appointed governor-general of Indo-China. He had wide jurisdiction over the various administrative units in the Indo-Chinese Union. Under him was a governor for the colony of Cochin China and chief residents for the four protectorates of Annam, Tongkin, Cambodia and Laos, as well as a chief administrator for the leased territory at Kwangchow Bay in China. He was assisted by a consultative body known

---

[4] For a further discussion of Russian and Japanese influence in Sinkiang and Mongolia, see pp. 547-549.
[5] Value of franc in 1938 was $.0287.

as the *Conseil de Gouvernement* composed of high-ranking officials, representatives of the *Conseil Colonial* of Cochin China (a partially elected body composed of French and natives of the colony), of chambers of commere and agriculture and a few Indo-Chinese chosen by natives holding high and responsible positions. This body, which met annually, could deal only with matters submitted to it by the governor-general, but he had to submit to it the budget and proposals concerning taxation. The chief residents were in turn assisted by councils consisting of the heads of the services and delegates from chambers of commerce and agriculture on which a few natives sat. A *Grand Conseil* was instituted in 1928 to discuss economic matters. By 1931 the number of natives on this body equaled the number of French.

The French wisely adhered to the principle of home rule in local and village communities and placed responsibility on the locally selected headmen. To enhance their prestige they were accorded honors and a position of importance. In contrast with the British system of indirect rule, which relied on reactionary chiefs of the old regime, the French placed their trust in a body of progressive and well-trained natives who realized that their power and authority rested upon their continued loyalty to the protecting power.

Despite a relatively advanced state of commercial development, the degree of representation granted to taxation was small; all real power gravitated into the hands of the French officials. The natives had almost negligible representation and that was restricted to a few not elected by popular vote but chosen by a comparatively small number of Indo-Chinese who occupied positions of responsibility in trade and agriculture. It was not until 1913 that anything like a representative body was created. The various councils mentioned above could not discuss or express opinions on political issues as they existed only for the expression of native views upon subjects relating directly and primarily to their immediate economic interests. The native intelligentsia resented their relegation to the lower ranks of the civil service and the inferior pay which they received when they discharged duties similar to those performed by higher salaried French officials.

In matters of fundamental importance or general application the laws of France were applied to the colonies by presidential decree. Local requirements were implemented by decrees issued by the governor-general, the more important of which had to receive the preliminary sanction of the *Conseil d'État* in Paris.

French rule in the area falls into three well-defined periods. From 1861-1879 there was the period known as the "rule of the Admirals" which was marked by forceful subjection and conquest of the peoples. It was replaced by a civil administration which pursued a policy of assimilation—political, economic and cultural —to France. The continued unrest and revolt which this policy aggravated were partially responsible for the gradual adoption of a policy of "association" or indirect rule after 1900. Increasing respect was paid to indigenous customs, laws and traditional forms of communal rule in local and village life, while the élite among the people were given a minor place on the various consultative councils. To 1940, however, economic assimilation still remained predominant through an assimilative tariff policy that distorted and warped the economy out of its Far Eastern setting to fit it in with French needs. After the outbreak of the war in Europe in 1939 certain liberal reforms were introduced to bind the colony more closely to France. The composition of the *Grand Conseil Economique* was modified to provide for the election of all members and the number of seats allotted to Indo-Chinese was increased. On April 1, 1940, a chamber of representatives was established for the first time in Cambodia.

How Acquired. By 1867, as stated above, the French had acquired Cochin China and Cambodia.[6] British advances in Upper Burma and efforts to open southwest China to British capital and trade stimulated the French imperialists to extend their control northward to the borders of China. The next step was taken with the signing of the Treaty of Saigon on March 15, 1874, in which France recognized the sovereignty and independence of Annam. The Chinese resisted this attempt to destroy their suzereign-vassal relationships with that kingdom. War finally broke out in 1884 and was brought to an end in 1885 by the Treaty of Peking, signed in June 9 of that year, whereby China abandoned all claims not only to Annam but to Tongkin as well.

---

[6] See p. 474.

In 1893 the kingdom of Laos was wrested from Siam. By 1897 all opposition within Indo-China, particularly along the China frontiers, was suppressed and France's conquest of Indo-China was virtually completed after years of military action, which is estimated to have cost the French people $150,000,000. In view of the fact that France had seized portions of Siam in rounding out its empire in Indo-China, it is not surprising that Siam or Thailand should take advantage of France's fall in June, 1940, to recover, after some fighting and with Japan's diplomatic assistance, in March, 1941, some 25,000 square miles of former Siamese territory from Indo-China.

Economic, Land and Labor Policies. The French engaged in expensive public works projects, including the construction of extensive irrigation projects, the improvement of communications through the construction of roads and railroads, and the modernization of the larger cities. There was a rapid expansion of trade under French initiative. In accordance with the principle of economic assimilation there was free trade between France and the colony. After 1928 the principle of tariff personality was applied to the colony to permit it to establish protective tariff measures in a limited way, but still continuing in the main the policy of economic assimilation to France. Under this policy France's share of the colony's trade increased from about 25 per cent in the period from 1911-1920 to over 50 per cent in 1938. The system of protection developed was designed to prevent foreigners from doing any business in the colony which Frenchmen could profitably undertake, with the result that foreign investments there were negligible. This was similar to Japan's policy in its Overseas Territories and stands in contrast to Dutch and British policies in their far eastern colonial areas. After the fall of France in June, 1940, the Vichy government, under pressure from Japan, granted to Indo-China on January 4, 1941, tariff autonomy to enable it to extend economic concessions to Japan in order to maintain its territorial integrity.

Lack of tariff autonomy for the colony up to 1941 and the continuance of free trade with the home country had the adverse economic effect of artificially raising costs of living for the Indo-Chinese, as they were forced to pay more for products from France or locally produced which they might have acquired more cheaply elsewhere. Moreover, the loss of revenues which ensued forced the adoption of monopolies in salt and opium and higher taxes generally in an effort to balance the budget and maintain fiscal independence of the mother country.

The land policy was one of almost utter confusion, replete with contradictions, inconsistencies and abuses. As late as 1940 a complete land survey had not been completed. On the one hand the French tried to protect the small peasant in his holdings, but ignorance of local custom frequently worked against the fulfillment of that policy. On the other hand the desire to entice colonists from the homeland and to encourage the development of large plantations was frequently abusive of native rights. Likewise the government's efforts to relieve the peasants of their perennial burden of various debts through the establishment of credit societies of one sort or another were accompanied in their administration by abuses that frequently defeated the purposes for which they were established. Too often the well-to-do native was the great beneficiary of these credit facilities to the exclusion of his needier compatriots. Much remained to be done to improve the lot of the small Indo-Chinese peasant by giving him greater security, a clearer title to his land and in general raising his standard of living.

The French made no move to initiate labor regulations for workers until 1913. The corvée was abolished in Tongkin only in 1923 and an inspectorate of labor conditions was created as late as 1926. In 1932 forced labor was generally prohibited. The right to strike was limited to certain circumstances. Trade unions did not exist. The laborers were too lacking in class consciousness and too widely dispersed to permit of ready organization. Work of women and children was limited by statute and the health of workers on plantations was safeguarded. In general, labor legislation was behind that in British Malaya and the Netherlands East Indies, though there was marked progress in this respect during the decade after 1930. Thus in December, 1936, a labor code was promulgated which provided for the ultimate enforcement of a 49-hour week for natives, collective bargaining and vacations with pay. It contained, however, no provisions for trade unions.

Social Services. Despite a rapid advance in medical and health services, they were still inadequate. Cochin China was best provided with these services. For a population of 23,000,000 there were available by 1935 only 6 large hospitals, 112 secondary hospitals and 344 medical posts, clinics and dispensaries. Only about 4 per cent of the 1931 budget was devoted to social welfare, most of which was spent on education. Nevertheless such services as were available were efficiently run. Annamese doctors proved themselves to be quite the equal of French doctors. Extensive vaccination and sanitary campaigns carried on throughout the union abated considerably the serious plagues and epidemics. The population of Annam, which was declining when the French came, was on the increase. In Cambodia the population increased threefold after it came under French protection. The problem of extending medical services and health measures to the fearful and superstitious people was one of education as much as of finance. The French were making laudable progress in solving both, after a long period of trial and error and of inefficiency, owing to frequent changes of policy and administration which characterize the history of French rule in Indo-China. At long last they were beginning to approach the British and the Dutch as successful colonial administrators.

From the outset of their control the French began to promote education. In 1935 there were about 400,000 students in schools, of which number 40,000 were girls. However, only about one-third of the boys of school age were receiving an education at that time. The most progress was made in Cochin China, where elementary education was made compulsory in 1927. At first, in accordance with the policy of assimilation, the French authorities developed education on French models and conducted it largely in the French language. With the adoption of a policy of association, primary education was promoted in the vernacular languages of the respective peoples. Up to 1926, however, they continued to promote higher education along French lines when the evils of that system became apparent in the production of a large class of pathetic, "cultural Eurasians" who knew little of their own or French culture. From members of this unadjusted group came many of the nationalist agitators. To counteract this tendency emphasis was placed on the study of Oriental humanities for those taking higher education. Also the increase in the number of professional schools and technical schools provided the élite among the Annamites with a means of livelihood other than that to be derived from entering the civil service. At Hanoi there was a university whose law and medical faculties had as high standards as were to be found in France. In 1922 at Hué and Hanoi schools were established emphasizing studies of Annamite law, folk lore, and history to placate the nationalists. In these centers an effort was made to link up Far Eastern history and culture with world history and world movements in general.

Defense Policies. The comparatively marked absence of racial prejudice, philosophically and administratively though not necessarily individually, exhibited by the French in their relations with their colonial natives, in comparison with other European colonial powers, led them to make use of native peoples in the military services to an exceptional degree. As early as 1892 natives were in command of militia units in Tongkin and Annam and were assisting the French in pacifying the countryside and eliminating banditry. During the first World War some 50,000 Annamese troops served effectively at the front. The threat of Japan's southward advance stimulated the development and modernization of the colony's defense forces. Efforts were made to establish munition and aircraft plants and in general to increase the economic self-sufficiency of the colony by encouraging a degree of industrialization and increasing its production of agrarian commodities.

For the defense of Indo-China an alleged well-equipped, largely native, army of 100,000 men was stated to exist. A project for the development of a naval base at Cam Ranh Bay was announced, though it is doubtful that much progress was achieved by the time war broke out in 1939. Moreover, French naval units in the Far East were small in number and antiquated. The French continued to lean heavily upon the protective arm of British sea-power in the Far East. It was generally thought that Japan, if freed of its military and naval problems in China, would find little difficulty in conquering Indo-China if it were opposed only by local French and native forces. Some British aid might possibly be counted upon, but any active American assistance seemed remote. After the defeat of France in the summer of 1940 the Japanese put increasing pressure on French authorities in a successful effort to secure military and air bases in Tongkin for the ostensible purpose of attacking the armies of Chiang K'ai-shek from that alleged point of advantage.

Thailand (Siam)

The expanding French and British empires in Indo-China and Burma respectively threatened to absorb the kingdom of Siam during the latter decades of the nineteenth century. The country was to escape, however, the fate of all the other countries of the Far East, with the exception of Japan, that of falling under the partial or complete control of Western powers. Finally after 1926 it emerged as an independent state. Its survival was due primarily to two factors. One was the fortunate occupation of the throne by the progressive King Chulalongkorn, whose long reign (1868-1910) was almost exactly coterminous with that of the reforming Emperor Meiji of Japan. Not only was he eager to modernize his country, but he was a shrewd statesman well able to play upon the mutual jealousies of the imperialist powers to the advantage of his own country.

The other factor which served to preserve Siam's independence was the periodic threat to the peace between France and Great Britain which their rivalries on the Indo-Chinese Peninsula occasioned. To avoid war and allay their mutual suspicions France in 1885 proposed the neutralization of Siam. This offer the British declined. The way was left open for further territorial aggrandizement at Siam's expense. After making threats to bombard Bangkok, the capital, the French secured a treaty in 1893 which transferred to their control all Siamese territory east of the Mekong River. At one stroke the French nearly doubled the area of their holdings in southeast Asia. Their demands did not stop at that point as in 1904, and again in 1907, they acquired additional Siamese territory. The British then took their turn and in 1909 they wrested from Siam four Malay states on the northern part of the Malay Peninsula.

With that seizure further territorial demands upon Siam came to an end. The country was left with only about half of its former territory. Though nominally independent it remained, however, a semicolonial state like China, as it still had fastened upon it "unequal" treaties which accorded Westerners special privileges, such as that of extraterritoriality. Continued reform along economic, social and legal lines by Chulalongkorn's successors and the country's contribution to the cause of the Allies after it had declared war upon Germany in 1917 led to the gradual relinquishment, under American leadership, of all restrictions upon the country's internal administrative independence. In 1920 the American government surrendered its privileges. The other nations quickly followed suit and by 1927 Siam had recovered its tariff autonomy and practically full control over all aliens in its midst. A few exceptional privileges to which the British and French continued to cling were finally given up in 1937. The country was left as free as most small countries to pursue its own domestic and foreign policies.

PORTUGAL

Macao and Timor

Portugal held after 1870 but two small pieces of territory in the Far East, remnants of an erstwhile "empire" that embraced half the world and within which it was claimed that only the Portuguese among all the Europeans might conduct trade and carry on missionary enterprises. Its far eastern holdings in the nineteenth and twentieth centuries consisted of Macao, on an island near Canton, China, and the eastern half of the island of Timor in the East Indies. Macao was occupied as early as 1557 but it was not until 1887 that China recognized Portuguese sovereignty over the place. It had an area of only six square miles and a population in 1936 of 200,000 of whom only 4,000 were Portuguese. Once the chief entreport of trade between China and Europe, it sank into relative insignificance in relation to nearby Hongkong in the nineteenth century. In 1936 its trade amounted to only about 25,000,000 *patacas* or about $14,000,000.

By treaty in 1859 the island of Timor was divided between the Netherlands and Portugal. The Portuguese portion covered an area of 7,330 square miles and had a population of 463,796 in 1936. The trade in 1937 amounted to a little over a million *patacas*. Each of these two Portuguese colonies was under the control of the metropolis. Each had a governor and enjoyed fiscal and administrative autonomy. Budgets, however, were adopted subject to the approval of the Minister for Colonies. Native labor was protected, and forced labor was forbidden except for public services, punishments and payment of taxes. A restricted amount of education for natives was offered by the missions.

JAPAN

Korea (Chosen)

AREA: 85,228 square miles
TRADE: 1936—Y1,355,730,000 [7]
    Exports: Y593,313,000
    To Japan proper: Y518,047,000
    Imports: Y762,417,000
    From Japan proper: Y647,918,000
INVESTMENTS: (1928) Y804,000,000 [8]

How Administered. The establishment in 1929 of a Ministry for Overseas Affairs indicated that the Japanese government did not consider the term "colony" appropriate but rather considered its holdings "Overseas Territories." However, as they were administered from Tokyo by imperial officers under laws more or less distinct from Japan Proper, the "Overseas Territories" had one of the basic characteristics of colonial government and their administration closely resembled that of the British crown colonies. A policy of direct assimilation was pursued—political, economic and cultural. Karafuto was already practically assimilated and Formosa was more nearly so than Korea. The trend of the administration was toward incorporation of Korea and Formosa into the prefectural and local systems of Japan. However, developing opposition within the areas opened the way to a possible evolution toward self-government. The Koreans had for some time clamored for representation in the imperial diet and the Formosans for their own diet, but in vain.

At the head of the Korean administration was a governor-general. After 1919 it was possible for civilians to become governors-general, but to 1940 no civilian had found his way to that post in Korea though several had in Formosa. The governor-general had far wider powers than the governors of prefectures in Japan Proper, as the imperial government did not go much beyond supervising the general outlines of colonial administration. He had legislative as well as executive functions, there being no legislative body, but he had to secure the sanction of the throne

[7] Value of Yen in 1936 was $.29.
[8] Value of Yen in 1928 was $.46.

for his decrees. He was assisted by a consultative body known as the central council made up of sixty-seven members, all of whom he nominated. The president of this council was a Japanese, but all other members were Koreans. Koreans were eligible to appointment in the lower ranks of the civil service, which formed a part of that of Japan Proper, but had no voice in forming policy. Beginning in 1919, following serious nationalist uprisings in Korea, a general liberalizing of colonial administration was initiated. In Korea it bore fruit in the establishment of a small degree of autonomy in the local districts after 1930. It provided for election, by a limited franchise, of councilors to town, village, municipal and provincial assemblies and advisory councils. In 1931 municipal councils were given limited legislative authority. The Koreans as a whole, however, had practically no voice in the conduct of the central administration. Since 1936 there has been a progressive militarization of the administration under the oppressive governorship of the extreme nationalist, General Jiro Minami.

How Acquired. Japan's active interference in Korean affairs during the modern period dates from just before the Restoration in 1867. The government's primary concern then as to the fate of Korea was strategic, fearing that it might fall from the weak grasp of its suzerain overlord, China, into the hands of a European power. A long and bitter quarrel ensued with China culminating in the war of 1894-1895, which resulted in China's acknowledgement of Korea's independence. Japan was then confronted by Russia, which contested its efforts to establish its predominant influence in the peninsula. The war with Russia followed in 1904-1905 as a partial result of this struggle, and left Japan with a free hand to deal with Korea as it chose. In 1910 it was formally annexed to the empire.

Economic, Land and Labor Policies. All Japanese colonies lay within Japan's tariff zone, hence a vast percentage of their overseas trade, running to over 75 per cent, was with the empire. Consequently the chief sources of revenue in the colonies were the monopolies and state enterprises. In addition, the Tokyo government subsidized Korea to the amount of about Y15,000,000 yearly. The total amount of subsidy granted the colony reached a figure over Y300,000,000 by 1940.

The government was glaringly remiss in bettering the lot of the peasants who comprised the greater part of the population.

Tenancy increased from 50 per cent to 60 per cent from 1919 to 1936. Eighty per cent of the peasants were in debt and paying interest at the rate of 3 to 4 per cent a month. There was an actual decline in living standards among the poorer peasants. Inadequate measures were taken to protect them against rapacious landlords, both Korean and Japanese. The government encouraged the colonization of Japanese farmers through the Oriental Development Company, which owned over 300,000 acres, including some of the finest rice land. It became the largest landlord in Korea. To acquire its land thousands of Koreans were forced out to make room for the Japanese farmers. About 20 per cent of the total area given over to rice cultivation was under Japanese control. Faced by intolerable conditions at home, Korean laborers have migrated in increasing numbers to Japan and Manchuria in recent years. Their number in Japan grew from 41,000 to 419,000 in the decade 1920-1930, while in Manchuria they increased from 55,000 in 1910 to nearly a million by 1940.

Japanese capital and industrial enterprises were finding it profitable to establish plants in Korea where labor legislation was still in a primitive stage of development and wage scales much lower than in Japan proper. By 1935 there were 5,635 plants employing 135,797 workers. Strikes were on the increase after 1930, owing primarily to the extremely low wages offered the Koreans in the mills and factories.

Social Services. As in Japan Proper, so in the colonies the Japanese have shown themselves to be apt students of the West in developing sanitary and medical services to eliminate epidemics and improve the general health of the population. In the development of "backward" colonial areas the introduction of modern health and medical services was as vital as improving communications, and as essential as pacifying and policing the natives. The inflow of capital was dependent upon the creation of a fairly healthy working class. Moreover, general health conditions had to be improved to make the country attractive to managerial staffs and their families from the homeland, as well as to the members of the civil service from the homeland. The increase in population in Korea and elsewhere resulted primarily from the development of these services rather than from the slight improvement made in the standard of living of limited sections of the population.

Before 1920, in accordance with the policy of cultural assimilation to Japan, efforts were made to force the natives to learn Japanese in the schools, while a distorted version of Korean history was taught. The obvious failure of that policy was evidenced in a rising nationalist movement which broke out into violence in 1919. These uprisings led to a relaxing of the former assimilation policy. The teaching of the Korean language was made obligatory in lower schools, together with more emphasis on Korean history and geography. The policy was again reversed in 1938 under pressure from chauvinistic army and bureaucratic circles that dominated Japan after 1931. Once again the teaching of the Korean language and history was subordinated to the study of Japanese. In 1937 there were 1,211,000 children in all schools in Korea, but there were twice as many children who could not attend, either because a sufficient number of schools was lacking or because they could not afford to pay even the nominal tuition fees. Under General Minami's reactionary administration after 1936 the amount of money allotted to education was reduced from the amount it had been under the more liberal rule of the preceding governor.

Formosa (Taiwan)

AREA: 13,889 square miles
TRADE: 1938—Y823,113,000 [9]

Exports:	Y456,454,000
To Japan proper:	Y420,104,000
Imports:	Y366,659,000
From Japan proper:	Y327,950,000

INVESTMENTS: 1928—Y355,000,000 [10]

How Administered. A civil administration was set up in the island in 1896 under a governor-general. In accordance with the more liberal colonial policy launched in 1919 all officials from the governor-general down have been civilians. The powers of the governor-general were practically identical with those of the one in Korea, except that he not only was subject to the control of the premier, but also checked in matters relating to finance and

[9] Value of yen in 1938 was $.28.
[10] Value of yen in 1928 was $.46.

communications by the respective home ministries concerned. His ordinance or legislative power was not so inclusive as the former. There were councils composed of mixed Japanese and Formosan (Chinese) membership, which, as in Korea, had only an advisory capacity.

How Acquired. As in the case of Korea, strategic considerations dictated an interest in Formosa at the time of the Restoration. Efforts to acquire the island finally achieved success as a result of the defeat of China in 1895.

Economic and Social Policies. From 1896 to 1904 the government received subsidies from Japan but since then, according to an official statement, it has been "fiscally self-sustaining." The government derived a major portion of its revenues from opium, salt, camphor, tobacco and alcohol monopolies. A further indication of the large degree to which the government participated in the economic exploitation of the island was seen in the formation, in 1936, of a Formosa Development Company. Half of the capital of this company was supplied by the government, largely in the form of real estate. It was organized to plant, on a large scale, cotton, cinchona trees (from which quinine is derived) and cocoa trees.

The social services were similar in nature and degree to those in Korea. Elementary education was given in both the vernacular and the Japanese languages, but middle and higher school education was Japanese in character. Universal education had not been attained, though the amount spent on education doubled between 1933 and 1938.

Karafuto (Island of Sakhalin)

AREA: 13,934 square miles
TRADE: 1937—Y180,750,000. All but Y523,000 was with Japan.[11]

How Administered. Karafuto was administered by a governor under direct control of the ministry of overseas affairs with wide powers over mining, forestry, taxation, railways and postal service. Thus it was a colony despite the fact that 318,321 of the total population of 326,946 were Japanese. The courts were integrated with the judicial system of Japan proper. The laws and ordinances

---

[11] Value of Yen in 1937 was $.28.

of Japan Proper were extended to the area so generally that it was almost completely assimilated to the mother country.

How Acquired. As a result of the war with Russia in 1904-1905 Japan acquired that portion of the island of Sakhalin which lies south of the fiftieth degree of latitude.

Social Services. The extension of health and medical services accompanied the economic exploitation of the colony. Schools on the model of those in Japan Proper provided education for some 57,000 pupils.

South Sea Islands

AREA: 830 square miles
TRADE: 1937—Y61,517,170 [12]

Exports:	Y38,252,645
To Japan:	Y37,864,371
Imports:	Y23,264,525
From Japan:	Y21,996,516

How Administered. The Japanese navy occupied the former German-held islands north of the equator in October, 1914, and established a military government.[13] A civilian administration was set up in 1918. In January, 1920, Japan was granted a class "C" mandate over the islands. The administration obtaining in 1940 was set up in April, 1922. It was under a governor, who was under the direct control of the ministry of overseas affairs. Communications were supervised by the ministry of communications in Japan and currency, banking and customs by the ministry of finance. In accordance with the provisions of a class "C" mandate Japan could and has extended its own laws to the islands.

How Acquired. Following upon a declaration of war against Germany in August, 1914, these islands were occupied by the Japanese navy. After the war the Japanese accepted a class "C" mandate over them under the supervision of the League of Nations. Despite the fact that Japan withdrew from the League in 1935, the mandate status remained in form. Considerable dis-

---

[12] Value of Yen in 1937 was $.28.

[13] The Marshall Islands were acquired by German traders during the 1860's and 1870's and taken under the protection of the German government in 1886. The Caroline Islands were bought by Germany as a bargain from Spain after the Spanish-American War.

pute arose in consequence of this development as to where sovereignty in a mandate lay, some ten different theories in all having been advanced. Realities have, however, overridden legal fictions and for all intents and purposes the islands were an integral part of the Japanese Empire and will remain so no doubt as long as the Japanese navy is predominant in Eastern Asia. While the number of natives increased under Japanese control, the number of Japanese in the islands was already in 1940 considerably in excess of the number of natives.

Economic and Land Policies. In the past, several private Japanese concerns dominated the economic life of the islands, but in 1936 there was organized the South Sea Development Company, founded by imperial ordinance, in which the government holds one-half the shares. Under the class "C" type of mandate Japan was not required to keep the door open to outside trade and investments. Phosphates, copra, sugar, dried bonito and alcohol accounted for 96 per cent of the exports, and 61 per cent of the imports consisted of cereals, cotton textiles, clothing, metal goods and lumber. Practically all this trade was with Japan.

The Japanese took over the liberal German methods for protecting the natives in their land. All transactions in real estate owned by the natives were subject to approval by the government.

Social Services. The extension of sanitary and medical services contributed to a slight increase in native population. Some 26 native schools extended education to about 3,000 native children. The native population was about 51,000.

Kwantung Leased Territory

This small leased territory of 1,435 square miles, located at the tip of Liaotung Peninsula in Manchuria, was important because of the dominant strategic and economic position which it gave Japan for exploiting Manchuria and North China. Japan acquired it after the Russo-Japanese war of 1904-1905 and forced an extension of the lease to 1997 in 1915, as a part of the Twenty-one Demands presented to China at that time. About 90 per cent of the population of over a million was Chinese, most of the rest being Japanese. Up to 1934 the territory was under the control of a governor. In that year a bureau was established at Hsinking, the new capital of Manchoukuo, which was under the control of

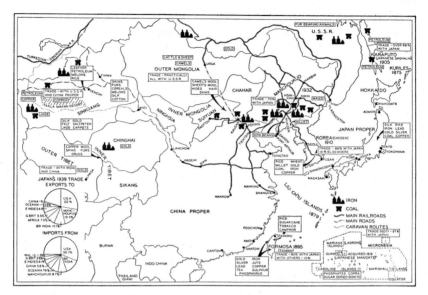

POLITICAL AND ECONOMIC MAP OF THE JAPANESE EMPIRE AND
GREATER CHINA, 1940

the Japanese ambassador there. The president of this bureau had charge of civil administration in the territory and supervised the business of the Japanese government-controlled South Manchuria Railroad Company which had its headquarters in the territory. Health and medical services, particularly as affects the Japanese, were well developed. Education for the Japanese was amply provided. For the Chinese the facilities were by no means comparable to those provided the Japanese. Most of the population lived in two cities—Dairen, the chief port of entry of goods to Manchuria, and Port Arthur, the naval base. Both were attractive modernized cities.

Manchoukuo

    AREA: 501,201 square miles
    TRADE: 1938—Y2,000,202,000—Japan's share 70.6 per cent [14]
    INVESTMENTS: 1936—Y3,400,000,000. Practically all Japanese [15]

---

[14] Value of Yen in 1938 was $.28.
[15] Value of Yen in 1936 was $.29.

How Administered. Manchoukuo is included here as this nominally independent state is in reality a Japanese protectorate administered under the indirect type of colonial rule. Under the organic law of 1934 the state was centralized in and organically assimilated to the throne after the pattern in Japan. A complete reorganization of the national administration was effected July 1, 1937. Three administrative branches were set up: a state council, a legislative council and the judicial system. It was a highly centralized state, the governors of provinces being under the direct supervision of the prime minister. While most of the higher posts in the administration were nominally held by "Manchurians" (i.e., Chinese) Japanese held key advisory positions in every department, while the general affairs board, the actual policy-forming body, was dominated by Japanese officials. In the civil service as a whole the number of Japanese approximately equalled the number of "Manchurians." They were predominant in the higher ranks of the service. Efforts to train a Manchoukuo army met with little success with the result that Japan had to garrison an estimated number of from three to four hundred thousand Japanese soldiers on the region. This was necessary partly to pacify it and partly to protect its frontiers from Chinese or Russian attacks.

How Set Up. The elimination of the former Chinese regime in Manchuria after September 18, 1931, and the setting up of the new state under Japanese protection and domination were work of the Japanese army and its civilian associates. In 1934 Manchoukuo was made a monarchy. The last reigning emperor of the former Manchu dynasty in China was enthroned at the new capital, Hsinking, in that year. Japan was first to recognize the new state, followed by San Salvador, Germany, Italy, Poland, the Dominican Republic, the Holy See, Spain and Hungary. Until 1940 all other states had refused to extend it *de jure* recognition, still considering the territory a part of the Chinese republic.

Economic and Social Policies. Economic life as well as the governmental activities were completely under control of the Japanese. Economic policies were dictated by the twofold objective of the Japanese army for setting up a form of state socialism designed to make the economy of Manchoukuo subservient to that of Japan and at the same time encourage the development of heavy armament industries to make the area the strategic base for pursuing Japanese military objectives on the continent. A series of state trusts and monopolies were set up in the fields of communications, mining, steel production, opium, oil. The forced development of these had more than doubled Japanese investments in the region between 1931 and 1940. One competent observer reached the conclusion that since 1931 the lot of the workers and peasants had grown worse under the increased taxation and forced labor practices which the Japanese employed to push through their militarized developmental schemes.[16]

Reflecting the continuing unrest under these exploitative measures was the large percentage of the budget apportioned the department of public peace, which in 1939 amounted to over 25 per cent. By way of contrast, less than 5 per cent of that year's budget went to the Department of People's Welfare, which covered public health measures and education. In 1938, according to official reports, 1,429,805 students were in primary schools and some 50,000 in higher, mostly technical schools. The study of the Japanese language was made compulsory.

Inner Mongolia

It was a part of Japan's continental policy to drive a wedge between China and the U.S.S.R. by extending indirect forms of control over the Mongols and Chinese of Inner Mongolia and to set up regimes favorable to themselves there and in Sinkiang as well. To win the support of the lama priests and the Mongolian princes they promised to help them retain their lands and their former positions of economic and political dominance. The provincial lines drawn by the Chinese in 1928, when they divided Inner Mongolia into the three provinces of Chahar, Suiyuan and Ninghsia, cut across the territories of the former Mongolian Leagues with a view to destroying the traditional divisions of power in the area and facilitate its reduction to direct Chinese control. Japan has professedly aimed at restoring these Leagues and has set up a puppet regime known as the United Leagues of Mongolia covering an area in Suiyuan and Chahar under tenuous Japanese military occupation. A Federal Council of Mongolian Borderlands was set up to consider problems arising in the area.

---

[16] Bisson, T. A., *Japan in China* (New York, Macmillan, 1938), pp. 383 ff.

Plans for economic development, designed to make the region a raw-material, chiefly wool-producing area for the Japanese interests, were drawn up. Continued effective Chinese resistance prevented the Japanese from establishing a permanent regime in Suiyuan by 1940, while Ninghsia and Sinkiang still remained beyond the orbit of their political and military influence. The province of Chahar, in the east, was well under Japanese control by 1940.

THE SOVIET UNION

Mongolia

Soviet Russia established over Outer Mongolia a virtual protectorate while at the same time recognizing Chinese suzerainty over the area. In contrast to Japanese policy in Manchoukuo, however, the Soviets have interfered but little in the internal affairs of the virtually autonomous state which they brought into existence in 1921. In that year there was established a Mongolian People's Republic which adopted a form of state socialism and overthrew the economic and social order under control of the lamas and princes of the *ancien regime*. To this revolutionary government the Soviets loaned money without interest, provided technical assistance for building factories and extended aid in training and equipping a mechanized Mongol army. In addition, they entered into close trading relations with it. This resulted in a reversal of the flow of virtually all trade, which went formerly through Inner Mongolia, from China to the U.S.S.R. All Chinese economic and trading interests were eliminated.

On April 8, 1936, the Soviets announced that they had entered into a mutual assistance pact with Outer Mongolia. Japan's efforts to open Outer Mongolia to its influence, in pursuance of a policy designed to unify the two Mongolias into an autonomous state under Japanese hegemony, inevitably drew the Soviet-sponsored government in Outer Mongolia and the Soviets together into an agreement to protect the area from an attack through Manchoukuo. Repeated border conflicts in the roughly defined area where Outer Mongolia meets Manchoukuo called forth direct military assistance from the U.S.S.R., which had, to 1940, successfully overcome the efforts of Japanese armed forces to "rectify" Man-

choukuo's border areas at Outer Mongolia's expense as well as
to enter into direct relations with Outer Mongolia. At the time
of the signing of the Moscow-Tokyo neutrality pact on April 13,
1941, there was also signed a frontier declaration in which Japan
pledged to respect the territorial integrity of Outer Mongolia,
and Russia that of Manchoukuo.

Sinkiang

Sinkiang, China's remote northwest province in Central Asia, is
bounded for the most part by Outer Mongolia and Russian Central
Asia on the north and west and by India and a British-dominated
Outer Tibet on the south. Its geographic situation made it the
center in the past of a mild form of inter-imperial rivalry between
Russia and England, the chief object of which was to see whether
their own frontiers in Russian Turkestan and India were vulnerable to each other. Chinese rule in the area had, therefore, never
been seriously impeded or challenged. After 1929 Soviet influence
in the province was on the ascendant. Increasing civil strife
after 1928 led finally to Soviet armed intervention, which helped
the Chinese government to restore order by 1933. After that Soviet
troops were withdrawn.

New policies and reform measures were introduced under
Soviet influence. The Russian principle of racial equality was
adopted. The military services were opened to all the peoples
of the province on equal terms with the Chinese. Schools were
opened to which all races were admitted. Economic reform
measures were initiated including efforts to establish a balanced
budget, elimination of irregular taxes, the development of agrarian
and mineral resources and the adoption of a three-year industrial
development plan which had been drawn up with the assistance
of Russian specialists. Russian money, machinery and technical
assistance were provided for the establishment of a printing plant,
tanneries, oil refineries and power plants. The opening of the
Turkestan-Siberian Railroad in 1930, which passes near Sinkiang,
helped to orientate an increasing proportion of the export trade
of the province to the Soviet Union.

Through the province runs the highway which forms the one
direct link between China and the U.S.S.R. Since the outbreak
of the war with Japan in 1937 considerable amounts of munitions

and other war supplies reached Chinese forces over this route. Japan aspired to cut this route and establish in the province a regime favorable to its interests, but by 1940 its military forces were unable to do so.

UNITED STATES

Philippine Islands

> AREA: 114,400 square miles
> TRADE: 1939—*Imports:* $122,750,000
> From U.S. over two-thirds
> *Exports:* $121,250,000
> To. U.S. over three-fourths
> AMERICAN INVESTMENTS: (1935) $200,000,000

How Administered. The Philippine Islands were administered in 1940 in accordance with the Tydings-McDuffie Independence Act passed by Congress on March 24, 1934. Under this act the Filipinos were to attain their independence on July 4, 1946. During the interim period they were to be under a Commonwealth government which was inaugurated on November 15, 1935. To the legislative powers granted the Filipinos under the Jones Act of 1916 the Independence Act added extensive executive powers subject to certain important checks over government loans, tariffs, immigration, and control of foreign affairs still retained by the United States government. A high commissioner, appointed by the President, exercised these reserved powers on his behalf. The citizens of the islands owed allegiance to the United States and their officials must recognize the supreme authority of the United States. The Filipinos drew up a constitution which provided for a presidential form of centralized government adapted from existing American and Filipino systems of government. The President was to be elected for a six-year term. There was a unicameral national assembly elected every three years by literate males over twenty-one years of age.

How Acquired. They were acquired as a result of the war with Spain in 1898. Their acquisition has been aptly characterized as the "impulsive manifestation of an essentially 'unripe' imperialism." Economic considerations played a minor secondary rôle. Well-grounded suspicions that the islands would fall into German hands after the war if left to Spain were the prime factor, together with a desire for sea power and prestige awakened by the writings of Captain Mahan and implemented by the assistant secretary of the navy, Theodore Roosevelt, and Senators Lodge, Beveridge and others. Added to this was the encouragement given by Great Britain, which preferred to see them in friendly American hands. To appease the American democratic conscience it was promised at the time of their acquisition that the Filipinos would be granted their independence as soon as they were prepared for it. The relative alacrity with which that promise was fulfilled was without parallel in the history of modern colonialism, as was the making of the promise itself.

Economic and Social Policies. The United States initiated a mutual free-trade system with the Philippines in 1909 and extended it in 1913. Under this regime the rapidly expanding foreign trade of the islands was predominantly with the United States. Since 1930 over 80 per cent of the exports have gone to, and 60 per cent of the imports have come from, this country. The effects of this policy were twofold. In the first place, the increasing importation of Filipino sugar and coconut oil led beet sugar, dairy farm and vegetable oil interests in this country to form a bloc in Congress which helped to force through the Independence Act. In the second place, it distorted Filipino economy out of its Oriental setting, stimulating the excessive development of a few agrarian products which unbalanced the one-time self-sufficiency of that economy. The latter development has necessitated the setting up of an elaborate arrangement designed gradually to adjust Filipino economy, with a minimum of hardship to the economic well being of the people, to the time when, upon the attainment of independence, Filipino exports will be confronted with the high American tariff wall. This process of adjustment has been made more difficult as the American Congress has not permitted the Filipinos to enter at once upon reciprocal trade agreements with other countries. The loss of the free-trade relationship with the United States would probably mean lower living standards and increased social unrest. As more and more of them came to realize this, a movement to retain some sort of dominion status under the United States flag gained momentum. Strategic considerations, arising from fear of conquest by Japan, economic if not political, contributed to the growth of that movement. A comparison of their relatively freer economic and political status under the American flag with that of the Koreans and Formosans under the Japanese flag has been made by enlightened Filipinos and the consequent lesson derived.

From the outset of American administration of the islands the Filipinos were protected on their land by a rigid restriction of land holding by corporations to about 2,500 acres and of individuals to 40 acres. These restrictions were carried over into the Commonwealth regime. Under its constitution, except for rights existing at the time of its inauguration, all public lands, minerals, and other natural resources were declared to be the property of the state and only Filipinos, or corporations in which they held 60 per cent of the stock, could exploit them. At present 98 per cent of the cultivated land is in the hands of Filipinos, mostly in the form of small holdings averaging three acres in extent. As regards labor, the present government is required to afford protection and to regulate relations between labor and capital.

Since the American occupation of the islands, sanitary and medical services were rapidly expanded, resulting in a practical elimination of epidemics of smallpox and cholera. Despite the fact that as much as 9 per cent of the budget has been devoted to this work in the past, much remains to be done to improve the general health of the population. To fulfill the promise to prepare the Filipinos for independence, educational facilities were rapidly extended. The number of students in schools increased from 227,000 in 1904 to 1,111,500 in 1928. This in relation to the population was over three times the number in schools in the Netherlands East Indies or in Indo-China. As much as 25 per cent of the budget was devoted to educational purposes in contrast to a figure that usually ran below 5 per cent in other far eastern colonial budgets. The chief criticism of the educational program in the past has been that it was too American in tone and content together with the fact that too much time and money were rather uselessly and inefficiently employed in teaching English in primary schools. With the passage of the Independence Act the content of education became more nationalized. It aimed to fit the Filipino for life in his native environment.

Defense Measures. Though Theodore Roosevelt was one of a small group of men largely responsible for the conquest and retention of the Philippines, he was a few years after the acquisition to call it the "Achilles heel" of American defense. And to the present it has remained that, there being as yet no adequate American naval base nearer than distant Hawaii to defend it. Only a few thousand American soldiers have been garrisoned there to maintain order in co-operation with Filipino scouts and a Filipino constabularly of fewer than ten thousand men. The Filipinos under their new government have launched a military program designed to create an army of 400,000 reservists by 1946 and to build up a small mobile fleet and an air force. These defense measures they hope will either make conquest by another nation so costly as to discourage the attempt or hold off such an enemy until the American navy might hopefully and at great cost fight its way to the islands. After the lapse of the Washington naval treaties in 1936, the United States could once again strengthen its naval position in the islands. President Quezon publicly announced that should America build a Gibraltar there, the Filipinos would not consider it an infringement upon their sovereignty after independence is secured in 1946. During 1940 the naval and air forces were considerably augmented and the decision was reached to strengthen naval bases at Guam and in the islands.[17] Naval strategists maintained that a base there would constitute a serious threat to Japan's lines of communication with its home bases should that country attack the islands. The question of the extent to which America would undertake to defend the islands against aggression after 1946 was intimately related to the larger issue as to the course of American policy in the whole Far East, and that in turn was highly conditioned by developments arising out of the European war which began in 1939. That war has not only thrown the status and future destiny of Europe, Africa, and the Near East into a high state of flux and uncertainty, but that of far eastern colonies, protectorates and countries as well.

---

[17] The island of Guam, the largest of the Mariana archipelago, has an area of 206 square miles. It lies about 1,550 miles east of Manila and 3,760 miles west of Honolulu. It was ceded to the United States by Spain by the Treaty of Paris of December 10, 1898. In 1930 it had a population of 18,509. It was a naval station under the jurisdiction of the Navy Department. The governor of the island was a naval officer appointed by the President. He exercised complete power. Elementary education was made compulsory even for the natives. Exports to the amount of $124,178 in 1939 consisted largely of copra and coconut oil. Imports came to $659,649 in the same year.

READINGS

Bell, Sir Charles. *Tibet—Past and Present,* 1924. Good on foreign relations.

Bell, Sir Hesketh. *Foreign Colonial Administration in the Far East,* 1928. One of the best comparative accounts.

Bousquet, G. H. *A French View of the Netherlands Indies,* 1940. A penetrating and critical analysis of Dutch rule.

Clyde, Paul H. *Japan's Pacific Mandate,* 1935. A comprehensive account.

Emerson, Rupert. *Malaysia, a Study in Direct and Indirect Rule,* 1937. A critical analysis of Dutch and British administration.

Ennis, Thomas E. *French Policy and Developments in Indochina,* 1936. A competent, well-documented account.

Ireland, A. *The New Korea,* 1926. Uncritical, but still valid on most administrative phases.

Kirk, Grayson L. *Philippine Independence,* 1936. A history of the American conquest and administration of the islands to the establishment of the Commonwealth government.

Landon, K. P. *Siam in Transition,* 1939. Valuable survey of important developments in all spheres in the past decade.

Lattimore, Owen. *Inner Asian Frontiers of China,* 1940. A provocative historical survey and analysis by an outstanding authority.

Lee, Hoon K. *Land Utilization and Rural Economy in Korea,* 1936. A statistical analysis of the agrarian policies pursued by Japan.

Roth, Andrew. *Japan Strikes South,* 1941. An up-to-date account of Japan's activities in Indo-China.

Sansom, G. B. *Japan: A Short Cultural History,* 1932. The standard one-volume survey.

Thompson, Virginia. *French Indo-China,* 1937. A well-balanced work.

Thompson, Virginia. *Thailand: The New Siam,* 1941.

Vandenbosch, Amry. *The Dutch East Indies, Its Government, Problems and Politics,* 1933. Rev. Ed., 1941. A standard work on the subject.

Winstedt, R. O. *A History of Malaya,* 1923. Best account from earliest times to 1909.

Wyndham, H. A. *Native Education in Ceylon, Java, Formosa, the Philippines, French Indochina and British Malaya,* 1933. A comprehensive comparative account.

Yakhontoff, V. A. *Russia and the Soviet Union in the Far East,* 1931. Useful.

Yanaihara, T. *Pacific Islands under Japanese Mandate,* 1939. An account by a Japanese authority.

CHAPTER NINETEEN

Nationalist Movements and International Relations in the Far East

THE RESULTS OF EUROPEAN EXPANSION

EuROPEAN EXPANSION in the Far East, as in other parts of Asia, resulted in the development of modern nationalist movements among a majority of the peoples of the region. These had for their common ultimate aim the overthrow of all alien control and the establishment of independent sovereign states, but they varied considerably in degree of development and intrinsic strength. This was primarily due to the widely divergent stages of historically conditioned, cultural maturity and of political consciousness prevalent at the time the Europeans came. It was secondarily determined by various factors such as the extent to which modern education had introduced Western ideas of national sovereignty, of social and political liberty and individualism; the degree to which a modern industrial order had developed, accompanied as in the West by the rise of a bourgeoisie whose economic interests were coterminous with a national economic order; and the extent to which modern means of communication had broken down family, tribal, village, and provincial ties and loyalties.

At one extreme in the scale of national development were the primitive peoples inhabiting the islands of the south Pacific under the control of Japan. Among them a modern nationalist movement could not be said to exist. At the other extreme stood Japan itself, where an intense form of modern integral nationalism found its fullest expression in the Far East. Imperialism, the ultimate expression of that type of nationalism, had also there found its highest development in an expanding empire which suppressed among the peoples drawn within its orbit that political and even cultural independence which the Japanese themselves most ardently cherished. Between these two extremes were the nationalist movements among the other racial and territorial groupings, representing various degrees of strength, maturity and progress toward political sovereignty. All of them emerged in their political manifestations as a direct consequence of European expansion into the region since the middle of the nineteenth century.

As a general rule these movements were launched by intellectuals, who, either in their native land or through residence in the West, had acquired some knowledge of Western social and political institutions as well as an awareness of the history of modern nationalism as it had developed and found expression among Western peoples. They strove to transplant among their own people the sentiments and ideals of this nationalism and its forms of expression through patriotic songs, flags and national holidays. Employing as far as available the modern means for propagandizing this artificially stimulated movement, through the press, the platform, the radio and systems of education, they sought to indoctrinate their own people with the commonly held beliefs and objectives of modern nationalists everywhere. Owing to the limited extent to which systems of education, as well as the modern press and other means of modern communication had developed in the Far East by 1940, with the exception of Japan and to a lesser degree the Philippines, together with the repressive policies pursued by the colonial powers, the sentiments of patriotic nationalism had not permeated thoroughly the peasants and laborers. This considerably limited the scope and intensity of the movements, confining them for the most part to sporadic outbreaks in the larger urban centers, which the colonial powers were able effectively to control.

Nationalist movements had, however, in most colonies and areas under partial alien control, spread beyond élite intellectual circles to native commercial and industrial classes whose interests were bound up in an expanding domestic and international trade, as well as in newly born industries that marked the spread of the Industrial Revolution in the Far East. An awareness of the benefits to be derived from a centralized government in the way of a stabilized uniform currency, the suppression of former barriers to internal transit of goods, and the potentialities in tariff autonomy for protecting their native industries, led them to lend support to the nationalist cause if only to be used immediately as a bargaining weapon with the colonial governments with which to extract concessions conducive to their own economic well-being. To the demands of this rising class of bourgeoisie, colonial governments in the Far East had to pay heed. By according them a voice, through various kinds of advisory councils, in measures directly affecting them, the colonial governments sought to appease them. Moreover, by opening up more places and higher positions in the civil service to the intellectuals and by granting an extension of facilities for education in the vernacular languages and in indigenous history, philosophy and culture they sought to meet the vociferous demands of nationalist agitators. Before attempting to appraise the significance of these nationalist movements as affecting the political status quo in the Far East as of 1941, it would be well first to review briefly the history and present status of these movements in turn.

Japan

With the above generalizations in mind, by way of background, let us first consider the nature and strength of nationalist movements in the Japanese Empire and in Japan's protectorate, Manchoukuo. It is not surprising that the one country in all Asia by 1941 that had risen to the position of a great world power was the first country to witness the earliest maturing of a nationalist movement. The creation of a highly militarized centralized state was predicated upon the inculcation into the people of that state of sentiments of supreme loyalty to it and a jealous guarding and asserting of its sovereign powers and prerogatives. There already have been discussed some of the factors and historic developments which have worked together for the emergence of modern

Japan.[1] The psychological factors and historical developments which paved the way for the rapid maturing of the modern nationalist movement after the Restoration in 1867 will now be briefly noted. The Japanese developed their civilization in comparative isolation upon four islands which lie only a few miles apart. Out of that geographic background emerged their racial homogeneity and cultural uniformity—factors which contributed greatly to enrich the soil in which modern nationalism flourished. Yet for centuries under a feudal regime the people had been torn apart by the intrigues and conflicts of the ruling feudal families. Suddenly within ten years after the Restoration the formal aspects of the feudal regime passed and internal armed conflicts ceased. The immediate occasion for this rapid transformation was the threat of conquest by the Westerners. However, it does not explain why the Japanese were able successfully to meet this threat whereas other far eastern peoples fell in varying degrees under Western control.

The explanation is to be initially sought in the past, particularly in the developments which occurred during the Tokugawa regime from 1603 to 1867, when that family, as Shoguns, dominated the country. Politically the Tokugawas gave the country over two hundred years of peace under the most highly centralized bureaucratic government in Japanese history. Under this regime domestic commerce developed to unprecedented heights and with its growth there emerged an urbanized class of bourgeoisie whose economic interests transcended old feudal barriers to trade and intercourse and who longed to enter into trade with other lands. Their financial support was drawn upon by the Restoration leaders to overthrow the feudal regime and to build up the new Japan.

Culturally also a most significant development occurred in that period which bears directly upon the rise of modern Japanese nationalism. In the seventeenth and eighteenth centuries there occurred a Japanese renaissance. It was initiated by scholars who delved into the history of indigenous institutions and religion, partially as a reaction to the "alien" Confucianistic political and social institutions which the Tokugawas were promoting to consolidate their centralized control over the whole country. The

[1] See pp. 491-494.

results of these studies appeared in a series of works which disclosed and extolled the peculiar virtues of Japanese culture as distinct from the profound and pervasive Chinese cultural and institutional as well as Buddhistic religious influences which had swept into the country centuries before, particularly after the seventh century. Features of Confucianistic and Buddhistic thought and institutions dominant under the Tokugawas were attacked, while Shintoism, the indigenous cult of Japan, was revived and admired. Then, too, they discovered anew that, according to their most ancient records, their imperial line was descended from the gods and had allegedly ruled the country up to the emergence of the feudal regime in the twelfth century. Thus it came about that the dominant feudal lords or Shoguns, who had for centuries preempted secular power, came to be pictured from the seventeenth century on as usurpers by the lesser feudal lords jealous of their power.

The work of the renaissance scholars prepared the way intellectually for the Restoration itself and for the new spirit of nationalism, which invoked in the people a supreme sense of loyalty and devotion to their alleged divinely descended and newly restored emperor. The rapidly expanding modern educational system was made the primary vehicle for carrying this new spirit to the people. National holidays were established, a national flag and song adopted, while textbooks were carefully prepared and edited with a view to awakening in the hearts and minds of Japanese children an awareness of the unique and unequaled virtues of Japanese culture and to instill in them a moral sense of supreme loyalty to their emperor-god, whom they fervently believed had descended from the Sun-Goddess. Shintoism, with its emphasis upon emperor and ancestor worship, was elevated to the virtual status of a state religion. A large number of the more important Shinto shrines were brought directly under the control of the government. The priests who functioned in these shrines were made members of the civil service. The result of it all was that no people in modern times have exhibited a greater degree of unity and loyalty nor a more intense spirit of at times chauvinistic, integral nationalism than the Japanese.

Japan's successful attainment of the status of a world power had a far-reaching influence upon nationalist movements among other peoples of Asia. The country's amazing victory over Russia in

1904-1905 was a source of great stimulation and encouragement to the leaders of less mature and more hopeless nationalist causes. What one Asiatic power had achieved in meeting and defeating a Western power other Asiatic peoples might be able to do in time. So, at least, they hopefully reasoned. Japan's imperialistic expansion since then lost to it this once-held position of inspiring leadership. Its influence on other Asiatic nationalist movements, particularly those in the Far East, did not cease, however, though its nature radically changed. The shadow of its expanding orbit of power, falling ever widely over far eastern regions during the 1930's, was a constant stimulus in a negative sense, to struggling nationalist causes in China and the south Pacific and even as far away as India. The rôle which Japan played in the rising nationalist movements in Asia after 1914 was similar, in other words, to that of the Western powers from the middle of the nineteenth century on.

Korea

Only in Korea, among their overseas territories, were the Japanese confronted with a nationalist movement of sufficient strength and maturity to present them with serious problems of control and repression. While racially akin to the Japanese and northern Chinese, the Koreans inherited certain racial characteristics that set them apart from other peoples of eastern Asia. Of more significance was their historical and cultural development and unity. While for centuries they were vassals of the Chinese Empire and while for a time the southern portion of the peninsula was under Japanese control, the Koreans had nevertheless retained a high degree of administrative independence and separatism. Moreover, they retained their own language, for which they created phonetic symbols, though Chinese characters were used in more formal administrative and literary styles. Though the roots of their culture were drawn from Buddhistic and Confucianistic China, this they remembered less than the fact that they passed this culture on to the one-time more backward Japanese, whose contemporary assumption of superiority with respect to them they bitterly resent.

Upon this historically conditioned foundation of racial, linguistic and cultural differentiation of which they were self-consciously aware, the Korean nationalists developed their movement since the annexation of the peninsula by Japan in 1910. The assimilation policy adopted by the Japanese, which involved a discouragement of the study of Korean language, history and culture, paved the way for the first general series of nationalist uprisings which broke out in 1919. Taking hope from the Wilsonian declaration of the principle of self-determination of peoples, Korean nationalists organized public demonstrations for independence with a view to enlisting the support of the Peace Conference at Paris. In order to legalize the movement the nationalists established a provisional government at Seoul, the capital, in April of that year. Driven from Korea by the Japanese, this "government" removed to Shanghai, from whence it continued to direct agitation for independence not only in Korea, but in Western countries as well.

Inability to enlist foreign support, lack of funds, and Japan's effective efforts at suppression through a mixed policy of force and conciliation, led to a rapid decline in the active aspects of the movement. Except for brief outbreaks in 1926 and 1929-1930 the movement has remained underground for the most part since that time. China's struggle against Japan after 1937 gave the movement new stimulus, resulting in the arrest of hundreds of Korean students and potential leaders. The Chinese nationalist government lent its support to the cause and a Korean brigade was attached to one of the Chinese armies fighting Japan. Though vigorously suppressed in Korea, nationalist organizations aiming at independence existed in China, Manchuria and possibly in Japan. By 1941 the Korean nationalists had wrested from the Japanese only a very limited degree of autonomous control in strictly local affairs.

Manchoukuo

In the protected state of Manchoukuo the Japanese did not adopt an avowed policy of assimilation as in Korea, but sought to create a new nation and a new nationalism for it. The vast majority of the population (97 per cent) who were in reality Chinese were not considered as such, but were called "Manchurians." By the employment of all the arts of modern propaganda through the school, the press and the radio, as well as by the establishment of nationalist holidays, the adoption of national songs and a flag, the Japanese strove to create a new sense of patriotic loyalty to the emperor, K'ang Te. All historical and cultural ties with China Proper were rigidly cut off. The youth were taught to think of Manchuria as a distinct geographical and cultural unit inhabited by a new race. A highly attenuated form of Confucianism, that went under the rubric of the "Kingly Way," was inculcated into the students for political as well as moral reasons. One of the principal organizations for promoting this new nationalism was the government-supported, but Japanese army-controlled, Concordia Society. Its purpose was to "ease the execution of the government's plans . . ." by working among and close to the people in order to ". . . complete the structure of the nation and mould the minds of the people."

As late as 1940 the multifarious activities of the Japanese designed to unify the new state through the creation of a synthetic Manchurian nationalism had apparently met with little success. Repeated outbreaks and uprisings indicated that even after nine years of military occupation the Japanese army had not succeeded in "pacifying" the people. A great majority of the Chinese in Manchuria were immigrants and still looked back to, and maintained when possible, contacts with their ancestral homes in China Proper. The struggle of the Chinese south of the Great Wall against Japan since 1937 further served to keep alive a desire to become politically reunited with the land where their ancestors dwelt.

China

The historical, political and social factors delaying China's emergence as a strong modernized state in contrast with developments in Japan have been outlined above.[2] Equally important in explaining this retarded rate of modernization was the slow growth and spread of the spirit of modern patriotic nationalism. The well-nigh insuperable obstacles to the development of an individualistic sense of patriotic loyalty to the concept of China as a national state, rather than as a universal empire, accompanied by a feeling of responsibility for protecting its sovereign rights

---

[2] For political developments under the republic see pp. 495-496.

and independence in a world of warring national states, were threefold. The first obstacle was the traditional subordination of the individual to the highly developed family system which demanded his prior loyalty and in which he found his status and security. Second, there was the adherence to the universalistic aspects of humanistic Confucianism, which caused the thinking and beliefs of the Chinese to transcend racial and geographical barriers and at the same time bolstered up the family system by its emphasis upon filial piety and ancestor worship. Finally, there was the persistence into the present century of highly localized economic and political interests which limited the horizons of most to the village and the province.

In its origins in the late nineteenth century and until the third decade of the twentieth century, the nationalist movement was essentially negative in character, being at one and the same time anti-foreign and anti-Manchu. The early leaders of the movement heaped upon the heads of the alien Manchus the blame for all the ills which beset their country as a result of European expansion. They set themselves, first, therefore, to the task of overthrowing the Manchus, and, under the leadership of Sun Yat-sen, of replacing the empire by a republic.

That first objective was nominally achieved in 1912 when the dynasty was overthrown. The failure, in the years which followed, to establish a strong national government which could recover from the Europeans and the Japanese its lost sovereign rights led to the realization upon the part of a more modernized group of Western-educated intellectuals that the emergence of a modern state in China was contingent upon a reinterpretation of the cultural, historical and literary heritage of the nation. To achieve this there came about in 1917 a movement to which its leaders, borrowing from Western history, gave the name "renaissance." A parallel movement, as we have seen, occurred in Japan nearly two centuries earlier. Its belated appearance in China goes far to explain the differing rates of modernization in the two countries. The leaders of the Chinese renaissance from the outset advocated the overthrow of Confucianism and the old family system to which it gave support. The way would then be cleared, they believed, for the rise of modern individualism. Individualism would in turn provide fertile soil for the growth of loyalties which, transcending family obligations, would center in a devotion to and a sense of security in the national state. Above all, they sought to implant the seeds of this modern individualism and its concomitant nationalism among the masses of the people, primarily through the developing modern system of education, as the only sure guarantee that the forces of "feudal" and bureaucratic reaction, sectionalism and provincialism would be overthrown.

One of the first phases of this renaissance to develop and bear fruit was that known as the "literary revolution" launched in 1917 by Hu Shih and Ch'en Tu-hsiu, two professors at the University of Peking. It aimed at the substitution for the traditional classic literary style known as *wen-li,* the writing and reading of which required years of study of the Confucian classics and other old literary masterpieces, a written form of the vernacular language known as *pai-hua.* The new medium of written expression, they contended, would enable the students more quickly to learn to read and write in a curriculum that emphasized modern subjects such as science, world history, politics, government, law and Western literature rather than the classics. It would hasten the spread of education and awaken the people to an awareness of China's dangerous international position and of the pressing internal problems confronting the nation. The movement met with surprisingly little opposition and within three years the vernacular language was being taught in the primary schools, while a large and rapidly growing number of books and magazines were appearing written in a *pai-hua,* which in the past had been confined only to Confucianist-despised novels and dramas.

Another phase of the renaissance known as the movement to "Reorganize the National Heritage" embraced an effort on the part of a large group of modern-trained historians, philosophers and archeologists to reinterpret, critically and comparatively, the whole of Chinese history, culture and philosophy as a necessary prelude to an effectual modernization of the thought life of the people. Traditional views of China's past were ruthlessly attacked, its alleged early chronology overthrown, its Golden Age dispelled; its mythical heroes were indiscriminatingly hanged and quartered; ancient schools of thought neglected for centuries were revived and extolled as being more in accordance with the logical, scientific and legalistic thought of the modern age than was Confucianism. As the old traditions and history were saturated with

Confucian thought and its moralistic emphasis, this phase of the renaissance constituted an indirect attack on Confucianism and the general social and governmental system which it had fostered.

The opposition to Confucianism as the embodiment of the old order by the more modernized of China's nationalist leaders presents something of a paradox. Usually nationalist movements cherish mythical heroes, and traditionally recount exploits of an uncritically viewed past. In Japan modern critical historians dare not question the belief that the emperor is the direct descendant of the Sun-Goddess or materially revise the ancient false chronology. It is not surprising to find, therefore, that the nationalist government was to reverse the former trend and order that respects be paid to Confucius on his anniversary, which has become once again a national holiday, or officially demand that the shadowy Huang-ti or Yellow Emperor continue to be pictured in textbooks as the recognized founder of the Chinese people.

The answer to the question as to when China will emerge from its present "semicolonial" status is to be found in large measure in an examination of the degree to which the spirit of modern nationalism has penetrated all classes of Chinese society. This much we may state, that by 1940 it animated a majority of the intellectuals and the students, the more modern elements among the bureaucracy under the nationalist government and important segments of the modern mercantile, industrial and financial communities whose interests were nation-wide in scope. However, it had affected significantly only that section of the working class resident in the larger urban centers where modern industry was still in the early stages of development, and had touched but a small fraction of the three hundred and fifty million peasants. The striking progress made by the nationalist government during the decade from 1927 to the outbreak of the war with Japan toward the achievement of political and economic unity on a national scale caused the nationalist movement to reach new heights of strength and intensity.[3]

Yet it should be borne in mind that less than one-fourth of the people were literate. The realization of the goal set by the nationalist leaders of building a modernized independent state was

---

[3] On political and economic developments after 1927 see p. 497.

inherently restricted by the degree to which the mass of the illiterate people could be educated and transformed into ardent, loyal as well as effective nationalistic citizens. To hasten this process the nationalist government introduced as required reading and study Sun Yat-sen's "Three Principles of the People," wherein he set forth his program for the rejuvenation and unification of China, into the curriculum of its expanding educational system. In the degree to which that system expands will China emerge as a unified, sovereign state. The Chinese still need peace and time in which to mature their nationalist movement.

Mongolia and Tibet

In theory the newly established Chinese republic accorded the inhabitants of the former empire's dependencies, Mongolia and Tibet, racial and political equality. This was symbolized in the adoption of the five-barred flag by the republic, each bar of color representing one of the five "races," Chinese, Manchus, Mongols, Tibetans and Mohammedans (in reality a religious rather than a distinct racial or territorial grouping) living in harmony and equality together. In practise, however, the successive governments set up under the republic, and more often local authorities who dealt with these areas with little supervision by the central government, pursued a policy that tended to assimilate these peoples and their lands. Pressure from Great Britain, Russia, and in recent years, Japan, upon these areas was a factor leading to the adoption of this policy of assimilation.

It is not surprising, therefore, to find that modern political nationalism had found expression among more modernized Mongolian and to a lesser extent Tibetan leaders. In 1912 and 1913 Mongolian and Tibetan leaders proclaimed their independence of China. In the years which followed they were unable to make good that declaration. Both Russia and Great Britain in their respective spheres of influence in Outer Mongolia and Outer Tibet continued to recognize these areas as autonomous parts of the Chinese republic. In Inner Mongolia and Inner Tibet the Chinese authorities under combined economic, military and political measures pressed forward with their assimilation policy, which aimed at transforming these regions into integral administrative parts of the republic.

The Mongols and Tibetans possessed those basic ingredients necessary for the emergence of the traditional, cultural type of nationalism. Each was a fairly homogeneous racial unit occupying for centuries a fairly well-defined geographical area. Upon this basis was built a differentiated culture, possessing its own language, customs and literary heritage. Furthermore, the peoples in each retained memories of past military strength and political independence. The Mongols could look back, for example, to the great Mongol empire created by Khublai Khan in the thirteenth century.

The failure of the more modernized leaders to transform this sentimental and cultural unity into a hard, intense political nationalism was attributable to a complex series of developments which can only be briefly hinted at here. In the first place, the remoteness of the two regions delayed the penetration of modern ideas, education, means of communication, the development of modern industry and the building up of a modern army capable of meeting the modernized armies of China, Great Britain, Russia or Japan. The conservative lamas and princes of Inner Mongolia instead of taking the lead, as did the ex-Samurai of Japan, in instituting a social and economic transformation of their territories, pursued a policy of compromise with the expanding exploitative forces emanating from China and lately from Japan, hoping, by playing one off against the other, to maintain their traditional privileged rôles. To bolster up their position they made an appeal to a conservative, traditional type of nationalism. The younger leaders, despairing of bringing about a social and economic revolution as a necessary prelude to the emergence of a strong unified state, in many cases left the region for Outer Mongolia. There they contributed to the building up of a revolutionized social, economic and political state under the influence of the Soviets. The development of a Greater Mongolia movement to unite the Mongols in a struggle against the reactionary lamas and priests within and the forces of imperialism from without awaits the future.

In Tibet the traditional leadership, under the influence of Great Britain since 1912, was more receptive to modern ideas than the reactionary leaders of Inner Mongolia. Under the dominant priests a slow modernization of the country was taking place. Forces were at work seeking to restore the traditional frontiers of the country in those sections of Inner Tibet which fell under dominant Chinese influence and control. One outstanding authority on Tibet has written as follows with regard to the outlook of the modern Tibetan: "The Tibetan of these days values freedom and desires emphatically to live his own life. . . . But there is one thing that he values even more highly than he values the territorial independence of his country, and that is his religion. He does not wish his country to be a powerful nation; in fact, he would be opposed to such a contingency. For deep down in the Tibetan mind is the idea that religion and worldly power are incompatible with each other. . . . [They do not wish] to utilize any foreign agency in order to 'develop' Tibet. . . . They know that the foreigner will exploit the resources of their country, thinking mainly of his own personal gain. . . . Tibet, indeed, wishes to develop, but to do so on its own lines and at its own pace. Above all, it wishes to live its own life, and preserve its own religion." [4]

While the nationalist movement in Tibet cannot be said to be a dynamic force, yet it is firmly rooted in a cultural and historically conditioned background. Moreover, among the more alert lamaist leaders it has found self-conscious expression in the political realm.

Indo-China

In Indo-China the French from the outset met with opposition to their rule as did the Japanese in Korea. Like the Koreans, the peoples inhabiting Annam, Tongkin and Cochin China had long been vassals of the Chinese Empire and under strong Chinese cultural, legal, literary and administrative influences. Nevertheless the Chinese dynasties had been wont to allow vassal kingdoms almost complete autonomous powers, with the result that they possessed, when the French came, all the elements essential to the existence of the traditional, cultural type of national consciousness. When the French sought through their assimilation policy to replace the loose type of relationship exercised by the Chinese by one which substituted French rule for the traditional

---

[4] Bell, Sir Charles, "Tibet and Its Neighbors," *Pacific Affairs*, Dec., 1937, pp. 432-33.

forms of control, they met with increasing opposition. When young modern, educated Annamese began to become acquainted with Western political theories and concepts of state sovereignty, there was introduced into Annam a modern, political nationalist movement about 1900 that has steadily grown in strength and potential significance. As elsewhere in Asia, the Japanese victory over Russia in 1905 gave the leaders of the new movement hope and inspiration. Students went to Japan to study and to learn the secrets of Japan's successful rise to the status of a world power. They returned to organize secret societies to agitate for the provision of more educational facilities, the opening up of more positions to Annamite intellectuals in the government and the "adoption of a decent manner toward the natives as a whole," as one Annamite patriot put it. The extremists in the national movement looked beyond autonomy under French overlordship to ultimate independence.

The first World War and the ideas of self-determination for all peoples to which it gave rise, further stimulated the movement. Communist influence in the form of the Comintern's policy of fostering nationalism among Asiatic workers and peasants made itself felt after 1924. A communist party was formed which was as much if not more nationalist in character and objectives than anticapitalist. The height of the communist movement was reached on February 9, 1930, when in a rebellion at Yen Bay two companies of Tongkinese troops killed six of their officers. Uprisings involving loss of life continued into 1931 in every part of the Indo-Chinese Union. The movement was ruthlessly driven underground by the French in the years which followed.

The nationalist movement as a whole was an important factor in leading the French to abandon their assimilation policy for the more liberal policy of association. It also led to the expansion of an educational system whose curriculum was based upon Annamite cultural, linguistic and literary heritage. More positions in the civil service were made available to the native intellectuals under its stimulus, while more representation in the formulation of government policies was provided through the organization of various advisory councils, chambers of commerce and agriculture and the participation by natives in municipal governments. Since the outbreak of the European war in 1939 the French, to assure Annamite loyalty, further liberalized the administration to provide more places on the various councils and assemblies for natives and made all positions on the grand economic council elective, though its powers were not increased. The future status of Indo-China and the fate of the nationalist movement was, in 1941, as much, if not more, dependent upon developments in world politics growing out of the European war as it was upon internal developments.

Malaya

The British in Malaya were at no time before 1941 confronted with a unified nationalist movement. As a large percentage of the population was made up of Chinese and Indian immigrants or their descendants and as they differed markedly racially, religiously and culturally from the native Malays, the prospect for the development of such a movement seemed remote. Among the Malays themselves there was no appreciable development of a racial and political consciousness. Their common Mohammedanism remained a negative potentiality as a basis for such a movement. The result was that the British were not forced to take steps leading to an autonomous status. They had difficulty, however, in controlling the more racially, culturally, and in recent years, politically conscious Chinese who maintained sentimental and economic connections with the homeland. Their ardent support of the Chinese nationalist cause, which in recent years led to boycotts of Japanese goods, was an increasing cause of concern and embarrassment to Britishers bent on maintaining good relations with Japan. Measures were taken to control and in some degree suppress political activities of the Chinese and, by required registration, to keep a careful watch over the schools which they had established whose curriculum was modeled upon that of the educational system of China.

Thailand (Siam)

When in June, 1939, Bangkok announced that henceforth the kingdom of the White Elephant would be called Thailand instead of Siam, there was officially born into the world a new and potentially disturbing irredentist movement. Having escaped only twelve years before from the restraints placed upon its adminis-

trative integrity by the Western nations, the nationalistic leaders
of the country were ready to revive the age-old dream of recovering dominion over all the Thai peoples scattered under the flags
of China, France and Great Britain. The war which broke out in
Europe in September, 1939, was to give them an early opportunity
to try to fulfill that dream. In September, 1940, taking advantage
of France's defeat and Japan's demands upon Indo-China for
military and air bases, Thailand put forward its claims to territory seized by France in the nineteenth century and succeeded
in recovering a portion of it, as we have seen.[5]

The emergence of this aggressive, politically self-conscious,
nationalist spirit dates back immediately to the internal revolution
of 1932. In that year a middle-class group of civil and military
leaders, aided by a self-styled People's Party, took control in Bangkok and forced the king to grant a constitution providing for a
senate and eventual universal manhood suffrage. It was this new
middle-class leadership which galvanized the latent though vague
racial and cultural consciousness and patriotism of the Thais into
an aggressive economic and political nationalism.

This new nationalism aimed not alone at an external irredenta
but an internal irredenta as well. When the revolutionary leaders
came to power they found 95 per cent of the country's business
in the hands of foreigners. Rice production, Thailand's principal
agrarian crop, was under Chinese control, as was the fishing in
Siamese waters. The foreign debt was held by Britishers.
The valuable tin mines, which were producing 9 per cent
of the world's tin, were in British and Chinese hands, as were
the other major export commodities of teak and rubber. The
Chinese controlled a large share of the retail business of the
country.

In the face of this situation the new regime launched a twofold program of transferring the chief export industries and
more of the retail business to Thai hands and of establishing a
more self-sufficient economy by reducing the excessive amount
of land devoted to rice cultivation for export markets. The large
number of Chinese in the country were the first to feel the effects
of this new economic nationalism. Innumerable regulations and
taxes were designed to restrict their entrance into the country and

---

[5] See p. 531.

to hamper the business activities of those already there. Many prominent and wealthy Chinese were forced to leave the country. The schools for those that remained were closed, their newspapers suppressed, and even the use of Chinese characters on shop signs was forbidden.[6]

Netherlands East Indies

The Malays inhabiting the Netherlands East Indies were more racially, culturally and of late politically conscious, particularly those on the island of Java, than those under British rule on the Malay Peninsula. Nevertheless, the modern nationalist movement that emerged under the leadership of modern trained intellectuals had not by 1940 effectively overcome the particularism of the separate islands nor of the traditional communities within them. The movement was further weakened by the absence of a unified leadership. While having its roots in a common racial, cultural and religious (Mohammedanism) heritage, its leaders sought to apply different measures to attain their ultimate goal, depending upon whether they represented traditional hereditary rulers; the modernized conservatives, who aimed at increased participation in the government on the part of the Malays and gradual development toward autonomy; or the more radical elements who, falling under communist influence in the twenties, sought to give a class-conscious, economic basis to the movement. It has been, furthermore, distracted by the weak Pan-Asiatic movement fostered predominantly by Japanese interests, a Pan-Malay movement and a Pan-Islamic movement. These movements, however, attained little vitality, while the communistic elements were effectively suppressed or driven underground by the Netherlanders. The more moderate elements, willing to co-operate with the Dutch, were encouraged by the gradual opening up of more and higher positions in the Malayan civil service to native intellectuals and the democratic trend evidenced in the creation of a hierarchical series of advisory and representative legislative bodies culminating in the Volksraad.

[6] See Thompson, Virginia, "Thailand Irredenta—Internal and External," *Far Eastern Survey*, Oct. 23, 1940, pp. 243-250.

The Philippines

The Filipino independence movement dates back to the 1870's. It had its spiritual and intellectual origins in the writings of the martyred patriot, D. José Rizal, who was executed by the Spanish authorities in 1896. Organized fighting broke out in the latter year under the leadership of Emilio Aguinaldo. The movement was temporarily suppressed in the following year when Aguinaldo and other leaders were exiled. Upon the outbreak of the Spanish-American War, Admiral George Dewey brought Aguinaldo back to the islands and aided him in launching new attacks on the Spaniards. The result was that when the decision was finally reached in Washington to retain all the archipelago, the American government was confronted with the task of suppressing the Filipino forces under his leadership. The Senate passed a resolution upon ratification of the peace treaty to the effect that the American government did not plan to annex the islands permanently, but would prepare them for self-government. In the light of this promise no effort was made to suppress the Filipino nationalist, independence movement. It continued to grow through the years, its leaders finding their way into the highest positions accorded Filipinos in the administration, while in response to their demands they were granted increasing responsibility in the conduct of the government from time to time. Finally, in 1934, as stated previously, the Independence Act was passed which promised the Filipinos their independence in 1946.

Strong and developed as was the Filipino nationalist movement and near as it was to achievement of its goal of political independence, yet many doubts arose in the minds of the Filipino leaders themselves as to whether, after they had passed beyond the protection of the United States, they would be able to maintain their independence in the face of Japan's southward expansion. Many Filipino economic and a few political leaders advocated some form of dominion status under the United States flag. Balked in their efforts to have the independence issue re-examined both in the islands and in the United States and alarmed at the greater freedom of action given Japan as a result of German successes in the first year of the European (1939-1940) war, some of these leaders advanced the idea of a Malayan Confederacy which would bring all the Malay peoples into some kind

of federation under the combined protection of Great Britain
and the United States. By linking their fate with that of other
members of the Malay race in the Netherlands East Indies and
in British Malaya they hoped to assure the continued protection
of the American and British navies. Capitalizing upon American
needs for the rubber and tin produced in the other Malay
areas, they hoped to induce the United States to participate in the
creation of this protected Malay Confederacy.

Nationalist Movements and the Second World War

In the light of this survey of modern nationalist movements
among the peoples in the Far East, which arose as a reaction
to European and later Japanese expansion, it is apparent that
modern nationalism has been one of the most potent forces
molding internal developments in far eastern countries and con-
ditioning the course of their relations with each other and with
the Western nations. In comparison with them other movements
such as Pan-Asiaticism, or Pan-Buddhism, fostered largely by
Japan for its own political ends, or communism, unless it subordinated its ultimate social and economic objectives to the ends
of political nationalism, have been weak.

Led for the most part by modernized intellectuals, these movements have sought to unify and to modernize the various countries
of the Far East. Nearly everywhere they were winning a successful struggle against sectionalism and provincialism as well as
against conservative aristocracies and reactionary bureaucracies.
Yet the greater number of them, representing a majority of the
population of the Far East, had not yet overcome the forces
of imperialism and the various forms of colonial subservience
that imperialism had fastened upon them. Only Japan and Thailand, among them, were completely independent countries in
1940, while the Philippines were scheduled to attain that status by
1946. The Chinese since 1937 had been waging a major war for
national liberation against Japan. Regardless of the outcome of
that conflict the special position held by Europeans in the country
since the nineteenth century seemed doomed. However, if Japan
succeeded in establishing its hegemony over the northern and
coastal provinces, China would fall under a more severe form of
external control derogatory of its national sovereignty than ever

before in modern times. The French, the British, the Dutch and the Japanese had never at any time promised their colonial subjects independence or even an autonomous status, though they had been granting them an increasing share in local government in the decades prior to 1940.

Developments arising out of the first year (1939-1940) of the European war by no means caused it to appear that the day when political nationalism would triumph in the Far East had been brought within view. While evidence was forthcoming in the first year of the war that the European colonial powers, under stress of war, would accord greater concessions to the demands of colonial nationalists to assure their loyal support, the conclusion of the present conflict is likely to see developments pursuing one of three main trends, no one of which assures political independence for the colonies. Either the pre-war status quo will be maintained, or there will be a redistribution of colonies in the Far East, or all European and American political and economic controls will be replaced by Japanese controls under an "Asia for Asiatics" movement. In any event, the goal of complete political independence will not be attained by all far eastern peoples in any predictable future. Should Japan be successful in setting up its version of an Asiatic Monroe Doctrine, it is apparent that it would mold political and economic developments to serve its own ends. Culturally, it would adopt measures designed to warp or control nationalist movements as it does in regions now under its control. It could scarcely hope to assimilate the peoples of the Far East with their diverse racial, cultural and religious backgrounds. Its own failure to assimilate the Koreans would appear to be evidence of that truism.

Consequently a traditional, cultural type of nationalism will probably continue to persist in the Far East regardless of post-war developments. And where it exists it will struggle to attain its political fulfillment and become, therefore, a constant source of unrest, agitation and periodic uprisings. Unrest within and continued competitive struggles among the great powers for hegemonic control over the subject peoples of the Far East are likely to determine the unhappy fate of the peoples in that part of the world, regardless of who is victor and who vanquished in the present European conflict. This is apt to be so unless perchance a stable economic and political world order will be established which accords to all advanced peoples racial, cultural, and religious equality and liberty and at least the promise of political independence.

THE EFFECT UPON INTERNATIONAL RELATIONS OF EUROPEAN EXPANSION INTO THE FAR EAST

At the outset of this section assaying the effects upon international relations of European expansion into the Far East since the mid-nineteenth century, it needs to be emphatically stated that these effects were constant and at times determinative upon the course of European diplomatic history. The term "Far East," born in a period of slower communications and more sporadic contacts, may give rise to the erroneous use of adjectives such as "tangential" or "peripheral," as descriptive of far eastern developments in relation to their influence on international relations.

It is true that developments in the Near East and in Africa more frequently disturbed the shaky foundations of the European "balance of power," bringing the nations repeatedly to the brink of war, than those in the Far East. Yet in the years from 1890 to 1904, when the European nations were making their decisions as to who was to be friend and who was to be foe in the apparently approaching holocaust, the animosities and fears arising out of their struggles for concessions in China and special positions in the whole Far East were to play a decisive rôle in determining the pre-war lineup. By the end of the nineteenth century the chief threat to England's position in India and in the Far East was an expanding Russia. Germany's policy of egging Russia on to further adventures in the Far East, so as to have a freer hand to pursue its own designs in the Near East, was one of the decisive developments which killed all hope of any kind of Anglo-German understanding, and led England to abandon a policy of "splendid isolation" by entering into an alliance with Japan in 1902. Then there followed the signing of the *Entente Cordiale* with France in 1904 and, when England reached a general understanding with Russia in 1907, the lineup of the powers for the first World War was consummated.

By 1860, as we have seen, Russia had completed its expansion eastward to the Pacific and had acquired a port and a potential

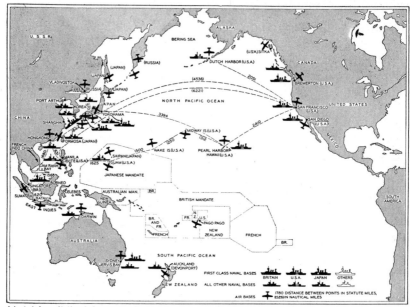

Adapted from National Geographic Society Map

MAP OF PACIFIC OCEAN INDICATING DIFFERENT MANDATED ZONES,
CHIEF NAVAL AND AIR BASES, ISLANDS, AND COUNTRIES, AS WELL AS
DISTANCES BETWEEN MAIN POINTS

Pacific naval base at Vladivostok. Not satisfied with the acquisition of these vast domains, the czar and his agents began in the
1880's to interest themselves in opening and exploiting Korea
and Manchuria. Then, too, they were in search of a warm-water
port further south, as Vladivostok is icebound three to four
months of the year. Both England and Japan watched these
movements with increasing uneasiness and met every Russian
advance with as effective a countermove as they could muster.
Thus Japan in the treaty of peace signed at Shimonoseki in March,
1895, after its victory over China, not only hoped that it had
established its supremacy over a Korea which China then recognized as independent, but had counteracted Russia's southward
expansion by occupying the tip of the Liaotung Peninsula in
Manchuria, thereby keeping Russia out of its strategic warm-
water ports. However, in the following month, there occurred
the famous tripartite intervention when Germany joined with

Russia's ally, France, in supporting Russian ambitions by order-
ing Japan to return the peninsula to China.

In the face of such overwhelming odds there was nothing for
Japan to do but to retrocede the area to China as gracefully as
possible. In the period of the scramble for concessions which
followed the Sino-Japanese War, Russia extracted from China
a lease over the peninsula in 1898. At Port Arthur, on the tip of
the peninsula, the Russians established a naval base. Not satisfied with that, they continued to interfere in Korean affairs, to the
growing alarm and resentment of Japan. In the years which
followed, efforts made by Japan to settle by negotiation their
respective spheres of influence in Korea failed. The Japanese were
finally to realize that they must some day fight Russia and began
to prepare themselves for such a conflict. Fearing that France
and Germany might again intervene, the Japanese like the British
found their position of "splendid isolation" growing increasingly
more uncomfortable, and began to cast about for an ally. Leaders
in both countries as early as 1898, sensing the mutuality of their
interests in the Far East, began to talk of an alliance.

In England, however, dominant government leaders still hoped
to reach an understanding with Germany which would lead that
country not only to abandon its policy of encouraging Russia in
the Far East, but even to restrain the Russians. Among the series
of agreements growing out of the period of the scramble for
concessions in China, by which the outbreak of a general European conflagration was narrowly avoided, was one signed between
England and Germany in 1900 providing for recognition of their
respective spheres of influence in China. When in 1901 England
appealed to Germany under the terms of this agreement for help
in restraining Russian advances in Manchuria, Germany declined.
This development contributed, together with issues arising out
of the Boer War and an expanding German naval program, to
the growing estrangement between the two countries. From then
on, the British government gave up all hope of securing German
assistance in thwarting Russia and turned reluctantly to Japan
as a second best ally.

The two nations rapidly reached an agreement. The first Anglo-
Japanese Alliance was signed in January, 1902. In 1904 war
broke out between Japan and Russia. The Treaty of Portsmouth
of September, 1905, which brought it to an end, left Japan

supreme in Korea and South Manchuria. Russian encroachment upon China was brought within bounds and its bid for sea power in the Pacific frustrated. Henceforth, Japan was to dominate the waters of Eastern Asia. Rebuffed in the Far East, Russian diplomacy again centered upon developments in the Balkans and the Near East. German advances and ambitions in both those areas had reached proportions which were alarming to both Russia and England. After reconciling their differences in Central Asia and the Middle East, they entered upon a formal understanding in 1907 which was at least indirectly aimed at Germany. In the same year czarist Russia abandoned all thought of a war of revenge upon Japan when the two countries signed an agreement recognizing their respective positions and interests in northeast Asia. The lineup of the Allies who entered into a war against Germany seven years later came about, therefore, as a direct result of the reconciliation of their erstwhile conflicting expansionist aims.

The World War of 1914-1918 had marked repercussions upon the respective positions and interests of the powers in the Far East. Germany's financial, commercial and missionary interests were seriously impaired and its special position in China and holdings in the Pacific eradicated. The special position which czarist Russia held in China Proper was voluntarily surrendered by the Soviet Union in 1924. France and England, tired by the war, were interested only in maintaining peace and the status quo in the Far East as elsewhere. Japan and the United States inherited the rôle of leadership in far eastern developments which Europe had held up to 1914 and lost in the war which followed. From the rôle of aggressors England and France fell to a position of passive defenders of the status quo in China and in their far eastern colonies.

It was in the Far East that the post-war lassitude of France and England, who were furthermore suffering from the effects of the depression which began in 1929, found its first expression in the negative policy of appeasement. When in September, 1931, Japan renewed its policy of continental expansion, both France and England, in failing to take a strong lead in protesting Japan's action, made it clear that as far as they were concerned Japan could have a free hand in Manchuria and even in North China. The Manchurian "incident" came before the League of Nations and was the greatest crisis in international affairs with which it had been confronted. The failure of France and England to endorse the use of sanctions, either of an economic or military character, resulted in the first serious breach of the post-war peace structure. Through this breach marched Italy into Ethiopia and Germany into the Rhineland. The failure to uphold the principles of the League of Nations Covenant and the Washington Treaties in the Far East had paved the way for the disastrous policy of appeasement in Europe which preceded the outbreak of war in September, 1939.

In the lineup of the nations in the European war in 1939, as in the case of the first World War, factors arising out of their interests in and relationships to each other in the Far East played their contributory rôle. The most significant change in that lineup was the decision of the U.S.S.R. to remain neutral. This considerably shifted the balance of power in Germany's favor at the outset of the war, as it was then relieved of the necessity of fighting upon two fronts. England's failure to win the support of the U.S.S.R. was its first major defeat on the diplomatic front in the second World War. In the years and months immediately preceding the outbreak of the conflict the Soviet Union had been one of the staunchest supporters of the system of collective security set up under the League. Germany's rearmament program was as much of a threat to its security as it was to that of England and France. Despite the sharp ideological and diplomatic issues that separated the two countries, it seems logical to assume that Great Britain and the U.S.S.R. should have readily reached an understanding which would have enabled them to present Germany with a united front as in 1914.

The reasons for England's failure to secure Russian support under these circumstances were substantially twofold in origin. In the first place, the Conservatives, who were in power in the years before the war, were unable to swallow their distaste for and fear of Communist ideology and domestic policies. Secondly, ostensible Soviet opposition to imperialism, and for a time active support through the Comintern of communist-nationalist movements in Asiatic colonial areas and in China, caused them to appear in the eyes of British imperialists as a more serious threat to the empire than a resurgent Germany which might be appeased by some territorial adjustments in Europe and the return of some of its former colonies. In the Far East they tended to support Japan's policy of controlling North China and Manchuria as a safeguard against the communization of the whole Far East. With a capitalistic, imperialistic Japan as well as with a Nazi Germany they believed they could compromise their differences and protect their interests.

England's distrust and fear of Soviet expansion in Asia as a threat to its position there is an old story, as we have seen. The decision to abandon "splendid isolation" at the end of the last century by seeking an ally to thwart Russia arose out of this traditional distrust. When Germany gave sufficient evidence that its policy was designed to keep Russia busy in the Far East so that it might have a freer hand in the Balkans and the Near East, England turned to Japan and entered into an alliance with that power in 1902. Japan's defeat of Russia three years later, resulting in the sinking of the Russian Baltic as well as far eastern fleets, destroyed in the minds of the British much of the old fear of the Russian Bear. Meanwhile an expanding Germany gave England and Japan cause for alarm, and by 1907 we find them cooperating diplomatically after reaching an understanding with respect to their positions in Asia. In the same year Russia and Japan delimited their respective spheres of influence in the Far East and Russia was freed to turn its major attention to the German threat in Europe.

Tory diplomats in the past few years, their vision distorted by their anticommunist prejudices, seemed to have lost sight of the fact that Russian foreign policy, perhaps more than that of any other European power except England itself, was dictated by the fact that more than half of its vast domain lies in Asia. Its far eastern possessions presented serious problems of defense in the face of an expanding Japan. Toward the end of the first World War Japan had occupied eastern Siberia as far west as Lake Baikal and only finally and reluctantly withdrew under the combined pressure of England and the United States at the Washington Conference in 1922. The dream of the conquest of the Siberian Pacific littoral continued to haunt the minds of Japan's strategists and industrialists in the years which followed. England, by its failure to stop Japan in its occupation of Manchuria and later invasion in China Proper, contributed acutely to the insecurity of the Soviets. Confronted in Europe and in Asia by two traditional enemies, who were piling up armaments at an alarming rate, the diplomacy of the Soviets necessitated the formulation of a policy which would avoid their being drawn into a simultaneous conflict on both fronts. Had the British been willing to restrain Japan in the Far East and thereby strengthened the Soviets' hand there, the way would have been opened to closer collaboration in meeting the German threat in Europe. As a result, England in 1939 might again as in 1914 have had Russia, even a communist Russia, as an ally.

In view of the fact that the United States and Japan had succeeded to the positions of leadership in far eastern developments formerly held by England and France before the first World War, it would be well briefly to consider their respective policies emerging out of their conflicting positions in the region. Not only have far eastern developments conditioned the course of European international relations, but they have had, as well, far-reaching effects upon American naval and diplomatic policies. While the broad principles which underlay the far eastern policy of the United States were the same as those which guided that policy in other parts of the world, the methods employed to apply them differed markedly. In the Far East these methods were positive in character, involving the United States directly in extra-American affairs with a persistence unparalleled in its relations with other parts of the non-American world.

The primary reason for this has been the striking contrasts in the political and naval situations which confronted the nation across the Atlantic and across the Pacific. Behind the protective shield of British seapower this country has been content to leave European affairs to Europeans, except when that wall was threatened as during the first World War or as during the European war that broke out in September, 1939, or again when the Monroe Doctrine was not fully or adequately respected by European nations. Throughout the nineteenth century Anglo-American relations gradually improved until by the end of that century a firm foundation of understanding and co-operation had been laid which not only covered the Atlantic but was extended also into the Pacific. The formulation and enunciation of the Open Door policy by John Hay in 1899 and 1900 had the close co-operation and support of the British. The decision to retain the Philippines after the Spanish-American War was done with the full approval and support of the British, who much preferred their occupation by a friendly America than by a threatening Germany, into whose hands it was believed they would have fallen had they been left to Spain.

It was the absence of a developed balance of power in eastern Asia, enforced by a dominant naval power up to the time of the first World War, which provided the occasion for and in degree necessitated this direct and active participation by the United States in far eastern affairs. The cornerstone of that policy has been the Open Door for commercial and financial interests in the development and exploitation of the markets and resources of China as well as for missionary interests and the preservation of China's territorial and administrative integrity as the best guarantee that the door would remain open in the future for American enterprises. American efforts to maintain that Open Door were first directed against Russian threats to close it in Manchuria until 1905. After that time Japan was the chief threat to that policy in its aim at establishing its hegemony over all China and recently in the South Pacific. Significantly enough, however, Washington voiced no opposition to Japan's acquisition of Korea, nor to France's seizure of Indo-China nor of England's strengthening of its position in Malaya. Having indulged in a bit of imperialistic adventuring in the seizure of the Philippines, the United States was in no position effectively to oppose the acquisition of territory around the periphery of China or of the islands in the South Pacific. As far as Japan's objectives with respect to Korea were concerned, President Theodore Roosevelt, as early as 1905, entered into a secret "agreed memorandum" with Prime Minister Katsura, which stated that in return for Japan's guarantee of respect for the American position in the Philippines, he would not oppose Japan in Korea. Thus did he seek to protect what he had come to call the American "Achilles heel," for the acquisition of which he had been primarily responsible.

American naval policy after the first World War was designed primarily to support American far eastern policy. Naval construction and strategy were based upon problems arising from the operation of a fleet in the broad expanses of the Pacific against the only potential naval opponent in that vast area— Japan. The Washington Conference of 1921-1922, called at the behest of the American government, was at first to be only a naval disarmament conference. As England, previous to the calling of that conference, had agreed in principle to naval parity with the United States, no political issues arising out of our relations with England or the continent were raised. But it at once became clear that if Japan were to be induced to disarm to a degree and to stabilize its naval program, the whole political situation that had arisen in the Far East during the first World War, when the Japanese expansionists went ahead with their program on the continent, would first have to be taken into consideration. At that conference England abandoned its support of Japan through the Anglo-Japanese Alliance and co-operated with the United States in forcing Japan to disgorge part of its gains on the continent achieved during the war and to accept an inferior naval ratio of three to five. While this ratio left Japan supreme in the waters of eastern Asia, it still left the island empire too weak to threaten seriously the American position in the Philippines or that of the other colonial powers in southeastern Asia in the face of a combined Anglo-American naval action to protect such areas.

Japanese naval and political leaders accepted this limited sphere of dominance in the Far East with reluctance. After 1931 they virtually tore up the naval and political agreements reached at the Washington Conference. The status quo in eastern Asia was again upset and the naval race between the United States and Japan renewed. Since that year a major portion of the American navy has been stationed in the Pacific to watch and, if possible, by lending support to American diplomacy, to check Japan's expansion. The course of events in the first year of the European war of 1939-1940 opened new vistas of empire to Japan. The German occupation of France and the Netherlands and the threat to England seemed to present the Japanese with the opportunity of the century. So at least proclaimed their extreme imperialists. An opportunity to extend Japanese hegemony over the crumbling outposts of British, French and Dutch colonial empires in the Far East had arisen. The signing of a neutrality pact between Tokyo and Moscow on April 13, 1941, served to free Japan of the threat of a Soviet attack from eastern Siberia, thereby strengthening the country for an economic, political, and possibly military drive into southeastern Asia and the Netherlands East Indies. Despite the increasing threat to American security in the Atlantic, to which the possible seizure or partial destruction and dispersion of the British fleet gave rise, no decision had been reached, as late as the spring of 1941, to withdraw a major portion of the American fleet from the Pacific, where it remained as a check to possible moves by Japan to occupy colonial areas in southeastern Asia. What happened rather was that talk of building a two-ocean navy suddenly bore fruit when Congress approved the construction and voted the money for such an enlarged navy in September, 1940.

Whether the United States could, in the face of these developments, continue to pursue its traditional policy in the Far East with any hope of success without resort to force was highly problematical by 1941. The upholding of that policy in the years immediately preceding that year had required ever closer reliance upon the navy and the adoption of gradual steps leading to embargoes on shipment of vital materials, such as oil and scrap iron, to Japan. That such action might lead the nation to war was repeatedly pointed out by prominent leaders.

The 1939 European war had presented America with no less than three main lines of policy with respect to the Far East. Lacking the full support of England and of France in upholding the status quo in the region, the United States might temporarily back down in the face of Japanese aggression, as during the previous war. After the war was over, should England emerge victorious with its fleet intact, it might be possible, as at the Washington Conference, to bring united pressure upon Japan to disgorge its temporary gains.

A second line of action, and the one that was followed throughout the first year of the war, involved a continuation of traditional American policy, enforced by gradually increasing economic pressure upon Japan coupled with continued naval pressure maintained by leaving the navy in the Pacific. Should this prove to be insufficient to stop Japan from moving into the South Pacific, it appeared that it might become necessary, in event the war should drag on in Europe, for the United States to lease bases in Australia and other points in the South Pacific and even to station a portion of the fleet at the Singapore naval base. A third line of action, which seemed to have little likelihood of adoption, advocated immediate and complete withdrawal from the Far East and a retreat to a policy of hemispheric isolation and defense. Japan would then be freer to set up its own version of an Asiatic Monroe

Doctrine though still subject to check possibly, though not probably, by the Soviet Union and ultimately by the victors in the war in Europe.

He would indeed be a bold prophet in these uncertain times to assert which of these three possible alternatives American far eastern policy might follow. They have been set forth not with a view to making a prophecy, but rather to show how intimately related far eastern politics were to developments in all other parts of the world. Since the last part of the nineteenth century, the large stakes which the European nations and the United States held in the region in the way of prestige, of missionary and cultural interests, of investments, of markets, and their dependence upon its essential raw materials such as rubber and tin, antimony and tungsten, have made it inevitable that every major move in war and diplomacy was conditioned by their position in or ambitions with respect to that part of the world.

The Far East has repeatedly been the storm-center of world politics. In the past century England and France have each fought two wars with China, Japan has fought one war and is at present engaged in another struggle with that unhappy country. Japan has also fought a war with Russia. The United States found the theater of its war with Spain extended to the Philippines. More than a center for war itself, the Far East has contributed with the rest of Asia and of Africa to make of all wars *in* Europe in the modern period more than wars *about* Europe. And in so far as this is so, peace in Europe is dependent upon more than a settlement of European political and economic problems. It involves as well a settlement of problems arising out of the political and economic control exercised over colonial peoples and their resources in the Far East as well as in the Middle and Near East and in Africa.

READINGS

Bousquet, G. H. *A French View of the Netherlands Indies,* 1940. Especially good on nationalist movements.

Denlinger, S. and Gary, C. B. *War in the Pacific,* 1936. The strategic aspects of a possible American-Japanese naval war.

Far Eastern Survey. Fortnightly publication of the Institute of Pacific Relations, 129 East 52nd St., New York, N. Y. Invaluable for keeping abreast of current economic developments.

Foreign Policy Reports. Published by the Foreign Policy Association, New York, N. Y. Its periodic reports, some of which relate to economic and political developments in the Far East, are invaluable.

Griswold, A. Whitney. *The Far Eastern Policy of the United States,* 1938. A critical account of that policy since 1898.

Hindmarsh, A. E. *The Basis of Japanese Foreign Policy,* 1936. A sympathetic account of economic motivations.

Holland, W. L., (Editor). *Commodity Control in the Pacific Area,* 1935. A standard work on a pertinent subject.

Holtom, D. C. *The National Faith of Japan,* 1938. An authoritative account of the elevation of Shintoism to the status of a national religion.

Hudson, G. F. *The Far East in World Politics,* 1937. Readable, objective, balanced.

Hu Shih. *The Chinese Renaissance,* 1934. Brief account by one of its leaders.

Langer, W. L. *The Diplomacy of Imperialism, 1890-1902,* 2 vols., 1935. Has valuable chapters on the rôle of the Far East in European diplomacy.

McKenzie, F. A. *Korea's Fight for Freedom,* 1920. A sympathetic account.

Moon, Parker T. *Imperialism and World Politics,* 1926.

Morse, H. B., and MacNair, H. F. *Far Eastern International Relations,* 1931. A standard text.

Norman, E. H. *Japan's Emergence as a Modern State,* 1940. The best analytical and interpretative account.

Peake, Cyrus H. *Nationalism and Education in Modern China,* 1932.

Sun Yat-sen. *San Min Chu I* (The Three Principles of the People). Frank W. Price, Tr., 1927. Sun's program for the modernization and unification of China under a democratic Republic.

Wright, P. G. *Trade and Trade Barriers in the Pacific,* 1935. A statistical analysis of a pertinent problem.

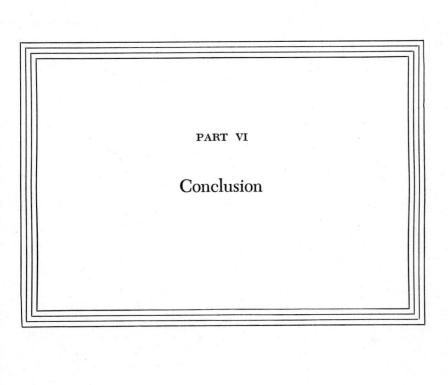

PART VI

Conclusion

CHAPTER TWENTY

An Evaluation of Modern Colonial Expansion Since 1871

A RETROSPECT of modern colonial expansion poses the inevitable query: "Are colonies worth while?" or "Do colonies pay?" and it is significant that a prolific literature has sprung up in recent years that has sought to provide a definitive "Yes" or "No." The answer, however, is not easy to find and any valid reply to the question must be careful to give both an adequate definition of "worth while" or "pay" and an understanding of the historic setting, the political and economic system, in which modern colonialism has functioned. The period 1871-1941 established certain definite standards of values, both in external and internal affairs, against which colonialism must be measured if any accurate estimate of its worth-whileness is to be obtained.

In the first place, the period 1871-1941 constituted an era of economic nationalism, of competitive, international trade, of the balance of power system in international relations. It was a time during which the game of power politics was cleverly and cease-lessly played and, hence, the national states found themselves involved in an unremitting struggle for ascendancy and mastery which demanded that national policies must supply the physical and economic foundations for ultimate victory. Furthermore, these foundations for national sovereignty were no longer confined to Europe, as they had been in the seventeenth and eighteenth centuries, but, because of the achievements of science and technology, had become extended to every part of the world where the forces of Western civilization had been and were being introduced.

Secondly, it must be emphasized that this was a time when, internally, the bourgeois capitalist class was enjoying the apogee of its power, both economic and political. It was the age of industrial and finance capitalism, of big business, and of the increasing participation of government in the promotion of business interests. In order to preserve and perpetuate its power, this class, once staking its ascendancy upon literal, *laissez-faire* economy, had found it essential, with the growth of national rivalry, to return to a neo-mercantilism, a protectionism which strove to create and monopolize its own markets, its own sources of raw materials and, further, to insure these by navalism, militarism and colonialism. In other words, the all-dominating business interests sought assistance from the national state in the ever growing, bitter competition; they demanded that the state employ its improved naval and military power against both the weapons of the native peoples and against other states.

Hence the expression "pay," in regard to colonies, came to possess specific meanings: provision for overpopulation of the home countries, the securing of sources of raw materials and foodstuffs, of opportunity for capital investment and the exercise of careers, as well as of a prosperous trade. At the same time, "pay" also meant the gaining of power, security and prestige for the national state itself in the balance of power system by giving it control over strategically situated overseas territory, naval bases, harbors and safeguards to its lines of communication. These factors all constituted, in the language of the expansionists themselves, the fundamental objectives of imperialism. Consequently, it is in harmony with the prevailing system of world economy during the period and also in the light of these definitions of "worthwhileness" that colonies must be evaluated.

Recent criticism of modern overseas expansion has sought to demonstrate by careful statistical study that colonies did not pay because they signally failed to meet those demands of the colonialists for outlets for overpopulation, for raw materials, for trade and commerce that would have redounded to the wealth and strength of the mother countries. Hence, this criticism must be examined.

THE POPULATION ARGUMENT

It has, indeed, been conclusively and correctly proved that the colonies did not supply "safety valves" for overpopulation in Europe. Concrete figures of various kinds may be cited to illustrate this fact to anyone's satisfaction. For instance, it has been shown that in 1933, there were in all only 4,500,000 whites in all the dependencies, protectorates, colonies and mandated territories put together; [1] that by 1936, the number of Europeans who had gone to Africa to reside permanently was equal only to six ten-thousandths of Europe's total population, and that fewer than four out of every thousand permanent emigrants from Europe had gone to European-controlled parts of Asia. Only about 22,000 Germans left the Fatherland to live in all the German colonies in Africa and the South Seas, during the thirty years of colonial activity from 1884-1914, and more Germans reside today in Yorkville, New York City, than ever made their homes in the German colonies. As for the Italians, there are more of them to be found in New York City within a quarter mile of Cherry Street than ever went to all the Italian colonies combined. Grover Clark, an authority on colonial statistics, wrote in 1936: "More people now live . . . in any one of a dozen medium-sized cities, like Amsterdam, or San Francisco, or Yokohama, than left all of Europe to settle permanently in all the European colonies in the past 50 years." [2]

Reasons for the apparent failure of colonial territories to attract Europeans are various. In the first place, there existed other and more desirable, more remunerative areas inviting those Europeans who wished to improve their condition. As statistics show, these went in large numbers to the Americas, especially to the United States, to Argentina and to Brazil—a steady and ever increasing stream until the first World War, after which it was checked by artificial means. For states in the Americas and Australia passed

---

[1] Moresco, E., *Colonial Questions and Peace*, pp. 96-100; *International Studies Conference*, 1939.

[2] Clark, Grover, *A Place in the Sun*, p. 85.

immigration laws for self-protection, and the totalitarian states have curbed emigration (except of Jews), either by keeping their nationals at home for nationalistic and military reasons, or else, like Italy and Japan, have attempted to send them to their own colonies only, an effort which has not succeeded as yet.

Again, to cite the obverse of the above reasons, primitive, backward parts of the world offer peculiar obstacles to white settlement. The physical difficulties of the habitat, as for example those that exist in tropical and subtropical Africa, loom large with their measure of disease, danger and low-subsistence level. Today also, economic means or resources, the large expenditure of capital in colonial areas, is a requisite for the European settler, for the modern colonizer cannot be the pioneer of past days. Demands for equipment and machinery are too insistent. The need for capital expenditure increases with the undesirability of the location. It is significant, in this respect, that the most extensive experiment in white settlement in colonial areas in recent years has been that of the Jews in Palestine. For the enormous work of settlement would not have been possible without lavish capital expenditure provided by the liberality of world Jewry to fulfill the ideal of a "National Home."

To the question, then, whether colonies during the modern period of expansion have "paid" as "safety valves" for overpopulation at home, the answer must be a decided "No," if based upon the statistics of European settlement in colonial areas and the reasons which explain their low figures. Nevertheless, in the minds of many advocates of colonialism, especially those in the

WHITES IN COLONIAL AND MANDATED AREAS ACCORDING TO
ADMINISTERING POWERS, 1935 *

	AFRICA	ASIA	OCEANIA	TOTAL
Belgium	18,500	....	....	18,500
France	1,361,596	32,705	22,397	1,416,698
Great Britain	48,702	298,907	5,220	352,829
Italy	50,500	10,000	....	60,500
Japan	....	1,996	....	1,996
The Netherlands	....	177,149	....	177,149
Portugal	41,864	3,500	....	45,364
Spain	136,797	....	....	136,797

*Adapted from Kuczynski, R., *Colonial Population*, London, 1937.

so-called Have-Not states, the argument has apparently not lost its force and hence as a psychological factor demands recognition.

As Sources of Raw Materials

Employed as one of the most potent arguments for colonial expansion, the claim that colonies are needed as sources of raw materials has likewise experienced weakening under recent expert analysis. Reference to the introduction to this book [3] will show how, at first glance, the maladjustment of distribution among the European countries of colonial raw materials and food supplies provides one of the most serious elements in the clamor for colonies. Because of this, there has arisen from the Have-Not states an insistent demand for the transfer to them of sovereignty over colonial areas where raw materials will make good or help to make good their own deficiencies.

Yet, as in the case of the population argument, analysis has made clear the following points in regard to colonial raw materials. First, the League of Nations Committee for the study of the problem, has shown that as a matter of fact, colonies produce only a small part of the world's raw material supply, that "the total present production of all commercially important raw materials in colonial territories (excluding dominions and other self-governing territories) is no more than about 3% of world production." It is probable, also, so say the experts, "that a similar calculation for the importance of colonial foodstuff production would yield a scarcely greater percentage of world food production." [4] Generally speaking, it is the noncolonial regions that supply the great quantities of vital commodities needed by the industrial powers. Hence, when the world is at peace, it is not difficult for any country to secure all the materials it may need, under a system of international trade.

In the second place, it is pointed out that a monopoly over colonial supplies of raw materials which does assume an advantage in time of war may be enjoyed only by that country with a navy strong enough to control its sea lanes, in which case it could procure its materials from neutral states, as Great Britain

---

[3] See pp. 20 ff.
[4] Moresco, E., *op. cit.*, p. 128.

was engaged in doing in 1939-41, even in the face of United States neutrality legislation.

Hence, it is maintained, colonies cannot be claimed to be of any great potential aid in the pursuit of economic self-sufficiency, except for a few commodities. The British Commonwealth of Nations is the only overseas empire which can be said to approach self-sufficiency and this is so by virtue of the mineral and agricultural wealth of the dominions and India, rather than that of the rest of the empire. Great Britain with the colonial empire alone is deficient in nonferrous metals, most textiles, petroleum and many essential foodstuffs. France, with her vast colonial empire, lacks basic material of coal, rubber, petrol, cotton. Belgium and the Netherlands, two great colonial powers, are also compelled to purchase abroad most of the materials for their industries. In the years 1930-1934 France took, on the average, 6.2 per cent of her raw materials from her colonies, Britain 7.8 per cent, Belgium only 3.7 per cent from the Congo.

As for foodstuffs, the case is somewhat stronger but not definitive: France, in 1934, derived 63.5 per cent of foodstuffs imports from her colonies, but 35.1 per cent came from Algeria, an integral part of France; in 1933, 90 per cent of the Congo's food exports went to Belgium; Great Britain derived about 8 per cent of foodstuffs from the colonies proper, but 38 per cent from the independent nations of the British Commonwealth. Moreover, countries controlling colonial sources of foodstuffs or raw materials often have preferred to buy elsewhere because of shipping or other costs. For example, very little of the petroleum of the Straits Settlements and Sarawak comes to the United Kingdom, but a considerable proportion of that from Trinidad and Tobadoes. Germany took almost as great a proportion of West African palm kernels as did Great Britain, while Germany and the United States together took as much of the Rhodesian copper as the United Kingdom. Britain took one-fifth of her rubber from countries other than the British colonies in 1934, and the United States is the largest purchaser of rubber from British Malaya and Ceylon. Under the system of international trade prevailing during the period 1870-1941, monopoly over colonial raw materials could be said to possess the advantage claimed for it by those who answer the question *Do colonies pay?* with an unqualified affirmative.

Colonial Trade

Again, the unmodified assertion that colonies pay because of the favorable trade statistics which they present and that, therefore, the possession of a colonial empire creates a profitable commerce bringing a stream of wealth back to the mother country is particularly vulnerable to criticism. It cannot be denied, of course, that colonies do afford real commercial advantages to the mother country: it is easier, for example, to pay for commodities bought from a colony in national currency than from elsewhere in foreign currency; it is easier to sell manufactured goods to a colony than to a foreign country; colonies provide the assurance of a preferential market. But the whole question of the value of trade and its resulting economic advantage to the colonial power is beset with many variables. To mention only the major ones: there is the time element—does trade pay now, has it paid in the past or will it pay in the future, is it actual or potential remuneration that is meant; then, the investment element—does it pay in proportion or relation to the outlay, which is of many kinds, expended upon or invested in the colony, the costs of acquisition, maintenance, protection, the capital risked; and finally, the payee factor must not be forgotten—whom does colonial trade pay a group, a class, the investor or the colonial power as a whole.

No analysis has satisfactorily answered all these questions, doubtless because it is impossible since their elements are so imponderable. Certain, it is, however, that the answers cannot be drawn off a balance sheet of trade statistics. All that can be done by way of solution is to indicate concrete examples and examine them in the light of the variables enumerated above.

In regard to the time element, it may be shown, for instance, that before the first World War, France's colonial trade was extremely profitable; it formed 25 per cent of her total imports and 29 per cent of her total exports; even up to 1931, after the war, the export balance was 990,000,000 francs. Beginning with 1932, however, there occurred a sharp reversal of imperial trade balances, so that in 1934 imports exceeded exports by 310,000,000 francs and in 1936 by 2,089,000,000 francs. Therefore, judged by trade during the depression period, the French colonial empire became an expensive luxury. It may also be shown that even during the period of France's profitable colonial trade, Algeria, a part of France, absorbed one-half of her total export colonial trade; and also that while the French imports from the colonies were cheaper than those obtainable elsewhere, France could still have secured these did she not hold colonies.

Again, the time element in colonial trade values may be illustrated from another angle by the German colonies. It is true that in 1914 the total German colonial trade had risen in value from 71,213,000 M. in 1904 to 263,400,000 M. But of this total, less than one-half, 110,000,000 M., was with the Fatherland and represented only one-half of 1 per cent of the nation's total foreign commerce. Yet, German colonialists argued that Germany had been engaged only thirty years in colonization, that time would bring an increasing return upon the total invested capital in the colonies of 505,000,000 M.; that the German colonial empire was potentially extremely valuable.

As an illustration of the economic value of colonies in relation to costs [5] and investment, the case of French Indo-China may be cited. For, from one point of view, French Indo-China may be said to have paid France. The colony has not only been economically independent in recent decades, but from the time of the first World War to 1930 as much as 17 per cent of the general revenues went to pay for French military expenses. During the first World War, Indo-China sent 50,000 laborers and 50,000 soldiers to France. Of a total of 27,000,000 gold francs contributed to France by its colonies during that war, Indo-China contributed just over half. As a source of supplies it was second only to West Africa. It has been capable of supplying France with large quantities of rice, maize, alcohol, sugar and, in recent years, rubber. Against this apparent recent advantage, however, there must be placed the cost of acquiring and maintaining Indo-China which, although figures are lacking, must have been considerable. For France assumed primary responsibility for military costs as well as for all deficits in the civil budgets of her colonial empire when they occurred and her total colonial charges increased from 127,000,000 francs in 1871 to 2,403,000,000 francs in 1931. As for the economic value of individual investments in Indo-China, it has been estimated that out of seventy Indo-Chinese holdings,

---

[5] Another difficulty lies in the correct estimates of costs in view of changing money values.

thirty-nine, representing capital investment of about 1,500,000,000 francs, have paid no dividends, while the remaining thirty-one, capitalized at 8,500,000,000 francs, have paid an average of 1.87 per cent.[6]

Again, balancing costs against return, from another point of view, it may be claimed that British Malaya, for example, whose modern administrative period dates from 1867 when the administration of the Straits Settlements was transferred from the India office to the colonial office in London, has paid and paid well, given the British Empire as it stood in September, 1939. For the revenue of Malaya is exceptionally high for the size of its population, owing to the world demand for its rubber and tin, which constitute its primary sources of revenue. This revenue and the sound credit status it enjoys enabled the area to be economically independent of the mother country. The growth of British, American and Japanese investments in recent years indicated that profitable investments were to be found there. The possession of this strategic naval and commercial position in the Far East by the British added greatly to the strength of their imperial structure and assured them, in time of peace and during a successfully conducted war, a source for two vital materials of modern industrial society—rubber and tin. On the other hand, the great cost of this colony must be remembered. Since the first World War, Singapore has become one of the most vital points in the British Empire line of defense. In 1938, one of the largest and strongest naval bases in the world was opened there. To the construction of the base and to imperial defense generally the colony, it is true, contributed handsomely in proportion to its size and population. Annual contributions ran to about Straits $5,000,000, while since the first World War a total sum of some Straits $100,000,000 has been contributed; but this is only in addition to the millions expended by Britain. In terms of defense, power and prestige, however, who can estimate whether or not this colony has paid?

On the other hand, the Italian colonial empire presented a liability rather than an asset, if estimated on the basis of trade in relation to costs. For Italy's colonial trade was always of minor importance; in recent years, it amounted to under 2 per cent of the total of all her foreign trade and before that to less than 1 per

<hr>

[6] Moresco, E., *op. cit.*, pp. 114-115.

cent, while she reported the largest colonial estimates of any colonial ministry and in twenty years expended 1,300,000 more lire in keeping control of her colonies than the amount of her total trade with them over a period of forty years. Yet, although financially a liability, Italy's colonies appeared strategically an asset. She felt the need to attempt to control the Mediterranean Sea, for 86 per cent of her sea-borne trade passed through it. She possessed no alternative route and it was peculiarly liable to blockade.

An interesting example nearer home which illustrates many of these variable factors in regard to estimating the value of colonies is provided by the Philippines. Have they paid the United States? The conquest of the islands from the Filipinos themselves after their formal transfer to American sovereignty cost 4,165 American lives and $175,000,000. In addition, it has been estimated that they have cost the American government $4,000,000 a year excluding interest on the acquisition costs. To that must be added the annual indirect cost of about $22,000,000 to American consumers for Philippine products, principally sugar, owing to the free-trade regime. On the other hand, American exports under this same free-trade regime, rose to as much as $90,000,000 in 1938. In addition, there is the return of a possible $10,000,000 a year to Americans on their investments in the islands, whose total is estimated at about $200,000,000. The resulting balance, whether it indicates profit or loss, would be relatively small in comparison with the total annual income and wealth of the United States. American investments in the Philippines represent only 1 per cent of the total foreign investments of the United States.

From the strategic point of view these tropical islands can potentially provide America with rubber and quinine and free it of dependence on foreign-controlled sources. In addition, the islands supply America with 8 per cent of its chromite and could supply more and all its Manila fiber necessary for naval cordage. The real answer to the question lies in the realm of the imponderables. Has American control resulted in bettering the livelihood of the Filipinos to a degree and with a rapidity that would otherwise have come about? Is the presence of an American naval base there vital to the maintenance of America's prestige in support of her far eastern policies? Will the defence of the Philippines draw us into a naval war with Japan?

One more factor requiring consideration in the discussion of trade and costs, as we have indicated above, is the question of who derives the advantage. The answer would seem to be the group most concerned, the industrialists, shippers, engineers, munition makers, private investors—in short, the capitalist class. Material in this book has already indicated the huge profits obtained from colonial enterprises overseas, were they loans to old-world potentates at from 20 to 30 per cent or even higher interest rates, tea plantations in India, copper mining in Rhodesia, oil wells in the East Indies, rubber plantations in the Belgian Congo. It was estimated by the *Economist* (Nov. 20, 1937), for example, that capital investment in the whole dependent British Empire yielded an annual income of about £38,000,000; and it has been calculated that Dutch investments in the East Indies grew from 750,-000,000 florins in 1900 to 3,500,000,000 in 1940, that the Dutch derived an annual return from the islands of 200,000,000 florins in direct, and 120,000,000 florins in indirect gains; and that one-tenth to one-fifth of the population of the Netherlands was directly dependent upon or interested in commercial or industrial development there. At the same time, it is pointed out that the amount of financial help which the colonial nation gives the colonies, in the way of loans, protection and other costs, bears heavily upon the taxpayer at home whether or not he is included in the investor class, in which case the advantage would seem to lie with the capitalist group again.

In addition, the point is made that the middle-class group, which includes many of the investors, is identical with the group which gains materially from the jobs with which the colonial empires provide them. The statement that the "British Empire is a gigantic system of outdoor relief for the British governing classes," made in the middle of the nineteenth century and variously attributed to James Mill and John Bright, holds true to some extent for all the colonial empires, especially the British and the Dutch, and on a smaller scale for the others. In the United Kingdom, for example, it has been estimated that there were rather under 2,000 persons who drew incomes between £250 and £1,000 per year from services, official and unofficial, in the colonies. Obviously, the figures are only approximate, but they have given rise to the criticism that one of the main advantages of the colonial empire to the middle class is that it enables "middle-class persons to live upper-class lives" on the condition of their removing to the tropics.[7]

In view of all the difficulties and variables of calculation which have been pointed out in the above discussion, it will be seen that it is almost impossible to give a definitive answer to the question *Did colonies pay?* during the period 1871-1940. However, with the various qualifications in mind, it may be safely hazarded that, given the political and economic conditions of the era, they did pay in immediate returns at stated times in terms of wealth and income, prestige, power and security, both for the nation at large and the dominating class which gained profit from them, and that they paid in some instances extremely well indeed.

Have Colonies Paid in the Long Run?

The question whether colonies have paid ultimately or in the long run would seem to demand a negative answer. For it is all too apparent that the imperialism of 1871-1940 has for some years been distinctly on the wane and because of the disquieting (to imperialists) reason that it bore within itself the seeds of its own destruction. In whatever areas it operated, as this book has sought to emphasize, its two inevitable results, nationalism and international strife, acted as a boomerang upon the interests of the colonial powers themselves. These universal consequences, disastrous as they were to the possession of overseas empires, inevitably followed from imperialism itself, in whose nature they were inherent. As we have observed, national revolts increased in Africa, the Near East, the Middle East and the Far East, in direct ratio to the extension of industrialization and Europeanization, the tools of colonialism; and where they had not already won autonomy, they were threatening the supremacy of the imperialist powers. At the same time, international rivalry and hostility grew apace in similar proportion to the acceleration of expansionism; passed beyond the compromise or colonial-deal stage and eventuated in the cataclysm of the first World War. Then, the peace terms of 1919 failing to effect an equitable colonial

---

[7] Barnes, L. *Empire or Democracy*, p. 88.

settlement, created instead a wider gulf between the Haves and
Have-Nots in overseas possessions, and helped lead inevitably to
the present European struggle.

Nothing illustrates more clearly the intensification of international rivalry as a cause of the waning of the "old colonialism"
of 1871-1940 than does the behavior of the three Have-Not
powers, Germany, Italy and Japan, during the ten years from
1930 to 1940. This may well come to be considered as a transitional period in the history of colonialism. By 1934, not only had
the old liberal system of multilateral trade, access to vital raw
materials and markets at equitable prices, been cut into by
monopolistic protectionism, to the extent that, as a system of
economy, it had ceased to be; but the corresponding rise of a
belief in autarkie and self-containment in the totalitarian states
threatened to destroy it forever. During the decade, each one
of the Have-Not powers launched an attack upon the system.
They were determined, apparently in their extremity of exclusion
from an adequate share of overseas territories, to strike a death-
blow against the old imperialist masters.

Thus Germany, bereft of her entire colonial empire by the
Treaty of Versailles, had, ever since 1919, smarted not only from
her loss but from the "insult" of the so-called "colonial lies" which
had accused her of inefficient colonial rule. The Allies justified
the seizure of all Germany's colonies by the statement that "Germany's dereliction in the sphere of colonial civilization has been
revealed too completely to admit of the Allied and Associated
Powers consenting to make a second experiment and of their
assuming the responsibility of again abandoning thirteen or
fourteen million natives to a fate from which the war has delivered
them." Accompanying the foregoing was a severe indictment of
German colonial rule on the grounds of cruelty, slavery, compulsory labor, and militarization. Brooding upon this injustice, the
German people were nevertheless forced to accept the official attitude of impotent resignation towards the lost colonial empire,
poignant witness to which was borne by the funereal evergreen
wreath before the tablet inscribed "the Colonies," set in the wall
of the *Feldhernhalle* in Munich. The German republic, 1919-1933,
had its hands too full with pressing domestic difficulties and occupied too weak a position in foreign affairs to enable it to accede
to the demands of the colonial societies and the expansionists, who

kept alive a strong unofficial colonial movement throughout those years.

This attitude of supine resignation on the part of the German government experienced a sharp reversal with the rise of Hitler and National Socialism. Waiting until the time was ripe to launch a vigorous colonial policy, the Hitler regime lent, nevertheless, the utmost support to the unofficial colonial movement, and there exists abundant evidence to prove that the Führer himself favored ultimately the recovery of the colonies.[8] Scrutiny of *Mein Kampf* reveals many criticisms of the colonial policy of the Hohenzollerns and many recommendations that Germany first expand upon the European continent, before turning overseas; but the conclusion is that the author intends to prosecute colonial expansion when the requisite conditions have been secured. One of these conditions, as the Führer states, is: "The German people possesses no moral right to colonial activity so long as it is not able to unite its own sons in a common state. Only when the boundaries of the Reich include even the last German . . . does there arise from the need of its own people the moral right to acquire foreign soil. The plow then gives way to the sword and out of the tears of war springs daily bread for posterity."

The years 1936-1938 supplied not only a significant satisfaction of the above requisite but gained for Germany a position in international affairs, strong enough to assert herself. Consequently a "wave of colonial consciousness" swept the country, both administration and people, and Hitler followed up his declaration in February, 1938, that "the claim for Germany's colonial possessions will be voiced from year to year with increasing vigor," by making the colonies the central theme of his sixth anniversary speech in January, 1939.

Moreover, the three chief arguments advanced by the Third Reich for colonies were: economic, based upon her need for raw materials, new markets, food, a wider area for her own currency circulation; political, which reflected her desire to be a world power; and emotional or nationalistic, which arose from her need of removing the stain upon her national honor. All these

---

[8] Townsend, M. E., "The German Colonies and the Third Reich," *Political Science Quarterly*, June, 1938.

arguments gained greater force as the idea of totalitarianism, of autarkie and self-sufficiency began to replace the old world order of international trade and constituted an attack upon it. Dr. Schacht, minister of economics, insisted, for example, that "the possession of colonial raw materials and raw materials territories is essential for an industrial nation." He deprecated the Open Door in colonial territories as wholly insufficient for Germany "which must have her own raw materials within her currency sphere." Hitler supported this argument with frequent references to Germany's poverty, the "heroic conception of wealth," the fact that Germany was bursting with population and ability.

In addition, as early as 1937-1938, during the Anglo-German discussions regarding a colonial settlement, Hitler announced that "the German colonies are not to be made the subject of bargaining," and, also, that Germany is not interested in a "general settlement" but in "direct bilateral agreements." That this position was a blow at collective security and the order of world economy then prevailing has been only too obviously confirmed by the outbreak of the 1939-1940 European struggle, in which Hitler has announced that he is out to "break the British Empire."

In the second place, Italy contributed her blow to the colonial organization existing since 1871 by striking at Ethiopia. As we have already observed, the powers, Britain and France, failed to control Mussolini either by their joint action within the framework of the League of Nations, by multilateral agreement, or even by unilateral arrangement. With their failure, the fifty-year practice of "keeping Italy in leading strings in Africa" came to an end.

Moreover, Italy joined Germany in the totalitarian effort to attack the existing imperialist structure by cementing the Rome-Berlin Axis and by echoing Hitler's demands for colonies in Africa, a consolidated plan which subsequent events at the outbreak of the current struggle have confirmed.

Japan, the third Have-Not power, struck earlier than either of the other two against the prevailing imperialist system in the Far East and has materially contributed to its disintegration in that area. For Japan launched upon her expansion program into territory near the homeland and in Manchuria primarily for reasons of strategic defense under the pressure of the steady advance of European nations to the Far East. Economic considerations were secondary and are still, at times, subordinate to military policy.

Her policies *vis à vis* China and southeastern Asia, on the other hand, have been dictated primarily by economic considerations. Mounting tariff barriers and a closing of doors to outside investments, the establishment of quotas on certain commodities in all parts of the world since the depression have driven Japanese interests to support the army's policies in China and the navy's plan for expansion in the South Pacific. Given a world of free trade, the Open Door for investments and the development of concessions and consequent access at all times to vital raw resources and markets at equitable prices, there would be little if any occasion or justification for an implementing of economic policies with military and naval force. It was not that kind of world, however, in which Japan rose to power. In view of that fact, incidentally, it cannot be said that Japan's expansion has not paid, for Japan has become a relatively wealthier, more powerful state than has China, which failed to progress along the parallel roads of militarization and industrialization that tend ever to coalesce and to create a policy of imperialist expansion. Now Japan is attempting not only to dominate the markets of China and to control her raw materials, but also is moving into Indo-China and casting ahead of her the threatening shadow of naval and economic domination of Malaya and the Netherlands East Indies. Since 1937, she has expended sums of money that have nearly doubled her total public indebtedness, which by 1941 had risen from ten to nearly twenty billion yen.

Many will contend that from the viewpoint of human and spiritual values Japan has already lost in her gargantuan efforts to swallow China. But from the economic aspect, the answer cannot yet be given. It may well be that the Japanese leaders have overreached themselves, that the Japanese Empire has already reached its zenith and henceforth will decline in power and extent. On the other hand, the drive for markets and raw materials in Southeastern Asia and the Pacific was beginning in 1940 to receive implementation by a vigorous naval policy of expansion. Should the second World War present a favorable opportunity, it is likely that Japan's economic and naval expansion will become one, and the whole Far East may fall under a virtual Japanese protectorate.

In addition to these open attacks upon the colonial system of 1871-1940 inflicted both by the subject peoples against their imperialist masters and by the Have-Not powers during 1930-1940 and continuing into armed struggle, there existed other evidences of the waning of modern imperialism. These were mainly the prolific literature of drastic criticism with which we have already dealt, and the promulgation of plans and remedies for its reform. To mention the chief of these, they were: the mandate system, contained in the League of Nations Covenant; the proposal of the return to Germany of her former colonies, which met serious opposition from Britain and France; and the plan to provide Germany with colonial territory at the expense of the smaller powers like Portugal and Belgium, which in turn excited their stern opposition. Also, another possible solution, which would have taken into account the claims of Japan and Italy as well as Germany, was that contained in Sir Samuel Hoare's speech before the League of Nations Assembly in September, 1935, in which he offered a proposal for international discussion of the redistribution of raw materials, an offer rescinded by Anthony Eden, the foreign secretary, in the House of Commons, February, 1936. The same idea was elaborated by Sir Arthur Salter in his book *Peace and the Colonial Problem* and given further and more detailed development in his suggestions for the distribution of colonial raw materials and the establishment of the colonial Open Door contained in Paul van Zeeland's Report of January, 1938.[9] Other suggestions, coming mainly from the opinion of the left, comprised the proposal to extend the mandate system to all colonies, which Leonard Barnes put forth in his book *The Future of Colonies;* and later his somewhat startling plan that Britain renounce her empire, outlined in his book *Empire or Democracy.*

With the outbreak of the conflict in 1939, all these proposed remedies, which indicated the crumbling of empire, were swept away overnight and the question of colonies as national assets has come to depend upon the form the future world order will assume, and what colonial sovereignty is going to mean in that new world, whatever it may be. Even if Great Britain should definitely win in the current struggle, the old multilateral trade system with her at the center, which had about disappeared in 1934, would scarcely ever be revived. And as the "old colonialism" of 1871-1934 was part and parcel of that system, it is not to be expected that it either could live again, especially as we have

[9] Full text in *The New York Times,* January 28, 1938.

seen what an active rôle it has played in bringing the whole structure of capitalist world economy to the point of crisis.

It may be that there will arise a new economy of some kind with
multilateral features and in it there will be "colonies" or areas
producing raw material and foodstuffs dominated by stronger
centers of trade manufactures and finance. If future peace is to
obtain, a positive, constructive peace and not a mere interlude
of exhaustion or of preparation for renewed warfare, it will depend upon the creation of a world-wide economic and political
order out of the present competitive chaos. Peace according to
the prevailing geo-political concept of Europe for the Europeans,
or Asia for the Asiatics, America for the Americans, is a snare
and a delusion. The dividing of the world into three or four areas
under four or five dominant powers, all striving for economic self-
sufficiency within their respective spheres, would result only in
affording to all the economic conflicts and political struggles
which have made war in the past, a larger stage upon which to
operate. The wars of 1914 and 1939 already have shown that
modern wars cannot be easily confined to one continent or to one
region of the world but tend ever to spread to global proportions.
This is primarily because the vital raw resources of the world,
both mineral and agricultural, have not been equitably and uni-
formly distributed among these geographic regions. Unless the
door is left open for trade, investments and access to vital resources in all parts of the world for the interests of all the nations,
conflict is bound to occur.

Peace must have more, however, than a world economic and
political order for its basis. In proportion to the degree to which
men enjoy economic and physical security do they demand individual, social, religious and political liberties. Unless the
dominant world powers are willing to be tolerant not only of the
variant cultural, religious and social backgrounds of the minority
groups within their borders, or of the weaker national states which
surround them, but also of the colonial peoples among whom the
sentiments of modern cultural and political nationalism have been
so rapidly spreading and who fall within their orbits of superior
economic political and military power, there can be no peace, but
only suppression, bitterness and revolt. For it needs to be borne
in mind that revolts among colonial peoples will assume an increasingly effective military aspect as industrialization of colonial

areas, greatly stimulated by the two great recent conflicts, places in the hands of those peoples the improved instruments of modern warfare. Until that day of liberty and tolerance arrives, all the areas of the "old colonialism" of 1871 to 1940 in Africa, the Near East, the Middle and the Far East, will only remain more so than in the past, contributing factors of world unrest and of periodic wars.

READINGS

Angell, N.   *Raw Materials, Population Pressure and War*, 1936.   Valuable, condensed.

Ashton, H. S.   *Clamor for Colonies*, 1936.   Over-popularized.

Barnes, L.   *The Future of Colonies*, 1936.   Plea for re-distribution.
     Empire or Democracy, 1939.   Program for renunciation.

Feiss, H.   "Raw Materials and Foreign Policy," *Foreign Affairs*, July, 1938.

International Studies Conference   *Peaceful Change: Procedures, Population Pressure, the Colonial Question, Raw Materials and Markets*, 1938-1939.   Careful surveys.

Kuczynski, R.   *Colonial Population*, 1937.   Statistical tables.

Langsam, W. C.   *In Quest of Empire. The Problem of Colonies*, 1939.

Leith, C. K.   *World Minerals and World Politics*, 1931.   Scientific treatment.
     "Mineral Resources and Peace," *Foreign Affairs*, April, 1938.

Royal Institute of International Affairs.   *The Colonial Problem*, 1937.   Detailed.
     Germany's Claims to Colonies, 1938.   Comprehensive.
     Raw Materials and Colonies, 1936.   Statistical, brief.

Staley, E.   *Raw Materials in Peace and War*, 1937.   Reliable.

Ward, B.   *The International Share-Out*, 1938.   Realistic.

Index

Index

625